PART 6 Sentence Style 421

23 Coordinate & Subordinate Sentences 422
a Relating equal ideas
b Distinguishing main ideas

24 Parallelism 434
a To coordinate series elements
b Parallelism with pairs
c To enhance coherence
d For lists & outlines

25 Sentence Variety 443
a Sentence length
b Sentence openings
c Sentence types

26 Emphasis & Conciseness 453
a Write with emphasis
b Write with conciseness

PART 7 Words 469

27 The Dictionary 470

28 Appropriate Words 478
a Denotation & connotation
b General & specific; abstract & concrete
c Formal & informal language
d Jargon
e Archaisms, neologisms, acronyms
f Regionalisms & dialect
g Euphemism
h Clichés
i Figurative language

29 Biased Language 496
a Racially & ethnically biased language
b Sexually biased language
c Other biased language

30 Vocabulary 504
a History of English
b Roots of words
c Meanings of prefixes & suffixes
d Stories behind words
e Context clues

31 Spelling 517
a Word meanings aid spelling
b Recognize homonyms
c Common spelling rules
d Forming plurals
e Unstressed letters
f Spelling with hyphens
g Steps to better spelling

PART 8 Punctuation & Mechanics 533

32 End Punctuation 534
a Periods
b Question marks
c Exclamation points

33 Commas 539
a Before coordinating conjunctions
b With introductory elements
c With nonrestrictive elements
d Between items in a series
e Separate coordinate adjectives
f With transitional words

g With absolute phrases
h With contrasting elements
i With dates, addresses, numbers, & titles
j With quotations
k For comprehension
l Avoid unnecessary commas

34 Semicolons & Colons
SEMICOLONS
a Between independent clauses
b With conjunctives & transitional phrases
c Separate complex clauses
d Separate items in a series
e Avoid semicolon errors
COLONS
f Introductory statements
g Introducing lists
h Introducing quotations
i Introducing appositives
j In salutations, headings, time, & titles
k Avoid colon errors

35 The Apostrophe 566
a The possessive case
b Not for possessives of pronouns
c In contractions
d Plurals
e Avoid apostrophe errors

36 Quotation Marks 573
a For direct quotations
b For quotes within quotes
c Lengthy quoted passages
d With poetry
e With dialogue
f With titles & definitions
g With words in special usage
h Misuses of quotation marks
i With other punctuation

37 Other Punctuation 581
a Dashes
b Parentheses
c Brackets
d Ellipses
e Slashes

38 Capitals 592
a First word of a sentence
b First word of a quotation
c First letter in a line of poetry
d Proper nouns & adjectives
e Titles & subtitles
f I & O
g Misuses of capitals

39 Italics 600
a For titles
b For words, letters, numbers, & phrases
c For foreign words & phrases
d For names of trains, ships, air & spacecraft
e For emphasis

40 Abbreviations 604
a Personal & professional titles
b Acronyms & abbreviations
c Symbols
d Documentation
e Other types of abbreviation
f For reference

41 Numbers 611

PART 9 Research

43 Understanding Research 622
a Getting ready
b Selecting a topic
c Primary & secondary sources
d Library resources
e Library searches on computers
f Research on Internet & WWW
g Field research
h Working bibliographies

44 Writing the Research Essay 665
a Restricting the topic
b Evaluating sources
c Reading critically
d Taking notes
e Developing a thesis
f Considering audiences
g Organizing the essay
h Drafting the essay
i Incorporating evidence
j Avoiding plagiarism
k Revising & collaborating
l Preparing the final manuscript

45 Documenting Sources 695
a MLA in-text citations
b MLA explanatory notes
c MLA Works Cited lists
d APA in-text citations
e APA content notes
f APA References lists
g CMS footnotes & bibliography
h CBE in-text citations
i CBE References lists

46 Two Research Essays 743
a MLA style
b APA style

PART 10 Writing in the Disciplines 779

47 Literature & the Arts 780

48 Social & Natural Sciences 802

49 Business Writing 819

50 Writing with a Computer 827

Appendices 838
Glossary of Usage 846
Glossary of Terms 854
Index 869

The SCRIBNER HANDBOOK for Writers

Second Edition

Robert DiYanni
Pace University

Pat C. Hoy II
New York University

Allyn and Bacon
Boston   London   Toronto   Sydney   Tokyo   Singapore

Vice President and Editor in Chief, Humanities: *Joseph Opiela*
Development Editor: *Allen Workman*
Marketing Manager: *Lisa Kimball*
Cover Administrator: *Linda Knowles*
Cover Designer: *Susan Paradise*
Composition Buyer: *Linda Cox*
Manufacturing Buyer: *Megan Cochran*
Production Administrator: *Susan Brown*
Editorial-Production Service: *Matrix Productions*

Copyright © 1998, 1995 by Allyn & Bacon
A Viacom Company
Needham Heights, Mass. 02194
Internet: abacon.com

Library of Congress Cataloging-in-Publication Data

DiYanni, Robert.
     The Scribner handbook for writers / Robert DiYanni, Pat C. Hoy II.—2nd ed.
     p.   cm.
     Includes bibliographical references and index.
     ISBN 0-205-19838-4
     1. English language—Rhetoric—Handbooks, manuals, etc.
     2. English language—Grammar—Handbooks, manuals, etc. 3. Report writing—
     Handbooks, manuals, etc. I. Hoy, Pat C. II. Title.
     PE1408.D59 1998
     808'.042—dc21   97-18962
                                                                          CIP

Printed in the United States of America
10 9 8 7 6 5 4   VHP   00 99

Credits begin on page 865, which constitutes a continuation of the copyright page.

Contents

Instructor Preface xv

Student Preface xxv

PART 1

The Writing, Reading, Thinking Connection

1 Writing—A Way of Expressing Ideas 2

a. Becoming a writer 2
b. An overview of the writing process 3
c. Accumulating evidence and formulating ideas 4
d. Assessing audience and purpose 6
e. Preparing to write 9
f. Organizing 12
g. Drafting and revising 17
h. Collaborating 20
i. Editing and proofreading 21

2 Critical Reading 24

a. Adjusting to different kinds of texts 24
b. Writing from reading 25
c. Analyzing what you read 33
d. Formulating an interpretation 35
e. Evaluating a text 37
f. Discussing your reading with others 40
g. Reading reflectively and critically 41
h. Interpreting a text: An example 42

3 Thinking 49

a. Comparing creative and logical thinking 49
b. Creative thinking techniques 50
c. Overcoming obstacles to thinking 58
d. Logical thinking 63
e. Understanding causality 68
f. Thinking about analogy in arguments 70

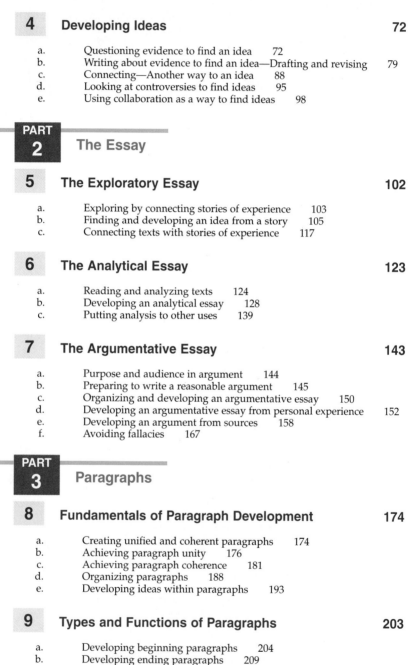

4   Developing Ideas   72

a.   Questioning evidence to find an idea   72
b.   Writing about evidence to find an idea—Drafting and revising   79
c.   Connecting—Another way to an idea   88
d.   Looking at controversies to find ideas   95
e.   Using collaboration as a way to find ideas   98

PART 2   The Essay

5   The Exploratory Essay   102

a.   Exploring by connecting stories of experience   103
b.   Finding and developing an idea from a story   105
c.   Connecting texts with stories of experience   117

6   The Analytical Essay   123

a.   Reading and analyzing texts   124
b.   Developing an analytical essay   128
c.   Putting analysis to other uses   139

7   The Argumentative Essay   143

a.   Purpose and audience in argument   144
b.   Preparing to write a reasonable argument   145
c.   Organizing and developing an argumentative essay   150
d.   Developing an argumentative essay from personal experience   152
e.   Developing an argument from sources   158
f.   Avoiding fallacies   167

PART 3   Paragraphs

8   Fundamentals of Paragraph Development   174

a.   Creating unified and coherent paragraphs   174
b.   Achieving paragraph unity   176
c.   Achieving paragraph coherence   181
d.   Organizing paragraphs   188
e.   Developing ideas within paragraphs   193

9   Types and Functions of Paragraphs   203

a.   Developing beginning paragraphs   204
b.   Developing ending paragraphs   209
c.   Developing middle paragraphs   212
d.   Linking paragraphs in an essay   215

PART 4   Grammar

10   Basic Sentence Grammar   220

a.   Recognizing subjects and predicates   220
b.   Recognizing objects and complements   223
c.   Recognizing and using phrases   226
d.   Recognizing and using clauses   232
e.   Using the basic sentence patterns   234
f.   Using different types of sentences   235

11   Verbs   240

Verb Forms

a.   Primary verb forms   241
b.   Auxiliary verb forms   243
c.   Regular and irregular verbs   246
d.   Other types of verbs   249
e.   Using *sit/set, lie/lay,* and *rise/raise*   251

Verb Tenses

f.   Simple tenses   254
g.   Perfect tenses   256
h.   Progressive tenses   257
i.   Verb tense sequences   260

Voice

j.   Uses of the active voice   262
k.   Uses of the passive voice   263

Mood

12   Nouns, Pronouns, and Case   270

a.   Understanding nouns   270
b.   Understanding pronouns   271
c.   Understanding pronoun case forms   274
d.   Using *who* and *whom*   277
e.   Using personal pronouns with compound structures   280
f.   Using personal pronouns with appositives   281
g.   Using personal pronouns with elliptical constructions   281
h.   Using *we* and *us* with a noun   282
i.   Using objective case forms with infinitives   283
j.   Using possessive case forms with gerunds   283

13   Adjectives and Adverbs   286

a.   Distinguishing between adjectives and adverbs   286
b.   Using adjectives with linking verbs   289

c.	Using adverbs with two forms	289
d.	Using *good/well* and *bad/badly*	291
e.	Using comparative and superlative forms	292
f.	Avoiding double negatives	295
g.	Avoiding overuse of nouns as modifiers	295
h.	Using possessive adjectives	296

14   Prepositions, Conjunctions, and Interjections   299

a.	Recognizing prepositions	299
b.	Using prepositions in writing	299
c.	Recognizing conjunctions	301
d.	Using interjections	304

15   Maintaining Agreement   306

Subject-Verb Agreement

a.	Making a verb agree with a third-person singular subject	306
b.	Making separated subjects and verbs agree	308
c.	Making subject and verb agree with a compound subject	309
d.	Making a verb agree with an indefinite pronoun subject	310
e.	Making a verb agree with a collective noun subject	311
f.	Making a verb agree with its subject rather than a complement	312
g.	Making a verb agree with relative pronoun subjects	313
h.	Making subject and verb agree in inverted sentences	313
i.	Maintaining agreement with singular words that appear plural	314
j.	Making verbs agree in titles and with words used as words	315

Pronoun–Antecedent Agreement

k.	Making a pronoun agree with an indefinite pronoun antecedent	318
l.	Making a pronoun agree with a collective noun antecedent	318
m.	Making a pronoun agree with a compound antecedent	318
n.	Checking for gender-specific pronouns	320

16   Grammar for ESL Writers   323

a.	Distinguishing count nouns from noncount nouns	323
b.	Recognizing and using determiners	325
c.	Using the articles *a, an,* and *the* correctly	326
d.	Choosing the correct quantifier for count and noncount nouns	329
e.	Using demonstratives correctly	331
f.	Using possessive forms of pronouns correctly	332
g.	Using correct word order for adjectives and other noun modifiers	334
h.	Distinguishing between present participle and past participle used as adjectives	336

i. Learning the forms of *be, have,* and *do*   337
j. Using the auxiliary verbs *be, have,* and *do* correctly   338
k. Recognizing and using modal auxiliaries   342
l. Using gerunds and infinitives   344
m. Recognizing common phrasal verbs and correctly placing their objects   348
n. Using prepositions to express time, place, or motion   351
o. Placing adverbs   352
p. Changing forms with indirect discourse   354
q. Using verb tenses in conditional sentences   356
r. Learning idiomatic expressions   358

PART 5   Clear and Effective Sentences

17   Sentence Fragments   364

a. Correcting sentence fragments   364
b. Revising phrase fragments   366
c. Revising compound predicate fragments   368
d. Revising dependent clause fragments   369
e. Using acceptable fragments   371

18   Comma Splices and Fused Sentences   373

a. Dividing clauses into separate sentences   374
b. Joining clauses with a semicolon   374
c. Joining clauses with a semicolon and a conjunctive adverb   375
d. Joining clauses with a comma and a coordinating conjunction   376
e. Converting two clauses into a single independent clause   378
f. Converting one of two independent clauses into a dependent clause   378
g. Using comma splices and fused sentences appropriately   379

19   Misplaced, Interrupting, and Dangling Modifiers   382

Misplaced Modifiers

a. Revising misplaced words   383
b. Revising misplaced phrases   384
c. Revising misplaced clauses   385
d. Revising squinting modifiers   386

Interrupting Modifiers

e. Revising lengthy modifiers that separate a verb from its subject   387
f. Revising modifiers that separate a verb from its direct object or a subject complement   387
g. Revising modifiers that split an infinitive   388
h. Revising modifiers that separate parts of a verb phrase   388

Dangling Modifiers

i.   Revising dangling word and phrase modifiers   390
j.   Revising dangling elliptical clauses   391

20 Avoiding Shifts and Maintaining Consistency   393

a.   Maintaining consistency of person and number   393
b.   Maintaining consistency in verb tenses   394
c.   Maintaining consistency in mood   396
d.   Maintaining consistency in voice   396
e.   Avoiding shifts between direct and indirect quotations   397
f.   Maintaining consistency in diction and tone   399

21 Pronoun Reference   403

a.   Making sure a pronoun refers to a single antecedent   403
b.   Keeping pronouns and antecedents close together   404
c.   Clarifying confusing references with particular
        pronouns   406

22 Mixed and Incomplete Sentences   412

Mixed Sentences

a.   Revising mixed sentences with incompatible grammatical
        patterns   413
b.   Revising mixed sentences with faulty predication   414

Incomplete Sentences

c.   Revising confusing elliptical constructions   416
d.   Revising sentences to include missing words   417
e.   Revising incomplete comparisons   418

PART 6 Sentence Style

23 Writing Coordinate and Subordinate Sentences   422

a.   Using coordination to relate equal ideas   422
b.   Using subordination to distinguish main ideas   427

24 Using Parallelism in Sentences   434

a.   Using parallelism to coordinate elements in a series   435
b.   Using parallelism with pairs   435
c.   Using parallelism to enhance coherence   438
d.   Using parallelism to organize lists and outlines   441

25 Achieving Sentence Variety 443

a. Varying sentence length 443
b. Varying sentence openings 447
c. Varying sentence types 449

26 Achieving Emphasis and Conciseness 453

a. Writing with emphasis 453
b. Writing with conciseness 459

PART 7 Words

27 Using a Dictionary 470

a. Exploring a dictionary 470
b. Using different types of dictionaries 474

28 Using Appropriate Words 478

a. Understanding denotation and connotation 478
b. Using general and specific, abstract and concrete words 481
c. Using formal and informal language 483
d. Avoiding jargon 485
e. Using archaisms, neologisms, and acronyms 486
f. Understanding regionalisms and dialect expressions 487
g. Avoiding euphemisms 490
h. Avoiding clichés 491
i. Using figurative language 492

29 Avoiding Biased Language 496

a. Avoiding racially and ethnically biased language 496
b. Avoiding sexually biased language 497
c. Avoiding other kinds of biased language 501

30 Enriching Your Vocabulary 504

a. Learning about the history of the English language 504
b. Recognizing the roots of words 507
c. Understanding the meanings of prefixes and suffixes 509
d. Learning the stories behind words 513
e. Using context clues 515

31   **Improving Your Spelling**   **517**

a.   Using word meanings to aid spelling   517
b.   Recognizing homonyms   518
c.   Applying common spelling rules   521
d.   Forming plurals   526
e.   Spelling words with unstressed vowels and consonants   527
f.   Spelling words with the hyphen   529
g.   Six steps to better spelling   529

**PART
8**   **Punctuation and Mechanics**

32   **End Punctuation**   **534**

a.   Using the period   534
b.   Using the question mark   535
c.   Using the exclamation point   537

33   **Commas**   **539**

a.   Use a comma before a coordinating conjunction that links
     independent clauses   540
b.   Use a comma to set off introductory elements   541
c.   Use commas to set off nonrestrictive elements   542
d.   Use commas between items in a series   545
e.   Use commas to separate coordinate adjectives   546
f.   Use commas to set off transitional and parenthetical
     expressions   547
g.   Use commas to set off absolute phrases   548
h.   Use commas to set off contrasting elements, *yes* and *no,*
     direct address, and tag questions   548
i.   Use commas with dates, addresses, place names,
     numbers, and titles   549
j.   Use commas with quotations   551
k.   Use commas to aid comprehension   552
l.   Avoid using unnecessary commas   553

34   **Semicolons and Colons**   **556**

Semicolons

a.   Use semicolons to signal a close relationship between
     independent clauses   557
b.   Use semicolons between independent clauses linked with a
     conjunctive adverb or a transitional phrase   558
c.   Use semicolons to separate long and complex independent clauses
     and those that contain commas   559
d.   Use semicolons to separate items in a series   559
e.   Avoid semicolon errors   560

Colons

f.	Use colons to introduce a statement that qualifies a statement in an independent clause	562
g.	Use colons to introduce a list	563
h.	Use colons to introduce long or formal quotations	563
i.	Use colons to introduce delayed appositives	563
j.	Use colons in salutations, memo headings, hours/minutes, titles/subtitles	564
k.	Avoid misuse of the colon	564

35 The Apostrophe 566

a.	Use apostrophes to form the possessive case of nouns and indefinite pronouns	566
b.	Do not use an apostrophe to form the possessives of personal pronouns and adjectives	568
c.	Use apostrophes in contractions and to indicate missing letters, numbers, or words	569
d.	Use the apostrophe to form the plural of letters, numbers, symbols, and words used as words	570
e.	Avoid using the apostrophe incorrectly	571

36 Quotation Marks 573

a.	Use quotation marks for direct quotations	573
b.	Use single quotation marks for quotes within quotes	574
c.	Set off lengthy quoted passages	574
d.	Use quotation marks with poetry	574
e.	Use quotation marks for dialogue	575
f.	Use quotation marks to enclose titles and definitions	575
g.	Use quotation marks for words used in special ways	576
h.	Avoid common misuses of quotation marks	577
i.	Follow established conventions for using quotation marks with other punctuation	577

37 Other Punctuation Marks 581

a.	Using the dash	581
b.	Using parentheses	584
c.	Using brackets	587
d.	Using ellipses	589
e.	Using slashes	590

38 Capitals 592

a.	Capitalizing the first word of a sentence	592
b.	Capitalizing the first word of a quotation	593
c.	Capitalizing the first letter in a line of poetry	594
d.	Capitalizing proper nouns and adjectives	594
e.	Capitalizing the titles and subtitles of works	597

f.   Capitalizing *I* and *O*   597
g.   Avoiding the misuse of capitals   598

39   Italics   600

a.   Using italics for titles   600
b.   Using italics for words, letters, numbers, and phrases
used as words   601
c.   Using italics for foreign words and phrases   602
d.   Using italics for the names of trains, ships, aircraft,
and spacecraft   602
e.   Using italics for emphasis   602

40   Abbreviations   604

a.   Abbreviating personal and professional titles
and academic degrees   604
b.   Using familiar acronyms and abbreviations   605
c.   Using the abbreviations *a.m., p.m., B.C. (BC), A.D. (AD),*
and symbols   606
d.   Using Latin abbreviations for documentation   607
e.   Using other types of abbreviations   607
f.   Using abbreviations for reference information   609

41   Numbers   611

a.   Spelling out numbers of one or two words   611
b.   Spelling out numbers at the beginning of a sentence   611
c.   Using figures according to convention   612

42   Hyphens   615

a.   Use hyphens to divide words at the end of a line   615
b.   Use hyphens with compound words   616
c.   Using hyphens with prefixes and suffixes   618

PART 9   Research

43   Understanding Research   622

a.   Getting ready to do research writing   623
b.   Selecting your topic   626
c.   Using primary and secondary sources   627
d.   Discovering the library's resources   628
e.   Searching for sources in the library and on computers   641
f.   Researching on the Internet and the World Wide Web   646
g.   Doing field research   657
h.   Compiling a working bibliography   661

44 Writing the Research Essay 665

a. Restricting your topic   665
b. Evaluating the usefulness of sources   667
c. Reading sources critically   668
d. Taking notes   670
e. Developing a reasonable thesis   679
f. Considering your audience   680
g. Organizing your essay   681
h. Drafting your essay   683
i. Incorporating evidence   684
j. Avoiding plagiarism and acknowledging sources   688
k. Revising your research essay and collaborating   692
l. Preparing the final manuscript   694

45 Documenting Sources 695

MLA Documentation Style

a. MLA style for in-text, parenthetical citations   697
b. MLA style for explanatory and reference notes   701
c. MLA style for the Works Cited list   703

APA Documentation Style

d. APA style for in-text, parenthetical citations   721
e. APA style for content notes   725
f. APA style for the References list   725

CMS Documentation Style

g. CMS style for footnotes (or endnotes) and bibliography   734

CBE Documentation Style

h. CBE style for in-text, parenthetical citations   738
i. CBE style for the References list   739

46 Reading Two Research Essays 743

a. Sample research essay in MLA style   743
b. Sample research essay in APA style   772

PART 10 Writing in the Disciplines

47 Writing about Literature and the Arts 780

a. Writing to understand a work   780
b. Writing to interpret a work   786
c. Writing to evaluate a work   792

d. Writing papers on literary works: The assignment 793
e. Two sample interpretations of literary works 794

48 Writing in the Social and Natural Sciences 802

a. Understanding methodology and using evidence in the social sciences 802
b. Considering purpose and audience for writing in the social sciences 804
c. Documenting sources in the social sciences 805
d. Understanding assignments and formats in the social sciences 806
e. Understanding methodology and using evidence in the natural sciences 810
f. Considering purpose and audience for writing in the natural sciences 811
g. Documenting sources in the natural sciences 813
h. Understanding assignments and formats in the natural sciences 814

49 Business Writing 819

a. Writing business memos and letters 820
b. Writing job application letters 823
c. Writing and formatting résumés 825

50 Writing with a Computer 827

a. Working with a word-processing program 827
b. Using a computer to generate ideas and to organize 828
c. Using a word processor for drafting and revising 829
d. Benefiting from available features 829
e. Designing documents 831
f. Creating and using visuals 835

Appendices

Appendix A
Preparing the Final Manuscript for Submission 838

Appendix B
Writing Essay Examinations 842

Glossary of Usage 846

Glossary of Terms 854

Credits 865

Index 869

Instructor
Preface

*T*his is a handbook for writers. It begins by discussing what writing is and how to do it well. It goes on to offer suggestions for writing essays, papers, and reports in different disciplines and for taking essay exams. It shows how an understanding of words and sentences, paragraphs and punctuation, grammar and usage helps writers with the work of writing.

We wrote *The Scribner Handbook for Writers* because we wished to create a college handbook that would be useful not only as a reference guide to grammar and language, but also as a guide to writing. We wanted to provide an accurate and comprehensive demonstration of how writers actually write. The discussions of writing we found in other handbooks seemed to oversimplify the often messy and complex process of writing. Instead of the realities of writing—and its intimate connections with reading and thinking—we found formulas and procedures that described a finished product rather than a method for showing students how to become involved successfully in the intricate and exciting process of writing college essays.

We wrote this book also because we wanted a college handbook to include discussion of the kind of reading and thinking required of students in college. We believe that reading and writing are mutually supportive and that they should be taught together. We also believe that there can be no real writing and no inferential, interpretive reading without creative and logical thinking. And so we have striven to connect reading with writing and writing with thinking. As a result, this *Handbook* is also about making connections.

The Scribner Handbook for Writers, thus, is both a complete handbook of English grammar, style, punctuation, and usage and a thorough guide to writing. Between the covers of the handbook, students will find what they need to use language accurately and effectively.

A Handbook that Shows How Writers Write

Writing Essays and Paragraphs

The first four chapters of this *Handbook* are about the connections among writing, reading, and thinking. Students will find in these chapters practical suggestions for doing the work of writing, especially for finding ideas and presenting those ideas convincingly to readers. Included are five techniques for discovering ideas: questioning, writing, connecting, exploring controversies, and using collaboration. Chapters 5–7 explain how to write three different types of essays: exploratory, analytical, and argumentative. These chapters contain exemplary student writing that demonstrates how writers discover and develop their ideas. These three writing chapters provide context-based demonstrations of how essays are constructed as student writers move from preliminary thinking to finished products. Taken together, the first seven chapters on writing offer clear, thorough, and honest presentations of the various writing processes students may use to write the kinds of essays their interests incline them toward and their college courses require.

Chapters 8 and 9 are devoted to writing paragraphs. We have provided two chapters on paragraphs because we believe that writing effective paragraphs is essential to successful academic writing. The first of our two paragraph chapters concerns the fundamentals of paragraph development. It describes strategies for achieving unity, coherence, and emphasis as well as techniques for organizing paragraphs efficiently and effectively. We have presented these organizational strategies as ways for developing ideas within paragraphs rather than as abstract organizational patterns. Our second paragraph chapter offers context-based demonstrations of how to write beginning, middle, and ending paragraphs for exploratory, analytical, and argumentative essays. This functional paragraph writing chapter includes advice on writing informational and transitional paragraphs, which are each presented with context-specific examples.

Reading: Process and Practice

We have devoted a complete chapter to reading because we believe that reading and writing are indissolubly interconnected and because we know that students need practice and guidance in how to get more out of what they read. Chapter 2, on critical reading, leads students to formulate a written interpretation of a text. Discussion of the experience of reading illustrates how to question a text, engage it on the writer's terms, and consider a writer's ideas and evidence in light of a reader's knowledge, experience, and values. The chapter demonstrates the recursiveness of reading while simultaneously introducing concepts of critical and creative thinking. It also invites students to participate actively in making meaning from the different kinds of texts they read. The principles delineated in this chapter are intimately connected with those explained in all of our writing chapters and are additionally reinforced in our chapters on research writing and on writing in the disciplines.

The Importance of Thinking

We have included a full chapter on thinking because we believe that much attention should be given to creative thinking in college writing courses. There is sometimes an overemphasis on logic at the expense of creative thinking. We want to redress that imbalance by providing a thorough discussion of the techniques of creative thinking. This chapter explains why creative thinking is necessary (especially in writing), and it provides specific techniques to help students think creatively in their writing. We also discuss critical and logical thinking. Here we introduce many of the terms and concepts important for writing argumentative essays. In addition to advice on avoiding common logical fallacies, students will find in our thinking chapter an approach to thinking critically that considers causality, authority and testimony, and the uses and limits of analogy as a strategy of argument.

In addition, we have integrated thinking into many sections of *The Scribner Handbook for Writers*. In the chapters on writing, for example, readers encounter repeated instances of student and professional writing where ideas are foregrounded and evaluated. The essay writing chapters show how students can construct essays that develop ideas in exploratory, analytical, and argumentative modes. Several chapters focus on how thinking and reading inform writing—especially Chapter 8, "Fundamentals of Paragraph Development," Chapter 44, "Writing the Research Essay," Chapter 47, "Writing about Literature and the Arts," and Chapter 48, "Writing in the Social and Natural Sciences." These chapters give students advice on enriching the ideas of their essays and developing and supporting the ideas with precision and care.

Grammar

Grammar is presented not as an isolated system, but as a living element of language intimately bound up with speaking, thinking, and writing. The focus remains on using grammatical structures and elements in writing. Examples of this practical focus include the numerous Usage Notes and Writing Hints students will find throughout the grammar section. Usage Notes guide students through some of the trickier aspects of applied grammar, emphasizing situations in which common problems occur. Writing Hints provide guidance in how to use different grammatical principles in academic writing. Along with an emphasis on using grammar in writing, students will encounter throughout these chapters a supportive, encouraging tone. They are shown how to use grammar to increase their repertoire of sentence forms, types, and patterns. They are also shown how to write grammatically rather than being presented with numerous examples of failings that need correction.

Coverage of grammar in *The Scribner Handbook for Writers* is extensive. The grammar chapters are arranged for maximum ease of use as a reference guide. Those who need work on grammatical structures or elements will find abundant examples and numerous exercise items that range not only across the academic disciplines but also across topics representing experiences from everyday life. The exercises and examples throughout these chapters balance the familiar and the new, the academic and the everyday, references to majority culture with various minority multicultural perspectives.

English as a Second Language

Chapter 16, "Grammar for ESL Writers," emphasizes the grammatical structures that many speakers and writers of English as a Second Language find troublesome. Carefully chosen examples offer students advice on usage coupled with clear explanations of basic grammatical concepts. Exercises provide numerous opportunities for students to practice using the various grammatical structures. Our ESL chapter includes an additional unique feature: a chart of common idiomatic expressions that students can use as a guide to the meanings that words and phrases acquire in nonliteral contexts. We believe that this chart will serve as a helpful tool for teachers unaccustomed to working with ESL students and a helpful resource for the students themselves.

Style: Playing with Words and Sentences

The Scribner Handbook for Writers deals extensively with style, a critical aspect of writing for college students but one often neglected or given only cursory treatment. Two examples of our special treatment of style include the extensive coverage of diction and the display of sentence structures in our chapter on parallelism. Our chapters on words offer detailed examples of how words are used in various social contexts, how they carry not only lexical and social intonations but also regional information and figurative implications. We have included a full chapter on language bias, devoting attention to avoiding gender and race bias in language, but considering as well how to avoid other forms of biased language such as that directed against age, region, religion, sexual orientation, and physical and mental characteristics.

Since understanding the connotation of words is crucial for students who are learning how to be more perceptive readers, more able writers, and better critical thinkers, we have created exercises that invite students to think about language, to analyze it, and to stretch their imaginations in a series of playful but instructive examples. We consistently connect our discussion of connotation (and the other aspects of diction) with reading, writing, and thinking.

One of the more unusual things we do in teaching sentence style is to set off parallel sentence elements in stacks or layers to provide a visual illustration of sentence organization. Our goal throughout the chapters on language and style is to help students express themselves with accuracy and grace.

Research

The four research chapters illustrate the complexity of the writing processes outlined in earlier chapters (especially Chapters 1–7) and they reinforce in cogent ways the important concepts developed in our reading and thinking chapters (Chapters 2 and 3). The first of the research chapters (Chapter 43) lays out the fundamentals of directed research. Primary emphasis is on showing students how to become efficient and effective researchers in the library, in the field, and in searching the Internet. Chapter 44 shows students how to make use of that research—how to restrict a topic, read and evaluate sources, take notes, develop a reasonable thesis, consider audience and organization, draft an essay, incorporate evidence, avoid plagiarism, and prepare a final manuscript. To make these two chapters more illustrative of the recursive processes of researching and writing, we show students how first-year student Ericka Kostka used library resources to become knowledgeable enough to write a research essay, and how she developed that essay.

In Chapter 45 students find the help they need to document their research essays and papers, whether they use MLA, APA, or a CBE format. Our coverage of these documentation styles is complete and up-to-date, offering thorough coverage of MLA and APA and numerous examples of documenting in the sciences and documenting electronic sources. In Chapter 46 students can see how to document both MLA and APA essays. Ericka Kostka's complete essay appears in MLA form along with extensive annotations that highlight principles of research and writing from earlier chapters. Excerpts from Rosette Schleifer's essay illustrate the basic format for APA papers and reveals the nature and scope of her research.

Teaching and Reference Features to Aid Understanding

Examples of Student Writing

The Scribner Handbook for Writers contains more extensive and more instructive student writing than any handbook or writing guide currently available. Five complete student essays appear in Chapters 4–7. Another full essay and a lengthy excerpt appear in the research writing chapters, one using MLA and the other APA documentation style. Five additional complete student papers appear in the disciplines writing chapters. In all, fourteen complete pieces of student writing, some of them fairly extensive, are complemented by numerous shorter examples of student writing ranging from a sentence or two to several paragraphs. These student examples provide a demonstration of how writers write. In showing the decision-making and revising processes in action, these writers help students understand the complex process of writing and its close connections to reading and thinking

In addition, this *Handbook* offers many excellent examples by reputable writers, ranging from sample sentences to complete brief essays. These models throughout the text reinforce key principles in the chapters on reading, writing, and thinking in the opening parts of the *Handbook*.

Engaging Exercises, Individual and Collaborative

Exercises in *The Scribner Handbook for Writers* are numerous and various. Students will find exercises ranging from readily accessible practice materials to intellectually provocative and challenging writing assignments that call for creative and critical thinking and that encourage students to stretch their imaginations. Many exercises can be performed individually while others invite collaboration. Teachers who use collaborative teaching strategies will find ample opportunity to encourage students to work together on exercises and assignments throughout the *Handbook*. In all collaborative exercises, student writers are encouraged to seek feedback from their classmates, to share ideas, to open themselves to other points of view—all with an eye to returning to their individual writing tasks with additional ideas for revision.

Artwork in Color as Cues to Thinking and Writing

Students will find that color reproductions of artwork—paintings by Picasso and van Gogh, and photographs by Richard Avedon and New York University student Anna Norris—are included as part of the pedagogy in our chapters on writing processes and writing in the disciplines. The inclusion of Richard Avedon's photo, for example, serves as a stimulus for a lesson in questioning one's way to an idea. The pedagogy that accompanies the artwork shows students how to use guiding questions to discover an idea.

Vincent van Gogh's *The Starry Night* is discussed in Chapter 47, "Writing about Literature and the Arts." Students are led into the painting through a series of carefully sequenced exercises that invite their personal responses, their observations and inferences, and their evaluation of the interpretive ideas of others. As with the photographs and Pablo Picasso's *Guernica*, which appears with a student essay in Chapter 6, van Gogh's painting is included to stimulate thinking. All four works of art serve as evidence for ideas that student writers develop in response to looking at artwork, learning about it, and thinking about what they see and learn in the context of their own lives.

The reproductions are an integral part of the pedagogy of Chapters 4, 6, and 47. Working through this pedagogy reminds students that learning to make observations from evidence is central to interpretation, and that moving from observations to connections and inferences can lead to viable and defensible interpretations. We have found that students write well about visual images when they are encouraged to look carefully at details, describe accurately what they see, and reflect thoughtfully on their observations. Students also seem to enjoy writing and thinking about paintings and photographs.

Charts and Lists for Ready Reference

More than one hundred fifty charts and lists are included in *The Scribner Handbook for Writers*. These compact reference aids—displayed in accessible categories on the back endpaper—provide handy summaries of key points for students to study and review as they learn and write. Some of the charts function as overviews, some as summaries, some as aids to memory. All offer a succinct visual counterpart to the discussions they abstract and condense.

Overall, these strategically placed charts are designed to make concepts and information optimally accessible to students.

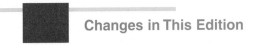

Changes in This Edition

Throughout this new edition of *The Scribner Handbook for Writers*, we have worked to maintain the elements that distinguished the first edition. We have added elements we believe will aid teachers in helping students become better writers, readers, and thinkers in a wide range of academic contexts.

In this second edition, we have tried to make our approach to using a handbook even more accessible. We have consolidated a number of chapters, streamlining the pedagogy to make it more user-friendly. The chapters on reading and thinking have been consolidated and moved to form a tight trinity with the initial chapter that presents an overview of the writing process.

We have reorganized the writing chapters to make a coherent and teachable unit. Two chapters from the first edition have been combined to make the present Chapter 4—an expanded treatment of "Developing Ideas." Chapters 5–7 have been tightened to provide guidance in writing essays typically required of college students—exploratory (personal) essays, analytical essays, and argumentative essays.

We have expanded our Writing Hints feature by adding a new writing/grammar connection to all grammar and sentence chapters—a new section called "Grammar and Writing." These end-of-chapter discussions show students how to focus on specific grammatical elements and to apply their newly acquired grammatical understanding to examples of their own writing.

Part Nine, "Research," has been updated to accommodate the latest developments in electronic information databases and CD-ROM technology. Our research essay model now includes examples of Internet sources. And Chapter 45, "Documenting Sources," explains how to document the newest additions to Internet and electronic media sources.

We have upgraded our discussion of business communication. We have expanded our discussion of writing with a computer. Chapter 50 includes new information on designing documents to take full advantage of word-processing technology to achieve the essential rhetorical concerns of communicative accuracy, efficiency, and effectiveness.

Supplements

SUPPLEMENTS FOR INSTRUCTORS

- *Instructor's Edition.* Annotations and teaching suggestions have been prepared by the authors with the help of Delma Porter of McNeese State University.

- *Instructor's Resource Guide. Teaching College Writing*, by Maggy Smith, of the University of Texas at El Paso, is available to adopters who wish to explore more teaching resources.
- *Diagnostic Tests and Exercise Bank.* Two diagnostic tests offer an analysis by common errors and are keyed to *Handbook* sections. Exercises supplement those found in the *Handbook*. (Also available in computerized formats.)

SUPPLEMENTS FOR STUDENTS

- *The Scribner Exercise Book for Writers.* This exercise book by Marie-Louise Nickerson of Bronx Community College provides numerous and varied exercises. Answer key available.
- *The CLAST Study Guide* prepares students for the Florida test in composition.
- *The TASP Study Guide* prepares students for the Texas test in composition.

COMPUTER-BASED AND MEDIA SUPPLEMENTS

- *The Scribner On-Line Handbook.* This electronic version of the *Handbook* allows topics to be quickly accessed by Contents, Index, or keyword. Available in IBM Windows format.
- *Diagnostic Tests and Exercise Bank.* Available in IBM and Macintosh formats.
- *"GrammarTeacher" Software* offers ten interactive lesson modules focused on common errors. Available in IBM Windows format.
- *Transparency Masters* for key instructional diagrams in the *Handbook.*
- *CompSite website* offers resources and instructional material for students and instructors, including helpful information on using computers for writing, techniques for using the Internet for research, and a forum for exchanging papers and writing ideas.
- *The Writer's Toolkit CD-ROM* offers a complete writing environment for planning, drafting, and revising. It provides a wealth of heuristic devices to assist students with a variety of writing activities. Available in IBM and Macintosh formats.

Acknowledgments

From beginning to end, writing *The Scribner Handbook for Writers* has been a collaborative effort. We acknowledge here the help we have given one another in writing this book. We wish to thank our collaborators around the country who evaluated our initial plans and drafts, offering sound advice.

We thank these reviewers for their constructive comments on various parts of the manuscript: Virginia Johnson Anderson, Towson State University; Deborah C. Andrews, University of Delaware; Linda Anstendig, Pace University; David Bartholomae, University of Pittsburgh; Patsy Callaghan, Central Washington University; John Chaffee, LaGuardia Community College; Carolyn Channell, Southern Methodist University; Joseph J. Comprone, Arizona State University West; Thomas A. Copeland, Youngstown State University; Bobby Cummings, Central Washington University; Carol David, Iowa State University; R. Scott Evans, University of the Pacific; James Farrelly, University of Dayton; Michael C. Flanigan, University of Oklahoma; Mark Gallaher, Freelance Ink; Chrysanthy M. Grieco, Seton Hall University; Christine Hult, Utah State University; Douglas Hunt, University of Missouri, Columbia; William B. Lalicker, Murray State University; Mark Lester, Eastern Washington University; Miriam P. Moore, University of South Carolina; William Peirce, Prince Georges Community College; Annette T. Rottenberg, University of Massachusetts, Amherst (Emerita); Alice M. Roy, California State University, Los Angeles; Barbara Stout, Montgomery College; John W. Taylor, South Dakota State University; Richard Veit, University of North Carolina, Wilmington; and Linda Woodson, The University of Texas at San Antonio.

Thanks also to many instructors who responded to surveys that were helpful to our design of this book: Libby Bay, Rockland Community College, SUNY; Kathleen Beauchene, Community College of Rhode Island; Peter G. Beidler, Lehigh University; Pam Besser, Jefferson Community College, Louisville; Wendy Bishop, Florida State University; Lynn Z. Bloom, University of Connecticut; John Boe, University of California, Davis; Alice Glarden Brand, SUNY Brockport; Alice Brekke, California State University, Long Beach; Stuart C. Brown, New Mexico State University; Thomas A. Brunell, Rutgers University, Newark; Dolores M. Burton, Boston University; Lee C. Carter, Wake Forest University; Donald A. Daiker, Miami University; John A. R. Dick, University of Texas, El Paso; Mimi Still Dixon, Wittenberg University; Jane Dugan, Cleveland State University; Penelope Dugan, Richard Stockton College of New Jersey; Lisa Ede, Oregon State University; Theresa Enos, University of Arizona; Christine Farris, Indiana University; Gary Fincke, Susquehanna University; John Fugate, J. Sargeant Reynolds Community College; Susan Galloway, St. Mary's University; Michelle Gibson, Ohio University; Muriel Harris, Purdue University; Andrea W. Herrmann, University of Arkansas, Little Rock; Rosalie Hewitt, Northern Illinois University; Elizabeth Hodges, Virginia Commonwealth University; Francis A. Hubbard, Marquette University; Sally L. Joyce, Keene State College; Joyce Kinkead, Utah State University; Mary Levitt, North Adams State College; Marty Lewis, University of Texas, Brownsville; Tom MacLennan, University of North Carolina at Wilmington; Lynne C. McCauley, Western Michigan University; Susan H. McLeod, Washington State University; Nikki Lee Manos, Marymount College, Tarrytown; T. A. Marshall II, Robert Morris College; Janet Marting, University of Akron; Emily P. Miller, Virginia Military Institute; Kevin Morris, Greenville Technical College; Robert M. Otten, Indiana University, Kokomo; Susan Palo, University of California, Davis; Deepika Petraglia-Bahri, Bowling Green State University; John Woodrow Presley, University of Michigan, Dearborn; Jeanie Page Randall, Austin Peay State University, Clarksville; Ruth Ray,

Wayne State University; Marjorie Roemer, Rhode Island College; Duane H. Roen, Arizona State University; William J. Schang, Ripon College; Charles I. Schuster, University of Wisconsin, Milwaukee; Nancy S. Shapiro, University of Maryland, College Park; Phillip Sipiora, University of South Florida; John W. Taylor, South Dakota State University; and Irene Ward, Kansas State University.

A number of colleagues deserve special thanks for their contributions, especially the following second edition manuscript reviewers, many of whom based their comments on use of the first edition: Linda Anstendig, Pace University; Chris Baker, Armstrong State College; Cherie Clark, Miami Dade Community College; Boyd Creasman, West Virginia Wesleyan College; Jack Ferstel, University of Southwestern Louisiana; Nancy Krimmel, Midlands Tech College; Lee Anne Mauno, Indiana University; Susan Moore, Scottsdale Community College; Viki Pettijohn, Southwest Oklahoma State University; and Carol Schiess, Boise State University. Thanks to Alleen Pace Nilsen of Arizona State University, who reviewed Chapter 29, "Avoiding Biased Language," making extensive suggestions and contributing generously to our work there. Thanks also to Margaret Bonner, who developed a rich chapter on English as a Second Language (Chapter 16). And thanks as well to those who helped us develop and revise our research documentation chapter, especially Joseph Law of Texas Christian University.

Special gratitude must also be expressed to two other professional colleagues: Bill Lalicker of Murray State University and Robert Funk of Eastern Illinois University. Professor Lalicker has been with us on this project from the beginning, when we presented our initial ideas for the book. He has reviewed each of our drafts, offering consistently wise counsel, which we have incorporated gratefully in our revisions. Professor Funk gave us the benefit of his extensive knowledge of grammar by scrupulously reviewing Chapters 10–15 and 17–26 and revising them to clarify explanations, add and replace exercises, and provide sound ways to illustrate grammatical and stylistic distinctions. We thank Bill Lalicker and Robert Funk for their help.

At Allyn and Bacon we have had the good fortune to work with Joseph Opiela. We also benefited from the perceptive assistance of development editor Allen Workman; from Susan Brown, our production administrator; from Lisa Kimball, our marketing manager; and from Doug Day, field marketing specialist in English.

Finally, we owe a profound debt of gratitude to our wives, Mary Hammond DiYanni and Ann Burns Hoy for their loving support and their patience during these years of labor. Thanks also to our children, Karen and Michael DiYanni, and Patrick and Tim Hoy, whose contributions appear in countless, anonymous ways in these pages.

ROBERT DIYANNI
PAT C. HOY II

Student Preface

How to Use this Book:
A Guide to Special Features

Quick Access Features for Reference

The Scribner Handbook for Writers is a reference work to consult about matters of grammar, punctuation, mechanics, and style as well as a guidebook for your writing processes. This section shows you the features that will help you locate the information you need to use this *Handbook*.

Use these information locators.

- Front endpapers: The compact contents chart provides an overview of the section and page numbers of key topics you will need.

- Main contents: A detailed listing of sections and pages for all topics.

- Revision symbols—back endpaper: This chart guides you to the revision symbols likely to be used by instructors or peers annotating your paper. The symbols are cross-referenced to appropriate *Handbook* sections, where you will see the symbols also used at the head of each page.

- A list of useful checklists, charts, and boxes—back endpaper: This listing is a convenient tool for locating the special boxed panels of checklists and guidelines for every stage of writing and revision.

Look for these features on each page:

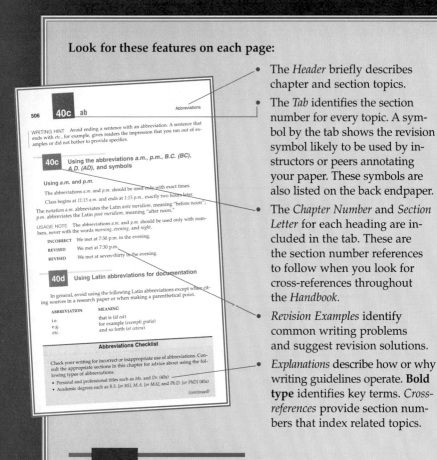

506 **40c** ab Abbreviations

WRITING HINT Avoid ending a sentence with an abbreviation. A sentence that ends with *etc.*, for example, gives readers the impression that you ran out of examples or did not bother to provide specifics.

40c Using the abbreviations *a.m.*, *p.m.*, *B.C. (BC)*, *A.D. (AD)*, and symbols

Using *a.m.* and *p.m.*

The abbreviations *a.m.* and *p.m.* should be used only with exact times.

Class begins at *11:15 a.m.* and ends at *1:15 p.m.*, exactly two hours later.

The notation *a.m.* abbreviates the Latin *ante meridiem*, meaning "before noon"; *p.m.* abbreviates the Latin *post meridiem*, meaning "after noon."

USAGE NOTE The abbreviations *a.m.* and *p.m.* should be used only with numbers, never with the words *morning*, *evening*, and *night*.

INCORRECT We met at 7:30 p.m. in the evening.

REVISED We met at 7:30 p.m.

REVISED We met at seven-thirty in the evening.

40d Using Latin abbreviations for documentation

In general, avoid using the following Latin abbreviations except when citing sources in a research paper or when making a parenthetical point.

ABBREVIATION	MEANING
i.e.	that is (*id est*)
e.g.	for example (*exempli gratia*)
etc.	and so forth (*et cetera*)

Abbreviations Checklist

Check your writing for incorrect or inappropriate use of abbreviations. Consult the appropriate sections in this chapter for advice about using the following types of abbreviations.

- Personal and professional titles such as Ms. and Dr. (40a)
- Academic degrees such as B.S. [or BS], M.A. [or MA], and Ph.D. [or PhD] (40a)

(continued)

- The *Header* briefly describes chapter and section topics.
- The *Tab* identifies the section number for every topic. A symbol by the tab shows the revision symbol likely to be used by instructors or peers annotating your paper. These symbols are also listed on the back endpaper.
- The *Chapter Number* and *Section Letter* for each heading are included in the tab. These are the section number references to follow when you look for cross-references throughout the *Handbook*.
- *Revision Examples* identify common writing problems and suggest revision solutions.
- *Explanations* describe how or why writing guidelines operate. **Bold type** identifies key terms. *Cross-references* provide section numbers that index related topics.

Handy Boxes Quickly Sum Up the Writing Steps and Guidelines That You Need

Users of *The Scribner Handbook for Writers* have taken advantage of the abundant box panels throughout the book. These distinctive panels do more than overview the high spots in grammar and writing—they sum up and provide step-by-step checklists to help walk you through the writing and revision processes that are most important. Especially in working with writing processes, you can start with the box summaries listed in the back endpapers, and then look at the text and student sample papers for a full understanding of how a writing process works. Take a look at the following examples, and then follow how these processes are explained in Chapters 2 and 44.

Tips for Incorporating Evidence

- Clearly introduce and conclude each summary, paraphrase, or quotation in such a way that readers know where it begins and ends.
- Ensure that the incorporated material blends smoothly into your sentences and paragraphs (see 44i-1). Avoid shifts in verb tense or awkward phrasing that would contrast sharply with the incorporated evidence, making your sentences difficult to read and understand.
- Provide a parenthetical citation within the essay to document the source of your evidence and avoid plagiarism. That in-text citation will correspond to the source list at the end of the essay (see Chapter 45).
- Explain the incorporated evidence so that readers can understand how the evidence relates to a paragraph's main idea and, when appropriate, to your thesis (see 44i-2).

also appear as a part of the parenthetical citation when more than one work by that author appears in your list of sources, or when you do not know the author. This parenthetical information signals for your readers the end of the incorporated material. (See Chapter 45 for more precise information on citing references.)

You will also want to integrate your sources so they blend smoothly into your paragraphs. Avoid awkward phrasing or indiscriminate shifts in verb tense that might distract the reader from your idea. To avoid such problems, be sure the tense of your verbs matches or is compatible with the tense of the verbs in the borrowed passage.

AWKWARD

Wildlife biologist John Weaver has made the observation that wolves would be released in Yellowstone wearing radio collars that "may be equipped with remote-controlled tranquilizing darts, a new device that could greatly facilitate the capture of problem animals" (qtd. in Cauble 29).

REVISED

Wildlife biologist John Weaver observed that wolves will be releas[ed in Yellow]stone wearing radio collars that "may be equipped with rem[ote-controlled] tranquilizing darts, a new device that could greatly facilitate t[he capture of] problem animals" (qtd. in Cauble 29).

Always consider reducing quoted material to the words you cons[ider es]sential. The fewer quoted words the less difficult the integration [ ]

When you introduce quotations, pay particular attention to [ ] of verbs. Write in the active voice. Your verb choice can conve[ ] clearly your attitude about the subject. Verb choice can also sug[ ]

Here are some guidelines for using supporting evidence in your paper.

---

or not—wince at the word "cripple," as they do not at "handicapped" or "disabled." Perhaps I want them to wince. . . .

As a lover of words, I like the accuracy with which it describes my condition: I have lost the full use of my limbs. "Disabled," by contrast, suggests any incapacity, physical or mental. And I certainly don't like "handicapped," which implies that I have deliberately been put at a disadvantage, by whom I can't imagine (my God is not a Handicapper General), in order to equalize chances in the great race of life. These words seem to me to be moving away from my condition, to be widening the gap between word and reality.

—Nancy Mairs, "On Being a Cripple"

---

3 Using a double-column notebook

To create a **double-column notebook**, simply divide your page in half. One half is for summarizing (see 2b-4) and interpreting what you read. Use this side of the page to record as accurately as you can your understanding of what the text says. Use the other side to respond to what you have read, to think about its implications, and to relate it to other things you have read or otherwise experienced.

The advantage of a double-column notebook is that it encourages you to be an active reader, to think about what you read and to make connections with your reading and experience rather than to consider a text in isolation. You can use the double-column notebook to think further about your earlier reactions, which you may have recorded in annotations or freewriting, and to sustain a conversation with the writer and with yourself. The accompanying chart outlines how to use a double-column notebook.

Highlights of the Double-Column Notebook

SUMMARY	COMMENTS
Summarize the text.	Respond to your summary.
Interpret the author's ideas.	Reflect on the author's ideas.
Explain the ideas succinctly.	Consider whether you agree or disagree—and why.
Identify important details.	Raise questions about the details you have observed.
Relate the details to the central idea.	Relate the text and the writer's main idea to other things you have read and to your own experience.

Here's an example of a box on critical reading.

Ways to Get Ideas and Develop Them into a Solid Essay

Users of *The Scribner Handbook for Writers* have a unique advantage in looking for reliable methods of developing writing ideas and applying them to successful writing assignments. This *Handbook* shows you how to select and apply any of five methods for discovering key ideas; how to use reading skills to find ideas from evidence (Chapter 2); how to use specific thinking skills to develop ideas (Chapter 3); how to work with your ideas to form a thesis with sound support (Chapter 4); and how to develop your ideas into essay projects of exploration, analysis, or argumentation (Chapters 5, 6, and 7). Here's an overview of five ways to develop ideas:

1. *Inferring ideas by creative and logical thinking and questioning of evidence.* Section 4a shows you how to look for key features and significant patterns within the evidence, to seek underlying relationships that weren't at first obvious but that can be used to build inferences and ideas for your paper, and to decide how you feel about the evidence before you.

2. *Letting your ideas evolve through stages of writing and revising.* Section 4b shows how you can work from sketchy freewriting or brainstorming exercises to find a usable starting point for your essay. This discussion also helps you test your intentions and the implications of your draft from new angles by redrafting, questioning, and connecting to alternate possibilities until you have a developed essay. Excerpts from a student essay and from a paragraph by E. B. White show you how this revising can be done.

3. *Looking for creative connections and relationships in your material to find ideas.* Section 4c shows how questioning and writing about evidence can lead to a connection-making process. This process will help you respond to one idea (an assignment or a provocative statement) in relation to another statement, image, text, or experience that has moved you. As you put together the ideas you discover when making these connections, you can form a significant essay that says something important to you.

4. *Discovering writing ideas from looking at controversies that interest you.* Section 4d shows you how to work with evidence about conflicting points of view. This section covers ways to line up opposing viewpoints and look for questions, weaknesses, and connections among

parts of the controversy until you have formed what can become a reasonable conclusion of your own. This section also shows how to use your conclusion as a basis or thesis for your own essay.

5. *Discovering writing ideas by experimenting and collaborating with others to test your thinking.* Section 4e shows you how you can develop your writing ideas through dialogue and interaction with others, in face-to-face work groups, in an Internet network group, or in informal peer groups. This collaborative approach can work either in undirected discussions with sketchy ideas, or at later stages of the writing process with exchanges of writing drafts and questioning sessions with peers.

Ways to Form Ideas into Essay Assignments You Will Meet in Your Courses

The Scribner Handbook for Writers shows you how to work within the forms your writing is likely to take for most of the assignments you encounter in college. The *Handbook* also shows how an essay evolves in stages rather than by any simple application of a formula. Whether your writing ideas evolve from personal experience, from a close reading of a text, or from observing and studying a set of objects, college essays that develop these ideas are likely to become one of these three types of essays:

Essays of Exploration (Chapter 5). An exploratory essay strives to share with readers the writer's process of inquiring into an interesting but often hard-to-define idea. When you write an exploratory essay, you develop an idea, often from experience that has become familiar in your or another person's life and you shape this experience into a coherent form that is often a narrative.

Essays of Analysis (Chapter 6). The main goal of analytical essays is to share with readers an interpretation of a "text"—a set of written, experienced, or observed events—that is complex and in need of explanation.

Essays of Argumentation (Chapter 7). Developing an argument in an essay involves a relatively formal process of building upon evidence to discover a claim that can be supported with careful reasoning. This process requires careful consideration of counterarguments and viewpoints, especially those that readers are likely to have in mind.

Full-Length Student Samples Show You Realistic Ways to Develop Essays

A distinctive feature of *The Scribner Handbook for Writers* is its exceptionally generous sampling of real student research papers and essays that have been developed using the methods described in the *Handbook*. You can learn how real writers build assignments by analyzing how the sample essays are constructed and by reading the *Handbook's* generous commentary about these essays. In research as well as essay writing, the *Handbook* offers a step-by-step demonstration of how revision and the process of rethinking ideas affects writing.

Two research papers using the MLA documentation style.

- Ericka Kostka develops evidence from written and electronic sources to write about the controversy over introducing gray wolves into Yellowstone National Park.

- Michele Carerra works with secondary sources to write about James Joyce's *The Dead*.

Two primary-source student papers on literary topics.

- Jennifer Stepkowski writes on Sylvia Plath's "The Mirror."
- Ruth Chung writes on Virginia Woolf's "Old Mrs. Grey."

Two research papers using other documentation styles.

- Rosette Schleifer does a research piece on intimate relationships.
- A team of students do research on recycling attitudes and actions.

Five student essays show samples of exploratory essays, analytical essays, and argumentative papers. Each of the five is shown in various stages of revision. Four student essays use visual examples (reproduced in the *Handbook*) as basis for their writing.

An argumentative paper by Dan Legerit shows one way through the revision process.

Applied Grammar Demonstrations Show You How the Rules Work in Real Writing Situations

The Scribner Handbook for Writers helps you look beyond the grammar rules to see why conventions of usage and grammar work to your advantage as you craft sentences that say what you mean.

- Grammar and Writing sections appear at the end of the key grammar and usage chapters. These boxed panels explain why the rules work to your advantage.

Grammar and Writing

Coordination and Subordination

You can apply what you know about coordination and subordination to your writing when you draft and revise your essays, papers, and reports. When you compose a draft, use coordinate and subordinate structures to clarify your expression of ideas and your presentation of information.

Use the charts on p. 426 and p. 431 to check for excessive use of either coordination or subordination in your writing when you revise. Too much of either grammatical form may create monotonous or unemphatic writing. Try for a blending of coordinate and subordinate grammatical structures.

The most important aspect of coordination and subordination for writers is also the most complex and challenging: using these grammatical structures logically. As you write and revise, check to see that your uses of *and* and *but, of if* and *because* (and other coordinate and subordinate conjunctions) link clearly expressed and logically thought-out relations among the parts of your sentences.

EXAMPLE:

                                                        but
She was never much of a musician, [and] she did briefly study piano and violin.

Because
. Her playing lacked musicality, [and] her teachers discouraged her from continuing her musical study.

---

244   **11b**   vb   Verbs

But I *do recognize* the name of the Secretary of State. [emphasis]

Did you *visit* the Acropolis? [question]

He *had* not *received* his magazine subscription as of last Wednesday. [negative]

USAGE NOTE   Some dialects use the base form *be* instead of *am, is,* or *are,* especially to express habitual or continued action. This usage is not standard, however, for college writing.

NONSTANDARD   He *be* the best player on the team.

STANDARD   He *is* the best player on the team.

NONSTANDARD   I *be* taking three math courses this year.

STANDARD   I *am* taking three math courses this year.

A **modal auxiliary verb** (such as *can, could, may, might, must, shall, should, will,* and *would*) combines with a main verb to form a verbal phrase. The modal auxiliary can refine the meaning of the main verb by indicating necessity, obligation, permission, possibility, and the like. Modal auxiliaries do not change form to indicate person or number and always combine with the base form of the main verb.

If she is to win the case, the defense lawyer *must undermine* the plaintiff's credibility. [necessity]

I really *should visit* my grandmother this weekend. [obligation]

You *may leave.* [permission]

If I *could manage* to get an interview, I know I *would prove* that I *could perform* the job. [possibility]

USAGE NOTE   Use the conditional auxiliary *would* only in an independent clause, never in an *if* clause.

                  INDEPENDENT CLAUSE   IF CLAUSE
NONSTANDARD   We *would* have helped if we *would* have known.

STANDARD   We *would* have helped if we *had* known.

WRITING HINT   Modal auxiliaries can combine with other auxiliary verbs to form complicated verb phrases that require careful attention.

When *have* comes after a modal auxiliary, as in "I could have gone," the *could have* is pronounced with stress on *could* and no stress on *have.* Thus, in speech *could have* sounds like *could of* and is sometimes incorrectly written that way. Be sure to write *have,* not *of,* in sentences like these.

You *should have* read the directions more carefully.

It *would have* saved you considerable time and energy.

- Writing Hints apply grammatical concepts to the writing of effective sentences.

- Usage Notes provide guidance on trickier aspects of applied grammar and common usage problems.

xxxi

Practical Processes and Priorities with Computer-Based Writing

- *Searching for fresh research material on the Internet.* Chapter 43 describes reliable guidelines, step-by-step processes, and applied examples of Internet research procedures. Section 43f shows you how using search engines can be a productive way to find information for your paper. This section also explains how to consider the tradeoffs of time and effort needed for Internet research by critically evaluating the flood of sources available on the Internet.

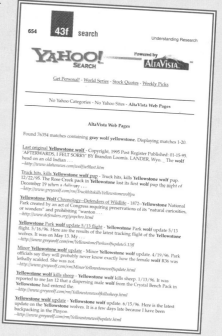

- *Writing with a computer.* Sections a–d in Chapter 50 offer practical guidance in word-processing procedures, both as a reminder to the less experienced and as a useful summary for those more experienced with word processing.

- *Designing documents with word-processing programs.* Sections d and e in Chapter 50 offer detailed examples of graphics and page design that need attention as writers become more proficient in using word processors.

Other Extras Give You Help Where You Need It

The Scribner Handbook for Writers helps you solve writing problems beyond the basics of developing and revising an essay. Here are some key areas where you can find helpful guidelines and examples:

- *Models and guidelines for the writing you'll use in the workplace.* Chapter 49 highlights résumés, job application correspondence, and business letters and memos.

- *Finding help with the English language for international students, regional speakers, or writers seeking to avoid biased language.* Chapter 16 gives a complete reference for international students needing a refresher on troublesome features of the English language. Chapter 28 provides helpful guidelines for regional and dialect speakers in making decisions about forms of English to use in writing. Chapter 29 addresses issues of biased language.

- *Getting extra help with grammar and usage trouble spots. The Scribner Handbook for Writers* provides extensive exercises, many of them fascinating thinking and writing activities, as well as supplements in key areas of grammar and usage.

The Writing, Reading, Thinking Connection

Writing

Learning and writing go hand in hand. You have to have something to say before you can learn to say it well. As you accumulate knowledge and learn to say what you mean, writing becomes its own reward. Your audience comes to understand what you have in mind and, if you are persuasive, may even be convinced to see things your way.

Writing leads to discoveries. As you write and think about your subject, you clarify your ideas and create meaning. But the writing process varies according to the kind of writing you are doing, your audience, and your purpose. For all types of writing, however, thoughtful reading and careful thinking will help you discover and clarify your ideas.

Reading helps you acquire and consider ideas for writing. Along with the factual information you absorb from reading, the ideas you encounter can provide evidence for your writing. As you write and read, you will consistently find yourself thinking about what others have written. Discovering ideas, reconsidering and evaluating them, is essential for academic work in the sciences, social sciences, and humanities.

When you write, you will need to think creatively and logically. Creative thinking helps you generate ideas; logical thinking helps you analyze and evaluate them. These two kinds of thinking complement and reinforce one another. Together, they enable you to improve your ability to read critically and write convincing essays.

Those essays are based on an idea—the leading thought (often called a thesis) that you are trying to convey to your readers. Ideas come from your analysis of evidence (lived experiences, books, essays, and articles assigned in your courses, even movies, poems, songs, and art objects that interest you). The leading idea you derive from your analysis of this evidence will be developed in your essay, using approaches shown in Chapter 4.

CHAPTER 1

Writing—A Way of Expressing Ideas

1a   Becoming a writer

Becoming a good writer depends on your becoming a good reader and thinker. Writing, reading, and thinking are so closely related that it is difficult to imagine one without the others. Knowledge provides the basis for your writing—knowledge that you gain from thinking or reflecting about what you read, experience, and observe.

You have been getting ready to write for a long time, storing up ideas in your mind. Every day you add to that storehouse, and when you write you bring together the fragments of stored knowledge to develop your own ideas—ideas that give you a reason for writing. You want your readers to understand those ideas.

Discovering ideas can be exciting. Studying and writing, you find that you know enough about a subject to make judgments and draw conclusions. You discover possibilities that no one else has imagined quite the way you have. With something to write about, you begin to understand that you are not a recorder, transcribing what others have said. Rather, you are a *thinker*—a writer with ideas of your own to express. You have the power to cause others to sit up and take notice. You know something, and you know how to say it.

To express your ideas well, you will need to acquire another kind of knowledge—knowledge about how to write. Like the awareness that leads to ideas, you can accumulate it through reading, and you can learn a great deal about writing by studying other writers. But to become a skilled writer—to know how to write—you have to practice. There is no other way. And, of course, you should couple practicing with a genuine desire to have the words say what you mean. You have to want to be understood.

As a writer, you often want to move as quickly as possible from coherent sentences to good paragraphs and then on to full-length pieces of writing such as interesting essays or reports. But you can gain a great deal by moving gradually and deliberately instead of leaping ahead too fast. Reviewing the fundamentals can help you write better. Another look at the basics about sentences can reveal not only how to write different kinds of sentences but also how to vary sentences to interest your readers and to help you develop ideas. Reconsidering the fundamentals of paragraph writing can show you how paragraphs, like good essays, vary according to purpose and rely on different kinds of evidence depending on the nature of your idea.

Reviewing these fundamentals, you can become aware of just how exciting words and syntax (the arrangement of words into sentences) can be. Consider these two sentences:

The woman walked down the trail.

The frail woman walked with a slight limp as she made her way down the narrow, winding trail, looking, as she went along, for the thief who had assailed her when first she turned round the bend, the thief who had been dogging her for nearly a mile as she made her way home, deep in the woods, way out beyond help and the telephone and the police.

Each of these sentences has its own special qualities. Neither is preferable. The simplicity and directness of the first, complemented by the surprising revelations of the second, suggest possibilities available to you as a writer. The first sentence conveys information. The second also conveys information but suggests as well an idea—the idea that movement deeper into the woods is movement toward isolation and danger. The writer does not declare that idea straight out but implies it in the details of the sentence. Like a good story, the second sentence draws you into it, inviting you to decipher its meaning. The sentence conveys more than the writer states.

When you write, you have options, endless possibilities for helping your readers understand what you have to tell them. The two preceding example sentences suggest how interesting the choices can be. Learning about the options and variations by writing and practicing, you will begin to discover how satisfying it is to find an idea and express it so that others know just what you know. Therein lie the writer's most gratifying rewards.

1b An overview of the writing process

The **writing process** often begins with a fleeting hunch about something you want to write about and ends with a completed essay. Writing that essay depends very much on your ability to think, read, and take notes, but it also depends on your capacity to complete a series of related tasks: accumulating evidence, formulating ideas, considering audience and purpose, preparing, organizing, drafting, revising, editing, and proofreading. We will look closely at these tasks in this chapter.

But to suggest that the writing process is linear—that you go through these tasks step by step, the same way every time—would be to deny its most important characteristic: flexibility. You may discover differences in the process almost every time you write an essay.

Writing an essay can be, and most often is, a messy business. Thinking and reading and drafting and rethinking and revising and rereading go on and on as you write. The process moves back and forth; it is recursive. It usually involves some false starts as well as botched endings, jumbled middles, and muddled ideas. Do not be dismayed by the complications. You will get better and more efficient as you learn to be more comfortable with the writing process and its interesting complications. All writers face them, no matter what their level of experience. In Chapter 4, you can watch E. B. White, a professional essayist, struggling to develop an idea in a single paragraph about the first moon walk. But you can tell that the struggle is accompanied by the pleasure of getting the words right, finally.

As you learn the different skills and the nature of the various tasks in the writing process, you will be less anxious about them; but relying only on that process still will not lead you to a good essay. You also have to concentrate on your writing. As you learn the essential skills and recognize the various writing tasks, you may even begin to enjoy this messy business of writing. The real pleasure comes when your readers understand what you want them to understand. That understanding is what you aim for; it is often your main purpose for writing.

1c   Accumulating evidence and formulating ideas

To become a good writer, you need the two kinds of knowledge you have just read about—knowledge about how to write and knowledge of a subject. You will accumulate knowledge about how to write as you study writing and as you write. You can acquire knowledge about a given subject much more deliberately, by way of experience, of course, but also through concentrated study. Let us consider briefly the subject *civil disobedience*—disobeying seemingly unjust laws through passive resistance—and how you might begin to acquire knowledge and evidence about it to gain insight that will lead to ideas.

Reading about civil disobedience, you discover that people often have to make complex choices in the face of the law. As you read and think about civil disobedience and then start to write about it, you discover how disobedience can be civilized and nonviolent, how it can affect lives, and how it can lead to violence, just as it can lead to changes in laws that a community considers unjust.

Studying such a controversial issue, you begin to realize that you have something to say about it that no one else has imagined quite the way you have. Your acquired knowledge provides the foundation for your ideas and eventually becomes the **evidence** you use in your essays.

Ideas and evidence have a symbiotic relationship; they feed off each other. Stephen Jay Gould, an evolutionary biologist, makes some interesting observations about his own science that should help you understand more clearly the relationship between evidence and ideas:

> Well, evolution *is* a theory. It is also a fact. And facts and theories are different things, not rungs in a hierarchy of increasing certainty. Facts are the world's data. Theories are structures of ideas that explain and interpret facts. Facts do not go away when scientists debate rival theories to explain them. Einstein's theory of gravitation replaced Newton's, but apples did not suspend themselves in mid-air pending the outcome. . . . In science, "fact" can only mean "confirmed to such a degree that it would be perverse to withhold provisional assent."
>
> —Stephen Jay Gould, "Evolution as Fact and Theory"

An **idea** accounts for evidence, provides a theory about it. An idea is your sense of what the evidence means, your explanation or interpretation of the facts. Your essay will be shaped and controlled by a leading idea (often called a **thesis**).

Think again about the topic *civil disobedience*. It is not a new concept. The United States was founded on disobedience, not all of it civil. Looking back at U.S. history, you can find numerous examples of important changes brought about by disobedience and revolution. But the term acquired new meaning during the civil rights demonstrations in the late 1950s and early 1960s in the United States when African Americans began to speak out against racial injustice. If, as a writer, you choose to look into the matter of civil disobedience, you might focus on what has already happened, or you might focus on what is going on in the United States today. Wherever you look, you will find **controversy**—disagreement about past events or about future courses of action. When you find such controversy, you are probably on the scent of an idea.

The evidence you assemble about civil disobedience leads to questions: Under what conditions is it permissible to break the law? What is justifiable violence? How should oppressed citizens respond to unjust laws? At first, such questions lead to a search for more evidence, but then those questions lead to answers, to your interpretation of what the evidence means. That interpretation is your idea, something you reason or intuit from the evidence. (See Chapter 3 for thinking processes that raise key questions. See Chapter 4 for processes that help you develop ideas.)

As a writer, your dual tasks are to create a good idea from the available evidence and to find an interesting way to express that idea, often in an essay. You can never be sure about that available evidence—where it will come from, what you will think about it once you find it, how you will use it in your essay. At the outset, you cannot predict where your search for evidence will take you. Every time you begin the process of writing an essay, you are on the trail of discovery, on the scent of something new, something you can discover and express in words.

An **essay** is your attempt to express an idea through writing so that readers can understand and accept what you have discovered. As you have just seen, the knowledge you acquire through study becomes the evidence you need in your essay to illustrate and develop your leading idea.

When you begin to decide how best to explain your idea and your reasons for believing it, you will have to select evidence from all that acquired knowledge. You have to consider what you know, think about your purpose, and think about what your readers need to know so that you can choose only the specific evidence that will help you present your idea. You will also have to organize your presentation into the form of an essay. (See Chapters 5–7 for more on writing different types of essays.)

1d   Assessing audience and purpose

1   How audience influences writing

Your readers, those people you are trying to reach with your writing, constitute your **audience**. The relationship between your audience's needs—based on its knowledge and level of expertise—and your own selection and presentation of evidence is important. Much of what you say and how you say it depends on whether your audience is a group of experts or a more general audience consisting of diverse people interested in your topic.

Even the way you organize your writing and the amount of detail you include (the terms you define, the amount of context you provide, the level of your explanations) depend in part on what your audience needs to know. If you are writing about civil disobedience for a group of historians, you can assume that because they are experts they know the meaning of civil disobedience and know its history. At the outset of your essay, you would need to remind them only of key points important to the development of your idea. But if you are writing about the same subject for a general audience with little expert knowledge (e.g., your English class), you may have to prepare your audience by filling in important background information and defining basic terms. You have to establish context so they can understand your idea.

As a writer, you must always consider what your audience needs to know to understand your essay. It pays to think often of that audience. Think about what assumptions you share with your readers and what you might disagree about. Use the Audience Checklist on p. 9 to help you think about your audience and make decisions on how best to communicate with that audience. (See 7a and 7b-4 for more on considering your audience.)

2   How to assess audience feedback

Often in a college course your instructor will be your primary audience, providing written feedback and guidance as you develop your papers. Your instructor may also designate classmates as your audience and at the same time ask them to be your collaborators. They will provide feedback during the time that you are drafting and revising. You will not have to imagine their response as you often do with other audiences. They will tell you how well they understand what you have written (see 1h, 4e, and 5b-1).

Your instructor and your classmates serve as important reminders that you rarely write just for yourself. Unless you are writing a personal journal, you are writing to reveal your thoughts to someone else, so you always have to put yourself to the test of your readers' understanding. To put yourself in your readers' place takes practice and skill at separating yourself from what you have written. But it is not only a matter of learning to stand apart from your drafts and see them objectively; it is also a matter of learning to spot gaps even as you write. Develop the good habit of pausing occasionally as you write to ask yourself whether you think your audience will be able to understand your point. For more ideas or tips on writing and rewriting with your audience in mind, see the Drafting and Revising Guidelines on p. 19.

3 How to influence an audience—Purpose and tone

You write for any number of reasons or **purposes**—to provide information; to persuade others to accept your point of view; to explain an event that you witnessed, a poem that you read, or a movie that you saw; to entertain— but beneath all of these reasons for writing is the desire to be understood. You also often write to get a response.

You may simply want your readers to know something—to respond by understanding—but you may also want to stir them to action. Whatever your purpose, you are not likely to accomplish it without carefully considering your own relationship to your audience. When you write, you not only provide evidence and explanation so that your audience can follow along and understand what you have to say; you also provide a crucial sense of your own attitude to that audience through the **tone** of your writing. Tone conveys your attitude toward your subject and your sense of how best to approach your audience according to your purpose. Tone, therefore, includes strategy. Let us consider a few of your options by examining four professional writers at work. All of these writers are targeting a general audience.

In the following example, the writer's tone is conversational, light, and humorous. The writer's purpose is to interest his readers in a subject of great interest to him—his own writing.

> Occasionally I write familiar essays. When I send them to editors, I usually explain that I am trying to write my way to a new car, adding that I have done well recently and have earned the front half of a station wagon, the automatic transmission, power brakes, and a luggage rack. Of course, that's not true. My essays will never earn me a new car. Besides I am happy with my 1973 Pontiac.
>
> —Samuel Pickering, "Being Familiar"

The tone of the following example is biting, witty, and angry, and the author's purpose is to evoke awareness. Carter is having a bit of fun about women's makeup, but anger lurks behind her playfulness, anger intended to evoke awareness and perhaps to change habits. Hers is a serious cultural argument.

> White-based lipsticks, colourless glosses, or no lipstick at all, were used in the 1960s. Now the mouth is back as a bloody gash, a visible wound. This mouth bleeds over everything, cups, ice-cream, table napkins, towels. Mary Quant has a shade called (of course) "Bloody Mary," to ram the point home. We will leave our bloody spoor behind us, to show we have been there.
>
> —Angela Carter, "A Wound in the Face"

In the passage that follows, the author uses a clear, unemotional tone. She also uses images to lull her readers into awareness and understanding about the relationship between the stark beauty of winter and winter's effect on the mind. The transparent, unemotional flatness here leads her audience to accept a revelation at the end of the paragraph.

> Winter is smooth-skulled, and all our skids on black ice are cerebral. When we begin to feel cabin-feverish, the brain pistons thump against bone and mind interrupts—literally invading itself—unable to get fresh air. With the songbirds gone only scavengers are left: magpies, crows, eagles. As they pick on road-killed deer we humans are apt to practice the small cruelties on each other.
>
> —Gretel Ehrlich, "The Smooth Skull of Winter"

Finally, the tone of the following passage is technical and academic but inviting. The author seeks to interest a general audience in a technical experiment, but without becoming so technical and formal that he turns away all but the experts. Heinrich tries to figure out how he will gather experimental data that will in turn allow him to explain how the sphinx moth regulates its body temperature during flight.

> My problem was now specific: Is heat loss regulated by way of the circulatory system? I couldn't stay away from the lab for more than a few hours at a time. Once I went to camp out for a weekend in the Sierras, but my mind was in the lab and I didn't see the birds or flowers. My measurements of heat production (oxygen consumption rate) and thoracic temperature showed that the moths thermoregulated by as much as tripling their rate of heat loss during flight at high air temperatures. But how could you measure heat loss facilitated by blood flow in a flying moth? Sphinx moths are extremely fast. You can't trail them in flight with instruments attached. I decided to mimic the overheating that normally occurs in flight and to control it myself.
>
> —Bernd Heinrich, "The Thesis Hunt"

The four preceding passages give you a glimpse of how you can vary tone to suit your purpose. Academic writing often has a formal and technical tone, and it should always be reasonable and objective, serious and thoughtful. It should also avoid contractions such as *they're*, *we'll*, and *you're*, and casual expressions such as "I'd thought long and hard about Sylvia Plath's images." Write instead, "Sylvia Plath expresses her sense of despair in a number of images that form a pattern within her poem," and then go on to discuss each of those images and explain the pattern in clear, direct analytical language.

Despite its formality, academic writing can, at appropriate times, accommodate humor, personal experience, and even satire. But it is not ordinarily as conversational or personal as Samuel Pickering's is in the preceding passage from "Being Familiar." Your tone will depend on your subject, but it will depend as well on your purpose and your sense of what your audience will be most receptive to. No formula specifies what tone to use for what effect. You will learn what is appropriate by experimenting, by practicing, and by studying how other writers use tone effectively.

The questions in the accompanying Audience Checklist will help you gain perspective on your audience and on your own writing.

1e   Preparing to write

As preparation for writing and for discovering ideas, you might begin to record your interesting experiences and your reflections about the books and articles you read. Most of the evidence for your essays will come from actual

---

Audience Checklist

- Who are my readers? Are they experts or are they generalists?

- What reasonable assumptions can I make about what my audience knows? Do I need to provide detailed background information? Can I assume that my audience will understand the technical terms and language?

- What sort of audience response do I hope for? Is my essay a call to action, to understanding?

- Will my audience's response be friendly or hostile? If hostile, what can I say to make my readers more receptive? What concessions can I make to them without compromising my own position? If my audience is friendly, how can I keep their interest?

- What can I discover by looking at my writing objectively—that is, by reading my writing as if I am a member of the audience? What evidence or explanations have I left out? What might my audience object to?

- What tone would be most appropriate and produce the desired effect with this audience?

experience and from reading, so it will pay to keep journals. It will also help to know other preparatory strategies.

1 Keeping a reading journal

Try to become an active reader who not only questions and thinks about what you read but also keeps ongoing records of those questions and reflections. Such written records may turn out to be your best source of ideas. Because remembering and reflecting can add to and enhance your preparation for writing, read with pen in hand. Keep track of your mind's play by noting what interests you and by jotting down your thoughts in a **reading journal** as you read.

The format for your reading journals can vary. If you are reading a book or copies of articles that you own, you can record your observations directly on the printed pages—highlighting or underlining what seems important, writing down questions that occur to you as you read, making note of connections you see within the piece you are reading and of connections with other books or articles you have read or with observations from your field research. The book or article itself becomes a journal that you can go back to, studying both it and your reflections all in one place. (See 2b-1 and 47a-1 for more information on annotating texts.)

At times you will need more space than the printed page provides. In that case, you can keep a journal in a separate notebook, on a pad of paper, or in your computer. This type of journal would consist of your **freewriting**. This is writing in which you let your mind play more expansively over what you have read, recording your thoughts in whatever way they occur. (See 2b-2 and 47a-4 for more instruction on freewriting and an example of it.) Or you can keep a double-column notebook in which you can align your reflections with your summary of the text you are reading. Simply divide your notebook pages so that in one column you summarize what you have read and in the facing column you reflect on what you have summarized. (See 2b-3 and 47a-5 for more on the double-column notebook.)

Reviewing your journals should help you get your bearings, suggesting the importance of what you have read and of your reflections about that reading. That record helps prepare you for writing, reminding you of how you made sense of what you read, of your questions, of tentative connections you made, of controversies that seemed intriguing, of other books you have read that seem to relate to the assigned or chosen reading. Most important, however, is that your reading journals help you discover your own ideas. (See Chapter 4 on writing as a way of developing ideas.)

2 Keeping a personal journal

You will not, of course, depend solely on evidence that you have gleaned from reading. Sometimes, when writing essays, you will make use of your own experiences, such as in an exploratory essay (see Chapter 5). Those experiences will actually constitute much of the evidence from which you develop ideas.

Keep a record of interesting experiences in a **personal journal**. You should be especially mindful of moments that stop you in your tracks and make you take notice—a little walled-in enclosure with a tiny headstone just off the side of a quiet country road; the shimmering effect of the breeze on the leaves of the birch trees outside your window; a scene you saw on television or at the movies; music you heard on the radio or at a concert. Think of yourself as a writer trying to remember the essence of what you have seen. You are less interested in creating a detailed report of what happened than in conveying what the event meant to you. You want to account for why it struck you so powerfully.

As you make notes about those events, remember to describe how you felt about them and what you thought about those feelings. Later, when you sit down to write, these memories may come back to mind when you least expect them, and if they do, you will be able to turn to your journal for details. As your mind plays over the moment and as you consider your recorded evidence, you may begin to connect those recorded events with books you have read, with other experiences, with movies or songs or visual images. Connecting those pieces of evidence can create the trace of an idea. (See 4c for more on connecting as a way of developing ideas.)

3   Using other preparatory strategies

Besides journal writing, a number of other important strategies can help you prepare to write and can lead you to develop ideas. The accompanying list identifies those strategies and refers you to the sections of the *Handbook* that discuss and illustrate them.

Preparatory Strategies that Will Lead You to Ideas

- Outlining and mapping (see 1f)
- Questioning (see 2b-1, 3b-6, 4a, and 47a-3)
- Writing to discover ideas (see 4b)
- Developing ideas by making connections (see 4c)
- Using controversy to find ideas (see 4d)
- Listing details and observations (see 47a-2)

EXERCISE 1–1 **Recording Your Ideas**

1. Create a reading journal. Select a textbook from your syllabus and read a portion of it. Then make a list of two or three major ideas you found in the book. Reflect on those ideas, writing down what you think about them. Finally, see if those ideas lead you to an idea of your own or to questions that you would like answered.

2. Create a personal journal. Make observations about interesting details for about a week. Remember also to keep track of how those observations affected you.

3. After you have kept your personal journal for several days, look back through it for connections between two events that you recorded, events that might not on the surface seem related. If you see such connections, add notes to your journal about them. Look back to your reading journal as well. Make notes about the connections you see between what you have been reading and what you have been observing. Let your imagination have free rein; let your mind play over this recorded evidence. Begin to write, preparing two typed pages in which you try to reveal your discoveries to a general audience.

1f   Organizing

After you have become knowledgeable about an assigned subject or one you have selected on your own, and after you have begun to develop an idea about your evidence (gathered from reading, field research, your own experiences and observations, and so forth), you will have to figure out how to convey that idea to your readers. To do this, you will have to answer two interesting questions:

1. How do I decide what evidence to select from all of the evidence I have accumulated?

2. In what order do I present the evidence to my readers?

The answers to these questions are quite simple: You select the evidence that will, in your mind, help your audience see what it is that you want to convey. You then present that evidence—along with your explanation of it—in a way that you think will make it easy for your audience to follow.

How then should you go about organizing your evidence and your essay? Each essay you write will have a basic, three-part organizational structure—a beginning, a middle, and an ending—that will give shape to your essay and help readers understand your idea. Each part of the essay serves a particular function:

The *beginning* introduces your leading idea.

The *middle* presents evidence and develops the idea.

The *ending* offers a closing perspective on the idea and reminds readers of your main supporting points.

The beginning and the ending lead readers into and out of the essay. They are relatively short and easy to organize. The middle can be more difficult because you have to deal with those vexing questions about selecting and presenting evidence.

Organizing an essay has to do with how you finally decide to present your idea. Will you provide historical background information—a context for understanding—just after your introduction, or will you spread the information throughout your essay? Will you present your best evidence first, or should you save it for last? Do you need to define an important term such as *civil disobedience* early in your essay, or will your audience already know a great deal about it? These kinds of practical, organizational decisions will depend on the kind of essay you decide to write, on the essay's purpose, and on your imagined or targeted or assigned audience—what the members of that audience already know about your subject, whether they are likely to be hostile or friendly to your idea, and whether you will try to get them involved in an inquiry about that idea or whether you want to do everything in your power to convince them of the truth of what you have discovered.

A number of organizational methods can help you present ideas and organize evidence within paragraphs of an essay. These methods include organizing from general to specific or from specific to general, climactic order, time order, and spatial order. Two of these methods—climactic order and time order—also have broad application to the organization of entire essays. They help you decide in what order to present your supporting ideas.

When you use **climactic order**, you present your least important idea first and move toward your most important, most convincing idea. Or, you present simpler ideas first and move toward more complex ones. The overall effect of using climactic order is to build your essay toward an emphatic climax. Climactic order is especially effective for analytical and argumentative essays (see Chapters 6 and 7). When you use **time order**, you present your ideas in accordance with a time sequence, narrating how the ideas themselves developed or accounting for the actual order in which events occurred. Organizing the presentation of your ideas will ultimately depend on your subject, your evidence, your essay's purpose, and your sense of how your audience will respond. (See Chapters 5–7 on developing different kinds of essays, and 8d on organizing paragraphs.)

1   Outlining

Outlining can help you organize your essay and present your ideas in a way that allows your readers to see how the parts of your essay fit together coherently. Readers who do not have to pause to figure out what you mean or why you ordered your evidence in a particular way are likely to keep reading.

An outline is a visual representation of how you expect to organize your essay. Although the outline is used primarily to organize the difficult middle portion of your essay, you can also use it to organize an entire essay, depending on your needs and the essay's length and complexity.

An outline can also be useful while you are writing a first or preliminary draft. Even after you have written your first draft, an outline can help you see what you have discovered, assess the effectiveness of your organization, and ask questions about your audience, such as these:

- Can readers follow this development without difficulty?
- Do I need to make adjustments for readers, such as rearranging the order of my paragraphs, providing more details, or offering additional explanation?

There are two main types of outlines—informal and formal. An informal outline is a sketch consisting of a few key terms or phrases listed in an order that will guide you as you write or as you think about what you have written. This type of outline does not follow the conventions of a formal outline. (See 1f-2 for examples of two types of informal outlines.)

Outlines can also be detailed and formal, written out in complete sentences (a *sentence outline*) or with words and phrases (a *topic outline*) and organized into units that show the structure of every section of the essay. A **formal outline** reveals the logical relationships among the various sections of the essay; those relationships are only suggested by an informal outline.

The following example of a conventional formal outline shows how to organize major and subordinate headings. As you can see, major headings are designated by roman numerals, while subordinate headings are signaled by indented capital letters, arabic numbers, or lowercase letters. The headings indicate the level of importance of your ideas and evidence and their relationship with each other. Note that outline headings should always contain at least two parts (e.g., if you have an *A* heading you should also have a *B* heading).

FORMAL OUTLINE FORMAT
  Leading idea
  I. First major idea
     A. First supporting idea
        1. First illustration or explanation (your supporting evidence)
        2. Second illustration or explanation
     B. Second supporting idea
        1. First illustration or explanation
        2. Second illustration or explanation
        3. Third illustration or explanation
  II. Second major idea
     A. First supporting idea
        1. First illustration or explanation

    2. Second illustration or explanation
      a. First additional illustration or explanation
      b. Second additional illustration or explanation
  B. Second supporting idea

As the formal outline shows, a well-developed essay often has a hierarchy of ideas—a leading idea that you are presenting and developing, along with a number of supporting ideas that contribute to your readers' understanding of the leading idea. Each subordinate idea must be illustrated or explained by evidence that clarifies it. The relationship of each supporting idea to the leading idea must also be clear if your essay is to be persuasive and coherent.

2 Mapping

Some writers like to use an outline to begin thinking and getting organized, but others prefer to use a different method—a diagram that results from keeping up with the mind as it plays over a given subject. **Mapping** can lead to sketchy, informal outlines, to drafting, and then, perhaps, to a more formal outline that will accompany the final essay submitted to the instructor. (Instructors often require that a formal outline accompany a research essay.)

You begin mapping by choosing a piece of evidence—a quotation, a discovery from an experiment, a recollected experience, a cliché—and writing it in the center of a blank piece of paper. Then you begin to think about it, keeping track, mapping the mind's play as in the accompanying example. The sample *mind map* traces how one student, Robin Dumas, was motivated to write an essay about skiing. By mapping her thoughts about a cliché—"Nothing lasts forever"—she came up with a subject and a question she wanted to answer. She went directly from her mind map to an informal outline because she got an idea about teaching intermediate skiers how to ski moguls—the small mounds that form on a ski slope and present a challenge to skiers. Robin saw right away how to organize her thoughts, but she could just as well have started another mind map, beginning with the words *Of course,* placing that new starting point in the center of the map and venturing out to other discoveries about skiing as her mind played over her experiences. What you do and how you get organized depend on what works best for you.

Writers who prefer to begin with a mind map often say they find a linear outline too structured and confining. They want to explore their imagination and express their findings in a diagram. But an outline is not necessarily confining; it can be quite flexible. An outline, like a mind map, can help you get organized and discover ideas. In fact, mind maps and outlines are useful, complementary techniques.

Robin went from mapping to this informal outline:

Purpose: To convince the intermediate skier that mogul skiing is within reach
Moguls
Turning and sliding
Riding the troughs
Rhythm

After mapping and outlining, Robin wrote a preliminary draft and then re-constructed what she had written (to think about it) by outlining again. She recorded her concerns within the outline so she could consider them with her instructor when they met to discuss her draft.

Beginning: Introduce readers to the subject of mogul skiing and the essay's purpose--to convince the intermediate skier that mogul skiing is within reach. Define <u>moguls</u>.

Middle: Approaching the mogul--like stopping.
Initiating the turn, reaching for the sky--nothing new for an intermediate.
Compressing, sinking down to earth--a brief rest on the way up again.
Repeating the process--up, down, around.
Getting the rhythm--speed in the troughs.

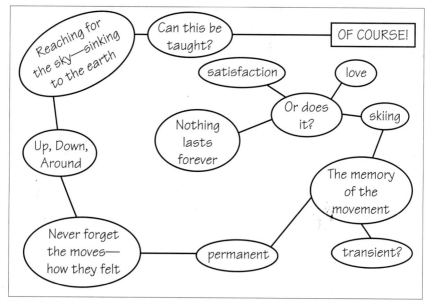

Example of a Mind Map

Concerns: Should I use sketches within my essay? Do I need photographs to illustrate each phase of the turning? How technical should the terms be? Do I need to get into the physics of it all?

Ending: Pull the essay together, emphasizing the ease of the transition from intermediate to expert. Point out the joys of skiing rather than the sore back and wobbly legs that follow. Reveal what it's like to sit in the lodge at the end of the day talking about skiing the bumps.

As you can see from Robin's more detailed informal outline, she has a good idea of how she intends to develop her essay. She will use this outline like a road map, aware that she will also navigate side roads and alternate routes to reach the final destination—a well-developed essay. She does not want to exclude alternate routes altogether, but, like all of us, she does want to be able to begin her essay with a clear sense of direction, reserving the right to change her course if necessary. Good writers know that changes in direction can lead to new insights and greater clarity.

Whether you prefer outlining or mapping to begin organizing an essay, you should always have three aims in mind: (1) to select appropriate evidence, (2) to organize your presentation effectively, and (3) to make your idea accessible to your readers. Often, outlining and mapping are combined with drafting (as in Robin's case) and revising.

EXERCISE 1–2   Mapping and Drafting

1. Select a cliché (*You can't teach an old dog new tricks; No pain, no gain; What can't be cured must be endured*) that you have been carrying around in your memory. Write it in the center of a blank piece of paper and circle it. Let your mind play over the cliché. Devise a mind map, keeping track of where your mind takes you, jotting down the thoughts and memories you associate with the cliché. Model your efforts on the mapping diagram in 1f.

2. Look at the evidence you recorded about your cliché on the mind map—your thoughts and associated memories—and see if you can form an idea, something new and fresh to say, about that old cliché (see 1c on evidence and ideas).

3. Write a draft paragraph about your idea.

1g   Drafting and revising

Writers almost never get the words right the first time. They are always drafting and revising. **Drafting** involves successive attempts to say what you mean and to say it clearly. **Revising** involves going over what you have written, rethinking it with an eye to whether your audience can understand you. Drafting and revising also lead to ideas (see 2b).

When you set out to write the draft of an essay, you are not trying to produce letter-perfect writing. It is to be expected that your punctuation and grammar might not be perfect and that your spelling may not always be correct. You will get a chance to fine-tune those details later in the writing process. You can make notations to correct any errors as you are revising. But deal with them when you edit and proofread your work (see 1i), not when you draft. When drafting, you want to write your way to a clear expression of your idea. This process takes time and, often, successive efforts. Trying to make everything perfect from the beginning will almost surely divert you from your larger purpose: developing your idea so that your readers can understand it. Because you are making discoveries even as you write, you should anticipate the need to revise. Nancy Sommers, a writing teacher and an authority on revision, calls her students' final essay "the last abandoned draft," emphasizing the recurring and, perhaps, never-ending need for revision.

You should always be writing to discover what you are thinking, writing to find your way. During your initial efforts to find an idea in your preliminary drafts, you may do no more than doodle, or you may write out elaborate notes; or you may just begin writing to find out what you are thinking, exploring as you write. You may use the ideas generated by your journal writing, freewriting, outlining, and mapping. Whatever your method, you will be reminded of a statement made earlier in this chapter: writing is a messy business. Much of it is preliminary and tentative. (For some examples of drafting and revising, see E. B. White's three revisions of a single paragraph in 4b and the student revisions of essays and parts of them in 5b-4, 6b-4, 6b-6, 7d-1, and 7d-2.)

Your first draft—your first effort to create the essay—is always an exploration, so you should expect to get off track. Your mind does not like to be controlled. Turn it loose with a pen in your hand or a keyboard at your fingertips, and you can expect it to take detours away from the main idea. Let that happen. Let your mind have free rein as you write the initial draft. (The accompanying Drafting and Revising Guidelines suggest what you should consider as you write. They also suggest how you might move from reading and thinking to writing and thinking, from drafting to revising, and back again.)

When you set your first draft aside for a few hours and return to it later to revise it, you can do so in a different frame of mind. Come back and ask probing questions: Does this draft make sense? Have I stayed on track? Was that diversion really illogical, or is there something in that wayward paragraph I need to think more about? As you read your draft, you will undoubtedly find problems: fuzzy sentences, a need for an illustration to help clarify a point, an important paragraph that needs to be moved, a connection that needs more explanation. You can also try reading your essay aloud; often you will become aware of errors that you could not spot reading silently. As you read aloud, you can also get a sense of whether your sentences flow well. A sentence that is hard to read aloud usually needs revising.

If you give your draft to a fellow student or collaborator to read, or talk about it with your instructor, you are likely to get additional insight about what you have done and what needs to be revised. Out of these helpful readings, you get direction for revising your draft and creating another one (see 1h, 4e, and 5b-1 on collaboration).

Revising leads to new writing and often results in reorganizing, more reading, gap filling—new drafts. As you draft and revise, you want to improve what you have already written. When you discover a gap in your explanation, you sometimes must do additional reading, which in turn leads to further reflection and additional changes. As you fill the gaps and make your presentation clearer, you can begin to pay attention to the way you use words, to the structure of your sentences, to the way in which your sentences flow from one to the other, and to the transitions between paragraphs. (See Chapter 28 on words, Part Six on sentence style, 8c on paragraph coherence, and 9c-2 on transitional paragraphs.)

How, then, you ask, does a writer know when to stop drafting and revising? There is no conclusive answer, but when you can say "yes" to the following questions, you have likely reached your final draft.

1. Can my readers follow my train of thought?
2. Have I made my points clearly and convincingly?
3. Have I included sufficient evidence to illustrate what I mean and to convince my readers?
4. Am I satisfied with what I have written?

Remember to refer to the Drafting and Revising Guidelines at this stage in the writing process.

Drafting and Revising Guidelines

- Read your first draft carefully, looking for signs of a good idea. Think about the evidence you have included in the draft. See what else it might suggest.

- As you read the first draft, think about your paragraphs. Can you see a clear relationship between each paragraph and the idea you are trying to develop in your essay? Are those relationships logical? (See Chapters 8 and 9 on paragraph development.)

- Pause over sentences that are not clear. Instead of editing out those sentences, stay with them. Create some space on your computer screen or on a piece of paper and write out what those confusing sentences make you think about. Then revise for clarity. (See Part Six on sentence style.)

- Consider key words in your draft. Will your readers know what they mean, or do you need to define them? Check the dictionary for the meanings of words and then revise if necessary. (See Part Seven on words.)

(continued)

- Begin another draft, taking your direction from the idea you discovered in the first draft. Think more about your audience now. Try to explain and develop your idea for that audience. Use the Audience Checklist. Think about whether a change in tone may help you interest and convince your audience. (See 1d-3 on tone.)

- As you write, pause occasionally to let your mind make connections with new evidence that occurs to you. Write about those connections to find out what they might have to do with the idea you are developing.

- Question your evidence. Consider what it might mean to someone whose ideas may differ from yours. (See 4a on questioning.)

- Stop. Put the draft aside for a few hours or, if you can, for a few days. Get some distance from your writing, and then reread what you have written. Think about the relationship between your evidence and your idea. Clarify wherever you can.

- If you have work groups in class, ask the group to read your draft and identify its strengths and weaknesses. If you do not have a work group, ask a classmate to read the draft. (See 1h and 4e on collaboration.)

- Write other drafts if you still need to clarify your thinking.

1h   Collaborating

During the processes of drafting and revising, you can benefit from the help of your instructor and your classmates—in the form of **collaboration**. Your instructor can assist you as you draft and revise, responding occasionally to your drafts and helping you answer tough questions and make important decisions. Your instructor may also ask you to do collaborative writing in a work group in class so that you and your classmates can help each other become better writers. You might work in a small group within the class at times specified by your instructor, or on a one-to-one basis outside of class, reading and responding to each other's writing. Nothing can spur you on like a friendly but critical collaborator who is willing to give you an honest reaction to your writing. That collaborator can save you the misery of self-doubt by pointing out strengths in what you have done. That person can also help you identify troubling gaps in your writing and offer constructive suggestions for improvement. Most writers thrive on collaborative feedback.

Writing is a lonely act only up to a certain point. Few good writers stay isolated from readers during the entire process. Collaboration can bring you out of hiding and remind you that you are writing for an audience, that there is someone outside your head who wants to understand what is going on inside.

The accompanying Guidelines for Collaboration will help you provide feedback about written texts. (Also see 1d-2 on audience feedback and 4e on collaboration as a way of developing ideas.)

Guidelines for Collaboration

- Work in a small group of two to five students so that everyone has a chance to be heard. Your task is to provide feedback to the other writers—a genuine response to what you have read. That feedback can be about ideas, about the cited evidence, or about the overall effectiveness of the student's text.

- Write the word *nice* in the margin or insert a check mark (✓) to identify the most satisfying parts of the essay: a fine sentence, a telling detail, a good paragraph, an arresting line of dialogue, a sentence or two that give you a clear sense of the essay's meaning.

- In the margin of the paper, write the word *gap* where you believe you need more information. If you are confused at some point, write a brief marginal note explaining what troubles you.

- Write specific questions in the margin as you read: *What do you mean? Please explain. What does this passage or this paragraph have to do with your leading idea?*

- Always write a note to the student (at the bottom of the page or on the reverse side) saying what you think the essay is about. Try to restate the essay's idea in your own words, whether that idea is expressed explicitly or implicitly.

- Offer constructive comments about how you think the essay could be revised. Refer back to the gaps or your marginal questions.

- Remember that as a collaborator, you are serving as both audience and editor—offering advice and feedback about your reaction to the essay. Be friendly and evenhanded, but talk back, giving your writer a chance to hear an audience response.

1i   Editing and proofreading

Once you have a typed final draft, you should edit and proofread it to identify and correct errors that might distract your readers. Surface errors in your writing are quite different from the problems you address while drafting and revising your essay. These surface errors have to do with grammar, spelling, usage, punctuation, mechanics, and format rather than with the

Editing Guidelines

Editing is important. Take time with it. Do not rush. When you are editing, check for the following types of errors. Refer to the chapters indicated for more information.

- Check your grammar (Chapters 10–16).
- Check your sentences (Chapters 17–26).
   —Do you avoid sentence errors such as fragments (Chapter 17) and misplaced and dangling modifiers (Chapter 19)?
   —Are your sentences parallel (Chapter 24), varied (Chapter 25), and concise (Chapter 26)?
- Check the appropriateness of the words you use (Chapter 28).
   —Do you avoid biased language (Chapter 29)?
   —Are all words spelled correctly (Chapter 31)?
- Check your use of punctuation marks (Chapters 32–37).
- Check your use of capitalization, italics, abbreviations, numbers, and hyphens (Chapters 38–42).

How to Proofread

- Carefully read the final draft, line by line.
- Use a ruler to help you stay focused on individual sentences and words rather than on your idea and how it is expressed.
- Try reading backward to stay focused on the details.
- Check the final draft against the edited draft, sentence by sentence.
- Read the final draft aloud to hear and detect any remaining errors.

During this final stage of proofreading, look for omitted words or letters, misspellings, punctuation errors, illegible type, and anything that does not look neat. Retype or reprint the essay if you find too many errors. See Appendix A for information on preparing and formatting the final draft.

more conceptual revision of your idea. During **editing** you read specifically to identify and correct surface errors; in **proofreading** you ensure that you have corrected those errors and that your final draft is in near-perfect shape. The accompanying guidelines will help you with these tasks.

If you use a computer when you are writing your paper, edit first on the computer screen using the computer's special features, such as the spell checker. (See Chapter 50 for more information about computer assistance when editing.) Then check the printed copy of your paper for errors. You can often spot mistakes in the printed copy that you did not notice on the computer screen.

EXERCISE 1–3   Revising and Collaborating

1. After setting it aside for a few hours or a day, look at your paragraph from Exercise 1–2. Reread it, and think about what you could change to make it easier for someone else to understand your idea. Make those revisions.

2. Write a letter to a friend explaining your idea. In the letter, try to interest your friend in the idea. Finally, ask for feedback: What do you like about the idea? Is it confusing? Did I convince you about my idea?

CHAPTER 2

Critical Reading

*T*he reading you do in college most often is critical reading; it requires careful analysis and thoughtful response. More specifically, **critical reading** involves reacting to what you read, analyzing it, interpreting it, and evaluating its ideas and assessing its values. The word *critical* in this approach to reading does not mean "being critical of" in the familiar sense of disapproval. Critical reading is more encompassing than this, involving a wider range of possible judgments and a deeper sense of understanding. This chapter provides an approach to reading that incorporates the major aspects of critical reading that are outlined in the accompanying chart.

Critical Reading: An Overview

- Adjusting to different kinds of reading material (2a)
- Writing while reading to record your reactions and reflections (2b)
- Analyzing the texts you read—observing details and connecting them (2c)
- Interpreting texts by making inferences and drawing conclusions (2d)
- Evaluating texts by judging their quality and considering their ideas and values (2e)
- Discussing your reading with others (2f)
- Reading reflectively (2g)
- Interpreting a text: an example (2h)

 2a   Adjusting to different kinds of texts

Reading a written text critically requires knowing what kind of work you are reading. Your expectations and response derive from the nature of the text you are reading and your purpose in reading it. Different kinds of texts require different ways of reading. You may skim a magazine article to pick up essential information.

You may read a popular novel swiftly to discover what happens. You read your textbooks more slowly, taking time to absorb information, understand concepts, and consider questions. You read a newspaper editorial or an article in a serious journal carefully to analyze its argument and evaluate the evidence used to support it.

In the same way that we analyze a written text we can analyze the constructed "text" of an object, an action, a work of art, or a historical event. Thus a **text** can be something made or socially constructed, something that happens, as well as something written. Texts include works of art such as paintings, drawings, sculptures, and architectural monuments. They also include historical events, such as the Vietnam War. And they include other kinds of actions and events such as sports contests, beauty pageants, social celebrations (such as wedding ceremonies and receptions), and public ceremonies (such as presidential inaugurations).

Later chapters will demonstrate techniques of analysis suited to interpreting unwritten texts (see 6c and 47b). A number of these analytical skills are analogous to those you use in reading a written text. For now, we will consider what happens when you read a written text.

You may read to collect information, to analyze, or to develop an argument. The students whose essays appear in Chapters 5–7 (on writing different types of essays) and in Chapter 44 (on writing research essays) read at different speeds and with varying degrees of deliberateness, depending on where they were in the writing or research process.

You take a slightly different approach to reading stories and poems than to reading informative essays and popular and scientific articles in periodicals. Fiction and expository prose make their points in different ways. Whereas expository writing presents ideas directly, fiction does so indirectly. In expository prose, the writer's ideas are usually stated and described explicitly. But in fiction you must often infer a writer's implied idea or interpret the meaning of a story or novel. Although you need to analyze and interpret both kinds of writing to some extent, you should expect to do more interpretative work, and thus spend more time, when you read imaginative literature. (See also Chapter 47.)

Complex material may require more than one reading. Rereading can take a number of forms. You might simply review a textbook chapter's major sections. Or you might reread one particularly complicated passage of a text. Or you might read an entire text a second (or even a third or a fourth) time, concentrating more on analyzing and assessing the work than on simply understanding its central idea. This is so whether the text is something actually written, or whether it is an object or an event you are interpreting.

2b   Writing from reading

You can expect much of your college reading to lead to writing assignments such as essays, research papers, and reports. To develop those assignments, it helps to write both while and after you read. React to what you read by making marginal notes or annotations (only if you own the text, of course). Afterward, do some reflective writing, such as freewriting. Either keep a double-column notebook or a reading journal, or write a summary. The kind of writing you do will be determined by your purpose. But whatever your purpose, you can begin responding to what you read by using the following writing techniques.

1 Reacting to a text with annotations

Annotations are brief notes you write about a text while reading it. You can underline and circle words and phrases that strike you as important. You can highlight passages. You can make marginal comments that reflect your attitude toward the text. Your annotations might also include arrows that identify related points, question marks that indicate your confusion, and exclamation marks to express your surprise. Annotations can be single words or brief phrases; they can be statements, exclamations, or questions. Depending on how extensively you annotate a text, your annotations may form a secondary text that reminds you of the text you are reading. Annotations used this way serve as an abbreviated outline of what the text says and what you think about it.

As you read the following passage, notice the various types of annotations and add some of your own.

Is beauty really essential? Seems exaggerated. Society defines norms of beauty. Women are pushed into overconcern with their appearance. Contrast: men _do_ well; women _look_ good.

To be called beautiful is thought to name something essential to women's character and concerns. (In contrast to men—whose essence is to be strong, or effective, or competent.) It does not take someone in the throes of advanced feminist awareness to perceive that the way women are taught to be involved with beauty encourages narcissism, reinforces dependence and immaturity. Everybody (women and men) knows that. For it is "everybody," a whole society, that has identified being feminine with caring about how one looks. (In contrast to being masculine—which is identified with caring about what one _is_ and _does_ and only secondarily, if at all, about how one looks.)

· · · ·

Contrast: _desire_ for beauty versus _obligation_ to be beautiful. Sontag politicizes the issue—beauty as means of oppression. Women + beauty = body parts.

It is not, of course, the desire to be beautiful that is wrong but the obligation to be—or to try. What is accepted by most women as a flattering idealization of their sex is a way of making women feel inferior to what they actually are—or normally grow to be. For the ideal of beauty is administered as a form of self-oppression. Women are taught to see their bodies in _parts_, and to evaluate each part separately. Breasts, feet, hips, waistline, neck, eyes, nose, complexion, hair, and so on—each in turn is submitted to an anxious, fretful, often despairing scrutiny. Even if some pass muster, some will always be found wanting.

· · · ·

<table>
<tr>
<td>

Doesn't author
exaggerate here
about perfection?
Nice distinction
here on beauty
and the sexes.

</td>
<td>

   In men, good looks is a whole, something taken in at a   3
glance. It does not need to be confirmed by giving measure-
ments of different regions of the body; nobody encourages a
man to dissect his appearance, feature by feature. As for perfec-
tion, that is considered trivial—almost unmanly.

</td>
</tr>
</table>

—Susan Sontag, "A Woman's Beauty:
Put-Down or Power Source?"

The types of annotations used most often include the following:

1. Restating the language of the text
2. Asking questions about the text
3. Challenging the text's ideas or details
4. Comparing and contrasting the text with other things

2   Reflecting on a text in freewriting

   Your initial impressions of a text, which you can record with annotations, will often lead you to further thoughts about it. You can develop these thoughts with **freewriting**. Like annotating, freewriting is an invention technique that serves as a source of ideas for writing. In freewriting, you record your ideas, reactions, or feelings about a text without arranging them in any special order. You simply write down what you think about the passage, without worrying about spelling or grammar. The point is to get your ideas down on paper and not to censor or judge your ideas prematurely. Freewriting, in fact, offers you a way to pursue an idea, to develop your thinking to see where it may lead.

   Both annotation and freewriting precede the more intricate and deliberative work of analysis, interpretation, and evaluation (see 2c–e). Annotation and freewriting also provide a convenient way to prepare for writing essays, papers, and reports. These two informal techniques work well together; the brief, quickly noted reactions of annotation complement the more leisurely paced reflections of freewriting.

   Here is an example of one reader's freewriting about the preceding annotated passage by Susan Sontag. Notice how the writer uses the freewriting exercise to reflect on and ask questions about the passage.

Example of Freewriting

   Interesting questions. Women do seem to think more about their looks than men do. But since it's men women wish to please by looking good, men may be responsible (some? much?) for women's obsession with appearance. How far have women bought into the beauty myth? How far are they responsible for obsessing about beauty? How about money and profit? And at whose expense?

   Why don't men <u>need</u> to be beautiful? To please parents--employers? To attract a mate? To be considered "normal"? Sontag says that beauty is irrelevant to men--

men judged by different measures--strength, effectiveness, competence. She doesn't mention power, money, status. She leaves things out--intelligence and moral qualities, kindness, decency, generosity. How important are these?

Distinction between <u>desiring</u> to be beautiful (perhaps to be desired or admired) and <u>needing</u> to be. There's nothing wrong with women wanting to be attractive, to look their best. The problem occurs when desire becomes <u>obligation</u>, wasting women's talents, minimizes them, keeps them subservient.

Parts and whole--are women concerned with <u>parts</u> of their bodies--certain parts? Their overall appearance? Their sense of self? Silicone breast implants? Cosmetic surgery generally? (But: men have nose jobs, facelifts, even pectoral implants.) Men are concerned with <u>some</u> parts of their bodies more than others.

What about the words used to describe good-looking women--or good-looking men? A "beautiful" woman but a "handsome" man. A "foxy" lady, a "gorgeous" woman (guy?), an "attractive" girl, a ??? And what of men? "Handsome" does most of the work. So too does "good-looking." Though we also have "pretty boy" and "hunk"--derogatory? Hmm. Statuesque? Powerfully built? A real he-man?

EXERCISE 2–1 Annotating and Freewriting

Annotate one of the following passages. Then develop your initial thoughts about the passage by freewriting.

1. Americans are at last realizing that the acquisition of goods is not the whole of life. Consumption, on one level, is turning insipid, especially as the quality of the artifacts themselves seems to be deteriorating. On another level, consumption is turning sour. There is a growing guilt about the masses of discarded junk—rusting automobiles and refrigerators and washing machines and dehumidifiers—that it is uneconomical to recycle. Indestructible plastic hasn't even the grace to undergo chemical change. America, the world's biggest consumer, is the world's biggest polluter. Awareness of this is a kind of redemptive grace, but it doesn't appreciably lead to repentance and a revolution in consumer habits.

   —Anthony Burgess, "Is America Falling Apart?"

2. I am a cripple. I choose this word to name me. I choose from among several possibilities, the most common of which are "handicapped" and "disabled." I made the choice a number of years ago, without thinking, unaware of my motives for doing so. Even now, I'm not sure what those motives are, but I recognize that they are complex and not entirely flattering. People—crippled or not—wince at the word "cripple," as they do not at "handicapped" or "disabled." Perhaps I want them to wince. . . .

As a lover of words, I like the accuracy with which it describes my condition: I have lost the full use of my limbs. "Disabled," by contrast, suggests any incapacity, physical or mental. And I certainly don't like "handicapped," which implies that I have deliberately been put at a disadvantage, by whom I can't imagine (my God is not a Handicapper General), in order to equalize chances in the great race of life. These words seem to me to be moving away from my condition, to be widening the gap between word and reality.

—Nancy Mairs, "On Being a Cripple"

3   Using a double-column notebook

To create a **double-column notebook**, simply divide your page in half. One half is for summarizing (see 2b-4) and interpreting what you read. Use this side of the page to record as accurately as you can your understanding of what the text says. Use the other side to respond to what you have read, to think about its implications, and to relate it to other things you have read or otherwise experienced.

The advantage of a double-column notebook is that it encourages you to be an active reader, to think about what you read and to make connections with your reading and experience rather than to consider a text in isolation. You can use the double-column notebook to think further about your earlier reactions, which you may have recorded in annotations or freewriting, and to sustain a conversation with the writer and with yourself. The accompanying chart outlines how to use a double-column notebook.

Highlights of the Double-Column Notebook

SUMMARY	COMMENTS
Summarize the text.	Respond to your summary.
Interpret the author's ideas.	Reflect on the author's ideas.
Explain the ideas succinctly.	Consider whether you agree or disagree—and why.
Identify important details.	Raise questions about the details you have observed.
Relate the details to the central idea.	Relate the text and the writer's main idea to other things you have read and to your own experience.

To get a better idea of how the double-column notebook is used, first read this passage from an essay by Katherine Anne Porter, and then examine the sample double-column notes that follow. Notice how one side of the two-column notebook summarizes and interprets Porter's idea and how the other side raises questions, offers judgments, and makes connections.

Adventure is sometimes fun, but not too often. Not if you can remember what really happened; all of it. It passes, seems to lead nowhere much, is something to tell friends to amuse them, maybe. "Once upon a time," I can hear myself saying, for I once said it, "I scaled a cliff in Boulder, Colorado, with my bare hands, and in Indian moccasins, bare-legged. And at nearly the top, after six hours of feeling for toe- and fingerholds, and the gayest feeling in the world that when I got to the top I should see something wonderful, something that sounded awfully like a bear growled out of a cave, and I scuttled down out of there in a hurry." This is a fact. I had never climbed a mountain in my life, never had the least wish to climb one. But there I was, for perfectly good reasons, in a hut on a mountainside in heavenly sunny though sometimes stormy weather, so I went out one morning and scaled a very minor cliff; alone, unsuitably clad, in the season when rattlesnakes are casting their skins; and if it was not a bear in that cave, it was some kind of unfriendly animal who growls at people; and this ridiculous escapade, which was nearly six hours of the hardest work I ever did in my life, toeholds and fingerholds on a cliff, put me to bed for just nine days with a complaint the local people called "muscle poisoning." I don't know exactly what they meant, but I do remember clearly that I could not turn over in bed without help and in great agony. . . .

I think it is a pastime of rather an inferior sort; yet I have heard men tell yarns like this only a very little better: their mountains were higher, or their sea was wider, or their bear was bigger and noisier, or their cliff was steeper and taller, yet there was no point whatever to any of it except that it had happened. This is not enough. May it not be, perhaps, that experience, that is, the thing that happens to a person living from day to day, is anything at all that sinks in? is, without making any claims, a part of your growing and changing life? what it is that happens in your mind, your heart?

—Katherine Anne Porter, "St. Augustine and the Bullfight"

EXERCISE 2–2 Beginning a Double-Column Notebook

Create your own double-column notebook by following Highlights of the Double-Column Notebook. You may use a passage from a reading required for one of your courses or choose a reading selection from this book. Then consider how your double-column notebook entries might prepare you to write an essay or report.

SUMMARY	*COMMENTS*
Porter argues that adventure is not very much fun, not much of it, and not most of the time. She criticizes her mountain-climbing experience by saying that she didn't learn anything from it and that it caused physical pain.	Perhaps she means that adventures provide only the illusion of fun. They are not fun when they occur; we make them fun only in retrospect. After all we invested time, money, energy, etc. in "having" those adventures.
Porter adds a twist: that many people's adventures do not really differ from hers. She suggests that the differences are of <u>degree</u> rather than of <u>kind</u>.	Her tone here is strongly condemnatory. Is she fair in reducing adventure to "climbing things"? My adventures, good and bad, involve more than this.
Adventure is only what <u>happens</u>, not what the happening <u>means</u>. For Porter, adventure alone is never enough. That is, adventure is only an external experience, which Porter distinguishes from <u>real</u> experience, what happens <u>after</u> the adventure is over. This real experience is not physical, but intellectual and emotional.	Her tone at times seems hesitant, questioning, as if she is thinking things out rather than insisting on her views. Yet she seems to believe what she is saying. Is this part of her persuasive strategy? Her concern with <u>real</u> experience links up with the idea that wisdom and maturity derive from reflecting on what happens to us.
Experience for Porter changes the mind and affects the heart and spirit. But adventure changes nothing—though it is the raw material that can be converted to real experience.	If this is the case, then isn't Porter being somewhat hard on <u>mere</u> adventure? If she converts adventure into <u>real</u> experience, hasn't she then redeemed adventure after all?
Experience is a way of seeing—a kind of perspective that leads to understanding.	Compare Porter's idea with Annie Dillard's on "Seeing" from <u>Pilgrim at Tinker Creek</u>?

Sample Double-Column Notebook

4   **Writing a summary**

A **summary** is a compressed version of a text in which you explain the author's meaning in your own words. You summarize a text when you need to give your readers the gist of what it says. A summary should present the author's text accurately and represent his or her views fairly. You build your summary on the observations, connections, and inferences you make while reading. Although there is no rule for how long or short a summary should be, a summary of a text is always shorter than the text itself.

Writing a summary requires careful reading, in part to assure that you understand a text well. Writing a summary helps you respond to a text by requiring you to analyze and consider its details. Your goal in summarizing a text is to render a writer's ideas accurately and fairly.

A **paraphrase,** which is similar to a summary, tends to be nearly as long as the text paraphrased. When you paraphrase a poem, for example, you explain its meaning in your own words, line by line or stanza by stanza. Unlike a summary, a paraphrase follows the order of ideas, images, and details in the original text. For more on summarizing and paraphrasing, see Chapter 44.

Writing a summary requires essentially two kinds of skills: identifying the idea of the text you are summarizing and recognizing the evidence that supports that idea. One strategy for writing a summary is to find the key points that support the main idea. You can do this by looking for clusters of sentences or groups of paragraphs that convey the writer's meaning. Because paragraphs work together, you cannot simply summarize each paragraph independently. You may need to summarize a cluster of paragraphs to convey the idea of a text effectively. (See Chapter 9 on how paragraphs work together.)

The accompanying chart explains what you need to do.

How to Write a Summary

1. Read the text carefully, looking for the main idea and important supporting points.
2. Write a sentence that identifies the writer's main idea.
3. Write a few sentences that explain the key supporting points from different paragraphs or paragraph clusters.
4. Write a draft of your summary by putting together the sentences you wrote for steps 1–3, in the order you wrote them.
5. Revise your summary by adding transitional words and phrases to link your sentences. Add introductory and concluding sentences as necessary.

Here is an example of the process at work on the passage about women's beauty by Susan Sontag (pp. 26–27).

General idea of passage: Women are seen as superficial and trivial, concerned with surface beauty rather than with deeper qualities of character. Women are viewed as beautiful objects, valued for how they look rather than for who and what they are.

Key supporting points:
- Women's preoccupation with their beauty is a sign of their self-absorption and inconsequentiality.
- Women's concern for beauty is a form of enslavement that results from their need to always care about their appearance, all the while being objectified as mere body parts.
- Men are less concerned about their appearance, especially with trying to perfect their outward look.

To create a smooth summary from these sentences, it is necessary to add introductory and concluding sentences. Transitional wording is also needed. Basically, however, you can follow the order devised for the passage as reflected in the sentences for the main idea and key supporting points.

Here is a revised version that avoids direct quotation from the original text. Also avoided are opinions or judgmental words and phrases. Notice, too, how the writer and text are identified in the opening sentence.

Revised Summary

In her essay "A Woman's Beauty: Put-Down or Power Source?" Susan Sontag explains how women's need to appear beautiful trivializes them, making them concerned with superficial appearances and identifying them as creatures preoccupied with how they look rather than who and what they really are. Sontag suggests that women's preoccupation with physical beauty is a sign of their self-absorption and lack of power. Through being taught to see themselves as mere body parts, women become both objectified and ridden with anxiety that their parts may not measure up. Unlike women, men are viewed for their good looks overall rather than for the beauty of their particular parts. Also unlike women, men are perceived as more serious, more sure of themselves, and more powerful than the women who anxiously labor to be beautiful to please them.

A final note: When you are working with readings for a research essay or project, you have a choice of summarizing, paraphrasing, and quoting the text. For advice about deciding when to summarize, paraphrase, or quote, see 44i.

EXERCISE 2–3   Writing a Summary

Write a summary of Katherine Anne Porter's comments about adventures on p. 30. (See 2b-3.)

2c   **Analyzing what you read**

After reacting to a text with annotations, reflecting on it in freewriting, and perhaps summarizing it or recording your thoughts about it in a double-column notebook, you can return to it for further analysis. When you **analyze** a text, you isolate and look closely at its parts (the beginning, middle, and ending of an essay or article, for example, or the sequence of events in a story). You focus on one element at a time, observing its details. Then you look for connections and relationships among those details. Your goal in analyzing a text is to understand it, to see how its parts fit together to make sense as a whole.

Your analysis of a text can only be as good as the evidence that supports it. And that evidence begins with what you notice or observe in the text. It is crucial, then, to learn to look carefully, to notice details, and to make accurate observations about the texts you read.

1   Observing details

The kinds of observations you make about a text will depend upon the kind of text you are reading. If you are reading a scientific report, you will observe its argument and the evidence that supports it. If you are reading a psychological abstract, you will attend to the purpose and limits of the study as well as to the kind of field research it may involve. In reading literary works (see 47a–b), you will consider such elements as diction and imagery (especially for poetry), character and conflict (especially for fiction and drama), and style and structure. Your instructor may also encourage you to focus on particular features of a text.

Here are some observations you might make about the Sontag piece.

- Sontag focuses throughout on surface beauty—on appearance.
- She distinguishes between beauty in women and men.
- She sees women's obsession with beauty as dangerous.
- She describes men as strong and competent.
- She italicizes certain words.
- She places some sentences in parentheses.
- She puts certain words in quotation marks.
- She punctuates heavily with dashes.

Look back at the passage about beauty by Susan Sontag (2b-1). Make your own observations about the ideas in Sontag's comments; select one sentence in each paragraph that crystallizes her thought. Next, make stylistic observations about Sontag's sentences: their type, length, and forms. Observe how Sontag punctuates her sentences and how she begins and ends paragraphs. Notice the kinds of observations you make when looking at different details in the passage. You might decide to consider the effects of such stylistic and rhetorical choices on the passage as a whole.

2   Connecting the details

It is not enough, however, simply to observe details about a text. You must also connect them with one another. To make a connection is to see one thing in relation to another. You may notice that some details reinforce others, or that the writer repeats certain words. Perhaps the writer sets up a contrast (as Sontag contrasts women's and men's attitudes toward beauty). Perhaps the writer uses personal experience as part of the evidence to develop or support an idea, as Betsy Miller does in her essay in Chapter 5. Or perhaps the writer relates something previously read to his or her experience, as Zack Wolfe does in his essay in 7e.

While you are noticing aspects of a text, you can also begin making connections among its details. Your goal is to see how the connected details help you make sense of the text as a whole. One way to do this is to group information in lists (see 47a-2) or in outline form (see 1f-1). This involves setting up categories or headings for related details. In reading the Susan Sontag passage, for example, you could create heads for "men" and "women" or for "style" and "ideas," and then group related details under them. Notice, for example, how the preceding list of observations can be divided in these ways (i.e., the first four items concern Sontag's ideas and the last four her style).

In addition, you should reread a text. Upon rereading, you may discover details you had not noticed on your initial reading and deepen your understanding of the text.

Making observations about a text and establishing connections among them form the basis of analysis. From that basis you begin to consider the significance of what you observe and proceed to develop an interpretation.

EXERCISE 2–4   **Making Observations and Connections**

Choose either the passage by Susan Sontag or the one by Katherine Anne Porter and make at least two new observations about it. Relate these observations to one another or to any you made earlier. As you begin to group your observations, identify the connections that emerge.

2d   Formulating an interpretation

An **interpretation** is your tentative or provisional conclusion about a text based on your analysis of it (your observations and connections). To arrive at an interpretation, you need to make inferences based on your observations. An **inference** is a statement you make based on what you have observed. You infer a writer's idea or point of view, for instance, from the examples and evidence he or she provides. Inferences drive the interpretative process. They push you beyond making observations toward explaining them and the text. Without drawing inferences you will not be able to arrive at an interpretation based on textual evidence. (For additional discussions of inference making, see 4a-1, 3d-1, and 3d-2.)

1   Making inferences

You make inferences in everyday life all the time, and there is nothing mysterious about the process of making them. If you see someone at 8 a.m. with a large ring of keys opening a classroom door in a university building, you may infer that he or she is a member of the school staff whose job it is to unlock classroom doors. You may, of course, be right or wrong about your inference, but you will have made a reasonable inference nonetheless.

The same is true when you make inferences about a text. Your inferences are a way of understanding the text by "reading between the lines," by discovering what is implied rather than explicitly stated.

The freewriting about the Sontag passage (2b-2) contains examples of inferences. Here are a few additional inferences a reader could draw from the Sontag passage.

- Sontag thinks the double standard by which women are judged for their beauty and men by other qualities is wrong (paragraph 1).
- She implies that few women can meet the high standards for beauty that society imposes (paragraph 2).
- She seems to approve of the way masculine beauty is considered as a sum of each feature of a man's appearance and implies that this would be better for women as well (paragraph 3).

Sontag does not say any of these things explicitly, but readers might infer them. Remember that an inference can be right or wrong, and thus different readers might debate the reliability of these or other inferences. The important thing is not to be afraid to make an inference because you think a particular inference might be challenged or questioned. Critical reading involves thinking. Thinking involves making inferences. Making inferences and thinking about what you read help you arrive at an interpretation of a text. This, ultimately, is your goal as a reader—to understand what the writer says explicitly and to determine what he or she further implies.

2   Arriving at an interpretation

The step from drawing inferences to arriving at an interpretation is small. An interpretation is a way of explaining the meaning of a text; it represents your way of understanding the text expressed as an idea. You might interpret Katherine Anne Porter's text (2b-3), for example, in the following way.

> Porter reexamines the meaning of the concept of "adventure" and argues that what are normally considered adventures are nothing of the sort, and that instead real adventures are experiences that affect us psychologically or intellectually.

This interpretation can be debated, and it can be further explained and elaborated. But in making such an interpretation of Porter's text, you would base it on the inferences you made when you read it.

Your goal in interpreting any text is to understand it so that you can explain its meaning accurately. Informative texts, such as newspaper reports about current events or textbook material about scientific processes, require factual understanding and accuracy. Literary texts demand accurate observations and defensible inferences. Persuasive interpretations are characterized by these qualities.

When you arrive at an interpretation, look back at the text's details to reconsider your initial observations as well as to review the connections you established to see if they still make sense. Consider whether your inferences are defensible—that is, whether you can offer support on their behalf. Look also to see if additional details can support your inferences, or whether you wish to make different inferences that may lead to another interpretation. Remember that you can alter your understanding of a text; you can revise your interpretation of it.

You may decide later, in fact, to interpret the text differently. In looking back at the Sontag passage (2b-1), for example, you might notice that the writer mentions society's responsibility for foisting certain ideals of beauty upon women. In thinking about the implications of that observation, you might make other inferences, which will lead you to an interpretation of Sontag's passage that emphasizes her attitude toward a society that forces such an ideal of beauty upon women. You arrive at your idea about the text's meaning (whether your original interpretation or a later revised one) by reaching a conclusion based on your inferences. These inferences, in turn, are based on your observations about the text and the connections you make among those observations. The accompanying chart presents an overview of the interpretive process—from observation to interpretive conclusion.

Steps to Interpretation

- Make observations about the details of a text (2c-1).
- Relate your observations, looking for connections (2c-2).
- Develop inferences based on the related observations (2d-1).
- Arrive at an interpretation based on your inferences (2d-2).

2e   Evaluating a text

In reading to interpret, you give the author a chance to make a point or to develop an idea without judging the merit of that point or the value of that idea. You thus recognize the writer's meaning as paramount and your primary aim to understand what the writer says. In reading to **evaluate**, however, you want to both understand and assess the writer's idea. If you find yourself disagreeing with the writer's idea, you may refuse to accept other dimensions of the text, including the values it reflects.

Evaluating a text involves making judgments about it. You consider its effectiveness, and you assess the cultural values it embodies. When you evaluate a text, then, you make two kinds of judgments: one about quality, the other about values.

Your evaluation of a text grows out of your interpretation of it. To make fair and reasoned judgments about a text, you first need to be clear about what it says. You can evaluate the quality of a text only after you understand its meaning. And you can evaluate the cultural values of a text only after you understand the cultural values it embodies or promotes.

Evaluating a text requires more than interpreting it reasonably. You also need to be alert to your own personal and cultural values. This is so in part because evaluation is affected by your likes and dislikes, by what appeals to you or repels you, as well as by your knowledge of what the text reveals. Your evaluation of a text may also be entangled with your feelings about its subject.

Consider the following brief passage by Ernest Hemingway, a vignette based on a war experience.

> While the bombardment was knocking the trench to pieces at Fossalta, he lay very flat and sweated and prayed oh jesus christ get me out of here. Dear jesus please get me out. Christ please please please christ. If you'll only keep me from getting killed I'll do anything you say. I believe in you and I'll tell every one in the world that you are the only one that matters. Please please dear jesus. The shelling moved further up the line. We went to work on the trench and in the morning the sun came up and the day was hot and muggy, and cheerful and quiet. The next night back at Mestre he did not tell the girl he went upstairs with at the Villa Rossa about Jesus. And he never told anybody.
>
> —Ernest Hemingway, *In Our Time*

In the process of interpreting this passage, consider your personal response to the events it describes. If you are repelled by the soldier's behavior, ask yourself why. Is it because he acts cowardly? Is it because he prays out of desperation? Is it because once out of danger he forgets his promise, or because he visits a prostitute? Perhaps you are not bothered by his behavior or by his language. Do not be surprised if your reaction to this text differs from the reactions of others—in fact, be prepared for it. Every reader has a unique perspective on what a text reveals and a unique set of personal values to bring to Hemingway's text.

Here is one reader's evaluation of the Hemingway passage. The evaluation includes judgments about both its effectiveness and the cultural and moral values the text suggests.

Evaluation

In his brief vignette from In Our Time, Ernest Hemingway describes some realities of war. The young soldier in the trenches is terrified of the artillery shells exploding near the trench, where he lies praying to God for deliverance. Instead of behaving heroically or courageously, the young soldier bargains desperately with God. His behavior is far from the ideal not only in the way he prays, but also in the way he breaks his promise. He is neither courageous nor honest. And his visit to a prostitute degrades the ideal of love as his earlier behavior degraded the ideals of war and faith.

The image of war Hemingway describes in the vignette is brutally realistic. He avoids glorifying war or idealizing the soldier's behavior. And yet even though some may find the soldier's behavior repugnant, Hemingway does not explicitly condemn that behavior. In fact, it might be argued that he helps readers understand the young soldier's predicament. His visit to the prostitute, given the circumstances, is convincing. The passage brings readers into the soldier's mind so they can understand how he feels. In its refusal to idealize war, it convinces us of its truth.

Evaluating this vignette or any text is not easy. Readers will disagree about both the cultural values this passage displays and about how well the writer has described the soldier's predicament. Readers will disagree in their judgments of the soldier, some finding his behavior inexcusable and morally reprehensible, others finding it neither extraordinary nor troubling—given the situation. Making your own judgments about the text is what is important. Equally important, however, is to make those judgments responsibly, by grounding your evaluation in a thoughtful consideration of meaning. (For more on interpreting and evaluating literary works, art works, and other kinds of texts, see Chapter 47.)

The accompanying Guidelines for Evaluation, along with the Steps to Interpretation (p. 37), will help you improve your ability to read critically. They will also help develop your ability to think critically.

Guidelines for Evaluation

- Consider your initial reaction to the text and why you react as you do.
- Interpret the text, using the Steps to Interpretation.
- Decide whether you agree with what the text argues or illustrates.
- Identify and respond to the cultural values the text presents.
- Decide whether the text relates an idea or an experience effectively.

EXERCISE 2–5   **Evaluating a Text**

Write one paragraph identifying the cultural values in the Sontag or the Porter passage. Write another paragraph in which you evaluate the strengths and successes of either text.

2f   Discussing your reading with others

One of the pleasures of reading comes from discussing what you have read with others. Although reading is usually thought of as a private affair (just you and the text existing quietly together), it is also a social act. Reading has a social dynamic not only because you bring to your reading a wide range of social experiences, but also because in reading you communicate with another person—the author. You may also find yourself bringing your reading into everyday social situations.

The social dimension of reading is important for interpreting many types of texts. In reading informative texts (reports of business or political plans, for example), you would discuss your understanding with others to ensure that you have understood them clearly and accurately. In reading persuasive texts, you would discuss your understanding with others perhaps to come to an agreement about the importance or value of its message or its argument.

Besides these basic social realities, you may be aware that in discussing what you read with others you discover different ideas in it, thereby enriching your understanding. Other people's responses to texts reflect their social histories and backgrounds just as your responses do. In the same way that doing collaborative work at different stages of the writing process helps you revise your writing, collaborating with other readers can help you revise your interpretations and evaluations of texts.

EXERCISE 2–6   Collaborative Evaluation

Once you develop an evaluation of the text by Sontag, Porter, or Hemingway, share it with two or three other students. Use group collaboration not only to argue your point of view but also to widen and deepen your appreciation of the text by hearing what others have to say about it.

EXERCISE 2–7   Responding, Interpreting, and Evaluating Texts—A Series of Related Assignments

1. Record your responses to a text your instructor assigned or to one you choose. Use freewriting or annotation to record your responses.
2. List your observations about the text.
3. Identify one or more connections or sets of relationships among the details on your list. Categorize the items and create headings for them.
4. List the inferences you can make on the basis of the textual details observed and the connections you established among them.
5. Prepare a double-column notebook entry on the text.

6. Write a summary of the text in which you offer an interpretation based on your evidence and inferences.

7. Write an evaluation of the text in which you discuss (a) how well the text achieves its purposes, (b) the cultural values the text displays, and (c) your assessment of those values.

2g   Reading reflectively and critically

When you read reflectively, you think about or reflect on what the writer is saying. One focus for your reflections should be other things you have read or learned that relate to the details the writer uses to develop her argument. You are encouraged, for example, to introduce into your response to the essay and commentary other works relevant to Ehrlich's essay (see 2h). Perhaps you will think of a popular song or an advertisement, of a scene from a film, or of something you read for a psychology or marketing course that resonates with her essay. Ehrlich herself refers to an advertisement, a film, and another writer's comment. You might bring into your consideration of Ehrlich's essay what you have learned about cowboys and the West from other sources.

Reflective reading moves one step beyond interpretation. In **reflective reading** you make comparisons between different things you have read. And you make comparisons between what you are reading and what you have learned from living. The *analysis* required for interpreting a text's internal workings and the *reflective reading* that takes you beyond the text's details together constitute *critical reading*.

1   Moving beyond the details of a text

As you read, if you consider another work you have read in relation to the one you are presently reading, you are reading intertextually. **Intertextual reading** (a type of reflective reading) involves connecting the text you are reading with other things you have read, seen, heard, or experienced. This does not mean that you avoid making internal connections among the details of a text. You need to make intra-essay connections to interpret any text. But instead of remaining bound by a text's details, you go beyond them. In doing this kind of reflective reading, you make your lived experience relevant to your reading and you make your reading relevant to your life.

Look back, for example, to the double-column notebook entry in 2b-3, which shows examples of a reader making connections between Katherine Anne Porter's ideas about adventure and the reader's own life and previous reading. Or just peek at Ehrlich's first sentence (2h), in which she refers to an advertisement for Marlboro cigarettes. You can move beyond the details of

Ehrlich's text by remembering this kind of ad or by recalling other advertisements (whether for cigarettes or other products, especially those that convey a particular type of masculine image). Perhaps you will recall instead a television commercial for Busch or Budweiser beer in which images of the West or of athletic contests convey attitudes and feelings the marketers wish to evoke. Of course, you will need to see how Ehrlich uses the image of the Marlboro cowboy to know how relevant your connections are. But you should try to avoid reading her essay (or any text) in a vacuum.

2   Rereading

Like writing, reading is a recursive process (see 1b). This means that as you read, you return mentally to what you have already read, circling back in thought even as you read ahead. You should find yourself holding in mind what you read at the beginning of a piece while you read the middle or end of it. In addition, as you read any particular text, you compare what it says with what you know and with what you have read elsewhere.

Rereading is a normal part of reflective reading. Whether you reread because the writer is explaining a complex idea, because you want to be sure you understand what is being said, or because you enjoy how the writer has expressed herself—or for some other reason—it is not unusual to reread parts of a text even before you have finished reading it. Nor is it unusual to reread a text in its entirety at a later time, giving it a second or even a third reading. Complex texts, in fact, require such repeated reading.

Whether you are reading a text for the first time or giving it a second reading, try to become more conscious of how your mind plays back over the text even as you move forward through it. Attend also to the ways your mind anticipates what is coming based on what you have already read. In doing so, you will become more fully aware of how you think. You will also make more observations about the text and establish better connections among your observations (see 2c).

You can use the guidelines in the accompanying chart to review this chapter's advice on critical reading. The chart should be consulted whenever you write about a text you are reading critically.

2h   Interpreting a text: An example

To read a text critically, you might want to break it down by paragraph or section and to summarize and interpret each chunk or unit. Your writing should include your observations about the writer's idea and the evidence used to support it, but it may also involve, for example, your evaluation of the argument or your questions about the evidence. In the sample interpretation that follows in this section, each paragraph of Ehrlich's essay is accompanied

---

Guidelines for Critical Reading

- Read actively, annotating the text.
- Read attentively, focusing on each paragraph or section.
- Interpret the text by observing and connecting details, drawing inferences, and formulating a conclusion.
- Evaluate the text, considering its effectiveness, its persuasiveness, and its cultural values.
- Reflect on the text and question it.
- Read intertextually, bringing in other texts and experiences.

---

by observations about the essay's details. The interpretation also includes references to connections among details in different paragraphs, such as the different places Ehrlich uses quotations as evidence. The sample interpretation illustrates the kind of careful reading and thinking you should do when reading (and writing about) a text.

Here is Ehrlich's first paragraph from "About Men."

About Men

In paragraph 1, Ehrlich corrects what she considers an inaccurate stereotype of the "cowboy." She begins with a reference to this stereotype (the Marlboro cowboy) and offers a more complex understanding of the image created by the ad. She works from the stereotype to show how the conventional image and idea are inadequate, how they oversimplify and misrepresent reality. In contrasting the conventional understanding of a cowboy's character with her own perspective, Ehrlich uses the cowboys' own speech to help characterize them.

When I'm in New York but feeling lonely for Wyoming I look for the Marlboro ads in the subway. What I'm aching to see is horseflesh, the glint of a spur, a line of distant mountains, brimming creeks, and a reminder of the ranchers and cowboys I've ridden with for the last eight years. But the men I see in those posters with their stern, humorless looks remind me of no one I know here. In our hellbent earnestness to romanticize the cowboy we've ironically disesteemed his true character. If he's "strong and silent" it's because there's probably no one to talk to. If he "rides away into the sunset" it's because he's been on horseback since four in the morning moving cattle and he's trying, fifteen hours later, to get home to his family. If he's "a rugged individualist" he's also part of a team: ranch work is teamwork and even the glori- 1 fied open-range cowboys of the 1880s rode up and down the Chisholm Trail in the company of twenty or thirty other riders. Instead of the macho, trigger-happy man our culture has perversely wanted him to be, the cowboy is more apt to be convivial, quirky, and soft-hearted. To be "tough" on a ranch has nothing to do with conquests and displays of power. More often than not, circumstances—like the colt he's riding or an unexpected blizzard—are overpowering him. It's not toughness but "toughing it out" that counts. In other words, this macho, cultural artifact the cowboy has become is simply a man who possesses resilience, patience, and an instinct for survival. "Cowboys are just like a pile of rocks—everything happens to them. They get climbed on, kicked, rained and snowed on, scuffed up by wind. Their job is 'just to take it,'" one old-timer told me.

A cowboy is someone who loves his   2 work. Since the hours are long—ten to fifteen hours a day—and the pay is $30 he has to. What's required of him is an odd mixture of physical vigor and maternalism. His part of the beef-raising industry is to birth and nurture calves and take care of their mothers. For the most part his work is done on horseback and in a lifetime he sees and comes to know more animals than people. The iconic myth surrounding him is built on American notions of heroism: the index of a man's value as measured in physical courage. Such ideas have perverted manliness into a self-absorbed race for cheap thrills. In a rancher's world, courage has less to do with facing danger than with acting spontaneously—usually on behalf of an animal or another rider. If a cow is stuck in a boghole he throws a loop around her neck, takes his dally (a half

Ehrlich's second paragraph, which continues to play off the stereotype she began with, increases our understanding of what a cowboy's life is really like. Here Ehrlich talks about "courage" and "heroism"—popular virtues associated with the cowboy. Instead of denying the importance of these virtues for cowboys, Ehrlich reinterprets them, explaining that cowboys act courageously not out of some macho need to prove themselves in the face of danger, but out of necessity, often on behalf of another cowboy or an animal. A key word for her in this respect is compassion, one of Ehrlich's apparent requirements for successful cowboy life. And for Ehrlich, compassion is linked with maternalism, which she associates with the cowboy's selflessness.

hitch around the saddle horn), and pulls her out with horsepower. If a calf is born sick, he may take her home, warm her in front of the kitchen fire, and massage her legs until dawn. One friend, whose favorite horse was trying to swim a lake with hobbles on, dove under water and cut her legs loose with a knife, then swam her to shore, his arm around her neck lifeguard-style, and saved her from drowning. Because these incidents are usually linked to someone or something outside himself, the westerner's courage is selfless, a form of compassion.

3   The physical punishment that goes with cowboying is greatly underplayed. Once fear is dispensed with, the threshold of pain rises to meet the demands of the job. When Jane Fonda asked Robert Redford (in the film *Electric Horseman*) if he was sick as he struggled to his feet one morning, he replied, "No, just bent." For once the movies had it right. The cowboys I was sitting with laughed in agreement. Cowboys are rarely complainers; they show their stoicism by laughing at themselves.

4   If a rancher or cowboy has been thought of as a "man's man"—laconic, hard-drinking, inscrutable—there's almost no place in which the balancing act between male and female, manliness and femininity, can be more natural. If he's gruff, handsome, and physically fit on the outside, he's androgynous at the core. Ranchers are midwives, hunters, nurturers, providers, and conservationists all at once. What we've interpreted as toughness—weathered skin, calloused hands, a squint in the eye and a growl in the voice—only masks the tenderness inside. "Now don't go telling me these lambs are cute," one rancher warned

Paragraph 3 makes explicit something that had been implicit up to this point: that cowboys endure considerable physical punishment. Listen to the comment of the movie character that Ehrlich quotes approvingly. And then look back to the old cowboy's comment at the end of paragraph 1. Notice, too, how Ehrlich uses the film Electric Horseman not to contradict its image of the cowboy (as she does with the Marlboro ad), but to endorse that image. Ehrlich also describes the cowboy's attitude toward his physical hardships, one she describes as stoical and self-mocking.

In paragraph 4, Ehrlich emphasizes the combination of qualities cowboys possess— a mixture of what have been traditionally considered masculine and feminine traits. Ehrlich describes this mixture of qualities a number of ways—by using the word androgynous, which means "having both male and female characteristics"; by identifying the complementary characteristics of toughness and tenderness; by calling the cowboy's balancing of these different qualities "natural"; and by illustrating this with the rancher's comment about the cute lambs.

In paragraph 5, Ehrlich enlarges the scope of her essay. She touches on a historical explanation for the behavior of western cowboys, explaining their chivalry as a transplanted southern trait and their standoffishness as a consequence of the scarcity of women in the West. We can speculate why Ehrlich might have included the final detail of this paragraph—the rancher tipping his hat and greeting her with a "Howdy, ma'am" rather than a handshake. It illustrates her point rather nicely. But you might wonder whether Ehrlich would prefer a handshake.

In paragraph 6, Ehrlich develops the point made in the preceding paragraph. She suggests that later generations of cowboys perpetuate the attitudes and behavior of the earlier ones. Echoing part of the conventional image she began with, Ehrlich suggests that cowboys do not have much to say to women, largely because they know neither what to say nor how to say it. The cowboy's lack of verbal facility, according to Ehrlich, appears less an inability to experience emotion than a lack of adequate language to express the complexity of his feelings. In a manner characteristic of this essay, Ehrlich illustrates her point with striking details.

In paragraph 7, Ehrlich seems to attribute the shyness and standoffishness of cowboys partly to the physical vastness of the West and partly to what she describes as its "social isolation." As she does earlier in the essay, Ehrlich sets up a contrast between inner and outer, between what cowboys feel ("impulse, passion, intuition") and how they act (according to norms of "respectability, logic, and convention"). Once more, she supports her point with a cowboy's spoken comment, which she uses to conclude her paragraph—

me the first day I walked into the football-field-sized lambing sheds. The next thing I knew he was holding a black lamb. "Ain't this little rat good-lookin'?"

So many of the men who came to the West were southerners—men looking for work and a new life after the Civil War—that chivalrousness and strict codes of honor were soon thought of as western traits. There were very few women in Wyoming during territorial days, so when they did arrive (some as mail-order brides from places like Philadelphia) there was a stand-offishness between the sexes and a formality that persists now. Ranchers still tip their hats and say, "Howdy, ma'am" instead of shaking hands with me.

Even young cowboys are often evasive with women. It's not that they're Jekyll and Hyde creatures—gentle with animals and rough on women—but rather, that they don't know how to bring their tenderness into the house and lack the vocabulary to express the complexity of what they feel. Dancing wildly all night becomes a metaphor for the explosive emotions pent up inside, and when these are, on occasion, released, they're so battery-charged and potent that one caress of the face or one "I love you" will peal for a long while.

The geographical vastness and the social isolation here make emotional evolution seem impossible. Those contradictions of the heart between respectability, logic, and convention on the one hand, and impulse, passion, and intuition on the other, played out wordlessly against the paradisiacal beauty of the West, give cowboys a wide-eyed but drawn look. Their lips pucker up, not with kisses but with immutability. They may want to break something she does on a number of other occasions as well.

Ehrlich's final paragraph reinforces her central idea: that cowboys are both maternal and paternal, that they possess characteristics associated with both sexes. Ehrlich suggests that cowboys often try to live up to the tough image and hide the tenderness inside. She also suggests that the gentleness of cowboys results from living intimately with nature, especially from being responsible for the animals' lives. Overall, the final paragraph seems less to advance Ehrlich's argument than to consolidate it. She pulls her idea together one last time.

out, staying up all night with a lover just to talk, but they don't know how and can't imagine what the consequences will be. Those rare occasions when they do bare themselves result in confusion. "I feel as if I'd sprained my heart," one friend told me a month after such a meeting.

My friend Ted Hoagland wrote, "No **8** one is as fragile as a woman but no one is as fragile as a man." For all the women here who use "fragileness" to avoid work or as a sexual ploy, there are men who try to hide theirs, all the while clinging to an adolescent dependency on women to cook their meals, wash their clothes, and keep the ranch house warm in winter. But there is true vulnerability in evidence here. Because these men work with animals, not machines or numbers, because they live outside in landscapes of torrential beauty, because they are confined to a place and a routine embellished with awesome variables, because calves die in the arms that pulled others into life, because they go to the mountains as if on a pilgrimage to find out what makes a herd of elk tick, their strength is also a softness, their toughness, a rare delicacy.

—Gretel Ehrlich

You can use the preceding example of a critical reading of Ehrlich's essay as a model. The accompanying guidelines, How to Enhance Your Experience of Reading, can also help you read and write about texts.

EXERCISE 2–8   Reading Intertextually

Following are two brief excerpts that are related, in different ways, to Ehrlich's essay. Read each passage and consider how it might tie in with what Ehrlich says in "About Men." Then write an essay in which you develop the intertextual relationships among the three texts.

1. I have always disliked being a man. The whole idea of manhood in America is pitiful, in my opinion. . . . Even the expression "Be a man!" strikes me as

insulting and abusive. It means: Be stupid, be unfeeling, obedient, soldierly, and stop thinking. Man means "manly"—how can one think about men without considering the terrible ambition of manliness? And yet it is part of every man's life. It is a hideous and crippling lie; it not only insists on difference and connives at superiority, it is also by its very nature destructive—emotionally damaging and socially harmful.

—Paul Theroux, "Being a Man"

2. I am demanding something of you that takes more courage than entering a battle: not to enter the battle. I am asking you to say *no* to the values that have defined manhood through the ages—prowess, competition, victory—and to grow into a manhood that has not existed before. If you do, some men and women will ridicule and even despise you. They may call you spineless, possibly even (harshest of curses) womanish. But your life depends on it. My life depends on it.

—Nancy Mairs, "A Letter to Matthew"

EXERCISE 2–9 **Writing an Argumentative Essay**

Write an argumentative essay in which you use Ehrlich's "About Men" as one kind of evidence to develop and support your idea. As other evidence, you may use the reading you did for Exercise 2–2, 2–3, or 2–4. (Before writing, you may wish to review Chapter 7 on writing argumentative essays.)

How to Enhance Your Experience of Reading

- Read actively, annotating the text.
- Read attentively, focusing on each paragraph or section.
- Reflect on the text and question it.
- Interpret the text by observing and connecting details, drawing inferences, and formulating a conclusion.
- Evaluate the text, considering its effectiveness, its persuasiveness, and its cultural values.
- Read intertextually, bringing in other texts and experiences.

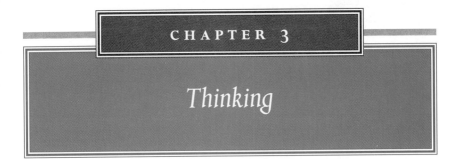

CHAPTER 3

Thinking

When we consider the act of thinking, logical thinking usually comes to mind. But another kind of thinking, creative thinking, is equally important. Both types of thinking are necessary for writing. Creative thinking helps you generate ideas and discover evidence to support them. Logical thinking helps you evaluate ideas and evidence that emerge in reading, in discussion, and in your writing. These two kinds of thinking serve different purposes and produce different results: they complement and reinforce one another.

3a Comparing creative and logical thinking

Creative thinking provides an alternative to logical thinking. Since these two kinds of thinking differ in important ways, you should know the values and limitations of each. Each kind of thinking has unique qualities. You use logical thinking, for example, to evaluate ideas. But to generate ideas to evaluate requires creative thinking.

Creative and logical thinking processes are complementary. Developing skill in using both types of thinking in everyday life, in school, and at work will help you develop your intellectual abilities.

Although you can use specific techniques to think both more creatively and more logically, creative and logical thinking are habits of mind, not simply techniques of thought. These habits need to be developed and applied if they are to become useful in your academic and professional life. The accompanying chart describes the major features of both creative and logical thinking.

EXERCISE 3–1   **Collaboration: Thinking about Thinking**

In discussion with your classmates, provide examples of when you used creative thinking to solve a problem or arrive at a decision.

Note: Sections 3a and 3b are based largely on the work of Edward de Bono, especially his *Lateral Thinking.* Section 3c is based largely on the work of James L. Adams, especially his *Conceptual Blockbusting.*

Overview of Creative and Logical Thinking

- Creative thinking puts things together; it synthesizes.

- Creative thinking generates new ideas.

- Creative thinking explores many alternatives; it is unconcerned with being correct every step of the way.

- Creative thinking is inclusive, admitting all ideas no matter how trivial or outrageous they may seem.

- Creative thinking is random. Moving backward as well as forward, in circles as well as in straight lines, it permits jumps beyond the next step in a logical sequence.

- Creative thinking forestalls judgment, deliberately delaying critical evaluation.

- Creative thinking is questioning, tentative, provisional. It adds the hypothetical, the "What if?" to logical thinking's "How?"

- Creative and logical thinking ask "Why?" In creative thinking, the "Why" stimulates further thought.

- Creative thinking encourages humor and fluidity; it is unsystematic and flexible.

- Logical thinking analyzes things, takes them apart.

- Logical thinking develops and evaluates ideas that have already been formulated.

- Logical thinking focuses on finding an answer and being correct at each step.

- Logical thinking is selective, screening out and eliminating unpromising possibilities.

- Logical thinking is linear and sequential. It moves from point to point in a straight line, allowing for no skips or gaps.

- Logical thinking encourages making judgments, assessing whether an idea or piece of evidence is valid.

- Logical thinking deals with "How?" and is more assertive, confident, sure of itself.

- In logical thinking, the "Why" answers a question or proposes a solution to a problem.

- Logical thinking prizes seriousness and rigor; it is systematic and methodical.

3b   Creative thinking techniques

Numerous techniques and strategies exist for developing the ability to think creatively. Some creative thinking techniques are especially conducive to group collaboration. One such is brainstorming, in which alternative solutions for analyzing problems are identified and considered. Thinking strategies, such as visualizing, can be used as specific techniques for individual brainstorming. Other techniques, such as establishing a quota of alternatives, are especially well suited to group collaboration.

The accompanying chart identifies some useful techniques for creative thinking.

Techniques for Creative Thinking

- Establishing a quota of alternatives (3b-1)
- Reversing relationships (3b-2)
- Using analogy (3b-3)
- Shifting attention (3b-4)
- Denying the negative, pursuing the possible (3b-5)
- Asking questions (3b-6)

---

1   Establishing a quota of alternatives

When you are trying to make a decision or solve a problem, you are often trying to choose the best solution from a number of options. You may be looking for the best bargain in a computer store or the most suitable companion for a date. In creative thinking, however, your goal is not to find the single best option but to generate several alternatives. One way to avoid becoming too easily satisfied with the first reasonable alternative you find is to establish a **quota of alternatives**, a set number of different possibilities. Even though you may find a very good solution initially, if you challenge yourself to find, say, four solutions, you may discover even better ones later. For instance, if you are required to select your own topic for a research paper, do not limit yourself to the first idea that comes to mind. Instead, think of three or four very different possibilities. And once you decide on a topic, avoid settling on the first approach you can think of. Consider different ways of developing and organizing your paper.

To practice applying the quota-of-alternatives technique, consider the following scenario and explanation.

> Each weekday morning, a woman takes the elevator in her office building to the tenth floor. She gets out there and walks up to the sixteenth floor, where her office is located. After work, she enters the elevator on the sixteenth floor and rides down to the first floor. She exits and heads home.

One possible explanation for the woman's behavior is that she uses the bathroom on the tenth floor, the only floor in the building with bathrooms.

Another is that she may stop to meet her supervisor who works on the tenth floor.

EXERCISE 3–2   **Providing Alternative Explanations**

Reread the preceding passage and think of two other explanations for the woman's elevator-riding behavior. Share your solutions with one or more of your classmates. Collect at least four explanations.

EXERCISE 3–3   **Using Alternatives in Reading**

Consider a poem or short story you have read recently, perhaps one you discussed in class. Develop three different potential interpretations of the work. Explain each interpretation in a paragraph.

EXERCISE 3–4   **Using Alternatives in Writing**

Look over a paper you wrote for one of your courses. Rewrite the introduction three different ways. For example, begin with a quotation, then with an anecdote, and finally with a question.

Do the same for the conclusion. Try various ending strategies, such as concluding with a question, a quotation, or a reference to something from your opening.

EXERCISE 3–5   **Preparing Multiple Drafts**

For your next writing assignment, prepare at least three drafts. Consider each draft a different way of approaching the assignment. Give yourself enough time to think of the different ideas and examples you will include in each draft.

---

2   Reversing relationships

When you **reverse relationships**, you approach your topic from several different perspectives to gain insight into your topic. It is as if you assume the identity of another person and try to explore your topic from his or her perspective. For example, if you were writing your views about a controversial issue, you might begin writing with an argument for one view and then switch tacks to argue the merits of an opposite position. This kind of mental shifting will help you understand counterarguments better and help you find convincing support for your views.

Reversing relationships will also help you reconsider your topic; to examine your topic with a different perspective. For example, instead of thinking of ice cooling the water in a glass, think of the water warming the ice. Instead of thinking of the legs of a table supporting its top, think of the legs suspended from the tabletop. Or think about the reverse relationship in Emily Dickinson's line "Much Madness is divinest Sense . . . Much Sense—the starkest Madness."

You might also want to reverse the relationships in the writing process. For example, you may want to write your ending before your beginning; you may want to begin writing about a topic before completing research about it; or you may want to outline your paper after you write it. These exercises can help you evaluate the strengths and weaknesses of your evidence and your argument.

Reversing relationships can also spur you to think more creatively by enabling you to break away from fixed ways of thinking. Like setting a quota of alternatives, reversing relationships can help you generate ideas for your course assignments.

EXERCISE 3–6   Reversing Relationships in Reading and Writing

---

Select *one* of the following for practice in reversing relationships.

1. In reading an article, an essay, or a chapter from one of your textbooks, begin with the final paragraph and work your way back to the beginning, one paragraph at a time.

2. In writing an essay, a paper, or a report, instead of trying to write your opening paragraph first, begin at the end and work backward from your conclusion. Write the opening paragraph last.

3. In preparing an outline for a paper or a report, write the outline last rather than first.

---

3   Using analogy

Writers often use **analogy**—a comparison of similar features of two different items—to clarify, illustrate, and explain difficult or confusing concepts. For example, when describing the control panel of an airplane, you might compare it to the dashboard of a car. To illustrate how knee joints work, you might compare them to door hinges and how they work.

Although using analogy in building logical arguments is discouraged, you should feel free to use analogy when thinking creatively because analogies can help you generate ideas for writing. For example, if you describe the control panel of an airplane in comparison to the dashboard of a car, you could come up with a way to organize that section of a paper. Or, if you compare knee joints to door hinges, you might begin to wonder how a delicate instrument can support seemingly impossible weight and remain flexible.

Analogy can help you approach a topic from a new perspective and, in turn, help you think about a topic differently. Consider how Phyllis Rose uses analogy to compare French cooking and torture in the following paragraph.

> The secret of torture, like the secret of French cuisine, is that nothing is unthinkable. The human body is like a foodstuff, to be grilled, pounded, filleted. Every opening exists to be stuffed, all flesh to be carved off the bone. You take an ordinary wheel, a heavy wooden wheel with spokes. You lay the victim on the ground with blocks of wood at strategic points under his shoulders, legs, and arms. . . . Who would have thought to do this with a man and a wheel? But, then, who would have thought to take the disgusting snail, force it to render its ooze, stuff it in its own shell with garlic butter, bake it, and eat it?

> —Phyllis Rose, "Tools of Torture"

EXERCISE 3–7   Using Analogy in Writing

Write a paragraph in which you develop an analogy of your own. If you like, you can use the analogy to illustrate a point. One suggestion is to think of something you know how to do well, then explain or describe how to do it by using an analogy. For example, skiing, swimming, grilling meat, shooting a basketball, taking photographs, drawing, and finding lost possessions are possible topics.

4   Shifting attention

Sometimes in writing you come to a dead end or run out of ideas because you focus too sharply on a single aspect of your topic. Deliberately **shifting attention** away from the dominant element of your topic can lead you to additional ideas. For example, in writing a paper about the effects of excessive drinking, you may be concentrating on an individual drinker. Shifting your focus to the effects of alcohol on the drinker's family and friends will stimulate further thought and additional ideas. So will a different kind of shift, one to a consideration of the broader social consequences of alcoholism. You might find yourself readjusting the focus of your paper, perhaps revising your initial purpose, point, and intended emphasis.

The following example shows how a shift of attention can lead to the solution of a problem.

> As a man is driving home from work, his car comes to a halt. Lifting up the hood, he notices that he has a broken fanbelt. His solution? He takes off his

necktie and ties it tightly in the fanbelt position. He drives a quarter mile to the nearest service station and replaces his fanbelt. With the money he saves on a towing charge, he buys a new tie.

EXERCISE 3–8 **Shifting Attention**

Read a short story or play that describes a relationship between two characters. Focus your attention closely on one character, considering that character as the more important of the two. Then shift your attention to the other, thinking of that character as the more important one.

5   Denying the negative, pursuing the possible

Whereas logical thinking tends to reject ideas, creative thinking encourages them. Instead of thinking that something will not work, that an approach to a problem is unrealistic or inadequate, that an idea is silly or erroneous, stop yourself. Say "Yes, perhaps," rather than "No." **Deny the negative.** Be careful not to reject an idea, regardless of its degree of promise, because a poor idea may lead to a better one. As you consider the limitations of one idea, a better one may emerge. You might discover, for example, that a mistake you made in writing up a lab report leads you to an unintended but lucky alternative solution. Asking "What if?" or "Why not?" can help you pursue possibilities. When you ask yourself "What if?" you open yourself to new ideas. When you ask someone else "Why not?" you invite discussion, perhaps even debate. Both techniques can lead you to a better understanding of ideas. Pursue the possible, even against the odds.

EXERCISE 3–9   **Denying the Negative, Pursuing the Possible**

For part of one day, record how often you hear people using the negative to deny a prospect or possibility. Notice, too, how often you do this yourself. On at least one of those occasions, wait, and consider how perhaps what is being denied may be possible after all. Or let the unpromising possibility sit for a while, and see if a better alternative comes to mind. Write about your experience.

6   Asking questions

Born inquisitive, we continue through childhood asking numerous questions. As we grow older, however, we begin to be more interested in answers than in questions. This is unfortunate because when we are no longer **asking questions,** we may cease looking for better answers.

It is easy to develop a questioning attitude. Without becoming obsessive about it, you can question your parents, teachers, friends, and especially yourself. You can practice asking questions by making a game of questioning assertions you encounter from television and radio, class lectures, your reading and conversations, even your own thoughts.

The most productive kinds of questions lead to further thought. Best are open-ended questions, which do not lead to a single, conclusive answer. Questions that hypothesize stimulate thinking. So do questions about questions (answering one question by asking another); they can help you develop the habit of thinking.

In thinking about how you might approach a writing assignment for one of your courses, for example, avoid deciding immediately on a topic and an approach. Instead, consider questions that provoke thinking, such as the following.

What are some possible topics I might choose?

Why should I choose topic *X* rather than topic *Y* or *Z*?

How can I approach the topic in a way that will satisfy the instructor's requirements? Can I approach the topic in more than one way?

How can I best maintain my interest in the assignment to increase the likelihood I will do a good job?

What if I were to do something different and unusual to fulfill the assignment? Would this be permitted? What might be the advantages? The drawbacks?

How can I make my paper interesting for the instructor to read rather than merely making it correct or accurate?

These general questions about approaching an assignment should be supplemented with specific questions tied closely to the particular issues, examples, facts, readings, and uses of evidence and experience you will introduce in completing the assignment. What is important, however, is that good questions get the creative juices flowing.

EXERCISE 3–10 Asking Questions

Choose an essay or a paper you wrote recently and reread it. Ask yourself questions as you read—about the assertions you make, the examples and evidence you use to support your assertions, and so on. Look also at whether the instructor who read your paper marked down any questions about it. Then rewrite the paper, incorporating the additional thinking generated by the answers to the questions you asked yourself or to those raised by your instructor (or both).

EXERCISE 3–11   Practice in Creative Thinking

Use the appropriate creative thinking techniques to complete the following.

1. Set yourself a quota of alternatives for improving your grades, for saving time, or for increasing the amount of reading you do.

2. Divide these six squares into four parts. Do it a different way each time.

3. Describe the following figure in as many different ways as you can. For example, discuss it as a table, a crosswalk, and so forth.

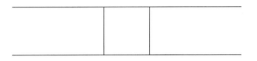

4. Think of two things that are normally considered opposites. Then write sentences in which you suggest a nonconventional, unorthodox view of their relationship. Example:

   truths/lies
   Some truths are the basest lies, some lies the most astonishing truths.

5. Provide three alternative solutions for each of the following situations.

   a. Shoplifting in large department stores

   b. Cheating on exams given in large lecture halls

   c. Graffiti in dorm bathrooms

6. Generate ideas for writing a report on some way to improve the quality of academic life or of dorm living.

7. Develop some strategies for avoiding negative thinking.

EXERCISE 3–12   Creative Writing and Collaboration

Following are the first four stanzas from the poem "Thirteen Ways of Looking at a Blackbird" by Wallace Stevens. Add three or more of your own stanzas and re-title the poem, "X Ways of Looking at a Blackbird."

Choose the one of your three stanzas that you like best. Put it together with other ways of looking at a blackbird supplied by other members of your class to create a collaborative poem.

I
Among twenty snowy mountains,
The only moving thing
Was the eye of the blackbird.

II
I was of three minds,
Like a tree
In which there are three blackbirds.

III
The blackbird whirled in the autumn winds.
It was a small part of the pantomime.

IV
A man and a woman
Are one.
A man and a woman and a blackbird
Are one. . . .

—Wallace Stevens, "Thirteen Ways of Looking at a Blackbird"

3c   Overcoming obstacles to thinking

To become a more creative thinker, you may need to overcome various obstacles to thinking: ingrained habits, fears, even anxieties. The accompanying chart outlines the major obstacles to creative thinking and suggests ways to conquer them. Recognizing these blocks to thought is the first step toward overcoming them. This section provides actual strategies to help you get past these obstacles and think more freely and creatively.

1   Overcoming perceptual blocks

Perceptual blocks inhibit our ability to make sense of what we are looking at. They interfere with our thinking by blocking what we can see. For example, upon first looking at Picasso's painting *Guernica* (see p. 140), you may be confused by the strangeness of its images. Your initial reaction may be simply to throw your hands up in frustration over not being able to understand the images. The key to getting beyond such a reaction and overcoming this perceptual block is to take a second, third, perhaps even a fourth look—

How to Overcome Obstacles to Thinking

OBSTACLES	WAYS TO OVERCOME OBSTACLES
Perceptual blocks	Practice observing and noticing (3c-1).
Cultural blocks	Become aware of cultural perspectives (3c-2).
Intellectual blocks	Study. Review. Prepare (3c-3).
Emotional blocks	Conquer your fears about mistakes (3c-4).
	Learn to tolerate ambiguity (3c-4).
Polarizing	Identify the middle ground (3c-5).

to keep looking until you can begin to make some sense of what you are looking at. For example, if you look at *Guernica* patiently and attentively, you can begin to see that the artist has depicted an apocalyptic scene. And you may also become disposed to think more seriously about what the work's images suggest. If you do some research on the painting, you will notice even more, because you will learn when and why Picasso painted it. You can use that knowledge to understand better what the artist accomplished (see p. 140).

Learning to see new things requires patience, effort, and practice. You have to prepare yourself to see. You have to learn to look. This is particularly important for academic work. Whether you are looking at a Renaissance sculpture or a modern painting; whether you are analyzing a social problem or identifying changes in someone's behavior; whether you are doing a lab experiment or observing qualities of style and form in Greek architecture; or whether you are learning to analyze cases in business law—you can describe and discuss only what you have noticed. One crucial element of your education, therefore, is to become more observant. The more you observe, the more you will have to think and write about.

It is certainly true that to notice qualities of Notre Dame cathedral in Paris or to appreciate the moves of Michael Jordan, you have to know something about architecture or basketball already. One pillar of observation, then, is knowledge. The more you know about something, the better you can appreciate it in its entirety. If you consider Picasso's *Guernica*, for example, without any knowledge of its connection to the Spanish Civil War, you miss an important part of the meaning of the painting.

2   Overcoming cultural blocks

Cultural blocks derive from ingrained habits of thinking that govern the minds of many people. Cultural blocks to thought may derive from your connection with particular ethnic, racial, and intellectual traditions as well as from your social class and gender. For example, men and women may sometimes have different life priorities partly, or even largely, because of their different biological, social, and sexual experiences. Similarly, people of different religions may be committed to radically different ideas about the role of children in society or the degree of respect given the elderly or the sick. Further cultural influences on thought include perspectives strongly tied to racial and ethnic attitudes and beliefs. Although none of us is locked into a particular way of seeing and thinking because of our race, class, gender, intellectual disposition, or ethnic background, each of us must be aware of the ways our culture and background may influence and possibly limit our perspective on an issue.

An example of a typical American cultural block is the tendency to value logical thinking more than creativity. Impatience with the techniques of creative thinking, such as delaying judgment or denying the negative, exemplify this attitude. So, too, do an impatience with error and an emphasis on being right all the time. Allied with these cultural attitudes is a lack of appreciation for the roles of play and chance in learning. Our educational institutions seem to distrust pleasure, to think that learning should be work rather than play. Play is suspect; pleasure is considered an irrelevant luxury in learning. These counterproductive ideas result from cultural blocks that need to be overcome.

Cultural blocks inhibit thinking. Some, such as the biased attitudes of prejudice and sexism, are dangerous and destructive. Moreover, one of the benefits of collaborating with others—in brainstorming, planning, group discussion—is comparing your cultural assumptions with theirs. Recognizing and acknowledging cultural blocks will help you avoid such inhibitions to constructive thought. (See 7f-2 on stereotyping and Chapter 29 on biased language.)

3   Overcoming intellectual blocks

Intellectual blocks involve obstacles to knowledge. You may find yourself unable to solve a problem because you lack information or because you have incorrect or partial information. When you buy a car, for example, you can be blocked by being unaware of various cars' performance ratings, repair records, or safety features. Or you may be blocked because you have only one-sided information—that presented by sales representatives for each of the auto models you are considering. Or, possibly, you may simply not know enough about cars to purchase one with confidence.

Perhaps you know quite a bit about a particular subject but still lack the skill to express your ideas effectively. How many times have you said to yourself, "I really knew more than I wrote on that essay, test, or paper. I just couldn't get it down on paper. I couldn't organize my ideas clearly."

To break through an intellectual block, you need either to acquire additional information or to deepen your understanding of the information you have. For example, if you are working on a paper about dreams and you find that you are stuck on a point, it may be time to do some more reading or to talk with someone about the subject. Sometimes getting past an intellectual block may be less a matter of acquiring more or better information than of gaining a new perspective on that information. If you are basing your paper on one theory about dreams, you may need to consider introducing alternative theories. Or, if you have been relying on traditional psychological explanations, perhaps you should look at some medical studies. In any case, you may need to look at the information you cull from your reading in more than one way. You may need to question it and analyze it to understand its significance on a deeper level.

The way to overcome intellectual blocks, then, is first to identify whether your block is caused by a lack of information, by too much information, or by an inadequate perspective on the information. You may then need to review, study, or read more to prepare yourself better before you continue writing.

4   Overcoming emotional blocks

Emotional blocks occur when feelings inhibit thinking. Such blocks include fears and anxieties. Emotional blocks often combine with intellectual blocks; in fact, the distinction between these types of blocks is minor.

Perhaps the biggest emotional block to thought is the fear of being wrong. This fear is grounded in how you think people will perceive you, especially what they might think of you if you make a mistake. As a result, you may be unsure about expressing ideas you are uncertain about. "What if I'm wrong?" you wonder. "What if people think my comment is foolish?" Such blocks can inhibit your ability to explore your topic and, as a result, may impede your creativity. The solution to such a problem is to develop confidence in yourself, to allow yourself the luxury of being wrong, and to realize that your primary academic goal is to learn and make intellectual progress, and that making mistakes and not knowing all the answers is normal.

Another emotional block to creative thinking is the inability to tolerate ambiguity, uncertainty, or confusion. Periods of confusion and uncertainty are often necessary for creative breakthroughs. You should be aware that you may have to create or at least tolerate chaos in your thinking before eliciting order from it. In writing a paper, for example, you should not expect simply to think of a thesis, neatly outline your organizational plan, develop your ideas, and then write a perfect essay in a single try. Instead, you should understand that a period of confusion, of trying out different ideas, of experimenting with different approaches to the subjects, and of writing some messy drafts is typical for professional writers as well as for students. (See 4b for E. B. White's drafts of a paragraph; see 5b–c, 6b, and 7c–d for examples of students drafting and revising exploratory, analytical, and argumentative essays.)

To think creatively, you have to overcome whatever inhibits your thought. You have to tolerate ambiguity, and you have to overcome the fear of being wrong. Few successful thinkers or writers get anything right the first time. Writers, scientists, artists, and creative people in all fields reconsider their work in the process of revising it.

5   Avoiding polarization

To **polarize** is to see things in terms of opposites, such as "us" and "them," thereby oversimplifying a situation. Polarizing involves setting up mutually exclusive categories without compromising and without exploring the arguments on either side. Polarized categories, like those in the following list, inhibit creative thinking.

yes/no	friend/enemy
right/wrong	win/lose
true/false	intelligent/stupid
now/never	freedom/tyranny

Do not be limited by such polarized categories. Look, instead, for the middle ground between opposite poles. To do that, you should establish a continuum that permits gradations between opposing perspectives. Think, for example, of being told that if you are not "for" something you are "against" it. Consider how such a forced choice often unfairly misrepresents the complexity of your feelings about an issue. You may want to say, "Wait a minute. I am for this part of the issue, but I am against that part of the issue." For instance, you may favor curtailing welfare care costs, but that does not necessarily mean that you support the president's plan for welfare reform. Conversely, to oppose the president's plan does not mean you are against keeping welfare costs in check. You need not be completely for or completely against a particular viewpoint or proposal. Often, your agreement or disagreement will represent one or another gradation or shade of conviction.

You can also see the complexity of problems and issues by introducing the **notion of degree.** Asking "to what extent" or "to what degree" is more productive than seeing a situation as "all-or-nothing." Asking yourself *to what extent* an idea is challenging, a book interesting, or a film entertaining is more fruitful than seeing the idea as *completely* challenging or not, the book as *absolutely* interesting or not, the film as *totally* entertaining or not. Considering degree or extent pushes you to make distinctions and to think independently. It helps you explore and think about possibilities and, ultimately, to become a critical and creative thinker, both on your own and in a collaborative group.

EXERCISE 3–13   **Avoiding Polarization**

Choose *one* of the following sets of polarized terms and draw a continuum, as shown in the example for *love/hate*. Identify three or four intermediate terms that represent the categories between the two opposites. Example:

```
 +———————+————————+————————+————————+————————+————————+———
 love      affection    good      mistrust    bad       dislike     hate
                        feeling               feeling
```

heroic/cowardly   success/failure
good/bad   proud/humble

EXERCISE 3–14   **Overcoming Blocks to Creative Thinking**

1. Describe a situation in which you had an opportunity to use creative thinking but did not. Or describe a situation in which you wanted to use creative thinking but could not. Explain what you might have been able to accomplish had you used creative thinking in that situation.

2. Think of something you do not do well but would like to do better. Consider why you do not perform this activity as well as you would like. Then think of three things you can do to improve your ability. Write about your analysis of the problem and your plan for improvement.

3. Identify three reasons why your most difficult academic course gives you trouble. Think of one possible emotional block that could be overcome and of one prospective intellectual block you could eliminate. Consider how you might go about improving your performance in this course.

4. Identify two cultural blocks to understanding that, if removed, would promote tolerance, improve social relationships, or enhance the academic environment.

  Logical thinking

Logical thinking involves reasoning carefully as you develop arguments in writing (see 7b). It also involves thinking critically about the validity of ideas and arguments when you read (see 2c–e). Three important aspects of logical thinking are inductive and deductive reasoning; causal explanation; and reasoning by analogy. Each of these elements of logical thinking is useful in understanding the forms an argument can take.

1 Using inductive and deductive reasoning

In **inductive reasoning,** you begin reasoning from particular instances about x, y, and z, and then you reach a general conclusion about those instances. Based on observation, inductive reasoning forms the basis for scientific experiment. **Deductive reasoning** works the opposite way. When you reason deductively, you begin with a general principle and then you apply it to one or more specific circumstances. Deductive thinking is based on general ideas and uses them to make predictions.

Inductive reasoning is useful in presenting the causes of particular events or circumstances. You might identify a series of events as contributing causes of the Balkan war or the collapse of communist rule in eastern Europe. Because inductive thinking depends upon probability, the connection between the evidence and conclusion is considered a probable cause. Conclusions reached through inductive reasoning are considered to be *probable, reliable,* or *unreliable,* rather than simply right or wrong.

The elements of inductive thinking are summarized in the accompanying chart.

Elements of Inductive Reasoning

- Begins with a specific observation
- Continues with additional specific observations
- Arrives at a general claim or a conclusion that is based on available evidence
- Attributes causes to events or circumstances, resulting in a hypothesis that can be tested further
- Offers probability rather than certainty

Deductive reasoning is syllogistic reasoning. A **syllogism** is an argument arranged in three parts: a major premise, a minor premise, and a conclusion. A *major premise* stipulates a general principle (e.g., that all spiders have eight legs), and a *minor premise* reflects a specific instance (e.g., that the creature crawling across your desk has six legs). Your *conclusion* that it is not a spider follows logically from these major and minor premises. Since these premises can be supported with relevant evidence, they can be considered reliable.

In many cases syllogistic reasoning depends on premises that are *assumptions* rather than facts. An assumption may or may not be based on evidence that makes it reliable. Consider the assumption behind the major premise in the following syllogism.

MAJOR PREMISE	If you wear Gap clothes to school, you will be accepted by the school's most popular group. (Assumption)
MINOR PREMISE	Jose wears Gap clothes to school. (Fact)
CONCLUSION	Jose will be accepted by the school's most popular group.

When a premise is an assumption rather than a fact, you must be able to support the premise with evidence. Because the major premise of this example rests on a shaky assumption (it cannot be supported with evidence), the argument is not true. In most instances, wearing Gap clothes (or any other brand or type of clothing) does not ensure automatic popularity. Since the assumption behind the major premise is unsupported, it is an unreliable premise and the argument based on it is not true. The syllogism, however, is valid because validity concerns the syllogism's structure, which is sound; that is, if you accept the major premise, and if the minor premise is accurate, then the conclusion follows logically.

Most arguments do not follow a formal syllogistic pattern. A newspaper editorial that supports the closing of military bases or a magazine column that argues for a student loan program run by the federal government would more than likely be presented with its major premise left unstated. One reason for avoiding syllogisms in everyday argument is that they sound rigid and formal. Writers typically express their arguments less formally to appeal to a wider audience.

An argument in which the major premise is left unstated is called an **enthymeme**. An enthymeme often appears as a conclusion supported by a single premise. Here is an example.

> More than half of all varsity football players do not receive a diploma after studying six years at this university. We have to do something to improve that figure, or we should eliminate the football program.

Laid out in syllogistic form, the argument looks like this.

MAJOR PREMISE	(*unstated*) Students, including football players, should earn a diploma within six years.
MINOR PREMISE	More than half of all varsity football players do not receive diplomas within six years.
CONCLUSION	We have to improve that figure or eliminate the football program.

You may agree or disagree about the reliability of the enthymeme's unstated premise. But the argument is easier to evaluate with the major premise stated. Be alert for arguments containing unstated premises; try to supply unstated premises so you can more easily assess their truth or reliability. Remember, too, that an argument is only as strong as its premises. If an argument's premises are faulty or if an argument includes unsupported assumptions, then it can easily be refuted. (See 7f on logical fallacies, which are sometimes the result of faulty syllogisms.)

The accompanying chart outlines the elements of deductive thinking.

Elements of Deductive Reasoning

DEDUCTIVE REASONING
- Begins with a general idea or major premise
- Continues with an additional minor premise applied to a particular case
- Concludes with a specific statement derived from the premise

DEDUCTIVE ARGUMENTS
- Can be reliable or unreliable, depending on how true or false the premise is
- Can be valid or invalid, depending on the structure of their syllogisms
- When reliable, provide certainty rather than probability

EXERCISE 3–15   **Analyzing Deductive Arguments**

Analyze the following deductive arguments. When necessary, supply the missing premises.

1. To improve the economy, the president should create public works projects and increase the number of available jobs.
2. I'm doing twice as much work today as I did ten years ago. I'd better slow down or I'll be endangering my health.
3. Students today do not read as much as they did in previous generations. How can we expect to have an enlightened citizenry unless they read more?
4. I think; therefore, I am.
5. She must be a good student since she is on the Dean's List.
6. Guns should be outlawed for civilians. The world has changed radically since the framers of the Bill of Rights included the right to bear arms.
7. Give me liberty or give me death.
8. When in Rome, do as the Romans do.
9. A political leader who cannot control his or her own family should not be given the responsibility of governing a state.
10. Alcoholic beverages destroy brain cells, so alcohol should be made illegal.

Construct a valid syllogism for each of the following minor premises. Example:

> The New York Mets lost more games in 1993 than in any year since the first year of the franchise.
>
> **MAJOR PREMISE**   Losing a large number of baseball games indicates that a team is in need of a major restructuring.
>
> **MINOR PREMISE**   The New York Mets lost more games in 1993 than in any year since the first year of the franchise.
>
> **CONCLUSION**   The New York Mets need a major restructuring.

1. Cigarette smoke is dangerous to the health of nonsmokers who breathe it.
2. Walking vigorously for twenty minutes a day provides excellent cardiovascular exercise.
3. Macy's reported substantial losses for the eight quarters of 1995 and 1996.
4. Speaking a foreign language can enhance one's pleasure when traveling abroad.
5. Interest rates have declined consistently in recent years.

---

2   Using inductive and deductive reasoning together

In practice, inductive and deductive reasoning work together and complement each other. Scientists, like other thinkers, use both inductive and deductive reasoning to construct arguments and reach conclusions. Consider the following account of the evolutionary connection between long-tongued moths and a species of orchid. In a story reported in the *New York Times,* Gene Kritzky, a scientist, hypothesized that a moth with a six-inch wingspan and a fifteen-inch tongue had to exist—even though there was no record of anyone ever having seen one. On the face of it, this may sound like an outrageous claim. But once you know that a type of orchid exists whose nectar lies fifteen inches deep into its flowery interior, then the existence of such a pollinating moth becomes more likely. The prediction becomes an even greater likelihood when you consider the following facts (Kritzky's evidence).

1. In 1862, Charles Darwin had made a similar prediction about the existence of a moth with a twelve-inch tongue, based on his discovery of a slightly smaller orchid (one with its nectar thirteen inches deep inside).
2. Darwin's orchid, like the one discussed in the *Times* article, was found in Madagascar.

3. Although the scientist who predicted the existence of this larger moth has not seen the larger orchid, someone else has seen and described it.

4. Both Darwin's and this larger orchid cannot be pollinated by small insects that crawl into it, for the orchids are structured so that if the insects go too deeply in they can never get out.

5. Forty years after Darwin's prediction, the moth whose existence he had hypothesized was found.

Darwin arrived at his prediction that such a moth existed partly from his observation of the deep orchid and partly from his knowledge that no known creature could pollinate such a deep flower. He reasoned inductively from particular circumstances, but he also reasoned deductively from the scientific law of natural selection that he had formulated. Darwin reasoned that species develop and change to enhance their opportunities for continued successful existence. Since moths with slightly shorter tongues pollinate slightly smaller orchids, then according to the principle of natural selection, a longer-tongued species would evolve to pollinate the deeper flower.

To reach their hypotheses, both Darwin and Kritzky worked from an unstated assumption: that orchids are pollinated by insects. They also worked from the general law that stipulates how insects adapt to their environment. Thus, since Darwin's reasoning has been proven correct with regard to this kind of moth and this orchid species, and since more than likely the same principle applies to Kritzky's example, it will be only a matter of time before the longer-tongued moth is found.

3e　Understanding causality

Sometimes you reason from effect to cause; sometimes you reason from cause to effect. In both cases, you rely on establishing a causal connection or causal relationship between two facts or events. **Causality** refers to a relationship between or among events in which one event is responsible for causing the others to occur. Single-cause explanations oversimplify. They cannot explain complex historical events or intractable social circumstances. Consider, for example, your decision to attend college, to take a particular course, to study with a particular teacher, or to prepare for a particular career. In these personal matters, you more than likely can point to specific advice you were given, experiences you had, or situations you heard about that influenced your various choices. To say, however, with absolute certainty that any single event "caused" you to make any of those personal decisions would be an oversimplification. Or consider that the causes of the recession in the United States in the early 1990s included tight credit, business failures, bank and trading scandals. More remote causes included junk bond trading in the 1980s, an escalating national debt, a sliding trade deficit, and a spiraling increase in consumer debt coupled with decreased savings.

Be aware that causality is rarely easy to establish. Since complex events have multiple causes, identifying those causes and deciding which are most influential often lead to disagreement. Scientists disagree, for example, about the causes of dinosaur extinction. Educators disagree about the causes of the decline in SAT scores. In developing an argument about these and other subjects, you need to establish the strongest causal relationship you can, even when you cannot prove the causal connection conclusively. The stronger you make a case for a causal connection, the stronger your argument will be.

One common danger in making causal arguments is confusing association with explanation. Just because one event is associated or linked with another does not mean that one caused the other. Thunder and lightning are both associated with certain kinds of rainstorms. But one of these storm elements doesn't cause the others. All are the result of specific atmospheric conditions. Because an association may or may not involve causality, it is wise not to assume a causal explanation unless you have good evidence to support it.

The criteria for what is considered adequate evidence in support of causal connections are not easy to apply. Since causality usually does not involve ironclad proof, readers and writers most often operate in the realm of likelihood and possibility. As a reader, you should consider carefully the evidence writers supply when offering causal explanations. As a writer, you should qualify your use of causality and offer causal explanations warily.

EXERCISE 3–17   Examining Causes and Effects

Choose *one* of the following events. Identify its causes in one list and its effects in another list.

1. The American Civil War
2. The United States' involvement in Vietnam
3. The increased number of health maintenance organizations (HMOs)
4. The collapse of the Berlin Wall
5. The rise in the salaries of professional athletes

EXERCISE 3–18   Using Causality in Writing

In two paragraphs, identify the causes of *one* of the following. Then explain its effects in another two paragraphs.

1. A personal decision (such as your choice of a major course of study)
2. A social problem (such as drug abuse, AIDS, or homelessness)
3. A natural phenomenon (such as global warming or earthquakes)

4. A scientific discovery (such as the discovery of X-rays)
5. A technological development (such as television or computers)

3f   Thinking about analogy in arguments

Writers often use an analogy to explain something unfamiliar to their readers by comparing it with something they are more familiar with. For example, you might liken a double play in baseball to a dance routine. To explain how the heart functions, you might draw an analogy between the heart and a water pump. Analogies help readers understand what writers mean. Conversely, they help writers clarify their thinking for readers.

Be careful, however, when you think about an analogy to develop an argument. Arguments based on analogy lack persuasive rigor because analogies offer neither conceptual explanations nor logical analyses of ideas. In other words, analogies do not prove a point. Instead, they provide alternative perspectives from which to analyze a subject. You can take an analogy only so far before the similarities between the two things compared end and the important differences emerge. A baseball double play, in some ways, is like a dance. But in other ways it is not. A heart is like a water pump, but only to a point.

Remember that analogies work best to generate and clarify ideas rather than to offer logically convincing explanations. (For a discussion of how analogy stimulates creative thinking, see 3b-3.)

Consider the following argument by analogy.

> It is clear that the decline of a language must ultimately have political and economic causes: it is not due simply to the bad influence of this or that individual writer. But an effect can become a cause, reinforcing the original cause and producing the same effect in an intensified form, and so on indefinitely. A man may take to drink because he feels himself to be a failure, and then fail all the more completely because he drinks. It is rather the same thing that is happening to the English language. It becomes ugly and inaccurate because our thoughts are foolish, but the slovenliness of our language makes it easier for us to have foolish thoughts.
>
> —George Orwell, "Politics and the English Language"

In arguing that the English language is in decline, Orwell suggests but does not identify a group of "political and economic causes." He proposes that an effect (the decline of English) can become a cause furthering that decline (originally an effect of those unidentified political and economic causes). He then introduces his analogy (a man who drinks) as a way of supporting his argument about effects becoming causes that further intensify the problem. As readers, we need to be clear, first, about the idea expressed in the analogy and, second, about how well the analogy supports Orwell's claim.

Just what does Orwell's analogy assert? That a person drinks because of some kind of unidentified personal failure (e.g., social, political, financial); and that the drinking that began as a consequence of a personal problem can become a cause rather than an effect. The drinking becomes a cause that accelerates the drinker's decline and failure. The drinking is now a cause of failure rather than one of its effects.

But is Orwell's analogy a persuasive part of his overall argument? Does the fact that an effect can become a cause, as the analogy demonstrates, apply to the decline of the English language in the way Orwell suggests? Does it "prove" that a decline was occurring among some users of English? Or does it instead clarify Orwell's idea, enabling us to better understand his point? (For discussion of false analogy as a logical fallacy, see 7f.)

EXERCISE 3–19   **Analogy and Argument**

Explain how the analogy in the first passage develops the writer's argument and how the analogy in the second passage clarifies the writer's explanation.

1. History is to the nation rather as memory is to the individual. As an individual deprived of memory becomes disoriented and lost, not knowing where he has been or where he is going, so a nation denied a conception of its past will be disabled in dealing with its present and its future.

   —Arthur Schlesinger, Jr., *The Disuniting of America*

2. The Big Bang picture of the universe can be understood in terms of a simple analogy. Think of a lump of rising bread dough with a few raisins scattered throughout. Imagine further that you are standing on one of the raisins in the dough, looking at the other raisins. What would you see?

   From your point of view, your raisin is stationary—you are not moving through the dough. On the other hand, if you looked at a neighboring raisin, you would see it moving away from you because the dough between you and it is expanding. In the same way, if you looked at a raisin that was twice as far away, it would be moving twice as fast as the nearer raisin, simply because there is twice as much dough to expand. No matter which raisin you looked at, it would be moving away from you, and the farther away it was, the faster it would move.

   —James Trefil, *Reading the Mind of God*

EXERCISE 3–20   **Using Analogy in Writing**

In one or two paragraphs, use an analogy to clarify or illustrate a point.

CHAPTER 4

Developing Ideas

In Chapter 1, you learned about the relationship between evidence and ideas. You began to see, in Chapters 2 and 3 how reading, thinking, and reflecting contribute to the accumulation of evidence, how ideas account for the meaning of that evidence, and how good writing eventually depends on such ideas. You learned that the act of writing does not follow a linear sequence moving cleanly from one step to the next. Instead, it is a recursive process that goes forward and loops back as you read and write and revise and read some more, always thinking and reflecting as you go along. By pursuing a number of avenues, you can come increasingly closer to developing the leading ideas that let you control your essay.

Developing ideas is an eternally interesting process. Ideas are never fixed; they have about them a certain elasticity. They can be stretched, modified, made more interesting. They are, as one student told us, "always capable of further analysis." Ideas come from a variety of sources: your reading, your consideration of a painting or a photograph, your own lived experiences. They take shape as your mind plays over such sources and begins to make sense of them.

This chapter presents you with five techniques that can help you formulate and develop ideas as you think about your evidence and begin your essays: questioning, writing, connecting, considering controversies, and collaborating. These five techniques should help you as you move *from* sources *to* ideas *to* essays. The techniques are highly effective when you use them concurrently, letting them guide your mind's play toward ideas. We begin with questioning, but we could just as easily begin with one of the other techniques. They are related, and, in practice, you are likely to use the techniques simultaneously. We separate them now so that you can more clearly understand them.

 Questioning evidence to find an idea

Questioning follows from a natural human curiosity about what something means. Much questioning can take place in your mind as you mull over the evidence you have collected, but writing about the evidence even before you have developed your idea often leads to more questions and helps you clarify what the evidence means. As you write, your mind surprises you; it reaches back into memory or leaps from one piece of evidence to another, making connections, helping you discover meaning.

Curiosity leads naturally to questions about meaning. Those questions often lead to the kinds of ideas you will need for your essays. Matthew Arnold, a nineteenth-century literary and social critic, associated curiosity with "a free play of the mind on all subjects, for its own sake." The phrase *for its own sake* suggests that the mind has its own delight, that it may be inclined to play over subjects just for the pleasure of thinking, free of bias. Perhaps you can hold Arnold's notion before you as a near-perfect state of mind for the writer curious about the meaning of things.

1   Inferring—A logical process

Ideas evolve in your mind as you consider the evidence, but the acts of mind that lead you from evidence to ideas are not part of a magical process. Although no formula ensures insight every time you examine a body of evidence, you can learn the logical process that leads from evidence to idea. (See 3d-1 for more on inductive reasoning.)

Consider this example: an elderly couple lives in the house across the street from you. For a week you notice that newspapers are accumulating in their yard. By the end of the week the grass needs mowing, and you know from past experience that the Spencers always keep their yard in perfect order. After noticing these changes, your curiosity is aroused, and you begin to pay attention to other signs around the house and to question their meaning. You wonder why the shades remain at the same position day after day and why the lights go out each night at the same time in all of the rooms except one. The Spencers do not come out for their usual walks in the late afternoon, and you do not see them in the reading room at the local library on Saturday morning. You wonder why. As you watch their house for other signs, you begin to make inferences about what might have happened to the Spencers. Those signs constitute your evidence, and you decide to try to figure out what it means.

Try always to formulate the simplest explanation that will account for the evidence. Here are four possibilities:

1. The Spencers have changed their habits.
2. The Spencers have gone away on vacation.
3. The Spencers are sick.
4. The Spencers have died.

These inferences are not forced by the evidence; they are not *necessarily* true. Put another way, the evidence itself does not spell out the answer; *you have to develop the theory or the idea that will account for the evidence.* As you gather more evidence—in this case, as you continue to observe what is going on around the Spencers' house—one of your ideas might become more plausible than another. You might, for example, read in the local newspaper that the Spencers won a trip to Asia. That piece of information would seem to confirm your second inference. But given what you know without that information, any one of your theories seems plausible, and without more evidence you have to consider which idea seems most convincing based on the available evidence. To reach a higher degree of certainty about your idea, you would have to gather more evidence.

The evidence you consider as a writer will often be less conclusive than that given here about the Spencers. Nevertheless, you attempt to develop an idea that accounts for the evidence you are examining. Rarely does an idea acquire the certainty of a fact.

Consider again civil disobedience (the topic we first looked at in 1c). If you read Thoreau's "Civil Disobedience," you may come away thinking that civil disobedience is not only a positive moral action but also a civic duty. If you then consider historical and contemporary events, such as the American Revolution and the more recent women's movement, you might reasonably conclude that civil disobedience leads to beneficial results. But if you look further, you can discover that civil disobedience does not always produce results pleasing to everyone. Demonstrators for and against abortion commit acts of civil disobedience, so whichever side you take, you see the other side as guilty of unjustifiable civil disobedience. In short, evidence gathered as a basis of writing is likely to be not only less conclusive than the details about the Spencers, but also fiercely contradictory. Considering and reconciling the evidence is part of the challenge and excitement of writing. (See 2d and 3d for more on inferences and interpretation.)

The accompanying Preliminary Questions to Ask Yourself about Evidence will remind you about looking for patterns and meaning in the evidence you evaluate. That evidence could be a written text, a painting, a photograph, or a real-life situation like the Spencers' disappearance. Follow one guideline at a time, giving yourself the opportunity to move deliberately, with an open mind. Remember, you are looking for an idea—a thought that the evidence suggests, a tentative answer to the questions you formulate. That tentative answer helps you make sense of evidence. It may change as you consider more evidence, eventually resulting in a leading idea for your essay.

2   Questioning a photograph—A student example

To illustrate how curiosity might lead you to interesting questions that can, in turn, guide you to ideas, let us consider a photograph that seems to offer, at first glance, little more than an arresting image of a young man in motion. His name is Killer Joe Piro; the photograph is by the well-known photographer Richard Avedon.

Preliminary Questions to Ask Yourself about Evidence

1. What do I first notice about the evidence? What is most obvious?
2. How do I feel about what I am seeing or reading?
3. Are any patterns obvious in the evidence?
4. When I look again, do I realize some deeper meaning that was not so obvious on first consideration? What can I logically infer about the evidence?

Instead of turning directly to the image itself, let Kristina Wilson's recreation of her first encounter with Joe Piro help you conjure up his image in your own imagination. When Kristina saw Avedon's photograph of Piro at the Whitney Museum in New York City, she had been dragged there on a Sunday morning by her father. Kristina would eventually study at New York University's Tisch School of the Arts, but that morning she had gone to the Whitney unwillingly. Piro grabbed her attention:

We inched our way through the huge gray, steel doors and eventually found our way into the exhibit itself. I walked through the entrance with my head down and my eyes averted, ironically making a show of my apathy. When something finally provoked me to look up--an elbow in my side, a person in front of me, what it was, I'm not quite sure--I came face to face with an image that has rarely left me since that morning.

A huge enlargement of Avedon's portrait of the dancer Killer Joe Piro confronted me, stared at me, commanded me to really <u>see</u> for once in my life. He threw his head back and his entire face rushed upward. His hair became a solid black mass with edges of velvet grain, and a cowlick of dagger-sharp spikes pointed downward from the left side of his head. A bit of his bangs fell forward onto his face, melding and becoming one with the shadows between the bridge of his nose and his left eye. Black eyes raced upward as well, reflections of light in the pupils carving burning paths in front of him like dividing lines on a highway. He seemed to have four eyes, six, and at the same time, none at all. Joe's nose, along with his forehead, cheeks and chin, were white hot, scorched into pure whiteness by intense light, and came together to make a negative-space cross. . . . His teeth were playing the same game as his eyes--multiplying and dividing until they became one and a thousand at the same time. Those white forms reached upwards and downwards like stalactites and stalagmites in the dank cave of Killer's mouth, interspersed with a few needle-thin light smears. His dynamic head rested upon a seemingly stable half circle of complete darkness, surrounded by a hint of white collar that disappeared into the stark white background and the deep black of

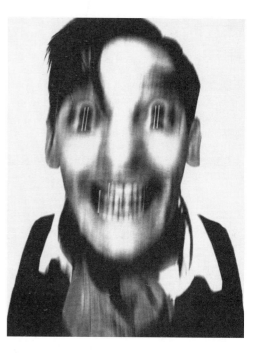

Photograph by Richard Avedon
Killer Joe Piro, dancer
New York City
January 3, 1962

Killer's sweater. An ascot ran down an inch or so from his chin, taking on the look of wood grain as it was smeared, as if by the hand of some small child, down into the darkness and off the print.

Never before had I been so enraptured by a single image, but Killer Joe sucked me in--into the massive fine grain that made up his blurring face, into his upward motion, and into photography.

I stood in front of him for a long time, trying to unlock his secrets--how was he moving? How had he been captured? How could *I* do work like this? I finally moved on to view the rest of the exhibit, which astounded me as well, but I kept finding myself in front of Joe again, as I do now.

3 Questioning to address the writing requirement

Kristina had been asked in a second-semester freshman writing class to select an image (a photograph, a painting, or a sculpture) and bring it to class, described in her own words so that others could see it as she saw it. The exercise was a preliminary step that would lead to an essay about the relationship between an artist and her or his work. To write the essay, Kristina would need an *idea;* to find an idea, she would need *evidence* to consider.

The recreated image—the word-picture brought by the student to class—was to be the first piece of evidence that students would investigate. Their task was to look at this initial piece of evidence—the image itself—to question it, and to look again to see what else it might reveal. That questioning should lead eventually to an idea.

Kristina's response—Questioning to find an idea

As you can see, Kristina's vivid description of the photograph ends with a series of interesting questions. Even as she describes her encounter with the photograph, she is already seeing Piro's image as a source of inspiration for her own work as a photographer. She sees motion and light.

In subsequent writing as she questions the photograph and tries to keep her mind on the essay requirement—the one that asks her to try to account for Avedon's relationship to the photograph—Kristina worries first about whether she has, in the two years since she first saw the photograph, "seen too much of Killer Joe, if I've exhausted a seemingly inexhaustible resource." She has a T-shirt with Joe on it, and a book about Avedon's photography by Jane Livingston. Killer Joe has "popped up" in her papers and conversations and her thoughts often. She worries about whether there is anything fresh to see. She questions whether too much knowledge gets in the way of seeing.

Looking at the photograph, she also begins to question whether her own work is being "polluted" by the opinions of others. That question leads to another, one more directly related to her essay assignment. Here is Kristina's account:

> In investigating the pollution that has occurred in my work, and in my view of Killer Joe, I begin to wonder if Avedon perhaps has the same problem. I would imagine that he does, and in much more profusion than I--after all, hundreds of critiques have been written about his work, and I have been privy to only a few. Avedon's portraits have been said to be about "being caught out of character, about the matter of transforming personality and disguising motive" (Livingston 11)-- a theory we can certainly find support for in his blurred, dynamic portrait of Killer Joe. Joe is most definitely being caught at something here--his entire body in motion and his eyes glaring maniacally at us.

Taking her cue from a 1995 PBS documentary that she had seen about Avedon's life, Kristina questions whether his photographs are not in some way self-portraits, whether all photographs are self-portraits, no matter what the subject. From the documentary, she recalls Avedon's struggle with "his strong Jewish roots coupled with his lack of native culture or religion and his sense of being the 'loneliest person on earth.'" She concludes tentatively: "So perhaps there is a piece of the photographer in his portrait of Killer Joe—the fleeting moment, the slight look of desperation in Joe's eyes, but I wonder—now that this fact has been revealed to him, how it is that he can continue to photograph so remarkably? How does he, how can *I*, get around knowing too much?"

Looking for a leading question or idea

That last question is the one that intrigues Kristina, and it is the one she tries to answer in her essay. Can photographers not be overwhelmed by too much self-knowledge and too much technical knowledge when they go out into the world to take their photographs? She concludes that they can get around knowing too much, that there is a way:

> Over time, old visions and theories will be worn down and pushed away by the gentle running of new ones over the old, like stones in a meandering stream. Eventually a small, polished smooth piece of something will remain, ready to be pulled out of one small branch of the massive, intricate system of waterways that are our minds.

Let's highlight the process that Kristina used and then infer additional guidelines for questioning evidence.

- Recall that Kristina began with evidence that she was genuinely interested in. Even though she had looked at that photograph of Piro many times, she chose to look at it again, to see if there was something there she had not seen before.
- She was also looking at the photograph in connection with the requirements of her writing course; that course gave her a line of inquiry, a question to begin with. As she looked and wrote about her questions, she asked more questions.
- She found two other sources of evidence: Jane Livingston's book about Avedon and the PBS documentary. Those sources came into play as she continued to question the photograph.
- Finally, the questioning led to an idea that she eventually developed in her essay, using as evidence the photograph as well as information from the Livingston book, the documentary, and several other essays that she read in the course.

EXERCISE 4–1   Questioning an Image

Select one of the paintings or photographs, other than the one of Killer Joe Piro. Using the guidelines on p. 79, question the image. Answer your own questions by writing about them. Keep a list of new questions that follow from your questions and your writing about them. Which question would you most want to keep investigating? What would you hope to learn from that investigation?

EXERCISE 4–2   Reconsidering *Killer Joe Piro*

Having read Kristina's description of Avedon's photograph of Killer Joe, what can you see in the photograph that Kristina did not mention? What does the image remind you of? What questions does it raise for you? Try to answer the most interesting of those questions by writing about it. Keep track of new questions and connections that come to you as you write.

EXERCISE 4–3   **Questioning Advertising**

1. Select from a magazine any advertisement for a beauty product. Question that advertisement using the guidelines above. Look especially for the way the written part of the advertisement fits in with the images it presents. Then consider how questioning led you to discover the advertisement's underlying assumptions about beauty. Discuss your responses to the photograph with others in the class. How do those responses help you *see* more?

2. Look at several other advertisements for beauty products. Question them and try to find an idea about them that you would like to investigate and develop in an essay.

Developing Questions from Evidence

1. Begin with evidence that interests you.
2. Study it. Look at it again and again to try to understand what it means. Use the guidelines about evidence on p. 75.
3. Think about the evidence and the assignment together. What questions do they suggest?
4. As you begin to ask questions, try to answer them in terms of what you already know. Write out these tentative answers. Then question your answers.
5. As you formulate answers, consider other related information that you remember or that comes from assigned readings in your course.
6. Look for the question that most intrigues you. Work with it; write about it. The answer to that question could turn out to be the idea you develop in your essay.

4b   Writing about evidence to find an idea—
                 Drafting and revising

     E. B. White, essayist, storyteller, and grammarian once said, "I always write a thing first and think about it afterward, which is not a bad procedure, because the easiest way to have consequential thoughts is to start putting them down." White seems to have followed his own sound advice in **drafting** several versions of one paragraph (attempting in writing to catch hold of an idea and to express that idea clearly). If you look carefully at his various drafts, you will see how, even in the construction of a single paragraph, White wrote and rewrote to clarify his thinking. (See 1g for a general discussion of drafting and revising.)

Watching White work his way through three drafts of a paragraph about the first moon walk, you will see that even professional writers do not get their ideas formulated on the first try. **Revising**—rewriting, redrafting, rethinking—is the watchword. White revises within a given draft to clarify a tentative idea that he is trying to express, and then he does more extensive revision from draft to draft as he becomes more certain about what he wants to say. Always, it seems, his desire to clarify and present an idea guides such revision.

Looking on the following pages at these drafts (three of the six drafts he wrote), you will see that White does not simply edit his work to correct errors or to make minor word changes within his sentences. Rather, he *explores* as he writes, trying to figure out exactly what that space walk he saw on television meant to him and what he wanted his audience to understand about what he saw.

White's drafts change considerably, and they suggest how you might also draft and revise. The accompanying guidelines, Writing to Discover and Clarify an Idea, give you a sense of what good writers do when they write to clarify an interesting idea.

1   White's first draft—Finding an idea

White began with what he saw on television one night in 1969, when Neil Armstrong and Buzz Aldrin stepped out of a lunar module onto the surface of the moon. That televised event constituted White's evidence.

Watching the astronauts, White was struck with a notion about the American flag that they planted on the moon. Thinking and writing about that notion, he clarified it and eventually turned it into a clear idea about universality and conquest. It took several drafts to get the words right.

Let us consider three of the six drafts of "Moon Landing" that White wrote. Look first at his initial draft. Although this first draft is rough, it lets you see how White got his initial thoughts down on paper and then modified them.

What can you learn about your own drafts from reading and thinking about White's? In his first draft, you can glimpse how a writer takes up one notion and then moves to another and then another, all in the space of one paragraph. White's first draft is his initial attempt to say something about the evidence, and he does not get the words right or the idea clarified in this first draft. Writers usually do not. You have to let your mind play over the evidence, to explore, to write down your thoughts, and to make mistakes. In this draft, White shows you how to wind your way to an idea.

Look carefully at how White compares preparing for a picnic and preparing for a trip to the moon. That connection sets his mind moving. At first, he emphasizes that the astronauts must have made fairly elaborate preparations for taking a little American flag to the moon. He devotes nearly two-thirds of his paragraph to developing that picnic analogy. But then he becomes *critical* about the planting of the flag and, when he does so, when he makes that *judgment* about the flag, he is on the scent of an idea.

white

comment

astronauts would never have reached their goal. But they sent along something that might better have been left behind —

Planning a trip to the moon, ~~isxessentiallyxno~~

~~differ~~ differs in no esstial respect from planning a trip
to the beach. You have to decide what to take, *along,* what to leave

behind. Should the thermos jug go? The child's rubber horse?
The dill pickles?
These are sometimes fateful decisions, on which the success or
failure   *outing*
~~isxhappixexxx~~ of the whole ~~expexixixx~~ turns. Something goes

along that spoils everything because it is always in the way.

Something gets left behind that spoils everything because it is
                                             were saddled with the
desperately needed for comfort or, safety. The men who had to
                                     for
decide what to ~~take~~ along to the moon must have pondered long and
hard, drawn up many a list. We're ~~not sure~~ they planned well, *n my*
when they included the
~~foxxthxyxeieexxedxtoxtakexalong~~ the little telescoped flagpole and
     artificially stiffened
the ~~stiffenxdx~~ American flag, ~~artifixxxlyxxxiffxxx~~d so that it
would fly to the breeze that didn't blow.
flew to the breeze that didn't blow. The Stars and Stripes on

the moon undoubtedly gave untold satisfaction to millions of
          But
~~Whx~~ As we watched the Stars and Stripes planted on the surface of

the moon, we experienced the same sensations of pride ~~and~~ that

must have filled the hearts of millions of Americans. But it

the emotion soon turned to *stone in my stomach*

~~This~~ was ~~our~~ *a* great chance, and we muffed it. The ~~xxxx~~ men who
                              were
stepped out onto the surface of the moon are in a class by
themselves---pioneers of what is universal. They saw the

earth whole---hust as it is, a round ball in a   But they ~~fittxed~~

colored the moon red, white, and blue0---~~good colors all---but~~

~~out of place in that setting.~~ The moon still ~~influences~~ the
                                  still
tides, and the tides lap on every shore, right around the globe.

White's First Draft   *(continued) still holds the Key to madness*

Kiss in every land

The moon stil belongs to lovers, and lovers are everywhere--not

just in America. What a pity we couldn't have planted some
             precisely   this unique, this incredible
emblem that ~~exactly~~ expressed the occasion, even if it were

nothing more than a white banner, with the legend: ~~XXXXXXXXXXXXX~~-y."
                                    that simply said E.
"At last!"

handkerchief, symbol of the common cold
Which, like the moon, belongs to all
mankind

White's First Draft

White thinks the planners and the astronauts "muffed it" when they planted the flag. Instead of being nationalistic, the astronauts should have done something with more universal appeal, something that would have been a more fitting tribute to all people. Having written his way to that idea, White begins to think about what the moon actually stands for, and his mind seems to reach out for a symbol as universal as the moon, "even if it [that symbol] were nothing more than a white banner."

The most striking feature of White's first draft is the way his mind moves from *picnic analogy* to *judgment* to *symbol*. One notion leads him to another, as he follows his own leads. But we can learn even more from his draft. White's corrections (both typed and handwritten) suggest that even as he wrote the draft, he moved away from his work to read it and think about it. On occasion, he realized that he needed to clarify what he had written, and he made those corrections you see—as he went along.

White was not content to let sentences stand as they were even though he was only drafting and laying out his idea. It was as if fixing a sentence allowed him to clarify his thinking and go forward. There is no better example of that kind of thoughtful revision than in the handwritten correction of the last sentence in this first draft. White makes the "white banner" more specific, more concrete; it becomes a "handkerchief, symbol of the common cold which, like

---

Writing to Discover and Clarify an Idea

1. Look carefully at the evidence, then begin writing about whatever notion strikes you as interesting.

2. At the outset, open your mind to intrusions—to new notions that want to be let into what you are writing.

3. Stop. Consider what you have written. See what your writing has revealed to you about the evidence.

4. Write another draft, beginning this time with your revelations about the evidence. See if you can clarify them by writing about them.

5. Make connections. If the revelation reminds you of other things you know or have read, write down those connections. See what they reveal to you.

6. Question your draft as if you are a member of your audience. Ask yourself questions about the relationship between the evolving idea and the evidence.

   • Is that relationship clear to an audience that has to read about it without the benefit of all that I know?

   • Are my intentions clear?

   • Are there deeper implications in the evidence than I have expressed, other aspects of the idea that need to be clarified?

   • What else might I learn about my idea if I examine my own draft according to Preliminary Questions to Ask Yourself about Evidence?

---

the moon, belongs to all mankind." That correction puts White on the track for a subsequent revision.

2   White's revised draft—Changing tone

Read White's revised draft. As you can see, the controlling idea about universality is again at the heart of White's paragraph, but he gets to that idea much sooner in the revised version and is much less harsh in his criticism of the flag planting. Nothing like "we muffed it" appears in his revision. White softens his tone—his expressed attitude about the event—even though he remains critical of the flag. (See 1d-3 on the relationship between tone and purpose.)

A lesson about audience is embedded in White's change in tone. He is trying to reach a general audience (see 1d-1), so he does not want to alienate his readers by criticizing too harshly that amazing accomplishment he witnessed on television. If his audience is proud of the accomplishment and White belittles it, he might turn readers away.

The following two versions of the same sentence reflect White's change in tone as he shifts from his harsh judgment to the idea about universality so closely related to that judgment.

white

comment

Planning a trip to the moon differs in no essential respect from planning a trip to the beach. You have to decide what to take along, what to leave behind. Should the thermos jug go? The child's rubber horse? The dill pickles? These are sometimes fateful decisions on which the success or failure of the whole outing turns. Something goes along that spoils everything because it is always in the way; something gets left behind that is desperately needed for comfort or for safety. The men who drew up the moon list for the astronauts planned long and hard and well. (Should the vacuum cleaner go, to suck up moondust?) Among the *inevitable* items they sent along, of course, was the little jointed flagpole and the flag that could be stiffened to the breeze that did not blow. (It is traditional among explorers to plant the flag.) Yet the two men who stepped out on the surface of the moon were in a class by themselves and should have been equipped ~~it~~ accordingly: they were of the new breed of men, those who had seen the earth whole. When, following instructions, they colored the moon red, white, and blue, they were fumbling with the past---or so it seemed to us, who watched, trembling with awe and admiration and pride. This moon plant was the last *chapter* scene in the long book of nationalism, one that could well have been omitted. The moon still holds the key to madness, which ~~its~~ is universal, still controls the tides that lap on shores everywhere, still guards lovers that kiss in every land under no banner but the ~~wide~~ sky. What a pity we couldn't have forsworn our little Iwo Jima scene and planted instead a banner acceptable to all---a simple white handkerchief, perhaps, symbol of the common cold, which, like the moon, affects us all.

White's Revised Draft

First Draft

The men who stepped out onto the surface of the moon were in a class by themselves—pioneers of what is universal, of men and women everywhere. They saw the earth whole—just as it is, a round ball in a dark sky.

Revised Draft

Yet the two men who stepped out on the surface of the moon were in a class by themselves and should have been equipped accordingly: they were of the new breed of men, those who had seen the earth whole.

Locate this sentence within White's revised draft, and try to figure out why the beginning word *Yet* is so important. How does it help change the tone of the entire paragraph? Think too about why White decides to call the astronauts a "new breed of men." Were they actually a new breed, or is this White's way of making readers think in a new way? Consider why the writer might have decided that the astronauts had "seen the earth whole" instead of as a "round ball in a dark sky."

White's subtle revisions of details are suggestive. He *speaks* to you indirectly through detail. White asks you to think and imagine as you confront his work.

White not only suggests something important about universality through these revised subtleties; he also makes other striking changes in the revised draft. In his last sentence, for example, the new phrase "Iwo Jima scene" clarifies his thinking about nationalism.

First Draft

What a pity we couldn't have planted some emblem that precisely expressed this unique, this incredible occasion, even if it were nothing more than a white handkerchief, symbol of the common cold which, like the moon, belongs to all mankind, that simply said: "At last!"

Revised Draft

What a pity we couldn't have forsworn our little Iwo Jima scene and planted instead a banner acceptable to all—a simple white handkerchief, perhaps, symbol of the common cold, which, like the moon, affects us all!

When White recalls Iwo Jima—a scene near the end of World War II when American soldiers raised the U.S. flag to signal victory and conquest (captured permanently in the Iwo Jima memorial sculpture at Arlington National Cemetery)—he has in mind nationalism, a symbolic, victorious act characteristic of postwar America. By changing "planted some emblem" to the more specific "Iwo Jima scene," White clarifies his judgment against the nationalistic act of flag planting and leans in the direction of a simpler, less-charged universal symbol—a white handkerchief—that does not make the astronauts look like American conquerors on the moon. Consider too how the words *pity* and *forsworn* convey White's judgment in the revised sentence.

White's revisions in this paragraph—his earlier emphasis on the idea about universality, his change of tone, the subtle alterations in detail, the addition of a new example—suggest the possibilities open to you as you revise your own work. Revision is never simply changing a word or a sentence here and there. It involves rethinking and reconstructing—*changing for the sake of clarifying and strengthening your presentation of the idea.*

3 White's final draft—Refining the idea

Scott Elledge, White's biographer, tells us that after White sent that revised version of the paragraph to *The New Yorker* (where the complete essay was published in 1969), he had a change of mind and composed three other drafts. White eventually phoned the final draft to his editor after he had telegraphed this message: "My comment [by which he means the 'revised draft' you just considered] is no good as is. I have written a shorter one on the same theme but different in tone."

```
white

comment

              The moon, it turns out, is a great place for
    men.  One-sixth gravity must be a lot of fun, and when Arm-
    strong and Aldrin went into their bouncy little dance, like
    two happy children, it was a moment not only of triumph but of
    gaiety.  The moon, on the other hand, is a poor place for flags.
    Ours looked stiff and awkward, trying to float on the breeze
    that does not blow.  (There must be a lesson here somewhere.)
    It is traditional, of course, for explorers to plant the flag,
    but it struck us, as we watched with awe and admiration and
    pride, that our two fellows were universal men, not national
    men, and should have been equipped accordingly.  Like every
                  and
    great river every great sea, the moon belongs to none and
    belongs to all.  It still holds the key to madness, still con-
    trols the tides that lap on shores everywhere, still guards the
    lovers that     kiss in every land under no banner but the sky.
    What a pity that in our moment of triumph we did not forswear
    the familiar Iwo Jima scene and plant instead a device acceptable
    to all:  a limp white handkerchief, perhaps, symbol of the
    common cold, which, like the moon, affects us all, unites us
    all.
```

White's Final Draft

Tone, as you have already learned, reveals a writer's relationship to his or her material. In White's final draft, you can see how he went even further to soften his tone and turn the moon walk into a festive occasion, marred only by the flag planting. Instead of blaming the astronauts, however, White shifts the blame for that nationalistic act to the planners. The astronauts were just doing what someone else told them to do. Now White tells us that the astronauts were "universal men, not national men" and that they "should have been equipped accordingly."

But perhaps the most significant lesson you can learn from White's final revision is about letting go of evidence that in the beginning of your exploration seemed so important but in the end has no place in the piece. The picnic analogy does not appear in White's final draft. At the outset, it led him to his idea, but as he began to emphasize that idea, the picnic analogy became less and less important. We know that it is in the background even in this final draft—in the lighthearted spirit of the paragraph—but packing and planning are much less important in the final draft. Festive sharing of a great moment occupies White's mind. He wants to make that moon walk a moment for everyone in the world.

White demonstrates in these three drafts how much freedom you have to revise as you write. His drafts show you as well *how to explore to find an idea and how to be responsible to both your idea and your audience.* The changes that he makes do not come automatically to any writer. They evolve as you write and think about your idea. Your aim, your purpose in writing (as you learned in Chapter 1), is to present your idea in such a way that your audience will be able to discern exactly what you mean. White's work reminds you that you have to stay with the task, sometimes through several drafts, to get the words—and the idea—right.

The same activities that led White to his idea while writing that single paragraph can also lead you to ideas when you write longer compositions. By writing drafts and revising, you can begin to discover and clarify your idea.

Questioning while writing

Curiosity leads you along from an initial hunch to questions about meaning. At the end of the first draft, White must have had in mind questions such as these: "What can I do to clarify my idea about universality?" "Am I being too tough on the astronauts?" "What is that flag planting all about?" "Why are Americans always staking a claim on territory?" "What would happen if we saw this event as something for everyone?" These are the kinds of questions you must learn to ask about your own writing. Such questions lead in turn to further revision and to clarification, as well as to more questions. The process is recursive, not linear. Ideas emerge as you write and mull over what you have written and as you write again, revising as your mind moves freely over the evidence. But remember: White did not follow any easy, clear-cut

rules in his revisions of his paragraph; only by writing and questioning and revising did he arrive at his final draft.

EXERCISE 4–4 Thinking about Drafting and Revising

1. Read back through each of White's three drafts and identify other revisions that seem significant to you. How exactly do these revisions help you understand White's idea? In two typed pages, describe the inferences you made about the writing process from studying White's revisions.
2. Consider the final draft of White's paragraph in terms of today's audience. Would his message about universality be undermined by his language? Does the term "universal men" contradict White's idea about universality? Did women have a place in all that moon planning and exploration? Revise White's final draft to eliminate the sexist language (see 29b).

EXERCISE 4–5 Drafting and Revising a Paragraph

1. Select an event that stirs your imagination—something you see on television, or read in the newspaper, or remember—and write a paragraph about it. Begin by writing freely about the event, letting your writing lead you to an idea. Then follow the guidelines in 4b (and White's example), and draft and revise until you have a paragraph that you want to present to your class about that idea.
2. Have your in-class work group or another classmate comment on your idea, questioning it as a way of helping you clarify it.

 4c Connecting—Another way to an idea

You have examined two techniques that lead writers to interesting ideas. That examination showed you how to begin thinking about evidence—how you can look at something as accessible as a photograph or a television event and begin to let your mind play over that material in search of an idea. Curiosity leads you to question the evidence, and questioning leads to the kind of writing that helps clarify ideas. Those two techniques—questioning and writing—can also lead you to make **connections,** to think about one thing in relation to another. Noticing relationships, you begin to notice ideas.

You saw the benefits of connecting when you looked at the way Kristina Wilson brought together the image of Killer Joe Piro, the Jane Livingston book on Avedon, and the PBS documentary. You also saw E. B. White connect a picnic with a lunar walk so that eventually he developed an idea about the flag the astronauts planted on the moon. For both writers, questioning, reading, writing, and connecting went hand in hand, as they often do.

As a general rule, you can better understand one thing by relating it to another. Noticing connections, you begin comparing and contrasting, accounting for likenesses and differences. Even when connecting similar subjects—the playing style of the Boston Celtics and the New York Knicks, the paintings of Picasso and Van Gogh, the corporate environment at Ford and General Motors—you begin to distinguish one from the other. In the process, you not only understand each of those subjects better but also begin to see that the comparison can lead you to ideas. Comparing and contrasting seemingly unrelated subjects, you may find even more interesting ideas.

1　Scientific research—Discoveries through connecting

Consider the unlikely connection between dolphins and chimpanzees that led to important scientific research. In "The Social Lives of Dolphins," William Booth, a science writer, relates a story about a place in western Australia where "wild bottlenosed dolphins swim into knee-deep water and allow tourists to stroke their flanks and feed them frozen fish." This site on the shores of Sharks Bay is now being compared to the Gombe Stream Reserve in Africa, where Jane Goodall studied chimpanzees. Researchers from the Gombe site were drawn to Sharks Bay because they were interested in comparing "the social lives of these two big-brained mammals."

The research into social communities began when two graduate students observed that dolphins at Sharks Bay showed evidence of "begging behavior similar to that exhibited by wild chimpanzees." Their comparison attracted the interest of other scientists and led to extensive research on the social lives of dolphins and chimpanzees. Here is a glimpse of some of their many findings about the way these mammals form communities.

> Within the community, dolphins have a tendency to associate with members of the same sex and age, except in the case of females and young calves. Mothers and offspring form some of the tightest bonds in the community, remaining together until the calf is weaned between the ages of three and four years.
>
> Indeed, like chimpanzees, sons and daughters may often closely associate with their mothers years after weaning. Wells [researching as far away as Florida] reports that he has watched older offspring return to their mother's side for the birth of a sibling. "They seem to want to check out the new arrival," says Wells.
>
> Female dolphins with calves are extremely cooperative. The mothers will often form "playpens" around youngsters and allow them to interact within the protective enclave. Episodes of "baby-sitting" are also common, where one female will watch another's calf while the mother is occupied elsewhere.

—William Booth, "The Social Lives of Dolphins"

Once you have read a few of these observations, you begin to make your own connections and ask your own questions. If chimpanzees exhibit social behavior similar to that exhibited by dolphins, what do these patterns of behavior tell you in general about big-brained mammals? Is their gender-related behavior learned or inherited? What might this information tell us about humans? These kinds of questions lead to further research and eventually to ideas. (See 4d for more on looking at controversies to find ideas.)

The simple connection made by the graduate students opened up a whole new world of research. You can see from that experience what you, too, might do. But you do not have to be off at a remote research site to reap the benefits of such connections. You need only be alert to your mind's work. When you think of a connection or a comparison, pursue it.

2   Academic exploration—A student connecting and searching

Let us turn now to the kind of connecting that can serve you in your courses, the kind of connecting that can lead you to a good idea of your own. Begin by thinking about what your mind can do for you if you allow it to move (sometimes leap) toward whatever connections it wants to make. Your precise understanding of what your mind has done will come after the fact, after you have written your thoughts down and turned back to see what your writing reveals to you. Joan Didion, a novelist and essayist, says, "I write entirely to find out what I'm thinking." Respecting that exploratory notion of Didion's, consider what can happen when you write with no other purpose at the outset than letting your mind make connections.

The writing assignment

We will consider work done by Anna Norris during a freshman writing class as a way of seeing how a process of connecting can lead to ideas. In her writing class, Anna was asked first to think and read about three abstract concepts—truth, representation, and value—and then to interpret what those concepts might mean to her in concrete terms, as a student or as a citizen living in the world.

In one of her other courses, Anna was studying photography, so she chose to think of those three abstract concepts as they might relate to her own photographs or to photography in general. Eventually she would need to find an idea related to those concepts so that she could write an essay for the writing course, but at the outset her primary business was connecting.

Anna's response—Reading, writing, connecting

As Anna began to think about the kind of representing that photographers do in their photographs—the way they represent themselves and the

Anna Norris, *Whispering Wall, Soho 1996*. Photograph by student, New York University, Collection of Anna Norris.

way they represent the world—she was able to call on reading that she was doing in her photography course and on her own experience. When she came to her writing instructor for an early conference, he suggested that she take preliminary notes about the connections that occurred to her as she thought and read about truth, representation, and value, and that she could take full advantage of the work and the reading she was doing in her other course. He encouraged her *to give free rein to her thoughts but to try to keep up with them,* making a list of ideas and reading notes as she worked. Here is an excerpt from Anna's list of notes based on her own photos, those of others, song lyrics, and her reading:

- Photography is a means to play and explore representation. It is done for the love of the medium itself—of fascination with pictures. From the beginning, love and fascination. My imagination, as in my photo of hands. The images [of hands] are fabricated, wispy, fanciful. [See Anna's photograph of hands within the photograph *Whispering Wall, Soho 1996.*]

- The photograph's truth is made up of nothing that has its representation in the surface of the image; any search for the truth behind the image would result in a synopsis of the method I used to arrive at these pretty fabrications.

- What's the use of pictures to anyone who didn't make them?

- Coffee table images. Stock photos. In their case, they gain meaning with context. As everything does, I would think. The story: the Polaroid show where my images were shown; images seem meaningless beyond the activity that went into them. Significance through context.

- "Meaning is discovered in what connects, and cannot exist with development." "When we find a photograph meaningful, we are lending it a past and a future" (quotes from book by Berger 89).

- "Photographs do not translate from appearances. They quote from them" (quote from Berger 96).

- "I have a photograph—preserve your memories, they're all that's left you"— Simon and Garfunkel, *Bookend's Theme*

- The muse of photography is memory—depend on and equally oppose the passing of time—stimulate and are stimulated by the interconnectedness of events (Berger 280).

- Don't look at this [photo of hands] with admiration, and then search for meaning! It is a trick of light, and the result of a playful period of time spent in the creation of this fabrication of mine. Watch what happens when the same sort of image, created in the same spirit, occupies a different space within a different context:

  POLAROID SHOW: assigned meaning, assigned worth
  OUTSIDE GALLERY: a place marker for the conflict with the city

- Collected and seen by a few people, the image's worth then is as an icon for something that happened to it. I can speak this way about [the photographs of hands] because they are my own photos, and though I can't really know their effect, I know the story and reasons for their conceptions.

This was not Anna's complete list, but it shows how her mind moved *from* general thoughts about photography *to* the quotations from *Another Way of Seeing* (John Berger's book) *to* Simon and Garfunkel *to* her own photographs and her thoughts about them. Obviously journal notes based on hearing Garfunkel and reading Berger influenced her thinking. (See reading journal, in 1e-1.) Probably journal notes on two or three other photographers and critics who appear in subsequent notes were important. (See 1e-2 on personal journals.)

Anna's idea—Connecting and more writing

It is productive for writers to read back through the notes, paying particular attention to key themes and ideas. In this example, notice the way Anna switches to her own photographs in the last section, beginning with "Don't look at this [picture] with admiration, and then search for meaning!" By that time in her thinking and writing, she had discovered an idea; it had evolved through the listing and the connecting and the writing. Some writers might accomplish these connections through mapping, listing, or outlining (see 1f).

Here in the beginning section of an essay she wrote later, "Photographic Assertions," you can see where the list and the idea led her. If you refer to the composite photograph of the hands that is included within *Whispering Wall*,

Soho 1996 (p. 91), you will see that this photograph of the hands is the image Anna refers to in the following passage:

Do not look at this image with admiration for some dreamed-up intrinsic value! It is a trick of light. Don't look at it with admiration for its aesthetics, and then search for meaning. Any search for the meaning of the image, as it stands here, would result in a synopsis of the method I used to arrive at this pretty fabrication. An explanation of the mechanics would not bring anyone closer to an understanding of the image's effects, or its worth to anyone else. This image, alone within the frame of a page, asserts very little.

The image exists as a medium; meaning will come from other sources. As John Berger explains, meaning lies in the connections that we make between an object or event or set of data, and its place within the set of information that we base our thoughts and judgments on, not in those things themselves, as isolated objects (89). Under this framework, it seems as if the photographer's role is inconsequential; why bother making an image at all, if perhaps a random object found in nature could spark just as valid a response at the viewer's whim? But the photographer's influence does not end with this isolated image, stranded, at the mercy of a viewer's set of individualized inferences and colorations; she still has the authority to change her image by placing it in a context. She then changes the image from a rectangle of light-sensitive materials, so contained in itself as to be bordering on solipsistic self-referentiality, into a powerful communicative medium.

If you look again at the *Whispering Wall* photograph, you can see the hands photo in a new context—the context of a city wall that gave it still another meaning. Anna's purpose in looking at her photos is to reveal her leading idea: *Seeing a photograph is complicated business. Isolated and alone a photograph may seem to represent one thing, but in a gallery show or in the context of a city, it may seem to represent another. Context changes meaning.*

In this next section of her essay, you can see Anna beginning to develop her idea:

With the understanding, then, that pretty pictures are worthless for their own sake, watch what happens when the same sort of image, created in the same spirit, occupies a different space within a different context. I make a Polaroid photograph of a delicate, wispy hand appearing twice on the pure black background as it moves across the frame. For a few months its only activity was in being taped to my wall as decoration, speaking nothing and asserting no new viewpoint. Then I made it a frame, as a way to make it seem more formal and serious and less like the playful experiment that it began as, and I entered it in a group show for exhibition in SoHo. The theme was "Instant Visions: Polaroid Photographs by and about Women in New York."

Now, without any change to the image itself, it becomes a representation of what it is to be a woman in New York. One might read the image as speaking of meditative, fanciful, ephemeral night-dreams that occupy a woman's mind as she escapes from daily drudgery. Perhaps it is the promise of learning to fly, before she realizes that she is still anchored by a body and its needs and her responsibilities. I could speculate to no end because within this established context, the image guides viewers to their own conclusions. Within this context the image held significance for someone; it sold within the first half-hour of the exhibition.

Connecting and writing led Anna to her idea about context and meaning. You can do what Anna did; the process is neither intimidating nor complicated. Yet there are no hard-and-fast rules to make that kind of connecting take place, just as there is no established, foolproof process that could lead Anna from her general comments about photography to the written texts and then to her idea. But there are some general principles embedded in her work that can help you make connections and discover ideas.

The accompanying Guidelines for Making Connections will help you. They encapsulate what Anna did. Follow one guideline at a time, giving yourself the opportunity to complete one before going on.

Guidelines for Making Connections

1. Begin always with an aspect of your chosen or assigned topic that interests you most. Select this aspect after you have thought about the topic and have perhaps done some reading about it.

2. List your thoughts, allowing your mind free rein as you make your list. As connections occur, jot them down. Connections can be to related thoughts, to course readings, to other kinds of texts—photographs, movies, poems.

3. Question your preliminary list. See if reading through that list all at once might generate new insights, new connections.

4. Give yourself space to write notes in the margins beside the list—add thoughts, other connections, questions.

5. Look over the list and the notes to see what you have discovered. Does that discovery stand up to the *test of a good idea:* When you state the idea outright, might it cause others to want to know more? Might there be a suggestion in it that needs developing and explaining so that someone else could understand it?

EXERCISE 4–6   Formulating Ideas

What other ideas do you see emerging from Anna's list (p. 91–92)? If you work within a discussion group in class, write down your ideas and compare them with ideas recorded by other members of your group. Try to reach some consensus about an idea related to context and meaning. If you are working alone, see if you can capture an idea of your own about context and meaning, in two or three sentences.

Art and Ideas

The reproductions of two photos and two paintings on these pages are featured in this *Handbook* as starting points for student writing projects described in Chapters 4, 6, and 47. In these chapters, you will see how student writers, responding to these works of art, were able to develop fresh ideas for writing. If you are tempted to develop your own writing ideas with these or some other images, you can find some useful guidelines in sections 2d, 2e, and 4a to help you get started analyzing and interpreting a text or image.

Photograph by Richard Avedon
Killer Joe Piro, dancer
New York City
January 3, 1962

Anna Norris, *Whispering Wall, Soho* (1996). Photograph by student, New York University. Collection of Anna Norris.

Pablo Picasso, *Guernica* (1937). Museo Nacional Centro de Arte Reina Sofia, Madrid. © 1997 Estate of Pablo Picasso / Artists Rights Society (ARS), New York.

Vincent van Gogh, *The Starry Night* (1889). Oil on canvas. 29″ x 36 1/4″. Collection, the Museum of Modern Art, New York. Acquired through the Lillie P. Bliss Bequest.

EXERCISE 4–7   Making Connections

1. Turn to Anna's photograph, *Whispering Wall, Soho 1996* (p. 91). The photograph is a picture of what she considered her "gallery," a wall in Soho where artists put pictures; she put hers there and left them for people to take or do with what they wanted. Consider the broader social context for "Whispering Wall" as Anna describes it: "During the time that I was operating my 'gallery,' a conflict came into play between the street artists and the New York City government, wherein the city repeatedly and illegally arrested artists for selling their works on the sidewalk." Make as many connections as you can between what Anna has told you and what you can see in the picture. Give your imagination free rein. Make a list of the connections. See if you can discover an idea of your own as you make connections and write about them.

2. Now look again at the photograph. This time, look with critic Joel Eisenger's remark in mind: "Captions change, the context of display changes, the times change. In the end, photographs have no fixed meaning; they float free of any anchor in discourse, offering endless possibilities for speculation." To what extent do you agree or disagree with Eisenger? Formulate a one-paragraph answer in light of Anna's story about the hands photo (described in 4c-2), Eisenger's remark, and your own experience with the way objects either change meaning in different contexts or stay relatively the same over time. Try to work both Anna and Eisenger into your paragraph.

EXERCISE 4–8   Comparing as a Way of Connecting

Consider two fields of study that interest you. Start by writing an impersonal and objective paragraph comparing and contrasting the two fields. Then prepare two or three other paragraphs about the fields, making these more subjective and personal. Recall how you first became interested in each of the fields. Next, consider the impersonal comparison in terms of the more personal exploration. What are the relative merits of each? Finally, let one of those personal accounts, the one you like best, lead you to other connections and ideas. Do not restrict the play of your mind in this final phase of the exercise. Let your mind take its own direction.

4d   Looking at controversies to find ideas

The writing examples presented thus far suggest not only how questioning, writing, and connecting can help you find an interesting idea but also how close at hand such ideas can be. You need not go far to find evidence based on your own experiences and observations, and it can lead you to an idea worth writing about.

But, of course, as a student you will have to find other types of evidence. You saw an example of the kind of evidence that comes from research when you considered the connections between dolphins and chimpanzees made earlier in this chapter (4c-1). Evidence from research may come from the field (as with the dolphins and chimpanzees), or it may be found in the library.

In many of your college courses you will be called on often to do directed research, which involves focused reading. Your instructor may ask you to write about a particular subject, such as civil disobedience, the Persian Gulf War, gun control, or environmental waste. Perhaps you choose a subject and write about it. Whatever your subject, questioning, writing, and connecting can serve you well as you try to find an idea related to evidence from research, but identifying a controversy related to your subject can also lead quickly to an idea. (See Chapters 43–46 for more on conducting research.)

1 Finding a thesis within controversies

Typically, when doing assigned research, you will be asked to develop a leading idea in the form of a **thesis**—a point of view about your subject. That thesis, like a good idea, is nothing more than your conclusion about what the evidence means. One effective way to discover your own point of view is to consider what others have written about your subject. In the sources you consult, look always for differing points of view because they usually signal a topic worthy of your consideration; they point to the heart of controversy.

For every controversial issue, you are sure to find special-interest groups that insist on your seeing the issue the way they see it. You have to sort out the issues and try to resolve the controversy.

Because neither you nor anyone else can be expected to have the range of experience each special-interest group represents, you have to supplement your own limited experience with research. You have to broaden your understanding of the issues, turning to other **sources** for help: books and articles; published interviews and personal interviews (i.e., those you conduct with experts and others affected by the issue or problem you are investigating); newspapers; government studies; documentaries; pamphlets; and any other source that might give you a clearer understanding of the controversy.

A thorough consideration of the appropriate and available sources should help you decide what you think about the controversy. Your reasonable conclusion will become the thesis for your essay.

Considering the gray wolf controversy

Let us see how a consideration of conflicting points of view can help you develop an idea. When Ericka Kostka, a student, began her research, she was concerned about the disappearance of the gray wolf from the United States. But she decided to limit her inquiry to Yellowstone National Park, even though the wolf problem exists elsewhere.

Ericka's research pinpointed several special-interest groups, chiefly environmentalists, who wanted to restore the wolf population, and stockgrowers, who feared the wolves would endanger their stock. As she uncovered the competing points of view, she had to weigh one against the other. To do so, she had to locate as best she could a reliable account of each group's vested interest. No single source provided a solution. Ericka had to search through written accounts for answers. That search gave purpose to her research, focused her effort, and led to an idea about the gray wolf.

2   Arriving at a thesis

Behind Ericka's search for a clear resolution of the wolf controversy was a guiding question that focused her research: To what extent does it seem reasonable, given the conflicting interests, to make an effort to restore the wolf population in Yellowstone? As Ericka gathered evidence and considered the conflicting points of view, that question kept her on track. It could not be answered with a simple "yes" or "no"; it required her to think about *reasonableness* as she developed her thesis.

To reach a conclusion, Ericka had to consider those opposing points of view. She had to learn enough about each special-interest group to know how to formulate her thesis—the idea that would give purpose and unity to her essay. Here is her thesis.

Given that evidence strongly indicates that wolf populations are important to the predator-prey balance of nature [in Yellowstone] and that the details of repopulation can be viable for both the gray wolf and its opponents, I believe that we should reverse the one-sided concessions to the stockgrowers that we forced upon a now endangered population.

Ericka did not bring the thesis to the assignment. Rather, it evolved through learning and writing, as she considered conflicting points of view, wrote about them, questioned them, and, finally, reached her own conclusion.

In Chapter 44, you can see in detail how Ericka questioned those points of view, resolved the controversy, and wrote a research essay to present and defend her thesis. Her complete essay appears in 46a.

3   Using your own investigations to resolve controversies

Ericka's methods can also serve you well when you do directed research to develop a thesis for your own essays. This recursive process, which takes you from library sources to drafting and back to the sources, moves back and forth until you can formulate a thesis that you feel confident defending. The accompanying checklist, Considering Controversies to Find Ideas, will guide you. (See also Chapter 7 on argumentative essays and Chapter 44 on the research essay.)

Considering Controversies to Find Ideas

1. Select a controversy that interests you.
2. Go to the library. Locate sources for conflicting points of view. (See Chapter 43 on researching.) Outline each special-interest group's concerns.
3. Question sources. Look for weaknesses and connections in the various arguments.
4. Begin to formulate what you think is a reasonable conclusion about the controversy. Write down your thesis and your reasons for believing it. List questions that still need to be answered.
5. Broaden your reading to help answer remaining questions and test your conclusion, making sure that you have not overlooked important evidence.
6. Modify your conclusion in light of the evidence and formulate your thesis—the clear-headed statement that you will set down and defend in an essay.

EXERCISE 4–9 **Locating and Investigating a Controversy**

---

1. Read the local or state newspaper for three or four days looking for a story about a controversial topic that is important enough to require coverage for more than one day. Read the coverage carefully, looking for signs of special-interest groups. List the groups and their opinions. Which group do you side with? Why?

2. Investigate one of the groups that you did not side with—by reading other newspapers, by interviewing people involved in the controversy, by discussing the subject with others in your writing class. Try to be open minded about that other group's point of view but question their ideas, looking for their value as well as their weakness. Write a paragraph about the other group's special interest. Question what you have said about the group's point of view. Does this preliminary research change your mind about the controversy? Explain.

4e Using collaboration as a way to find ideas

In Chapter 1, you learned about collaboration and were provided Guidelines for Collaboration (1h). The emphasis there was on collaboration during drafting and revising. Here we want to shift the emphasis to a period of time just before you begin drafting your essay or just after, when you are still trying to develop a good idea. During this searching stage, any one of several collaborators can help you: your instructor, the members of an in-class work group whose members follow one another's writing (on paper or online), or, if you do not work in groups, one of your classmates.

As you develop ideas, you can expect a collaborator to help you with your thinking and help you as you experiment with any of those other four techniques that can lead you to ideas: questioning, writing, connecting, or considering controversies. If you go back to review any of those techniques, you will notice collaborative exercises for each of them.

As a way of seeing how collaboration might help as you work with the other four techniques, let us consider again Kristina Wilson's work with the Avedon photograph, *Killer Joe Piro* (see 4a-2). In a very early draft of her essay based on her interest in that photograph, Kristina was trying to make connections with other texts that she was reading in her writing course. She had begun to question whether a photographer who knows too much, either about the art of photography or about herself as an artist, might be hampered while taking pictures. Might knowing too much interfere with picture taking or with seeing an art object?

Collaboration to share connections between ideas and reading

As Kristina explored this question, she made a couple of tentative connections with essays she had read by E. M. Forster ("Anonymity: An Inquiry") and C. G. Jung ("On the Relation of Analytical Psychology to Poetry"). Here is her draft paragraph that considers these connections:

> Of course, I wouldn't desire a purely aesthetic, untrained view of art either, even though Forster declared that "aesthetic experience is an end in itself, worth having on its own account." I would hope that perhaps a happy medium between the two could be reached, a state in which we could see without blinding ourselves in the process. As Jung revealed, "There are all sorts of ways in which the conscious mind is not only influenced by the unconscious but actually guided by it," and I long for the day in which we can be guided more in this fashion, and less by our selves.

Collaboration to clarify thinking and focus

One of her classmates who was collaborating with Kristina made this written comment at the end of the paragraph: "You're contending that our experiences are not part of our self. That our unconscious is our self—is that what you really think?" That reader included these additional comments at the end of Kristina's draft. Notice the balance between praise and suggestion:

Kristina--the description of Killer Joe is so amazing. You definitely pulled the reader into the Avedon piece and into your own piece. I think I held my breath. You connected everything so well. The Killer Joe part leads to your idea--how can one really see, without being tainted by experience, etc. or by seeing too much. You explore your self-portraits.

That was great === the journal entry was good--you posed questions to your self & therefore to the reader. Fitting Jung into that was fluid + clear. He supported you + you didn't force the incorporation. Then Gablik + Forster fit in really well, in assisting your thinking. Overall--it's great you have a clear idea, + it's well supported by the image you used, your experience, + texts. The only thing I see that needs work is, besides a conclusion, I was caught off guard + a bit distracted w/the section on page 5--the section with "Family Matters." I think you can possibly use another example to make it more effective, if you agree. Also towards the end, I would bring Avedon's piece back, but maybe you're going to do that in the conclusion.

You did do a good job of reflecting. The texts lead you to exploring the idea, they don't control you or the idea.

Collaboration to discover ideas through writing

Kristina talked with her fellow collaborator in class after each of them had read the other's draft. Kristina wrote another draft and deleted the paragraph on "Family Matters" that her collaborator had questioned. She added a long concluding section and revised the Forster paragraph as follows:

On the other hand, E. M. Forster looks at our mind's role in our interpretation of art from the opposite perspective. If our thought-processes are "undisciplined and uncontrolled by the eye," he asserts, "we may take just the same course through dreamland . . . and never experience anything new." Forster's theory, I think, remains true only if we are speaking of a completely disinterested individual, such as a tourist who is dragged along from museum to museum by some member of his family, and whose only concern is in getting back to his hotel. This traveler is merely a bystander, not an observer--all he sees when he looks at a painting, or a photograph, or a statue is the desire to go to his hotel room and relax. The undisciplined yet interested mind, however, is free to see a myriad of things in any work of art, in any aspect of life. This mind sees the very essence of the work itself, untainted by the critic's views or their own old expositions. It sees.

It is unlikely that Kristina could have made the changes she did in her essay without the helpful comments from her collaborator. Two minds working for a while on the same problem enhanced their thinking and led Kristina to a clearer formulation of her idea and, in turn, to a better essay.

The Essay

Audience, Purpose, and the Essay

*A*n essay is a trial, a writer's attempt to entice an audience to think about an idea. The way you as a writer present that idea depends on your audience and purpose. But all essays have organization: a beginning that introduces the main idea; a middle that considers the idea and presents the evidence; and an ending that unifies the essay and reminds the reader about the idea and its importance. In Part Two, you will learn how this three-part structure varies according to the essay's purpose, but you will also see how, despite variations, beginning, middle, and ending give shape and clarity to an essay.

Your purpose will often dictate the kind of essay you write. If you want your audience to think about the stuff of everyday, including your own experiences, and you wish to maintain a casual and conversational tone, you would write an *exploratory essay* (Chapter 5). It would likely ramble a bit while making its case.

If you want to reveal your discoveries about the relationships within something you've read or seen (characters in a short story, shapes in a painting, or scenes in a television show), and if you then want to indicate what those relationships have to do with the meaning of a piece, you would write an *analytical essay* (Chapter 6). It would rely on a straightforward presentation and defense of your idea.

If your purpose is to convince an audience of your position on a controversial issue or topic (e.g., the gray wolf population in Yellowstone ought to be restored), you would write an *argumentative essay* (Chapter 7). It is likely to be straightforward and address the positions of the various special-interest groups involved in the controversy.

All essays have a common purpose: the clear and interesting expression of an idea. As you consider how to develop exploratory, analytical, and argumentative essays in Chapters 5–7, you will see how writers vary the way they develop their ideas.

CHAPTER 5

The Exploratory Essay

The **exploratory essay** has an ambling, storytelling quality. Its tone suggests that you are inviting your reader to sit back and listen, that your idea will not unfold predictably but will follow the twists and turns of your mind playing over the evidence. The evidence is often a story of experience, but it could just as well be an allusion to or a story about a book you have read or a movie you have seen.

Although an exploratory essay has a beginning, a middle, and an ending, it offers, nevertheless, more organizational freedom than the analytical or argumentative essay. An exploratory essay can refer to almost anything that might cause your readers to pay attention—a painting, song, movie, poem, or book—so long as what you write about helps readers understand your main idea. Those surprising mental turns and the meaningful connections help generate reader interest just as they help clarify your idea.

Exploratory essayists ruminate, ponder ideas almost for the pleasure of the process, and move to the full expression of those ideas without insisting. They would not argue, for example, that final examinations be abolished and then offer three reasons—in three paragraphs—for doing so. A short, insistent argumentative essay can be effective, especially when those three reasons are sound and when the paragraphs develop cogent, supporting points. But that argumentative essay lacks the searching quality of the exploratory essay, which is more like an inquiry about an idea than a defense of it. The accompanying Features of the Exploratory Essay outlines the main characteristics of such an essay.

The *purposes* for writing exploratory essays vary, but primarily these essays give readers a chance to observe writers in the act of thinking about an idea, working it out, while they are presenting it. The exploratory essay fosters inquiry. Writers often use it as a way of trying to get at an idea that is not susceptible to rigorous proof; such ideas are, nevertheless, susceptible to rigorous analysis, and they are important. The two student writers whose work appears in this chapter are looking into the power of the imagination and the nature of learning. They have no interest in arguing a particular point; instead, they want to explore an idea and reach a tentative conclusion large enough to account for their discoveries.

Audiences for exploratory essays usually consist of generalists (1d-1), but they are generalists who enjoy the art of playful, inquiring discourse, readers who are interested in elusive but important subjects that call on a writer to experiment and to make odd, but relevant connections as a way of clarifying an idea. Specific audiences could range from a class of student writers to readers of familiar essays or academics assembled at a scholarly conference. Such readers have an interest in following how a well-informed writer plays seriously with a complex, compelling idea, using an essay form that can accommodate stories of experience as well as a whole array of other kinds of evidence.

Features of the Exploratory Essay

- Develops an idea in an interesting, informal way.
- Permits the essayist to make far-reaching connections that clarify the idea.
- Encourages the use of experience and other texts as evidence.
- Encourages the essayist to use various kinds of evidence to add new dimensions to the idea, enriching it and making it more interesting as the essay evolves.
- Seems more like an inquiry into meaning than a proof.
- Has a beginning, a middle, and an ending.

5a Exploring by connecting stories of experience

You may recall from Chapter 4 how Anna Norris connected stories about her photographs with written texts to find and develop an idea about the way meaning is affected by context (see 4c). By following Anna's example and Betsy Miller's complete essay (which we will refer to throughout the first part of this chapter), you can learn to connect your own memories of experience and begin to create your own exploratory essay. Writing this kind of essay involves more than connecting memories; but the process is no more complicated at the outset than telling an interesting story. Remember that one way to distinguish a storyteller from an essayist is the way they tell stories: a storyteller aims mainly to entertain; an essayist selects stories as evidence, using them to illustrate ideas as well as to entertain. Essayists make connections and discover relationships among their seemingly unrelated experiences, and in the process, they find meaning or significance in them. A story used effectively in an exploratory essay does just what data gathered from research does in an argumentative essay—it helps you develop your idea.

Although writers occasionally create an exploratory essay out of a single story, they more often connect two or more stories to illustrate their idea.

Remember that a story is not an essay. Tacking a moral onto the end of a story does not create an exploratory essay; it creates a story with a moral tacked onto the end. As you study Betsy Miller's essay in the first section of this chapter, you will see how she links two and then three stories together, clarifying and enriching her idea as she develops it. In the second section (5c), you will see Alexandra Johnes connect written texts and stories to develop an idea about learning.

By considering Betsy's composing process as well as the distinguishing features of the essay she creates, you will learn how to apply the accompanying Guidelines for Developing an Exploratory Essay. You can, of course, create such an essay in other ways, but the composing process that led to Betsy's essay encourages exploration. By examining her work, we can pinpoint the major features of the exploratory essay.

Guidelines for Developing an Exploratory Essay

- Recall an experience that continues to excite or haunt you. Re-create that experience in writing (see 5b).
- After you write your version of the experience, think about what it means. Locate the idea in your story of experience (see 5b).
- Use collaboration to develop and revise your idea (see 5b-1).
- Let that experience and that idea serve as a lodestone—a magnetic force—pulling in another experience related to the idea you discovered in the first experience (see 5b-2).
- As you write, begin to link your stories of experience. You can also include references to other texts that occur to you as you connect your stories and develop your ideas (see 5a and 5c).
- At this point you are drafting the middle of an exploratory essay, making discoveries about your idea, even as you write and figure out how the stories and other texts might fit together (see 5b-1–4).
- Attempt the beginning of your essay after you know more about what the evidence means to you (see 5b-4). Write a beginning for your essay that will grab your readers' interest and introduce your idea. Add to your essay as you write and think of new evidence that can help you clarify your emerging idea (see 5b-5–6).
- Write an ending for your essay that further explains the idea (see 5b-6).
- Revise your essay again, going back to clarify the meaning of your evidence as you develop your idea. Think about audience and purpose, making sure that your readers know enough to understand your idea.
- Select a short title, one that will catch your readers' attention. Aim to find a word or two that captures the essence of your idea. Reread your essay in light of your title. Does the title work with your essay? If not, revise it.

In her first-year college writing class, Betsy Miller was asked to write, in three typed pages or less, about an experience that still lingered in her memory, one that still clung to her imagination. She was asked to render that story so that her readers could *experience* it themselves, could know what it was like to have been there when it happened. In the process of writing it, she went through many of the thinking and writing processes described in Chapters 3 and 4. Here is her first story.

Betsy's first story

My two youngest brothers always get to open a few presents on Christmas Eve. Daniel, my youngest brother, celebrated his third Christmas this year. He joyfully pranced around the living room, surrounded by many gifts that most children his age, including Daniel, normally find fascinating. But only one present held Daniel's attention that evening: the Batman costume from Aunt Pat. Ever since he had unwrapped the gift and discovered what it was, he had dragged the box containing the costume around the living room, demanding that someone help him put it on. Finally, catching the attention of his mother, she helped Daniel, and he suddenly turned into Batman, running around the living room and shooting his family members with tiny plastic arrows from his knuckle gun. His glossy red hair poking out the sides, Daniel peered through the eyes of his Batman mask with a look of confidence and determination, ready to conquer any villains posing a potential threat to the successful completion of his mission, whatever it might be.

Tired of playing dead every time Daniel pegged me with one of his arrows, I began to read the box that had contained the Batman costume. A warning sign on its side caught my eye:

WARNING

Vest is not really bulletproof.

Cape will not enable user to fly.

I chuckled as I read the note of caution, then burst into laughter as I realized its absurdity. How could anyone think that a little piece of nylon could send them soaring into the air? My whole family joined me in laughter after I read the warning to them, as they too considered how silly it was. That is, everyone except Daniel. Although understanding the words I had said, he found no humor in them. Instead of joining in the laughter of the rest of his family, Daniel continued to prance about the room, completely absorbed in the fantasy of the world to which his Batman costume had flown him.

Each day, Daniel lives the excitement of a different world, one of which he is the sole creator. That night, Daniel was Batman. He ran about the room, stalking his prey and deftly conquering each one with his batlike agility--the thin, black cape streaming behind him. That night, there was no one in Daniel's world more powerful than he.

1   Using collaboration to find an idea

The students in Betsy's composition class were organized into work groups whose purpose was to comment on one another's writing or to collaborate. (See 1h and 4e for more on collaboration.) Betsy read her story to the other five members of her group, all of whom had written stories. Each student was to tell Betsy what he or she thought the story was about and whether it contained an idea. Betsy was to listen without comment to the group's responses, which follow.

I think the story is about how silly we are when we are young.

The story doesn't seem to be about being silly; it seems to be about Betsy's cruelty to her younger brother—the way we react to younger brothers and sisters when we get tired of playing the games they ask us to play. Then we say something to them to get even, and we hurt their feelings.

Well, I see all of that, but that last paragraph, that last part of the story, seems to be about Daniel and the power of his imagination. After all, Betsy tells us, "That night, Daniel was Batman."

Good point, but I think the story is really about the stupidity of warning labels. I read something the other day about those labels on mattresses and sofas, the ones you're not supposed to take off. You know, the ones that will get you fined. I see some of that absurdity in what Betsy tells us in her story.

At the end of the collaborative session, Betsy and the other students were asked to think about their own stories, to reflect on their meaning, and to see if they could infer ideas from them. The session helped the students gain a clearer sense of what their stories were really about, or could be about if told in a slightly different way. For their next class, the students were asked to let the emerging idea serve as a lodestone to pull in a second story that could clarify, illustrate, and enrich the idea.

2   Writing and connecting to find out what you are thinking

Essayists must seek ways to help readers understand their ideas. No individual story tells us everything we need to know about the idea. Each story reveals something a little different; each has its part to play in the essay.

After thinking about her classmates' comments, Betsy began writing her second story. She explored as she wrote, letting her two stories come together.

She sensed that they were connected, and while she was drafting she wrote without worrying about what idea or ideas would bring them together in the essay. (See 4b and 4c for more on writing and connecting as ways of finding ideas.)

Daniel's cape was very much on Betsy's mind as she wrote; in fact, she had decided to wear the cape herself, in an imaginary way, and to think also of her friend David decked out in his own cape while they played dodgeball. Her aim was to clarify her thoughts about the transforming power of imagination. Here is her second story.

Betsy's second story

As David and I frolicked about the dodgeball court during recess in the third grade, there were no real Batman capes streaming behind us, but we soared just as high as Daniel did that Christmas Eve. We were completely absorbed in the thrill of competing against other dodgeball teams, focusing solely on our movements and the rules of the game. Nothing else in the whole world mattered to us on that wonderful afternoon except our game of dodgeball.

In my continuous quest to sharpen my dodgeball skills, I took it upon myself to ask David for some personal help in developing my ball-throwing technique. In his carefree manner, he remarked to me that it was all in the wrist and demonstrated exactly how he used his wrist to produce such power. In his blue and white school uniform, shirt untucked as usual, he smiled gleefully and hurled a ball across the court, hitting the wooden kick board on the opposite side with a resounding thud. Pleased by the fascination I showed toward his unique ability, he smiled, messed up my hair, and darted across the court to retrieve the ball and give me a try. Despite the simplicity and the clarity of his explanation, I never quite caught on to David's art of ball throwing, but I treasure my memory of him and me soaring, supported by our capes, together through our world of dodgeball.

A skiing accident over Christmas vacation took away David's ability to walk, ripping from him the cape that had allowed him to soar through his world of athletics, dominating every sport he undertook. Instead, he was forced to cope with life as a paraplegic during the prime of his athletic career. David's skiing accident forced him to picture himself in a wheelchair, a picture that he found too difficult to accept. After losing his ability to fly in his world of athletics, the one he loved most, David was not able to climb back on the rest of his cape. He wheeled himself off a pier into Lake Washington this month, taking his life and the love of many with him.

3   Getting at the idea through creative thinking

Betsy has still not found the precise leading idea that will hold her essay together, but she is getting closer. As E. B. White did in the paragraph you considered in Chapter 4, Betsy is thinking as she writes. As she explores, she seems to be asking her readers to believe that the cape her little brother wore is a cape that all of us might want to keep wearing past childhood. She suggests that such a cape can empower everyone. But she also becomes keenly aware that such empowerment may not always sustain us. David, according to Betsy's speculations, lost the cape we create in our imagination—his ability to fly. Nevertheless, Betsy seems to be holding on to the idea that there is some life-sustaining power in it. She seems to believe that imagination itself can lift us above the mundane and the tragic. That idea evolved out of the writing and the connections she began to explore between the cape her brother wore on Christmas Eve and the capes she imagined she and her friend David had also worn on the dodgeball court.

These two writing activities—the recovery of a memory and the working out of its relationship to another memory—have led Betsy closer to an idea. But even at this point in her drafting, she is still not ready to pin down the idea and limit it because she is not yet clear about all of its implications. Nevertheless, she is ready to try a beginning for her essay that may help her refine the idea even more.

4   Beginning the essay

The **beginning** of an essay—also known as the *introduction*—is an invitation to the reader. It not only guides the reader into the essay by alluding to the idea, but also makes the reader want to continue reading.

In the drafts of her two stories of experience, Betsy presented her evidence and developed her idea in what will become the middle of her essay. Now that she has a clearer sense of that idea, she wants to try to introduce it to her readers.

Because the beginning forecasts what will follow, it is difficult to say exactly *when* you should write it. If you have not begun to select and consolidate your evidence, whether that evidence consists of stories or research data, it makes little sense to try to write a beginning. First get a feel for the evidence. Write a bit of the middle, as Betsy has done. Explore. Think and write concurrently about the evidence.

A good rule of thumb is to write a draft of your beginning only after you have begun to collect your evidence and to consider what you want to say about it. You can revise the beginning as you collect more evidence and refine your idea.

Your beginning should make it easy for the reader to understand your idea and how you will develop it. You need not say, "In this essay, I am going to develop the idea that imagination can empower us long past childhood, and I am going to develop that idea by telling you two or three stories so that you will be able to see what I mean." Most readers prefer something subtler— an inviting hint, perhaps. In the beginning of Betsy's essay, which follows, she says, "But I still try to hold onto my cape." That tells her readers that she has not given up on the imagination's power to let her fly "high above my worlds." By placing that statement near the end of her introduction, Betsy invites her readers to go on reading the rest of the essay, where they can discover why she continues to "hold onto" her cape. That statement also leads readers smoothly and logically into the middle.

Consider Betsy's first try at a beginning. As you read, notice how she picks up the threads of her idea from the two stories and tries to clarify her idea.

Betsy's beginning: First draft

I soar across the vast terrain of my world, a world about which I know everything there is to know, supported by my cape. My cape has several forms; it has accompanied me across many lands, each my own creation. It has brought me much comfort and pleasure throughout my life, instilling within me a great love for flying. My closest companion, it has always supported me in the past. But it is growing tired now, and I fear that someday it may no longer be able to take me flying across my worlds at my whim. The many forms of my cape are slowly being pulled out from under me, sending me tumbling down to the earth where I am confronted by a new world, one that is far more frightening, and intriguing, than the ones I have created for myself in the past. But I still try to hold onto my cape. Only my cape can take me flying high above my worlds, the ones about which I know everything there is to know.

In her beginning, Betsy emphasizes the importance of the cape and her changing relationship to it. We sense that it is becoming more difficult for her to hold onto the simple idea that the cape empowers her. You know from Betsy's two stories—the one about her younger brother and the other about David's accident—why she is having to rethink her idea. The cape did not do for David what it did for her brother. Nevertheless, Betsy continues to write about the power of the imagination. That idea is implicit in her beginning; she does not spell it out, but she hints at it. When readers unfamiliar with the two stories read her introduction, they get a feel for what will follow. After they read the essay, they can go back to the beginning and discover how much Betsy has told them without giving away too much of the essay. (Also see the revised version of Betsy's beginning in 5b-5.)

5   Developing and revising the essay from the middle

An essay is a unified effort to express an idea, and its beginning and middle are dependent on one another. In the beginning, you give readers a sense of what your evidence means; in the **middle,** you present and evaluate that evidence, letting readers gain insight from your thoughts about what the evidence means.

When you write an exploratory essay and use stories as evidence, the stories themselves—if told effectively—illustrate something important about your idea. But often, no matter how well you tell the stories you link together, you need to add some *explanation* to make sure that your readers know what you know. Readers have to understand why you are telling the stories, what those stories have to do with your idea. The same is true when you present research data or other forms of evidence. It is never enough just to present the evidence; you have to explain it as well.

Revising the essay from the middle

After composing her middle and a draft of her beginning, Betsy could very well decide to finish her essay using only the stories about David and Daniel as evidence. She would need only to write an ending that in some fresh, informed way alludes to her idea and accounts for what her stories imply and what her exploration means. (Endings are discussed more fully in 5b-6.)

But Betsy has not stopped thinking about her idea, so she is not ready to write an ending. Instead of being satisfied with the two stories, she continues to revise what she has already written, trying to clarify the relationship between her stories and her idea.

As she reads her draft and thinks about how to revise it, Betsy is keenly aware of her readers. She wonders whether they can understand her idea. In fact, she tries to put herself in her readers' place and questions her own writing as if she is reading her draft for the first time, thinking of it impersonally and objectively. She asks herself these questions.

- What is each of my stories about?
- What does each story have to do with my idea?
- Is the relationship between the stories clear?
- Does the beginning both capture the essence of my stories and forecast my idea?

As you play the role of reader, you may find confusing sentences that need to be rewritten, and you may discover the need for more explanation at various points in the essay. You might also find that the need for more explanation leads to the need for more evidence—that is, for another story or for a different kind of evidence. Asking and answering questions inevitably lead to revising and more writing. That was Betsy's experience, and you will no doubt find it to be the case when writing your own essays. Revising generates new thoughts as well as clearer sentences and paragraphs. (See 4a and 1g for more on questioning and revising.)

Continuing the exploration

Revising led Betsy to tell a third story in the middle of her essay. Her new story about fire fighting (p. 113, paragraphs 6–7) helped clarify a notion that she only touched on in the story about her friend David—that the worlds of fantasy and reality sometimes clash violently. Betsy was not yet satisfied that she had completed her exploration; she had not expressed some aspects of her idea about fantasy, so she kept writing, letting the stories she recalled give her further insight as she wrote. Betsy's third story also led her to rewrite the beginning after her idea became clearer to her. Such revision is consistent with good writing practice. You will always make adjustments, writing and rewriting, as you go along.

Revising the beginning

After additional work on the middle, you will often revise the beginning, accounting more accurately for what readers should expect to find in the essay. Betsy's readers—the members of her work group—gave her the following advice after reading her beginning: "Reconsider your beginning. See if you can become much less dependent on the word *cape*. Decode that word; help us understand what it stands for in your mind. Keep working to reveal your idea that is embedded in that word. You're onto something good!" Here is Betsy's revised beginning.

Betsy's revised beginning

Flying is a passion of mine. I have treasured its comfort ever since the first time   1
I soared above the imperfect world of reality in the land of my imagination,
supported by the powerful, mysterious force of flight. The marvelous phenomenon
of flight lifts me out of the present, carrying me to a world of my creation. And in
transcending the constraints of time, my flights create a mockery of the incompleteness, the relentlessness of the world from which they snatch me. I do not
remember where my first journey took me. I was so young that I do not remember
the journey at all, only the wonderful feelings I found on my trip. I was comfortable,
happy, optimistic, confident, powerful. And each time I fly, these feelings that I
cherish come to me once again. I doubt that I have ever left the ground on any of
my journeys; my flights are not of the physical sort. But they are very real in my
mind. They are real in the way they inspire me to tackle the world of reality with a
renewed enthusiasm, conquering its imperfections with the power inside me that I
find on my adventures. My flights help change the way I picture my life; they help
construct who I am.

EXERCISE 5–1   Close Reading and Writing

1. How has Betsy's idea in the first beginning changed in the revised beginning? Write a paragraph about the differences. Cite specific evidence from Betsy's two paragraphs to make your case more convincing.

2. Where in Betsy's revised beginning do you find a hint about David's story? Cite the words or sentences that anticipate the dangers of flight. What can you infer about Betsy's attitude toward such dangers? What is your evidence for that inference? Has Betsy's attitude about such dangers changed

from that expressed in the first version of the beginning? Explain your answer.

Returning to the middle

Let us go back to the middle of Betsy's essay. In it, you will reencounter the stories about Daniel and David; you will also find the new story about fire fighting. Read through the final draft of Betsy's middle twice. On the first reading, try only to get a sense of how Betsy finally connects all of the parts together, and let her lead you along. Then reread the revised beginning before you move on to the middle. As you read the middle, pay particular attention to the underlined sentences and phrases, which give you a sense of how Betsy offers explanations along the way that tie her stories together and make her idea clearer. Here is the middle of Betsy's essay, which she tentatively titled "Flying."

Betsy's middle: Final draft

My two younger brothers always get to open a few presents on Christmas Eve. Daniel, the youngest, celebrated his third Christmas this year. Convinced that the best gifts always come in large packages, he chose the presents he wished to open that evening solely on this condition. He was surrounded by stuffed animals, a race car track, a train set, and a few other gifts that, due to their size, made maneuvering about the living room a challenge. But only one present held Daniel's attention that evening: the Batman costume from Aunt Pat. Ever since he had unwrapped the gift and discovered what it was, he had dragged the box containing the costume around the room, demanding that someone help him put it on. Finally, receiving the needed help from his mother, Daniel turned into Batman, running around the living room and shooting his family members with tiny plastic arrows from his knuckle gun. His glossy red hair poking out the sides, Daniel peered through the eyes of his Batman mask with a look of confidence and determination, ready to conquer any villains posing a potential threat to the successful completion of his mission, whatever it might be.

Tired of playing dead every time Daniel pegged me with one of his arrows, I began to read the box that had contained the Batman costume. A warning sign on its side caught my eye:

WARNING

Vest is not really bulletproof.

Cape will not enable user to fly.

I chuckled as I read the note of caution, then burst into laughter as I realized its absurdity. How could anyone think that a little piece of nylon could send them soaring into the air? My whole family joined me in laughter after I read the warning to them, as they too considered how silly it was. That is, everyone except Daniel. Although understanding the words I had said, he found no humor in them. Instead of joining in the laughter of the rest of his family, Daniel continued to prance about the room, completely absorbed in the fantasy of the world to which his Batman costume had flown him.

Each day, Daniel experiences the excitement of a different world, one where he is the biggest, smartest, most powerful creature of all. That night, Daniel was Batman. He ran about the room, stalking his prey and deftly conquering each one with his batlike agility--the thin, black cape streaming behind him. That night, there was no one in Daniel's world more powerful than he. [4]

Many of my flights have placed me in the shoes of someone else, just as Daniel became Batman that evening. Some of my favorite people to be when I was little were cowboys, Olympic athletes, astronauts, singers, police officers--each unique in a different way. The people in my adventures were quite varied. But they all had something in common: they were all heroes of a sort. They were all good at something that, in pursuing their talent, brought them pleasure, confidence, success. The person I liked to be the most was a firefighter. Conquering the powerful flames that have so often destroyed beautiful monuments and taken away lives is a heroic act that has always fascinated me. In my role as a firefighter, I concentrated my actions on trying to defeat nature's attempt to create tragedy, to stop nature from taking away its own creations. [5]

Despite the remarkable capacity for imagination that most children have, pretending to fight fires when I was a child was a challenge. Melinda Morbeck, my childhood comrade, and I tried many approaches to creating a fire that appeared convincing enough to warrant our battling against it, but rarely were we satisfied with our attempts to create fictitious fires. Wrapped up in our fantasy of being fire's archenemies, Melinda and I decided we were prepared to fight a real fire, so we torched one of the rhododendrons in my backyard. The powerful, destructive force of the fire took control and, before we even began to combat the flames, the fire had spread to the other rhododendrons and to the fence behind them. Within minutes, the scream of sirens announced the arrival of a fire truck, and real firefighters took over our unfinished mission. By the time they conquered all of the flames, all the rhododendrons were gone along with most of the picket fence surrounding the yard. [6]

During the following week, which Melinda and I spent in our rooms, I reflected on our brush with disaster--the violent collision of fantasy with reality. Our flight had taken us to a pleasant, fascinating world in which we were the heroes, the most powerful, skillful fighters of nature's wrath. But a vivid reminder of reality was displayed for us in the form of a very real fire, one that took over my backyard. Our flight took Melinda and me to a world of fantasy that, like all the worlds that can be reached by flying, is not totally separate from the one everyone shares. Fantasy [7] cannot be entirely freed from the imperfect, unpredictable world of the present, a world in which I do not have total control over my future or my happiness. But I do have this control when I fly to my worlds, and the pleasant feelings I find there stay inside me when I am forced to return to the apathetic, uncontrollable world of reality.

On a beautiful spring afternoon during my third-grade year, my friend David Ingham and I frolicked about the dodgeball court at our school, perfecting our roles as professional dodgeball players. Even though there were no real Batman capes streaming behind us, we soared just as high as Daniel did that Christmas Eve. We were completely absorbed in the thrill of competing against the other dodgeball team, focusing on our movements and the rules of the game. Nothing else in the whole world mattered to us on that wonderful afternoon except our game of dodgeball.

In my quest to sharpen my dodgeball skills, I took it upon myself to ask David for some personal help in developing my ball-throwing technique. In his usual carefree manner, he remarked to me that it was all in the wrist and demonstrated exactly how he used his wrist to produce such power. In his blue and white school uniform, shirt untucked as usual, he smiled gleefully and hurled a ball across the court, slamming the wooden kick board on the opposite side. Pleased by the fascination I showed, David smiled, messed up my hair, and darted across the court to retrieve the ball and give me a try. Despite the simplicity and the clarity of his explanation, I never quite caught on to David's art of ball throwing, but I treasure my memory of him and me flying together through our world of dodgeball.

But I am afraid my flights with David are over. A skiing accident over Christmas vacation left him paralyzed from the waist down. The tragic intervention of reality took away his ability to soar through his world of athletics and dominating every sport he undertook. Instead, he was forced to cope with life as a paraplegic during the prime of his athletic career. David's skiing accident forced him to picture himself in a wheelchair, a picture that he found too difficult to accept. After losing his ability to fly in his world of athletics, the one he loved most, David chose to escape the cruel, apathetic world that had robbed him of his pathway to comfort, his source of happiness. David wheeled himself off a pier into Lake Washington this month, taking his life and the love of many with him.

But the direction of time is not all bad. Even though it prevents David from coming back, it soothes me by pushing the horror, the terrible shock of his death farther and farther away from me as each day goes by. And when I think about David now, the joy we shared so often together is gradually overcoming my sorrow at this loss. The good feelings I have for him are stronger, more persevering, than the sad memory of his death. The passage of time has helped me focus on the joy we shared rather than on the tragic, inexplicable reality of his death. I could not fly through my worlds of comfort and happiness for a while after David died. But I have gradually regained my ability to soar into worlds that transcend reality and carry me for a brief time out of my constraining, unpredictable life. Each time I fly, I find comfort again. All the while, the sad memories of events in the past keep being pushed farther away from me, farther back in my memory until they are only shadows. Flying reminds me of my losses, but it helps me rediscover who I am. The worlds I create in my imagination restore my sanity, my stability, my identity.

EXERCISE 5–2   Understanding the Essay

Read Betsy's beginning and middle twice and answer the following questions.

1. Reread Betsy's beginning. How does she foreshadow what will follow in the middle? Link specific parts of the beginning to specific parts of the middle.

2. Identify the three stories Betsy tells in the middle of her essay. How does each story contribute to her idea?

3. Paragraphs 7 and 11 contain a great deal of explanatory material (underlined). In what ways does that material help you understand Betsy's idea? Write a paragraph or two to explain your answer.

4. In two or three sentences write what you think Betsy's idea turns out to be.

6   Ending the essay

The **ending** of an exploratory essay should take readers back to the beginning, reminding them in some way about the development of the idea. But the ending should not merely repeat what has already been said. It should sum up in a way that gives readers a fresh perspective on the idea.

In preparation for writing an ending, you should reread the entire essay and try to let that reading guide you as you attempt to capture the essence of it all. The ending is your last chance to make your reader see it your way.

The following paragraph is Betsy's ending. The underlined portions reflect traces of her idea; they serve as reminders, stitching the parts of the essay together.

Betsy's ending

Daniel, my younger brother, will be four years old this month. He will soon   12
embark on another year of his own soaring. One day, he will come to understand
that a little piece of nylon cannot support his weight in flight. But even then, he
will still be able to fly, as long as he holds on to the memory of its comfort. For now,
Daniel will find nothing funny in a warning label on the box of his Batman costume
trying to tell him that he cannot fly with his cape. Maybe the cape won't let him fly
across the living room for all to see. But who knows what Daniel can do in his world?

Betsy returns to her younger brother as a way of reminding readers about the childlike nature of flying. But she does much more: she reminds readers that the comfort people might derive from the kind of flying she is promoting depends on their ability to remember the comfort they got from such flights of fancy as children. It is that comfort that will sustain them later in life, long past their realization that "a little piece of nylon cannot support [their] weight in flight." In short, Betsy repackages her idea in the ending and offers readers a new perspective on the idea.

The ending, like the beginning and the middle, is an integral part of the essay. Beginning, middle, and ending constitute a unified attempt to express an idea. The accompanying chart (Considering the Essay's Beginning, Middle, and Ending) will help you focus when you write your beginnings, middles, and endings for your essays.

Considering the Essay's Beginning, Middle, and Ending

The Beginning
- Write the first draft of the beginning only after you have collected evidence and considered what you want to say about it—after you have a good sense of your essay's idea.
- Try to draw your reader into the essay with an anecdote (a brief, pointed story) that highlights your essay's idea. Or simply explain what the essay is about.
- Be sure the beginning foreshadows the whole essay, but without revealing the details and surprises that follow.
- Make sure you know where your beginning ends.

The Middle
- Make sure the middle follows smoothly and logically from the beginning.
- Present your evidence and give your reader a sense of what it means.
- Whether your evidence includes stories or data garnered from research, be sure to explain the relationship between that evidence and your idea.

The Ending
- Read through the entire essay, and try to capture the essence of what you have written.
- Sum up the idea in the ending, but do not merely repeat what has gone before; reveal a fresh perspective on your idea.
- Draw into the ending selected details that have appeared earlier in the essay to remind your reader of important aspects of your idea.

EXERCISE 5–3   **Writing an Exploratory Essay**

Re-create a moment from memory—an experience—that still interests you, a moment that lingers in your imagination. Re-create that memory in the form of a story. (Aim for two or three typed pages, double spaced.) Then follow Features of the Exploratory Essay to create a four- to six-page exploratory essay in which you reveal what that story and others mean to you.

5c   Connecting texts with stories of experience

As you learn to write more complex, and perhaps more interesting, exploratory essays, you will begin to move beyond your immediate experience to enrich the presentation of your idea. This section considers how Alexandra Johnes developed an idea about learning by combining stories of experience with other evidence—five published essays.

Alexandra's initial work resembled that done by Betsy Miller (5b) in that she combined stories of experience as a way of finding and then developing an idea. The class was working on a common subject—education—and they read together a number of short exploratory essays, some by students, some by professional writers. You will see later how Alexandra makes use of some of those essays.

1   Writing a letter as a way of enriching an idea

Reread the Guidelines for Developing an Exploratory Essay on p. 104 to refresh your memory about the process: developing a story of experience, questioning it to find an idea, and then combining it with other stories to clarify the idea. Alexandra did all of those things before her teacher asked her to move beyond stories of experience to other kinds of evidence. The new, added requirement was to write a letter to a friend (not in her class), to make use of her initial stories in that letter, and to connect those stories with other kinds of evidence that might help the friend understand the idea about education that was beginning to take shape in her mind. Alexandra and the other students were encouraged to give their imaginations free rein as they made meaningful connections during their letter writing (see 4c for more on connecting).

Here is an excerpt from the beginning of Alexandra's letter in which she recalls a book she has read and links it with stories of experience as a way of investigating and enriching her idea about education:

Dear Eva,

Have you read <u>The Moviegoer</u> by Walker Percy? I've been thinking a lot about the search lately, about what it means to be looking for something, to be looking for purpose.

When I think back to my three years at M--, I think I'll always remember late night conversations the most, above and beyond any class discussion. I realized that among the mass of things I learned there, I learned the most from simply being part of the community.

The wonderful thing about college thus far has been that all of a sudden all those elements in life that were once considered distractions can be integrated into my education. For the first time what I'm thinking about doesn't seem so wholly at odds with what I'm studying.

But there's more to it than that. It's not all that simple. I guess maybe what I've been reveling in since I've been here is not so much college, per se, but rather growing up and having things fall into place, make sense.

Damian's older sister, Trisch, the one who's a professional ballroom dancer, has been a positive example for me. She was telling me that if her students found out how long she'd been studying ballroom, they'd think she was a fraud, since she only started ballroom in her senior year of college and was teaching less than a year later. But, because of her extensive background in both music and dance, she picked it up very quickly. Her being a ballroom dancer makes a lot of sense out of the pattern of her life. Perhaps when she started dancing or playing the cello, her friends and family were wondering what the point was, or why she was taking it so seriously, but now that she's a dance teacher, it would almost seem ridiculous if she hadn't done those things. See, I'm a firm believer that if you just keep following your heart, it will lead to a logical and happy place.

As for me, I thought about and studied a lot of different things when I was at M--, but they always seemed to be attached somehow to popular culture. When I studied feminism in my civil rights class, I wrote about the Wonderbra. I wrote about movies for the school newspaper. When I gave the Baccalaureate speech at graduation, I framed my speech around Susan Powter, the blonde head-shaven woman who does the Stop The Insanity! infomercials. But the point isn't, yeah, I'm finally in college and can write about pop culture or yeah, I'm finally studying film. It's about having a certain cohesion to your life--but simply because it's cohesive doesn't mean it requires any less work.

I went to Las Vegas over Thanksgiving, and as a pop culture connoisseur, I was fascinated with the experience. However, it was not until I wrote an ethnography paper in class, and slaved and slaved over it, that I think I fully understood the experience and what it meant to me. I had to work my thoughts and work that essay. Simply because pop culture is something I think a lot about, or have a passion about, does not mean that I've figured it all out.

So that's what I'm trying to write to you about. I'm trying to write to you about working to figure things out, working to search for answers like Binx does in The Moviegoer, working to see and understand more clearly.

Alexandra does not tell her friend much about the details of *The Moviegoer;* she doesn't need to. She tells her enough to let her know how the book was helping her explore her thoughts about education and learning. It provided another story or example for her, as Trisch's career had done. What she needed here was not to write a review about the book, but to let the evidence in the book serve as a springboard for thinking.

There is a telling point about the way Alexandra explored this connection in the letter: she does not use all the details of the letter's connection in her final essay. She does not need to; she needed the letter's ideas as a way of pushing her thinking, much as a journal writer may do. (See 1e-2 and 2b.) Later, in her drafting, she found other connections.

2   Multiplying the connections

As students moved from the ideas in the letter to their early drafts, they were encouraged to make other connections with the essays they were reading in class. Here is an early draft paragraph where Alexandra tried to bring together several essays to make a point about the limitations of following only your passions when trying to learn. Notice how sketchy the connection is with the Ehrlich essay and with an essay by Jane Tompkins about Indians; they came to her while drafting. She will develop them in the final draft. You will see the paragraph in final form in the next section (5c-3):

And while this road [down which I followed my passions] did bear fruitful advantages, the greatest disadvantage was that I missed out on what I call "free learning," or learning without expectations. In Walker Percy's essay "The Loss of the Creature," Percy argues that a tourist can never really "see" the Grand Canyon as it really is, because his or her vision will be tainted by pre-existing expectations. Similarly, in --?-- essay "Indians, ---", in her desperate search for the most valid account of the history of the American Indians, she dismisses every one, ultimately not "seeing" any of them. And in Gretel Ehrlich's "Looking for a Lost Dog," Ehrlich. . . . In each case, the subject, in looking for something in particular (the Canyon as expected, the real history of the Indians), misses seeing the reality of what is right in front of them.

Just before this paragraph Alexandra had made another sketchy note to herself about her reading. Remembering a student essay the class had read earlier, she wrote the author's name in brackets: [David Gray in here somewhere]. Let us see now how she developed that connection and how that connection established a context for the paragraph you have just read.

3   Developing the essay from the middle

Alexandra's essay "Passionate Learning" suggests that school is a kind of game that students should enter into playfully and responsibly, but that even if they do, they will discover that following their passions may still not be satisfying enough. Here is a central section from the middle of her essay that lets you see her combining her analysis of David Gray's essay with stories of her own experience and with those other written texts she cited in her rough draft.

In his essay "Dulcis Est Sapientia," David Gray points out that
> the mind does not register, or does not make sense of, information where it is not accompanied by another factor, a will to understand. . . . [B]y making sharp divisions in what knowledge we consider "useless" or "useful," we set up barriers, we put on intellectual blinders which keep us from steering off the familiar one-way track to understanding. (3)

He suggests that while he is perfectly capable of learning Swahili, he would never be able to because it does not seem useful to him: "I can see no connection between Swahili and any other knowledge I have."

Gray is pointing out that learning requires a will to learn, and that this will derives from the degree to which we can relate the prospective knowledge to knowledge we already have. He argues that "education should stress the context of ideas above the mere presentations of facts." He would have liked to use me as an example. My education history is a case in point. I only truly learned when I could connect my learning to myself, to my own personal agenda. However, where Gray would see my experience as cause to reorient the way education approaches students, I also see it as cause to reorient the way students approach education, and in the larger sense, to reorient the way people approach the world.

Gray is pushing to make learning a more natural, and thus easier and more enticing, process for students. And while this goal is a valiant attempt to draw people more into education, a much needed action, it also makes students lazy. Because, while we may be able to bundle education into a cuter and cuter package, we cannot do the same to our surrounding environment. Teachers can help students make connections, but once in the real world students must perform this task themselves. And this task does not come naturally; it requires work.

This revelation came to me recently when I found myself immersed in my passions but only understanding them minimally. Having followed my heart, I landed this fall at film school. In a directing class, my professor casually asked me what the theme was of one of my favorite scripts, and I found, much to my embarrassment, that I didn't quite know it exactly. In fact, I couldn't communicate very well at all what it was about, the script that I loved so much. I had eaten up its surface meaning. Unfortunately, and embarrassingly enough, this scenario seems to be part of a trend. I understand very little about those things which I am most passionate about. I am not very versed at putting my passions into words. This habit of mine is of particular concern in considering film as a medium of pop culture. Too often we absorb meanings of popular culture without ever knowing exactly what meanings we have absorbed.

Furthermore, only following my heart, only learning when I could relate new knowledge to previous knowledge, limited me from learning for learning's sake. In Walker Percy's essay "The Loss of the Creature," he argues that a tourist can never "see" the Grand Canyon as it really is because his or her vision will be tainted by preexisting expectations. Similarly, in Jane Tompkins's essay "Indians," Tompkins, in her desperate search for the most valid account of the history of the American Indians, dismisses every one, ultimately not "seeing" any of them. In "Looking for a Lost Dog," Gretel Ehrlich comes to realize that in her search for her dog, she misses experiencing her journey. In each case, the subject, in looking for something in particular (the Canyon as expected, the real history of the Indians, the dog), misses seeing what is there.

Similarly, in looking at new knowledge only as it related to old knowledge, I missed out on seeing the knowledge as it stood on its own. I saw it only as it related to my immediate state of mind, to my immediate place on my personal path. The same "familiar one-way track to understanding" that Gray wants to tap into locked me inside of it, blocking a clear view of the outside world. I evaluated all of new knowledge in terms of its usefulness to my understanding of myself. I saw each piece as a prospective answer to my personal pondering; if the piece did not offer some sort of resolution, I dismissed it as being irrelevant.

What I'm leading to is this: Life takes work.

There is more to this fine student essay about games and learning and passion. With her ending paragraph, Alexandra managed to put all her ideas and evidence in perspective:

> To recognize that life takes work is to accept the rules of the game and thus, to have self-respect. As Joan Didion says, people with self-respect know the price of things. They
>> are willing to accept the risk that the Indians will be hostile, that the venture will go bankrupt, that the liaison may not turn out to be one in which every day is a holiday because you're married to me. They are willing to invest something of themselves; they may not play at all, but when they do play, they know the odds. (149)

People who respect themselves "are willing to accept the risk" that the teacher might be wrong, that their hearts may take them in the wrong direction. "They are willing to invest something of themselves;" they may choose not to play the games at all, but when they do play, they play in <u>full awareness</u> of the rules. They know the odds. They know that it takes <u>work</u> to play well.

Alexandra reminds you just how far you can take the exploratory essay. It can admit a variety of evidence—experience, books, essays, movies—and a host of ideas that are hard to get at but fun to think about. This form of the essay can treat serious subjects in an exploratory way and can lead to exciting discoveries. It lays the foundation for more formal writing by showing you how such writing must be grounded in expansive yet rigorous thinking.

EXERCISE 5–4   **Writing an Exploratory Essay with Written Texts**

Select an area of inquiry—education, seeing, some aspect of pop culture—and recall and re-create a moment from your own experience related to that area of inquiry. Then follow Guidelines for Developing an Exploratory Essay on p. 104 to create an exploratory essay of four to six pages in which you develop an idea related to your area of inquiry. Include in your essay two or three written texts that help you develop your idea.

CHAPTER 6

The Analytical Essay

You can write an **analytical essay** about a written text (essay, poem, novel), a work of art (painting, sculpture, photograph), a performance (movie, play, opera, sporting event), a family, a social group, a historical event, a psychological concept—anything complex enough to interpret. Let us think of all these different subjects—the written text, the art object, the performance—as *texts* to be investigated and interpreted by you, the essayist. Your first task will be to figure out *what* the text means; but to get to meaning, you will also have to pay attention to *how* the text works, how it conveys meaning. Your essay will eventually analyze the relationship between the text's meaning and the way you think the text conveys that meaning.

Although the texts you analyze will have concrete, unchangeable characteristics, every text is open to new and exciting interpretations. The words of an essay, the brushstrokes of a painting, and the frames of a movie objectively exist in the same way for all people, but you analyze each of them from your unique vantage point. You may find different ways of making sense of what you see or read. And you can certainly expect that everyone will interpret differently. Making sense depends in part on your understanding of how the text works, how it reveals itself to you as you study it. Making sense also depends on the knowledge and experience you bring to your analysis. Confronting the text is where the fun and the challenge of analysis lie. In the play between your imagination and the text, you find an idea, an interpretation you want to stake a claim on and write about. That claim, like the leading idea in an argumentative essay, has more certainty in it than the idea for the exploratory essay. Much of the working out of the claim takes place in drafts and does not show up in the final essay. It shows less process and more results.

Like the exploratory essay, the analytical essay has a beginning, a middle, and an ending. The analytical essay, however, is more direct than the exploratory essay. Its pace is brisker, its tone more businesslike and formal. The analytical essay is more of a presentation than an exploration. Instead of ambling along like a good story, it moves directly to the interpretive idea and the explanation of that idea. Your aim in an analytical essay is to convey what you learned through the analysis of a text.

The *purposes* for writing analytical essays vary, but primarily these essays give readers a chance to see the results of rigorous analytical work that you have done as part of the drafting. That work usually depends on the critical reading, questioning, and interpretation of a text of some kind. The process of that reading, questioning, and interpreting is less evident in the analytical essay than in the exploratory essay, but the process is reflected indirectly by the way you establish relationships between the text you have read and what you have to say about that text, between your evidence and your claim. Writing analytical essays helps you learn the process of analysis and allows you to practice making use of that analysis.

As you will see later in this chapter, the skills you learn while writing analytical essays can also be used in exploratory essays. Sometimes analyzing a particular text sets your mind working on a subject that is more suitable for an exploratory essay than an analytical one. In 6c-3, for example, you will see how one student uses analysis to help develop the beginning of an exploratory essay.

Audiences for analytical essay could be either specialists or generalists (1d). If the analytical process focuses on the interpretation of a literary text (or some other academic text), the audience might be either students studying literature or teachers and scholars working in that discipline. If the analysis focuses on a performance of some kind—drama, movie, sporting event—the audience would more than likely be generalists with a deep interest in the subject under consideration. Thinking about that audience will certainly help you decide how much technical detail to include in your analytical essay as well as the assumptions you can make about what members of the audience already know and just how they might resist your interpretation of the text. The accompanying Features of the Analytical Essay outlines the main characteristics of the analytical essay.

Features of the Analytical Essay

- Focuses on the writer's interpretation of a text—what it means and how it conveys meaning.
- Develops an idea about that interpretation in an interesting, formal way.
- Is more like a defense of the idea than an inquiry about it.
- Depends primarily on the text itself for evidence.
- Has a beginning, a middle, and an ending.

6a   Reading and analyzing texts

In preparing to write an analytical essay, read or view the text carefully. **Critical reading** involves paying close attention to the text so that you can notice its features, raise questions about it, and come to some understanding about what you think it means. (See Chapter 2 on strategies for critical reading, and 4a on questioning.)

The text you are analyzing will become part of your evidence. Coming to terms with that evidence—understanding it—is not a straightforward, linear process; it is recursive. As you develop your analytical essay, you are likely to move back and forth between reading the text you are analyzing and writing your essay. Writing about a text you are reading can lead to a clearer understanding of that text. As you develop your analytical essay, you will probably read the text, write a bit, return to the text, revise—moving between your evolving essay and your evidence until you create an analytical essay that accounts for your interpretation.

This chapter will give you a clearer sense of how that recursive process works. You will look at how Jim Foley, a writing teacher, and Ruth Chung, a student, analyze two very different texts. Jim analyzes the game of baseball; Ruth analyzes an essay by Virginia Woolf. You will see that as different as their respective texts are, the principles of analysis and the nature of their writing tasks are essentially the same. Their work will provide a set of guidelines that will give you direction when you analyze a text and write about it.

The accompanying chart, Analytical Methods and Objectives, outlines the principles of analysis and will help you stay focused on your analysis. (See also 2c and 2d on analysis and interpretation.) Let us turn to the tasks of analyzing and writing about the results of your analysis.

Analytical Methods and Objectives

- Think of the analytical process as an attempt to take a text apart so that you can bring it together again in your mind's eye. Breaking down a text and the interpretive process involved in putting it together again yield insight.

- Read the text closely so that you understand how it works and what you think it means. Notice details and their relationships to one another within a selected text.

- As you read the text, work to discover and question the text's inherent ideas— what you think the text is about (see Chapters 2 and 3).

- If the text reminds you of other texts or ideas that you have read, analyze those texts and ideas. Curiosity about the connections you make can lead to clearer understanding of the text you are analyzing (see 4c).

- Your primary objectives are to understand the text being analyzed and to account for that understanding in an essay.

1   Reading the game of baseball

Jim Foley is a writing teacher with a long-standing love of baseball. To help his students learn about analysis, he chose the game of baseball as his text. Jim was interested in the effects of the *designated-hitter (DH) rule* on the game. His analysis of those effects led him to interesting ideas.

Before looking at those ideas, let us consider Jim's text (the game of baseball) and the tasks he faced as he set out to read and understand that text. Those tasks will be similar to the ones you face each time you read a text. Your reading will be influenced by the knowledge you bring to the text.

Jim was not a newcomer to the game of baseball. He was familiar with his text, and that gave him a head start. The knowledge he already had provided the foundation for his analysis. Because Jim was interested in writing about the game in general rather than about a particular game, he had to have more than rudimentary knowledge. He needed to know the characteristics of baseball—that it is a game with nine players, six of whom occupy the infield (first, second, third base; shortstop between second and third; pitcher on the mound; catcher at home plate) and three of whom occupy right, left, and center fields. Jim also had to have knowledge of how the game is played so that he could look beyond these basic elements to what he considered the game's essence—hitting, fielding, and teamwork.

Jim's text was both temporal and dynamic. It included all the games of baseball that he had seen or played. He also had to know the DH rule, its origin, its purpose, and the characteristics of games played with and games played without the rule. Finally, against the backdrop of all this knowledge, Jim had a specific analytical task to perform: to assess the DH rule's effect on the game.

2   Analyzing the game of baseball

As Jim considered the impact of the DH rule, he did what writers often do. He thought about one thing in terms of another: the game before the rule and the game after the rule. Making that comparison, Jim spied an idea.

Before the DH rule was put into effect in the American League, every player on the team had to bat in a fixed order; if a pinch hitter was called into the line-up to bat for another player, that player had to be replaced. In short, the manager had to decide whether sending in a pinch hitter at crucial times to replace the pitcher (usually the worst hitter on the team) would be more advantageous than having the pitcher in the line-up. Under the DH rule, the designated hitter could bat for the pitcher at any time, and the pitcher could keep playing. Part of the rationale for the DH rule was that fans would be happier because there would be more hits and more scoring with the pitcher out of the batting order.

Jim, it turns out, had a different idea about the effect of the DH rule. In the two paragraphs that follow, he analyzes the game of baseball and shows his readers how the game works under the influence of the DH rule. Look especially at the italicized sentences in the first paragraph and at the entire second paragraph to see how Jim moves beyond his foundation of knowledge to interpret the game of baseball.

> *The baseball fan celebrates complexity over simplicity. For the fan, the richness of the game lies in its network of endless possibility.* Should the runner on first base break with the pitch so as to remove the possibility of the double play? Might it not make more sense to have him steal? Or should we call for the batter to bunt? Would a hit-and-run play do the trick? *Any time an element which contributes to this network of possibility is removed from the game, baseball is the poorer for that removal, and the true fan laments the change. Such is the case with the DH rule.* Because that infamous offensive liability, the pitcher, no longer comes to the plate, an entire array of managerial responses designated to compensate somehow for that embarrassment has been rendered needless. Not having to plan around the pitcher's inexorable slouch towards home plate with bat in tow, the manager need not longer worry about how to minimize the pitcher's usually depressive effect on the team's offensive effort. The manager has one less thing to manage—*as do those thousands of surrogate managers, the fans.*
>
>   The richness of baseball owes in large measure to its potential for a perfection it never achieves. The ideal baseball game is a thing of the mind. Real baseball games only approach it, only whet the appetite for the ideal. In the ideal game, all the pitchers can hit. In the real game, after swatting pathetically at the ball three times, most of them sit down. The gap between the ideal game and the real one is often wide and frustrating. It's supposed to be. To attempt to narrow the gap by introducing an interloper, the designated hitter, is cheating somehow. It borders on free substitution and all those other diluting tendencies associated with sports such as football, basketball, and hockey—sports where specialization is cultivated, where special teams have become the rule rather than the exception.
>
>   —Jim Foley, "Networks of Possibility"

Out of Jim's analysis of the game and the rule, he renders judgments and offers explanations to account for them. Writing about those judgments, he gives us insight into his understanding of the game.

   Watching only one baseball game could not have given Jim the insight reflected in those two paragraphs. Nor would he necessarily have come to those conclusions had he watched a hundred games of baseball. The ideas in those two paragraphs—that the essence of baseball is an endless network of possibilities and that baseball is a game of the mind—were ideas that came out of Jim's imagination as he analyzed and interpreted the game of baseball, modified by the DH rule.

The following working assumptions, which governed Jim's analysis, provide the foundation for analyzing any text:

- Reading the text thoroughly leads to an understanding of how the text works.
- Understanding how the text works leads to an understanding of what the text means.
- Understanding a text's meaning leads to ideas.

But these working assumptions do not account for all that goes into the process. They do not account for Jim's knowledge of the game of baseball, for example. He clearly understands the DH rule. Yet his assessment—especially in the two paragraphs you just read—reflects more than an understanding of the rules; it also indicates that Jim has the knowledge of a fan who has watched a lot of baseball and has thought a lot about it. Jim's analysis, then, depends on his knowledge derived from personal experience as well as on that acquired from reading about the DH rule.

6b   Developing an analytical essay

You just saw how one writer's knowledge and analysis of a text—baseball—led to interesting ideas. Now let us see how such an analysis might take place from start to finish—from analyzing a text to writing an essay about it.

This time the analysis is of a written text, "Old Mrs. Grey," a brief essay written by Virginia Woolf. Ruth Chung, a student, selected the essay as her text for analysis because she found it interesting and intellectually challenging. Every time Ruth read the essay and made discoveries about how it works, she became more interested in it. For Ruth, reading and rereading "Old Mrs. Grey" was not unlike Jim Foley seeing many baseball games. Each reading led Ruth to more knowledge about the text and a clearer sense of its meaning.

When you are aiming to create an analytical essay, the process of reading is always followed by the process of writing. The processes of reading and writing inform and depend on one another. The accompanying Guidelines for Developing an Analytical Essay will help you create your own essay.

1   Reading Woolf's "Old Mrs. Grey"

Before Ruth Chung could begin to write her essay about "Old Mrs. Grey," she had to read Woolf's essay carefully and question it. She used the Developing Questions from Evidence guidelines on p. 79 in Chapter 4 as she read the essay.

Read Woolf's essay from start to finish, making notes of your own in the margins or in a reading journal. Later, you can compare your response with

Guidelines for Developing an Analytical Essay

1. Read the text. Notice details within the text—a vivid image, phrase, word, anything that strikes you. Keep track of insights and connections in a reading journal or double-column notebook (see 1e-1, 2b-3, and 47a-5). Restate anything you do not understand into focusing questions that you will try to answer as you read and reread (see 4a).

2. Reflect on your questions and observations, and think about *how* the text works and *what* it means.

3. Reread the text, considering your observations in relation to one another. Note the connections you find (see 4c).

4. Select one detail from the text that interests you, and write a paragraph or two explaining what that detail has to do with the meaning of the text. In the Norris photograph reproduced on the color insert, an interesting detail might be the various kinds of images within the photograph. In a poem, it might be the repetition of a phrase. In an essay, such as "Old Mrs. Grey," it might be a group of striking images. These paragraphs of exploration, analysis, and reflection will likely become a part of the middle of your essay.

5. Let the analysis of one selected detail lead you to analyzing other related details. These groupings or clusters of details often lead to deeper insight about a text. Keep writing to reveal the relationship between the text's details and its meaning. This analysis will also become a part of the middle of your essay.

6. Think about your readers. Can they follow your analysis? Do you need to include more analysis and explanation so that readers can understand what the details have to do with your interpretation? Do you need to include more details?

7. Collaborate and revise with your readers in mind. (See 1d on audience, 1h and 4e on collaboration, and 1g on revision.)

8. Write a beginning for your essay that focuses readers' attention on the points that your analysis will reveal. Make sure your readers can understand the idea (or the thesis) of your analytical essay.

9. Revise the middle—the analysis about detail and meaning as well as your interpretation—of the essay.

10. Write an ending that offers a final perspective on your interpretation.

Ruth's to see if you followed a similar process. Keep in mind that this is an essay you are reading, not a short story. Woolf makes her argument in subtle ways, using storytelling just as an exploratory essayist might and incorporating visual details, or images, to allow you to see part of what she conveys. As you read through Woolf's essay for the first time, place a check mark in the margin when some detail in the text seems vivid and interesting. Pay attention to the way Woolf repeats some of the details. Think about meaning as you read.

Old Mrs. Grey

Virginia Woolf

There are moments even in England, now, when even the busiest, most contented suddenly let fall what they hold—it may be the week's washing. Sheets and pajamas crumble and dissolve in their hands, because, though they do not state this in so many words, it seems silly to take the washing round to Mrs. Peel when out there over the fields over the hills, there is no washing; no pinning of clotheslines; mangling and ironing; no work at all, but boundless rest. Stainless and boundless rest; space unlimited; untrodden grass; wild birds flying; hills whose smooth uprise continues that wild flight.

Of all this however only seven foot by four could be seen from Mrs. Grey's corner. That was the size of her front door which stood wide open, though there was a fire burning on the grate. The fire looked like a small spot of dusty light feebly trying to escape from the embarrassing pressure of the pouring sunshine.

Mrs. Grey sat on a hard chair in the corner looking—but at what? Apparently at nothing. She did not change the focus of her eyes when visitors came. Her eyes had ceased to focus themselves; it may be that they had lost the power. They were aged eyes, blue, unspectacled. They could see, but without looking. She never used her eyes on anything minute and difficult; merely upon faces, and dishes and fields. And now at the age of ninety-two they saw nothing but a zigzag of pain wriggling across the door, pain that twisted her legs as it wriggled; jerked her body to and fro like a marionette. Her body was wrapped round the pain as a damp sheet is folded over a wire. The wire was spasmodically jerked by a cruel invisible hand. She flung out a foot, a hand. Then it stopped. She sat still for a moment.

In that pause she saw herself in the past at ten, twenty, at twenty-five. She was running in and out of a cottage with eleven brothers and sisters. The line jerked. She was thrown forward in her chair.

"All dead. All dead," she mumbled. "My brothers and sisters. And my husband gone. My daughter too. But I go on. Every morning I pray God to let me pass."

The morning spread seven foot by four green and sunny. Like a fling of grain the birds settled on the land. She was jerked again by another tweak of the tormenting hand.

"I'm an ignorant old woman. I can't read or write, and every morning when I crawls downstairs, I say I wish it were day. I'm only an ignorant old woman. But I prays to God: O let me pass. I'm an ignorant old woman—I can't read or write."

So when the colour went out of the doorway, she could not see the other   8
page which is then lit up; or hear the voices that have argued, sung, talked for
hundreds of years.

The jerked limbs were still again.   9

"The doctor comes every week. The parish doctor now. Since my daugh-   10
ter went, we can't afford Dr. Nicholls. But he's a good man. He says he wonders I don't go. He says my heart's nothing but wind and water. Yet I don't
seem able to die."

So we—humanity—insist that the body shall still cling to the wire. We put   11
out the eyes and the ears; but we pinion it there, with a bottle of medicine, a
cup of tea, a dying fire, like a rook on a barn door; but a rook that still lives,
even with a nail through it.

EXERCISE 6–1   **Questioning the Essay**

Reread Woolf's essay and devise your own questions about textual details. For example, Ruth wondered what Woolf meant by *our*—by humanity's—relationship to
Mrs. Grey. In your reading journal, keep track of your questions and any details
from the text that help you respond to those questions (see 1e-1 on the reading
journal).

2   Questioning "Old Mrs. Grey"

During her second reading, Ruth thought about the three-part structure
of Woolf's essay—the beginning, middle, and ending that all essays have.
Ruth was looking for suggestions in Woolf's first paragraph, her beginning,
that pointed to something in the middle of the essay (see 4a for more on questioning). In more specific terms, Ruth noticed in paragraph 1 that Woolf repeats the words *boundless rest* twice; she refers to *space unlimited* and *wild flight.*
Ruth saw traces of those images of freedom and expansiveness in the rest of
the essay, and she wanted to know what they suggest about Mrs. Grey. She
looked for references to freedom as she read through the essay and noticed
that although Woolf brings up the notion of freedom, she also alludes to the
notion of entrapment. Ruth wondered just what those details about freedom
and entrapment reveal about Mrs. Grey's state of mind.

Ruth also noticed that Woolf often compares two things as a way of
revealing more about one of them. For example, in paragraph 3, Woolf compares Mrs. Grey's predicament to that of a marionette. Ruth asked herself a
series of questions about that comparison: Why does Woolf make that
comparison? How does she use it and extend it within the essay? What does
she gain by extending it beyond the paragraph where she first suggests
it? What keeps jerking on those imaginary strings attached to Mrs. Grey?

Are they really imaginary? Do we—humanity—have anything to do with the jerking?

Ruth was struck by the images of flight and freedom that occur throughout the essay. She was particularly interested in the birds in paragraph 1 and the rook (the black bird) in paragraph 11. She wondered what those birds have to do with Mrs. Grey. Ruth also noted Woolf's use of the light and fire in paragraph 2 and the many references to Mrs. Grey's eyes in paragraph 3. She wanted to see whether those details reappeared in other places within the essay.

The last paragraph seemed different from the rest of the essay. Ruth reread the essay for details that might help her understand how Woolf's ending relates to what goes before it.

3   Analyzing textual details—The middle

As Ruth reflected on her questions, she was struck by Mrs. Grey's desire to escape pain and suffering, and Woolf's use of certain details to highlight her suffering and longing. Ruth's focusing question, the question that led her to consider the meaning of the entire essay, became: What is the relationship between these textual details about suffering and longing and Woolf's suggestion in the last paragraph about who causes the suffering? The answer to that question would more than likely become Ruth's thesis—the idea she would explain and defend in an analytical essay.

Ruth discovered that the details about suffering and longing fell naturally into groupings—details about the house, light, pain, mental anguish, and blame. She started to write the essay's middle to discover the relationships between the textual details in each of those groupings. Ruth wrote first about how Woolf uses the house and landscape to convey Mrs. Grey's state of mind. Here is Ruth's first middle paragraph.

Ruth's first middle paragraph: An analysis of textual details

Throughout the essay, Woolf uses Mrs. Grey's house and the landscape outside   2
to describe the old woman's mental state. Woolf's description of the house and the rolling fields and hills seems to be just another picturesque view of England's countryside. From the context of Mrs. Grey's pain and her desire to die, however, the house, with its door wide open, may represent her body on the verge of death. The comparison may run still deeper. Woolf describes Mrs. Grey's mind as open and ready to be enveloped and swallowed by death's rays. It also follows that the image of the fields and hills, described as places of "stainless and boundless rest; space unlimited; untrodden grass; wild birds flying," comes to represent the pure, unblemished paradise, the haven from pain for which Mrs. Grey yearns. It could also simply be a representation of death, a state of being (or not being) that

everyone must eventually face, a time when "even the busiest, most contented suddenly let fall what they hold."

In this paragraph, Ruth is beginning to sort through the details she selected from the text. Notice that she sometimes provides a **summary** of (explains in her own words) what she observes in the text: "Woolf describes Mrs. Grey's mind as open and ready to be enveloped and swallowed by death's rays." At other times, Ruth uses Woolf's words, placing them in quotation marks to indicate that they come directly from "Old Mrs. Grey." Ruth combines summaries and quotations as she analyzes how Woolf uses the image of the house to represent Mrs. Grey's state of mind. (See Chapter 44, especially 44d-1 and 44i, for more on summarizing, quoting, and incorporating evidence.) As Ruth continued to write and think about the textual details, she realized that Mrs. Grey was longing to die. She discovered that Woolf indicates that longing in her references to light. Ruth continued her analysis, focusing on Woolf's use of light.

Ruth's analysis of other textual details

Woolf further describes Mrs. Grey's longing for death using light as a symbol to   3
enhance our understanding of that longing. Through the seven-foot-by-four opening of Mrs. Grey's front door, sunshine pours in from the outside, putting "embarrassing pressure" on the fire burning in the grate, which appears "only as a small spot of dusty light feebly trying to escape." Here, the fire burning in the grate may represent the appeals and delights of life, which have become dreary to Mrs. Grey when compared to the lure of the afterlife, the sweet respite of death, as represented by the streaming sunshine from outside. Mrs. Grey is so enamored by the prospect of going to such a paradise of rest and relief that living for the present becomes pointless; it seems silly to do the week's wash "when out there over the fields over the hills, there is no washing; no pinning of clotheslines; mangling and ironing; no work at all."

The idea of a new life dawning is also represented by "morning spreading seven   4
foot by four green and sunny," which tries to infiltrate the house and beckons to Mrs. Grey through the front door. Mrs. Grey welcomes this light as much as she welcomes death, but the light has not yet been able to permeate the whole house. She has put so much hope into this state of rest that "when the colour went out of the doorway, she could not see the other page which is then lit up." This "other page" represents Mrs. Grey's present chapter of life, which has potential, even in her pain, to be enjoyable and fulfilling. But Mrs. Grey can see this life only as she sees the fire burning in the grate, which becomes dim in the light of her suffering and pain. She is so weary of her life that "her eyes had ceased to focus themselves. . . . They could see but without looking." It isn't that she is physically blind, but that her pain is so great that it is all she can see. It could also be that nothing in her

present life seems to be worth looking at because she cannot appreciate the little pleasures of life: "She had never used her eyes on anything minute and difficult; merely upon faces, and dishes and fields."

Ruth brings textual details into her paragraph to help account for how Woolf uses those details in her essay. Throughout the three middle paragraphs, Ruth remains focused on Mrs. Grey's longing for death, and she repeatedly demonstrates how the textual details substantiate her claim. Revealing that relationship between the textual details and the thesis is Ruth's primary writing task, just as it will be yours when you write an analytical essay.

4 Collaborating to enrich the analysis

Although these are fine analytical paragraphs, Ruth's work group had some questions about them (see 4e for more on collaborating). Students wanted to know more about the relationship between the textual details and Ruth's idea about Mrs. Grey's longing for death. They were not so much interested in more details as they were in more analysis, more thinking.

As a way of illustrating how that kind of feedback from the work group can lead to revision and a richer analysis, let us look at a place in Ruth's third paragraph that caught the work group's attention.

Here, the fire burning in the grate may represent the appeals and delights of life, which have become dreary to Mrs. Grey when compared to the lure of the afterlife, the sweet respite of death, as represented by the streaming sunshine from outside. Mrs. Grey is so enamored by the prospect of going to such a paradise of rest and relief that living for the present becomes pointless.

The first sentence in this excerpt is Ruth's first interpretative leap in the paragraph, her first attempt to analyze and explain the textual details about light from Woolf's essay. When the members of the work group read that paragraph, they wanted to know more about what Ruth meant in the sentence. They suggested that she separate that sentence from the one following it—creating blank space on the computer screen or page on which she was writing—and fill in the space with more analysis or explanation. Ruth's revisions appear here underlined.

Ruth's revision

Here, the fire burning in the grate may represent the appeals and delights of life, which have become dreary to Mrs. Grey when compared to the lure of the afterlife, the sweet respite of death, as represented by the streaming sunshine from outside. <u>That sunshine is actually life-giving even though it is calling Mrs. Grey to death. Death, Woolf seems to be suggesting, is preferable to the life of pain that</u>

Mrs. Grey must endure. There is a sweeter, more peaceful life in death. The sunlight outside the door beckons, offering promise, relief, "stainless and boundless rest." Mrs. Grey is so enamored by the prospect of going to such a paradise of rest and relief that living for the present becomes pointless.

In her revision, note how Ruth more fully explains the connections she sees within Woolf's essay.

EXERCISE 6–2   Analyzing and Revising

1. Look back through Ruth's three middle analytical paragraphs and select a spot where you would like more explanation about one of her interpretative sentences. Revise that section by filling in what you think Ruth is suggesting. Add only your thoughts, not more textual detail.

2. Each of Ruth's paragraphs ends with a quotation. Select one of those paragraphs and, after the quotation, add a sentence or two of explanation that helps readers see more clearly what you think the quotation means. Write your explanatory sentences in the context of what you think Ruth is trying to say in the paragraph. In essence, help Ruth complete her paragraph.

5   Writing the beginning

Ruth's analysis of Woolf's essay leads her finally to a consideration of the intensity of Mrs. Grey's pain and weariness. After writing about the images of pain scattered throughout the essay, Ruth turns to Woolf's last paragraph and her claim that humanity is responsible for prolonging Mrs. Grey's suffering. All of Ruth's analysis (about the house, light, pain and mental anguish, and blame) becomes the middle of her essay. In the middle, Ruth offers her interpretation of "Old Mrs. Grey," her idea about how the textual details of the essay suggest that Mrs. Grey would be better off dead and that humanity needlessly prolongs her suffering. That idea is the thesis of Ruth's essay—the point she must defend.

Having written the middle of her essay, Ruth is ready to write a beginning that will interest readers in her analysis of "Old Mrs. Grey" and, at the same time, suggest her thesis. Here is the draft of her beginning.

Ruth's beginning

In her essay "Old Mrs. Grey," Virginia Woolf paints a picture of a ninety-two-year-old woman whose supreme desire is to die. There is no action or movement in this portrait; Mrs. Grey merely sits alone in a corner of her house. Woolf's short, page-long description not only depicts the sufferings of a single individual but of the old and the grey in general. And yet it is clear that the purpose of this piece is

1

more than the extraction of sympathy. Woolf expresses her view that a life of such suffering is not worth living. She asserts that the physical and mental agonies of old age should not be prolonged on humanitarian grounds.

Ruth's direct, succinct beginning orients readers; it gives them a sense of Woolf's essay and indicates what Ruth thinks it means. Although Ruth's introduction is good as is, she could improve it by giving her readers some clues about what the middle of her essay, where she substantiates her thesis about suffering and the reward of death, will contain. Readers usually like to know early on how textual details will contribute to their understanding of an essay's idea.

You can often convey how the textual details support your interpretation in a single thesis sentence such as: *Woolf does not make this assertion straight out; rather, she makes it through the suggestive details in her essay.* Ruth could place that sentence at the end of her beginning paragraph, pointing the way to her own analysis of Woolf's use of suggestive details.

6   Writing the rest of the middle and the ending

The ending for an analytical essay, as for every essay, must account for what has gone on in the middle. It cannot, of course, rehash all of the detailed analysis, but it must represent the essence of that analysis and provide a fresh perspective—yours. Because the ending must express a full understanding of the middle, you should write it last or when you are almost finished with your analysis.

Drafting the middle

To understand Ruth's ending, you need to see the rest of her analysis—the final three paragraphs of the middle. Here are paragraphs 5, 6, and 7 of the middle. They focus on the intensity of Mrs. Grey's pain. After writing and revising these middle paragraphs, Ruth was able to move on to two drafts of an ending (as we will see later).

Ruth's final three middle paragraphs

However, it is not fair to take Mrs. Grey's suffering lightly either, for she suffers   5
excruciating pain. Woolf compares her pain to a sadistic snake: "a zigzag of pain, wriggling across the door, pain that twisted her legs as it wriggled; jerked her body to and fro like a marionette." Woolf also speaks of a sharp, cutting pain by describing Mrs. Grey's body as being "wrapped around the pain as a damp sheet is folded over a wire . . . spasmodically jerked by a cruel invisible hand." The startling image of Mrs. Grey that these comparisons create, of her body writhing, twisting like a live wire, shows the sufferings the elderly must endure and explains Mrs. Grey's state of mind, her unexpected eagerness for death.

Woolf gives readers further insight into Mrs. Grey's mental anguish by taking us into her mind as well as allowing us to hear what she has to say. Mrs. Grey looks back to her active childhood, her entrance into the adult world, and the time spent with her eleven brothers and sisters. But these memories can only bring her sorrow and loneliness when she compares those times to the present. She is literally jerked back to reality by a convulsion: "The line jerked. She was thrown forward in her chair." Her old body is sick and deteriorating and all of her siblings have died; she has even survived her husband and her children.   **6**

The tone of Mrs. Grey's voice as she mumbles is not bitter, for she has no energy to complain. Woolf's fragmented sentences reflect Mrs. Grey's tiredness as though she doesn't have even enough energy to speak: " 'All dead. All dead. . . . My brothers and sisters. And my husband gone. My daughter too. But I go on.' " Her words also have an almost Mother Goose-rhyme quality to them: " 'I'm an ignorant old woman. I can't read or write and every morning I crawls downstairs, I say I wish it were day . . . ' " This suggests a regression into a childish state, or into senility, but the words are coherent, expressing her feelings of debilitation and inadequacy. While her words have no hint of bitterness in them, they evoke pity. Her daily supplications to God--" 'O let me pass' "--show how desperately she yearns to be relieved of her suffering. The thought of Mrs. Grey crawling downstairs and falling into bed by herself every day is especially poignant and helps readers understand Mrs. Grey's fatigue and loneliness.   **7**

Drafting the ending

The first draft of Ruth's ending is the weakest part of her essay. As you will see, she has not completed her analysis. She tries to finish that analysis and end her essay in the same paragraph. Avoid this common pitfall; essays require a separate ending.

Read the following paragraph with this question in mind: How well does Ruth's ending account for the analysis presented in her essay?

Ruth's ending: First draft

In the last paragraph of her essay, Woolf concludes by seeming to lay the blame for Mrs. Grey's suffering on humanity, again using comparisons. She asserts that it is the hand of humanity that jerks so cruelly on the wire of pain, that "puts out the eyes and the ears," that "pinions" the bodies of the elderly on those wires of pain by trying to keep them alive. The elderly are like tortured birds, pinned to a barn door, like "a rook that still lives, even with a nail through it." Woolf suggests that we, humanity, are responsible for prolonging their sufferings by caring for them and by trying to ameliorate their lives "with a bottle of medicine, a cup of tea, a dying fire." In a way, it seems as if Woolf is not really blaming humanity for the sufferings of the elderly but merely reprimanding us for not being aware of them.   **8**

Or perhaps she is merely voicing her own ambivalence about the issue of euthanasia. And yet her strong language in the last paragraph and in other parts of the essay accuses us of being the active perpetrators of a crime, a crime that we could not help. If Woolf's intention for this essay was, indeed, to lay the blame on us for Mrs. Grey's pain, it is an invalid and unfair indictment, for Woolf demands that we be selfish and inhumane in order to be humane, to help the elderly by turning our backs on them. Woolf does not realize that even we, who accept the suffering of our parents and grandparents, accept it for our own futures as well as an immutable fact of life.

This is how Ruth's instructor evaluated her ending: "Ruth, you may have tried to do too much in this paragraph. You try to complete your analysis of 'Old Mrs. Grey'; you react to Woolf's idea about euthanasia and blame within the context of your own analysis; and, finally, you turn away from your focused analysis and judge Woolf's idea in an entirely new context." The final two sentences of Ruth's ending provide the basis for another kind of essay, perhaps an exploration or an argument about who is to blame for the suffering of the older generation. Ruth's essay is supposed to be about *how* Woolf develops her idea in "Old Mrs. Grey," not about the appropriateness or reliability of that idea. Remember always to stay focused on your thesis.

Consider Ruth's revised ending. Her one long paragraph becomes two. The first of the revised paragraphs completes the analysis Ruth was doing in the middle of her essay; the second revised paragraph constitutes the ending of her essay.

Ruth's revised ending

In the last paragraph of her essay, Woolf concludes by laying blame for Mrs. Grey's suffering on humanity. Again, she makes her point using comparisons. She asserts that it is the hand of humanity that jerks so cruelly on the wire of pain, that "puts out the eyes and the ears," that "pinions" the bodies of the elderly on those wires by trying to keep them alive. The elderly are like tortured birds, pinned to a barn door, like "a rook that still lives, even with a nail through it." Woolf suggests that we, humanity, are responsible for prolonging their sufferings by caring for them and by trying to ameliorate their lives "with a bottle of medicine, a cup of tea, a dying fire." Our efforts to alleviate suffering inflict and prolong pain.   **8**

Perhaps Woolf is not really blaming humanity for the sufferings of the elderly but merely reprimanding all of us for being unaware of what we might be doing to cause such suffering. Perhaps she is merely voicing her own ambivalence about euthanasia. And yet her strong language in the last paragraph and her suggestive details throughout the essay suggest that Mrs. Grey is suffering unmercifully and that she longs to walk out that door of her house into those expansive fields to a new and deserved freedom. She longs to take flight, not to stay "pinioned" to a barn door. Woolf wants us to think about Mrs. Grey's pain and her desire, and she   **9** wants us to realize that our kindnesses toward the elderly may be misdirected. Woolf wants us to know that helping Mrs. Grey may very well mean helping her die.

EXERCISE 6–3 Analyzing the Revision

1. Are the two revised paragraphs more or less effective than the first draft of the ending (6b-6)? Explain your answer.
2. Now read Ruth's entire essay (paragraphs 1–9). Assess how effectively Ruth makes her case about the textual details and the idea she thinks Woolf is presenting. Annotate each paragraph, indicating where you think Ruth does her analysis convincingly. When you think she needs to show either more thinking or more textual detail within the paragraph, mark those spots with the word *gap*. Bring your notes to class, where you should try to reach a consensus about the changes Ruth might consider for her final version of the essay.

EXERCISE 6–4 Developing an Analytical Essay

Select a text (a work of art, performance, or essay) and read or study it. You want to look into the way the text works. Make notes as you read or study. Write out questions as they come to you. As you look over your preliminary analysis, see if you can ask a focusing question—one that will take you to the heart of the text. Then, following the Guidelines for Developing an Analytical Essay on p. 129, write your own four- to six-page analytical essay about the text.

6c Putting analysis to other uses

The methods Ruth Chung used in developing and writing her analytical essay—close reading, noticing textual details, questioning, grouping textual details, writing to discover meaning, quoting textual details in the essay to support and illustrate the interpretation—do not pertain exclusively to analytical essays. You can acquire these skills and use them to write other forms of essays as well. For example, let us look at how one student, Kristen Hughes, used an analysis of Picasso's painting *Guernica* to lead her to an idea that became the basis for an exploratory essay. (Analysis can also provide the foundation for argumentative essays, as you will see in Chapter 7.)

1 Questioning Picasso's *Guernica*

Before looking at the results of Kristen's analysis, try analyzing *Guernica* (reproduced on p. 140 and also on the color plate) on your own. Recall how

Pablo Picasso, *Guernica* (1937). Museo Nacional Centro de Arte Reina Sofia, Madrid.
© 1997 Estate of Pablo Picasso/Artists Rights Society (ARS), New York.

questioning led Kristina Wilson to an idea about Avedon's photograph, *Killer Joe Piro,* in Chapter 4 (see 4a, especially Developing Questions from Evidence on p. 79). Begin with nothing more than *Guernica,* looking at it and questioning it. Then we will consider how additional knowledge gained through research might enhance what you see in the painting.

2 Adding to your knowledge by using sources

You can make the analysis of texts more interesting by doing research. Using the evidence you find in outside sources often helps you gain insights that clarify your own interpretation of a text.

Consider how some outside knowledge might change the way you think about *Guernica.* You can find such background information quickly if you go to the library and explore its resources. (For help in using the library, see Chapter 43 on research skills.) For now, let us consider two sources. H. W. Janson, an art historian and critic, tells us in his *History of Art* that Picasso was "inspired by the terror-bombing of Guernica, the ancient capital of Basques in northern Spain. . . . The destruction of Guernica was the first demonstration of the technique of saturation bombing which was later employed on a huge scale in the course of World War II." (The bombing occurred during the Spanish Civil War.) The German planes, according to Edmund Burke Feldman—another art critic—were flying for Generalissimo Francisco Franco, who would become Spain's dictator. Guernica was defenseless and was not a military objective; the bombing was an experiment. How does that information alter the way you think about *Guernica?*

3   Using analysis in an exploratory essay

Picasso painted *Guernica* in 1937. More than fifty years later, Kristen Hughes stood before the painting in Spain. She had traveled there a year or so before her first year in college. The painting remained in her memory, and in her first-year writing class, she recalled it as she was searching her mind for an idea for an essay. When she visited the museum, Kristen learned that the painting was supposed to represent Picasso's reaction to war.

When Kristen began to think about the painting, she consulted the works of Janson and other art critics to get more information. But as she began to think and write about the painting, questioning and analyzing it, she was not interested solely in the painting's historical roots, nor was she interested in writing an analytical essay accounting for her interpretation of the painting's textual details. Instead, she wanted to explore how the painting seized her imagination as she looked at it, the way it impressed her in a very personal way. Thinking about that painting, she was not much different from E. B. White reflecting on the moon walk he had seen on television (see 4b). The painting and the moon walk served as catalysts for these two writers.

Kristen's analysis led her to see traces in the painting of an idea that she was trying to come to terms with. She decided, finally, to write an exploratory essay about heroism. Here are the thoughts that served as the beginning of her essay.

Kristen's beginning

In Picasso's <u>Guernica</u>, a bull stands implacably over a screaming woman with a dead child in her arms. Above and aloof from her and the other broken humans below, that bull may represent the German Luftwaffe, which bombed the small town of Guernica in 1937, the ruthless Franco, or even the masculine pursuit of war itself. The bull's eyes remain expressionless despite the chaos and destruction around him; his ears and horns are simple and sharp. As I looked up at the bull a few years ago in Madrid, I found I hated and feared his strength, his virile indifference to the pain in the faces of the other figures in <u>Guernica</u>; yet I also felt awe and admiration. In a perverse way I love his pride and his independence. Sometimes I wonder if there is any of him in me. I wonder too if I want him there.

The process of analysis helped Kristen study the painting and think about its historical background, but she was more interested in the idea that emerged from the analysis. What she wanted to resolve was whether a destructive form of masculinity might have something to do with her becoming a hero in her own right. Her analysis of the painting led her to an idea about what it might mean to become her own hero.

In her essay, Kristen tries to figure out whether she thinks it appropriate to internalize that fierce independence she associates with masculinity or whether she ought to keep it at bay. She eventually reaches this conclusion.

I am finding a new Hero in myself to follow. She can be violent at times, because she can be everything; but she will always be sorry. No matter how hungry her heart, indifference will not suit her. She has an indomitable will but is never proud for long.

The aspect of the hero that Kristen comes to terms with is no longer altogether masculine, no longer something outside herself. What Kristen asks us to consider is the possibility of a new kind of heroic "She," an idea she expressed in an exploratory essay, that evolved out of her analysis of Picasso's painting.

EXERCISE 6–5 Doing Analysis

Select a painting or a family photograph and "read" it, noting details. Think about the context in which it was created. Try to determine what outside influences might have affected the artist or the photographer. If you select a painting, you may have to do some research in the library to find out more about it. If you select a family photograph, you may want to ask family members what they see in it or what they know about it. Think about what might have been going on outside the frame of the photograph—what was not included in the picture itself. Write two or three analytical paragraphs that account for what you see.

CHAPTER 7

The Argumentative Essay

*I*n an **argumentative essay** a writer tries to *persuade* readers to adopt his or her point of view about a given issue. The subject can range from local problems to national and international ones—from a local school district's busing plan, to a nation's educational goals, to international concerns about arms control.

A good, persuasive **argument** is usually built from an interesting, substantial, and often controversial topic. You need not go far to find controversy; our diverse culture seems to thrive on it. Issues dealing with race, gender, war, technology, and education, for example, suggest controversies that seem never to be resolved. When you choose a topic to write about, or have one assigned by your instructor, you will investigate it, develop your ideas about it, and write an argumentative essay that presents and substantiates your point of view—the thesis that you will defend in a clear-headed and reasonable way.

As you begin thinking about your topic and considering the availability of evidence, you will act as a newspaper reporter, asking questions and looking for answers. But unlike a reporter, you will find that your task involves more than rendering reports; you will also have to reach the conclusion that will become the thesis for your essay. To reach it, you will have to consider the way other investigators have thought about the topic. Their written work will become one of your sources.

Your investigation might require you to conduct research in the library, to go out into the community to interview experts, to go into the field or the laboratory to conduct experiments, or simply to rely on your own experiences. Your investigation yields information that helps you reach a conclusion about your controversial topic. That conclusion is the leading idea that will become the thesis for your essay. Given the nature of the topics that lend themselves to argument, your thesis will always be subject to further analysis; it will need thinking about again in light of changing conditions and the availability of new evidence. So you need not think that you will be developing the final and definitive answer to these long-standing controversies. Rather, you will present a clear-headed conclusion that takes into account the available evidence and contributes to the dialogue about the controversy.

Often, if you are writing an argumentative essay for a course, your instructor will specify the range and nature of your investigation. On other occasions, however, you will have to decide on your own what sources you need to consider so you can clarify your perspective on the controversy and develop and defend your thesis. This chapter will suggest how to do this investigative work and how to use evidence effectively when you write your essay. You will see how two students develop their argumentative essays; one student will rely primarily on personal experience (7d), the other on written texts (7e). (Also see Part Nine for more detailed information on research.)

7a   Purpose and audience in argument

When you write an argumentative essay, your primary *purpose* is to present and defend your conclusion about a controversial issue so that you can influence change. That conclusion can lead to more controversy—on campus, in the local community, or in the nation—but it can also lead to social or institutional change. For example, you might try to persuade a community to change its attitude about winning and losing or its voting habits. Or you might try to persuade an organization to change the way it makes decisions. You might even try to influence the critical reception of a new book through a persuasive argument about its value.

In exploratory and analytical essays (Chapters 5 and 6), you show your readers how you think about an idea or a text; your allegiance is to your way of seeing and to the text you examine. In an argumentative essay, your allegiance shifts to a more rigorous, perhaps more formal persuasiveness that necessarily includes a consideration of your audience's values. In an argumentative essay, you must consider conflicting points of view as you develop and present your own position. You want your readers to know that you have been thorough, that you know what other investigators have proposed, and that you have a better solution. You also want your readers to agree with your position, and often, you want them to change not only their minds but also their behavior. Although argumentative essayists need not try to change the world, they often write about public issues that affect private lives. Their conclusions, if adopted, can have important, lasting consequences.

Arguments require an especially keen attentiveness to *audience* because your goal is to convince that audience of your conclusion; you do not want to invite your readers' opposition or hostility. However, the challenge for you as a writer is that not all audiences will agree with your point of view. To be persuasive, you need to show a real concern about how your readers might think about a given subject as well as how they might react to the way you think about that subject. Remember that all audiences—whether hostile or friendly, whether you know them well or have no idea how to persuade them— respond to logic and reasonableness. (See 7b-1 for more on reasonableness.)

7b   Preparing to write a reasonable argument

Preparing to write an argument is a lot like preparing to write any of the other types of essays (see 1f and Chapters 5 and 6). However, written arguments do have some specific requirements. The accompanying chart, Features of the Argumentative Essay, lists the principles that apply to all good arguments. You can use the chart as a model in building an argument and as a checklist to test the effectiveness of your completed argument.

Features of the Argumentative Essay

- It conveys a reasonable conclusion—often called a *thesis* or a *claim*—about a controversial topic.
- It presents supporting evidence that is always incorporated, explained, and documented clearly and precisely.
- It considers and often presents the conflicting points of view about the controversy.
- It reflects thorough research.

---

1   Being reasonable

Formal logic specifies rules for being reasonable, and you will benefit from keeping those rules in mind as you write. They will help you maintain a fair and reasonable argument rather than an unbalanced, hotheaded, or fallacious one. Chapter 3 discusses logical thinking in detail and explains how to use the principles of reasoning effectively. There, you will see how induction and deduction contribute to a sound argument (3d), and how to use causality and analogy in constructing arguments (3e and 3f).

Your informed judgment can also tell you a great deal about the reasonableness of your arguments and the soundness of your evidence. You must take the time to question yourself about your own point of view and to imagine what will seem logical and reasonable to your audience. Controversies often push opponents into extreme positions—my way is right, your way is wrong—when in fact, a much more reasonable solution often lies somewhere between the extremes.

Audiences also respond well if you adopt a fair-minded and reasonable tone in your arguments. Exaggeration and anger will work against you. For example, never use name calling as a tactic (you should not refer to your opposition as *stupid* or *ludicrous*). You should also avoid wording that sounds pompous or borrowed or that overstates your case and thereby distorts the truth. Russell Baker, a syndicated columnist, makes fun of such language in his retelling of the story of Little Red Riding Hood. Instead of saying "Grandmother, what large ears you have," Little Red Riding Hood says, "In reference to your ears it is noted with the deepest respect that far from being underprivileged, their elongation and enlargement appear to qualify you for unparalleled distinction." An inappropriate tone revealed through extremes of language can be humorous, as in this example, but it can also quickly undermine the credibility of a written argument. You should always choose your words carefully. (See also Chapters 28 and 29.)

2   The nature of your evidence

Argumentative essays require you to be rigorous and analytical as you sift through your evidence and think about how to develop your argument. Be thorough and open minded—look at the whole controversy so that you do not overlook important evidence. Jumping to conclusions tends to lead to using evidence that supports preliminary and, perhaps, unfounded bias for a particular solution. Combine open-mindedness with rigorous investigation so that you can acquire sufficient knowledge to develop a reasonable thesis.

One important way to test how thorough you have been is to ask yourself how other investigators might react to your thesis. If you have read or listened to others who have entered the debate about your chosen subject, you should be able to anticipate their objections and counter them once you know enough about the subject. Ignoring other points of view can only weaken your argument by suggesting to readers that you have considered no other position except your own. That kind of single-mindedness makes your viewpoint seem unreasonable.

Although you will get much of your information about your topic by investigating the way special interest groups think about and defend their views about the controversy, you will also have to seek out experts, looking always for those who have the least bias. Expert testimony—like that given in courts of law—can help you establish the reasonableness of your thesis. Such testimony is valuable as long as it is credible. To be credible, the person providing the testimony must operate within his or her area of competence or expertise. The testimony must also be accurate, current, and representative. You should scrutinize testimony with the same kind of logical analysis and careful questioning you bring to other forms of evidence (see 4a).

3   The nature of your argument

As you consider your evidence and its relationship to your thesis, you can also benefit from a systematic way of thinking about that relationship. Remember that the conclusion you draw from the evidence depends on your inferential skills—the skills that permit you to draw out the conclusion that makes sense of the evidence. That conclusion cannot be forced; it will probably not seem self-evident. As you look at the evidence (much of it conflicting) and try to reach a reasonable conclusion about it, you will have to give it considerable thought. As you continue to examine new evidence, your conclusion about the meaning of that evidence will continue to change until you have completed your research and examined all of your evidence. At that point you are ready to formulate the final thesis for your essay.

Building a relationship between evidence and thesis

In *The Uses of Argument*, the philosopher Stephen Toulmin provides a relatively simple but logical and rigorous way for you to think about that important relationship between your evidence and the conclusion you draw from it. Toulmin does not give you a foolproof way of reaching a reasonable conclusion; no one can do that. But thinking the way he does will help you be more reasonable. Identifying three important elements that are common to most arguments—a claim, support, a warrant—Toulmin places heavy emphasis on the *claim* that an argument makes. In the language that we have been using in this handbook, a *claim* is nothing more than a thesis, or the lead idea you have formulated and that you want to defend. Toulmin identifies three types of claims: claims of fact, claims of value, and claims of policy. Support, or evidence, to substantiate these three different kinds of claims will vary according to the claim.

Claims of fact suggest the truth of some condition that can be substantiated but that requires considerable research to do so: *The apparent epidemic of drug sales in Washington Square Park is on a par with other epidemics during the last three decades.* Claims of fact like this one about current drug sales and past epidemics require that you find existing evidence that can be verified but that may be very difficult to acquire. Even that verifiable evidence will need interpreting.

Claims of value express acceptance or denial of a standard of taste or morality: Good Morning, Vietnam *is the finest movie to come out of America's longest war.* A claim of value such as this one requires considerations of taste and morality; such considerations depend primarily on reasonableness and consensus about taste and morality rather than on verifiable, factual evidence.

Claims of policy assert that a particular policy or way of doing business should be adopted: *Curbing the drug epidemic in Washington Square Park requires more police patrols, more neighborhood effort, and increased support from local businesses.* Claims of policy require evidence that strongly suggests that the proposed policies have a reasonable chance of working; that they have worked elsewhere under similar circumstances.

You can see, however, that no matter how much evidence you accumulate to support these different kinds of claims, you can rarely build an absolutely airtight case. Your task is to be as reasonable as possible, not to be absolutely right. How convincing you are will depend on the quality of your evidence and the reasonable way you establish that relationship between the evidence and your thesis, between the support and the claim.

Warrants may, at first, be a little more difficult to detect and visualize than claims and support, but your understanding of them should help you write more convincing arguments. **Warrants**, in Toulmin's language, are "bridges" that establish connections between claims and support. They are essential to our understanding of the relationship between claim and support.

A warrant can be either implicit or explicit. When implicit, it resembles an enthymeme (3d-1), a formal syllogistic argument in which one of the premises is missing; it is implied. Consider the claim of value that we mentioned earlier: Good Morning, Vietnam *is the finest movie to have come out of America's longest war.* That complicated claim requires two kinds of support: evidence that will allow us to understand that movie's value in terms of other fine movies to come out of the war; and evidence that will establish the meaning of *finest.* Against the latter claim, you might amass evidence to establish the movie's realistic portrayal of the unusual war. Your support could come from your own analysis of the movie, from your interviews with veterans who could comment on the movie's realism, and from your comparison of that movie with other war movies.

But as sound as all of that evidence might be when you collect it and analyze it, the effectiveness of your argument will also depend on an unstated warrant that your reader will have to agree to accept: a war movie's ultimate value depends on its realistic portrayal of the war. If your reader does not accept that warrant, your argument will not be very persuasive. The movie's portrayal of violence, human relationships, and human development under stress, or the haunting beauty of its images, might be much more important to some viewers than its realism. For those viewers, realism alone would not make the movie the finest of its kind, no matter how much support you might offer to substantiate your claim.

If you think of your own arguments in terms of Toulmin's claim, support, and warrant, you can help yourself avoid common structural pitfalls: weak relationships between claim and support (thesis and evidence) and a failure to understand and account for the assumptions upon which your argument is based.

Troubleshooting an argument

You can avoid other common pitfalls—*logical fallacies* that undermine otherwise soundly constructed arguments—just by being aware of them and by considering them as you question your own written work during drafting and the final preparation of your essay. These logical fallacies appear at the end of this chapter (7f) and remind you of common mistakes associated with the misuse or insufficiency of evidence. For instance, you need to know that it is unreasonable to generalize from a single example; doing so results in a fallacy known as *hasty generalization*. To be logical and reasonable, you need to do your investigative work thoroughly and to draw conclusions that your evidence supports. Do not leap far beyond your evidence. Persuasive argumentative essays must be built on the relationship between solid evidence and reasonable conclusions. Turn to section 7f for more on logical fallacies.

4   Devising a thesis for a reasonable argument

For any argument to be reasonable and effective, the thesis—the conclusion to be defended in the essay—needs to fit the evidence. Let us see how a thesis can, with careful consideration, come to account for the evidence and represent a more reasonable argument. The topic, in this example, is how best to use a high school's library budget. One special-interest group in the community wants to build new storage space for books that few people consult; the other group wants to weed out the older books and spend most of the money for new books. These two groups are locked in a standoff, recognizing no middle ground.

Gloria Rodriguez had worked in the school library during summers in high school and spent additional summers there after going to college. From the day she started working, she heard about the storage problem. At home, she heard her father, a history teacher, complain about too few books in the library, while her mother, a member of the local school board, tried to decide how to allocate the library's funds. Because Gloria found herself in the midst of that controversy and listened to many sides of the debate, she was in a good position to write an argumentative essay that presented her own thesis about the controversy for her college composition class.

Gloria did not need to go far to find evidence that related directly to the issues. She used her own experience, but she also conducted research. The local papers published the budget information. The librarian had been keeping track of the dwindling storage space for the past ten years and had good records. Gloria interviewed her father and other teachers to get their views about gaps in the library's holdings. She also interviewed her mother about those gaps and the need to control expenditures.

Considerations of audience

Gloria had to be rigorous and thorough in her research so that she would not overlook important considerations as she reached her thesis. In its basic form, that thesis is a straightforward declaration.

The library must create additional space so that its collection can be supplemented.

But her declaration leaves Gloria vulnerable to alternative warrants—to explicit arguments based on different and more carefully considered premises.

Counterattacks can go back and forth as long as rival interest groups conceal their warrants from one another. A solution that includes explicit warrants offers a much greater chance for success, providing that the warrants have been carefully considered and are based on a logical relationship between the evidence and the claim.

Gloria's solution addresses this problem by providing precise and open warrants that directly acknowledge the positions rival interest groups have taken. Her solution also accounts for a better fit between claim and evidence than her first version did.

> Although our local library has a significant problem with dwindling storage space, gaps in the social studies, science, and fiction collections make it imperative that additional books be purchased. Placement of low-circulation books into secondary storage at an alternative location and a concerted effort by the librarian to replace bulky periodicals with microfilm can create sufficient space for supplementing the collection for five more years.

This second version of the thesis is an expanded version of the first, but it seems much more reasonable because it reflects Gloria's investigative work; it also reflects her keen sense of audience—especially those people in her hometown who have a vested interest in the outcome of her argument. She is making every effort to take into consideration the various special-interest groups so that her opponents know their points of view have been taken into account.

When you develop your own thesis, try always to ground it in the investigative work that you have done and offer the most reasonable conclusion that you can based on the evidence. Be specific and reasonable, anticipating the response of those who disagree with you. To avoid simple declarations that invite resistance, make your warrants as clear as your claim.

7c　Organizing and developing an argumentative essay

The accompanying Guidelines for Developing an Argumentative Essay take into account the necessary give and take between concerned interest groups. The guidelines also indicate that researching and writing lead to questions that in turn lead to more research and writing.

You can see, too, that your ability to detect the give and take between special-interest groups remains an important part of your researching and revising. In class, ask members of your work group or someone else to help you imagine the kind of opposition you will face from these special-interest groups. In doing this, you will know better how to take different viewpoints into account as you reach your conclusion and as you continue to refine your argument.

You need not follow the accompanying guidelines in sequence. Rather than providing a step-by-step system for developing an argument, they offer general considerations that will help you maintain focus. You will see in 7d and 7e how these guidelines helped Dan Legereit and Zach Wolfe create argumentative essays.

Guidelines for Developing an Argumentative Essay

- Select a controversial subject that interests you.
- Consider other points of view. Be fair to all sides of the argument during research by doing the following:
  - As your evidence begins to lead you to a conclusion, search for contradictory evidence.
  - Question your own evidence just as you question other investigators' conclusions.
  - Avoid jumping to conclusions, and never be satisfied if your evidence leads to only one way of seeing your topic.
  - Try to imagine how your audience will interpret your evidence. (See the Audience Checklist on p. 9 in 1d.)
  - Let the principles of logic guide your effort (3d). Consider your argument in terms of Toulmin's claim, support, and warrant (7b-2).
- Write a short account explaining what you have discovered about your controversy. Sketch out the various points of view.
- Based on the evidence you have gathered (from experience, reading, interviewing, and observing), formulate a tentative thesis, one that you will reconsider and modify as you do more reading, writing, and analysis.
- Think about your audience. Begin to map out in your mind how to present your argument. Consider what background information your audience will need to understand your point of view and the other points of view you will take into account. Make a tentative outline of how you think you will develop your argument (see 1f on organizing). The way you organize your evidence will help determine just how convincing your argument will be.
- Write a draft beginning, and go on to develop the middle of your essay. Write an ending.
- Present your argument to your work group or to another classmate. Ask your readers to resist your argument and to indicate weak spots—places where they cannot understand your point or where they would like to see more evidence or explanation. Also ask them to identify your thesis. (See 1h and 4e on collaboration, and especially the Guidelines for Collaboration on pp. 20–21.)
- Reflect on your draft and revise it based on the feedback you receive.

7d Developing an argumentative essay from personal experience

Dan Legereit's teacher asked his composition students to develop an argumentative essay from their own personal experiences. They were free to use whatever sources they chose, but they were not required to do formal field or library research. The students were asked to be reflective and reasonable throughout their essays.

As a way of discovering a thesis, students were to select an experience from memory that had a controversial, complex lesson attached to it. Dan's lesson is in the story of what happened when he got into a fight with his best friend. Here are his beginning paragraphs.

Dan's beginning paragraphs

When I was ten years old, I remember getting into a fight with my best friend   1
Richard. I don't remember what the fight was about, but it must have been
important because when I was ten I was pretty small and Richard was big,
very big.

During the fight I remember all the neighborhood kids forming a large circle   2
around Richard and me. There was no way out, I couldn't run, I couldn't hide, and I
sure couldn't find a rock large enough to crawl under. I was in serious trouble. I
decided to go for it, and I fought as best I could. But it was hopeless. It was like the
Heavyweight Champion of the World versus TV's Pee Wee Herman. I didn't have a
chance, so I took another strategy. I put up a good fight for awhile, I took my licks,
and my body began to ache all over. When a few stars appeared I quit, I gave up.
The word around the neighborhood for the next couple of days was that I was a
loser, I had quit in the middle of a fight.

During the fight I realized the only way for me to win was to quit. If I continued
to fight who knows what would have happened. We both won, and we both lost. I
didn't win the fight, but I won the chance to live another day. I won because all the
injuries I suffered were not that bad, only a black eye and a bloody lip, and I
learned a lesson. Sometimes quitting is the best way to win.

Dan has little difficulty thinking of the social implications of the lesson and writing about them. He can see, too, that his thesis—the lesson he derives from that experience—will not please everyone; it is controversial.

1 Using examples to build the argument

Dan knows that he has to consider other points of view, but his initial concern is to focus on his thesis. He wants to broaden its applications.

As Dan thinks of examples to illustrate the benefits of quitting and writes about them, he also begins to think about an audience that will be inclined to see quitting as failure. He begins to sense his readers' resistance.

The examples also help Dan see more clearly how to broaden his thesis. He is learning as he writes, clarifying for himself just what the examples might mean. He is testing reasonableness, developing more clearly the relationship between his evidence (in this case, the examples) and his thesis. Here are two middle paragraphs from Dan's first draft.

Dan's middle paragraphs: First draft

At the end of the movie <u>War Games</u>, the computer, after many minutes trying   4
desperately to win, quits playing. Then the computer says, "Funny game, nobody can win." It must be a myth that computers are never wrong, because in war the only way to win is never to either start or to quit before everyone is a loser.

Coming in first and being the best you can are not the qualities of a winner.   5
Winning requires giving and taking. Sometimes we have to give in a little more than our egos want, but if we look at the situation in a reasonable way, quitting may be the best way out. In the Vietnam War thousands of Americans lost their lives. If America had withdrawn (quit) earlier, many thousands of men and women might be with us now. I'm not saying we should let others take advantage of us and let others run all over us, but in some situations we gain more by being losers, by being quitters. Look at the Orlando Magic basketball team; they were losers. But because they won the right to draft Shaquille O'Neal, I'll bet they will be better off in the future.

Dan has come up with two **premises,** or supporting ideas, to reinforce his main point that quitters can win (see 3d-1 for more on premises). The first premise, developed in Dan's beginning, evolved from a moment in his life when he fought up to a point and then quit; by quitting, Dan believes he won. His second premise, developed in the two preceding middle paragraphs, evolved in his mind as he reflected on a movie about computer war games. The movie provides a background for Dan to restate and reinforce his idea that quitters can win, but this time the context is war, not a personal fight.

Dan also touches on the Vietnam War, making an interesting point about lives saved by quitting. The last lines of the second paragraph refer to basketball and specifically to the Orlando Magic's winning a certain advantage by having a losing season.

In these two paragraphs, Dan makes connections that will give readers a chance to see how his thesis might apply in situations other than a personal fight. He extends the range of his idea through four examples: the personal fight, the movie about war games, the Vietnam War, and the Orlando Magic basketball team. These examples illustrate the truth of what Dan is trying to get his readers to accept. Yet as he offers those examples, his idea remains fixed: quitters can win, and they do. Relying only on repetition, Dan passes up opportunities to be more reflective, either about his particular examples or about his thesis. You can easily overcome this pitfall by getting objective feedback or by imagining what your readers might say. (See 4e on collaboration.)

When you become involved in creating your argument, you need to pause and imagine that your audience might resist your point of view; imagine readers talking back to you and questioning what you are saying. For example, after reading his first two middle paragraphs, Dan imagines his audience asking him, "Can you think of any occasions when quitters lose? What about partial victories gained from quitting, and partial losses? What about the cost in war of quitting in order to save lives versus the cost of losing a nation to avoid human sacrifice? What about the Persian Gulf War?" Dan need not address all of these questions in a short argument, but by showing awareness of them and acknowledging the limitations of his thesis he could make his readers more inclined to accept what he says.

The argumentative form of the essay encourages directness; it asks that you make your case with evidence that reiterates and reinforces the main point of the essay. Whether your evidence consists of examples (as in Dan's essay) or other types of evidence, you need not make the same point repeatedly; instead, use your evidence to enlarge readers' sense of the thesis so its broader implications become clear.

2   Reflecting and revising

The first of Dan's draft middle paragraphs seems unfinished, but it does not need more evidence from the movie; it calls instead for more reflection about war and the circumstances under which Dan believes quitting might constitute winning. You have seen that in his first draft Dan touches on war in his first paragraph and then gets back to it near the middle of the second paragraph. One of his classmates read those paragraphs and suggested that Dan revise the first paragraph by bringing the Vietnam War into it to make his argument more convincing. In his revision, Dan develops the war idea and reconsiders the paragraphs—trying to be more thoughtful and reasonable as he thinks of his audience.

Revised middle paragraphs

At the end of the movie War Games, the computer, after many minutes trying desperately to win, quits playing. Then the computer says, "Funny game, nobody can win." But the computer seemed wrong to me because in war, sometimes, the only way to win is to quit before everyone is a loser. In the Vietnam War thousands of people lost their lives. If America had withdrawn (quit) earlier, many men and women might be with us now. That war went on for years and years, and at the end America lost anyway, claiming a "peace with honor." But I wonder about the lives of all those soldiers who came back home to a nation in turmoil, and about all those lives that were lost because no one in Washington could find a way to bring the war to a close. Stopping earlier could have been a way of winning--saving lives and relieving the suffering of those who came home to chaos.

Vietnam was, of course, a different kind of war from the so-called great wars. I 5 can see the merit of not stopping the fighting until there was a traditional victory in Germany during World War II. The nation had a clear and decisive reason for waging that war. Quitting would not have been appropriate until Hitler was finished off. But coming in first and winning in the traditional sense are not the only qualities of a winner. Winning requires giving and taking. Sometimes we have to give in a little more than our egos want, and if we look at the situation in a reasonable way, quitting may be the best way out. Looking back at the Vietnam War, it is difficult to tell why we stayed in it so long.

I'm not saying we should let others take advantage of us and let others run all 6 over us, but in some situations we gain by stopping. This is true in peace as well as in war. Cutting losses, even in business, can be cheaper in the long run than sticking with a losing project. Business analysts urge us to think about "sunk costs"--the money that's already been spent--and to think about how long it will take to recover those costs and turn a profit. Often, it is better to absorb the costs and abandon a project that seems likely to reap only modest returns.

Even in the competitive arena of professional sports, losing turns out to have its 7 benefits. Consider the Orlando Magic basketball team. A few years ago they were losers. But because of their losses, Orlando won the right to draft Shaquille O'Neal, and they certainly improved their lot. The draft rule that gives a losing team an advantage seems aimed at restoring some kind of balance in the league; it gives teams a way to improve so that competition across the league remains high. The loser rule plays into balance and fairness and, of course, competitiveness.

EXERCISE 7–1   **Evaluating the Revisions**

What is the effect of the revisions Dan made in paragraphs 4–7? Compare Dan's first draft (see 7d-1) to these revised paragraphs. Is his argument becoming more or less convincing? Explain your answer.

3   Outlining to see what you are thinking

Making an informal outline before you begin writing can sometimes help you get started. But as you have seen in this and preceding chapters, sometimes it is best just to start writing; you often do not know what you think about a subject until you start writing about it. Once you have done some writing, it is a good idea to create an outline from what you have put down on paper to reveal the structure of your thinking. An outline can show you interesting possibilities for revising and reorganizing your essay or for filling in gaps in your thinking. (See 1f on outlining and mapping.)

Here is a brief outline of Dan's work thus far.

Dan's outline

Thesis: Sometimes quitting is the best way to win.

Example 1: The fight at age ten.

First Premise: Stopping can be logical, even necessary for survival.

Example 2: War--the movie, Vietnam, World War II

Second Premise: Vietnam was not like WW II, where the objectives and the necessity were clear; quitting could have saved lives in Vietnam without altering the outcome.

Example 3: Business and sunk costs

Third Premise: Taking a loss sometimes saves money in the long run.

Example 4: Orlando Magic

Fourth Premise: Even in professional sports, losing sometimes pays off because there is a principle of balance and fairness at work along with the competitiveness.

This outline helps Dan see that each of his examples adds another dimension to his idea about quitting. They are not merely repeating the same point—and yet Dan does not claim too much for any one of them. Each example seems logical, and together they are interesting and compelling—in a word, persuasive.

EXERCISE 7–2   **Questioning the Premises**

1. Consider each of Dan's premises and reread his paragraphs. List any questions you have about his premises. Think of your questions as a way of talking to Dan, of giving him the advantage of better understanding his opposition.

2. Consider Dan's argument about quitting and winning in terms of Toulmin's claim, support, and warrant (7b-3). How does the argument measure up? Is there an implied warrant about the importance of winning that remains unexamined? Or do you find Dan's argument convincing, his support sufficient? Explain.

4   Organizing the essay

Dan now needs to put his thinking and writing into perspective. He needs to write a beginning and an ending that clearly state his thesis. He also needs to think about how to organize the middle of his essay.

When Dan discussed this draft with his instructor and with the members of his work group, they were encouraging about his revisions. One student suggested that the first three paragraphs would make a fine beginning for the essay as they do what a good beginning must: create interest and reveal the thesis. The instructor asked Dan to add another sentence or two at the end of paragraph 3 that would make readers want to read on into the middle of the essay. Dan finally decided to end the paragraph this way: "I won because all the injuries I suffered were not that bad, only a black eye and a bloody lip, and I learned a lesson. Sometimes quitting is the best way to win. It would be years before I learned how far reaching and sane that lesson could be."

As Dan considers the middle of the essay, he is concerned about the order of the three remaining examples. He knows that if he wants to end on a strong note, he should move from the least convincing example to the most convincing one. He thinks about moving the Magic example first, followed by the business example, and then ending with the paragraphs on war. But he decides finally to keep the order he had worked out as he drafted; it is logical, and he likes the way the war paragraphs follow naturally from the beginning about the fight. He is also pleased that the Magic paragraph is interesting in its own right; that point about balance and fairness and competitiveness seems to have a broader application that he wants to try to bring into the ending of the essay.

So Dan's essay is falling into shape. He has a beginning (paragraphs 1–3, with the added sentence at the end of paragraph 3) and a middle (paragraphs 4–7, as drafted). As a way of getting himself prepared for writing the ending, Dan rereads his essay, getting a clear sense of his whole argument so that he can wrap it up for his readers, giving them a thought-provoking closing perspective. Here is what Dan wrote after a couple of drafts.

Dan's ending

There is something pleasing about the notion that quitting can be a lot like winning. Thinking about the oft-quoted Green Bay Packer coach Vince Lombardi, I wonder whether his claim makes sense any more. Winning may still be everything, but there are more interesting ways to think about winning than clobbering an opponent, whether in a street fight like the one I had with Richard, or in a major war like the one in Vietnam. That loser-rule in basketball, like my idea about quitting, seems to have far-reaching applications. We would be a lot better off if we focused on balance and fairness and on cutting our losses rather than on always going for the big win. Sometimes, we stand to lose too much by winning the old-fashioned way.

EXERCISE 7–3   Writing Your Own Argumentative Essay from Personal Experience

Recall a heated discussion you had about some controversial issue that concerns you—a discussion that left you dissatisfied. Or recall a discussion that you overheard on campus or at work that caught your interest. Following the Guidelines for Developing an Argumentative Essay on p. 151, write an argumentative essay about that controversial issue. Develop the most reasonable response you can about the issue based primarily on your own experience.

7e   Developing an argument from sources

You have seen how Dan Legereit created an argumentative essay based initially on a fight he had as a ten-year-old. His evidence was familiar to him—his fight, a movie he had seen, his thoughts about war, and his interest in the Orlando Magic basketball team.

Let us look now at another kind of argument. This argument also evolves from a student's personal interest in a problem, but the evidence for the essay comes primarily from other essays that Zach Wolfe read in his composition class. Those essays will constitute his sources, and he will use them to develop his thesis. Other types of sources, include books, articles, surveys, field interviews, and so forth. (See Chapters 43 and 44.) In a different class and with a different assignment or purpose, Zach might consult other types of sources to make his argument.

In his essay Zach links a problem he experienced in the Texas school system with two essays he later read: E. B. White's "The Ring of Time" and Martin Luther King, Jr.'s "Letter from Birmingham Jail." The Texas school problem, which interests Zach because it almost prevented his graduation from high school, involved transferring tax money from affluent suburbs to poor inner-city and rural areas. At that time, the problem had threatened the shutdown of the area's schools. Months after Zach's high school graduation, while reading White's essay, he began to think again about the problem in Texas. He began to see more clearly how passive attitudes can have serious political and social consequences. He was making connections between his own life and the texts he was reading.

In the same composition class, Zach read Martin Luther King, Jr.'s "Letter from Birmingham Jail" and found interesting connections there, too—connections between race and privilege, time and passivity, and the problem in Texas that had almost kept him from graduating. His larger argument, however, eclipses the problems in White's essay, in King's essay, and in Texas. The larger argument—the one he will write about—is about the effect of passivity on social progress. Zach's point—his thesis—is not very complicated: *apathy retards progress*. His thesis becomes interesting in the way he develops it by using essays he read in class.

Let us examine how Zach develops his thesis. Look for the way the essay works and for the way Zach makes his case using the other essays. Recall these principles of analysis outlined and illustrated in Chapter 6.

- Reading a text thoroughly leads to an understanding of how the text works.
- Understanding how a text works leads also to an understanding of the meaning of the text.
- Understanding the text's meaning, in turn, leads to ideas.

You should also look to see how Zach uses his sources (the essays)—how he summarizes them, how he incorporates them into his essay, and how he brings them together to illustrate his thesis.

1   Using controversy and causality

In exploring the controversy (to redistribute Texans' tax money from wealthy school districts to poorer ones or not), Zach comes to a conclusion about the dangers of voter apathy. He arrives at his conclusion only after carefully reading White's and King's essays and reflecting on the causes and consequences of voter apathy.

Zach, like any serious scholar, researcher, or argumentative essayist, is looking back at the controversy to try to make sense of what happened, connecting events or sources that may lead to a greater understanding of the controversy. In this case, Zach is interested in **causality**—the logical relationship between a consequence and its possible causes (see 3e). He is more interested in what contributed to or caused the Texas school crisis than in the actual fight over money and the redistribution of wealth.

To suggest why voters might remain passive even though the consequences of their apathy may be serious, Zach knows he will have to develop a thesis from what he remembers about Texas voters as well as on his reading of White's and King's essays. His interpretation of his experiences and readings thus comprise his evidence; he does not have conclusive or verifiable evidence, such as a voter survey, to bolster his argument. Nonetheless, Zach is confident about his idea. He knows that without hard evidence he will have to make his case indirectly, with an **implied thesis.** This is a common practice in arguments based on interpretation rather than on conclusive evidence. Zach's decision to use an implied thesis also grew out of audience considerations—the voting audience might not like to be told directly to reexamine their voting habits. Zach could persuade his audience by getting them to see the consequences of their behavior without making them feel threatened by the revelations made in his essay.

Zach titles his essay "When Good People Do Nothing." Here are his beginning paragraphs.

Zach's beginning paragraphs

Though I passed all my classes, I almost didn't graduate from high school. 1
During my senior year the Texas Supreme Court declared the state's public school
system unconstitutional and set a deadline for the state legislature to come up with

a financing plan that would not discriminate against poor school districts. The court threatened to shut down every public school if the legislature failed to draft an equitable financing plan. The legislators did not want to acknowledge the fundamental problem--making the school system fair would mean transferring tax money from affluent suburbs to poor inner-city and rural areas. Doing this equals political suicide for most politicians. Taxes upset voters, but transferring wealth from rich to poor is even more upsetting because it involves a more radical change.

E. B. White develops a related point in his essay "The Ring of Time": people resist real change. But White's essay has another less apparent purpose that warrants analysis. Many people oppose change, it suggests, but even those who support change do not always actively promote it; they are passive. In 1954 when the Supreme Court ruled racially segregated schools unconstitutional in <u>Brown v. Board of Education</u>, few southerners supported integration. White himself supports integration but admits his own passivity in the matter. He does nothing, except write his essay, to promote change. But to the extent that his essay implicitly attacks hypocrisy by showing why both resistance to change and passivity are so seductive, it is a political act that points to a political weakness.

2

Although Zach's beginning only hints at his thesis, it draws us into the essay as a good beginning must. Notice that as Zach introduces White, he also introduces the idea of passivity. We do not yet know what he will make of that idea, but we are alerted to what will become the essay's central focus. As Zach orients us, he also suggests how he will use his evidence (the text by White).

Reconsidering Ruth Chung's analysis of Virginia Woolf's essay "Old Mrs. Grey" in Chapter 6, notice how Zach intends to use White's text in a different way. Ruth's focus is on how Woolf's essay conveys its point. Both Zach and Ruth have read their respective texts with analytical rigor, though Zach uses White's essay as evidence. He will apply White's analysis of the racial problem in southern Florida in 1956 to a different but related social problem in Texas in 1989. Zach sees the similarities between the two events, and that is the point he wants to make in his essay. Moreover, White's essay remains timeless; in Zach's mind, it pertains to Texas in 1989 as well as to Florida in 1956. That connection is crucial to Zach's argument; it helps him clarify his thesis about passivity.

2 Linking thesis and evidence—Using E. B. White's essay

As you read the first few middle paragraphs of Zach's essay, look for the way he presents White's ideas to clarify his own. Pay careful attention to how Zach links or establishes a relationship between his evidence (White's essay) and his own thesis. In the middle of his essay, he must develop that thesis and make its implications clear. Because his readers may or may not be familiar with White's essay, Zach faces a problem common to every writer: deciding which evidence is essential to his argument and needs to be explained and which to leave out. In this case, Zach needs to decide how much of White's essay to include in his own. He can make wise choices only by keeping his readers in mind, so he asks himself, "What do my readers need to know to understand White's point and to see how I am using White in my essay?" Here is how Zach responds to those questions as he develops his argument.

Zach's middle paragraphs

In his essay, White first demonstrates the relationship between conceptions of time and attitudes toward change. His essay begins with a scene from the South--from Fiddler Bayou, Florida, in 1956. Watching a performer ride a horse around a practice ring, White marvels at her youthful aplomb--she makes it look easy. He savors the apparent timelessness of the scene. "Time itself began running in circles," he writes (18). But this circular view of time shatters when he thinks that the girl will inevitably become an old woman. Like the circus scene, the sights and sounds of the bayou hide the advance of time. During his visit to Florida, White observes this effect. The sun rises slowly. Even the dampness of the air seems to encourage languor. The bayou scene and the circus scene both tempt one to deny the passage of time, to deny change. "We all instinctively avoid it," White observes, "and object to the passage of time and would rather have none of it" (21).   3

Although the connection is not explicit, the next section of White's essay, in which he considers racial integration, challenges this inertia and resistance to change. His argument against segregation is brief and simple; it mocks the "separate-but-equal" argument. Blacks, White observes, come to the ballpark and sit in a "separate but equal section of the left-field bleachers and watch negro players . . . using the same bases as the white players instead of separate (but equal) bases" (20). White implies that segregation is as silly as separate bases for black baseball players. When he tells his Finnish cook that the backseats of the bus are for black people, she calls the arrangement silly. White points out that this is a useful approach, considering that most people are "more touchy about being thought silly than they are about being thought unjust" (21). Although "the sense that is common to one generation is uncommon to the next," as White observes, common sense is a potent weapon, and White uses it here to criticize the opponents of integration (21).   4

But White intends not only to criticize opponents of change, but to show why passivity is so seductive. In the circus tent, the bareback rider's hypnotic circling makes White forget the passage of time. The girl distracts him from reality. "The enchantment," he writes, "grew not out of anything that happened or was performed but out of . . . a ring of ambition, of happiness, of youth" (18). His attraction to these three qualities reflects nostalgia, a longing for the happiness of the past. The girl--"cleverly proportioned, deeply browned by the sun, dusty, eager,   5 and almost naked"--allows the crowd of onlookers to escape from their boredom (18). Watching this casual ride around the ring, they temporarily escape reality. White writes of slipping into a "trance." He shows how easy it is to deny the passage of time, to deny change, especially when this denial is encouraged by nostalgia and by appeals to the senses.

White uses sensory details to show the seductiveness of doing nothing, and he makes us aware of the fact. He mentions the dominance of the letter s in the "sound of the sea and sand, in the singing shell, in the heat of sun and sky, in the sultriness of the gentle hours, in the siesta" (19). Do these sights and sounds of the South literally encourage passivity, or do they merely symbolize it? White seems to suggest that they do both. Either way, these scenes make the reader consider that people pursue change as slowly as the sun moves across the sky and that they long for the reliable sameness of that movement. In Florida, White says, "the sun does not take command of the day until a couple of hours after it has appeared in the east" (20). Daybreak comes slowly here, like every other change. The dampness of the air makes lethargy desirable in an almost sexual way. White artfully describes the humid Florida days. "Matches refuse to strike . . . the newspaper wilts in your hand . . . envelopes seal themselves," and "postage stamps mate with one another as shamelessly as grasshoppers," he writes (20). He allows the reader to see and feel how this appealing environment prevents things from happening--towels drying, matches lighting.

In addition, White confronts his own passivity, the fact that he supports racial integration but does not take any direct action to achieve it. His image of himself lying in bed in the morning sets the tone: "As the first light seeps in through the blinds I lie in bed half awake" (19). This leisurely image is a stern metaphor for White's position in society--he observes and comments, but he does not act--which he then acknowledges directly: "To a beachcomber from the North the race problem has no pertinence, no immediacy" (20). Thus, although White does not like segregation in public places, he never boycotts these places. He watches baseball games at the ballpark, walks down the beach, and rides the bus.

But White prevents the reader from simply feeling indignant or superior. The sights and sounds of Fiddler Bayou seduce White, but White seduces his readers with the same details. He does this by beginning his essay with a seemingly innocent scene, in which he never mentions segregation. Only after making us feel how easy it is to resist change does he raise the issue of segregation. White shows that the same impulse that allowed the circus rider to entrance him also allows people to resist social changes like integration. The Supreme Court decision of 1954 alone could not single-handedly overcome this resistance. The two sections of White's essay may appear unrelated--the first section is sometimes reprinted alone--but both are necessary to understand White's seduction and analysis. Without the second section, "The Ring of Time" would be a description of an interesting scene; but without the first section, the essay might merely strike readers as an argument against segregation. By combining the two sections, White forces readers to examine their own reluctance to pursue change.

Paragraphs 3–8 constitute Zach's reading of White's essay. If Zach has summarized White effectively, capturing the essence of White's essay in a few words, and if he has selected appropriate details and quotations to illustrate key points, and incorporated and explained that material well, readers should be able to follow his thoughts and understand his argument without having to read White's essay. (See 2b-4 and Chapter 44 for more on summarizing, quoting, and incorporating evidence.)

Because Zach is taking ideas and words from White's essay and using them, he must document, or give credit, to the original source. Zach uses the Modern Language Association (MLA) style of documentation (see 45a–c). The page numbers in parentheses throughout this section of Zach's essay (known as parenthetical citations) correspond to pages in the text or anthology that contains White's essay. At the end of the essay, Zach will include a Works Cited list so that interested readers can consult the texts he has used. The list of Works Cited must contain each of the texts Zach summarizes, paraphrases, or quotes. A reader matching parenthetical citations and entries in the Works Cited list will know exactly where to turn for more information. (See Chapter 45 on documentation.) Failure to credit sources used constitutes plagiarism, or theft. (See 44j on how to avoid plagiarism.)

EXERCISE 7–4 **Analyzing Zach's Middle Paragraphs**

---

1. Identify places in Zach's account of White's essay that seem unclear to you. Write a note about each place, explaining your confusion. Comment on whether the quotations clarify what Zach is telling you about White or confusing you.

2. In his middle paragraphs, Zach does not mention the problem in Texas. What can you infer about that problem from this section of Zach's essay? Should Zach be more explicit, or do you find it easy to make the connections he implies indirectly? Explain your answer.

3. Reread the first and last few sentences of each paragraph. How do the sentences help you understand and advance Zach's argument?

4. Paragraph 8 differs from paragraphs 3–7 in an important way. Reread it in light of all the paragraphs that come before it, including Zach's beginning paragraphs. What is the primary purpose of paragraph 8?

---

3   Linking thesis and evidence—Using Martin Luther King, Jr.'s essay

Before looking at the way Zach uses Martin Luther King, Jr.'s essay, let us reconsider the important tasks that all writers working with sources must confront: reading, summarizing, quoting, and explaining a text that will be used to make a point in an argument. Reading, summarizing, quoting, and explaining enable you to link your thesis and evidence. Zach is very good at these related tasks; it may help you to observe how he accomplishes them as he writes. Zach assumes you have not read the texts he refers to; he thus provides sufficient detail from both essays so you can follow and understand his argument. He keeps the reader in mind.

In the next section of his essay (paragraphs 9–10), Zach focuses on King's "Letter from Birmingham Jail," a 1963 appeal to eight clergymen who had criticized King for encouraging civil disobedience. Zach finds that his evidence from the King essay is easier to incorporate because King is more explicit about discrimination than White. Zach does not need to interpret King's point; he needs only to give readers sufficient detail to allow them to understand that point. As you read the following paragraphs, notice how Zach compares White's and King's views of time and passivity.

More of Zach's middle paragraphs

"The Ring of Time" thus addresses some of the same issues as Martin Luther   9
King, Jr.'s famous "Letter from Birmingham Jail." King argues that white moderates (like the clergymen who criticized him for taking action) oppose change by doing nothing, and that this opposition comes from a faulty conception of time. He writes: "I had also hoped that the white moderate would reject the myth concerning time in relation to the struggle for freedom" (504). These moderates think that change will eventually come if time is simply allowed to pass. "Such an attitude," King writes, "stems from a tragic misconception of time, from the strangely irrational notion that there is something in the very flow of time that will inevitably cure all ills" (505). This misconception differs from the one that White examines, by which people see time as a circle, in which nothing permanently changes; but when people accept either notion, they do nothing.

For both White and King, the enemies of positive change are not just the Ku   10
Klux Klan and the Birmingham police; they also include people who support civil rights and integration but remain passive:

> We will have to repent in this generation not merely for the hateful words and actions of the bad people but for the appalling silence of the good people. Human progress never rolls in on wheels of inevitability; it comes through the tireless efforts of men willing to be co-workers with God, and

without this hard work, time itself becomes an ally of the forces of social stagnation. (King 505)

While King and his followers face dirty jail cells and police attack dogs, so-called moderates tell him to wait. In his "Letter," King eloquently criticizes their reluctance to pursue change actively. In "The Ring of Time," White seeks both to criticize and to understand, in a way more typical of an essayist than an orator. He is not in the thick of battle, as King is, but he uses this very fact to explore the attractiveness of resisting change and to show how that kind of resistance can encourage passivity even among people who claim to want change.

EXERCISE 7–5   **Analyzing Zach's Middle Paragraphs**

1. In paragraphs 9–10 Zach introduces Martin Luther King, Jr. to enrich his discussion about time and passivity. What do King's comments add to your understanding of White's essay and of Zach's? Explain your answer.
2. Here, as in paragraphs 3–8, Zach does not mention the problem in Texas. Should he? Why or why not?
3. Look carefully at the block quotation in paragraph 10. Does Zach need to include all of it, or could he get by with less of it? Explain your answer.
4. Reread paragraphs 9–10. Notice how Zach reintroduces White in his discussion of King. Is his approach effective? Try reading the paragraphs by removing all references to White. What is lost? Explain your answer.

---

4   Writing the ending

The ending of an argumentative essay makes a final appeal to readers to accept the thesis. It gives a fresh perspective on the argument, pulling together the various threads that are developed in the middle of the essay. In his ending, Zach chose to add a new dimension to his argument.

Zach's ending

The Texas voters fear change because it reminds them of Communist and   **11** totalitarian states where tax structures place a heavier burden on the wealthy than on the poor. One can reply to this fear that the only way to avoid the two dangers of totalitarianism--centralized power and mass ignorance--is to ensure equal education, which guarantees that power will not become concentrated in the hands of a few wealthy people and empower individuals by giving them an important commodity, information. Some voters would probably even agree with this argument. But even those who support change, as White shows, may not do anything to further it.

Works Cited

King, Jr., Martin Luther. "Letter from Birmingham Jail." <u>Current Issues and</u>
<u>Enduring Questions</u>. Ed. Sylvan Barnet and Hugo Bedau. Boston: Bedford-
St. Martin's, 1990. 498–512.

White, E. B. "The Ring of Time." <u>The Contemporary Essay</u>. Ed. Donald Hall. New
York: St. Martin's, 1984. 145–52.

In his ending paragraph, Zach returns to the topic of the Texas voters. He makes claims about their fears, yet he offers no direct evidence to substantiate that claim. He has not polled the Texas population; he has not referred to any surveys, newspaper articles, or editorials. His entire argument is made by suggestion, as he asks readers to consider the Texas voters in the way that White and King considered passive citizens in their essays.

Zach also introduces a new dimension about totalitarianism and communism in his ending, as if he has been considering it throughout his essay. If he has, he has not made his readers aware of it. This bold move is followed at the end of the essay with very modest claims about the voters themselves. He uses the qualifying words *probably* and *may not* (in his closing sentences) to soften his claim. Zach seems to be trying to balance boldness and moderation as a sign of good judgment.

When you write your own argumentative essays, be cautious about making new claims in your ending that you did not substantiate in the middle of your essay. Sometimes such claims might seem justified, but they rarely are. It makes little sense to leap beyond your own analysis in closing. Even when readers might agree with your new claim, they will find it distracting because it suggests that you have lost track of your argument. Nevertheless, the ending is not just a repetition of what comes before it.

EXERCISE 7–6   **Questioning Zach's Ending**

---

1. Readers consider a successful argument reliable and are willing to accept it. Are you inclined to accept Zach's claims? Why or why not?

2. Consider Zach's argument about voter apathy in terms of Toulmin's claim, support, and warrant (7b-3). How does the argument measure up? Is there an implied warrant about apathy that remains unexamined? Are there other warrants? Explain.

3. How can Zach strengthen his argument without changing his approach? Explain your answer.

---

5   Rethinking and revising

Zach's work group has some interesting suggestions for his revision of the essay. As impressed as they are with how he cites White and King, the group wants to know more about the voters in Texas. They want to know how Zach came to think about the connection between the ideas in the two essays and the Texas voters. In other words, the work group wants more evidence and clarification about that connection.

Specifically, the work group suggests that Zach reconsider paragraph 11 (his ending) as the first of two or three paragraphs that begin a new third section in the middle of the essay. The additional paragraphs could give specific information about voter apathy in Texas based on Zach's observations during that turbulent period when he thought he would not graduate from high school. (See 7d-1 on using personal experience as evidence.)

The work group also wants Zach to write a new ending that will explain the connection of the three middle sections on White, King, and the Texas voters. His work group gives him the guidance he needs to revise his essay and make it more persuasive. (See 1h and 4e on collaboration.)

EXERCISE 7–7   **Writing Your Own Argumentative Essay from Sources**

Each day for about a week, read the editorial page of a state or national newspaper. Look for a controversy that interests you and has some immediate connection with your own experiences (although you need not be directly involved in it). Read three or four different accounts of the controversy by different writers. Then develop your own response to the controversy based on those readings. Recall other texts—essays or articles that you may have read—that remind you of the controversy. Also use your own experiences. Following the Guidelines for Developing an Argumentative Essay on p. 151, develop an argumentative essay that presents your response to the controversy.

7f   Avoiding fallacies

A *fallacy* is an error. A **logical fallacy** represents an error or mistake in logic. These mistakes most often occur when writers fail to establish a clear relationship between the claims they are making and the evidence they present (or fail to present) to substantiate those claims. Often the errors are not immediately apparent because the warrants or premises that account for the relationship between evidence and claim are missing, unstated. When the errors are deliberate, something tricky may be going on: a fallacious argument constructed to conceal the weakness of its evidence or the shallowness of its claim. The following list of common fallacies should help you detect errors in logic in your own writing and in what you read.

Checklist of Common Logical Fallacies

- **Hasty generalization:** A conclusion based on insufficient evidence.
- **Stereotyping:** Assuming without sufficient evidence that members of a group think or behave alike.
- *Either-or* **thinking:** Limiting possible explanations to two.
- **Illogical causality:** Assuming that an event is caused by another simply because one event occurs after the other.
- *Non sequitur:* A statement that does not follow logically from another.
- **Begging the question:** Assuming as true what needs to be proven.
- **Circular reasoning:** Asserting the same point in different words.
- **Special pleading:** Arguing without considering opposing viewpoints.
- **Red herring:** Introducing an irrelevant or distracting consideration into an argument.
- **Appeal to ignorance:** Assuming something is true because the contrary cannot be proven.
- **Playing prejudices:** Appealing to the prejudices of an audience.
- **Character attack:** Attacking a person's character rather than addressing the issue at hand.
- **False analogy:** Making an illogical connection based on irrelevant similarities.

---

1   Hasty generalization

A **hasty generalization** relies on inadequate evidence. Jumping to conclusions too quickly, before considering additional or alternative information, leads to hasty generalizations.

> For our Victorian Novel course, we read ten enormous novels, including Dickens's *Bleak House* and Eliot's *Middlemarch,* which like the others are nearly a thousand pages. It seems as if all Victorian novels are that long.

2   Stereotyping

Stereotyping, a form of hasty generalization, involves making assumptions about things, places, or people based on insufficient evidence. For example, you might describe Los Angeles as crime ridden when many sections of Los Angeles are quite safe. Or you might assume that Italians are quick tempered, that women drive poorly, or that college professors are absentminded. These examples of stereotypical thinking make unwarranted assumptions about an entire group of people based on the characteristics of some. (See Chapter 29 on biased language.)

3   *Either-or* thinking

Sometimes called *false dilemma*, **either-or thinking** limits the solutions to a problem to two—either *A* or *B*. Other alternatives are ignored.

Either the Democrats band together now behind one of the declared candidates, or they will kill each other off politically and ensure an easy Republican victory in the next presidential election.

Either-or thinking is limiting. It oversimplifies complex issues, reducing them to extreme explanations that ignore viable alternatives. (See 3c-5 on ways to overcome *either-or* thinking.)

4   Illogical causality

Illogical causality results from the assumption that because one event happens after another, the first causes the second. This is faulty cause-and-effect reasoning (see 3e), called *post hoc, ergo propter hoc* (Latin for "after this, therefore because of").

In 1991, under coach Bill Parcells, the New York Giants won their division, their league championship, and ultimately the Superbowl. The following year, under Ray Handley, the Giants, with a mediocre 8 and 8 won-lost record, did not make it even to the first round of the playoffs. Handley must be a poor coach, one who is responsible for the Giants' slide into mediocrity.

5   *Non sequitur*

Non sequitur is Latin for "it does not follow." A *non sequitur* is a conclusion that does not follow logically from an argument's premises—usually unstated.

I worked hard during the entire term. I deserve an *A* for the course.

Here the unstated premise—"students who work hard all semester should get an A"—is probably unreliable.

6   Begging the question

To **beg the question** involves assuming the truth of an issue without providing evidence or arguments in its support.

Hondas are reliable because they are Japanese cars.

7   Circular reasoning

To engage in **circular reasoning** is to assert the same idea in different words, but without introducing evidence or reasons in support.

> The growing popularity of aerobic exercise shows that people are becoming increasingly interested in aerobics.

8   Special pleading

In **special pleading** a speaker or writer presents a one-sided argument, completely ignoring contradictory information and opposing perspectives. Special pleaders present their case without indicating the existence of contrary evidence or the possibility of alternative views.

> Doberman pinschers are a good breed of dog. They are alert, highly trainable, and elegant.

9   Red herring

Introducing a **red herring** into an argument deliberately sidetracks the discussion by bringing in an irrelevant matter.

> "Officer, you shouldn't be giving me a ticket for illegal parking when criminals are roaming the streets at this very moment, killing people. The police ought to spend their time solving more important problems and preventing crimes instead of wasting it by harassing law-abiding citizens."

10   Appeal to ignorance

In an **appeal to ignorance** a speaker or writer argues that a situation is true merely because strong contrary evidence is lacking. Such an appeal assumes that a claim must be true simply because it cannot be disproved.

> God must have created the world in six days because scientists can't prove that He didn't. In fact they can't prove that God does not exist, which means, of course, that He does.

11   Playing prejudices

This fallacy (often labeled *ad populum,* Latin for "to the people") appeals to people's emotion, to popular feeling, and to prejudice, rather than to reason.

In speaking to middle-class voters, a candidate for political office criticizes the incumbent on the basis of the incumbent's wealth, connections, and private school education, which she argues make her opponent insensitive to the needs and concerns of middle-class people like herself.

12   Character attacks

One of the most common fallacies, *ad hominem* (Latin for "to the man"), is an attack on an individual's character, attributing motives to that person that he or she may not possess. It is an attempt to discredit an idea by attacking the person presenting it rather than by addressing the issue at hand.

Senator Martino argues that we should attempt to control the budget deficit by cutting spending in the military and social services sectors. But the senator has had serious problems handling his personal credit. Why should we listen to his views on the nation's economic plan when he can't manage his personal finances?

13   False analogy

A **false analogy** misleads by comparing situations that are more unalike than similar. False analogies are also sometimes based on irrelevant similarities.

If we add proficiency in a foreign language to the graduation requirements, we will deter students from attending this university, just as we did when we added math and science requirements ten years ago.

EXERCISE 7–8   Identifying Fallacies

Identify the fallacies of reasoning in the following statements. Explain what, if anything, may be wrong or illogical in each statement.

1. If we don't do something about the problem of overpopulation soon, the planet simply will be unable to accommodate the spiraling increase in people with sufficient food or adequate living space.
2. Those who are ignorant of history are condemned to repeat it.
3. He is the best senatorial candidate: he is tall and good looking; he is an eloquent speaker; and he gets along well with his colleagues.
4. Something horrible must have happened to them. They would have called if they were going to be this late.
5. Joanne's intelligence is her outstanding quality. Even though she is attractive and socially graceful, her mental ability is her strongest asset.

6. People are not really free. They only think they are. Their lives are actually determined by forces that control them without their being aware of it. No one can prove that he or she is impervious to the multitude of influences that bombard us throughout our lives.

7. Astrologers must know what they're doing. My horoscope for the past week has been right on target.

8. If you don't buy this CD player now, it won't be here tomorrow. And besides, prices are expected to go up next week.

9. Students should grade themselves in their courses. After all, no one knows better than they do how hard they have worked and how much they have learned.

EXERCISE 7–9   Uncovering Fallacious Reasoning

1. Reconsider either Dan Legereit's or Zach Wolfe's essay in terms of the Checklist of Common Fallacies on p. 168. Do you detect any fallacious reasoning in their essays? If so, how does it undermine the argument's effectiveness? Explain.

2. Find examples of fallacies in newspaper and magazine advertising, television commercials, and political speeches. Identify the fallacies you find, and explain why the reasoning is invalid.

Paragraphs

Understanding Paragraphs

A **paragraph** is a coherent unit of thought that can be easily identified on the printed page as a block of words beginning with an indentation. That block of words usually consists of a group of related sentences that work together to express an idea.

There is no single easy formula that you can follow to write effective paragraphs; in this respect, writing good paragraphs is like writing good essays. You must understand the fundamental characteristics of paragraphs, know what they are used for, how they can work together, and how their purposes differ. Chapters 8 and 9 will teach you how to develop paragraphs and the ways that different kinds of paragraphs work together to create essays.

Each paragraph you write, no matter what its purpose, should be a self-contained unit. It has to make sense on its own. But when a paragraph is also part of an essay, it has to be related or linked to other paragraphs to help express the essay's overall meaning.

There are a variety of different types of paragraphs. Beginning paragraphs introduce the essay. Ending paragraphs bring closure to the essay by pulling ideas together. Middle paragraphs develop the ideas and give substance to the essay.

To be an effective writer, you must understand paragraph variety and purpose and be able to write paragraphs and link them together to create meaning for your readers.

CHAPTER 8

Fundamentals of Paragraph Development

*I*n effective paragraphs, unity and coherence go hand in hand with a tight organization and the development of an idea. Everything in a paragraph helps achieve those four requirements of effective paragraphing: the flow of the sentences; their variety; the paragraph's evidence, including details, examples, and images; and the way in which evidence and explanation are arranged and presented.

8a   Creating unified and coherent paragraphs

A **unified paragraph** develops a single idea. A **coherent paragraph** is one in which all of the parts—sentences, evidence, thinking, explanations—come together in a near-perfect fit to express that idea. To write unified and coherent paragraphs you need to stay focused and make all parts of the paragraph stick together.

Following is a unified and coherent paragraph taken from a speech given before the United Nations by Václav Havel, president of the Czech Republic. As you read the paragraph, notice how Havel carries forward the idea expressed in the first sentence, how each sentence builds on the one before it, and how the sentences clarify and amplify the meaning of that first sentence.

Without a global revolution in the sphere of human consciousness, nothing will change for the better in the sphere of our being as humans, and the catastrophe toward which this world is headed—be it ecological, social, demographic or a general breakdown of civilization—will be unavoidable. If we are no longer threatened by world war or by the danger that the absurd mountains of accumulated nuclear weapons might blow up the world, this does not mean that we have definitely won. We are still incapable of understanding that the only genuine backbone of all our actions, if they are to be moral, is responsibility. Responsibility to something higher than my family, my country, my company, my success—responsibility to the order of being where all our actions are indelibly recorded and where and only where they will be properly judged.

—Václav Havel, "Global Responsibility"

Although the first sentence contains the germ of Havel's idea, his meaning is not altogether clear until you reach the end of the paragraph, where you learn what he means by a "revolution in the sphere of human consciousness." There, at the end of the paragraph, he calls for a higher sense of responsibility among nations as he brings the ideas of revolution and responsibility together. Each sentence in the paragraph enlarges our sense of Havel's idea.

When the parts of a paragraph do not fit together, the paragraph seems out of kilter, confusing. The defect usually results when a writer fails to stay focused or fails to clarify the relationships among the sentences in the paragraph. Consider this paragraph from an editorial that argues against limiting terms for members of Congress.

> As a college student in a constant struggle to balance coursework, extracurricular activities, and sleep, I often find it difficult to keep up with a constantly fluctuating world. However, there has always been something that never seems to change, American politics. It still seems to be as ineffective as ever. The stagnation on Capitol Hill has led to a situation where most of the exigencies of this country are not being met. It has turned into a bureaucratic black hole where everything is proposed but nothing is done. Most people suffer from intense feelings of anger and frustration when it comes to the government. It is easy to understand and sympathize with these people, many of whom have decided to wage a war on Congress. Recently, however, it seems as though the people's anger has been misdirected. It seems as though many have been swept up in the entire anti-incumbent fever.

> —Anshul Patel, student (draft paragraph)

In the first two sentences, Anshul seems to be trying to relate a personal experience to a problem he senses in politics, but he neither makes that relationship clear nor establishes its importance. He is not focused; he does not lead his readers to the paragraph's main point about anti-incumbent fever. Now consider what happens when he focuses his argument.

> As a result of the November 3rd election, at least 110 new faces will join the 103rd Congress. According to the *Congressional Quarterly,* this turnover, affecting nearly a quarter of the House, is the largest since 1948. The turnover was largely due to the anti-incumbency fever that swept the nation earlier this year. The stagnation on Capitol Hill had disillusioned most people in the electorate. Their anger was further fueled by revelations that hundreds of members of Congress had routinely overdrawn their House Bank accounts without penalty. The checking scandal and others like it seemed to symbolize just how out of touch senators and representatives were. All of this disenchantment lit a fire under the movement for term limits. The movement culminated on November 3rd when voters passed term limitation bills in fourteen states. However, it seems as though most people were so frustrated with Congress that they jumped onto the term-limitation bandwagon unaware of all its implications. Their anger was misdirected by term limiters who took full

advantage of America's disgust with its government. It is imperative that we realize that term limitations will only worsen the situation on Capitol Hill.

—Anshul's revised paragraph

This focused paragraph is also unified; every sentence leads to the next, carrying the reader forward to Anshul's main idea—in this case, expressed in the last sentence of the paragraph (reread Václav Havel's paragraph, where the main idea appears in the first sentence). The sentence containing a paragraph's main idea is referred to as a **topic sentence.** Topic sentences provide focus and clarify meaning; they contain the essence of each paragraph. These sentences can also point beyond the paragraph to the essay itself. Anshul's main idea will be developed and defended in the middle paragraphs of his essay.

When writing your own paragraphs, keep them unified and coherent. Your readers will expect you to stay focused, to explain your evidence clearly, to guide them from sentence to sentence, and, ultimately, to express a clear idea.

8b   Achieving paragraph unity

You can achieve paragraph unity by staying focused on the main idea expressed in your topic sentence and by clearly explaining the relationship between your evidence and the idea you are developing.

1   Staying focused on the idea

When you lose track of your paragraph's main idea and begin to digress, you create disunity in your paragraphs and confusion for your readers. One of the surest ways to keep your paragraphs unified is to stay focused on your main idea so that everything you put in the paragraph contributes to your readers' understanding of that idea.

Here is a paragraph that seems unsure of its controlling idea. Readers, therefore, have to guess about the paragraph's meaning, choosing between at least two possible ideas. About halfway through this draft paragraph, the writer seems to change her focus, moving from one idea to another. See if you can detect the shift.

> On the left side of the room, facing in from the doorway, is my boudoir. There is a bed and a vanity in the corner. It's kind of fun; I can play the leading lady who gives her long golden tresses one hundred strokes before retiring for the night. Only I don't have long hair. And it's not blonde. Besides, the mirror is all but obscured by photos, postcards, and other miscellany. There's my family, my best buddies, and the men in my life: Dizzy, Charlie Parker, and the Count.

—Cindy Fujita, student (draft paragraph)

Cindy begins the paragraph on an interesting note, calling her bedroom a "boudoir"—a woman's bedroom or private sitting room. In this particular boudoir, Cindy can "play the leading lady" as she fantasizes about combing her "long golden tresses." This first part of the paragraph suggests that the bedroom is a place for acting out fantasies. But about halfway through the paragraph—starting with "Only"—Cindy veers from fantasy into reality. She confesses that she does not have long blonde hair and that the mirror, the photos, and the postcards get in the way of the fantasy. So at the end of the paragraph, readers are confused about what Cindy thinks about her bedroom. Is the bedroom a place of fantasy or a place that brings Cindy to her senses?

To answer that question, you would have to read Cindy's full essay, where she writes about the importance of fantasy; that is her essay's main idea. Thus, her paragraph should stay focused on fantasy. A revised, unified paragraph will have to fit in with the rest of the essay's paragraphs and show readers how the boudoir enhances Cindy's fantasies.

> On the left side of the room, facing in from the doorway, is my boudoir, nothing so private as to be shocking, but special, very special, nevertheless. There is a bed and a vanity in the corner. It's kind of fun. I can play the leading lady who gives her long tresses one hundred strokes before retiring for the night, and when I look in my mirror it doesn't faze me that I see short, black hair. All around my face in the mirror, I see my friends, their faces, and their messages sent me from around the world. There's my family, my best buddies, and the men in my life: Dizzy, Charlie Parker, and the Count. As I sit and stroke my hair, I hear them playing for me, hear the sax and the piano and know that in this lair, I am the leading lady, waiting for them . . . or they are waiting for me to join them—out through the back door, only steps away from that other world.

> —Cindy's revised paragraph

Unifying the draft paragraph required little more than a clear sense of what the evidence in the "boudoir" was supposed to suggest. Cindy had to decide whether the mirror was a help or a hindrance, whether the pictures and postcards distracted her from her fantasy or enhanced it. Once she decided, she could explain how the mirror and images contributed to her idea about fantasy. She could stay focused, bringing the two parts of the paragraph together into a unified whole.

As a writer, you can make your selection of detail—your evidence—say what you want it to say. The choice is yours. But a paragraph must be unified, the relationship between evidence and idea clear. Also, the complete essay must be unified. In this case, Cindy's essay needed a paragraph about the merits of fantasy. The accompanying chart, Rules of Thumb for Writing Unified Paragraphs, lists some general principles to follow for keeping your paragraphs unified.

Rules of Thumb for Writing Unified Paragraphs

- Be sure your paragraphs focus on one idea and state that idea in a topic sentence (8b-1).
- Place your topic sentence effectively within your paragraph. Let the purpose of your paragraph and the nature of your evidence guide you (8b-2).
- Let your paragraph's evidence—the selected details, the examples—illustrate or clarify the idea expressed in your topic sentence (8b-3).
- Make sure you explain the relationship between your evidence and your idea so that it is clear to readers (8b-3).
- Think about unity among paragraphs when writing essays. Be sure your paragraphs are related, that they fit together and clarify your essay's idea.

EXERCISE 8–1   **Writing Paragraphs**

1. Select a space that intrigues you—a room, a spot outdoors, a state of mind— and write a paragraph about it. When you begin writing, do not worry about an idea; try only to convey through selected details what the space is like. Then look at what you have written and decide what you want your readers to know about that space. Revise your paragraph so that it conveys your idea about the space. Bring both versions of your paragraph to class for consideration by your work group or by another reader.

2. Read both versions of your paragraph to the work group or aloud to yourself, and explain the differences between the two versions. Explain why you made the changes you did.

3. Exchange revised paragraphs with a classmate. Read one another's paragraphs and comment in writing about whether the evidence (the selected details) is explained sufficiently to allow you to understand the idea of the paragraphs. (See 1h and 4e on collaboration.)

---

2   Placing the topic sentence

The topic sentence, which states the paragraph's main idea, can be placed anywhere in the paragraph, depending on how you want to lead your readers to understand your main idea. Consider the following options for placing the topic sentence.

Topic sentence at the beginning of a paragraph

If you place your topic sentence at the beginning of a paragraph, as Václav Havel did (8a), your readers will know immediately what your paragraph will be about. They will then be able to see how each subsequent sentence contributes to the development of your main idea.

This placement will serve you well when you are writing argumentative essays (see Chapter 7) or responding to essay examination questions (see Appendix B). In those cases, you are defending your position on a given subject; it is helpful if your readers can see prominently at the outset what your idea is.

Topic sentence at the end of a paragraph

Placing the topic sentence at the end of a paragraph, as Anshul Patel did (8a), lets you lead your readers through your evidence and your reasoning to your conclusion. You withhold that clarifying topic sentence until the end to leave readers with a clear and emphatic reminder of your main idea.

This placement is effective when you use stories as evidence and want to lead readers through a fairly complex inquiry, as you would in an exploratory essay (see Chapter 5). In this type of essay, you want to maintain some suspense; you do not want to give away your idea at the outset and undercut your effort to hold your readers' attention and to lead them to understanding. When you clarify meaning at the end of the paragraph, you leave readers with a clear sense of what the stories mean to you and what they have to do with your idea.

Occasionally you will want to lead your readers through your accumulated evidence to an idea that is difficult to grasp unless they first consider the evidence. In such cases, you present your evidence and explain it as you go along, guiding your reader to see what you see as you develop your idea. In the following paragraph, the main idea (a judgment about the Sioux Indians) does not become clear until the last sentence of the paragraph.

> In 1890, the year of the final defeat of the Sioux at Wounded Knee, the Ghost Dance was sweeping the plains. Begun by a few leaders, especially the Paiute seer Wovoka, the Ghost Dance promised its practitioners among the warriors that the buffalo would return and the white man would be defeated. Ghost Dancers believed that their ceremonial dancing and the shirts they wore would make them proof against the white man's bullets. Among the Sioux warriors at Wounded Knee, the willing suspension of disbelief was complete. It made the warriors reckless and abandoned, throwing normal caution and survival strategy to the wind.

—Diana Hume George, "Wounded Chevy at Wounded Knee"

Everything in this paragraph contributes to our understanding of that last sentence. That topic sentence calls attention to the unity of the paragraph because it lets us see how every other sentence in the paragraph contributes to its meaning.

A final note: topic sentences that appear at the end of an essay's beginning paragraph often become the essay's thesis—the main idea that gets developed in much greater detail in the middle of the essay. (See 9a for more on paragraph development.)

Topic sentence in the middle of the paragraph

Occasionally, you will need to prepare your readers with some background information before they can understand your topic sentence, and then you will want to offer further evidence and explanation before you bring the paragraph to a close.

Here is an example of an effective paragraph on the legacy of a mother's hard work. The topic sentence falls near the middle of the paragraph.

> But she did not raise me to respect her way of offering love and to believe that hard work is often the irreducible factor for survival, not something to avoid. Her woman's work produced a reliable home base where I could pursue the privileges of books and music. Her woman's work invented the potential for a completely different kind of work for us, the next generation of Black women: huge, rewarding hard work demanded by the huge, new ambitions that her perfect confidence in us engendered.
>
> —June Jordan, "In Our Hands"

You can see from this paragraph that it is often difficult to identify precisely which is the topic sentence. The second and third sentences are so closely connected that one seems to be saying much the same thing as the other. But you can see that even though the third sentence is long and complex, it simply amplifies and clarifies the second sentence (the topic sentence) by placing it in a larger context. That is the way unified paragraphs work; everything in them contributes to the meaning expressed in the topic sentence.

Implied topic sentence

A paragraph's main idea need not be stated explicitly; it can be implied. Paragraphs with implied topic sentences ask more of readers because the details of the paragraph only suggest the main idea. The reader must infer that idea from the details. Sometimes, however, the main idea appears in a preceding paragraph, thus eliminating the need to restate it in the paragraph that follows. At other times, the main idea of a paragraph will be so obvious to readers that stating it in a topic sentence is unnecessary.

The following paragraph with an implied topic sentence is easier to understand if you have some knowledge of the rest of the essay. But if you pay attention to the details, you can infer a great deal from them. The paragraph recounts the writer's experience and reflections as she paddled around a lake observing the change of season from summer to fall. See if you can infer the paragraph's main idea.

> As I drift aimlessly, ducks move out from the reeds, all mallards. Adaptable, omnivorous, and hardy, they nest here every year on the two tiny islands in the lake. After communal courtship and mating, the extra male ducks are chased away, but this year one stayed behind. Perhaps he fathered a clutch on the sly or was too young to know where else to go. When the ducklings

hatched and began swimming, he often tagged along, keeping them loosely together until the official father sent him away. Then he'd swim the whole circumference of the lake alone, too bewildered and dignified to show defeat.

—Gretel Ehrlich, "This Autumn Morning"

It may help you to know the main idea of Ehrlich's essay, stated in an earlier paragraph: "To long for love, to have experienced passion's deep pleasure, even once, is to understand the mercilessness of having a human body whose memory rides desire's back unanchored from season to season." With that sentence in mind, you can see more easily how Ehrlich sees her own plight in the duck's as the season turns from the dryness of summer to the fullness and fecundity of autumn. Ehrlich, too, finds herself alone, longing and bewildered but too "dignified to show defeat."

Paragraphs like Ehrlich's work together within an essay; they are like the sentences within a paragraph working together to express ideas. Ehrlich's implied idea is much easier to grasp if you keep in mind the idea that holds her essay together. Essay and paragraph are unified, and she never loses track of her main idea—either in the paragraph or in the essay.

3   Explaining the idea

As you have just seen, developing paragraphs around a single idea, often expressed in a topic sentence that you can present in a variety of ways, helps you achieve paragraph unity. However, you need to be sure that you do not rely solely on your topic sentence to carry the weight of your idea. Always offer sufficient explanation throughout a paragraph to make your idea clear to your readers. And be sure that the sentences in your paragraph include evidence—examples and details—that is clearly related to your idea. (See 1c on evidence and ideas.) Remember: your aim is always to ensure through adequate explanation that your readers understand what you are trying to say. (See also 8e on paragraph development.)

Reread June Jordan's paragraph. Notice that without the amplification and explanation of Jordan's main idea in the final sentence, we would know nothing about her mother's effect on that "next generation of Black women." Always explain your main idea so that readers will know what you want them to know.

8c   Achieving paragraph coherence

So far, we have concentrated on paragraph unity. But unity alone does not make a good paragraph. The key to focusing and explaining your idea is a coherent presentation. Let us now consider five ways to fit the various parts of a paragraph together to express your idea coherently. Refer to the accompanying chart, Ways to Achieve Paragraph Coherence, for an overview of these methods.

Ways to Achieve Paragraph Coherence

- Use pronouns to replace nouns (8c-1).
- Repeat and develop key terms (8c-2).
- Link sentences with transitional words (8c-3).
- Create visual clarity (8c-4).
- Use parallel structures (8c-5).

As you think about the guidelines and begin to understand what each one means, keep in mind that they represent techniques experienced writers eventually use almost unconsciously. Be aware of these techniques; try them as you write. In the long run, you will find yourself using them automatically.

1 Using pronouns

Let us begin with a paragraph that has unity of idea but lacks coherence. Something in this paragraph makes it difficult to read. The sentences, even though related to one another, stand apart. There is no easy movement from one sentence to another. See if you can detect the cause of the problem as you read out loud Patrick Cleburn's paragraph from an essay entitled "Leadership."

> During the attack, Lieutenant Sothoron did something very important. Lieutenant Sothoron gave the saving performance. Although Sothoron had been schooled in leadership and knew about the skills of soldiering, what Sothoron did that night was like drama. It was more like drama than leadership. Sothoron became someone else. Sothoron wore the mask of the warrior. That night in Vietnam, Lieutenant Sothoron played out his appointed part. Other soldiers participated in the fight, but Sothoron was responsible for what happened. He inspired them.

—Patrick Cleburn, student (draft paragraph)

The main idea in Patrick's paragraph is clear: Lieutenant Sothoron gave an unusual performance in combat, and his performance inspired other soldiers. Everything fits together; everything contributes to the unified expression of the idea. But the halting, choppy rhythm of the paragraph makes it difficult for the reader to grasp that idea.

One way to create smoother transitions from sentence to sentence is to substitute a pronoun for a noun. (See 12b for more on pronouns.) In Patrick's paragraph, for example, try substituting the pronoun *he* for either *Sothoron* or *Lieutenant Sothoron*. The pronoun should serve as a linking device, pulling the sentences together and making the paragraph easier to read and understand.

However, you should make sure the reader can always identify the person for whom the pronoun stands (its antecedent). Simply substituting pronouns for nouns can result in confusing sentences if pronouns do not clearly refer to particular antecedents (see Chapter 21).

Notice the way the pronouns—italicized in Patrick's revised paragraph—improve the rhythm and link the sentences, making the paragraph more coherent.

> During the attack, Lieutenant Sothoron did something very important. *He* gave the saving performance. Although Sothoron had been schooled in leadership and knew about the skills of soldiering, what *he* did that night was like drama. It was more like drama than leadership. Sothoron became someone else. *He* wore the mask of the warrior. That night in Vietnam, *he* played out his appointed part. Other soldiers participated in the fight, but Sothoron was responsible for what happened. *His* performance inspired them.
>
> —Patrick's revised paragraph

EXERCISE 8–2   Using Pronouns

1. Try other pronoun substitutions in Patrick Cleburn's revised paragraph. Can you substitute *he* for *Sothoron* in other places without creating confusion?
2. Write a paragraph about one of your heroes or heroines. Try to convey to your readers the one thing that you think is most important about that person. After you complete your draft, revise to make the paragraph more coherent, paying particular attention to the way you use pronouns.

2   Repeating key terms

Repeating important terms can positively affect paragraph coherence. In the revised paragraph about Lieutenant Sothoron, you can see that the terms *leadership* and *drama* are very important to the paragraph's idea. The term *leadership* appears twice to remind readers of the importance of that concept. These two terms appeared in the first version of the paragraph, too, but the unnecessary repetition of the name *Sothoron* so dominated the paragraph that the other words were somewhat obscured, and coherence was destroyed.

In the revised version of Patrick's paragraph, you can see more easily how the key terms *leadership* and *drama* contribute to the paragraph's main idea. As you reread the paragraph, notice how Patrick develops the notions of leadership and drama by introducing other related words, such as *soldiering, mask, warrior,* and *performance,* to help you understand his idea. You need not simply repeat a single term to reap the benefits of repetition—including related words can also clarify meaning and give the paragraph a forward momentum while drawing the parts into a coherent whole.

As a general rule, repeat words sparingly. Use repetition to develop your idea and to keep readers' attention on the paragraph's evolving meaning. Avoid excessive repetition; it can obscure your idea and create paragraphs that are difficult to read (as is the first draft of Patrick's paragraph with its repetition of *Sothoron*).

EXERCISE 8–3   Repeating and Developing Key Terms

1. Select one of the following words and write for ten minutes about that word: *woman, man, paragraph, heroism, leadership.* Do not feel obligated to define the word as the dictionary would; rather, use the word in a sentence and keep writing, trying to illustrate what the word means to you.

2. Look over what you wrote in the preceding exercise and identify what seem to be key terms in the passage. Pick out an idea that you see embedded in the passage, and think about the relationship between the key terms and the idea. Write a paragraph repeating the key terms to help you develop your idea.

3   Linking sentences with transitional expressions

Often, you can create coherence within a paragraph by linking closely related sentences with **transitional expressions.** Such linking often tightens paragraphs and clarifies meaning. Transitional words such as *although, therefore, thus, but,* and *yet* indicate the relationships among sentences and among the ideas in sentences; they refer to surrounding sentences, pulling the paragraph together. (See 14c and 25b-1 for more on transitions.) The accompanying chart provides a select list of commonly used transitional words and expressions.

As a writer, you cannot simply turn to a list of transitional expressions, select two or three of them, and insert them in paragraphs to create coherence. Rather, you must use transitions to convey a relationship that already exists among ideas. Transitions, by themselves, cannot create such relationships.

Consider the following paragraph about the differences between masculine and feminine discourse. In it, David Reich links sentences by using transitional words, but you can also see that those words signify the relationship among ideas about the two types of discourse. Those transitional words (shown in italics) and the movement of his thinking pull David's paragraph together and make it more coherent.

> *Another thing* that makes masculine discourse unimportant in a literary way, *besides* the fact that it is so marginal, is that it is, according to Joyce Carol Oates, "a story without words." Boxing, *for example,* allows for the "public

embrace of two men who otherwise, in public or in private, could never approach each other with such passion." *But* however communicative the embrace, the language of masculinity is emphatically a physical language and not a language of words, *so that* masculinity, for the most part, is not a literary idea in the same way that femininity is. Civilized conversation, *though,* tends more toward words and ideas—the province of femininity rather than masculinity. *Because* feminine discourse has something to say about words and ideas, *whereas* masculine discourse has very little to say, women are bound by expectations and subtexts that they themselves didn't create, *while* men are more free to approach civilization from a "neutral" perspective, to live first of all as human beings and only secondarily as manly men.

—David Reich, student

Consider how difficult it would be to follow David's paragraph without the transitional words. Reread the paragraph and skip over the transitional words and consider the difference. Without them, the sentences bear no clear relationship to one another; as a result, the paragraph is incoherent. It makes little sense and does not clearly reflect David's judgments about masculine and feminine discourse.

Transitional Words and Expressions

To Suggest Continuity and Sequence
again, also, and then, besides, finally, furthermore, in the first place, moreover, next

To Illustrate with Examples
after all, for example, for instance, specifically, such as, that is, the following example

To Suggest Comparison
also, in the same way, likewise, once more, similarly

To Indicate Contrast
although, but, despite, even though, for all that, in spite of, instead, nevertheless, notwithstanding, on the contrary, on the other hand, yet

To Show a Result
as a result, because, consequently, hence, so, then, therefore, thus, to this end

To Signal Time
after a few days, after a while, afterward, at that time, before, earlier, immediately, in the meantime, in the past, lately, later, now, presently, shortly, simultaneously, since, when

(continued)

To Indicate Place
above, below, beyond, closer to, elsewhere, nearby, opposite, out there, there, to the left, to the north, to the right, under

To Offer Concessions
although, but I admit, granted, it may seem that, let me concede that, of course

To Clarify and Conclude with Emphasis
as we have seen, finally, in any event, in conclusion, in other words, in summary, let me reiterate, notwithstanding, on the whole, therefore, thus, to put it differently, to sum up

---

EXERCISE 8–4 **Writing and Revising Using Transitional Words**

Respond to David Reich's paragraph in one of your own, developing the idea about either masculine or feminine discourse. Include both your ideas and David's in your paragraph. Revise for more coherence, using transitional words to link your thoughts.

---

4 Including visual details

Often, when you are trying to make your reader understand an idea in a paragraph, it helps to provide visual details or images. Joseph Conrad, the novelist, said he only wanted to make his readers *see*. Psychologists tell us that images elicit ideas. Because visual details can clarify meaning, they can also pull ideas in a paragraph together and make it more coherent.

In the following paragraph, novelist Toni Morrison relies on visual details to get at an elusive concept; she tries to make you, the reader, see what she means by "flooding."

> You know, they straightened out the Mississippi River in places, to make room for houses and livable acreage. Occasionally the river floods these places. "Floods" is a word they use, but in fact it is not flooding; it is remembering. Remembering where it used to be. All water has a perfect memory and is forever trying to get back to where it was. Writers are like that: remembering where we were, what valley we ran through, what the banks were like, the light that was there and the route back to our original place. It is emotional memory—what the nerves and the skin remember as well as how it appeared. And a rush of imagination is our "flooding."

—Toni Morrison, "The Site of Memory"

Morrison uses the image of flooding both literally and imaginatively to help readers visualize and understand the idea that writers are always trying to get back to some original place and to remember and render it. The visual detail of the flood not only clarifies the idea; it also makes the paragraph coherent because it draws together the ideas of remembering, flooding, and imagining in a way that shows you their close relationship.

EXERCISE 8–5   Writing with Images

Think of something you care a great deal about but that is hard to get across to someone else—a mathematical concept, a scientific principle, a notion about love, the texture of someone's hair, a political principle—and write a paragraph about it, using one or two images or visual details to help you clarify what you think.

5   Using parallelism

Repeating parallel structures is yet another way to make your paragraphs coherent. **Parallelism** results when you repeat a grammatical form. You can use parallel structures within your paragraphs to call attention to an important aspect of your idea and to create a pleasing, emphatic rhythm that underscores your idea and carries your reader forward.

Consider the italicized parallel phrases in the following paragraph. As you read the paragraph, listen to the words to hear how rhythm develops through repetition and how that rhythm moves through the paragraph and helps you stay focused on the accumulating meaning. Sound and sense combine to create coherence.

> Animals give us their constant, unjaded faces and we burden them with our bodies and civilized ordeals. We're both humbled by and imperious with them. We're comrades who save each other's lives. *The horse we pulled* from a boghole this morning bucked someone off later in the day; one stock dog refuses to work sheep, while another brings back a calf we had overlooked while trailing cattle to another pasture; *the heifer we doctored* for pneumonia backed up to a wash and dropped her newborn calf over the edge; *the horse that brings us home safely* in the dark kicks us the next day. On and on it goes.
>
> —Gretel Ehrlich, "Friends, Foes, and Working Animals"

Note the way Ehrlich identifies a "job" of each of the working farm animals, and how each of the working animals makes more work for the humans. The humans have to pull the horse out of a boghole, but later in the day, the horse bucks off the human. That pattern of work begetting work repeats itself throughout the paragraph and suggests some tension within the "odd partnership" between humans and animals that Ehrlich is writing about. The

parallel structures in the paragraph contribute to our understanding of its meaning and help pull the parts of the paragraph together coherently. (See also Chapter 24 on parallelism.)

EXERCISE 8–6   Working with Parallel Structures

1. Underline the parallel structures in the following paragraph. Then write a paragraph of your own explaining how those parallel structures contribute to coherence and meaning.

> Women of Color in America have grown up within a symphony of anger, at being silenced, at being unchosen, at knowing that when we survive, it is in spite of a world that takes for granted our lack of humanness, and which hates our very existence outside of its service. And I say symphony rather than cacophony because we have had to learn to orchestrate those furies so that they do not tear us apart. We have had to learn to move through them and use them for strength and force and insight within our daily lives. Those of us who did not learn this difficult lesson did not survive. And part of my anger is always libation for my fallen sisters.
>
> —Audre Lorde, "The Uses of Anger"

2. Start drafting a paragraph in which you try to achieve coherence by repeating a grammatical structure at least three times. Begin without a particular plan in mind. Through writing, discover a word, phrase, or clause worth repeating. Then write a coherent paragraph that uses your discovery.

8d   Organizing paragraphs

Paragraphs must be organized so that readers can follow the development of your idea and can understand the relationship between your evidence and the idea. Logically organized paragraphs are coherent paragraphs. A disorganized paragraph is difficult for your readers to comprehend. Always remember that your aim is to make it easy for your reader to follow your thinking.

The five organizational patterns identified in the accompanying chart represent logical and familiar ways to order paragraphs. Whether you have thought much about them or not, they have probably been serving you well for a long time. Think about them now as organizational options available to you.

In all likelihood, you will not sit down and decide that a paragraph needs a general-to-specific order or a climactic one. Instead, you will probably decide subconsciously how to organize paragraphs as you are writing or after you have done some drafting. Once you write your initial draft paragraph, always stop and think about how you have organized it. And then when you revise, use the organizational pattern that seems most appropriate for your purpose. Let your purpose and an organizational pattern shape your revision.

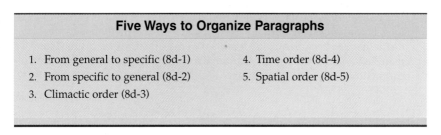

Five Ways to Organize Paragraphs

1. From general to specific (8d-1)
2. From specific to general (8d-2)
3. Climactic order (8d-3)
4. Time order (8d-4)
5. Spatial order (8d-5)

1 From general to specific

Paragraphs using the **general-to-specific order** move from a general statement of a problem to a very specific solution, or they move from a general claim about a fairly broad subject to a more specific claim about it. Here is an example of the latter.

> What we casually call "English," less and less defers to England and its "gentlemen." "English" is no longer a specific matter of geography or an element of class privilege; more than thirty-three countries use this tool as a means of "intranational communication." Countries as disparate as Zimbabwe and Malaysia, or Israel and Uganda, use it as their non-native currency of convenience. Obviously, this tool, this "English," cannot function inside thirty-three discrete societies on the basis of rules and values absolutely determined somewhere else, in a thirty-fourth other country, for example.
>
> —June Jordan, "Nobody Means More to Me than You
> and the Future Life of Willie Jordan"

This paragraph begins with the general claim that the English language cannot be too narrowly associated with England and class privileges. The paragraph ends with a very specific claim that adhering to such a restricted view of English would make the language unfit for use in all those other countries Jordan alludes to.

2 From specific to general

Paragraphs that use the **specific-to-general order** move from some specific detail (or group of details) to a general conclusion. Here is such a paragraph from an essay by Loren Eiseley, an anthropologist.

> I have seen a tree root burst a rock face on a mountain or slowly wrench aside the gateway of a forgotten city. This is a very cunning feat, which men

take too readily for granted. Life, unlike the inanimate, will take the long way round to circumvent barrenness. A kind of desperate will resides even in a root. It will perform the evasive tactics of an army, slowly inching its way through crevices and hoarding energy until someday it swells and a living tree upheaves the heaviest mausoleum. This covert struggle is part of the lifelong battle waged against the Second Law of Thermodynamics, the heat death that has been frequently assumed to rule the universe. At the hands of man that hoarded energy takes strange forms, both in the methods of its accumulation and in the diverse ways of its expenditure.

—Loren Eiseley, "The Last Neanderthal"

Eiseley begins this paragraph with a specific detail about a tree root bursting a rock face. But what really interests him is the force of life that expresses itself in that bursting. From his initial observation, he begins to generalize, explaining as he goes along how that hoarded energy manifests itself and what happens to that energy in human hands.

The specific-to-general pattern serves Eiseley well, leading him logically from a simple observation about a particular detail to a more general conclusion about that detail.

EXERCISE 8–7   Organizing Your Own Paragraphs

Try to develop two different paragraphs about the same topic—sewing, running, fighting, creating, or eating, for example. Use the general-to-specific pattern in one paragraph and the specific-to-general pattern in the other. Does one pattern seem more appropriate than the other for organizing your particular idea? Explain your answer.

3   Climactic order

It often makes good sense to present a paragraph in **climactic order,** moving from the least important information to the most important, leaving the most telling bit of knowledge for the end. Here is an example.

So it was that I stood above the mat and heard myself sigh and then felt myself let go, dropping through the quiet air, crutches slipping off to the sides. What I didn't feel this time was the threat of my body slipping into emptiness, so mummified by the terror before it that the touch of air preempted even death. I dropped. I did not crash. I dropped. I did not collapse. I dropped. I did not plummet. I felt myself enveloped by a curiously gentle moment in my life. In that sliver of time before I hit the mat, I was kissed by space.

—Leonard Kriegel, "Falling into Life"

Climactic ordering is particularly useful within a single paragraph when your idea is too complex to present all at once. In that case, you need to introduce an aspect of that idea and then develop it as you go along, saving your most important point until the very end of the paragraph.

What is true for paragraphs is true for entire essays. An effective argumentative essay will almost always present the least important evidence first and the most important last, becoming more convincing and emphatic as it moves along (see 7c).

EXERCISE 8–8   Writing Toward a Climax

1. Reread Kriegel's paragraph carefully and then answer these questions.
   a. What is the effect of the last sentence on the sentences that come before it?
   b. How does the last sentence change your sense of their meaning? Explain your answer.
   c. Consider what the paragraph might be like if it began this way: "The first time I fell after I contracted polio, it felt as though I had been kissed by space." Which version seems more effective to you? Explain your answer.
2. This paragraph is from Kriegel's essay (it follows the paragraph from 8d-3). Read this paragraph and answer the questions that follow it.

   My body absorbed the slight shock and I rolled onto my back, braced legs swinging like unguided missiles into the free air, crutches dropping away to the sides. Even as I fell through the air, I could sense the shame and fear drain from my soul, and I knew that my sense of my own cowardice would soon follow. In falling, I had given myself a new start, a new life.

   —Leonard Kriegel, "Falling into Life"

   To what extent is this paragraph organized like Kriegel's earlier paragraph? Do the paragraphs themselves follow a climactic order? Explain your answer.
3. Write a paragraph that is organized climactically. Use one of the topics identified in Exercise 8–7 or another of your own choosing.

4   Time order

The passage of time provides a context for understanding. You no doubt use it to explain how an event happened. Time, or chronology, helps us order events. Using **time order** to organize your paragraphs also makes it easier for readers to follow along with your thinking. You lead your readers through time to your idea.

Consider the following paragraph, in which the references to time are underlined.

I have lived this way <u>since</u> I abandoned the city. <u>Before</u> that, I began my day by bending to the mail slot of the front door of Fig Tree House and picking up the *Guardian* and the *Times* of London, and <u>before</u> that by stepping onto the fragrant front porch of our house on Upperline Street in New Orleans and picking up the *Times-Picayune*. I had trained <u>all my life</u> to be a city person, learning tennis manners and cocktail English. <u>When</u> I reached New Orleans, I assumed, as the people of that city do, that I would <u>never</u> move again. I became as mellow as an Orleanian, and was happy. <u>Then</u> I fled. There was an interlude in London, but even <u>then</u> I was in the act of flight. I landed in the Ozarks, in my native state. A rocky hillside farm became my home.

—Roy Reed, "Abandoning the City"

The chronological sequencing provides order in Reed's paragraph and helps you sense the significance of the idea that Reed associates with time passing—the idea that after all this time and traveling, after spending years training himself to be a city person, he had to return to the farm to find home.

You, too, can use chronology to orient your readers and help them understand your idea. Time may have something to do with your idea, as it does for Reed, or it may simply be an ordering device for your paragraph.

EXERCISE 8–9 **Using Time Order**

Write a paragraph explaining how you completed a challenging task such as conducting a chemistry experiment, preparing a meal, or programming a VCR. Revise your paragraph to organize it chronologically.

5 Spatial order

Often you want your readers to survey a place so that they can actually see what you want them to see. You may want them to see the space from a distance, from close up, or from top to bottom so that they can understand what happened there. Or you may want to "put them into" a space so they can know what it felt like to be there. Such arrangements use **spatial order,** and they go hand in hand with descriptive paragraphs—those that appeal to the senses and evoke sight, touch, taste, or smell to create ambience, or those that try to describe a place exactly as it is without emotional overtones. Vivid or exacting descriptions of a space orient readers and help you clarify your idea about that place or what happened there. (See also 8e-9 on description.)

Notice how description and spatial ordering work together in this paragraph to give you a sense of what is happening in the room.

One of the women from the cluster has walked away. Moving along the side of the studio, she maneuvers to avoid the clutter of easels and stacks of paintings. She pauses near the platform at the front of the studio. Meanwhile, among the others the discussions have ended and have been replaced by the gathering of pencils, charcoal, and paper. At the platform, the woman has begun to transform herself. As the clothes fall away from her body and she stretches out upon the platform, she becomes a model. The others become artists, intently observing. I become tense.

—Senta Wong, student

EXERCISE 8–10 Bringing Order and Idea Together

1. Reread Senta Wong's paragraph. How do her selection of detail and her description of the room make the revelation in the last sentence effective? Explain your answer. Then change the time order of the paragraph by moving the last sentence to the beginning of the paragraph. How does that change your response to the paragraph? Explain your answer.

2. Re-create in words a space or place where something unusual happened to you. Orient your readers by using spatial order, but also try to convey through your description and selection of details the effect of that experience.

8e Developing ideas within paragraphs

In addition to the methods you have considered for achieving paragraph unity and coherence and for organizing paragraphs, other traditional and familiar techniques are available for developing ideas within paragraphs. Without a well-developed idea in which the relationship between the idea and the evidence is clearly explained, paragraphs run the risk of being dull and ineffective; they do little more than relay information. Fully developed ideas not only make paragraphs more interesting, but also bind the parts of a paragraph together. (See 8b-3).

Rarely do you use just one developmental technique within a paragraph. As you will see, a paragraph can combine several techniques or can depend more on one technique than another. The important thing to remember is that you have options, and that as you learn the techniques and practice using them, they will, over time, become second nature. You will be able to use them without thinking about them just as you write various kinds of sentences without announcing to yourself beforehand that you will create a simple sentence, a compound one, or even a compound-complex one. The accompanying chart lists ten ways you can develop ideas within your paragraphs.

Techniques for Developing Ideas within Paragraphs	
• Enumeration (8e-1)	• Comparison and contrast (8e-6)
• Illustration by example (8e-2)	• Classification (8e-7)
• Definition (8e-3)	• Division and analysis (8e-8)
• Cause-and-effect analysis (8e-4)	• Description (8e-9)
• Process analysis (8e-5)	• Analogy (8e-9)

1 Enumeration

A basic method for developing paragraphs involves listing or enumerating a series of points. But when you develop paragraphs using enumeration, take care not simply to list your points without explaining or connecting them.

In the following paragraph, the British philosopher Bertrand Russell accounts for why he sought love.

> I have sought love, first, because it brings ecstasy—ecstasy so great that I would often have sacrificed all the rest of life for a few hours of this joy. I have sought it, next, because it relieves loneliness—that terrible loneliness in which one shivering consciousness looks over the rim of the world into the cold unfathomable lifeless abyss. I have sought it, finally, because in the union of love I have seen, in a mystic miniature, the prefiguring vision of the heaven that saints and poets have imagined. This is what I sought, and though it might seem too good for human life, this is what—at last—I have found.
>
> —Bertrand Russell, "What I Have Lived For"

Notice that Russell explains each reason as he gives it, avoiding the pitfall of merely listing for the sake of providing a list. His list develops and explains his ideas about the nature and rewards of love.

EXERCISE 8–11 **Writing a Paragraph by Enumerating**

Write a paragraph in which you list your reasons for something you believe, you think, or you are planning to do. Be sure to explain your list and the relationship among the elements of the list as you develop an idea.

2 Illustration by example

In using **illustration** in paragraphs to develop an idea, provide concrete and specific examples to help clarify that idea for your readers.

In the following paragraph, the writer relies on examples to illustrate her point about the way old trading posts are nurtured and preserved in New Mexico and Utah.

> Other posts retain a dilapidation that seems equally nurtured—and as historic. The corrals at Salina Springs stand knock-kneed with the force of the sly, artistic wind. Near Little Black Spot Mountain, Pinon Post is a faded store that trades, nonetheless, with more than 150 weavers who bring in rugs for the wholesalers who come through. In Utah, the Oljeto Trading Post is a slow-motion collapse of mud and wood. Inside, the post assumes credibility with the now rare bullpen where customers stand in front of high counters and point to goods stacked precariously to the ceiling: canned food, medicine, a sewing machine, fan belts, bolts of cloth, videos, and tires. Another original bullpen is at the Hubbells Trading Post, a National Historic Site cleverly leased by the Park Service to an experienced trader.
>
> —Sharman Apt Russell, "Trading Posts"

Notice that the examples in Sharman Russell's paragraph are not merely decorative; they illustrate the idea announced in the first sentence (the topic sentence) of the paragraph. Although Russell uses a number of examples, you may often find that a single example, developed fully with explanation, can suffice. Whether you need to use one or several examples depends on the quality of your examples and on the way you present them—how clearly you use them to illustrate your idea. Think about your reader to judge sufficiency. (See 1d on audience.)

EXERCISE 8–12 Writing Paragraphs Using Examples

Write two paragraphs that include examples to illustrate some idea. For your first paragraph, use a single extended example. For your second paragraph, use three to five examples. Which paragraph do you prefer? Explain your answer.

3   Definition

When you use **definition,** you explain the meaning of a word or a concept in a variety of ways. You can identify the word or thing as a member of a class, thus categorizing it. (A bird, for example, is a warm-blooded, egg-laying creature that flies.) You can distinguish the word or thing from other members of its group by further specifying its unique characteristics. (The bird is also a feathered vertebrate.) And you can say what the word or thing is by saying what it is not. (A bird is not a mammal, nor is it an invertebrate.)

You can use definition to develop paragraphs, but when you define a concept, always identify and discuss its essential elements or characteristics. Consider here how Joan Didion uses definition to explain her ideas about self-respect.

To have that sense of one's intrinsic worth which constitutes self-respect is potentially to have everything: the ability to discriminate, to love and to remain indifferent. To lack it is to be locked within oneself, paradoxically incapable of either love or indifference. If we do not respect ourselves, we are on the one hand forced to despise those who have so few resources as to consort with us, so little perception as to remain blind to our fatal weaknesses. On the other, we are peculiarly in thrall to everyone we see, curiously determined to live out—since our self-image is untenable—their false notions of us. We flatter ourselves by thinking this compulsion to please others an attractive trait: a gist for imaginative empathy, evidence of our willingness to give. *Of course* I will play Francesca to your Paolo, Helen Keller to anyone's Annie Sullivan: no expectation is too misplaced, no role too ludicrous.

—Joan Didion, "On Self-Respect"

When you use definition to develop a paragraph, your task is not to quote the dictionary, not to give a terse definition; rather, it is to develop a definition of your own that in itself becomes an idea about the concept or the thing you are focusing on. Didion's idea about self-respect outgrows a single sentence; an idea evolves as she continues to define and explain just what she means by the term.

EXERCISE 8–13   Writing Paragraphs Using Definition

1. Write a paragraph in which you define an object by placing it in a class and distinguishing it from other members of the same class. Possible objects include a fork, a shovel, a pencil, a dollar, a dog, a computer, a guitar, an encyclopedia, a baseball, or a tree.

2. Write a paragraph in which you define a concept by identifying and briefly explaining its essential characteristics or qualities. Possible concepts include justice, courage, success, love, honesty, adversity, anger, or beauty.

4   Cause-and-effect analysis

Use **cause-and-effect analysis** to develop a paragraph when you want to explain how or why something happened the way it did (the causes) and the results or consequences of what happened (the effects). If you explain in a paragraph why you came to college and chose your present course of study, you would be considering the causes of your current situation. If you consider the consequences of your decision—that you are happy being away from home, that your courses are exciting, and that you wish you had more friends who shared your interests—you would be considering the effects of your actions. A single paragraph usually emphasizes either causes or effects, but inevitably the two are linked, as you will see in the following paragraph, which emphasizes causes.

For any trend, there are as many reasons as there are participants. This person runs to lower his blood pressure. That person runs to escape the telephone or a cranky spouse or a filthy household. Another person runs to avoid doing anything else, to dodge a decision about how to lead his life or a realization that his life is leading nowhere. Each of us has his carrot and stick. In my case, the stick is my slackening physical condition, which keeps me from beating opponents at tennis whom I overwhelmed two years ago. My carrot is to win.

—Carll Tucker, "Fear of Dearth"

The causes in this paragraph are here for a reason: they provide background for your understanding of the effect. Tucker runs. He has his reasons for running, just like those other "participants" he mentions. Cause and effect go together to develop Tucker's idea about motivation.

EXERCISE 8–14 Writing Paragraphs Using Causal Analysis

1. Write a paragraph analyzing the causes of a social or political problem. Then write a paragraph analyzing its effects.

2. In a pair of paragraphs, discuss the causes and probable effects of an important decision you have made or one you need to make.

5 Process analysis

Developing a paragraph using **process analysis** involves explaining how to do something step by step, or explaining how something works or how something happened. Process analysis essentially involves giving directions. Paragraphs developed by process analysis are usually arranged chronologically or spatially.

The following paragraph explains how Chicano literature changed. The paragraph is arranged in chronological order.

The early stages of Chicano literature were full of identity assertions: "I am Joaquin, lost in a world of confusion," or "I am a Quetzal who wakes up green with wings of gold, and cannot fly," or "I am the Aztec Prince and the Christian Christ," or "I do not ask for freedom—I *am* freedom." But Chicano literature has gone beyond its beginnings. It no longer simply asserts and defines an identity. It now paints its context and carries out its visions. The identities of crazy gypsy, Aztec Angel, Mud Coyote, and Crying Woman of the Night now go beyond their own definitions to live out their lives in the more fully developed mythological and social context of Chicano literature.

—Carmen Tafolla, "Chicano Literature: Beyond Beginnings"

In this paragraph, the idea that Chicano literature changed is reinforced by process development.

EXERCISE 8–15   **Writing a Paragraph Using Process Analysis**

Explain in a paragraph how something is made (bean bags, ice cream, pizza), how something works (a VCR, camera, pinball machine), how something is done (how birds build nests, how a certain sport is played, how photographs are developed, how an orchestra or band rehearses for a performance). In your paragraph, try to develop an idea as you account for the process.

6   Comparison and contrast

Comparison and contrast involve setting one thing off against another to gain a clearer picture of both. Comparison involves seeing similarities. We compare for many reasons: because our minds are built to see things in relation to one another, because we have been taught to do so, and because comparison works so well. We contrast to see differences more clearly. Comparison and contrast are natural ways to develop paragraphs and to help your reader understand your idea.

Here is a paragraph that uses comparison and contrast to develop an idea about how the different characteristics of American and Chinese homes point to differences in cultural outlooks.

> Americans have a sense of space, not of place. Go to an American home in exurbia, and almost the first thing you do is drift toward the picture window. How curious that the first compliment you pay your host inside his house is to say how lovely it is outside his house! He is pleased that you should admire his vistas. The distant horizon is not merely a line separating earth from sky, it is a symbol of the future. The American is not rooted in his place, however lovely: his eyes are drawn by the expanding space to a point on the horizon, which is his future. By contrast, consider the traditional Chinese home. Blank walls enclose it. Step behind the spirit wall and you are in a courtyard with perhaps a miniature garden around a corner. Once inside his private compound you are wrapped in an ambiance of calm beauty, an ordered world of buildings, pavement, rock, and decorative vegetation. But you have no distant view: nowhere does space open out before you. Raw nature in such a home is experienced only as weather, and the only open space is the sky above. The Chinese is rooted in his place. When he has to leave, it is not for the promised land on the terrestrial horizon, but for another world altogether along the vertical, religious axis of his imagination.
>
> —Yi-Fu Tuant, "American Space, Chinese Place"

In developing a paragraph using comparison and contrast, you can proceed in one of two ways. You can discuss the first element of the comparison in its entirety (in the preceding example, the American home) and then discuss the second element (the Chinese home), as Tuant does. Or you can take up each point of difference and compare and contrast each in turn, alternating, as you develop the paragraph. John McPhee does this in the following paragraph about oranges.

> An orange grown in Florida usually has a thin and tightly fitting skin, and is also heavy with juice. Californians say that if you want to eat a Florida orange you have to get into a bathtub first. California oranges are light in weight and have thick skins that break easily and come off in hunks. The flesh inside is marvelously sweet, and the segments almost separate themselves. In Florida, it is said that you can run over a California orange with a ten-ton truck and not even wet the pavement. The differences from which these hyperboles arise will prevail in the two states even if the type of orange is the same. In arid climates, like California's, oranges develop a thick albedo, which is the white part of the skin. Florida is one of the two or three most rained-upon states in the United States. California uses the Colorado River and similarly impressive sources to irrigate its oranges, but of course irrigation can only do so much. The annual difference in rainfall between the Florida and California orange-growing areas is one million one hundred and forty thousand gallons per acre. For years, California was the leading orange growing state, but Florida surpassed California in 1942, and grows three times as many oranges now. California oranges, for their part, can safely be called three times as beautiful.
>
> —John McPhee, "Oranges"

McPhee uses this comparison and contrast of oranges grown in California and Florida to develop his idea about the effect of weather on the growth of oranges.

EXERCISE 8–16 Writing Paragraphs Using Comparison and Contrast

1. Develop an idea in a paragraph by comparing two things on the basis of common features. Stress the similarities. Possible topics include athletes and dancers, eating and learning, cooking and thinking.
2. Develop an idea in a paragraph by contrasting two things. Stress their differences. Possible topics include age and youth, training and education, the eating habits of dogs and cats.

7   Classification

Classification enables you to organize or order information that might otherwise confuse or overwhelm you or your audience. To *classify* means to group or categorize things according to their similarities. Classified ads organize goods for sale and services for hire. Each of us can be classified according to sex, race, religion, socioeconomic status, and age, among other things.

Classifying involves sorting, distinguishing one thing from another. It results in clarity particularly when used to develop ideas in paragraphs.

In the following paragraph E. B. White uses classification to distinguish among three different New Yorks so that he can make an important point about the third New York.

> There are roughly three New Yorks. There is, first, the New York of the man or woman who was born here, who takes the city for granted and accepts its size and its turbulence as natural and inevitable. Second, there is the New York of the commuter—the city that is devoured by locusts each day and spat out each night. Third, there is a New York of the person who was born somewhere else and came to New York in quest of something. Of these three trembling cities the greatest is the last—the city of final destination, the city that is a goal. It is this third city that accounts for New York's high-strung disposition, its poetical deportment, its dedication to the arts, and its incomparable achievements. Commuters give the city its tidal restlessness, natives give it solidity and continuity, but the settlers give it passion. And whether it is a farmer arriving from Italy to set up a small grocery store in a slum, or a young girl arriving from a small town in Mississippi to escape the indignity of being observed by her neighbors, or a boy arriving from the Corn Belt with a manuscript in his suitcase and a pain in his heart, it makes no difference: each embraces New York with the intense excitement of first love, each absorbs New York with the fresh eyes of an adventurer, each generates heat and light to dwarf the Consolidated Edison Company.
>
> —E. B. White, "The Three New Yorks"

Classification, like the other techniques for paragraph development, is nothing more than a way of thinking, a way of analyzing and making sense of your evidence. In the preceding paragraph, White is not interested in the act of classifying for its own sake; he is interested in using classification so that you, his audience, can understand his idea about the different New Yorks and can see more clearly what he wants to say about those "settlers" who interest him so much. Classification serves him well, just as the climactic order of the paragraph does; they are means to an end—the clear presentation of an idea.

EXERCISE 8–17   Writing a Paragraph Using Classification

Classify three of the following: books, houses, ice cream, restaurants, sports fans, classical music, rock music. Then select one of those classifications that interests you most and develop an idea about it in a paragraph.

8   Division and analysis

Division and analysis involves taking something apart or breaking it down into component parts so that you can put it back together to understand its significance. Analysis also carries with it the obligation to make sense of those parts, to try to understand their relationship to one another.

The following paragraph uses division and analysis to point out gender bias in our language.

> My first meaningful introduction to "the power of language" occurred at a rally for women's rights in Los Angeles that highlighted the not-so-subtle chauvinism in the English language. I was surprised to discover that the rally was not going to offer plans for the reintroduction of the Equal Rights Amendment or a call to elect more women to political office. Instead, the day's key speech was on gender-bias in the English language. When the rally began, the speaker at the podium read aloud the words on a sign above the podium: "Spell it with a *Y*; *WOMYN*." Turning to the audience, she shouted, "And why not spell it with a *Y*? We must break away from the male bias in our language. So many of our words are based on a male model—*their, her, they, she* all have the word *he* in them; *son* is the base of *person; lad* is the base of *lady;* and *man* is the base of both *human* and *woman*. Now is the time for us to reclaim our language! We do not need *men* to define ourselves; we can stand on our own. That is why I say: Spell it with a *Y!*"
>
> —Jessica Yellin, student

In this paragraph, dividing words into their component parts yields, through analysis, an idea about the bias that is built into the English language. When you use division and analysis, do so to reveal an idea, as Jessica did. Turn your ideas into effective paragraphs and essays. (See 6b on analytical essay development.)

EXERCISE 8–18   Writing a Paragraph Using Division and Analysis

Take some ordinary object or process—a bicycle, computer, telephone, or chair; or writing a paragraph, performing a laboratory experiment, or working out a math problem. Break that object down into its component parts, or consider the process in terms of its associated tasks, as a way of understanding the object or the process. Consider the implications of what you learned through division and analysis, and write a paragraph about your discovery.

9   Description and analogy

Description involves appealing to the senses of sight, taste, touch, and smell to convey an experience or a place. Reconsider McPhee's comparison-and-contrast paragraph about oranges (8e-6); almost every sentence in that paragraph describes something about oranges or the relationship between oranges and the weather. The paragraph also uses causal analysis; McPhee's idea has to do with the causal relationship between the weather and its effect on oranges. In White's paragraph about New York (8e-7), he describes three different New Yorks, so that classifying and describing go hand in hand in that paragraph.

Analogy is the comparison of one thing with another, dissimilar thing. Writers often use analogies and develop extended analogies so that readers can gain insight into an idea that is difficult to grasp. Although an entire paragraph might be built on an analogy, it is more common to see analogy used with other techniques to develop an idea.

Notice how the following paragraph develops an extended analogy between violinists and painters, but it also depends on description and process analysis to convey its idea.

> Violinists use the bow in the same way painters use the paint brush. Violinists employ many different bowing techniques just as painters use a variety of brush strokes. The violinist may arrive at a passage in the music where a strong sustained sound is required. One of the most difficult techniques involves controlling the bow while pulling it slowly across the string. The violinist must maintain the friction of the bow on the string without producing unintentionally raucous sounds. The sound must not waver; it must be round, sustained, clear, and rich. Painters use a similar technique when they have to decide whether to use heavy or light strokes to produce a desired effect. The artist must know before putting brush to canvas what the end result will be. While painting, the artist visualizes the length and thickness of the stroke, and the resulting mark on the canvas corresponds to the texture of the violinist's sound. Both artists perfect these techniques of touch to enhance the effectiveness of their artistic performances.

> —Karen Elizabeth, student

EXERCISE 8–19   Writing a Paragraph Using Description and Analogy

1. Think of an unusual relationship between two dissimilar things and write a paragraph in which you develop the relationship, extending it whatever way you can. Use narration and description to help you develop that analogy.

2. Reread Loren Eiseley's paragraph in 8d-2. Identify and list the various organizational and developmental techniques that Eiseley uses in that paragraph. Write a paragraph explaining how Eiseley's use of analogy helps you understand his idea.

CHAPTER 9

Types and Functions
of Paragraphs

As you learned in Chapter 8, good paragraphs must be unified and coherent, orderly and well developed. But paragraphs rarely stand by themselves.

Paragraphs have interesting relationships with one another, especially when they work together to build an essay. If you have read Part Two of the *Handbook,* you already know that essays generally have three parts: beginnings, middles, and endings (see Chapters 5, 6, and 7). Each of those parts contains a varying number of paragraphs, depending on the essay's subject, its purpose, the complexity of its idea, and its overall length.

As a rule of thumb, a three- to four-page typed essay will contain one or two beginning paragraphs, three to five middle paragraphs, and one or two ending paragraphs. Each paragraph will contain between one hundred and two hundred words. A longer research essay will likely conform to these same proportions, but the length of the middle can vary considerably (see Chapter 46).

An essay, like a single paragraph, must be coherent and unified. The essay's components—words, sentences, and paragraphs—must fit together, and the essay itself must stay focused on a controlling idea or thesis. The accompanying chart outlines how each kind of paragraph helps create that unity and coherence.

Types of Paragraphs

- **Beginning paragraphs** start the essay. They create interest and introduce the idea (9a).
- **Ending paragraphs** close the essay and pull its parts together to provide a final perspective on the idea (9b).
- **Middle paragraphs** develop the idea. They can be either informational or transitional (9c).

You will see that even a particular type of paragraph can vary from one kind of essay to another. For example, the conversational and informal beginning paragraphs in exploratory essays will differ from the formal, efficient beginning paragraphs in argumentative essays. In this chapter, you will consider those differences and others as you learn more about the types and functions of paragraphs.

9a   Developing beginning paragraphs

A **beginning**—sometimes called an **introduction**—performs important functions in an essay. It can consist of one or more paragraphs, depending on the length of the essay and the complexity of the idea. The paragraphs themselves can be brief (a couple of sentences), or they can be longer, as the following two introductions to essays illustrate.

> In the spring I was born naked. I was stuffed into a chamois cloth and presented to my mother.
>
> —China Forbes, student

> If reduced to its elements, the entire human body is worth approximately forty-seven dollars and twenty-three cents. We are primarily composed of hydrogen, oxygen, and carbon. The prices of these elements do not fluctuate on the common market, so only half of our elemental value is derived from traces of rare metals such as lanthanum that have poisoned our systems. In this respect, those who have died after smoking for several years or have been exposed to toxic waste and mercury poisoning derive a final revenge by being worth perhaps a dollar or two more than those who die untainted. Unless a research laboratory wishes to reconstruct an entire skeleton, or, like Lenin, one is able to secure a permanent postmortem position, the value of human composition is embarrassingly low.
>
> —Tracy Grikscheit, student

The beginning of an essay extends an invitation to readers and creates interest in what will follow in the middle of the essay. It also alerts readers to the essay's idea. The development of that idea is always the essay's central purpose.

The beginning also states or implies how the essay will evolve or be organized, foreshadowing the whole essay—its subject, its idea, its development. But the beginning will do so in different ways, depending on the type of essay. The accompanying chart lists guidelines for writing introductory paragraphs.

1   Beginning paragraphs in exploratory essays

Beginning paragraphs in exploratory essays are generally colloquial and inviting because their subjects are familiar. They read more like stories than

Guidelines for Writing Beginning Paragraphs

- Invite your readers into your essay with interesting stories, anecdotes, arresting details, a quotation, a question, or revealing background information.

- Do not fill your paragraph with vague generalizations. Do not depend on your thesis statement to convey all that your readers need to know. Also, be subtle when stating your intentions; do not say, "In this essay I am going to prove . . . ," or "The purpose of this essay is . . . ."

- Be mindful of your audience. Tell them what they need to know to understand your idea.

- State your idea explicitly or suggestively.

- Provide some indication of how the middle of the essay will develop the idea.

- Be confident about your idea. Avoid apologies for it or for not knowing enough about it. For example, do not say, "I have spent hours thinking about this idea, but I am still not certain about how to present it."

- Organize your beginning in a familiar way. Beginnings often move from a general discussion of an interesting subject to a specific idea about that subject so that the idea or thesis appears near the end of the paragraph in the position of emphasis. But there are other effective ways to organize your paragraphs (see 8d).

- Use the techniques of narration, description, and illustration to develop your paragraph so that readers can better understand your idea. (See 8e on paragraph development.)

- Avoid citing a dictionary definition as a way of starting your essay.

- Check to see that your beginning is unified and coherent (see 8a–c).

formal arguments—more like an inquiry about an idea than a defense of a conclusion. These beginnings usually reveal the essay's idea and overall plan of development subtly; readers must infer idea and order.

As you read this beginning paragraph from an essay entitled "Curious," see what you can infer about the essay's idea and the idea's development.

> As I watched intently through the missing window of the abandoned barn, the musty walls surrounding me faded rapidly in the evening light. I was beginning to doubt I would see a deer that day. Suddenly, I heard steps that seemed thunderous because all other sounds were filtered out of my head. My nerves tensed as I readied my bow. Abruptly, a doe appeared in the clearing. My mind raced in anticipation of what might be following her. Soon after, her twin fawns drifted into view. I held my breath, hoping a trophy buck would complete the family picture, but I was sure they were the only ones accompanying her. I did not realize at that moment that the doe had more to

offer than the buck. Her curiosity would give me a new experience, a thrill I could not anticipate.

—Karl Schmidt, student

This beginning is typical of an exploratory essay. It sounds as if Karl is merely recounting a personal experience when in fact he is providing background so that readers will be able to understand his idea and its unfolding. The subject of deer hunting is familiar. But the idea itself—his reason for writing the essay—is not so familiar. Karl only hints at that unusual and interesting idea in the last two sentences of the beginning paragraph, yet he implies a great deal about idea and order in those sentences.

Karl's essay is an attempt to lead readers to believe that it is possible to experience a deer; that is the idea behind his narrative account. That account—moving chronologically—provides the order for the middle of the essay, where Karl explains how the doe became more interesting than a buck would have been to him. (See 8d-4 on time order in paragraphs, and 5b-4 on beginnings in exploratory essays.) The accompanying chart outlines the features of the introduction to an exploratory essay.

Features of Beginnings in Exploratory Essays

- Entice readers
- Follow familiar organizational patterns
- Tell a story

- Hint at the essay's idea
- Introduce the story line that orders the middle of the essay

2 Beginning paragraphs in analytical and argumentative essays

Beginning paragraphs in analytical and argumentative essays differ from those in exploratory essays because they require a clearer statement of the idea and a tighter organization. Their language is usually more direct and formal, even when they use an anecdote to capture readers' attention because readers of analytical and argumentative essays want to know specifically where they are headed. (See 6b-5, 7d, and 7e-1 on beginnings in analytical and argumentative essays.)

As you read this beginning paragraph from an analytical essay, try to identify the writer's idea and plan for developing the middle of the essay.

Colonel Robert Gould Shaw knew what it meant to be noble and brave. Few white men in history have shown more courage and dedication in trying to give the black man his rightful place in America. Shaw did not put black men on a pedestal; he did not make speeches for them; he led them into combat while he faced much opposition for doing so. Prejudice was evident in the Northern army, and he had to overcome this prejudice just so that his black soldiers would have the right to fight for their own freedom. Shaw lost his life in the War between the States, and so did half of his regiment. History had largely forgotten him and his men until the poet Robert Lowell wrote "For the Union Dead" in 1964, about one hundred years after Shaw's men led their valiant charge against a Confederate fort. Then, in 1989, the movie *Glory* gave us another view of Colonel Shaw. Both the poem and the movie tell us what Shaw did during his time, but they seem to be showing us as well what we have not done in our time. These two works complement each other while presenting images of Shaw that remind us of the racial problems we face every day in America.

—Tim Burns, student

In this beginning paragraph, he arouses readers' interest by providing historical background about Colonel Shaw. Tim also gives important information about how Robert Lowell's poem and the movie *Glory* revived interest in Shaw and how the poem and the movie complement one another. This background information helps Tim's readers understand his idea—the interpretive claim he makes in the final sentence of the paragraph about the way Shaw is presented in the poem and in the movie. That sentence is the thesis, or main idea, for Tim's essay; he will develop it in the essay's middle.

Tim's thesis sentence not only contains the idea or thesis that he will develop, but also suggests how he will order and develop the middle of his essay. There he will analyze the images of Shaw presented first by the poem and then by the movie. What Tim does in this paragraph is typical of beginning paragraphs in analytical and argumentative essays. The accompanying chart outlines the features of the introduction to such essays.

Features of Beginnings in Analytical and Argumentative Essays

- Entice readers
- Follow familiar organizational patterns
- Provide the background information necessary for understanding the essay's thesis or main idea
- Include an explicit statement of the thesis
- Reveal, either explicitly or implicitly, how the essay will be developed

EXERCISE 9–1   Analyzing and Writing Beginnings

1. As you read the following beginning from an exploratory essay, try to figure out the essay's idea. Then answer the questions that follow it.

> I spy on my patients. Ought not a doctor to observe his patients by any means and from any stance, that he might the more fully assemble the evidence? So I stand in the doorways of hospital rooms and gaze. Oh, it is not all that furtive an act. Those in bed need only look up in order to discover me. But they never do.
>
> —Richard Selzer, "Four Appointments with the Discus Thrower"

   a. What can you infer about the "I" in this paragraph—about the narrator's profession and behavior? How does he feel about spying?

   b. Considering your answers to the preceding questions and taking into account the title and the last two sentences of the beginning paragraph, what can you infer about the essay's idea? Explain your answer.

2. Read the following beginning from an analytical essay, and then answer the questions that follow it.

> A short, delicate portrait of a patient—this is the first impression one has of Dr. Richard Selzer's essay "Four Appointments with the Discus Thrower." Selzer's persona (the "I" in his essay) is an inquisitive physician, looking in on his patient, who is a blind man lacking legs, seriously ill and about to die. The doctor describes his encounters with him before and after his death. This patient, known only as "Room 542," would be an ordinary, if unusually unfortunate, sufferer were it not for his odd habit of throwing his breakfast plate at the wall every morning.
>
> Selzer is a subtle presence in this portrait; as in a story, his meaning isn't obvious. . . . His entrances into the essay's meaning are the doctor's words themselves, starting with his references to himself as a "spy"—a man "looking for secrets"—and the criminal undertone of the piece. It becomes clear that the doctor is commenting upon the crimes being committed against Room 542, the indignities Room 542 is enduring, and the strength of his character. But Room 542 is not, ultimately, the subject of the submerged meaning in the essay; the doctor is the subject. The doctor is judge, jury, and executioner in his essay; and he returns a verdict of guilty against himself.
>
> —Brandt Kwiram, student

   a. Can you detect from Brandt's beginning how he will develop his essay?

   b. Brandt entitled his essay "The Patient Doctor." What does the title suggest to you about Brandt's idea—the claim that he makes in his essay?

3. Reread one of your own essays. Revise your beginning based on what you now know about beginnings (see the checklists in 9a).

9b Developing ending paragraphs

An **ending**—sometimes called a **conclusion**—has a close, functional relationship to a beginning. Together, beginnings and endings frame an essay; one leads into the essay, the other leads out of it. The ending also pulls all of the parts of the essay together, unifying the essay, and it reminds readers about how the idea or thesis was developed in the middle of the essay.

Perhaps the most important point to remember about an ending is its relationship to the rest of the essay. Because the ending of an essay depends on what comes before it, many of the details that appear in the ending point back into the essay, reminding readers of key aspects of the idea developed in the middle. Readers look for a final, fresh perspective on the idea and its development in the ending.

The characteristics for endings in exploratory, analytical, and argumentative essays are essentially the same. The accompanying Guidelines for Writing Ending Paragraphs will help you regardless of what type of essay you are writing. But do note that the endings in exploratory essays (see Chapter 5) will differ somewhat because of their familiar, personal quality and their implicit way of developing ideas.

1 Ending paragraphs in exploratory essays

To see how endings in exploratory essays work, look at the following example. Nicholas Seaver ends his exploratory essay, entitled "Why I Row," this way.

> Each rower has such a personal demon. However late I stay after practice, however many extra workouts I do, I am never the last one out of the boathouse. On my way out of the training room, I pass two or three oarsmen still on the ergometers, and I wonder at the force that drives them. And so might you wonder, next time you see a crew shell gliding by, and you look closer at the oarsmen, at their lips curled over their teeth in a devilish grimace and their eyes fixed wide open.
>
> —Nicholas Seaver, student

In this ending paragraph, Nicholas refers to a demon that he introduced at the start of his essay, before the beginning. There he quotes a brief passage from George Orwell's essay "Why I Write": "Writing a book is a horrible, exhausting struggle, like a long bout of some painful illness. One would never undertake such a thing if one were not driven on by some demon whom one can neither resist nor understand." Because Nicholas starts and ends by mentioning this demon, you can surmise that he has had something to say about the demon in the middle of his essay.

Nicholas's ending also harks back to his beginning paragraph, where he promises to develop the idea that rowing has two faces; one of those faces, the one he writes about in the essay's middle, is this demon's. The last sentence of the ending invites the reader to wonder what that face might look like.

The ending of Nicholas's essay contains other reminders of ideas developed in the middle: the workouts, the "force that drives" the rowers, the general sense of dedication and teamwork that makes the rowers exert themselves. You cannot understand all of these details without reading the middle of the essay, but you can surmise that these selected details in the ending paragraph are included to remind you, the reader, of Nicholas's idea about rowing's two faces. These references to the middle and the beginning of the essay pull the essay together and make it coherent.

Guidelines for Writing Ending Paragraphs

- Remind readers about the essay's idea or thesis, but avoid merely restating what you said in your introduction. Provide a fresh perspective on your idea.

- Include details and phrases from the beginning and the middle that underscore key points. Use those details to remind the reader how you developed your idea, but avoid mere repetition.

- Remain focused on the idea you developed in the essay. Do not veer off in a new direction or present new evidence.

- If you call for a course of action, make sure it is reasonable and justified in terms of the evidence you presented.

- Avoid logical fallacies (see 7f).

- Avoid apology and bravado. Moderate, reasonable conclusions appeal to your readers' good judgment.

- Check to see that your ending is unified and coherent (see 8a–c). Also ensure that your ending makes the essay more coherent by pulling all of its parts together.

---

2   Ending paragraphs in analytical and argumentative essays

Endings for analytical and argumentative essays are essentially the same. Only the essays themselves differ in purpose and subject matter (see Chapters 6 and 7).

Tim Burns's paragraph serves to illustrate an effective ending, whether the purpose of the essay is analysis or argument. Tim's analytical essay—you saw his beginning paragraph in 9a-2—comparing Robert Lowell's poem "For the Union Dead" and the movie *Glory*, ends this way.

"For the Union Dead" and *Glory* each represents Colonel Shaw in different but complementary ways. For Lowell, he is a static image, sitting atop his horse, waiting for the "blessed" bubble to break, waiting for things to change. Lowell hints at his stiffness, associates it with other New Englanders, and suggests to us through his images of destruction around Boston that we might take notice of Shaw and his men and take stock of ourselves. The movie lets us see the horse and the rider begin to move. The images become dynamic, and we have a chance to watch Shaw's transformation. He becomes a fierce, compassionate leader of his men. They follow him into battle, fighting for their freedom. But the movie does not leave us content with this heroic image of Shaw. It asks another question, a probing one, about the meaning of *glory*. As we look back on the movie's ending, we know that Shaw and his men may have died in vain, because when we look around us, we still see much of what Lowell saw in 1964. We see racial problems and strife. Not enough has been done. But we know, because of Lowell's images and those in the movie, that there is a better way. Shaw points us in the right direction.

—Tim Burns, student

Reading this ending paragraph independent from the essay, you cannot possibly understand all of the essay's details. You do not know, for example, who Colonel Shaw is. You do not understand the reference to the "blessed" bubble. You have no sense of how *Glory* revealed Shaw's transformation into a "compassionate leader of his men." But you do gain a clear sense that Tim's essay has revealed how Lowell's poem and the movie not only illuminate one another, but also offer a timeless message about racial strife in the United States. That point—Tim's thesis—stands on its own, but it grows out of those details.

If you reread Tim's beginning paragraph, you can see how he provides essential background information about Colonel Shaw's command of black soldiers during the Civil War, about Lowell's poem, and about the movie *Glory*. That beginning paragraph also includes the thesis that Tim will develop in the middle of his essay.

In the middle paragraphs, Tim develops his analysis by showing how Lowell's static images of Shaw come to life in the movie and by reminding us of our own failures in dealing with racial strife. The selected details in Tim's ending point back into his analysis. Whether in argument or analysis or exploration, we need the middle paragraphs to understand all of the ending, and we need the ending to put the entire essay in perspective.

EXERCISE 9–2   **Analyzing and Writing Endings**

---

1. Read an analytical or argumentative essay from Chapter 6 or 7 (Ruth Chung's analytical essay in 6b; Dan Legereit's argumentative essay in 7d; or Zach Wolfe's argumentative essay in 7e). Explain how the essay's ending ties in with its beginning and middle.

2. Find an argumentative essay in a magazine. Analyze it and explain how well the writer relates the ending to the beginning and middle.

3. Select one of your own essays and rewrite the ending based on the Guidelines for Writing Ending Paragraphs on p. 210.

9c   Developing middle paragraphs

Middle paragraphs, which appear in the body of an essay between the beginning and the ending, develop the essay's idea. There are two types of middle paragraphs: **informational paragraphs,** the most common, provide evidence and analysis necessary for understanding the essay's idea; **transitional paragraphs** serve as a bridge between informational paragraphs or between sections of informational paragraphs.

1   Using informational paragraphs

Informational paragraphs—also called topical or substantive paragraphs—do the major work of developing an essay's idea. Each informational paragraph develops an aspect of that idea. Each, therefore, has a narrower focus than the essay itself. Informational paragraphs must be viewed in relation to one another to understand an essay's idea.

Consider the following informational paragraph. As you read it, try to determine how well the paragraph follows the accompanying Guidelines for Writing Informational Paragraphs.

> Authenticity has many guises, each contributing something essential to our calm satisfaction with the truly genuine. Authenticity of *object* fascinates me most deeply because its pull is entirely abstract and conceptual. The art of replica making has reached such sophistication that only the most astute professional can now tell the difference between, say, a genuine dinosaur skeleton and a well-made cast. The real and the replica are effectively alike in all but our abstract knowledge of authenticity, yet we feel awe in the presence of bone once truly clothed in dinosaur flesh and mere interest in fiberglass of identical appearance.
>
> —Stephen Jay Gould, "Counters and Cable Cars"

Gould's paragraph begins with the topic sentence, a claim about authenticity. In the second sentence, he narrows his interest from authenticity to "authenticity of *object*." He then provides contrasting evidence about "replica making" using one well-chosen example—a dinosaur skeleton—as evidence to illustrate and clarify his point about the power of an object that is authentic. Gould's final sentence repeats the paragraph's main idea in a fresh, interest-

ing way, leaving you with a clear sense of what he thinks is the relationship between authenticity and awe, or what he calls in the first sentence, "our calm satisfaction with the truly genuine."

Guidelines for Writing Informational Paragraphs

- Use informational paragraphs to develop an idea. Such paragraphs should contribute to your readers' understanding of the central idea or thesis of an essay.

- Let your readers know what the paragraph will be about. Convey your paragraph's idea implicitly or in a topic sentence. If using a topic sentence, you can place it anywhere in your paragraph, but remember not to rely on it exclusively to carry your idea. The topic sentence will provide your paragraph with unity and focus, but the other sentences in the paragraph develop the idea contained in the topic sentence (see 8b).

- Use evidence in informational paragraphs to substantiate your idea and make your paragraphs convincing. Think of evidence as the foundation for your paragraph. That evidence can come from a variety of sources: experience, observations, books, experiments, interviews, newspapers. Evidence can be presented in the form of examples, illustrations, quotations, charts, graphs, and dialogue. Thinking also functions as evidence. There is no magic formula for what you must put into a paragraph, but evidence will help you clarify your idea; it also lends authority to what you have to say, and it helps you create interest. Try to have enough evidence to convince your audience that you know what you are writing about.

- Organize your paragraph to present your idea effectively (see 8d).

- Keep an eye on paragraph length. Although paragraph length is determined by a variety of factors—subject, purpose, and the complexity of your idea, for example—a good rule of thumb is to limit your paragraphs to two hundred words to ensure that you do not lose track of your main idea. Longer paragraphs often need to be divided to guarantee that focus and to enable your readers to follow your idea. Occasionally, you may even want to narrow or limit your idea within an informational paragraph to give readers a precise and specific sense of the idea. (See how Stephen Jay Gould narrows his idea in the paragraph here.)

- Be sure a clear relationship exists between the idea in your informational paragraph and the essay's idea.

- To bring informational paragraphs to a close, consider restating the paragraph's idea and purpose in a fresh and interesting way. Remember that the last two or three sentences of a paragraph are often the most important. If you have gotten your reader interested at the outset and as you presented your evidence, chances are that those last few sentences can clarify the entire paragraph, pulling idea and evidence together. The result: you leave the reader with a sure sense of the paragraph's idea and of the paragraph's relationship to the larger essay.

EXERCISE 9–3　**Revising an Informational Paragraph**

Select one of the essays you wrote for a course this semester. From the middle of that essay, choose an informational paragraph that you think is weak. Revise the paragraph using the Guidelines for Writing Informational Paragraphs.

2　Using transitional paragraphs

Transitional paragraphs are bridge paragraphs that link or pull sections of an essay together to make it more coherent (see 9c). These paragraphs often repeat or summarize information that has already appeared, or they point readers to the next part of an essay. In either case, transitional paragraphs provide clarification and focus.

Transitional paragraphs can be brief, consisting of one or a few sentences, or they can be as long as a typical informational paragraph. Whether long or short, transitional paragraphs serve to emphasize an idea, to make readers pause and think before proceeding to the next paragraph. They can alert readers to a significant shift in the development of the idea, or they can serve as a reminder of what the essay covered in a preceding paragraph. The accompanying chart provides guidelines for writing effective transitional paragraphs.

As you read the following excerpt from the beginning of an essay by Ellen Goodman, try to identify the transitional paragraph.

There was a time in my life, I confess, when I thought that the only inherent differences between men and women were the obvious ones.

In my callous youth, I scoffed at the mental gymnastics of sociobiologists who leaped to conclusions about men and women from long years spent studying bugs. I suspected the motives of brain researchers who split the world of the sexes into left and right hemispheres.

But now, in my midlife, I can no longer deny the evidence of my senses or experiences.

Like virtually every woman in America who has spent time beside a man behind a wheel, like every woman in America who has ever been a lost passenger outward bound with a male driver, I know that there is one way in which the male sex is innately different from the female: Men are by their very nature congenitally unable to ask directions.

The historical record of their unwillingness was always clear. Consider, for example, the valiant 600 cavalrymen who plunged into the Valley of Death . . . because they refused to ask if there wasn't some other way around the cannons.

Consider the entire wagon train that drove into the Donner Pass . . . because the wagon master wouldn't stop at the station marked Last Gas before the Disaster.

Consider even my own childhood. My father—a man with a great sense of humor and no sense of direction—constantly led us on what he referred to as "scenic routes."   7

But for centuries we assumed that this refusal was a weird idiosyncrasy. We never dreamed that it came with the testosterone.   8

In recent years, I have from time to time found myself sitting beside men who would not admit they were lost until I lit matches under their fingertips in an attempt to read maps in a box canyon.   9

—Ellen Goodman, "In the Male Direction"

Goodman introduces her idea about men in the first four paragraphs. In the next three paragraphs, she offers what she calls the "historical record"—her account of men's follies, their failures. The transitional paragraph, her eighth, points in two directions—back toward the idiosyncratic nature of male habit that leads to costly blunders, and forward toward something in the very nature of maleness. The word *testosterone* alerts you to the idea Goodman will develop in the next section of her essay—the link between blunders and testosterone. That pointing backward and forward characterizes good transitional paragraphs and illustrates how they link ideas in sections of the middle.

Guidelines for Writing Transitional Paragraphs

- Use transitional paragraphs to refer to what has come before—to summarize and clarify the idea from the previous paragraph or section of paragraphs.
- Use transitional paragraphs to point ahead, to anticipate and foreshadow an aspect of the idea that will be developed in the subsequent section of the essay's middle.
- Use transitional paragraphs to simplify rather than complicate your idea.

EXERCISE 9–4   **Writing a Transitional Paragraph**

Select one of the essays you wrote for a course this semester. Reread the essay, looking for a place in the middle to insert a transitional paragraph that would clarify what you said and point to what follows. Write that paragraph.

9d   Linking paragraphs in an essay

The excerpt from Ellen Goodman's essay demonstrates how informational and transitional paragraphs work together to develop an idea. But for an entire essay to be unified and coherent, all of its parts—beginning, middle, and ending paragraphs—must be unified and coherent and must work together to present and develop an idea.

The same techniques that work to organize and develop individual paragraphs (see 8c–e) can be used to achieve unity and coherence between paragraphs within an essay. Let us consider a student essay, looking at the beginning (one paragraph), one of the sections from the middle of the essay (four paragraphs), and the ending (two paragraphs) to see how beginning, middle, and ending paragraphs work together to present and develop an idea within the essay.

The essay is entitled "The Voice in the Looking-Glass." Notice how the student, Maile Meloy, uses two quotations—called epigraphs—at the head of her essay to stimulate thought about her idea. As you read the following excerpt from her essay, think about how the title, these quotations, and all paragraphs work together to suggest an idea about women and image making.

> A woman must continually watch herself. She is almost continually accompanied by her own image of herself. Men look at women. . . . Women watch themselves being looked at.
>
> —John Berger, *Ways of Seeing*
>
> The girl was ugly. I was bored during the whole journey.
>
> —Casanova, *History of My Life*

From the moment I became conscious of cause and effect, I have been conscious of the importance of my own appearance. Little girls (and little boys) learn early that the way women are treated is determined by the way they appear. John Berger, in *Ways of Seeing*, has gotten it right. *It is a woman's ever-present task to monitor her image, not to survey a situation to determine the appropriate action, as a man does, but to survey herself and define by her presentation the way she wishes others to act toward her. . . .*

We are taught our meticulous self-observation; it is a learned activity. At the onset of puberty, among the other ridiculously sexist boy-catching hints we receive, girls are often instructed to "learn how to take a compliment." We are expected to accept another person's sense of us as they have expressed it and to consider it a reward. By accepting it, we add it to our expectations of ourself—our checklist as we glance into the mirrors of shop windows, listen to ourselves speak, or choose our clothes, opinions, and other accessories.

When a girl "takes a compliment," she accepts the reward and accepts, as well, the requirement that earned her the compliment. Both become internalized. She now needs to be able to earn that other person's sense of her from herself. She practices her "disarming smile" in mirrors, concentrates on "poise," and makes sure she's being "a good listener." Not all compliments are "taken," of course, although they may be acknowledged with a polite "thank you." Some are discarded because they do not fit her image as the watcher in her sees it, and these rejects can be disconcerting as they suggest discrepancy between the internal surveyor and the external one, but true compliments, the ones that congratulate a girl's or woman's mutable, monitored perception of herself, are internalized and added to the checklist.

Sometimes the internal surveyor goes out of control. I have been haunted 4
for several days by the image of one of the homeless people in the city. She sits huddled in a doorstep in a beige coat with a scarf tied around her head, and she clutches a large white plastic bag. The first time I saw her I found myself staring, wondering at her face, which was colored a deep pink. As I neared her I could make out the cakey texture of makeup, and I caught the sweet chemical smell of the pink powder that covered her entire face: forehead, wrinkled cheeks, lips, eyes, eyebrows, and ears, that was smeared across the lapels of her coat and mixed with the pattern of her headwrap. I fixed my eyes back on the sidewalk, which was covered with white face powder, and braced for the inevitable request for money. It didn't come. She didn't even notice me; her eyes were riveted to a spot in the corner of the doorstep. I glanced back at that spot as I passed, expecting to see a mirror into which she was staring so intently. There was nothing there. Only the concrete wall stared back at her.

Later in the day she was gone, and only a white outline of her seated form 5
remained in the scattered face powder on the sidewalk, along with a sandwich in a baggie that someone must have given her, abandoned there with one bite taken. Disconcerted, I sought my own reflection in a shop window, to replace that of the trembling, staring, caricature of female vanity I had seen that morning. Even as I caught my own eye, I saw the irony in my means of escape. This poor, ill woman, to whom her own made-up self is more important than food, exists at the outer edge of the obsession with appearance that women learn from childhood.

I do not want to be John Berger's pathetically trapped woman, to "appear" 6
merely, and to be nothing more than a composite of other people's perceptions of me. I do not want to value appearance over action, but I cannot escape the habit of constantly having one eye on my own image. In mirrors and windows, in photographs, in other people's glances, and in my own mind I am haunted by images of myself. I am continually critiquing my appearance, my reactions, my gestures, and my speech. I am already caught in the queen's looking glass, already in conspiracy with the made-up old woman in the street.

A Stephen Sondheim character sings of his mistress, "Look at her looking, 7
forever in that mirror. What does she see?" He need not ask, for she sees through his eyes. She sees herself as lover, as desirable object, and as rival before she sees herself as a woman. She sees herself in relation to him and in light of his expectations, and she sees her imperfections in that light. She sees

Snow White fading and growing old and yet she clings to the facade. It is what she knows.

—Maile Meloy, student essay

The first paragraph—the essay's beginning—effectively draws the reader in without giving the entire essay away. It introduces the thesis, or main idea (shown in italics at the end of the paragraph), about a woman's "ever-present task to monitor her image." That notion of self-monitoring is then developed further in the essay's middle paragraphs. In the portion of the middle that you see here (paragraphs 2–5), Maile deepens our understanding about those images that seem to govern her life and produce devastating effects. She uses her own experience and knowledge as evidence. In an earlier section of the middle (not shown), Maile examines how women monitor and size up one another.

Notice how within her middle paragraphs, Maile achieves paragraph unity; she stays focused on her main idea about self-monitoring and continues to explain it even as she enlarges our sense of what it means. (See 8b-1 on staying focused and 8b-3 on explaining the idea.) Notice too how she expands the idea while making those middle paragraphs more coherent. She repeats and varies the key word *checklist* (explicitly in paragraphs 2 and 3; implicitly in paragraphs 4 and 5) to clarify how pervasive is the monitoring in a woman's mind. (See 8c-2 on repeating key terms.) She also relies on visual details to heighten our awareness of the effects of self-monitoring. (See 8c-4 on using visual details.)

Although each middle paragraph develops Maile's main idea, notice that none of these paragraphs is heavy-handed; the analysis is suggestive, balanced, and reasonable—in a word, convincing. One paragraph leads to another until you see the unity and coherence of the whole essay.

In the two paragraphs that make up the ending (paragraphs 6 and 7), Maile makes an explicit judgment about the idea she is developing. Notice how those ending paragraphs do what good endings should do: pull together all parts of the essay (including the epigraph) and clarify Maile's idea about those images that haunt and often govern a woman's life. You can also surmise from the details used in the ending that Maile developed the notion of Snow White and the looking glass in that portion of the essay's middle that you did not see. She is using those details to remind readers how she developed her idea in the complete essay.

EXERCISE 9–5   Analyzing and Writing about Coherence and Unity

---

Review sections 8a, 8b, and 8c, and then reread paragraphs 2–5 from the middle of Maile's essay. As you reread those middle paragraphs, make a list of the ways Maile achieves coherence among them. Make a separate list of how she makes the paragraphs cohere with other parts of the essay. Write a paragraph about how her efforts to achieve coherence contribute to the essay's unity.

Grammar

What Is Grammar?

Grammar is a system of principles that govern the way a language works. Grammar describes how words relate to each other, particularly how they function in sentences. In the opening sentence of this paragraph, for example, the noun *grammar* is the subject—what the sentence is about. The verb *is* links the subject with something said about it—that it is *a system of principles that govern the way a language works*. The words in this and any sentence can be identified as parts of speech—such as verbs, nouns, prepositions, and so forth—and are related to other words in the sentence according to grammatical function—such as predication (saying something about the subject) and modification (describing or limiting a word or group of words).

Grammar also conveys a sense of what is correct or acceptable in speaking and writing according to a set of conventions or rules. When we speak of "correct grammar," we mean the usage standards our culture has adopted from the practice of educated speakers and writers. This meaning of *grammar* refers to matters of proper and acceptable usage. For example, although you may use the word *ain't* in informal conversation, you would not use it in college papers and in professional writing (unless you had a special reason for doing so). And although you can find sentence fragments (grammatically incomplete sentences) in advertisements, the conventions of academic and professional writing limit their use.

Knowing how to use grammar accurately will give you confidence in both speaking and writing. Understanding grammar will enable you to construct sentences that express your ideas clearly, accurately, and effectively. It will also help you understand the writing of others.

CHAPTER 10

Basic Sentence Grammar

A **sentence** is traditionally defined as a group of words that expresses a complete thought. The thought a sentence expresses involves a grammatical relationship established between a subject and a predicate. The **subject** indicates what the sentence is about—its central topic. The **predicate** indicates something about the subject; it makes a statement or asks a question about it. Notice the subjects (S) and predicates (P) in these sentences.

⌐S⌐ ⌐P⌐
Bees buzz.

⌐—S—⌐ ⌐————————P————————⌐
The rain fell heavily through the night.

⌐—————S—————⌐ ⌐—————P—————⌐
The dense low-lying fog rolled across the meadow.

The accompanying chart outlines the parts of speech and indicates where you can find comprehensive coverage of each item in the *Handbook*.

10a Recognizing subjects and predicates

The subject of a sentence is always a noun, a pronoun, or a verb or clause that functions like a noun or pronoun. The predicate always contains a verb; often it also contains other words, such as prepositions, adjectives, adverbs, nouns, and pronouns.

Consider the following examples.

SUBJECT	PREDICATE
Spiders	have eight legs.
The American Civil War	lasted from 1861 to 1865.
Many economists	predict a quick end to the recession.
Many older voters	reacted unenthusiastically to the tax hike.

The subjects of these sentences vary. In the first sentence, the subject is a plural common noun. The subject of the second sentence is a proper noun identifying a particular war. In the third sentence, the subject is a plural common noun modified by the adjective *many*. The subject of the fourth sentence is a plural common noun modified by the adjectives *many older*.

The predicates in the preceding four sentences all include a single verb: *have, lasted, predict,* and *reacted.* Each predicate, however, also includes additional words, such as *eight* (an adjective modifying *legs*) and *legs* (a noun completing the meaning of the verb *have*); *from* (a preposition indicating duration of time); and *enthusiastically* (an adverb modifying the verb *reacted*).

The Parts of Speech

PART OF SPEECH	FUNCTION	EXAMPLE
Verb (See 11a)	Indicates action or state of being.	*spend, walk, see, care, be*
Noun (See 12a)	Names a person, place, thing, concept, or quality.	*John Smith, Pocahontas, home, child, coin, history, hope*
Pronoun (See 12b)	Takes the place of a noun.	*I, you, he, she, us, him, them, ours, who, anyone, myself, herself*
Adjective (See 13a)	Describes (modifies or qualifies) a noun or pronoun.	*hungry, rich, old, solid, desperate, neat*
Adverb (See 13a)	Describes a verb, adjective, or another adverb.	*often, quietly, cheerfully, nevertheless*
Preposition (See 14a)	Indicates the relationship between a noun or pronoun and another word in a sentence.	*into, from, to, with, above, at, behind, by, during*
Conjunction (See 14c)	Links or joins words, phrases, and clauses.	*and, but, or, after, until, therefore, however*
Interjection (See 14d)	Expresses surprise or emotion.	*Oh, Ah, Wow, Hey*

1 Subjects

The **simple subject** of a sentence is the single noun or pronoun that is its central subject. A simple subject appears most often as a single word, though it can also be a multiword proper noun such as *Golden Gate Bridge*. The **complete subject** of a sentence is the simple subject plus any additional modifying words or phrases. In the following example, the complete subject appears in italics and the simple subject is labeled SS.

┌─ SS ─┐
The majority of women painters from antiquity until the early twentieth century have suffered neglect if not outright dismissal.

Compound subjects identify two or more subjects used in a single sentence. A compound subject includes two or more simple subjects joined by a coordinating conjunction (*and, but, or, nor, for*) or by a correlative conjunction (*both . . . and, either . . . or, neither . . . nor, not only . . . but also*).

Mary Cassatt and Jean Renoir were two Impressionist painters who frequently painted scenes of women with children. *Neither Cassatt nor Renoir,* however, was considered as influential an Impressionist as Claude Monet.

2   Predicates

The **simple predicate** of a sentence is its verb. The **complete predicate** includes the verb plus its modifiers, complements, and object. Together the simple predicate and the complete predicate indicate something about the subject. In the following examples, the complete predicate appears in italics and the simple predicate is labeled SP.

SP
┌─┐
Our graduating class *used a Hawaiian theme for the senior prom.*

The simple predicate may include an auxiliary or helping verb along with the main verb. (See 11b on auxiliary verbs.)

┌── SP ──┐
They *were awaiting his arrival.*

Compound predicates include two or more verbs that have the same subject. The verbs may be joined by either a coordinating conjunction (*and, but, or, nor, for*) or a correlative conjunction (*both . . . and, either . . . or, neither . . . nor, not only . . . but also*).

The performers *danced and sang* enthusiastically, though with little effect on the audience.

In some sentences, a compound predicate may be separated by other intervening words.

Hurricane Andrew *reached* the southern coast of Florida at mid-morning *and battered* it mercilessly.

EXERCISE 10–1   **Recognizing Subjects and Predicates**

Identify the subjects and predicates in the following sentences. Underline the simple subject once and the simple predicate twice. Example:

> <u>Charles Darwin</u> <u>published</u> *The Origin of Species* in 1859.

1. Darwin acknowledged the provisional nature of evolution and affirmed the existence of natural selection.
2. Scientists regard debates on fundamental issues as a sign of intellectual health.
3. Evolutionary theory is now enjoying an upsurge of interest.
4. Creationists deny the premises of evolutionary theory.
5. Scientists continue to debate the validity of Darwin's theory.

10b   Recognizing objects and complements

In addition to a subject and a predicate, a sentence may include other elements, such as the object of the verb and the subject or object complement.

1   Direct and indirect objects of verbs

The **object** of a sentence may be either a direct object or an indirect object. The direct and indirect objects of the verb form part of the complete predicate of a sentence.

A **direct object** is a noun or pronoun that receives the action of the verb in a sentence. Only transitive verbs (see 11d-2) can take objects.

┌── DO ──┐
The United Nations inspectors examined the weapons.

A direct object of a verb frequently answers the question *What?* or *Whom?* about the verb. (The inspectors examined *what?* The weapons.)

┌── DO ──┐
The new policy affected the students. [The new policy affected *whom?* The students.]

An **indirect object** of a transitive verb identifies the recipient to whom or for whom (or for what) the action of the verb is done.

┌ IO ┐ ┌ DO ┐
Bill sent Ingrid flowers.

┌──────── IO ────────┐
The president of the company gave her administrative staff

┌──────────── DO ────────────┐
an inspiring motivational speech.

Direct and indirect objects can be simple, one-word objects or longer, more complete objects.

EXERCISE 10–2 Recognizing Direct and Indirect Objects of Verbs

Identify the direct and indirect objects of the verbs in the following sentences by underlining and labeling them DO or IO. Not all of the sentences will have both a direct and an indirect object. Example:

                      ┌ IO ┐ ┌───── DO ─────┐
The college awarded <u>my uncle</u> an <u>honorary degree</u>.

1. Give me liberty or give me death.
2. The novelist George Eliot abandoned her work for several years.
3. Charlotte Brontë put down her pen.
4. The audience appreciated the performer's explanations.
5. A painting in my grandmother's living room has always intrigued me.
6. I'll take a pastrami on rye and an Italian combo wedge with everything.
7. My grandmother sent my mother the traditional Egyptian engagement present of jewelry.

EXERCISE 10–3 Using Direct and Indirect Objects of Verbs in Writing

Write a paragraph in which at least three of your sentences contain an indirect object. You can choose your own topic or select one of these: something you own and value; something that annoys you; something you recently learned about; a news event; a historical event.

2 Objects of prepositions

In addition to direct and indirect objects of verbs, a sentence may include an object of a preposition. An **object of a preposition** is usually a noun or pronoun that follows the preposition and completes its meaning. The object of a preposition is a part of the prepositional phrase of a sentence. (See 14a on prepositions.)

$$\overset{\ulcorner OP \urcorner}{}$$
Bill bought flowers for Ingrid.

The president gave an inspiring motivational speech to

$$\overset{\ulcorner \text{———} OP \text{———} \urcorner}{}$$
her administrative staff.

As you can see in these examples, the object of a preposition may be one word or several words.

WRITING HINT   An indirect object (IO) always comes before a direct object (DO) in a sentence.

         IO   DO
They reserved us a table.

But the same meaning can usually be expressed in a prepositional phrase beginning with *to* or *for* and placed after the direct object.

             OP
       DO
They reserved a table for us.

Notice how this change—from indirect object to object of a preposition—emphasizes the recipient (*us*) more than the direct object (*table*). (See 26a on emphasis.)

3   Complements

A **complement** is a word or group of words that completes the meaning of a subject or a direct object by renaming or describing it. It may be either a subject complement, which completes the meaning of a linking verb (see 11d-1), or an object complement, which completes the meaning of a transitive verb (see 11d-2).

A **subject complement** (SC), which may be a noun or an adjective, follows a linking verb and identifies or describes the subject of the sentence.

      SC (noun)   SC (adj.)
His sister is a newscaster.   These muffins are delicious.

The most common linking verbs are the various forms of the verb *to be: am, is, are, was, were, has been, should be,* and so forth. Other common linking verbs include *appear, become, seem,* and, in some contexts, *feel, grow, look, taste, smell,* and *sound.*

His nephew *should be* a private investigator.

Your story *sounds* phony.

To distinguish between its two possible forms, a subject complement can also be called a **predicate noun** or a **predicate adjective**.

An **object complement** (OC), which can be a noun or an adjective, follows the direct object (DO) and renames or describes it.

                       ┌DO┐ ┌OC (noun)┐

The papers declared the play a hit.

                       ┌DO┐ ┌OC (adj.)┐

Wool socks will keep your feet warm.

EXERCISE 10–4   Identifying Subject and Object Complements

In the following sentences, underline and label the subject complements (SC) and object complements (OC). Example:

                               ┌OC┐

Her parents considered her <u>a genius</u>.

1. The fans thought the Mets season a disaster.
2. The rebels were experts in demolition.
3. The conclusion of the election was inevitable.
4. Home prices remained low, but only for a little while.
5. Mortgage interest rates were high.
6. His intentions were hardly honorable.
7. Olympic officials declared the second-place runner the winner after disqualifying the reigning champion of the long-distance event.

EXERCISE 10–5   Using Subject and Object Complements in Writing

Write a paragraph in which you employ subject and object complements. You may choose your own topic or one of these: a favorite or difficult course; a best friend; a book you read; a concert you attended; an idea that intrigues you.

 10c   Recognizing and using phrases

A **phrase** is a group of related words that does not form a complete sentence. Phrases might lack a subject or a predicate or both. Typically, phrases are embedded in sentences, adding information that clarifies, specifies, and illuminates the point of a sentence. Phrases, then, serve as modifiers. They also expand basic sentence patterns.

Consider the following example.

The next trout-fishing season will begin in early April.

The subject of this sentence is a noun phrase, *The next trout-fishing season*. The predicate is a verb phrase, *will begin*. Concluding the sentence is a prepositional phrase, *in early April*. The prepositional phrase functions here as an adverb, indicating when the season will begin.

1   Noun, verb, and prepositional phrases

Noun phrases

A **noun phrase** consists of a noun and its modifiers. A noun phrase can function as a subject (S), object (O), or complement (C) in a sentence.

$$\overset{\text{— S —}}{\textit{Warm sunny weather}} \text{ was predicted for } \overset{\text{— O —}}{\textit{the weekend}}.$$

$$\overset{\text{— S —}}{\textit{The Webers}} \text{ entertain } \overset{\text{— O —}}{\textit{many guests}} \text{ in } \overset{\text{— O —}}{\textit{their spacious home}}.$$

$$\overset{\text{— S —}}{\textit{Long cafeteria lines}} \text{ are } \overset{\text{— C —}}{\textit{a familiar sight}}.$$

Verb phrases

A **verb phrase** consists of a main verb and its auxiliary verbs. A verb phrase functions as the predicate in a sentence or a clause.

He *could have done* worse.

If we *had known* earlier about the low cost of food and lodging, we *would have planned* to stay longer.

Prepositional phrases

A **prepositional phrase** consists of a preposition, its object, and any of the object's modifiers. A prepositional phrase can function as an adjective or an adverb.

ADJECTIVE   The car *in the driveway* needed repair.

ADVERB   Tiger lilies grew *beside the road.*

On rare occasions, a prepositional phrase may function as the subject of a sentence.

Into the deepest part of the Ecuadorian jungle is the last place he had planned on going.

EXERCISE 10–6   Practice with Prepositional Phrases

Write a paragraph in which you use prepositional phrases in at least three sentences. Choose a topic of your own or one of these: a certain place (a campus hangout, your neighborhood), an object (a coin, photograph, tree, or flower) or a process (how to cook spaghetti, prepare for a hike, or teach someone to swim).

 2   Verbal phrases

Verbal phrases consist of a verbal and related modifiers, objects, or complements. **Verbals** are verb forms that do not function as verbs in sentences; rather, they function as nouns or as modifiers, mostly as adjectives. As such, they cannot stand alone. The three types of verbals are participles, gerunds, and infinitives. For more on verbals, see 11d-3.

Participles functioning as adjectives:

They waited as the *chugging* train finally arrived.

We heard the *excited* tone in her voice.

Gerunds functioning as nouns:

Swimming is enjoying a resurgence of international interest.

Without soap there wasn't much sense in *showering.*

Infinitives functioning as nouns, adjectives, and adverbs:

NOUN   Her goal was *to excel.*

ADJECTIVE   We had plenty of time *to waste.*

ADVERB   The chef was eager *to cook.*

Participial phrases

A **participial phrase** consists of a present or past participle and accompanying modifiers, objects, or complements. Participial phrases function only as adjectives, modifying nouns, or pronouns.

The cat *crouching behind the sofa* is Garfield, not Dolce.

Having saved for a year, they set out to shop for furniture.

Gerund phrases

A **gerund phrase** consists of a gerund with related modifiers, objects, or complements. Gerund phrases always function as nouns, whether as a subject or subject complement, a direct or indirect object, or an object of a preposition.

SUBJECT	*Playing baseball professionally* has always been his dream.
DIRECT OBJECT	He enjoyed *eating home-cooked meals.*
OBJECT COMPLEMENT	They did not want him *driving after he veered off the road.*
OBJECT OF A PREPOSITION	They were tired of *commuting two hundred miles a day.*

Absolute phrases

An **absolute phrase** consists of a noun or pronoun and a participle or complement, along with any related modifiers or objects. Absolute phrases modify entire sentences rather than particular words in those sentences. An absolute phrase can appear in many places in a sentence, but it is always set off by commas (see 33g).

Excitement over his girlfriend's return increasing by the minute, he found he could concentrate on little else.

The plane, *its engines thoroughly inspected,* was ready to take off.

The plane was ready to take off, *its engines having been thoroughly inspected.*

Infinitive phrases

An **infinitive phrase** consists of an infinitive with its related modifiers, objects, or complements. Infinitive phrases can function as nouns or as modifiers.

NOUN	*To give* is *to receive.*
ADJECTIVE	College is a good place *to meet new friends.*
ADVERB	*To succeed in college,* read widely and reflectively.

EXERCISE 10–7   **Using Verbal Phrases in Writing**

Write a paragraph that includes at least three sentences with verbal phrases. Choose a topic of your own or one of these: why you like to travel, shop, play sports; how you learned to swim, ski, drive, play the guitar.

Appositive phrases

An appositive renames the word or words it follows. An **appositive phrase** is a noun phrase that renames the noun or pronoun it immediately follows. Appositive phrases are usually set off from the rest of the sentence by commas (see 33c).

Toni Morrison, *author of several novels,* won the Nobel Prize for Literature.

The movie, *a fast-paced adventure story,* won rave reviews.

EXERCISE 10–8   Using Absolute Phrases in Writing

Combine the following pairs of sentences by converting the second sentence into an absolute phrase and attaching it effectively to the first sentence. Remember to use a comma (or commas) to set off the absolute phrase from the rest of the sentence. Example:

Our cat lay contentedly by the fire. Her tail moved from side to side like a metronome.

Our cat lay contentedly by the fire, her tail moving from side to side like a metronome.

1. Buildings crumbled along Market Street. Their foundations were damaged by the earthquake.
2. The game was officially halted in the fifth inning. The rain had persisted for over an hour.
3. There are remains of old Spanish forts everywhere. Their adobe walls are dissolving into dust.
4. We were now ready to talk business. The meal was finally finished.
5. Janetta sits at her desk. Her head is lowered over a pile of medieval art reproductions.

EXERCISE 10–9   Using Appositives in Writing

Combine the following sentence pairs by rewriting the second sentence in each pair as an appositive. Remember to set off the appositive phrases with commas if necessary. Example:

Bill watches television every night except Wednesday. Wednesday is his bowling night.

Bill watches television every night except Wednesday, *his bowling night.*

1. Black lung affects countless miners in Pennsylvania and West Virginia. Black lung is an incurable disease of the respiratory system.

2. Scientists have found the fossil of the oldest known vertebrate. The oldest known vertebrate is a jawless fish.
3. Brother Jim has been repeatedly denied a speaking permit by the university. Brother Jim is a preacher from Indiana.
4. Ben and Jerry are encouraging Americans to overeat for peace. Ben and Jerry are ice-cream makers who donate part of their profits to pacifist activities.
5. With the increased popularity of Caribbean cooking, plantains are replacing potatoes on American menus. Plantains are exotic bananas.

---

3   **Using phrases in writing**

You can use phrases to expand and develop your sentences by emphasizing particular details and creating emphatic endings. Consider the following examples.

My mother sat *on the patio sheltered by wisteria.*

Sheltered by wisteria, my mother sat *on the patio.*

Notice how both the prepositional phrase *on the patio* and the participial phrase *sheltered by wisteria* supply interesting detail to the sentence *My mother sat.* Notice, too, how shifting the phrase *sheltered by wisteria* to the beginning of the sentence changes the emphasis and, to a certain degree, the meaning of the sentence.

Look at the following sentence, and notice how it changes as phrases are added to it.

The mare's restless shuffling kicks up dust, which catches the light as it floats down.

The mare's restless shuffling kicks up dust, which catches the light as it floats down *to stick on the horse's sweating flanks.*

The mare's restless shuffling *in the hay* kicks up dust, which catches the light as it floats down *to stick in a gray film on the horse's sweating flanks.*

In this last version, the emphasis remains the same, but the added phrases expand and enrich the sentence.

EXERCISE 10–10   **Building Sentences with Phrases**

Expand each of the following short sentences by adding phrases. Example:

A girl stands.

In a darkened hallway stands a girl *in a pink sweater.*

1. Her smile is a mask.
2. Her photograph caught my attention.

3. Perfection is what I strive for.
4. Reality slapped me across the face.
5. He knew now what he had to do.

10d   Recognizing and using clauses

A **clause** is a group of words that contains a subject and a predicate. An **independent clause** can stand alone as a sentence.

Rosa loves lasagne.

A **dependent clause** cannot stand alone because it begins with a subordinating conjunction (see 14c-3) or a relative pronoun (see 12c).

Because Rosa loves lasagne

To form a complete sentence, a dependent clause must be joined to at least one independent clause.

Because Rosa loves lasagne, her mother makes it often.

(See also Chapter 17 on sentence fragments.)

1   Adjective clauses

An **adjective clause** modifies a noun or pronoun in another clause, although it usually appears immediately after the word it modifies. Adjective clauses are also typically introduced by a relative pronoun—*who, which, that, whose,* or *whom* (see 12b). When a dependent clause begins with one of these words, it can also be referred to as a **relative clause.**

Sappho is the ancient Greek poet *who lived on the island of Lesbos.*

Her poetry, *which exists mostly in fragments,* is lyrical, emotional, and erotic.

2   Adverb clauses

Adverb clauses modify verbs, adjectives, or other adverbs. They typically provide details about how, where, when, why, under what conditions, with what consequences, or to what extent an action occurs. They are introduced by subordinating conjunctions.

If you can make the first cut, you have a good chance to make the team.

His salary was increased *when the sales results were tabulated.*

WRITING HINT   Although adverb clauses often occur at the beginnings of sentences, they can be used in other places as well. Changing the position of adverb clauses in your sentences is one way to avoid monotony. It is also a way to vary the emphasis and rhythm of your sentences. Consider the following examples.

The band members went out for pizza *after they finished performing.*

After they finished performing, the band members went out for pizza.

Barbara McClintock continued her experiments with corn *even though her scientific work had long been ignored.*

Even though her scientific work had long been ignored, Barbara McClintock continued her experiments with corn.

See 33b and 33c for more information on punctuating adverb clauses.

3 Noun clauses

A **noun clause** can serve as a subject, an object, or a complement within a sentence. Noun clauses typically begin with a relative pronoun, such as *who, whom, whoever,* or *whomever,* or with a subordinating conjunction such as *when, where, whether, why, how, what,* or *whatever.*

SUBJECT	*That he complained* surprised me.
DIRECT OBJECT	Homer's *Odyssey* describes, in considerable detail, *how and why Odysseus' journey home from Troy took him ten years.*
SUBJECT COMPLEMENT	The administrative response to faculty demands for smaller classes was *that they were too costly.*
OBJECT OF A PREPOSITION	Don't listen to *what he says.*

EXERCISE 10–11   Using Clauses in Writing

Expand each of the following brief sentences by adding one or more dependent clauses. Example:

Only one person remained.

As the lights finally went out in the hall, only one person remained.

1. The old dog still barked loudly.
2. The church was being repaired.
3. They sat inside for more than two hours.
4. She always tried to look her best.
5. The sun shone through the branches of the newly planted cherry tree.

10e   Using the basic sentence patterns

You can use the basic grammatical elements described in 10a and 10b to construct many kinds of sentences. You can also combine and arrange the grammatical elements to create different types of sentences (see 10f).

The accompanying chart outlines the simplest and most common sentence patterns. They form the core of all sentences in English.

The basic sentence patterns begin with a subject and, except for the first pattern, conclude with an object or complement. Every sentence you read and write will contain combinations of these sentence elements, but not always in the sequences illustrated in the chart. Interrogative sentences (see 10f-1), inverted sentences (26a-5), and more complex types of sentences (10f-2; 25c), for example, follow different patterns.

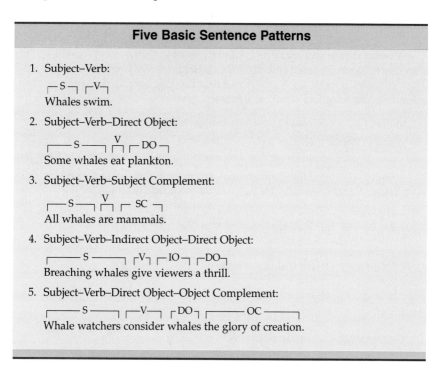

Five Basic Sentence Patterns

1. Subject–Verb:

   ⌐S⌐ ⌐V⌐
   Whales swim.

2. Subject–Verb–Direct Object:

   ⌐——S——⌐ ⌐V⌐ ⌐DO⌐
   Some whales eat plankton.

3. Subject–Verb–Subject Complement:

   ⌐——S——⌐ ⌐V⌐ ⌐ SC ⌐
   All whales are mammals.

4. Subject–Verb–Indirect Object–Direct Object:

   ⌐———S———⌐ ⌐V⌐ ⌐IO⌐ ⌐DO⌐
   Breaching whales give viewers a thrill.

5. Subject–Verb–Direct Object–Object Complement:

   ⌐———S———⌐ ⌐V⌐ ⌐DO⌐ ⌐——OC——⌐
   Whale watchers consider whales the glory of creation.

EXERCISE 10–12   **Using the Basic Sentence Patterns**

In the following sentences, label the subjects (S), verbs (V), subject complements (SC), direct objects (DO), indirect objects (IO), and object complements (OC) as appropriate. Then use the sentences as models for writing sentences of your own that incorporate subjects, verbs, subject complements, direct objects, indirect objects, and object complements.

1. Many readers enjoy a good detective story.
2. Literary historians give Edgar Allan Poe credit for inventing the modern detective story.
3. Poe's detective hero was a Frenchman.
4. Poe named his detective C. Auguste Dupin.
5. Dupin appeared in only three of Poe's stories.
6. Dupin became the model for a long line of popular successors, including Sherlock Holmes.

 Using different types of sentences

Sentences can be classified in various ways. One way to classify them is by function; a sentence can, for example, make a statement, pose a question, give a command, or convey a strong emotion. Another way to classify them is by grammatical construction, such as simple, compound, complex, or compound-complex.

1   Functional sentence types

In addition to understanding and using the five basic sentence patterns outlined in 10e, you can use the four types of sentences: declarative, interrogative, imperative, and exclamatory. Each type of sentence performs a different function. A **declarative sentence** makes a statement. An **interrogative sentence** asks a question. An **imperative sentence** gives a command or makes a request. An **exclamatory sentence** expresses strong feeling.

DECLARATIVE   War reparations were required.

INTERROGATIVE   How effective were they?

IMPERATIVE   Consider what happened in their aftermath.

EXCLAMATORY   What a powerful speech that was!

Declarative sentences

Most of the sentences you write are declarative sentences; they describe, explain, analyze, or argue a position. Whether you are describing how to paint with watercolors, explaining how a free-market economy works, or arguing for the elimination of the death penalty, you rely heavily on declarative sentences. Such sentences make assertions, state facts, present opinions, offer evaluations, identify problems, and present solutions. Most of the sentences in this book, including the majority of the examples, are declarative.

Interrogative sentences

Although interrogative sentences are used sparingly in academic and professional writing, they can enhance writing by creating a personal tone—one that involves readers and stimulates them to think. Consider how the following passage, written by a student, blends interrogative sentences with declarative ones to develop an idea.

> I am a clown and my makeup and mask are all that I am. My mask represents how far I will go to stay in character, to do what is expected of me. Like an artist perfecting her creation, I constantly check to see that I am doing what I should, what is expected, what my role requires. How long, I wonder, will I continue to wear this mask? Is it already too late for me to tear it off and become the person I want to be? My mask has grown almost too comfortable. I have become, it seems, too adept at performing the roles expected of me. Perhaps I will always remain a clown.
>
> —Nancy McArthur, "Beyond the Smile of the Clown"

Imperative and exclamatory sentences

Imperative and exclamatory sentences are used only infrequently in academic writing. Imperative sentences can direct readers to consider a point or evaluate an idea. Think, for example, of how often you are asked in this *Handbook* to "look at" or "consider" an example, or to "notice" how a writer achieves an effect. Too many imperative sentences, however, can create an insistent and overbearing tone.

Exclamatory sentences have their place in conversation, but outside of some kinds of descriptive and narrative writing, in which you may provide your reactions to an experience, you will rarely need them. Exclamatory sentences can make your writing appear overly charged and emotional.

EXERCISE 10–13   Identifying Functional Sentence Types

Identify each of the following sentences as declarative, interrogative, imperative, or exclamatory.

1. What an unusual family they are!
2. Learn a foreign language now before it's too late.
3. To what extent has this experience been engaging?
4. Until the committee renders its decision, no further action can be taken.
5. Can health costs be limited by the strategies proposed?

2   Grammatical sentence types

Grammatically, sentences can be classified as simple, compound, complex, and compound-complex. This classification is based on the way sentences use dependent and independent clauses. A clause is a group of words with a subject and a predicate. An independent clause can stand alone as a sentence; a dependent clause cannot. (See 10d.)

Simple sentences

A **simple sentence** consists of a single independent clause without any dependent clauses.

You can see the mountain.

Note that a sentence is still classified as a simple sentence even when it has a compound subject or predicate (or both) and includes modifying words and phrases.

You and your friends can see the mountain on your next trip.

You can see the mountain and climb to the top.

In the distance, you can barely see the outline of the mountain through the low-hanging clouds.

Compound sentences

A **compound sentence** consists of two or more independent clauses (IC) without any dependent clauses.

── IC ──
He wanted to attend the lecture, *but*

── IC ──
he had already promised to go to dinner with friends.

── IC ──
Naomi and her sister, Ruth, once swam competitively;

── IC ──
now, *however,* they rarely swim at all.

Complex sentences

A **complex sentence** consists of a single independent clause (IC) with one or more dependent clauses (DC).

── DC ──
When he heard that his brother had been wounded in the Civil War,

```
┌─────────────────────── IC ───────────────────────┐
```
Walt Whitman left home to find him and nurse him back to health.

```
┌──────────────── IC ──────────────┐ ┌──── DC ────┐
```
Michael Jackson embarked on a music career when he was a child.

```
┌──── IC ────┐ ┌──────────── DC ────────────┐
```
Few of us are confident that world peace will occur any time soon.

Compound-complex sentences

A **compound-complex sentence** consists of two or more independent clauses (IC) and at least one dependent clause (DC).

```
┌──────────────── IC ────────────────┐ ┌──── DC ────┐
```
Franz Schubert wrote his first song, "The Erlkönig," when he was eighteen,

```
┌──────── IC ────────┐ ┌──── DC ────┐ ┌── DC ──┐
```
and he continued to write songs until age thirty-one, when he died.

```
┌──── IC ────┐     ┌──────── IC ────────┐
```
The book was long, *but* it provided enjoyable reading

```
┌──────────────── DC ────────────────┐
```
because it had surprising action and complex characters.

EXERCISE 10–14 **Using Different Kinds of Sentences**

The sentences in the following paragraph have been simplified. Revise the paragraph to add sentence variety, such as by adding phrases and different kinds of clauses and by combining some of the sentences. Create an effective mix of simple, compound, complex, and compound-complex sentences in the paragraph. You may find it necessary to add or drop some words.

> For a long time, psychologists have wondered about memories and what they are. They have also wondered where memories are stored in the human brain. Memory has been studied intensely. That's because it is the basis of human intelligence. According to one psychologist, memory is an umbrella term. It covers a whole range of processes. These occur in our brains. In particular, psychologists have identified two types of memory. One type is called declarative memory. It includes memories of facts. These include names, places, dates, even baseball scores. We use it to declare things. That's why it's called declarative. The other type of memory is called procedural. This type of memory is acquired by repetitive practice. It is also acquired by conditioning. It includes skills like riding a bike or typing. We need both types of memory in our daily living. We need facts. We also use a variety of skills.

Grammar and Writing

Using Different Types of Sentences

You can put your knowledge of grammar to work in your writing immediately. One practical application you can make now is to vary the types of sentences you write, especially when you revise your writing.

You can begin by looking over one of your recent papers. Identify the kinds of sentences it contains: declarative and interrogative, for example, and simple, compound, and complex. Next, identify the ways your sentences begin—with article and noun, for example, or with adjectives.

If you find the same sentence type repeatedly, you can revise to vary your sentences. Mix simple sentences among complex ones; add an occasional interrogative sentence among your declarative ones. If you find the same kinds of sentence beginnings, you can vary them as well. Begin some sentences, for example, with an adverb or a prepositional phrase. Begin others with article and noun.

In short, use grammar to improve your writing.

Example

Reporter Bill Moyers investigated the field of mind-body medicine for three years. Moyers was skeptical at first, but he found that the link between mind and body has powerful effects on physical and mental health. Moyers was motivated in part by the death of his father when he first began the project.

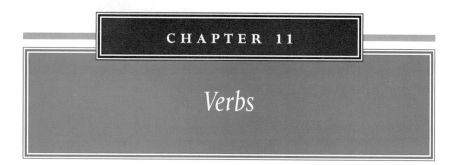

CHAPTER 11

Verbs

A **verb** is a part of the complete predicate that indicates an action (He *kissed* his mother), an occurrence (The responsibility *fell* on my shoulders), or a state of being (She *seems* tired). Different forms of a verb are used to indicate person, number, tense, voice, and mood. A verb's form also conveys information about the action within a sentence. The accompanying chart outlines some important characteristics conveyed by verbs.

Verb Characteristics		
Person	Indicates who or what experiences or performs the action—the person speaking, the person spoken to, or the person or thing spoken about.	**first person:** I *walk.* **second person:** You *walk.* **third person:** He/She/It *walks.*
Number	Specifies how many subjects experience or perform the action.	**singular:** It *walks.* **plural:** They *walk.*
Tense	Signals the time of the action. (See 11f–i.)	**past:** I *looked* out the window. **present:** I *look* out the window. **future:** I *will look* out the window.
Voice	Indicates whether the subject performs or receives the verb's action. (See 11j–k.)	**active voice:** The audience *watched* the performers. **passive voice:** The performers *were watched* by the audience.
Mood	Denotes the attitude expressed toward the verb.	**imperative:** *Listen* to me! **indicative:** You *are listening* to me. **subjunctive:** I wish you *would listen* to me.

> *Verb Forms*

11a   Primary verb forms

All English verbs, with the exception of *be*, have five primary forms.

BASE FORM	PRESENT TENSE	PRESENT PARTICIPLE	PAST TENSE	PAST PARTICIPLE
look	looks	looking	looked	looked
walk	walks	walking	walked	walked
watch	watches	watching	watched	watched

The **base form** (or **simple form**) is the form cited in dictionaries. The base form is also used for the present tense when the subject of the verb is *I, you, we, they,* or a plural noun.

Mary and Robert *look* at ruby rings.

I *talk* and you *listen.*

Mom and Dad *argue* about politics.

The **present tense** (or **-s form**), which is produced by adding *-s* or *-es* to the base form, indicates action in the present when the subject is third-person singular (*he, she, it* or a singular noun).

He *smiles* and she *returns* his smile with one of her own.

The instructor sometimes *dines* alone and *reads* a book.

USAGE NOTE   All singular nouns and many indefinite pronouns take verbs with the *-s* form in the present tense. (See 12a on nouns and 12b on indefinite pronouns.)

The judge clearly *believes* the defendant.

Everybody *wants* the deadline for the paper extended.

Each player *remains* responsible for staying in shape.

The **present participle** indicates continuing action. It is created by adding *-ing* to the base form of the verb. In order to function as the main verb in a sentence, a participle must be accompanied by a form of the verb *be.*

Mark *is anticipating* a good grade this semester.

They *were awaiting* instruction from the director.

When a present participle functions as the grammatical subject or object in a sentence, it is a **gerund** (see 10c-2).

> *Swimming* is good exercise. [*Swimming* is the subject of the sentence.]

> Karen enjoyed *fishing*. [*Fishing* is the direct object of *enjoyed*.]

A present participle can also function as an adjective in a sentence.

> *Accepting* the award, the actor was clearly overjoyed. [*Accepting* modifies *actor.*]

> The defense furnished *supporting* evidence. [*Supporting* modifies *evidence.*]

The present participle does not change form to indicate person or number in a sentence.

The **past tense** usually indicates action that occurred in the past. A verb's past tense can almost always be recognized by its *-d* or *-ed* ending. The past tense does not change form to indicate person or number.

> Paul *agreed* with her about the causes of inflation.

> They *persuaded* him to reconsider his opinion.

Some irregular verbs form their past tense in other ways and are called **irregular verbs** (see 11c and 11f-2).

> He *was* not happy about the change.

> His aunt and uncle *went* to Paris and *saw* the Eiffel Tower.

The **past participle** is identical to the past tense form of the verb, except in some irregular verbs (see 11c). Like the present participle, the past participle must be accompanied by a form of the verb *be* to function as the main verb in the sentence and does not change form to indicate person or number. The past participle is a part in the perfect verb tenses (see 11g) and the passive voice verbs (see 11k). It can also function as an adjective.

> Each *had waited* for the other to initiate the conversation. [past perfect tense]

> Nearly everyone *was helped* by the extra-credit question. [passive voice verb]

> Only occasionally will I eat an *overcooked* steak. [adjective]

USAGE NOTE   In speech the *-d* and *-ed* endings of past tense verbs are often dropped or given very little stress, as in *He asked me to leave* or *She composed a piece for the piano*. As a result, some people tend to forget these endings in writing.

In your writing, be sure to include the *-d* and *-ed* endings where they are needed, and avoid nonstandard forms of the past tense and the past participle. (See 11c.)

EXERCISE 11–1   **Selecting Standard Verb Forms**

Revise the following sentences so that the verbs conform to standard English usage. Some sentences may be correct as written. Example:

> *lives*
> Clarice ~~live~~ in New Harmony, Indiana.

1. After the party is over, we walking directly home.
2. I smile as I ate a piece of cherry pie.
3. Accountants and other tax advisors work long hours in March and early April.
4. Children asking many questions that are difficult to answer.
5. We observe an accident on our way out of town.
6. Yesterday Darrell receive an important call from his advisor.
7. Most students complete their assignments on time.
8. I answers him, "You will have to solve the problem by yourself."
9. The coach knows that I am ill, but she still expect me to show up for practice.
10. My roommate joke all the time about cafeteria food.

 Auxiliary verb forms

Some verb forms do not make sense as main verbs of a sentence without the aid of an **auxiliary verb** (or a **helping verb**). The most common auxiliary verbs are *be, have,* and *do.* (See the accompanying chart, Forms of *be, have,* and *do.*) The combination of an auxiliary verb with a main verb creates a **verb phrase** that typically indicates complete, continuing, or future action.

> VERB PHRASE
> AUXILIARY MAIN VERB
> The movie *is being filmed* in downtown Boston. [continuing action]

> VERB PHRASE   VERB PHRASE
> AUXILIARY MAIN VERB   AUXILIARY MAIN VERB
> I *have practiced* so that the magic trick *will succeed.*
> [completed action/future action]

Verb phrases are also used for emphasis, for questions, and for negative statements.

But I *do recognize* the name of the Secretary of State. [emphasis]

Did you *visit* the Acropolis? [question]

He *had* not *received* his magazine subscription as of last Wednesday. [negative]

USAGE NOTE   Some dialects use the base form *be* instead of *am, is,* or *are,* especially to express habitual or continued action. This usage is not standard, however, for college writing.

NONSTANDARD	He *be* the best player on the team.
STANDARD	He *is* the best player on the team.
NONSTANDARD	I *be* taking three math courses this year.
STANDARD	I *am* taking three math courses this year.

A **modal auxiliary verb** (such as *can, could, may, might, must, shall, should, will,* and *would*) combines with a main verb to form a verbal phrase. The modal auxiliary can refine the meaning of the main verb by indicating necessity, obligation, permission, possibility, and the like. Modal auxiliaries do not change form to indicate person or number and always combine with the base form of the main verb.

If she is to win the case, the defense lawyer *must undermine* the plaintiff's credibility. [necessity]

I really *should visit* my grandmother this weekend. [obligation]

You *may leave.* [permission]

If I *could manage* to get an interview, I know I *would prove* that I *could perform* the job. [possibility]

USAGE NOTE   Use the conditional auxiliary *would* only in an independent clause, never in an *if* clause.

	INDEPENDENT CLAUSE	*IF* CLAUSE
NONSTANDARD	We *would* have helped	if we *would have* known.
STANDARD	We *would* have helped	if we *had* known.

WRITING HINT   Modal auxiliaries can combine with other auxiliary verbs to form complicated verb phrases that require careful attention.

When *have* comes after a modal auxiliary, as in "I could have gone," the *could have* is pronounced with stress on *could* and no stress on *have.* Thus, in speech *could have* sounds like *could of* and is sometimes incorrectly written that way. Be sure to write *have,* not *of,* in sentences like these.

You *should have read* the directions more carefully.

It *would have saved* you considerable time and energy.

Also be careful when using *ought to*. It is awkward to use in the negative (with *not*). Combinations such as *shouldn't ought to* and *hadn't ought to* may be common in spoken English, but in writing *ought not to* is standard. You may want to use *should not* or *shouldn't* instead.

Forms of *be, have,* and *do*

The verbs *be, have,* and *do* have irregular forms. If you are unfamiliar with their forms, you will need to memorize them.

BASE FORM	PRESENT TENSE	PRESENT PARTICIPLE	PAST TENSE	PAST PARTICIPLE
be	I *am* he/she/it *is* we/you/they *are*	*being*	I/he/she/it *was* we/you/they *were*	*been*
have	I *have* he/she/it *has* we/you/they *have*	*having*	I *have* he/she/it *had* we/you/they *had*	*had*
do	I *do* he/she/it *does* we/you/they *do*	*doing*	*did*	*done*

EXERCISE 11–2   **Using Auxiliary Verbs**

In the following sentences, fill in each of the blanks with an appropriate form of *be, have,* or *do.* Example:

Paul Simon's songs __have__ become classics.

1. Liz _____ cooking dinner for her friends tonight.
2. Last week, Cliff _____ promised us roasted leg of lamb.
3. But this week, Cliff _____ offered to do the dishes.
4. Catherine _____ cleaned her apartment for our comfort.
5. How _____ he manage to scale the wall in five seconds?
6. I _____ hoping to see you before you left for Vermont.
7. My sister _____ not understand my sense of style.
8. Rob _____ talking with his girlfriend for hours last night.
9. He _____ tend to go on and on when he tells a good story.

11c Regular and irregular verbs

Regular verbs form the past tense and past participle by adding *-d* or *-ed* to the base form. The base form, past tense, and past participle are called the **principal parts** of the verb.

BASE FORM	PAST TENSE	PAST PARTICIPLE
call	called	called
follow	followed	followed
burn	burned	burned

The principal parts of **irregular verbs** do not follow the *-d* or *-ed* pattern in forming their past tense and past participle. Many irregular verbs form their principal parts by changing an internal vowel: *begin, began, begun; ring, rang, rung.*

Some irregular verbs do not change at all. Their base form is also used in the past tense and as the past participle: *bet, bet, bet; cost, cost, cost.* Some irregular verbs such as *go* and *am* change radically: *go, went, gone; am, was, been.* The only way to learn these irregular verbs is to memorize their principal parts.

If you are uncertain about which verb form is correct, consult a dictionary. All good dictionaries list the base form, past tense, and past participle of irregular verbs. Many of the most common irregular verbs appear in the accompanying chart. Memorize any irregular verbs whose parts you have trouble with.

EXERCISE 11–3 Using Irregular Verbs

For each irregular verb in parentheses, provide the appropriate past tense or past participle. Check the list of irregular verbs for any you are unsure about. Example:

Snow had *(fall)* fallen throughout the night.

1. The population of California has *(grow)* _____ dramatically in the last decade.

2. After the phone had *(ring)* _____ a dozen times, he finally *(wake)* _____ up and answered it.

3. Annie Proulx has *(write)* _____ an award-winning novel called *The Shipping News.*

4. Bobby Bonilla *(swing)* _____ at a high fastball and *(drive)* _____ it over the center field fence.

5. When Pablo Morales *(swim)* _____ the hundred-meter butterfly at the Barcelona Olympics, he *(show)* _____ everyone that he *(can)* _____ still compete with the best swimmers in the world.

6. She *(ride)* _____ the horse with confidence and grace. It looked as if she had *(ride)* _____ all her life.

7. The cat has *(eat)* _____; I *(feed)* _____ it this morning.

8. The lawyers for the defense have *(prove)* _____ conclusively that their client could not have *(steal)* _____ the jewelry.

9. The tank had *(spring)* _____ a leak.

10. The book had been *(read)* _____ many times.

Common Irregular Verbs

BASE FORM	PAST TENSE	PAST PARTICIPLE
arise	arose	arisen
awake	awoke	awaked *or* awoken
be	was	been
become	became	become
begin	began	begun
bite	bit	bitten
blow	blew	blown
break	broke	broken
bring	brought	brought
build	built	built
burn	burned *or* burnt	burned *or* burnt
burst	burst	burst
buy	bought	bought
can	could	could
catch	caught	caught
choose	chose	chosen
come	came	come
dig	dug	dug
dive	dived *or* dove	dived
do	did	done
draw	drew	drawn
drink	drank	drunk
drive	drove	driven
eat	ate	eaten
fall	fell	fallen
fight	fought	fought
find	found	found
fly	flew	flown
forget	forgot	forgotten *or* forgot
forgive	forgave	forgiven
freeze	froze	frozen
get	got	gotten *or* got
give	gave	given

(continued)

BASE FORM	PAST TENSE	PAST PARTICIPLE
go	went	gone
grow	grew	grown
hang (suspend)	hung	hung
hang (execute)	hanged	hanged
have	had	had
hear	heard	heard
hide	hid	hidden
know	knew	known
lay	laid	laid
lead	led	led
leave	left	left
lend	lent	lent
lie	lay	lain
lose	lost	lost
make	made	made
mean	meant	meant
meet	met	met
pay	paid	paid
ride	rode	ridden
ring	rang	rung
rise	rose	risen
run	ran	run
say	said	said
see	saw	seen
send	sent	sent
set	set	set
shake	shook	shaken
shine (glow)	shone	shone
shine (polish)	shined	shined
shoot	shot	shot
shrink	shrank	shrunk
sing	sang	sung
sink	sank	sunk
sit	sat	sat
sleep	slept	slept
speak	spoke	spoken
spend	spent	spent
spring	sprang	sprung
stand	stood	stood
steal	stole	stolen
stink	stank *or* stunk	stunk
swear	swore	sworn
swim	swam	swum
swing	swung	swung
take	took	taken

(continued)

BASE FORM	PAST TENSE	PAST PARTICIPLE
teach	taught	taught
tear	tore	torn
think	thought	thought
throw	threw	thrown
wear	wore	worn
wring	wrung	wrung
write	wrote	written

EXERCISE 11–4   **Using Irregular Verbs in Sentences**

Write two sentences for each of the following verbs. Use each verb first in the past tense and then as a past participle (with *have* or *had*). Example:

>*take:* I *took* the last seat. Michelle *had taken* the first one.

1. bring   3. freeze   5. ring   7. draw   9. see
2. choose   4. hide   6. break   8. forget   10. shake

 Other types of verbs

In addition to regular and irregular, two other important verb classifications are linking verbs and transitive verbs or intransitive verbs.

1 Linking verbs

A **linking verb** joins the subject of a sentence to a subject complement, which describes or renames the subject. Linking verbs usually describe states of being, not actions.

Columbus *was* an explorer with a plan.

King Ferdinand *remained* uncertain.

Queen Isabella *felt* confident about Columbus's chances of success.

In these examples the verbs (*was, remained, felt*) link their subjects (*Columbus, King Ferdinand, Queen Isabella*) to the subject complements (*explorer, uncertain, confident*). (See 10b-3 for more on subject complements.)

Common linking verbs include all forms of the verb *be: am, is, are, was, were, be, being,* and *been.*

He *is* the greatest.

We *are* hungry but soon we *will be* famished.

I *am* unable to agree and she *is* unwilling to compromise.

Linking verbs often describe the senses. These sensory verbs include *look, sound, taste, smell,* and *feel.* They are almost always completed by adjectives that describe the subject of the sentence.

This food *smells* and *tastes* delicious.

The child's blanket *felt* soft and warm.

Other common linking verbs convey a sense of existing or becoming, such as *appear, become, remain, seem, get,* and *grow.* These linking verbs are often completed by adjectives that describe the subject.

The grass *appears* brown and dead.

The congregation *remained* silent.

She *got* angry.

2 Transitive and intransitive verbs

A **transitive verb** transfers its action from a subject to a direct object. A transitive verb must have a direct object to complete its meaning.

She *bought* the car. [The meaning of the verb, *bought,* is completed by the direct object, *car.*]

An **intransitive verb** does not take a direct object.

He *blushes* easily. [The meaning of the verb, *blushes,* is complete in itself.]

Some verbs can be used both transitively (He *sees* his mistake) and intransitively (He *sees* poorly). You can see the difference between transitive and intransitive uses of a verb in these examples.

TRANSITIVE   Angela *climbed* the mountain.

INTRANSITIVE   Angela *climbed* expertly.

TRANSITIVE   Paul *speaks* German.

INTRANSITIVE   Paul *speaks* well.

3 Verbals

Verbals are verb forms that typically end in *-ing* or *-ed.* Verbals can function as nouns (*skiing* is fun) or as modifiers (the *stolen* goods, the desire *to succeed*).

A verbal cannot stand alone as the main verb in a sentence. *The clown smiling* and *the books read* are not complete sentences but sentence fragments (see

17a). A verbal must always be accompanied by an auxiliary verb when it serves as the predicate of a sentence.

Since verbals cannot stand alone as sentence predicates, they are called **nonfinite** (unfinished or incomplete) **verbs.** **Finite** (finished or complete) **verbs,** on the other hand, can serve as sentence predicates. For verbals in tense sequences, see 11i-1–2.

There are three kinds of verbals: participles, gerunds, and infinitives.

Participles function as adjectives. The present participle is the *-ing* form of a verb: *wishing, hearing, touching.* Although some verbs have irregular past participles (see 11c), the past participle of regular verbs is the *-d* or *-ed* form: *wished, heard, touched.*

He watched as the *falling* snow dropped quietly around him.

She noticed the *distracted* look on her father's face.

Gerunds, like the present participle, also end in *-ing.* Gerunds, however, function as nouns.

Hiking is very popular nowadays.

This institution now prohibits *smoking.*

Infinitives can function as nouns, adjectives, or adverbs. An infinitive consists of the word *to* plus the main or base form of the verb.

NOUN He wanted *to win.*

ADJECTIVE She had no more money *to spend.*

ADVERB The writer was ready *to revise.*

The three kinds of verbal phrases are participle phrases, gerund phrases, and infinitive phrases. (See 10c-2.)

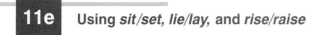

11e Using *sit/set, lie/lay,* and *rise/raise*

Three irregular verb pairs sometimes cause confusion: *sit* and *set; lie* and *lay;* and *rise* and *raise.* Part of the confusion derives from each pair's similar spellings, and part comes from the related meanings of each pair. (For *lie* and *lay,* the problem is compounded because the present tense form of *lay* is the same as the past tense of *lie.*) In order to distinguish between the pairs of words, you should think of them as either transitive verbs or intransitive verbs.

Sit is an intransitive verb (see 11d-2) and thus does not take an object. *Sit* means "to be seated." *Set* is a transitive verb and consequently takes an object. *Set* means "to put or place."

INTRANSITIVE Our cat *sits* on the windowsill. [present tense of *sit*]

TRANSITIVE He always *sets* his notes on the podium. [present tense of *set*]

INTRANSITIVE	They *sat* against the wall. [past tense of *sit*]
TRANSITIVE	The explanation *set* her mind at rest. [past tense of *set*]
INTRANSITIVE	They were *sitting* in the front row. [present participle of *sit*]
TRANSITIVE	Marc was *setting* the table when the phone rang. [present participle of *set*]

Lie is an intransitive verb and means "to recline." *Lay* is a transitive verb meaning "to put or place."

INTRANSITIVE	I often *lie* down after dinner. [present tense of *lie*]
TRANSITIVE	She *lays* down the law in our house. [present tense of *lay*]
INTRANSITIVE	I *lay* down before dinner last night. [past tense of *lie*]
TRANSITIVE	She *laid* the tray on my lap. [past tense of *lay*]
INTRANSITIVE	The lion was *lying* in its pen. [present participle of *lie*]
TRANSITIVE	The workers were *laying* bricks. [present participle of *lay*]

Rise is an intransitive verb and means "to get up." *Raise* is a transitive verb meaning "to lift up."

INTRANSITIVE	She *rises* early to begin writing. [present tense of *rise*]
TRANSITIVE	Your question *raises* another issue. [present tense of *raise*]
INTRANSITIVE	We *rose* late and had to hurry. [past tense of *rise*]
TRANSITIVE	He *raised* his arm and waved goodbye. [past tense of *raise*]
INTRANSITIVE	The foam was *rising* in the glass. [present participle of *rise*]
TRANSITIVE	They were *raising* their voices in celebration. [present participle of *raise*]

Forms of *sit/set, lie/lay, rise/raise*

	BASE FORM	PRESENT TENSE	PRESENT PARTICIPLE	PAST TENSE	PAST PARTICIPLE
INTRANSITIVE	sit	sits	sitting	sat	sat
TRANSITIVE	set	sets	setting	set	set
INTRANSITIVE	lie	lies	lying	lay	lain
TRANSITIVE	lay	lays	laying	laid	laid
INTRANSITIVE	rise	rises	rising	rose	risen
TRANSITIVE	raise	raises	raising	raised	raised

EXERCISE 11–5 Using *sit/set, lie/lay,* and *rise/raise*

Choose the appropriate verb for the context of the sentence. Example:

He (*rises*/*raises*) his hand in salute.

1. Mr. Anderson just (*lies/lays*) there staring at the wall.
2. After a while she (*rose/raised*) her head up and then (*set/sat*) on the edge of the bed.
3. (*Rise/Raise*) *High the Roofbeam, Carpenters* is the title of a book by J. D. Salinger.
4. Christians believe that Jesus (*rose/raised*) from the dead on the third day after his death.
5. He had (*laid/lain*) in the shade long enough. If his aunt saw him (*laying/lying*) there, she wouldn't like it. So he (*set/sat*) his drink aside and picked up the hedge clippers.

EXERCISE 11–6 Using *lie/lay, sit/set,* and *rise/raise* in Writing

Write a paragraph in which you use the present tense form of *lie/lay, sit/set,* and *rise/raise.* Then rewrite the paragraph changing all the verbs to past tense forms. Possible topics include getting up in the morning; going to bed at night; attending class during the day.

Verb Tenses

Tense indicates when the action of a verb occurs, whether in the past, present, or future.

PAST TENSE	She *wrote.*
PRESENT TENSE	She *writes.*
FUTURE TENSE	She *will write.*

These three tenses are called simple tenses to distinguish them from the perfect, progressive, and perfect progressive tenses. Perfect tenses indicate completed action: She *has written.* Progressive tenses indicate action occurring over time: She *is writing.* Perfect progressive tenses combine the sense of both continuity and completion: She *had been writing.*

Verb Tenses

VERB TENSES	REGULAR VERB	IRREGULAR VERB
Simple present	He *cooks*	She *eats*
Simple past	He *cooked*	She *ate*
Simple future	He *will cook*	She *will eat*
Present perfect	He *has cooked*	She *has eaten*
Past perfect	He *had cooked*	She *had eaten*
Future perfect	He *will have cooked*	She *will have eaten*
Present progressive	He *is cooking*	She *is eating*
Past progressive	He *was cooking*	She *was eating*
Future progressive	He *will be cooking*	She *will be eating*
Present perfect progressive	He *has been cooking*	She *has been eating*
Past perfect progressive	He *had been cooking*	She *had been eating*
Future perfect progressive	He *will have been cooking*	She *will have been eating*

 Simple tenses

The **simple tenses** are the most familiar and the most frequently used in speech and writing. They refer to action in the basic time frames of past, present, and future.

 Present tense

The **present tense** designates action occurring at the time of speaking or writing: *She lives in Toronto.* It is used to indicate habitual actions: *I exercise every morning.* It is also used to express general truths (*Time flies*) and scientific knowledge (*Light travels faster than sound*). In addition, the simple present can refer to future events: *The program airs next Saturday.* And it is conventionally used in discussing literary and artistic works that have been created in the past: *Michelangelo's sculpture of David stands more than eighteen feet high; Georgia O'Keeffe's paintings of flowers express an intensely passionate vision of life.*

Forms of the simple present

SINGULAR   I *work.* You *work.* He/She/It *works.*

PLURAL   We *work.* You *work.* They *work.*

In the present tense, the -*s* ending always appears on the third-person singular form.

Present tense also has some special uses:

* to indicate future time:

We *travel* to Italy next week.

Michael *returns* in the morning.

* to describe works of literature and the arts:

Hamlet *avoids* avenging his father's death for one reason.

Van Gogh *portrays* a sleeping village beneath a roiling sky.

See 47d for more on using verb tenses when writing about the arts.

2   Past tense

The **past tense** indicates action that occurred in the past and that does not extend into the present: *Bill worked on his history report for more than a month.* Unlike the simple present tense, the simple past tense has no additional special uses.

Forms of the simple past

SINGULAR   I *worked.* You *worked.* He/She/It *worked.*

PLURAL   We *worked.* You *worked.* They *worked.*

In the past tense, the verb ending remains the same in all singular and plural forms.

3   Future tense

The **future tense** indicates action that has not yet begun: *Julia will try to get us all free tickets for the game.* Verbs in the simple future tense almost always contain the auxiliary verb *will.*

Forms of the simple future

SINGULAR   I *will work.* You *will work.* He/She/It *will work.*

PLURAL   We *will work.* You *will work.* They *will work.*

USAGE NOTE   *Shall* sometimes replaces *will* in the first-person form to express determination or resolve: *I shall not fail; We shall overcome.* **Shall** is often used for first-person questions that request an opinion or seek consent. *Shall we see a movie this weekend? Shall we begin?* To use *will* in these cases would change the meaning considerably. In addition, *shall* appears frequently in commands (*Thou shall not kill*) and stipulations (*Skiers shall leave the slopes before dark*).

11g   Perfect tenses

The **perfect tenses** express more complex time relationships than do the simple tenses. They generally indicate an action that has been completed before another action begins or an action finished by a specific time. Perfect tenses consist of a past participle preceded by the present, past, or future form of the auxiliary verb *have.*

1   Present perfect tense

The **present perfect tense** indicates that an action or its effects, begun in the past, either ended at some time in the past or continues into the present.

I *have enjoyed* many movies in recent years.

They *have agreed* to iron out their differences.

We *have eaten* the plums.

She *has spoken* to the manager already.

Forms of the present perfect (*have* or *has* + past participle)

SINGULAR   I *have worked.* You *have worked.* He/She/It *has worked.*

PLURAL   We *have worked.* You *have worked.* They *have worked.*

2   Past perfect tense

The **past perfect tense** designates an action that has been completed prior to another past action. It indicates a time further back in the past than the present perfect tense or the simple past tense.

He *had planned* to travel this summer until airfares skyrocketed.

They *had expected* to wait a few years to purchase their home; however, with mortgage interest rates declining, they decided to act now.

We *had done* everything possible.

The group *had sung* its last song when the lights went out.

Forms of the past perfect (*had* + past participle)

SINGULAR   I *had worked.* You *had worked.* He/She/It *had worked.*

PLURAL   We *had worked.* You *had worked.* They *had worked.*

3   Future perfect tense

The **future perfect tense** indicates that an action will be completed at some future time.

I *will have finished* reading *Emma* by the time of the final exam.

By the weekend, she *will have prepared* for the holiday celebrations.

Forms of the future perfect (*will have* + past participle)

SINGULAR   I *will have worked.* You *will have worked.*
                  He/She/It *will have worked.*

PLURAL   We *will have worked.* You *will have worked.* They *will have worked.*

11h   Progressive tenses

Progressive tenses indicate action that is continuing in the present, past, or future. They are constructed with a present participle (the *-ing* form) and the present, past, future, present perfect, past perfect, or future perfect form of the verb *be*.

Each of the six progressive tenses corresponds to one of the three simple and three perfect tenses.

1   Present progressive tense

The **present progressive tense** conveys a sense of ongoing action.

I *am requesting* financial aid for next year.

We *are attempting* to resolve some thorny interpersonal conflicts.

Forms of the present progressive (*am, is,* or *are* + present participle)

SINGULAR   I *am working.* You *are working.* He/She/It *is working.*

PLURAL   We *are working.* You *are working.* They *are working.*

2   Past progressive tense

The **past progressive tense** conveys a continuing past action.

They *were driving* through the mountains when they heard the news about the fall of the Berlin Wall.

Forms of the past progressive (*was* or *were* + present participle)

SINGULAR   I *was working.* You *were working.* He/She/It *was working.*

PLURAL   We *were working.* You *were working.* They *were working.*

 3   Future progressive tense

The **future progressive tense** suggests continuing action in the future.

I *will be listening* with my heart in my throat as my daughter performs at her violin recital.

They *will be trying* for the third time to make the Olympic bobsled team.

Forms of the future progressive (*will be* + present participle)

SINGULAR   I *will be working.* You *will be working.* He/She/It *will be working.*

PLURAL   We *will be working.* You *will be working.* They *will be working.*

4   Present perfect progressive tense

The **present perfect progressive tense** indicates an action that began in the past and continues into the present.

Christine *has been running* her own business for more than ten years.

She and her friend Sam *have been working* together harmoniously all that time.

Forms of the present perfect progressive (*have been* or *has been* + present participle)

SINGULAR   I *have been working.* You *have been working.*
He/She/It *has been working.*

PLURAL   We *have been working.* You *have been working.*
They *have been working.*

5   Past perfect progressive tense

The **past perfect progressive tense** suggests a continuing action that ended before another action.

He *had been studying* Italian for years before he ever visited Italy.

They *had been sending* relief supplies to Sarajevo when the United Nations curtailed the shipments.

Forms of the past perfect progressive (*had been* + present participle)

SINGULAR   I *had been working.* You *had been working.*
He/She/It *had been working.*

PLURAL   We *had been working.* You *had been working.*
They *had been working.*

6   Future perfect progressive tense

The **future perfect progressive tense** indicates a continuing action that will end at a future time.

In ten minutes I *will have been reading* for four consecutive hours.

By the time she is twenty years old, she *will have been dancing* for more than three-quarters of her life.

Forms of the future perfect progressive (*will have been* + present participle)

SINGULAR   I *will have been working.* You *will have been working.*
He/She/It *will have been working.*

PLURAL   We *will have been working.* You *will have been working.*
They *will have been working.*

WRITING HINT   Always check your verb tenses when you edit and proofread your writing. Look at sentences where you have shifted tenses to ensure that those shifts are necessary. Avoid shifts between past and present tenses.

INCONSISTENT   Smithers *is* a loyal employee. He rarely *left* the office until all his work *was* completed.

CONSISTENT   Smithers *is* a loyal employee. He rarely *leaves* the office until all his work *is* completed.

INCONSISTENT   Later I *started* to think about the assignment. I *realize* that I *am* procrastinating again.

CONSISTENT   Later I *started* to think about the assignment. I *realized* that I *was* procrastinating again.

EXERCISE 11–7   **Using Verb Tenses**

For each of the following sentences, provide the correct tense form for the verb in parentheses. Example:

When the night class ended, everyone (*head*) <u>headed</u> for the parking lot.

1. Because of the heavy rains that (*fall*) _____ this past week, low-lying areas (*flood*) _____ .

2. The demand for a good product or service (*increase*) _____ when the price is right.

3. If you begin work right after college, you (*work*) _____ for a quarter century by the time you (*be*) _____ in your mid-forties.

4. Once a book engages your attention, it (*become*) _____ difficult to put down.

5. Martin Luther King, Jr. (*preach*) _____ many memorable sermons and (*give*) _____ a number of historic speeches.

6. Our copy of *Road and Track* (*arrive*) _____ late for the third straight month.

7. If it snows again today, it (*snow*) _____ nineteen days out of the past twenty.

8. Thousands of Romanian gypsies (*leave*) _____ Germany unwillingly in the early 1990s.

9. In Walt Disney's *Fantasia*, Mickey Mouse (*be*) _____ a leading character.

10. By six this evening, we (*hear*) _____ the results of the vote.

EXERCISE 11–8   Using Perfect and Progressive Verb Tense Forms

Write a paragraph in which you use perfect tense verbs and progressive tense verbs. Possible topics include a sport you watch or play; an activity you enjoy; an experience you had; an event from the news.

 Verb tense sequences

In writing and speaking you often combine a range of verb tenses to discuss your point. You have to keep the time relationships among events clear by carefully choosing your verb forms to reflect a logical sequence of tenses. **Tense sequence** refers to the relationship between the tense of a verb in an independent clause and the tense of a verb in a dependent clause. These verb tenses must follow patterns so that a passage is clear and makes sense. Consider the following examples.

> When I *study*, I often *listen* to music. [Because the two actions occur simultaneously and because they are habitual acts, the verbs are both in the simple present tense.]

> If I *get up* now, I *will have* time for breakfast. [The two acts occur in sequence, the first in the present and the second in the future; the verbs, thus, are in present and future tenses, respectively.]

> Few people *know* what actually *happened*. [This sentence refers to the knowledge of the present about an event of the past.]

Few people *knew* what actually *happened*. [This sentence refers to what people knew at the time the event occurred rather than to what people know now.]

Here is an example in which the sequence of tenses is unclear and does not make sense.

Our friends *travel* often because they *enjoyed* it. [If the enjoying is past, then why do the friends still travel? The two actions are not sensibly related.]

Here are two better alternatives.

Our friends *travel* often because they *enjoy* going to new places.

Our friends *traveled* often because they *enjoyed* going to new places.

1 Infinitives and verb tense sequences

An infinitive in the present tense consists of *to* and the base form of the verb (*to discover, to ask*). Use the present tense infinitive to indicate a time equivalent to or a time later than that of the main verb.

EQUIVALENT TIME	He refuses *to vote* in the upcoming election. [His refusing and voting are both happening in the present.]
LATER TIME	They had planned *to attend* the party. [The planning occurred before the attending.]

An infinitive in the past tense consists of *to have* followed by the past participle of the verb (*to have worked, to have written*). Use past (or perfect) infinitives to indicate action earlier than that of the main verb.

They seem *to have gone* home early.

2 Participles and verb tense sequences

A **present participle** (the *-ing* form of the verb) shows action that occurs at the same time as that of the main verb, whatever the tense of the main verb.

Giving his students a second chance, the teacher *retested* them on the course work covered up to that point. [The teacher's giving occurs at the same time as the retesting.]

The **present perfect participle** (*having* + past participle) reflects action that occurs before that of the main verb.

Having convinced the jury, the defense lawyers rested their case. [The defense lawyers convince the jury, then rest their case.]

The **past participle** shows action that occurs before that of the main verb or at the same time as the main verb.

Convinced by the evidence the defense lawyers presented, the jury decided on a verdict of not guilty. [The jury is convinced before it decides.]

EXERCISE 11–9 Using Verb Tense Sequences

Examine the sequence of verb tense in each of the following sentences. Correct any verb tense sequences that are incorrect. Example:

Gabriele will attend the party after she ~~will complete~~ her accounting problems.

1. Robert Redford directed his first movie after he had acted in many others.
2. During the years Redford was learning his craft as an actor, he also learns much about directing.
3. Firefighters believe that to perform their work properly, they needed sufficient training and proper equipment.
4. I will have gone if I can. But I won't go if I could not have.
5. Unprepared for the test's level of difficulty, the students decided to boycott it rather than take it.
6. Trying hard to impress his new boss, Tom had made a few mistakes.
7. Having worked hard all summer as a waiter at a steakhouse, he decided to take a long weekend trip with his friends before returning to college.
8. Unless both parties of the dispute begin to listen to one another seriously, the current unhappy state of affairs continues.
9. Being seen at the popular club is all that will matter to them.
10. Being seen at the popular club was all that matters to them.

Voice

Voice refers to the relationship between the subject and the verb. If the subject performs the action, the verb is in the **active voice.** (Alice *opened* the bottle.) If the subject is acted upon, the verb is in the **passive voice.** (The bottle *was opened* by Alice.)

11j Uses of the active voice

Use the active voice when you want to emphasize who or what performed the action.

Active and Passive Voices

VERB TENSES	ACTIVE	PASSIVE
Present	She *invites* us.	She *is invited.*
Past	She *invited* us.	She *was invited.*
Future	She *will invite* us.	She *will be invited.*
Present Perfect	She *has invited* us.	She *has been invited.*
Past Perfect	She *had invited* us.	She *had been invited.*
Future Perfect	She *will have invited* us.	She *will have been invited.*

Michael *ate* the fudge royale ice cream.

Writers typically prefer the active voice because it makes for tighter, more vigorous prose. For example, consider the difference between the preceding active voice example and its passive voice counterpart.

The fudge royale ice cream *was eaten* by Michael.

The first sentence, written in the active voice, emphasizes Michael and what he did; the second sentence emphasizes ice cream and is longer than the first.

To invigorate your writing, use the active voice as much as possible. When you revise and edit your drafts, check for passive voice verbs you can rewrite in the active voice. You will not only strengthen your prose but reduce its wordiness as well (see 26b).

Notice how Barbara Tuchman effectively uses the active voice in the following paragraph, which emphasizes the subjects and their actions.

> One learns to write, I have since discovered, in the practice thereof. After seven years' apprenticeship in journalism I discovered that an essential element for good writing is a good ear. One must *listen* to the sound of one's own prose. This, I think, is one of the failings of much American writing. Too many writers do not listen to the sound of their own words. For example, listen to this sentence from the organ of my own discipline, the *American Historical Review:* "His presentation is not vitiated historically by efforts at expository simplicity." In one short sentence five long Latin words of four or five syllables each. One has to read it three times over and take time out to think, before one can even make out what it means.
>
> —Barbara Tuchman, "In Search of History"

11k Uses of the passive voice

The passive voice indicates that the grammatical subject of a sentence receives the action of the verb. In fact, it reverses the relationship between subject and verb established in the active voice. Verbs in the passive voice always include a form of the verb *be* immediately preceding the past participle of the main verb.

Use the passive voice when the performer of an action is either unknown or considered relatively unimportant.

The car radiator *was repaired* while its owner went to lunch.

The game *was played* outdoors under a sunny, cloudless sky.

It *was decided* that some form of community service would be required.

The passive voice is sometimes used to avoid acknowledging responsibility.

It *was decided* that discounts would no longer be available. [Who decided?]

As a reader, you may wish to know who or what is responsible for a particular action and thus need to question speakers or writers who use the passive voice in this way. However, in situations where the event is more important than who or what caused it, the passive voice is especially useful. Descriptions of historical events and scientific developments, for example, often contain passive voice verbs. Notice how passive voice verbs enable the writer of the following passage to emphasize the historical importance of investment capital rather than the individuals involved in the events described.

Investment capital was used to finance development in the British Isles and abroad. In America, the Louisiana Purchase of 1803 was financed by two private London banks, Hope's and Baring's. Railways, harbors, and services of all kinds in cities round the world were financed from London, and designed by British engineers using plants and equipment made in Britain. The Galleria, the great shopping arcade of Milan, was a London project. But inevitably city capital was also used to help finance the growth and rebuilding of London itself.

—Mark Girard, *Cities and People*

EXERCISE 11–10 Working with Active and Passive Voice Verbs

Underline the active and passive voice verbs in the following sentences. Then rewrite the sentences so the active verbs become passive voice and the passive verbs become active voice. Explain the difference between the two versions for each sentence. Example:

The book *was read* by the class over a period of weeks.

The class *read* the book over a period of weeks. [changed to active voice; *The class* is emphasized in the active voice]

1. The roast was eaten by my brother and his roommates.
2. Thousands of manuscripts were hand-copied by monks in the Middle Ages.

3. The game was won by the Mariners in the ninth inning.
4. It was decided that there would be a tuition increase of 10 percent.
5. The answers on *Jeopardy!* are given by the host and the questions are provided by the contestants.
6. The contestants' answers, however, must be phrased as questions.
7. Historians presented other explanations for the event.
8. Scientists offer conflicting accounts of the origin of the universe.
9. American automakers were pressured to improve the quality and value of their products by intense foreign competition.
10. A lot of fun was had by all of us.

EXERCISE 11–11 Using Active and Passive Voice Verbs

Select a recent paper you wrote for one of your classes. Identify each verb in the paper as active or passive. Consider in each case whether you can tighten and strengthen your writing by converting some of the verbs in one voice into the other.

Mood

The **mood** of a verb refers to the writer's attitude toward what is being said or written. Verbs in the **indicative mood** state a fact, declare an opinion, or ask a question.

Columbus *is* generally *credited* with discovering America. [states a fact]

The contribution Columbus made to history *needs* reexamination. [declares an opinion]

Did Columbus *think* he had arrived in India, when he had actually landed in Central America? [asks a question]

Verbs in the **imperative mood** give directions or express requests or commands. Imperative verbs, which never change form, can appear without an explicit subject (*you* is understood as the subject).

Mr. James, please *give* this letter to Mrs. Jones.

Michael and Karen, *stop* that shouting right now!

Study the first four chapters for tomorrow's test.

Verbs in the **subjunctive mood** express wishes, stipulate demands or requirements, and make statements contrary to fact. They often appear in clauses introduced by *that* or *if*.

I wish that I *were* six feet two instead of five feet eight.

The course requires that a student *attend* class faithfully and *complete* written work on schedule.

If everyone *were* a liar, communication would be impossible.

Use the base form of the verb for the present tense of the subjunctive.

The first consideration is that the core curriculum *be* established.

The second concern is that it *remain* in place for at least five years.

In using the past tense of the subjunctive of *be,* use *were* for all subjects. (All other verbs are identical in the past indicative and past subjunctive.)

If I *were* you, I would accept the offer.

If you *were* smart, you would accept the offer.

If we *were* not so comfortable, we might strive for more.

The subjunctive mood is also important for indirect discourse (see p. 354). Use the subjunctive when making a strong suggestion or a recommendation.

We suggested that Mary go to the doctor.

The recommendation was that Jay apply for early admission.

Uses of the Subjunctive

1. When expressing a wish:

    I wish he *were* more upset by what has happened.

    Gwen sometimes wished that her friends *were* still unmarried.

2. When expressing a state contrary to fact in an *if* clause:

    If the new medication *were* to be proven safe, many of the restrictions governing its use would be lifted.

    If the public works project *were* approved, many people would find jobs.

3. When using clauses beginning with *as if* and *as though:*

    The captain of the football team acted as if he *were* a hero.

    During the 1980s, some stockbrokers traded high-risk "junk" bonds as though they *were* safe investments.

4. When expressing a demand, request, or recommendation in clauses beginning with *that:*

    The preacher suggested that she *make* a generous contribution.

    The position requires that all candidates *be* college graduates.

The Conditional

Although the conditional is not actually a mood of verbs, it is often confused with the subjunctive and thus deserves consideration along with the subjunctive mood.

Using conditional sentences

A **conditional** sentence does one of three things:

1. It indicates a relation between cause and effect.
2. It makes a prediction.
3. It speculates about what might occur.

Focusing on questions of truth, conditional sentences typically begin with *if* or an equivalent word, such as *when* or *unless*. Conditional sentences contain clauses that depend on one another, with the truth of one clause dependent on the truth of the other.

If you come home tomorrow, I will take you out to dinner.

Notice that the conditional clause, introduced by *if*, is in the present tense. This is a simple statement of a possibility that could become a fact. The conditional differs from the subjunctive, which states a condition contrary to fact but is also often introduced by *if*.

If you were here now, I would take you out to dinner.

In this example, it is clear that the *you* referred to is not present. Notice that the verb in the main clause follows the rules for verb tense sequence that govern the subjunctive (see p. 266).

Not all conditional sentences, however, begin with *if*. Some sentences that stress a factual relation between clauses begin with *when*.

When instructors *are* absent, they *request* substitutes.

This sentence suggests that when something happens (*instructors are absent*), something else happens (*they request substitutes*). In sentences that suggest a link between past events, use the past tense.

When instructors *were* absent, they *requested* substitutes.

In writing sentences that make predictions, you can usually use the present tense in the subordinate clause and the future for the main clause.

present   future

Until students *complain* about absent teachers, nothing *will be done* about the problem.

In writing sentences that speculate about future possibilities, follow one of these two procedures.

1. For unlikely though possible present events, use the past tense in the subordinate clause and *would, could,* or *might* with the main form of the verb for the main clause.

      past   *would* + verb

If gamblers *had* more money, they *would gamble* more often.

Use the same forms for impossible and contrary-to-fact events in the present:

      past   *might* + verb

If education *were* free, more students *might seek* it.

2. For impossible past events, use the past perfect tense in the subordinate clause and *would, could,* or *might* with the present perfect tense for the main clause.

            past perfect

If the City University of New York *had never imposed* tuition, more students

could, would, or *might* + present perfect

could (would or *might) have attended* what was once the largest free university system in the country.

EXERCISE 11–12   Using the Subjunctive

Revise the verbs in the following sentences that are not in the appropriate subjunctive form. Some sentences may be correct as written. Example:

          were
She moves as if she ~~was~~ a professional dancer.

1. If Dr. Shank was named to the committee, I would resign.
2. He treated her as if she was still a child.
3. The student senate recommended that the fees are lowered.
4. Thomas would give me his ticket if he were a true friend.
5. They proposed that David speaks on their behalf.

Grammar and Writing

Using Strong Verbs

You can put your knowledge of verbs to use in your writing in many ways. First, you can check your writing for accuracy in using verb forms. You can also check for correctness in using tenses, especially verb-tense sequences. And you can make sure that verbs reflecting different moods—indicative, imperative, subjunctive—carry the appropriate tenses.

You can improve your writing by focusing closely on the verbs you use most often. Look over a recent piece of writing and underline or circle the verbs. Check to see if you rely heavily on certain verbs, such as forms of *be, do,* and *have.* Check, too, for other recurring verbs. Then revise by supplying more varied verbs, making them as specific and concrete as possible.

EXAMPLE

On the first day of my trip I [had] *experienced* a headache, but I [had] *ate* a big breakfast
anyway before I [had to] meet *ing* my friends at our campsite.

Focus next on verb voice—active or passive voices. Change some of your passive voice verbs to active voice—especially those that use *is, was, are,* or *were.* Strive here, too, to choose specific concrete verbs.

EXAMPLE

Many kinds of stories are included in the book, but the ones I am most interested in are about love.

REVISED

The book includes many kinds of stories, but those about love interest me most.

CHAPTER 12

Nouns, Pronouns, and Case

 Understanding nouns

A **noun** names a person (*singer, Whitney Houston*), place (*city, Miami*), thing (*car, Volvo*), concept (*justice*), or quality (*depth*). Nouns can be common or proper. **Common nouns** refer to classes—to any person, place, thing, concept, or general quality. **Proper nouns** name specific persons, places, things, concepts, or qualities.

COMMON NOUNS	PROPER NOUNS
judge	Ruth Bader Ginsberg
city	Indianapolis
dog	Fido
book	*Madame Bovary*
philosophy	Platonism

Nouns can also fall in a continuum of "abstract" or "concrete." **Abstract nouns** name concepts, ideas, or qualities—that is, things not experienced by the senses. An abstract noun is usually not preceded by an article (*a, an, the*) unless it is modified (see 16c). **Concrete nouns** refer to things we know through our senses of sight, hearing, touch, taste, or smell.

ABSTRACT NOUNS	CONCRETE NOUNS
happiness	smile
religion	priest
fertility	egg

Nouns can be either singular (naming one) or plural (naming more than one). Plurals are typically formed by adding *-s* or *-es* to the singular noun form: *flute/flutes; war/wars; potato/potatoes* (see 31d). Some nouns, however, have irregular plural forms: *mouse/mice; tooth/teeth*. Nouns derived from French, Greek, and Latin sometimes retain the plural of the original language: *alumnus/alumni; crisis/crises*. Many such nouns have two plural forms—the original foreign plural (*curricula*) and one that follows the regular English pattern for making plurals (*curriculums*). Your dictionary will provide information about irregular plural forms.

In addition to proper or common, plural or singular, a noun can be classified as count, mass, or collective. A **count noun** is a noun that can be counted and has a regular plural form: *book/books; brick/bricks.* A **mass noun** (sometimes called a **noncount noun**) is a noun that cannot be counted and, thus, cannot be made plural: *dust, news, health, peace, money, research, homework.* Qualifiers such as *some, much,* and *amount* often accompany mass nouns: *some dust, much news, an amount of money.* A **collective noun** names a group and usually keeps a singular form: *team, family, herd, school, crowd.*

Nouns are usually introduced by determiners. **Determiners** act like markers, or signals, that a noun will soon follow. A determiner limits the meaning of a noun and comes before any adjectives that describe the same noun. In the phrases *his new car* and *that green coat,* the words *his* and *that* are determiners. Although many words, including possessives, can act as determiners in a sentence, the most common by far are the **articles** *a, an,* and *the. The,* which introduces a particular noun, is a **definite article.** *A* and *an,* which introduce general nouns, are **indefinite articles.** The indefinite article *a* is used before words beginning with a consonant (*a minute, a new book*); *an* is used before words beginning with a vowel or an unpronounced *h* (*an old book, an hour*).

USAGE NOTE   When putting an indefinite article before a letter or a set of letters (such as an acronym or an abbreviation), choose *a* or *an* according to how the first letter is pronounced (not whether the letter itself is a consonant or a vowel).

> *a* U.N. resolution (*U* is pronounced "yoo.")
>
> *an* NRA member (*N* is pronounced "en.")
>
> *a* CD player (*C* is pronounced "see.")
>
> *an* F in math (*F* is pronounced "ef.")

12b   Understanding pronouns

Pronouns take the place of nouns that precede or follow them in sentences. The noun that a pronoun refers to is called its **antecedent.** (See 15k–m.)

> The *doctor* would operate only if *she* had a good prognosis for success. [The antecedent of the pronoun *she* is the noun *doctor.*]
>
> The *dog* waited for *its* owner at the apartment entrance. [The antecedent of the pronoun *its* is the noun *dog.*]

You can use pronouns to introduce variety in sentences, to avoid repeating the same nouns. You can also use them to make your sentences and paragraphs more coherent (see 8c-1). In using pronouns, be sure that they agree with their antecedents in gender and number (see 15k–n).

Pronouns

Type of pronoun	Function

PERSONAL

I, me, my, mine
we, us, our, ours
you, your, yours
he, she, it, him, her, his, hers, its
they, them, their, theirs

Refer to people or things.

They moved to a bigger apartment.

Theirs is bigger than *ours*.

I want *him* to find *us* a new apartment.

DEMONSTRATIVE

this, that, these, those

Point to the nouns they replace.

These are the freshest tomatoes.

INDEFINITE

all, another, any, anybody, anyone, anything, both, each, either, everybody, everyone, everything, few, many, more, most, much, nobody, none, no one, nothing, one, several, some, somebody, someone, something

Refer to unspecified people or things, or to quantity.

Everyone came, but hardly *anyone* ate.

No one knows about *everything*.

A *few* drank *some* wine.

RELATIVE

that, what, whatever, which, whichever, who, whoever, whom, whomever, whose

Introduce clauses that modify nouns or pronouns.

He is a speaker *whose* voice carries.

Whatever you do, do not say *who* told you.

INTERROGATIVE

what, whatever, which, whichever, who, whoever, whom, whomever, whose

Introduce questions.

Who was there?

Which route should we take?

REFLEXIVE

myself, yourself
himself, herself
itself, oneself
ourselves, yourselves
themselves

Refer back to the subject of the clause in which they appear.

They surprised *themselves*.

You have no one to blame but *yourself*.

INTENSIVE

(same as reflexives)

Emphasize their antecedents.

I will do it *myself*.

RECIPROCAL

each other, one another

Indicate mutuality or reciprocity.

They helped *one another*.

Pronouns are classified as personal, demonstrative, indefinite, relative, interrogative, reflexive, intensive, and reciprocal. **Personal pronouns** refer to people or things. They show distinctions among three grammatical "persons": first-person pronouns (*I, we*) refer to the speaker or writer; second-person pronouns (*you*) refer to the person addressed or spoken to; and third-person pronouns (*he, she, it, they*) refer to the person or thing that is being spoken or written about.

> *Our* children like to be independent, but when *they* get into trouble *they* expect *us* to bail *them* out.

Demonstrative pronouns (*this, that, these, those*) point to the nouns they replace.

> *This* is the museum where I bought *those* prints for your birthday.

Indefinite pronouns refer to unspecified people or things (such as *any, anybody, everything, nobody, somebody*). They also express a quantity (such as *all, both, each, few, most, none, one, some*). Indefinite pronouns do not require an antecedent.

> *Nobody* claimed the prize.

Relative pronouns (such as *who, whom, which, that*) introduce clauses that modify nouns or pronouns.

> The letter *that* just arrived is from an old friend *who* lives in Spain.

Some relative pronouns (such as *what, whoever, whichever, whatever*) are indefinite and do not require an antecedent in the sentence.

> Order *whatever* you want from the menu.

Interrogative pronouns (such as *who, which, what*) introduce questions.

> *Who* is the political leader of Malawi, and *what* is his title?

Reflexive pronouns (such as *myself, yourself, himself, herself, itself, yourselves, themselves*) refer to the subject of the clause in which they appear.

> The performers are sure of *themselves* when they are on stage.

Reflexive pronouns are used as direct objects or objects of a preposition.

Intensive pronouns emphasize their antecedents. They have the same form as reflexive pronouns, but they do not perform a grammatical function in a sentence. In fact, an intensive pronoun can be removed without changing the meaning of the sentence.

> He vowed to raise the money *himself.*

Reciprocal pronouns (*each other* and *one another*) refer to separate parts of a plural antecedent.

> Sven and Reena helped *each other* complete the grueling experiment.

> The team members encouraged *one another* throughout the competition.

EXERCISE 12–1 Identifying Pronouns

In each of the following sentences, underline the pronoun once and its antecedent twice. Some sentences may not have antecedents. Example:

Barry and Sylvia bought their tickets at the stadium.

1. Miguel will figure out a solution himself.
2. These are my folders, those are yours.
3. The audience that applauded the panelists also thanked them.
4. When the workers finished setting up for the carnival, they headed home.
5. Do you know who is responsible for granting waivers from required courses?
6. Until then, whatever you would like is fine with us.
7. Somebody tore the pages right out of the book.

12c Understanding pronoun case forms

Pronouns change form to reflect their function in a sentence. The function of a pronoun, its role in a phrase or clause, is indicated by its **case**. Pronouns may appear in the subjective (or nominative), objective, or the possessive case (see the accompanying chart, Pronoun Case).

Pronoun Case

Personal pronouns

Singular	SUBJECTIVE	OBJECTIVE	POSSESSIVE
First person	I	me	my, mine
Second person	you	you	your, yours
Third person	he, she, it	him, her, it	his, her, hers, its

Plural			
First person	we	us	our, ours
Second person	you	you	your, yours
Third person	they	them	their, theirs

Relative and interrogative pronouns

	SUBJECTIVE	OBJECTIVE	POSSESSIVE
	who	whom	whose
	whoever	whomever	

USAGE NOTE   Possessive personal pronouns never include an apostrophe. *Its* is a possessive pronoun. *It's* is a contraction of *it is* or *it has*. Similarly, *whose* is a possessive pronoun; *who's* is a contraction of *who is* or *who has*.

1   Subjective case forms

Use the **subjective case** form of a pronoun when it is the subject of a clause, is a subject complement, or is an appositive to a subject or a subject complement. (See 10a-1 for subjects, 10b-3 for complements, and 10c-2 for appositives.)

SUBJECT OF A CLAUSE

We can be either cooperative or confrontational. [independent clause]

Since *he* is the best choice, Bill should get the job. [dependent clause]

SUBJECT COMPLEMENT

It is *they* who ought to be doing this work.

The last people to leave the room were *he* and *I*.

APPOSITIVES

Two players, *Carol* and *I*, represented the team.

USAGE NOTE   In conversation, you may sometimes use objective case forms of pronouns when formal written grammar requires subjective case forms. For example, in responding to a question such as, "Are you Carmela Shiu?," you might answer, "Yes, that's *me*," rather than "Yes, that's *I*." *Me* sounds more natural because that form of the pronoun is used more often in speech. However, *I* is grammatically correct in this instance. In informal situations, you have considerable flexibility with this usage. In formal writing, however, use the grammatically correct case forms for all pronouns.

2   Objective case forms

Use the **objective case** form of a pronoun when it is the direct or indirect object of a verb or verbal, when it is the object of a preposition, or when it comes before an infinitive verb.

PRONOUN AS OBJECT OF A VERB OR VERBAL

Some restaurant wines are so expensive that only connoisseurs order *them*.

When he handed *her* the flowers, she gave *him* a warm smile.

PRONOUN AS OBJECT OF A PREPOSITION

With *him* I always have a good time.

Everything was a joke to *them*.

PRONOUN BEFORE AN INFINITIVE

It was hard for *them* to hear the speech over the protesters' chants.

My mother never asked *us* to clear the table.

3 Possessive case forms

Use the **possessive case** form when a pronoun indicates ownership. Possessive pronouns can appear as adjective forms (*my, your, his, her, its, our, their*), which occur before nouns or gerunds; and as possessive forms (*mine, yours, his, hers, its, ours, theirs*), which replace possessive nouns.

In O. Henry's story "The Gift of the Magi," a young husband sells *his* watch to buy *his* wife a fancy comb to use on *her* abundant hair.

They gave away *their* tickets for the game.

The pleasure is *mine*.

Ours is the hardest but most wonderful challenge of all.

WRITING HINT   In your writing, when a pronoun appears before a gerund (an *-ing* verbal used as a noun), use the possessive case: We have tasted *their* cooking. In this example, *cooking* is used as a noun and is the direct object of *have tasted*. If a pronoun appears before a participle, use the objective case: We have watched *them* cooking. In this second example, *cooking* is used as a participle to describe *them*.

EXERCISE 12–2 Supplying Missing Pronouns

Supply the pronouns that have been eliminated from the following passage.

I am a writer. And by that definition, _____ am someone who has always loved language. _____ am fascinated by language in daily life. _____ spend a great deal of _____ time thinking about the power of language—the way _____ can evoke an emotion, a visual image, a complex idea, or a simple truth. Language is the tool of _____ trade. And _____ use them all—all the Englishes _____ grew up with.

　　Recently _____ was made keenly aware of the different Englishes _____ do use. I was giving a talk to a large group of people, the same talk _____ had already given to half a dozen other groups. The nature of the talk was about _____ writing, _____ life, and _____ book, *The Joy Luck Club*. The talk was going along well enough, until _____ remembered one major difference that made the whole talk sound wrong. _____ mother was in the room. And _____ was perhaps the first time _____ had heard _____ give a lengthy speech, using the kind of English _____ have never used with _____—all the forms of standard English that _____ had learned in school and through books, the forms of English _____ did not use at home with _____ mother.

Just last week, I was walking down the street with _____ mother, and _____ again found _____ conscious of the English _____ was using, the English _____ do use with _____. _____ were talking about the price of new and used furniture and _____ heard _____ saying this: "Not waste money that way." _____ husband was with _____ as well, and _____ didn't notice any switch in _____ English. And then _____ realized why. It's because over the twenty years _____ have been together, _____ have often used that same kind of English with _____, and sometimes _____ even uses _____ with _____. _____ has become _____ language of intimacy, a different sort of English _____ relates to family talk, the language _____ grew up with.

—Amy Tan, "Mother Tongue"

EXERCISE 12–3   Using Pronoun Case

Fill in each blank with the appropriate form—subjective, objective, or possessive—of the pronoun in parentheses. Example:

The police officer gave (*he*) __him__ a stern warning.

1. Betty's friends urged (*she*) _____ to quit smoking.
2. I watched (*they*) _____ playing soccer.
3. His co-workers were angry at (*he*) _____ refusal to join the strike.
4. The first two contestants, Tonya Sanchez and (*I*) _____ , were scheduled to appear at the same time.
5. Laurel's mother gets annoyed at (*we*) _____ because we call each other late at night.
6. The last piece of pizza is mine, not (*you*) _____.
7. This chair has one of (*it*) _____ legs missing.

12d   Using *who* and *whom*

It is not always easy to decide between the pronouns *who* and *whom* when writing a sentence. *Who* and *whoever* are subjective forms used when the pronoun is the subject of a sentence or clause. *Whom* and *whomever* are objective forms used when the pronoun is the direct or indirect object of a verb or the object of a preposition.

Who gave me this paper? [*Who* is the subject of a sentence.]

Whom will the new tax plan benefit most? [*Whom* is the object of a verb.]

The coach praised *whoever* performed well in practice. [*Whoever* is the subject of a dependent clause.]

Give the letter to *whomever* it is addressed. [*Whomever* is the object of the preposition *to*.]

1   Using *who* and *whom* at the beginning of questions

You can decide whether to use *who* or *whom* at the beginning of a question simply by answering the question with a personal pronoun. If you can answer with a subjective case pronoun (*I, he, she, we, they*), use *who* in the question. If you can answer with an objective case pronoun (*me, him, her, us, them*), use *whom* instead.

Who was at the party? [*They* were at the party. Since *they* is a subjective case pronoun, *who* is the correct form.]

Whom did you ask for help? [I asked *her* for help. Since *her* is an objective case pronoun, *whom* is the correct form.]

Who did you say is coming to the game? [*He* is coming. *He* is subjective case; therefore, *who* is the correct form.]

Whom do you believe? [I believe *her*. *Her* is objective case; therefore, *whom* is the correct form.]

USAGE NOTE   The distinction between *who* and *whom* at the beginning of questions applies to writing but not to speech. In everyday conversation (and in some kinds of informal writing), it is acceptable to use *who* at the beginning of questions like "*Who* will I show it to?" and "*Who* did you bring?"

You can use the guidelines in the accompanying chart to help you decide whether to use *who* or *whom* in questions.

2   Using *who* and *whom* in dependent clauses

In a dependent clause, the case of a pronoun depends on how it functions in that clause. Use *who* or *whoever* if the pronoun functions as the subject of the clause. Use *whom* or *whomever* if the pronoun functions as an object within the clause. It makes no difference how the clause as a whole functions in the sentence; usage is determined by how the pronoun functions in its clause.

She was the candidate *whom* the electorate found most compelling. [*Whom* is the object of the verb *found*. The objective case pronoun is required even though the entire clause refers to the word *candidate*, itself a subject complement.]

Deciding When to Use *who* or *whom* in Questions

1. Ask the question with both forms of the pronoun.

    Who/Whom deserves the biggest bonus?

    Who/Whom should we recommend for promotion?

2. Answer the question with a personal pronoun.

    She/Her deserves the biggest bonus. [Use the subjective personal pronoun.]

    We should recommend he/*him* for promotion. [Use the objective personal pronoun.]

3. Select *who* or *whom* based on the case indicated by the personal pronoun in your answer.

    Who deserves the biggest bonus? [Subjective case, *who*, is correct.]

    Whom should we recommend for promotion? [Objective case, *whom*, is correct.]

Provide pencils and paper for *whoever* may need them. [*Whoever* is the subject of *may need*. The subjective case pronoun is required even though the entire clause is the object of the preposition *for*.]

You can use the accompanying chart to help you decide whether to use *who* or *whom* in dependent clauses.

Deciding When to Use *who* or *whom* in Dependent Clauses

1. Identify the dependent clause.

    Many voters did not know *(who/whom) the minor party candidates were*.

    Most voters, however, know *(who/whom) the major candidates represent*.

2. Separate the subordinate clause, convert it to a statement, and choose a personal pronoun that fits the statement.

    They/them were the minor party candidates. [Use the subjective personal pronoun.]

    The major candidates represent *they/them*. [Use the objective personal pronoun.]

3. Select *who* or *whom* based on the case of the appropriate personal pronoun.

    Many voters did not know *who* the minor party candidates were. [Subjective case, *who*, is correct.]

    Most voters, however, know *whom* the major candidates represent. [Objective case, *whom*, is correct.]

EXERCISE 12–4   **Deciding When to Use *who* and *whom***

For each of the following sentences, underline the correct relative pronoun for use in academic writing. Example:

From *who/whom* did you receive this advice?

1. *Whoever/Whomever* gets home first will have to walk the dog.
2. *Who/Whom* are you to talk like that to her?
3. Richard Nixon was a president *who/whom* was nearly impeached.
4. I want to work for *whoever/whomever* best appreciates my particular talents.
5. She wondered if she could find someone *who/whom* she could get along with.
6. *Who/Whom* do you wish to consider for your advisor?
7. If there were soon to be a benevolent dictator, *who/whom* do you think the likeliest candidate would be?
8. He is someone *who/whom* would try the patience of a saint.
9. There are always those *who/whom* you will have to win over to your cause.
10. *Who/Whom* did this message come from?

 12e   **Using personal pronouns with compound structures**

Deciding on a pronoun for use in compound structures (two or more words joined by *and*, *or*, or *nor*) can be tricky. For compound subjects and objects, use the personal pronoun you would use if the paired word and conjunction were not there. For compound subjects use *I/we/he/she/they;* for compound objects use *me/us/him/her/them.*

SUBJECTS

Michael and I went to see the Red Sox play at Fenway Park. [*I* went to see the Red Sox. Use the subjective personal pronoun. When using compound structures place the first-person pronoun *I* after the other subject.]

SUBJECT COMPLEMENTS

The candidates for class president were *Mariah and she.* [The candidate was *she; she* was the candidate. Use the subjective personal pronoun.]

The next president of the glee club is likely to be *Casey or I.* [*I* am likely to be the next president. Use the subjective personal pronoun.]

OBJECTS

The candidates endorsed by the environmental lobby included Al Gore and *him*. [The candidates endorsed by the environmental lobby included *him*. *Him* is part of the direct object and is in the objective case.]

The president offered a cabinet post to Rodriguez and *her*. [The president offered a cabinet post to *her*. As part of the object of a preposition, *her* is in the objective case.]

The accompanying chart lists guidelines to follow when deciding whether to use a subjective or an objective pronoun in compound structures.

12f   Using personal pronouns with appositives

An **appositive** is a noun, noun phrase, or pronoun that renames the noun or pronoun it immediately follows. A pronoun appositive takes its case from the function of the noun it renames.

Three prominent defense attorneys—F. Lee Bailey, Roy Black, and *she*—boycotted the awards ceremony. [The appositive renames the subject, *attorneys*, so the pronoun is in the subjunctive case.]

The proposed wage increases, unfortunately, never included both groups of workers—the office staff and *us*. [The appositive renames *workers*, the object of the preposition *of*, so the pronoun is in the objective case.]

12g   Using personal pronouns with elliptical constructions

An elliptical construction is one in which some words have been intentionally omitted.

I attend films more frequently than stage plays. [The sentence is understood as *I attend films more frequently than I attend stage plays*.]

When an elliptical construction ends with a pronoun, mentally fill in the missing words of the elliptical construction to determine its grammatical function in the sentence. Once you know the pronoun's grammatical function, you can determine its case.

My father has considerably more mechanical aptitude than *I* [have]. [*I* is the subject of the implied verb *have*.]

Her sister is more artistic than *she* [is]. [*She* is the subject of the implied verb *is*.]

Deciding on Subjective or Objective Pronouns in Compound Structures

1. Separate each element of the compound structure.

   Bill and *she/her* attended the concert.

   Bill attended the concert.

   She attended the concert.

   I attended the concert with Amy and *he/him*.

   I attended the concert with Amy.

   I attended the concert with *him*.

2. Identify the case of the pronoun's function in the new sentence.

   She attended the concert. [*She* is the subject of *attended;* use the subjective.]

   I attended the concert with *him*. [*Him* is the object of *with;* use the objective case.]

3. Use the appropriate pronoun in the compound structure.

   Bill and *she* attended the concert.

   I attended the concert with Amy and *him*.

Miranda likes her cats more than [she likes] *us*. [*Us* is the direct object in the implied complete clause *than she likes us*.]

12h Using *we* and *us* with a noun

You may occasionally use the pronouns *we* or *us* before a noun to help establish the identity of the noun. If the noun is the subject or subject complement of a clause, use *we*.

> *We* athletes should stick together. [*Athletes* is the subject of the sentence; the pronoun paired with it should be in the subjective case—*we*.]

If the noun is a direct object, an indirect object, or an object of a preposition, use *us*.

> The administration never bothered to consult with *us* students. [*Students* is the object of *with;* the pronoun paired with *students* should be in the objective case—*us*.]

To decide whether to use *we* or *us* before a noun, mentally drop the noun and see if the pronoun itself should be in the subjective or the objective: *We should stick together; The administration never bothered to consult with us*.

USAGE NOTE   In conversation it is acceptable to use objective case pronouns after *as, than,* and forms of *be.* In writing, however, you should use the subjective case.

> I am not as clever as *she.*

> You are much shorter than *he.*

> It was *I* who called last night.

If these sentences sound unnatural, try expressing the idea in a different way.

> I am not as clever as *she* is.

> You are much shorter than *he* is.

> *I* was the person who called last night.

12i   Using objective case forms with infinitives

Use objective case pronoun forms as both subject and object of an infinitive.

subject of infinitive

The instructor asked *her* to conduct the class.

object of infinitive

The committee decided to invite *them.*

12j   Using possessive case forms with gerunds

Use the possessive case pronoun form immediately before a gerund. (A gerund is the *-ing* form of a verb used as a noun; e.g., *hiking* is exhilarating. See 10c-2 and 11d-3.)

gerund

They were disappointed with *his* cooking.

Before a participle (an *-ing* verb form used as an adjective), use an objective case form. (See 10c-2 and 11d-3.)

participle

I observed *them* kissing. (emphasis is on *them*)

To emphasize the action rather than those performing the action, use a possessive case pronoun form.

I observed *their* kissing. (emphasis is on *kissing*)

EXERCISE 12–5 Choosing the Appropriate Pronoun

Underline the appropriate pronoun in the following sentences. Example:

The possibility of *him*/<u>*his*</u> leaving never occurred to me.

1. It was unlike *they*/*them* not to call.
2. *Whoever*/*Whomever* wants to attend the play may do so.
3. She is someone *who*/*whom* other people like to be around.
4. The only players *who*/*whom* did not score were *he*/*him* and Ernie.
5. Leah reads novels more often than *I*/*me*.
6. When we were children, we had teachers *who*/*whom* made us study for hours.
7. The subject of *them*/*their* moviegoing never came up.
8. The government needs *we*/*us* taxpayers.
9. Television comedies appeal to *whoever*/*whomever* enjoys a good laugh now and then.
10. *He*/*Him* and his brother drove across country last August.
11. His father disapproved of *his*/*him* lifting weights.
12. The instructor asked *we*/*us* to stop talking.

Grammar and Writing

Controlling Pronoun Case

You can apply your knowledge of pronouns to your writing by focusing on pronoun case forms. Begin by checking over a recent paper for uses of *who* and *whom* and of *we* and *us*. Next, check to see that you have used *he* and *him, she* and *her,* and *they* and *them* correctly. Check as well for pronoun forms preceding any *-ing* verb forms.

Revise one of your papers to reflect appropriate use of pronoun case. Use the charts, guidelines, and usage notes of this chapter as you revise.

EXAMPLE

During [Vincent van Gogh's] last illness, [he] painted furiously, filling
       his   *Vincent van Gogh*
[them] with thick brushstrokes of brilliant color.
his canvases

The painter's brother Theo, who helped support Vincent financially, also
tried to help sell [his] paintings. [Their] close bond is evident in [Vincent's]
                  The brothers'   *their*
letters to [Theo].
     each other   *Vincent's*
                 his brother's

CHAPTER 13

Adjectives and Adverbs

*A*djectives and adverbs are modifiers. They describe, limit, or qualify other words. You can use adjectives and adverbs to add detail to your writing and to make it more vivid. Notice how Kay Boyle uses these modifiers, which we have set in italics, in the following sentence.

> The street that lay between the park and the apartment house was *wide* and the *two-way* stream of cars and busses, some with their headlamps *already shining*, advanced and halted, halted and poured *swiftly* on to the tempo of the *traffic signals' altering* lights.
>
> —Kay Boyle, "Winter Night"

Boyle could have written something simpler and less visual.

> The street was wide and the cars and busses advanced and poured on to the tempo of the traffic lights.

Boyle's original sentence, with its specific modifiers, helps us better imagine the scene than does the alternative sentence.

13a Distinguishing between adjectives and adverbs

Adjectives modify nouns and pronouns. **Adverbs** modify verbs, adjectives, or other adverbs. In the following example, the adjective *fearful* modifies the noun *children* and the adverb *quietly* modifies the verb *entered*.

The *fearful* children entered the house *quietly*.

Here is another example with the adjectives italicized and adverbs in bold print.

> I've come upon animals **suddenly before** and felt a *similar* tension, a *precipitate* heightening of the senses. And I have felt the *inexplicable* but **sharply** *boosted* intensity of a *wild* moment in the bush, where it is not until some minutes **later** that you discover the source of the electricity—the *warm* remains of a *grizzly* bear kill, or the **still** *moist* tracks of a wolverine.
>
> —Barry Lopez, "The Stone Horse"

Adjectives answer the questions *which?*, *how many?*, or *what kind?*

The *yellow* crocuses were the *first* blooms of *last* spring. [which crocuses? *yellow;* which blooms? *first;* which spring? *last*]

Several days passed before they found the body. [how many days? *several*]

Curious students are a joy to teach. [what kind of students? *curious*]

Some adjectives are formed by adding one of the following suffixes to nouns.

NOUN	SUFFIX	ADJECTIVE
charity	-able	charitable
style	-ish	stylish
dirt	-y	dirty
atom	-ic	atomic
season	-al	seasonal
pain	-less	painless
danger	-ous	dangerous
thought	-ful	thoughtful

Adjectives are also formed from verbs.

VERB	SUFFIX	ADJECTIVE
scare	-y	scary
hesitate	-ant	hesitant
notice	-able	noticeable
construct	-ive	constructive

However, many common adjectives have no identifying suffixes: *good, hot, little, young, fat.*

Participles and infinitives sometimes function as adjectives.

The *surprised* children looked at their *smiling* parents.

Philip had trouble deciding which car *to buy.*

Adjectives usually precede the nouns or pronouns they modify. Sometimes, however, they follow the words they modify.

The *beautiful ripe* fruit sat on the counter.

The fruit, *ripe* and *beautiful*, sat on the counter.

Adverbs answer the questions *when? how? how often?* or *where?*

I went to a Red Sox game *yesterday.*

We were *anxiously* awaiting the results of the final examination.

Although she is a chef, Margaret *rarely* cooks her own meals.

Karen sat *behind* me in chemistry class.

Adverbs are often formed by adding the suffix -*ly* to adjectives.

ADJECTIVE	ADVERB
glad	glad*ly*
careful	careful*ly*
unjust	unjust*ly*

But an -*ly* ending on a word does not necessarily identify it as an adverb. Some adjectives, such as *lonely* and *timely*, also end in -*ly* (a *lonely* child; in *timely* fashion). Moreover, some adverbs that indicate time or place do not end in -*ly*: *here, there, now, often, seldom, never.*

Adverbs can either precede or follow the verbs, adjectives, or other adverbs they modify.

The waiter *carefully* set the dishes of steaming food on the table.

Although he worked *quickly*, he never rushed.

Adverbs can sometimes be shifted to the beginning or end of a sentence, depending on the rhythm or emphasis a writer wants to achieve.

Carefully, the waiter set the dishes on the table.

The waiter set the dishes on the table *carefully*.

EXERCISE 13–1   Identifying Adjectives and Adverbs

In the following sentences, underline the adjectives once and the adverbs twice. Draw an arrow from each adjective to the word it modifies and from each adverb to the word, phrase, or clause it modifies. Example:

The snow fell <u>swiftly</u> in <u>thick</u> tufts, like <u>new</u> wool washed before the weaver spins it.

1. She was an old woman now and her life had become a network of memories.
2. The blankets her grandmother had woven so skillfully were neatly laid over the bedpost.
3. Eagerly they awaited the return of their ancestral artifacts.
4. He remembered sleeping warmly on cold windy nights, wrapped in the carefully stitched quilts.
5. Whenever a bird screeched raucously, he shivered violently.

EXERCISE 13–2   Using Adjectives and Adverbs

Transform the following words to adjectives; then transform the adjectives to adverbs. (You can consult a dictionary if necessary.) Finally, use the newly formed adjectives and adverbs in sentences. Example:

courage (*noun*); courageous (*adjective*); courageously (*adverb*)

Several *courageous* citizens identified the mobster in court.

They *courageously* stood up for my right to read whatever I want.

1. reason   2. help   3. act   4. fool   5. hero

13b Using adjectives with linking verbs

A modifier that follows a linking verb modifies the subject of the verb, and, therefore, is always an adjective. Linking verbs can be forms of *be* (such as *am, is, are, was, were, will be,* and *has been*), sensory verbs (such as *appear, feel, look, seem, smell, sound,* and *taste*), or verbs of becoming (such as *become, grow, prove,* and *turn*). When adjectives follow linking verbs, they function as subject complements. (See 11d-1 for more on linking verbs.)

When functioning as linking verbs, these sensory verbs are followed by nouns or adjectives, never by adverbs. When the verbs express action, however, they can be followed by adverbs.

The sauce *tasted* delicious. [linking verb with adjective]

The cook *tasted* the sauce regularly. [action verb with adverb]

13c Using adverbs with two forms

Some adverbs have two acceptable forms—a short and an *-ly* form. Sometimes the two forms have the same meaning; pairs such as *cheap/cheaply, deep/deeply, loud/loudly, quick/quickly, sharp/sharply,* and *slow/slowly,* for example, are interchangeable in informal conversation. But because the short form is informal, you will want to use the *-ly* form of the adverb in academic writing.

INFORMAL   They were cheering as *loud* as they could.

FORMAL   However *loudly* they cheered, the noise of the crowd absorbed their cheers into a grand clamor of approval.

INFORMAL   Drive *slow* through the intersection.

FORMAL   She drove *slowly* through the intersection.

In other pairs, the short and the *-ly* forms of the adverb have different meanings. When using adverbs such as *high/highly, late/lately, near/nearly,* or *wrong/wrongly,* be sure not to confuse those meanings.

Lately, their attendance had improved, though earlier they had often come late. [*lately* means "recently"; *late* means "not on time"]

As they drew *near* the theater, they realized they had *nearly* forgotten to call home. [*near* means "close to"; *nearly* means "almost"]

When you cannot tell from its form whether a word is an adjective or adverb, you should determine its function in the sentence. Remember that adjectives modify nouns or pronouns; adverbs modify verbs, adjectives, or other adverbs.

EXERCISE 13–3   Choosing Modifiers

1. Underline the appropriate modifier—adjective or adverb—in each of the following sentences. Example:

   Their *courageous/courageously* action saved many lives.

   a. In the midst of storewide confusion, the salespeople remained *calm/calmly*.
   b. The snow began falling *light/lightly* and then *steady/steadily* intensified.
   c. Remember to drive *slow/slowly* as you come through Devil's Pass.
   d. Before competing in a marathon bicycle race, the racers know to eat *hearty/heartily* portions of pasta.
   e. It is important not to arrive *late/lately* for the meeting.

2. In the following sentences, label the italicized *-ly* words as adjectives [ADJ] or adverbs [ADV]. Examples:

                         ADJ
   She played a *lively* melody on the piano.

                           ADV
   They went along *unwillingly* with the plan.

   a. They were charged with *disorderly* conduct.
   b. I *successfully* completed my first year as an intern.
   c. Edith guessed *correctly* that she had been given the job.
   d. Our accountant made a *costly* mistake in our tax return.
   e. We were more than *slightly* upset with him.

EXERCISE 13–4   Using Adjectives and Adverbs in Writing

Write a descriptive paragraph of six to twelve sentences in which you use adjectives and adverbs to enhance your description. Choose adjectives and adverbs that help your readers imagine that they can see, hear, smell, taste, and feel what you are describing. Possible topics include your room; your neighborhood; a place on campus; a scene in nature; a concert; a scene from a movie.

13d   Using *good/well* and *bad/badly*

Some writers confuse the adjective *good* with the adverb *well* and the adjective *bad* with the adverb *badly*. Use the adjectives *good* and *bad* to modify nouns or pronouns: *a good time; a bad play.* To modify verbs, adjectives, or other adverbs, use *well* and *badly*: *she speaks well; he hears badly.*

As adjectives, *good* and *bad* follow linking verbs.

The turkey looks *good.*

The chicken smells *bad.*

As adverbs, *badly* and *well* follow action verbs.

They both behaved *badly* throughout the proceedings.

They skate *well* enough to become professionals.

Well can be both an adjective and an adverb.

They looked *well* when we last saw them. [adjective meaning "healthy" and modifying *They*]

He performed *well* during the competition. [adverb meaning "effectively" and modifying *performed*]

EXERCISE 13–5   Using *good/well* and *bad/badly* Correctly

In the following sentences, correct the misuse of *good/well* or *bad/badly*. Some sentences may be correct as written. Example:

well

She no longer skates good.

1. It was a good time; it was a bad time.
2. It did not go good; it did not go badly.
3. It could have gone better, but it was not badly.
4. They invested their money good, so good that they doubled their investment.
5. Good high school and college athletic prospects do not always turn out well as professionals.

13e Using comparative and superlative forms

Adjectives and adverbs appear in three forms: **positive, comparative,** and **superlative**. The positive or simple form is the form most commonly used in speech and writing. The comparative and superlative forms of adjectives and adverbs are used to make comparisons.

POSITIVE	COMPARATIVE	SUPERLATIVE
hungry	hungrier	hungriest
small	smaller	smallest
useful	more useful	most useful
usefully	less usefully	least usefully

He was *hungry* at six o'clock, *hungrier* at eight, and *hungriest* at ten.

Although ours was a *useful* suggestion, Barbara's was even *more useful*, and Sharon's was the *most useful* of all.

Most one-syllable adjectives and many two-syllable adjectives add the suffixes -*er* and -*est* to form their comparative and superlative forms: *smooth/ smoother/smoothest; tough/tougher/toughest*. All adjectives ending with -*ful*, such as *useful*, and all adjectives with three or more syllables add the words *more* and *most* before the positive to form the comparative and superlative: *momentous/more momentous/most momentous*. Most adverbs of two or more syllables and most adverbs ending with -*ly* add the words *more* and *most* before the positive to form the comparative and superlative. Adverbs and adjectives that show negative comparison use the words *less* and *least* before the positive form: *loudly/less loudly/least loudly*.

These general principles have some exceptions. For example, some adjectives use *more* in the comparative (*more severe; more remote*) but add -*est* in the superlative (*severest; remotest*). If you are unsure about whether to use -*er/-est* or *more/most* to form the comparative and superlative forms of adjectives and adverbs, consult your dictionary.

1 Distinguishing between comparatives and superlatives

Use the comparative forms of adjectives and adverbs to compare two things. Use their superlative forms to compare three or more.

ADJECTIVE—COMPARATIVE	Hebrew is a much *older* language than English.
ADJECTIVE—SUPERLATIVE	Chinese is one of the world's *oldest* languages.
ADVERB—COMPARATIVE	Juanita's approach will resolve the problem *more effectively* than Hwan's.

ADVERB—SUPERLATIVE   Hilda's solution will solve the problem *most effectively* of all.

2   Checking for double comparisons

A **double comparison** is a nonstandard form that uses two comparative adjectives when only one is necessary. Use only one form of the comparative, not both, to make a particular comparison; that is, use either *-er* or *more*, but do not use both together.

FAULTY   Mozart's symphonies are *more better* known and *more often* recorded than his string quartets.

REVISED   Mozart's symphonies are *better* known and *more frequently* recorded than his string quartets.

FAULTY   Of the sixty-seven students in the class, Carol came *most closest* to a perfect score on the physics exam.

REVISED   Of the sixty-seven students in the class, Carol came *closest* to a perfect score on the physics exam.

EXERCISE 13–6   Using Comparative and Superlative Forms

Choose between the comparative and superlative forms of the adjective or adverb pairs in the following sentences. Example:

It is *better/more better* to be cooperative than confrontational.

1. Of the three proposals, theirs was the *more/most* sensible.
2. Paris is the European city *more/most* often visited by Americans.
3. Which is the *larger/largest* of the twin towers?
4. The fall of the Berlin Wall was the *more/most* stunning event of all.
5. They used to work out *more/most* regularly and with *greater/greatest* intensity than they do now.

EXERCISE 13–7   Using Comparative Forms of Adjectives and Adverbs in Writing

---

Write a paragraph in which you use the comparative and superlative forms of at least two adjectives and two adverbs. Include at least one adjective and adverb before the word(s) it modifies and at least one following the word(s) it modifies.

---

3   Checking for incomplete comparisons

Sometimes in speaking and writing we use incomplete comparisons, such as "the book was better" or "the service was worse." In the context of conversation it might be understood that the book was better than the movie or that the service was worse than the food. In academic writing, however, it might not be clear. You need to provide sufficient context to make all your comparisons clear when you write. (See 22e-1.)

INCOMPLETE	The doctors who participate in the program are wealthier.
COMPLETE	The doctors who participate in the program are wealthier than those who do not.
INCOMPLETE	Some believe that Einstein was the greatest.
COMPLETE	Some believe that Einstein was the greatest physicist in history.

4   Using irregular comparatives and superlatives

Some adjectives and adverbs change form to indicate their comparative and superlative degrees. The accompanying chart lists these irregular modifiers.

Irregular Comparative and Superlative Forms of Adjectives and Adverbs

Adjectives

POSITIVE	COMPARATIVE	SUPERLATIVE
bad	worse	worst
good	better	best
ill	worse	worst
little	less	least
many	more	most
much	more	most
some	more	most

Adverbs

POSITIVE	COMPARATIVE	SUPERLATIVE
badly	worse	worst
ill	worse	worst
well	better	best

13f Avoiding double negatives

A **double negative** is a nonstandard form using two negatives where only one is necessary. Although few speakers of English would misunderstand "I do not have no money," the statement is nonstandard because it contains two negatives and only one is necessary. The adverbs *barely*, *scarcely*, and *hardly* and the preposition *but* (meaning "except") are negative and should not be used with other negatives.

FAULTY   We couldn't *hardly* see the band. Their music did*n't never* reach the back rows of the stadium.

REVISED   We *could hardly* see the band. Their music *never reached* the back rows of the stadium.

OR: Their songs *would never* be heard in the back rows of the stadium.

Although double negatives were once acceptable in English (Shakespeare used them for emphasis), using them in your writing may lead your readers to believe you are careless. You should therefore revise any double negatives that creep into your writing.

WRITING HINT   In standard written English, you can combine two negatives to make a positive understatement.

Her resignation was *not unexpected*.

He was *not displeased* with his performance.

You can use such double negatives as these when the alternative positive statement (*Her resignation was expected*; *He was pleased with his performance*) would be too strong.

Some other negative combinations are also acceptable in writing.

We *cannot* afford *not* to speak out.

13g Avoiding overuse of nouns as modifiers

A noun can function as an adjective, modifying another noun.

turkey dinner	night shift	wheat bread	college student
crowd control	day care	mother figure	film critic

The meaning of such familiar terms is clear. Occasionally, however, a string of nouns used as adjectives either obscures meaning or becomes cumbersome; if this happens, you need to revise for economy and clarity.

AWKWARD	To enhance company morale, management introduced a series of *employee relations communications strategies.*
REVISED	To enhance company morale, management developed strategies to ensure communication between employees and supervisors.

EXERCISE 13–8   Using Irregular Adjectives and Adverbs

Make any necessary corrections to the irregular adjectives and adverbs in the following sentences. Some sentences may be correct as written. Example:

well

Laurence Olivier performed very ~~good~~ in his Shakespearean roles.

1. One of the best films I ever saw was Laurence Olivier's *Hamlet.*
2. It was even more good than the very good version with Mel Gibson as Hamlet.
3. Some other filmed versions of Shakespeare's play are not bad, but they are not as well as either Olivier's or Gibson's version.
4. One of the worse Shakespearean characters Olivier ever portrayed was the bad king, Richard III. Of his many Shakespearean roles, Olivier's portrayal of Richard III contains perhaps his better Shakespearean acting.
5. His portrayal does not compare badly with others', but his portrayal of King Lear in a later film, when Olivier was at the end of his career, is decidedly worst than his more youthful performances.

EXERCISE 13–9   Working with Nouns as Modifiers

Rewrite the following noun phrases to make their meanings clearer. Example:

annual human rights progress statements
annual statements on the progress of human rights

1. arms control impact statements
2. teacher education program analysis
3. a real estate law specialist
4. student dining hall policy committee meetings
5. English language deterioration concerns

13h   Using possessive adjectives

Some possessive forms of personal pronouns also function as adjectives; they modify nouns and indicate ownership.

My idea might differ from yours. [*My* is a possessive adjective modifying the noun *idea*. *Yours* is a possessive pronoun.]

His goal was to become a millionaire by age thirty. [*His* is a possessive adjective modifying the noun *goal*.]

If they don't get *their* act together soon, the directors of the company will be fired. [*Their* is a possessive adjective modifying the noun *act*.]

USAGE NOTE   In your writing take care to distinguish possessive adjectives from contractions and other words that are pronounced the same or similarly.

POSSESSIVE ADJECTIVE	The plan has *its* merits.
SOUND-ALIKE CONTRACTION	*It's* simple and workable.
POSSESSIVE ADJECTIVE	*Your* hands are cold.
SOUND-ALIKE CONTRACTION	*You're* not nervous, are you?
POSSESSIVE ADJECTIVE	*Their* house has been sold.
SOUND-ALIKE CONTRACTION	*They're* sure to be disappointed.
SOUND-ALIKE ADVERB	You won't find anyone *there*.
POSSESSIVE ADJECTIVE	*Whose* ticket is this?
SOUND-ALIKE CONTRACTION	*Who's* going to the game?

EXERCISE 13–10   Working with Possessive Adjectives

Underline the correct word in each of the following sentences. Example:

> They spend all *their*/they're time together.

1. The cat drank *its*/*it's* milk and washed *its*/*it's* paws.
2. We told him that *your*/*you're* daughter was in law school.
3. It is *your*/*you're* own fault if *your*/*you're* out of money.
4. Six members have paid their dues; *their*/*they're* the same people who do all the work.
5. *Its*/*It's* a nice jug, but *its*/*it's* handle is broken.

Grammar and Writing

Managing Modifiers

You can use your knowledge of modifiers to improve your writing. Look over a recent paper to see what kinds of modifiers you included. Use this chapter's charts and guidelines to check the correctness of your adjective and adverb forms. Check especially for uses of irregular adjectives and adverbs, such as *good* and *bad*, *well* and *ill*.

Then reread your paper to see how many modifiers you used. Do you have a tendency to overuse modifiers? If so, cut back on them. Could your writing benefit from adding an occasional modifier? If so, add a few.

Whatever changes you make, strive for a heightened awareness of what each modifier contributes to your writing. Ask yourself how each modifier clarifies the idea or conveys the attitude or feeling you wish to express.

EXAMPLE

The [numerous] casualties extensive[ly] suffered by both sides in the Civil

War Battle of Gettysburg filled the battlefield with bodies sprawled in
    delete
[agonizingly awkward] contorted positions. The only signs of life were
        hordes of buzzing   rigid
supplied by flies around the bodies.

CHAPTER 14

Prepositions, Conjunctions, and Interjections

  Recognizing prepositions

Prepositions are used extensively in speaking and in writing. A **preposition** shows the relationship between a noun or a pronoun (the object of a preposition) and another word or group of words in a sentence. A word is a preposition only if it is followed by an object and modifiers to form a **prepositional phrase.** The word *in*, for example, can function both as a preposition and as an adverb.

We found the letters *in* the mailbox.

Letters of support have been pouring *in*.

Prepositions can be used to indicate time, place, destination, possession, as well as other relationships among words in a sentence.

TIME   The lights came on *during* the intermission.

PLACE   The lamp stood *in* the corner *behind* the chair.

DESTINATION   They were heading *toward* the center of the city.

POSSESSION   That was the argument *of* the opposition.

The accompanying chart lists the most common prepositions.
    In addition to the common single-word prepositions, there is also a group of **compound prepositions** made up of two or more words. The accompanying chart lists some familiar compound prepositions.

14b **Using prepositions in writing**

A preposition appears before its object—that is, the noun or pronoun it connects with another part of the sentence. The preposition, its object, and any related modifiers form a prepositional phrase. A prepositional phrase almost always functions as an adjective or an adverb in a sentence.

The girl dived *into* the pond. [preposition *into* + object of preposition *the pond* = prepositional phrase]

299

Common Prepositions

about	below	inside	since
above	beneath	into	through
across	beside	like	throughout
after	between	near	till
against	beyond	of	to
along	by	off	toward
among	down	on	under
around	during	onto	until
as	except	out	up
at	for	over	upon
before	from	past	with
behind	in	regarding	without

Common Compound Prepositions

according to	by way of	in spite of
along with	due to	instead of
apart from	except for	in view of
aside from	in addition to	next to
as well as	in case of	on behalf of
because of	in front of	out of
by means of	in place of	with regard to

She wore a pink swimsuit *with* lavender stripes. [preposition *with* + object of preposition *lavender stripes* = prepositional phrase]

In both examples, the prepositions link words within the sentence. In the first example, the preposition *into* links its object *pond* to the verb *dived;* the phrase functions as an adverb because it modifies the verb. In the second example, the preposition *with* links its object *stripes* to the noun *swimsuit;* the phrase acts as an adjective because it modifies the verb.

Prepositions are indispensable in writing, but take care not to overuse them. Some sentences can be improved by using adjectives, verbs, and gerunds instead of prepositional phrases.

WORDY	IMPROVED
It was a day of sunshine.	It was a sunny day.
He gave an explanation for his mistake.	He explained his mistake.
We began a period of study for the exam.	We began studying for the exam.

(See also 26b-8.)

USAGE NOTE   In speech, people sometimes use extra prepositions.

We met *up with* the director at noon.

Their garage is *out in back of* the house.

You can streamline your writing by eliminating such unnecessary prepositions.

We met the director at noon.

Their garage is behind [*or* in back of] the house.

USAGE NOTE   Prepositions usually come before their objects. But in informal English, prepositions are sometimes placed after their objects. In conversation, these "deferred" prepositions frequently occur with questions, relative clauses, and passives.

Who are you talking *about?*

This book is the one that I'm interested *in.*

His problem has been taken care *of.*

In formal writing you should avoid putting prepositions at the end of a clause or sentence.

About whom are you talking?

This book is the one *in which* I'm interested.

We have taken care *of* his problem.

EXERCISE 14–1   Working with Prepositions in Your Own Writing

Refer to the preceding lists of prepositions. Compose a paragraph that includes at least five different prepositions.

14c   Recognizing conjunctions

Conjunctions link words, phrases, and clauses to one another. The four types of conjunctions are: coordinating conjunctions, correlative conjunctions, subordinating conjunctions, and conjunctive adverbs. (See also 23a-1 and 23b-1.)

1   Coordinating conjunctions

Coordinating conjunctions connect parallel words, phrases, and independent clauses within a sentence. The accompanying chart identifies the coordinating conjunctions and their functions. Coordinating conjunctions connect words, phrases, or clauses that have parallel grammatical structures and that have equally important meaning within the sentence. (See 23a-1 and 24b-1.)

CONNECTED NOUNS	Margaret Atwood writes <u>novels</u> *and* <u>short stories.</u>
CONNECTED VERBS	Maya Angelou might <u>sing</u> *or* <u>recite</u> her poems in public.
CONNECTED PHRASES	Some poets' work was <u>neglected in their time</u> *yet* <u>revered in our own.</u>
CONNECTED CLAUSES	<u>Robert Frost wanted to achieve popularity as a poet,</u> *but* <u>he longed to be admired by the critics as well.</u>

An easy way to remember the coordinating conjunctions is with the mnemonic *FANBOYS*. In this aid to memory, each letter stands for a different conjunction: *for, and, nor, but, or, yet, so.*

Coordinating Conjunctions

CAUSE OR REASON	*for*	She ate, *for* she was hungry.
ADDITION	*and*	He listens to jazz *and* blues.
NEGATIVE CHOICE	*nor*	I didn't answer the door, *nor* did I peek out the window.
CONTRAST	*but*	The task was difficult *but* not impossible.
CHOICE	*or*	We will *or* we will not.
CONTRAST	*yet*	They were eager *yet* afraid.
RESULT	*so*	He wanted it, *so* he bought it.

2 Correlative conjunctions

Like coordinating conjunctions, **correlative conjunctions** also connect words, phrases, and clauses that have parallel grammatical structures and that have equal emphasis. But as the accompanying chart shows, correlative conjunctions occur in pairs. (See 24b-2.)

Place each of the paired correlative conjunctions directly before the word, phrase, or clause it introduces.

He wanted *neither* <u>to eat</u> *nor* <u>to sleep.</u>

He was undecided *whether* <u>to continue graduate study in English</u> *or* <u>to redirect his energies toward business or medicine.</u>

Correlative Conjunctions

both . . . and	not only . . . but also	neither . . . nor
either . . . or	whether . . . or	just as . . . so

3 Subordinating conjunctions

Subordinating conjunctions introduce dependent (or subordinate) clauses and indicate the relationship of the dependent clause to the main clause of a sentence.

> *Even though* the deadline for financial aid had passed, her parents decided to submit an application anyway.

This sentence could be written with the clauses in reverse order to increase sentence variety (see Chapter 25) or to change the emphasis within the sentence (see 26a).

> Her parents decided to submit an application *even though* the deadline for financial aid had passed.

The accompanying chart lists common subordinating conjunctions and their uses.

Common Subordinating Conjunctions

CAUSE	as, because, now that, since
COMPARISON	as if, than
CONDITION	if, if only, provided that, unless
CONTRAST	although, even if, even though, though
MANNER	as, as if
PLACE	where, wherever
PURPOSE	in order that, so that
TIME	after, before, until, when, whenever, while

4 Conjunctive adverbs

Conjunctive adverbs emphasize a close relationship in meaning between two independent or main clauses. They indicate a specific, logical connection between the ideas expressed in the two clauses they connect.

The books had not arrived; *however,* they were due within the week.

He was angry and upset; *moreover,* he was also terribly disappointed.

They were denied admission to the medical school; they applied, *therefore,* to the graduate program in anatomy and physiology.

Conjunctive adverbs can appear in different places in a clause. Because they are adverbs, they can be shifted to create emphasis and provide variety.

Richard Cory had wealth, status, power, and good looks; *nevertheless,* he went home one night and put a bullet through his head.

Richard Cory had wealth, status, power, and good looks; he went home one night, *nevertheless,* and put a bullet through his head.

WRITING HINT   Avoid beginning too many sentences or independent clauses with conjunctive adverbs. Positioning the conjunctive adverb farther into the independent clause makes for smoother writing.

EXERCISE 14–2   Using Conjunctions

Write four sentences, each containing two independent clauses connected by one of the following words: *and, but, consequently, for, however, moreover, or, otherwise, then, yet.* Possible topics include watching television; preparing a meal; applying for a job; doing research; meeting someone new; making an important purchase.

Then rewrite your four sentences, using one independent clause and one dependent clause in each sentence. Use some of the subordinating conjunctions listed in the preceding chart.

Common Conjunctive Adverbs

also	furthermore	likewise	otherwise
anyway	hence	meanwhile	similarly
certainly	however	moreover	still
consequently	incidentally	nevertheless	then
finally	indeed	next	therefore
further	instead	now	thus

14d   Using interjections

Interjections are emphatic words or phrases that express surprise or emotion. They appear much more often in speech and dialogue than in expository writing, and they appear far less in formal and academic writing than in informal writing. They do not express a grammatical relation to other parts of a sentence; thus, they tend to stand alone as fragments.

Okay, already!	Help!	Wow!	Well!	What a night!
Ouch!	Hah!	Hey!	Oh!	No!

Wow! That was some dinner!

Hah! I knew I'd figure it out sooner or later.

EXERCISE 14–3   Using Conjunctions

Write a paragraph in which you include three sentences using coordinating conjunctions and three more sentences using subordinating conjunctions. Then write a second paragraph in which you include three sentences using correlative conjunctions and three sentences using conjunctive adverbs. Possible topics include bird or people watching; going to the beach; applying for a loan; meeting an old friend; buying something unimportant or frivolous.

Grammar and Writing

Controlling Prepositions and Conjunctions

Although only little words, prepositions and conjunctions can make a big difference in your writing. You can apply your knowledge of how these little words function by concentrating on them when you revise your writing.

Examine a recent paper, circling the prepositions and underlining the conjunctions. Look to see if you join many clauses with coordinating conjunctions such as *and* and *but*. You may wish to replace some of those with subordinate conjunctions. You may also wish to use an occasional conjunctive adverb, such as *therefore* or *however*.

You can strengthen your writing by reducing the number of prepositions you include. Heavy use of prepositional phrases often accompanies excessive use of passive voice verbs. Focusing on prepositions helps you identify ways to make your writing both more efficient and more effective.

EXAMPLE

The latest development in [the] technology [of] (television) has resulted in

[the increased promise of] sharper images. However, these new and sharper

images will reveal the imperfections of television newscasters.

CHAPTER 15

Maintaining Agreement

*I*n grammar there are two kinds of **agreement.** A subject and verb in a sentence must agree with one another in person (first person, second person, third person) and in number (singular or plural).

> A professional tennis *tournament* usually *involves* six rounds of play. [third-person singular]

> The seeded *players* sometimes *receive* a first-round bye. [third-person plural]

> Someday *we want* to attend Wimbledon. [first-person plural]

Likewise, a pronoun must agree with its antecedent (the noun it refers to) not only in person and number, but also in gender (masculine, feminine, or neuter).

> Our *parents* grow many kinds of vegetables in *their* garden.

> *Mom* grows *her* Halloween pumpkins and *Dad* takes great pride in *his* meaty tomatoes.

Subject–Verb Agreement

Making a verb agree with a third-person singular subject

In English, regular verbs take the same form in the first- and second-person singular, in the first- and second-person plural, and in the third-person plural. The only form that varies, and the form that may cause agreement problems, is the third-person singular form of the verb. (See 11c for more on regular and irregular verbs.)

	SINGULAR	PLURAL
FIRST PERSON	I think	We think
SECOND PERSON	You think	You think
THIRD PERSON	He/She/It thinks	They think

To make a present tense verb agree with a third-person singular subject, add -*s* or -*es* to the base form of the verb.

> The instructor *believes* her students are well prepared for the final.

> She *flosses* her teeth every day.

Two verbs—*have* and *be*—are exceptions to this rule. *Have* changes to *has* in the third-person singular of the present tense. *Be* changes to *is* in the third-person singular. (See 11b for more on forms of *have* and *be*.)

Nouns used as subjects are in the third person. To confirm that you are using the correct verb form with a noun subject, replace the noun with a third-person pronoun. If you can substitute *he, she,* or *it,* then you need the third-person singular form. If you can substitute *they,* use the third-person plural form.

> Product endorsement (*generate* or *generates?*) even more income.

> [It] *generates* even more income.

> Five-set matches (*last* or *lasts?*) more than three hours.

> [They] *last* more than three hours.

Notice that the -*s* or -*es* ending on a noun indicates a plural noun, while the -*s* or -*es* ending on a verb designates a singular verb.

> The movie *requires* sustained and careful attention. [singular subject; verb takes -*s* ending]

> Both movies *require* sustained and careful attention. [plural subject; verb lacks -*s* ending]

USAGE NOTE   *Be* is the only verb that changes in number in the past tense. *Was* is used with first- and third-person singular subjects.

> I *was* watching a team-tennis match on cable last night.

> Jimmy Connors *was* the only player I recognized.

Were is used with all plural subjects and with *you.*

> The matches *were* only one set apiece.

> You *were* always a fan of Bjorn Borg, were you not?

EXERCISE 15–1   **Working with Third-Person Subjects**

Rewrite the following sentences, changing singular subjects to plural and plural subjects to singular. Then change the verbs to agree with their subjects. Example:

A video *game costs* twenty-five cents for three minutes of play.

Video *games cost* twenty-five cents for three minutes of play.

1. Archaeologists study buildings, tools, and other artifacts of ancient culture.
2. An adult student has extra responsibilities to cope with.
3. An anthropologist always looks for signs of social change and development.
4. A high cholesterol level increases the risk of heart attack.
5. Film critics spend a lot of time in the dark.

15b   Making separated subjects and verbs agree

Sometimes a subject and a verb are separated from one another by words or phrases.

A box of oranges (*arrive* or *arrives?*) at the house once a month.

Low scores on the S.A.T. (*discourage* or *discourages?*) students from applying to certain colleges.

In these examples, the subjects are separated from their verbs by prepositional phrases. When this happens you may be inclined to make the verb agree with the noun closest to it (*oranges arrive; Test discourages*). However, the words nearest the verbs in these sentences function as objects of prepositions, not as the subjects of the sentences. The verb form in each sample sentence must agree with its subject.

A box of oranges *arrives* at the house once a month.

Low scores on the S.A.T. *discourage* students from applying to certain colleges.

When using expressions such as *accompanied by, together with, in addition to, like,* and *as well as,* check your sentences carefully to maintain subject–verb agreement. Be sure your verb agrees with the subject of the sentence, not with the word closest to it.

The Dodger first baseman, along with most of his teammates, refuses to get his hair cut short.

The Eiffel Tower, like many famous monuments, symbolizes the city in which it is located.

EXERCISE 15–2   **Maintaining Agreement between Subjects and Verbs**

In each of the following sentences, underline the subject and then circle the verb that agrees with it. Example:

One of the many bird species *is/are* in danger of extinction.

1. The honor of the occasion *is/are* entirely theirs.
2. It *give/gives* me hope to see them display such determined effort.
3. The coach, along with her players, *was/were* going out for pizza.
4. In some schools, members of the administration, as well as members of the faculty, *teach/teaches*.
5. Three of the four questions *is/are* challenging.
6. Bonsai trees *require/requires* careful pruning.
7. The participants in the ceremony *is/are* first-year college students.
8. Many movies made in the past year *contain/contains* violent scenes.
9. In many households, a VCR, as well as cable, *is/are* attached to at least one television.
10. The music *was/were* composed by George Gershwin.

15c   Making subject and verb agree with a compound subject

A **compound subject** is made up of two or more subjects joined by a conjunction. Compound subjects connected by *and* usually take a plural verb.

Tom and Jerry *are* a famous pair of cartoon characters.

Liberty, equality, and fraternity *have* long *been valued*.

However, when parts of a compound subject function as a single unit or refer to the same person or thing, the subject is considered singular, and the verb should also be singular.

Ogilvy and Mather *is* known as a creative advertising agency.

Apple pie and ice cream *has been* a favorite American dessert for years.

Her best friend and staunchest supporter *had proved to be* her mother, not her roommate.

When a compound subject is preceded by the adjective *each* or *every*, use a singular verb form.

Each sentence, phrase, and clause *needs* to be crafted with care.

Every candidate and criminal suspect *deserves* a fair hearing.

With compound subjects connected by *or, nor, either . . . or,* or *neither . . . nor,* the verb may be singular or plural. When both parts of the subject are singular, the verb is singular.

No food or drink *was* provided.

Neither the referee nor the tournament director *knows* when play will resume.

When both subjects are plural, the verb is plural.

Either the workers or the owners *will need* to make concessions.

But when one part of the subject is singular and the other is plural, the verb agrees with the subject closer to it.

To enroll, either junior standing or referrals from two faculty members *are* required.

Neither he nor his sisters *were* convinced by their father's arguments.

Neither the players nor the coach *wants* the season to end.

WRITING HINT   If one of the subjects joined by *or* or *nor* is singular and one is plural, place the plural subject closest to the verb to avoid awkwardness.

AWKWARD   Either the committee members or the president *is* misinformed.

REVISED   Either the president or the committee members *are* misinformed.

When the joined subjects are pronouns that take different verb forms, it is better to avoid having to make a choice. Rephrase the sentence.

AWKWARD   Neither you nor I (*am* or *are?*) ready for the test.

REPHRASED   Neither of us is ready for the test.

15d   Making a verb agree with an indefinite pronoun subject

An **indefinite pronoun** is one that does not refer to a specific person or thing. Most indefinite pronouns take a singular verb. (The accompanying chart lists common indefinite pronouns that take singular verbs.)

Everybody *is* coming.

Everyone who can help with the preparations *should* arrive early.

Indefinite Pronouns Taking Singular Verb Forms

another	either	neither	other
anybody	everybody	nobody	somebody
anyone	everyone	no one	someone
anything	everything	nothing	something
each	much	one	

Some indefinite pronouns take plural verb forms: *both, few, many, others,* and *several.*

Both *were* destroyed by the 1966 flood in Venice.

Few, if any, *were* missed by the best students.

Still other indefinite pronouns can be either singular or plural, depending on the noun or pronoun they refer to: *all, any, enough, more, most, none,* and *some.*

SINGULAR Enough of the tuna casserole *was* left for me to have a substantial lunch the next day. [*Enough* refers to the singular noun *casserole.*]

PLURAL Enough of the dishes *were* clean so that I didn't have to wash the others right away. [*Enough* refers to the plural noun *dishes.*]

SINGULAR Some of the writing *is* excellent.

PLURAL Some of the test questions *were* ambiguous.

15e   Making a verb agree with a collective noun subject

A **collective noun** names a group of people or things. They include such words as *group, class, team, committee, herd, crowd, number, audience,* and *family.* Because collective nouns describe a group that is considered a single unit, they usually take singular verbs.

The class *has performed* well throughout the term.

An audience *shows* its pleasure by applauding.

At times, collective nouns can be considered plural rather than singular. When emphasizing the individual members rather than the group as a whole, use a plural verb form.

The herd *cross* the road one at a time. [The emphasis falls on the individual members of the herd.]

The jury *are* expected to return to their homes upon completing their work on the case. [The individual jury members will return to their own homes.]

WRITING HINT   Since use of a plural verb with collective nouns such as *committee* and *jury* may sound incorrect, you can add a prepositional phrase or a plural word like *members* after the collective noun: The *committee members are* debating the proposal. The *herd of cattle cross* the river.

USAGE NOTE   The collective noun *number* can take either a singular or plural verb. When used with the article *a,* its verb is plural.

A number of classical works *are* repeated every season in concerts throughout the world.

When used with the article *the,* its verb is singular.

The number of well-read teachers *is* diminishing every year.

EXERCISE 15–3   Checking for Subject–Verb Agreement

Revise the errors in subject–verb agreement in the following sentences. Some sentences may be correct as written.

1. Both first place and fourth place was won by runners from our team.
2. Neither the chief negotiator nor the strikers accepts the latest proposal.
3. My first serious and unforgettable crush was on my third-grade teacher.
4. Each of the employees have agreed to a pay cut.
5. A number of new stores has left the mall.
6. The number of stores leaving the mall increase every month.
7. The faculty has not been able to decide among themselves.
8. Everyone in our family like pineapple pizza.
9. None of the speakers expects us to question their facts.
10. Chunks of granola and a spoonful of honey turns ice cream into a breakfast treat.

15f   Making a verb agree with its subject rather than a complement

Be sure a linking verb agrees with its subject and not with a complement.

The repeated humiliations of minorities *are* a stain on our nation's image. [The verb, *are*, agrees with the plural subject *humiliations*, not with the singular complement *stain*.]

An important influence in politics today *is* minorities. [The verb, *is*, agrees with the singular subject *influence*, not with the plural complement *minorities*.]

However, if the parts in the last example were reversed, the verb would be the plural *are* rather than the singular *is*.

Minorities *are* an important influence in politics today. [The subject is now *minorities*, which takes the plural verb *are*.]

15g   Making a verb agree with relative pronoun subjects

When the relative pronoun *who, which,* or *that* acts as the subject of a dependent clause, the verb in the clause must agree in number with the pronoun's antecedent.

Success is the goal that *drives* many students to study hard. [*That* refers to *goal*, a singular noun, and takes the singular verb *drives*.]

Success, self-satisfaction, and a desire to please one's parents are elements that *motivate* students to perform their best. [*That* refers to *elements*, a plural noun, and takes the plural verb *motivate*.]

When the phrase *one of the* comes before the relative pronoun, you need to check the intended meaning of the sentence.

Cheryl is one of the team members who always *stay* late for extra practice. [Cheryl and some of her teammates stay late. *Who* refers to those who stay late for extra practice, and hence takes a plural verb.]

Cheryl is the only one of the team members who *comes* to practice an hour early. [Only one player comes early—Cheryl. The antecedent of *who* is *one*, which takes a singular verb.]

Askold is one of those people who *hate* spectator sports. [*Who* refers to people, including Askold, and thus takes a plural verb.]

15h   Making subject and verb agree in inverted sentences

In a sentence written with **inverted word order** (an inverted sentence), the subject follows the verb rather than precedes it. To maintain subject–verb agreement in inverted sentences, be sure that the verb agrees with the subject of the sentence, not with a nearby noun.

Beneath the papers *was* the address book she had been looking for. [The subject is *address book,* not *papers.*]

Among the junk collected for the tag sale *were* a grandfather clock and an antique chair. [The compound subject is *a grandfather clock and an antique chair,* not *junk* or *sale.*]

Inverted subject–verb order also occurs when sentences begin with *there* or *here.*

There *are* similarities between them. [The subject is *similarities;* the verb is plural.]

There *is* the essential issue of authority. [The subject is *issue;* the verb is singular.]

Here *are* the grade reports for our department. [The subject is *reports;* the verb is plural.]

Here *is* the latest report on storm damage. [The subject is *report;* the verb is singular.]

Take particular care with the contractions *there's* and *here's.* Remember that the *'s* stands for *is*—a singular verb.

INCORRECT   *There's* still ten or twelve people without a ticket.

CORRECT   *There are* still ten or twelve people without a ticket.

EXERCISE 15–4   Checking Subject–Verb Agreement

Revise the errors in subject–verb agreement in the following sentences. Some sentences may be correct as written.

1. There was only ten minutes remaining in the game.
2. I paid the costs of shipping, which were minimal.
3. Here is some free tickets to the game.
4. The cultural achievements of ancient Greece is the subject of my report.
5. Sula is one of those people who thrives on competition.

 15i   **Maintaining agreement with singular words that appear plural**

Some nouns that look plural, such as *athletics, economics,* and *mumps,* are singular in meaning and take a singular verb.

Athletics *is* an important source of revenue at many universities.

Economics *predicts* the outcomes of some elections.

Mumps *is* essentially a childhood disease.

Some nouns that look plural, such as *politics* and *statistics,* may be used as either singular or plural nouns under certain circumstances.

SINGULAR   Politics *fascinates* me. [*politics* is a field of study or a set of ideas]

PLURAL   His politics *are* very different from mine. [*politics* refers to beliefs or views]

USAGE NOTE   The word *data,* the plural of *datum* (meaning "fact"), is often used as a singular noun. Scientists, for example, frequently think of data as a single collection of information rather than as individual facts. Although some writers and authorities retain the traditional use of *data* as a plural noun, others accept *data* in the singular as well.

SINGULAR   We cannot make a decision until all *the data has* arrived.

SINGULAR   Here *is the data* you need.

PLURAL   Our *data indicate* that it is time to make a change.

PLURAL   These *data strengthen* your argument.

When you think of data as a body of information, use the word with a singular verb form. When you think of data as a set of different facts, use it with a plural verb form.

15j   Making verbs agree in titles and with words used as subjects

Titles of books, films, and other works take a singular verb—even when those titles appear plural or contain plural words.

"The American Geographies" *is* a wonderful essay written by Barry Lopez.

"Father and Son" *is* a poem by Stanley Kunitz.

In the same way, a word referred to as a word takes a singular verb form, even though the word may be plural.

The word "receivables" *is* used in business to mean an asset due to one business from another.

Use the accompanying chart for questions you may have about subject–verb agreement.

Summary of Subject–Verb Agreement

- Normal agreement:

  Rocks *endure;* time *passes.*
- Third-person singular subject (15a):

  The day *dawns.*
- Subject separated from verb (15b):

  The books with the missing pages *lay* in the gutter.
- Compound subject (15c):

  Rocks and trees *dot* the landscape.

  A long story or a short play *is* required of every creative-writing major.
- Indefinite pronoun subject (15d):

  Everybody *listens* and all *hear.*
- Collective noun subject (15e):

  A crowd *gathers.*
- Relative pronoun subjects (15g):

  The group that *finishes* first *wins.*
- Inverted sentence subjects (15h):

  Under the trees *lies* our lazy dog.

  There *are* no trees in our yard.
- Plural form, singular meaning subjects (15i):

  Mathematics is a challenging major.
- Titles and words used as subjects (15j):

  Trees and Forests is the standard text.

  Oxen is the plural of *ox.*

EXERCISE 15–5   Revising for Subject–Verb Agreement

Correct the errors in subject–verb agreement that you find in the following sentences. Some sentences may be correct as written.

1. Each of us were too tired to finish the race.
2. The committee is intending to meet next week.
3. More upsetting than the things they said were the manner in which they said them.
4. A good hot meal and a good night's rest is all I need.
5. Dorothea Lange's photographs of people who were dispossessed during the Depression still convey considerable emotional power.

6. John Steinbeck's novel *The Grapes of Wrath* describe the effects of the Depression on a single family.

7. There are no team members who does not deserve the coach's criticism.

8. Mathematics are not as popular a major as it once was.

9. In an election year politics are a hot topic.

10. The study of foreign languages is resuming a former place of prominence in the university curriculum.

EXERCISE 15–6 Reviewing Subject–Verb Agreement

In the following passage about television commercials, underline the correct verb in each italicized pair.

> Television commercials (*is/are*) a form of religious literature. . . . I do not claim, for a start, that every television commercial (*has/have*) religious content. Just as in church the pastor will sometimes call the congregation's attention to nonecclesiastical matters, so there (*is/are*) television commercials that (*is/are*) entirely secular. Someone (*has/have*) something to sell; you are told what it is, where it can be obtained, and what it (*cost/costs*). Though these may be shrill and offensive, no doctrine (*is/are*) advanced and no theology invoked.
>
> But the majority of important television commercials (*take/takes*) the form of religious parables organized around a coherent theology. Like all religious parables, they (*put/puts*) forward a concept of sin, intimations of the way to redemption, and a vision of Heaven. They also suggest what (*is/are*) the roots of evil and what (*is/are*) the obligations of the holy.
>
> —Neil Postman, "The Parable of the Ring around the Collar"

Pronoun–Antecedent Agreement

To avoid repeating nouns in writing, you can use pronouns to stand in for them (see 12b). In doing so, you must be sure that each pronoun agrees with the noun it refers to (its **antecedent**). Pronouns and antecedents must agree in person, number, and gender. Consider the following examples.

> The cab driver cut through the traffic as if *she* were slalom skiing. [*Driver* is the antecedent of *she*, which is third-person, singular, feminine.]

> Although *they* were placed in a glass case, the awards meant little to him. [*Awards* is the antecedent of *they*, which is third-person, plural, neuter.]

Making a pronoun agree with an indefinite pronoun antecedent

An **indefinite pronoun,** such as *somebody* or *anything,* refers to an unspecified person or thing. Most indefinite pronouns are singular (see 15d for a list of indefinite pronouns).

SINGULAR   *Everybody has* his or her opinion.

SINGULAR   If *someone is* guilty, he or she should confess.

WRITING HINT   It is becoming increasingly common to hear people say "Everybody has their opinion" and "If anyone is available, they will be called." In such instances plural personal pronouns (*their* and *they*) are matched with singular indefinite pronouns (*everybody* and *anyone*). However, in academic and professional writing, use a singular personal pronoun or rewrite to avoid the agreement problem altogether.

Everybody has *an* opinion. [*an* opinion, not *their* opinion]

If someone is guilty, *that person* should confess. [*that person* instead of *he* or *she*]

 Making a pronoun agree with a collective noun antecedent

When a collective noun such as *team* or *class* refers to the group as a unit, the collective noun takes a singular pronoun.

The class had to organize *its* own trip, without administrative assistance.

When a collective noun refers to the individual members of the group, it takes a plural pronoun.

The group decided to split up and go *their* own different ways.

15m **Making a pronoun agree with a compound antecedent**

A **compound antecedent** has two antecedents joined by a conjunction. Compound antecedents can be either singular or plural. Those joined by *and* are plural and require a plural pronoun.

The man and his dog took *their* daily stroll through the park.

When a compound antecedent is preceded by the word *each* or *every*, or if the sense of the compound is clearly singular—as when two words joined by *and* refer to a single person—use a singular pronoun.

Every college and university has *its* own identity.

Oedipus's wife and mother, Jocasta, killed *herself* when she realized who Oedipus was and what he had done.

For compound antecedents connected by *or, nor, either . . . or,* or *neither . . . nor,* the pronoun should agree with the nearer of the two antecedents.

Either the lead singer or the orchestra members must decide to follow *their* conductor's tempo directions.

Neither Jocelyn nor Kate could find *her* rocket.

If one of the antecedents is singular and the other plural, put the plural antecedent closest to the antecedent to avoid awkwardness.

AWKWARD   *Neither* my friends *nor* my brother could stifle *his* laughter during the performance.

REVISED   *Neither* my brother *nor* my friends could stifle *their* laughter during the performance.

You can use the accompanying guidelines to review pronoun–antecedent agreement.

Summary of Pronoun–Antecedent Agreement

- Normal pronoun–antecedent agreement:
  The tree shed *its* leaves, each of *them* a bright orange-red.
- Indefinite pronouns as antecedents (15k):
  Each tree has *its* own distinct shape.
- Collective nouns as antecedents (15l):
  The speech team is having *its* best season in years.
  The family cannot settle *their* differences.
- Compound antecedents (15m):
  The oaks and the sycamore shed *their* leaves early.
  Either the elm or the birch retains *its* leaves through late fall.

USAGE NOTE A third-person antecedent should not be referred to by *you*. This shift can occur when you forget that you are writing in the third person and begin to address the reader directly.

INCONSISTENT If a person wants to lose weight, *you* must exercise regularly.

CONSISTENT If a person wants to lose weight, *he or she* must exercise regularly.

If people want to lose weight permanently, *they* must exercise regularly.

A person who wants to lose weight must exercise regularly.

Checking for gender-specific pronouns

Generic nouns and indefinite pronouns (such as *everyone* and *someone*) refer to both men and women, not to one sex or the other. Traditionally in English, when an indefinite pronoun or a generic noun served as the antecedent for a personal pronoun, that pronoun was the generic (or generalized) *he*.

Did anyone neglect to bring *his* money for the trip?

The person who organized this conference knew what *he* was doing.

Using the generic *he* in these examples, however, is sexist because it excludes women. The first example singles out males as most likely to forget their money. The second example assumes that the conference organizer must have been a male. The accompanying checklist details how you can avoid using sexist pronouns. (See Chapter 29 for more on avoiding biased language.)

EXERCISE 15–7 **Maintaining Agreement between Pronouns and Antecedents**

Revise the following sentences so that pronouns and their antecedents agree.

1. Every student is required to bring their registration cards to the first meeting of each class.
2. Each secretary has her own word processor.
3. The jury announced their verdict.
4. The committee unanimously agreed on its selection for Provost.
5. Neither Yankees fans nor the team's administration was willing to support the proposed trade of Don Mattingly for Howard Johnson.
6. Anyone who wants to study abroad for a term should meet with their advisor to discuss the details.

7. Either a hot fudge sundae or a slice of warm pecan pie could work their magic on me.

8. Will each doctor please take his seat?

9. Every flower and tree has their distinctive beauty.

10. One of the board members explained their point of view to the student paper.

Avoiding Sexist Pronouns

To avoid sexism, use alternatives to the generic *he*.

1. Use masculine and feminine pronouns together.

   Has anyone forgotten *his or her* money for the trip?

   The person who organized this conference knew what *he or she* was doing.

   This option can create awkwardness when numerous references to *he or she* and *him or her* occur, so use it sparingly.

2. Construct sentences that avoid the problem of sexist pronoun usage. Instead of using a singular antecedent, use the plural.

   Did any *people* neglect to bring *their* money for the trip?

   The *organizers* of this conference knew what *they* were doing.

   Or rewrite the sentence to eliminate the second pronoun.

   Did anyone neglect to bring money for the trip?

   The person who organized this conference did an outstanding job.

EXERCISE 15–8   Revising for Agreement

Revise the following paragraph to eliminate problems in subject–verb agreement and in pronoun–antecedent agreement.

College students are not the only ones who experiences frustration in trying to write well. Almost every writer agonizes over some of their sentences when they know their work will be read by a critical audience. Writing well is a painful process. Sometimes it goes smoothly, but inevitably you come to the difficult passages. And even the smooth passages that seemed almost to compose itself needs revision after all. A student will have a healthier attitude toward their composition course if they understand that even the professional writer shares your feeling of agony as he tries to develop an extensive piece of writing for critical readers. Neither the first-year college student nor the professional writer escape the pain of writing.

Grammar and Writing

Maintaining Agreement

What you have learned about grammatical agreement can pay immediate dividends when you write. Check a recent paper for agreement between subjects and verbs and between pronouns and their antecedents.
Look to see whether subjects agree with their verbs in person and number,
using the chart on p. 316 for guidance. Examine your pronouns for agreement with their antecedents using the chart on p. 319.

Essentially, you will be checking for grammatical accuracy. But you
may also notice that your meaning may be unclear. In such cases, you may
revise by changing pronouns to nouns or by changing singular subjects and
verbs to plural—or vice versa.

EXAMPLE

> The Vietnam Veterans Memorial, one of architect Maya Ying Lin's notable
>
>   has
> works, [have] become the most frequently visited monument in the coun-
>
> try. This memorial and Lin's Civil Rights memorial in Atlanta invite[s]
>
> viewers' involvement in the experience of remembering the dead.

CHAPTER 16

Grammar for ESL Writers

*I*f English is not your native language, you may find some of its features troublesome. This chapter provides practice in English grammatical structures that cause difficulty when English is a writer's second language (ESL).

16a Distinguishing count nouns from noncount nouns

To use nouns and determiners correctly, you must first know whether a noun is a *count* or a *noncount* noun (sometimes called a *mass noun*). (See 12a for a more complete discussion of nouns.)

A *count noun* refers to people, places, or things that are counted separately. Count nouns may be singular or plural. You may use a determiner such as *a* or *an* with a count noun.

Twenty-two *students* signed up for English 101.

One *student* never came to class. She was a transfer *student*.

A *noncount noun* is a noun that cannot be counted separately, such as *air, water,* and *wealth.* Noncount nouns do not have a plural form.

The *light* in the lecture hall was dim, and the *air* was pleasantly cool. Haroun had little *sleep* the night before.

Do not use *a* or *an* or a number before noncount nouns.

INCORRECT   We had *a rice* for dinner.

INCORRECT   We had *rices* for dinner.

REVISED   We had *rice* for dinner. *It* was delicious.

Words that indicate measures or portions can be used to show plural quantities of noncount nouns.

He ate *three bowls* of rice for dinner.

Please pick up *two pounds* of chicken at the supermarket.

The movers left *a few pieces* of furniture on the sidewalk.

Categories of Noncount Nouns

Groups of objects: homework, information, mail, news
Abstract words: courage, envy, health, time
Activities and sports: ballet, football, hockey, research, walking
Fields of study: anthropology, astronomy, engineering, photography
Foods: corn, fruit, lettuce, pasta, veal
Gases: air, nitrogen, oxygen, smog
Languages: Arabic, German, Japanese
Liquids: blood, coffee, gasoline, milk, tea
Materials: concrete, glass, iron, leather, polyester
Particles: pepper, rice, salt, sand
Weather: cold, ice, lightning, rain, sleet, snow, steam, sun

The distinction between count and noncount nouns differs from language to language. A noncount noun in English may well be a count noun in another language. The following English noncount nouns are count nouns in other languages. Take special care to use these nouns correctly.

advice   information   furniture   garbage   homework   housework
jewelry   luggage   mail   money   news   work

> **INCORRECT**   Do you have enough *monies* for your trip?
>
> **REVISED**   Do you have enough *money* for your trip?

Some nouns can be either count or noncount, depending on the use. A few examples follow; you should note others as you encounter them.

NONCOUNT NOUNS	COUNT NOUNS
This *bread* is delicious. I ate three pieces.	The Italian bakery sells delicious *breads*. [kinds of bread]
This is strong *coffee*.	Stan bought five *coffees* to go. [five cups of coffee]
Lin has beautiful *hair*.	Investigators found two *hairs* at the crime scene. [individual hairs]
Sid has no *experience* as a teacher.	They had interesting *experiences* on their trip. [separate experiences]
We had hardly any free *time*.	Hsiao-mi took the test three *times*. [on three occasions]

EXERCISE 16–1   **Working with Count and Noncount Nouns**

Underline the correct use of the noun in the following sentences. Example:

Richard needs *information*/*informations* about computers.

1. Firefighters exhibit their *courage*/*courages* every time they answer an alarm.
2. The company thinks I have more than enough *experience*/*experiences* to qualify for the job.
3. We had some funny *experience*/*experiences* last summer.
4. Over the weekend, my brother watched six full games of *football*/*footballs* on television.
5. Our history professor generously shared her *knowledge*/*knowledges* with us.

16b   Recognizing and using determiners

A **determiner** is a word or group of words that introduce a noun. Some determiners signal that a noun is to follow; other determiners indicate quantity. There are four types of determiners.

1. **Articles** indicate whether or not a noun refers to a specific person, place, or thing. The articles *a* and *an* are **indefinite articles** that refer to general nouns. The article *the* is a **definite article** that refers to specific nouns. (See 16c for a discussion of articles.)

   We saw *a* movie last night. *The* movies of Charlie Chaplin are classics.

2. **Quantifiers** (such as *one*, *some*, and *a lot of*) indicate how much or how many of a noun. (See 16d for a discussion of quantifiers.)

   Several filmmakers from Taiwan have received the Palme d'Or award.

3. **Demonstratives** (*this*, *that*, *these*, and *those*) point to a noun and distinguish it from others. (See 16e for a discussion of demonstratives.)

   This picture is beautiful. *That* argument is insupportable.

4. **Possessive adjectives** (such as *my*, *your*, *his*, *hers*, and *its*) indicate ownership of a noun. (See 16f for a discussion of possessive adjectives.)

   My ideas differ from yours.

   Do not use more than one determiner with each noun.

   INCORRECT   *The my book* is over there.

   REVISED   *My book* is over there.

Use singular determiners with singular nouns and plural determiners with plural nouns.

INCORRECT   Gretta read *a books* over the weekend.

REVISED   Gretta read *a book* over the weekend.

REVISED   Gretta read *several books* over the weekend.

16c Using the articles *a*, *an*, and *the* correctly

English has two kinds of articles: the **indefinite articles** *a* and *an* and the **definite article** *the*. In deciding whether to use *a*, *an*, or *the*, you must first determine whether the noun is indefinite or definite. A noun is indefinite when neither the writer nor the reader has a specific person, place, or thing in mind.

Let's try to find *a parking place*. [any parking place, not a specific one]

Could we open *a window*? [any one of several windows]

I love *music*. [music in general]

A noun is **definite** when both the writer and the reader know which specific person, place or thing it refers to.

Where is *the parking lot*? [a specific lot]

I opened *the window*. [the only window]

I love *the music* of the Jazz Age. [a particular style of music]

Next determine whether the noun is a noncount noun or a count noun (see 16a). Use the accompanying chart to decide on how to assign articles to count and noncount nouns.

Choosing the Correct Article

NOUN TYPE	IF INDEFINITE	IF DEFINITE
Singular count noun cat, hour	Use *a* or *an*	Use *the*
Plural count noun cats, hours	Use no article	Use *the*
Noncount beauty, time	Use no article	Use *the*

Using *a* or *an* with singular count nouns

Use *a* or *an* with every indefinite singular count noun.

INCORRECT   I wore *hat* today.

REVISED   I wore *a hat* today.

Every singular count noun must be preceded by a determiner. If the context does not require *a* or *an*, use another determiner. (See 16b for more on types of determiners.)

INCORRECT   We found *suitcase.*

REVISED   We found *a suitcase.*
                      We found *the suitcase.*
                      We found *our suitcase.*

WRITING HINT   Use *a* before a consonant sound. Use *an* before a vowel sound. Note that it is the initial sound, not whether the first letter is a consonant or a vowel, that determines whether *a* or *an* should be used.

a delicious meal; *a* history examination

a unique painting; *a* university [the *u* is pronounced like the consonant *y*]

an appetizer; *an* umbrella

an honest waiter; *an* hour later [the *h* is silent]

Using *the*

You can use the definite article *the* with all nouns—singular count nouns, plural count nouns, and noncount nouns.

When to Use the Definite Article *the*

- Use *the* when the noun has been mentioned previously. After the noun has been introduced, the reader knows which person, place, or thing it refers to.

  Early one morning, *a* child wandered into the Fifth Precinct station on Manhattan's Lower East Side. *The* child was shoeless and seemed to be lost. [*The child* was described in the preceding sentence.]

- Use *the* when the person, place, or thing is unique or generally known.

  The weather is getting stranger every year. [There is only one phenomenon we refer to as the weather.]

  I have never seen *the* Grand Canyon. [There is only one Grand Canyon.]

  Many immigrants pursue *the* American Dream. [The concept is generally known.]

- Use *the* when the context makes it clear which person, place, or thing is being referred to.

  The sick baby is crying. [There is one sick baby.]

  The flowers on your desk are beautiful. [There is one arrangement of flowers on the desk.]

  (continued)

- Use *the* when a clause or an adjective limits the noun so that it is clear which one is being referred to.

  Schindler's List was the best movie I saw in 1993. [There can only be one *best* movie.]

You can use one *the* for two or more nouns joined by *and*.

Dan circled *the* correct answer. [There is only one possible correct answer.]

People congregated on *the* porch and deck.

Insects flew amid *the* flowers, trees, and shrubs.

Using plural count and noncount nouns without an article

Do not use an article with plural count nouns or with noncount nouns when you make a generalization. A **generalization** is a statement based on or a conclusion derived from a limited number of examples.

INCORRECT   *The friends* are important.

REVISED   *Friends* are important.

INCORRECT   *The love* makes the world go around.

REVISED   *Love* makes the world go around.

USAGE NOTE   You will often come across generalizations with count nouns preceded by *a/an,* or *the* or even without an article.

A hamster is a wonderful pet.

The hamster is a wonderful pet.

Hamsters are wonderful pets.

There is no one rule for deciding how to phrase a generalization. However, you can avoid errors when you make generalizations with count nouns simply by using plural count nouns without an article.

INCORRECT GENERALIZATION
                 The vegetable is good for you.

INCORRECT GENERALIZATION
                 A vegetable is good for you.

REVISED   *Vegetables* are good for you.

Never use an article when you make a generalization with a noncount noun.

INCORRECT   Animals need *the oxygen* to survive.

REVISED   Animals need *oxygen* to survive.

WRITING HINT　You can often use indefinite plural count nouns and noncount nouns either without any determiner or with a quantifier.

Please buy *tomatoes* when you go to the store. [no determiner]

Please buy *some tomatoes* when you go to the store. [the quantifier *some*]

Water leaked all over the basement. [no determiner]

A lot of water leaked all over the basement. [the quantifier *a lot of*]

(See 16d for more on using quantifiers with nouns.)

EXERCISE 16–2　Choosing the Correct Articles

Complete the following sentences using the noun or phrase in parentheses and, if needed, the articles *a, an,* or *the*. Example:

　　(*help*) ___The help___ that you gave me was desperately needed.

1. (*children*) _____ sometimes require a lot of attention, and adults should realize this.
2. (*music*) I listen to _____ to relax.
3. (*best music*) _____ for relaxing is Keith Jarrett's.
4. (*advice*) She likes to give _____ , but she does not like to receive it.
5. (*dog*) It is your turn to walk _____ .

16d　**Choosing the correct quantifier for count and noncount nouns**

　　Quantifiers such as *several* and *a little* are words and phrases that indicate the amount or quantity of a noun. They tell how much or how many.

a few teachers	*not many* books	*some* lunch
several new students	*a lot of* classrooms	*many* pieces

　　Some quantifiers can be used only with noncount nouns and others with only count nouns (see 16a). Still others can be used with both. Refer to the accompanying chart when choosing a quantifier.

USAGE NOTE　Be aware of the difference between the quantifiers *a few* and *few*, and between *a little* and *little*. *Few* and *little* generally have a negative connotation. These words suggest "too few" or "too little."

He has only been here a week, but he has already made *a few* friends. [He has succeeded in making friends in a week.]

Choosing the Correct Quantifier

QUANTIFIERS WITH COUNT NOUNS	QUANTIFIERS WITH NONCOUNT NOUNS	QUANTIFIERS WITH BOTH COUNT AND NONCOUNT NOUNS	
a few dollars	*a little* money	*enough* jobs	*enough* work
too many problems	*too much* advice	*some* chairs	*some* furniture
forty minutes	*a great deal of* time	*a lot of* rings	*a lot of* jewelry
a number of bags	*a lot of* luggage	*any* minute	*any* time
several games	*little* time		
many tasks	*not much* energy		
a couple of sentences			

He has been here a year, but he still has *few* friends. [He has failed at making friends in a year.]

We had *a little* money to buy gifts. [We had money to buy some gifts.]

We had *little* money to buy gifts. [We did not have much money to buy gifts.]

WRITING HINT   Use the quantifier *any* with both noncount and count nouns in questions and negative sentences.

Do we have *any bread*?

We do not have *any bread.*

Are there *any tomatoes*?

I cannot find *any tomatoes.*

Use *how much* to ask about quantity with noncount nouns. Use *how many* to ask about quantity with count nouns.

How much bread do we need?

How many tomatoes should I buy?

EXERCISE 16–3   Working with Articles and Quantifiers

Revise the following passage. Underline and correct errors in the use of articles and quantifiers. Insert omitted articles or quantifiers. The first two errors have been corrected for you.

He had a nice apartment with ~~much~~ ^{many} rooms. Everyone stayed in ^{the} kitchen, even though living room and a dining room were spacious and inviting. His place was simple and functional. He had bought a few furniture from some friends who had lived in large house together but then had to move to small dorm rooms. When he invited friends over to his apartment, they stayed long and talked about any things, such as what they wanted to do with their lives and how they would make living.

16e   Using demonstratives correctly

Demonstratives are determiners that indicate the distance of a noun, in either space or time, from the speaker or writer. The demonstratives are *this*, *that*, *these*, and *those*. The following guidelines will help you use demonstratives correctly.

    1. Use *this* and *these* to indicate that a noun is close to you in either space or time. Use *this* with noncount nouns and singular count nouns. Use *these* with plural count nouns.

INCORRECT	*These information* from the post office is very helpful.
CORRECT	*This information* from the post office is very helpful.
INCORRECT	These *bell* rings beautifully.
CORRECT	This *bell* rings beautifully.
INCORRECT	*This statistics* are inaccurate.
CORRECT	*These statistics* are inaccurate.

    2. Use *that* and *those* to indicate that a noun is distant in either space or time. Use *that* with noncount nouns and singular count nouns. Use *those* with plural count nouns.

INCORRECT	*Those coffee* you made yesterday tasted delicious.
CORRECT	*That coffee* you made yesterday tasted delicious.
INCORRECT	*Those magazine* had an interesting article about the economy.
CORRECT	*That magazine* had an interesting article about the economy.
INCORRECT	In *that days* only men received an education.
CORRECT	In *those days* only men received an education.

EXERCISE 16–4   Choosing the Correct Demonstrative

Underline the correct demonstrative in each sentence. Example:

    Nearly all the kids I taught were well behaved and smart. Why did <u>*that*</u>/*those* fact surprise my nonteaching friends?

1. Born in 1981, *those/that* students were heirs of the Reagan administration.
2. They had many gifts, and *these/those* gifts helped them survive the often cruel world of the Bronx.
3. My students all watched television because they had nothing else to do. I did not bother mentioning *this/that* problem to their parents.
4. One morning a student swallowed a penny. *That/Those* day there was no one on duty in the office.
5. The Teaching for America project was a stunning success its first year. *That/Those* same year, however, the program was abandoned.

 16f   Using possessive forms of pronouns correctly

Possessive adjectives precede the nouns they modify and indicate ownership or a relationship. The possessive forms of pronouns substitute for noun phrases; they do not precede nouns. Use possessive adjectives, not possessive pronouns, to modify nouns. Although the forms of possessive adjectives are similar to those of possessive pronouns, their functions differ.

> *My* ideas differ from *yours*. [*My*, a possessive adjective, modifies the noun *idea*. *Yours*, a possessive pronoun, substitutes for the phrase *your ideas*.

> *Her* hobby is woodworking. *His* is gardening. [*Her*, a possessive adjective, modifies the noun *hobby*. *His*, a possessive pronoun, substitutes for the phrase *his hobby*.]

The possessive adjectives and possessive forms of the pronoun are listed in the accompanying chart.

Possessive Adjectives and Possessive Forms of Pronouns

POSSESSIVE ADJECTIVES	POSSESSIVE FORMS OF PRONOUNS
my, your, his, her, its, our, their	mine, yours, his, hers, its, ours, theirs
It was *my* idea.	The idea was *mine*.
It is *her* hat.	The hat is *hers*.
Our problems are minor.	The minor problems are *ours*.
That is *their* house.	That house is *theirs*.

Keep the following tips in mind when using possessive forms in your writing.

- Use the apostrophe to form the possessive of indefinite pronouns such as *one*, *anyone*, and *nobody*. (See 12b for more on indefinite pronouns, and 35a-1, 35b, and 35e on using apostrophes.)

  One's memory sometimes falters after the age of fifty.

  Diego is *everyone's* favorite uncle.

  You are *nobody's* fool.

- Use *whose* to ask about possession. You can use *whose* in a sentence with or without a noun. Do not confuse *whose* with *who's*, the contraction for *who is*.

  INCORRECT   *Who's* idea was it?

  REVISED   *Whose* idea was it?

- Do not use an apostrophe with possessive adjectives or possessive forms of pronouns.

  Possessive adjectives

  INCORRECT   The cat left *it's* dinner untouched.

  REVISED   The cat left *its* dinner untouched.

  Possessive pronouns

  INCORRECT   That is not my telephone ringing; it is *your's*.

  REVISED   That is not my telephone ringing; it is *yours*.

- Never write its'. There is no such form.

(For more on possessive forms of pronouns, see 12b–c.)

EXERCISE 16–5   **Working with Possessives**

Underline the correct possessive forms in the following sentences. Example:

Who's/*Whose* research paper is this?

1. That research paper is *mine*/*mines*, not *theirs*/*theirs'*.
2. The cat uses *its*/*it's* tongue to clean itself.
3. It was *nobodys*/*nobody's* fault.
4. *Ours*/*Ours'* was not the only complaint.
5. *Your*/*Yours* was the best response to that question.

16g   Using correct word order for adjectives and other noun modifiers

Use the accompanying chart to determine typical word order when you use two or more descriptive adjectives.

Noun modifiers other than adjectives typically occur in a particular order. Use the accompanying chart to help you determine the word order for noun modifiers, including adjectives.

WRITING HINT   Avoid using a long string of adjectives with one noun.

> **AWKWARD**   My cousin Hilda is a pretty, serious, lively, intelligent girl who is always ready to help out.
>
> **REVISED**   My pretty cousin Hilda is a serious, intelligent girl who is lively and is always ready to help out.

Noun **modifiers** are words added to nouns to describe them and to make their meaning precise. In addition to adjectives (ADJ), noun modifiers include determiners, such as articles (AR), quantifiers (QUAN), demonstratives (DEM), and possessive forms of pronouns (PP).

> ┌PP┐   ┌ADJ┐
> I remember her green summer dress.

> QUAN ADJ   AR
> There are some ripe peaches in the refrigerator.

> AR   ADJ   ADJ
> It was an interesting and stimulating idea.

> AR QUAN ADJ   DEM
> Yesterday was the first cold day we have had this winter.

No more than three noun modifiers are generally used with a noun.

This section gives practice in the correct use of adjectives and participles used as adjectives. (See 13a–b and 13e for more on adjectives, and 10c-2 for more on participles.)

USAGE NOTE   Adjectives always have the same form. They do not change to agree with the number or gender of the noun they modify.

> **INCORRECT**   She wore a *red* dress and matching *reds* shoes.
>
> **REVISED**   She wore a *red* dress and matching *red* shoes.

Word Order of Adjectives and Other Noun Modifiers

1. **Determiner:** *a, an, the, these, those, your, their, Sue's, anyone's, many, a few, a little, some, too much, too many*
2. **Words indicating order or number:** *first, initial, second, next, final, last, one, twenty*
3. **Adjectives expressing opinion or judgment:** *easy, attractive, dedicated*
4. **Adjectives indicating size or length:** *small, large, tall, long, short*
5. **Adjectives indicating shape or width:** *round, square, circular, oval, wide*
6. **Adjectives indicating condition:** *broken, dilapidated, smooth-running*
7. **Adjectives indicating age:** *old, young, new, modern, antique*
8. **Adjectives indicating color:** *blue, green, yellow, aquamarine, amber*
9. **Adjectives indicating nationality or religion:** *Spanish, Chinese, Muslim*
10. **Adjectives indicating material:** *plastic, stone, wood*
11. **Nouns used as adjectives:** *dining room, student*
12. **The noun**

Examples:

   1   2   6   11   12
Those last warm summer nights in September remind me of my childhood.

  2   4   5   10   11   12
Six large oval mahogany kitchen tables were delivered to the wrong house.

   1   3   9   12
A number of remarkable Italian restaurants can be found in Boston's North End.

  1   12   1   3   7   8   12
My brother refurbished that sleek vintage green Mustang.

EXERCISE 16–6   **Using the Correct Word Order for Adjectives**

The adjectives in the left column modify the noun to their right, but they are not in the correct order. Rearrange the adjectives in proper order. Example:

    serious/much   thought
    much serious   thought

1. colorful/many/deep-sea   creatures
2. exciting/special/her   surprise
3. used/old/many   books

4. dining/wooden/room   table
5. corduroy/threadbare/green   pants

Write about someone you know well in a paragraph or two. Include a description of the person's clothing or other belongings that characterize him or her. Use as many adjectives as you can. Ask your instructor or a native speaker in your class to check the word order of the adjectives you use.

 16h   Distinguishing between present participle and past participle used as adjectives

Both the **present participle**, such as *irritating* and *pleasing*, and the **past participle**, such as *irritated* and *pleased*, can function as adjectives in a sentence. When used as adjectives present and past participles have very different meanings. Participles that describe feelings or states of mind can be troublesome for nonnative speakers, as the following examples illustrate.

INCORRECT   I was *embarrassing*.

REVISED   I was *embarrassed* by his behaviors. [the past participle used as an adjective]

REVISED   It was an *embarrassing* moment for me. [the present participle used as an adjective]

INCORRECT   It was an *interested* film.

REVISED   It was an *interesting* film. [the present participle used as an adjective]

REVISED   The *interested* audience did not speak during the showing of the film. [the past participle used as an adjective]

Keep the following in mind when you use participles as adjectives.

• Use present participles (*boring, intriguing, fascinating, exhilarating*) to describe people, places, or things that *cause* a feeling or state of mind:

The book was *thrilling*. [The book caused this feeling.]

New York is an *exhausting* city. [The place causes this feeling.]

• Use past participles (*bored, intrigued, fascinated, exhilarated*) to describe people, places, or things that *experience* that feeling:

Kyung Hua is *fascinated* by English. [She experiences a feeling of fascination.]

The tourists will be *exhausted* by noon. [They will experience exhaustion.]

- Take special care when using the following participles:

PRESENT PARTICIPLES	PAST PARTICIPLES
amazing	amazed
annoying	annoyed
boring	bored
depressing	depressed
exciting	excited
exhausting	exhausted
fascinating	fascinated
frightening	frightened
interesting	interested
satisfying	satisfied
surprising	surprised

INCORRECT	Kyung Hua was *surprising* by her parents' arrival.
REVISED	Kyung Hua was *surprised* by her parents' arrival.
INCORRECT	*The Grapes of Wrath* offers a *fascinated* view of life during the Great Depression.
REVISED	*The Grapes of Wrath* offers a *fascinating* view of life during the Great Depression.

See also 10c-2 for more on the present participle and the past participle.

EXERCISE 16–8   Writing with Participles

In two or three paragraphs, describe a movie you saw recently. Explain what it was like and how you felt about it. Use present and past participles to describe the movie and your reaction to it. Ask your teacher or a native speaker in your class to check the participles in your description.

16i   Learning the forms of *be, have,* and *do*

The verbs *be, have,* and *do* are used frequently, both as main verbs and as auxiliary verbs. Since they are irregular, you must memorize their forms.

Remember that all English sentences require a main verb. Do not omit the verb in a sentence that has a complement, a word that describes the subject. (See 11d-1 on linking verbs.)

INCORRECT	He late.
REVISED	He *was* late.

INCORRECT   They never wrong about prices.

REVISED   They *are* never wrong about prices.

Keep in mind the changes required for third-person singular forms of *be, have,* and *do.* Use the accompanying chart for reference.

Forms of *be, have,* and *do*

BASE FORM	PRESENT TENSE	PRESENT PARTICIPLE	PAST TENSE	PAST PARTICIPLE
be	I *am* he/she/it *is* we/you/they *are*	*being*	I/he/she/it *was* we/you/they *were*	*been*
have	I *have* he/she/it *has* we/you/they *have*	*having*	I *have* he/she/it *had* we/you/they *had*	*had*
do	I *do* he/she/it *does* we/you/they *do*	*doing*	*did*	*done*

16j   Using the auxiliary verbs *be, have,* and *do* correctly

The **auxiliary verbs** (also called **helping verbs**) *be, have,* and *do* combine with a base form or a participle to create a verb phrase.

As a child I *was told* to study.

I *have learned* a lot about national politics this year.

I *do know* about the surprise party.

Progressive tenses, perfect tenses, the passive voice, negatives, and questions are all formed with auxiliaries. (For more on auxiliary verbs, see 11b.)

Progressive tenses

The **progressive tense** is used to indicate an action that continues in the past, the present, or the future. Use the appropriate form of *be* and the present participle to create the progressive tenses. (See 11h for more on progressive tenses.)

Remember the following points when you use the progressive tenses.

- The form of *be* must agree with the subject.

INCORRECT	Bob *are going* to class even though he feels sick.
REVISED	Bob *is going* to class even though he feels sick.

- Do not omit a form of *be* with the progressive tenses.

INCORRECT	We *starting* a new school club.
REVISED	We *are starting* a new school club.

Some verbs are used rarely in the progressive. They occur in the following categories. You must learn which verbs they are to use them correctly.

LINKING VERBS
be, become, exist, seem

VERBS THAT SHOW POSSESSION
belong, have, own, possess

VERBS THAT SHOW PERCEPTION
feel, hear, see, smell, taste

VERBS THAT SHOW FEELINGS, PREFERENCES, AND INTELLECTUAL STATES
believe, forget, hate, imagine, intend, know, like, love, need, pity, prefer, remember, suppose, understand, want, wish, wonder

INCORRECT	That book *is belonging* to Yokari.
CORRECT	That book *belongs* to Yokari.

Perfect tenses

The **perfect tense** is used to indicate an action that has been completed before another action begins, or an action finished by a specific time. Use the appropriate form of *have* and the past participle to create the perfect tenses. (See 11g for more on the perfect tenses.)

Akiko *has visited* the United States three times. [This sentence uses the present perfect tense to indicate that her visits began and ended sometime in the past. In the present perfect, the past participle of the main verb follows the present of *have*.]

She *had wanted* to visit the Deep South last February, but visited Australia instead. [This sentence uses the past perfect tense to indicate that she wanted to travel to the Deep South sometime before she went to Australia. In the past perfect, the past participle of the main verb follows the past participle of *have*.]

Remember the following points when you use the perfect tenses.

- The form of *have* must agree with the subject.

INCORRECT	My brother *have seen* every Clint Eastwood movie.
CORRECT	My brother *has seen* every Clint Eastwood movie.

- Do not omit a form of *have* when you use the perfect tenses.

    INCORRECT   Professor Lewis *gone* on sabbatical.

    CORRECT   Professor Lewis *has gone* on sabbatical.

- Use the past participle of the main verb, not the past tense, to form the perfect tenses.

    INCORRECT   Abdul and Sara *have ran* in the Boston marathon several times.

    CORRECT   Abdul and Sara *have run* in the Boston marathon several times.

When you are not sure how to form the past participle, check your dictionary. If the past participle and the past tense have different forms, the dictionary will give both forms. Also consult the chart in 11c.

USAGE NOTE   The present perfect tense after *since* requires a specific time. The present perfect after *for* requires a span of time.

We have been visiting this campground *since 1989.*

We have been visiting this campground *for ten years.*

Passive voice

In the **passive voice**, the grammatical subject of a sentence receives the action of the verb. Use the passive voice when the subject is unknown or considered relatively unimportant. (See 11j–k for more on verb voice.)

My brother *was elected* class president. [The emphasis in this sentence is on *My brother* rather than those who elected him.]

The passive voice combines the past tense of *be* and the past participle. Keep the following points in mind when you use the passive voice.

- The past participle never changes, but the auxiliary *be* must agree with the subject.

    INCORRECT   Many home-based businesses *was created* in the 1980s.

    CORRECT   Many home-based businesses *were created* in the 1980s. [The auxiliary *were* agrees with the plural subject *businesses*.]

- Use only transitive verbs in the passive voice. Transitive verbs, such as *kiss* and *hit,* are verbs that take a direct object (see 11d-2).

    ACTIVE   Brazilians *speak* Portuguese.

    PASSIVE   Portuguese *is spoken* by Brazilians.

- Intransitive verbs, such as *smile* and *occur,* do not take an object. They cannot be used in the passive voice.

    INCORRECT   A strange thing *was happened* yesterday.

    REVISED   A strange thing *happened* yesterday.

USAGE NOTE   Verbs using the word *get* are often heard in informal, spoken English. Such usage is correct. However, for more formal, written English, use the passive voice as described in this *Handbook*.

LESS FORMAL   The bank robber *got arrested* yesterday.

MORE FORMAL   The bank robber *was arrested* yesterday.

(For more on formal and informal usage, see 28c.)

Negative sentences and questions

Negative sentences and many questions combine a form of *do* with the base form of a verb.

Please *do not forget* to turn off the air conditioner.

Did you *hear* what I said?

Keep the following points in mind when you use *do* in negative sentences and questions.

- Remember that the third-person singular in the present tense uses the form *does*.

Does Jim often arrive late?

No, but maybe he *does not* know about this meeting.

- Use the present tense form of the main verb after *do*.

INCORRECT   *Did* you *saw* anything interesting?

CORRECT   *Did* you *see* anything interesting?

EXERCISE 16–9   Using *be, have,* and *do*

Complete the following sentences by adding the correct form of *be, have,* or *do*. Example:

Joel and Ethan Coen __are__ young, prize-winning filmmakers.

1. The brothers _____ a weird sense of humor, which characterizes their films.
2. In 1979, Ethan _____ working as a typist and Joel _____ editing horror films.
3. They started to talk about screenplays at that time, and they _____ worked together ever since.
4. Ethan _____ all the typing when they talk.
5. One of their films, *Barton Fink,* _____ awarded the Palme d'Or in 1991.

16k Recognizing and using modal auxiliaries

A **modal auxiliary** is an auxiliary verb that is used with a main verb to indicate necessity, obligation, permission, or possibility.

Wang *should wear* a suit to his interview tomorrow.

They *might offer* him the job.

Modals give information about the speaker or writer's attitude toward that verb. Modals have only one form. The accompanying chart indicates how to use modals.

Using Modals		
MODAL	MEANING CONVEYED	EXAMPLE
can, could	ability	Carla *can* run five miles. I *could* run last year, but I *cannot* run today.
should	advisability	It is going to rain. You *should* take an umbrella.
must, have to	necessity	We *must* remember to go to the library. We *have to* return some books.
not	prohibition	You *must not* park in front of the police station.
must, must not	logical necessity	This letter *must* be from Svetlana. I know no one else in Moscow. The Smiths *must not* know our new telephone number.
will, would	intention	I think I *will* go to the movies tomorrow.
may, might, could	possibility	Fred is sick. He *may* or *may not* come to the meeting today.

Keep the following in mind when you use modals in your writing.

• Do not use the third-person singular -*s* ending with a modal.

INCORRECT Glen *musts* register soon, or he will not get into the class.

CORRECT Glen *must* register soon, or he will not get into the class.

• Always use the base form of the verb, not the infinitive or past tense, after a modal.

INCORRECT	Sid and Maria *could to speak* English last year.
INCORRECT	Sid and Maria *could spoke* English last year.
CORRECT	Sid and Maria *could speak* English last year.

- When the modal is followed by another auxiliary verb (*be, have,* or *do*), use the base form of the auxiliary verb. (See 16j for more on forms of *be, have,* and *do*.)

INCORRECT	The package *could not been delivered.*
REVISED	The package *could not be delivered.*

- Do not use more than one modal with any main verb. Use one of the following phrases as a substitute for the second modal.

MODAL	SUBSTITUTES
can	be able to
must	have to
should	supposed to, be obliged to

INCORRECT	Sylvia *might can* pass the history test this semester.
CORRECT	Sylvia *might be able to* pass the history test this semester.

- Use the perfect tense after *could, would,* and *should* to relate something that did not happen. Do not substitute *of* for *have* in this structure.

INCORRECT	I *could of* worked last summer, but I decided to attend summer school instead.
CORRECT	I *could have* worked last summer, but I decided to attend summer school instead.

(For more on modal auxiliary verbs, see 11b.)

EXERCISE 16–10 Revising Errors with Modals

Correct the errors involving modals in the following passage.

Great blue herons are beautiful birds that used to be hunted for their feathers. They could had become extinct, but they were saved at the last minute by conservation laws. Game wardens such as Arthur Knight of the Chesapeake Bay area have protected them fiercely since then. Knight would has arrested his own brother for illegal hunting, say residents of his small town. Herons are fascinating birds for birdwatchers. An adult heron cans stand motionless while it watches for fish, and then can strikes with lightning speed. Young birds have a hard time learning this skill, however. Many would died of hunger without their parents' help. Besides fish, herons should also can able to find frogs and insects to supplement their diet. For that reason, they must to have a vital habitat.

—Adapted from Richard J. Dolesh, "The Great Blue Heron"

16l   Using gerunds and infinitives

Infinitives and **gerunds** are verbals—verb forms that function as nouns. An infinitive or a gerund can be used as a subject, an object, or a complement in a sentence. Take care to use the correct verb forms when using verbals as objects.

Attending college can be an exciting experience. [The gerund *attending* is the subject of the sentence.]

We enjoy *hearing* the lectures. [*Hearing* is the direct object of the verb *enjoy*.]

To see is *to believe*. [*To see* is subject of the sentence; *to believe* is the complement.]

Using infinitives as objects

Refer to the accompanying chart for guidelines on how to use infinitives as objects.

How to Use Infinitives as Objects

- Certain verbs are followed by an infinitive.

afford	consent	have	plan	swear
agree	decide	learn	pretend	threaten
arrange	deserve	manage	refuse	try
claim	fail	offer	seem	wait

Some students *fail to balance* their academic and recreational activities.

Other students *learn not to be* outdone by those pressures.

Note that *not* precedes the infinitive in the negative form.

INCORRECT   Tsilya *wants going* to Europe this summer.

REVISED   Tsilya *wants to go* to Europe this summer.

- Some verbs are followed by a noun or pronoun and then the infinitive.

advise	command	force	order	teach
allow	convince	hire	persuade	tell
cause	encourage	instruct	remind	urge
challenge	forbid	invite	require	warn

The city *hired* an investigator *to find* the causes of the accident.

Jorge *persuaded* his employer *to give* him time off to attend classes.

(continued)

- Other verbs may be followed either by a noun or pronoun and an infinitive, or directly by an infinitive.

allow	expect	help	want
ask	force	need	would like
cause	get	permit	

One student *asked to leave* the room.

The professor *asked* the disruptive student *to leave* the room.

The university *expects* Kara *to repeat* the course. She *expects to do* well.

- When the verbs *let*, *make*, and *have* mean *"allow," "cause,"* or *"require,"* they are followed by a noun or pronoun and the base form of a verb (the infinitive without *to*).

INCORRECT	Sue *has* her children *to read* or play games in the afternoon.
CORRECT	Sue *has* her children *read* or play games in the afternoon.
CORRECT	Sue *does not let* her children *play* video games.
CORRECT	Video games *make* her children *behave* aggressively.

Using gerunds as objects

Refer to the accompanying chart for guidelines on using gerunds as objects.

How to Use Gerunds as Objects

- Certain verbs are followed by gerunds.

admit	delay	imagine	practice	resist
allow	deny	keep	quit	risk
appreciate	discuss	mention	regret	stop
avoid	dislike	mind	remember	suggest
cannot help	enjoy	miss	report	tolerate
consider	finish	postpone	resent	understand

Sigeru Miyamoto *suggested changing* the nature of video games.

He *enjoyed creating* games with stories like fairy tales.

INCORRECT	Sal *denied to drink* before he drove his car that night.
REVISED	Sal *denied drinking* before he drove his car that night.

(continued)

- Many verbs followed by gerunds may also include a possessive form indicating the person performing the action.

appreciate	deny	mention	regret	risk
cannot help	enjoy	mind	report	suggest
consider	forgive	postpone	resent	tolerate
delay	imagine	prevent	resist	understand

We *understand* your *wanting* to go right now.

The company *appreciated* Sam's *changing* his vacation schedule.

The letter didn't *mention* his *not being* able to attend the meeting.

- Remember that only gerunds may be the objects of prepositions. Many English phrases consist of a noun, a verb, or an adjective plus a preposition. Always use a gerund after one of the following phrases. However, this list is not complete. You should add to it as you encounter more such phrases.

accuse someone of	be responsible for	fear of
apologize for	be tired of	interest in
approve of	be used to	look forward to
be afraid of	believe in	object to
be capable of	depend on	talk about
be interested in	dream of	think about

Greg *talks about changing* jobs, but he never does anything about it.

We would not *dream of leaving* without you.

Suwattana *is capable of handling* the project by herself.

Choosing an infinitive or a gerund

Some verbs may be followed by either a gerund or an infinitive. However, the meaning of the sentence may change depending on which form is used. See the accompanying chart for guidelines on working with verbs that take both infinitive and gerund objects.

Verbs Followed by Either Gerunds or Infinitives

- A few verbs may be followed by either an infinitive or a gerund with no change in meaning.

attempt	hate	omit
begin	like	prefer
continue	love	start

(continued)

Keith *continued to apply* for student loans.

Keith *continued applying* for student loans.

Students *begin to look* for jobs before graduation.

Marcia *began looking* for work in May.

- Some verbs of perception (*hear, look at, notice, see, smell, watch*) may be followed by either the base form (the infinitive without *to*) or the gerund. However, the meaning changes slightly depending on which form you use.

Jake *saw* two men *rob* that house. [He watched the whole incident.]

Jake *saw* two men *robbing* that house. [The robbery was in progress when he noticed it.]

- Some verbs change meaning depending on whether a gerund or infinitive object is used. These verbs are:

forget   stop
remember   try

Notice the different meanings for the infinitive and gerund with these verbs.

INFINITIVE	I *forgot to buy* groceries. [I forgot to buy them.]
GERUND	I *forgot buying* groceries. [I forgot I had bought them.]
INFINITIVE	I *remembered to meet* him after work. [I did not forget to meet him after work.]
GERUND	I *remembered meeting* him in January. [I remember that I met him in January.]
INFINITIVE	I *stopped to talk* to Myra. [I quit what I was doing to talk to Myra.]
GERUND	I *stopped talking* to Myra. [I ended my conversation with Myra.]
INFINITIVE	Please *try to open* the window. [Attempt to open the window.]
GERUND	*Try opening* the window to cool off the room. [See if opening the window works to cool off the room.]

- When the verbs *allow* and *permit* do not have a noun or pronoun object, they are followed by a gerund. When they do have a noun or pronoun object, they are followed by an infinitive.

WITHOUT NOUN OR PRONOUN OBJECT
The city *does not allow parking* on certain streets.

WITH NOUN OR PRONOUN OBJECT
The police officer *did not allow Hassan to park* in front of the library.

EXERCISE 16–11　Choosing Gerunds and Infinitives

Underline the correct form of the object in the following sentences. Example:

Some people need *facing/to face* risks in order to feel good.

1. These people enjoy *participating/to participate* in sports such as hang gliding.
2. While most of us only think about *windsurfing/to windsurf*, the risk takers actually do it.
3. Shekeina Hale decided *finding/to find* a high-risk sport because she wanted a challenge.
4. A friend advised her *trying/to try* skydiving.
5. "At first I was terrified," she said. "But I stopped *being/to be* afraid after my first jump."

EXERCISE 16–12　Writing with Gerunds and Infinitives

In one or two paragraphs describe an important experience in your life. Use verbs followed by gerunds or infinitives. Ask your teacher or a native speaker to check your use of gerunds and infinitives.

16m　Recognizing common phrasal verbs and correctly placing their objects

A **phrasal verb** is a verb phrase consisting of a verb and one or two prepositions or adverbs. (See also 10c, and 14a on prepositions, and Chapter 13 on adverbs.) Phrasal verbs often express an idiomatic, or nonliteral, meaning. (See 16r on learning idiomatic expressions.) That is, the complete phrasal verb has a different meaning from the meaning of each of its individual words. For example, when you use the two words *step* and *up* separately, they mean to take a step in a particular direction.

The lottery winner *stepped up* onto the stage to claim the prize.

However, the phrasal verb *to step up* means to increase, or to go faster.

Pat has decided *to step up* her training for the Olympics.

As you can see from the example of *step + up*, not every combination of verb plus preposition or adverb is a phrasal verb. However, you can test whether a combination is a phrasal verb by trying to substitute a similar verb in the phrase. If the phrase is a true phrasal verb, substitution is impossible.

POSSIBLE   The lottery winner *climbed up* onto the stage to claim the prize.

IMPOSSIBLE Pat has decided *to climb up* her training for the Olympics.

Since many phrasal verbs are idiomatic, or nonliteral, you must be careful that they convey your intended meaning.

You should also check your understanding of the phrasal verbs in the accompanying chart by consulting your dictionary, by asking your instructor, or by asking a native speaker about the meaning.

Some Common Phrasal Verbs

INTRANSITIVE (DO NOT TAKE A DIRECT OBJECT)

act up	get on	run out
break down	give in	stay up
catch on	grow up	step in
cut in	hang on	wear off

TRANSITIVE (TAKE A DIRECT OBJECT)

call on	give up	take off
do over	*grow up*	tear down
figure out	hand in	throw away
get in	look up	turn on
get on	pay back	turn down
get over	*run into*	*watch out for*

Note: The verbs in italics are inseparable.

USAGE NOTE   Phrasal verbs tend to be colloquial, or informal. As such, they may be unacceptable for academic writing, though acceptable in everyday conversation. Check the usage descriptions in your dictionary for two- or three-word verbs you are unsure about. If the phrasal verb is marked *slang*, or *colloquial*, you may also wish to use a one-word alternative.

INFORMAL   After her arrest, Lisa stopped *hanging out* with drug dealers.

REVISED   After her arrest, Lisa stopped *associating* with drug dealers.

INFORMAL   The band was *turned on* by the prospect of going abroad.

REVISED   The band was *enthusiastic* at the prospect of going abroad.

Notice how in the last example, the preposition *at* replaces *by*. When you substitute a one-word alternative for an overly informal phrasal verb, you may need to make other minor adjustments in your sentence as well. (For more on using informal language in writing, see 28c.)

Like other verbs, phrasal verbs may be either intransitive or transitive. An **intransitive verb** (including an intransitive phrasal verb) does not take a direct object.

> We were encouraged to *hang on* to our goals. [*Our goals* is the object of the preposition *to*, not the phrasal verb *hang on*.]

A **transitive verb** (including a transitive phrasal verb) takes a direct object.

> They *picked out* some new clothes. [*Some new clothes* is the direct object of *picked out*.]

Transitive phrasal verbs may be *separable* or *inseparable*. Inseparable transitive phrasal verbs must always keep the verb and particle (a word such as *for, on,* or *up*) together. In using these verbs, you cannot place the object between the verb and the particle.

> INCORRECT   The police are *looking* them *for*.
>
> REVISED   The police are *looking for* them.

In using *separable transitive verbs*, you may place a noun object (NO) either after the verb and the particle or between the verb and the particle. But you cannot place the particle after additional words in the sentence. Notice how the separable transitive verb *look up* is used in the following example.

> INCORRECT   Chris *looked* the word in the dictionary *up*. [The particle *up* does not come immediately after the noun object.]
>
> REVISED   Chris *looked* the word *up* in a dictionary. [The particle *up* comes immediately after the noun object.]
>
> REVISED   Chris *looked up* the word in a dictionary. [The parts of the phrasal verb are kept together, and precede the object.]

If the object is a pronoun, place it between the verb and the particle.

> INCORRECT   Chris *looked up* it in a dictionary. [The pronoun *it* is placed after the particle.]
>
> REVISED   Chris *looked* it *up* in a dictionary. [The pronoun *it* comes between the verb and the particle.]

EXERCISE 16–13   Working with Phrasal Verbs

Complete the following sentences using the phrasal verbs and objects in parentheses. Change verb tense when necessary, and place objects in their correct position. Example:

The overall project is complex, but we can (*break down/it*) into smaller parts. We can *break it down* into smaller parts.

1. That math problem was not difficult. I (*figured out/it*) in just a few minutes.
2. The radio is loud. Could you (*turn down/it*), please?
3. Jerrilyn met an old friend today. She (*ran into/him*) on the bus.
4. Ned is in a bad mood because he is sick. It is difficult to (*get along with/him*) when he is like that.
5. This novel is fascinating. I cannot (*put down/it*).

16n Using prepositions to express time, place, or motion

A **preposition** indicates the relationship between a noun or a pronoun and another word or group of words in a sentence. The prepositions that can be used to indicate relationships of time, place, and motion are sometimes confused. Use the accompanying guidelines when using the prepositions to indicate time, place, and motion in a sentence. (See 14a for more on prepositions.)

A Guide to Using Prepositions to Indicate Time, Place, or Motion

TIME

To indicate time, use the prepositions *in, on,* or *at.*

in the 1990s	*in* September	*in* a few minutes	*in* the morning
on Monday	*on* Labor Day		
at midnight	*at* 7:30 a.m.	*at* lunch time	

PLACE

To indicate place, use the prepositions *in, on,* or *at.*

in Mexico City	*in* the shower	*in* my room	*in* Kansas
on the desk	*on* Mt. Hood	*on* the river	*on* a plane
at the movies	*at* the station	*at* the bookstore	*at* home

MOTION

To indicate motion, use the pronoun *into.*

into the night	*into* our house	*into* agreement	*into* a fight

EXERCISE 16–14 Using Appropriate Prepositions

Underline the correct preposition in each of the following sentences. Example:

I went to pick up my brother *in/on/at* the airport.

1. Three books were *in/on/at* the shelf.
2. I saw a cute puppy *in/on/at* the store window.
3. We noticed them as soon as they came *in/into* the room.
4. She lives *in/on/at* Main Street *in/on/at* Muncie, Indiana.
5. The public television station broadcast a moving documentary *in/on/at* Monday evening about veterans who served *in/on/at* Vietnam.

16o Placing adverbs

An **adverb** is a word that modifies a verb, an adjective, another adverb, or an entire sentence. Adverbs are used to indicate viewpoint, order, intensity, manner, place, or time. Adverbs can be placed at the beginning, in the middle, or at the end of a sentence. They can appear before or after a verb, or between an auxiliary verb and a main verb. (See Chapter 13 for more on adverbs.)

Quickly, they tried their key in the front door.

The coach has *never* given up on his team.

They skied down the icy slope *carefully.*

We *rarely* stay up late.

He looked *anxiously* in her direction.

An adverb cannot be placed between a verb (V) and its direct object (DO).

INCORRECT   We watched *silently* the rain.

REVISED   We watched the rain *silently.*

Use the accompanying chart to help you decide on the placement of adverbs.

WRITING HINT   Place adverbs appearing in negative statements after the negative words.

Professor Josiah does not *always* return papers on time.

Our needs were not *adequately* provided for.

For questions, place the adverb some place after the subject of the sentence.

S
Will you *always* remember me?

S
Can you do this for me *now*?

Adverb Placement

- Adverbs conveying the writer's **viewpoint** should be placed at the beginning of the sentence.
  Fortunately, both sides came to an agreement and the strike ended.
  Surprisingly, she opted to visit her sister rather than her brother over vacation.
- Adverbs indicating **order** or **sequence** should be placed either at the beginning or at the end of the sentence.
  First, we will consider the causes of the war.
  We will examine justification for the war *last.*
- Adverbs indicating **intensity** should be placed immediately before the modified words.
  The decision *completely* surprised us.
  Their actions were *entirely* justified.
- Adverbs indicating **manner** can be placed immediately before the modified words or at the end of the sentence.
  The sleuth *silently* entered the room.
  The sleuth entered the room *silently.*
- Adverbs indicating **place** are usually placed at the end of the sentence.
  She planted snapdragons *here.*
  The hurricane uprooted trees *everywhere.*
- Adverbs indicating **time** are placed either at the beginning or at the end of a sentence. These adverbs always follow any adverbs that indicate manner and place.
  Yesterday, the baseball team won its first game.
  We completed our work *quickly.*
  It rained *hard here last* night.

EXERCISE 16–15 Revising with Adverbs

Rewrite the following sentences using the adverbs shown in parentheses. Example:

He did not see me or find out about my fear. (*luckily*)
Luckily, he did not see me or find out about my fear.

1. This is my first experience riding the New York subway and I am terrified. (*alone/completely*)
2. I need to go to the train station, but I am afraid I will get lost on my way. (*there*)
3. Before I left the apartment, I studied a subway map. (*carefully*)
4. I got on the wrong train and got lost. (*quickly*)
5. I got off the subway and took a taxi to the train station. (*miserably*)

EXERCISE 16–16   **Writing with Adverbs**

In two to three paragraphs write about a time when you did something difficult. Use adverbs in your description. Ask your teacher, another student, or a native speaker to check the word order of the adverbs you use.

16p   Changing forms with indirect discourse

Changes in word order and verb tenses often create problems when writers use indirect speech or indirect discourse (see 20e). When you record a speaker's or another writer's words exactly, you use quotation marks around them (see Chapter 36). This is **direct discourse**. When you do not quote someone else's exact words but instead report what was said using **indirect discourse**, you do not use quotation marks.

DIRECT DISCOURSE	Meteorologist Kurt Manner said, "Weather patterns have changed all over the world."
INDIRECT DISCOURSE	Meteorologist Kurt Manner remarked that weather has changed all over the world.

When you convert direct discourse into indirect discourse, you should keep the accompanying guidelines in mind.

Converting Direct Discourse to Indirect Discourse

- Change the simple present tense of direct discourse to the simple past tense.

DIRECT	He said, "Scientists *discover* traces of aluminum in the town's water supply."
INDIRECT	He said that they *discovered* aluminum in the town's water.

(continued)

- Change the present progressive tense of direct discourse to the past progressive.

  DIRECT   He said, "Scientists *are discovering* traces of aluminum in the town's water supply."

  INDIRECT   He said that they *were discovering* aluminum in the town's water.

- Change the present perfect and the simple past of direct discourse to the past perfect.

  DIRECT   He said, "Scientists *have discovered* traces of aluminum in the town's water supply."

  INDIRECT   He said that they *had discovered* aluminum in the town's water.

  (For more information on verb tenses, see 11f–i and 16h.)

- Change *will* to *would, may* to *might,* and *can* to *could.*

  DIRECT   He said, "Scientists *may discover* traces of aluminum in the town's water supply."

  INDIRECT   He said that they *might discover* aluminum in the town's water.

- Change *have to* and *must* to *had to.*

  DIRECT   He said, "Scientists *must discover* traces of aluminum in the town's water supply."

  INDIRECT   He said that they *had to discover* aluminum in the town's water.

- Report *yes/no* questions with the word *if* or *whether.* Use sentence word order, not question word order, with indirect questions. Do not use the words *do, does,* or *did* in an indirect question.

  DIRECT   He asked, "*Did* scientists discover traces of aluminum in the town's water supply?"

  INDIRECT   He asked *if* they discovered aluminum in the town's water.

- Report questions seeking information with *who, what, when, where, how,* or *why.*

  DIRECT   He asked, "*When* will scientists discover traces of aluminum in the town's water supply?"

  INDIRECT   He asked *when* they would discover aluminum in the town's water.

- Report invitations and commands with the infinitive.

  DIRECT   He said, "*Discover* traces of aluminum in the town's water supply."

  INDIRECT   He told them *to discover* aluminum in the town's water.

EXERCISE 16–17   Recording Viewpoints Using Direct and Indirect Speech

Interview several classmates about a topic in the news. Write two or three paragraphs in which you use both direct and indirect speech to report what they say.

16q Using verb tenses in conditional sentences

A conditional statement describes one event that must be true for another event to exist. A conditional sentence usually contains two clauses, an independent clause and a dependent clause (see 10d). The dependent clause in a conditional sentence typically begins with a word such as *if, when, whenever,* or *unless.*

┌─ DEPENDENT CLAUSE ─┐ ┌─── INDEPENDENT CLAUSE ───┐
Unless he arrives soon, we will have to leave without him.

When you write conditional sentences that include more than one clause, you must pay attention to the sequence of tenses you use in the independent and dependent clauses. (See 11i on verb tense sequences.) Use the accompanying chart to help you decide which tenses to use when describing real or unreal conditions in the past, present, or future.

Sentences with the verbs *hope* and *wish* are like conditional sentences. They too are used to write about uncertain situations.

I hope I can pass that test. [I might or might not be able to pass it.]

I wish I could pass that test. [I probably cannot pass it.]

Follow these guidelines for using verb tenses with *hope* and *wish.*

- Use the past tense to express a wish about the present or future.

   I wish I *knew* the answer. [I do not know the answer.]

   I wish I *were* going with you tomorrow. [I am not going with you tomorrow.]

- Use the past perfect to express a wish about the past.

   Jana wishes she *had stayed* in school. [She did not stay in school.]

   Veronica wishes she *had* not *bought* that new car. [She did buy that new car.]

- Use the present or future tense to express hopes.

   I hope you *have* a great time on your vacation.

   I hope I *will be* able to find a job after I graduate.

EXERCISE 16–18 **Writing with the Words *hope* and *wish***

Write three sentences for each of the following:

1. Describe what you hope will happen when you graduate from school.
2. Tell about something you wish were true about your life right now.
3. Write about something you wish had or had not happened in the past.

Guidelines for Using Verb Tenses in Conditional Sentences

- **Sentences that express real, factual conditions.**

  If the moon is full, the ocean tide runs high.

  In these sentences, the conditions stated in both the dependent and the independent clauses actually exist or did exist. Use the same tense in both clauses.

  INDEPENDENT CLAUSE   DEPENDENT CLAUSE

  Carlos bit his fingernails whenever he got nervous.

- **Sentences that express future real conditions.**

  If we leave now, we will get to the theater on time.

  These sentences predict situations that are likely to occur. Use the words *will, may, can, should,* or *might* followed by the base form of the verb in the independent clause; use the words *if* or *unless* plus a present tense verb in the dependent clause.

  INDEPENDENT   DEPENDENT
  CLAUSE   CLAUSE

  We will go to the party unless it snows.

- **Sentences that express present and future unreal conditions.**

  If we won the lottery, we would be rich.

  These sentences tell about unlikely or untrue situations in the present or future. Use the words *would, could,* or *might* followed by the base form of the verb in the independent clause; use the word *if* plus the past tense of the verb in the dependent clause.

  INDEPENDENT CLAUSE   DEPENDENT CLAUSE

  Nagash would study French if he had more time.

- **Sentences that express unreal conditions.**

  If you had filled the gas tank yesterday, we would not have run out of gas.

  These sentences tell about situations that failed to occur in the past. Use *would have, could have,* or *might have* followed by the past participle of the verb in the independent clause; use *if* plus the past perfect tense of the verb in the dependent clause.

  INDEPENDENT CLAUSE   DEPENDENT CLAUSE

  If I had taken one more course, I would have earned a minor in philosophy.

16r   Learning idiomatic expressions

Idiomatic expressions (or **idioms**) are phrases that do not take the literal meaning of the individual words that combine to form them. For example, *to get one's hands on* means to get possession of; it does not mean literally to put one's hands on something.

To get one's hands on something conveys a concrete image, something specific that you can see in your mind's eye. Because many idioms convey images, they have become a popular means of expressing an idea. And because they are popular, many idioms are clichéd. Since many idioms are informal expressions, they may be more appropriate for conversation than for academic writing.

Common Idiomatic Expressions

IDIOMATIC EXPRESSIONS USING *DEAD*

- to be dead on one's feet (to be exhausted)

  After working behind the ticket counter for ten hours, Jaime *was dead on his feet.*

- dead center (in the exact middle)

  You cannot miss the administration building; it is in the *dead center* of campus.

- to be dead tired (to be exhausted)

  Maurice *is dead tired* because he got no sleep last night.

- dead silence (absolute quiet)

  Dead silence greeted the news of Ruth's elopement.

IDIOMATIC EXPRESSIONS USING *END*

- to keep up one's end (to do one's share of the work)

  They asked Anne to leave the drama club because she did not *keep up her end* of the work.

- to make ends meet (to earn just as much as it costs to live)

  When Jack and Maya were first married, they could barely *make ends meet.*

IDIOMATIC EXPRESSIONS USING *HARD*

- to be hard up (to be short of money or to be poorly provided for)

  Ironically, during the spring floods, we were *hard up* for fresh water.

- to have hard feelings (to have an angry or bitter feeling)

  After their divorce, Chip's parents *had nothing but hard feelings* for one another.

(continued)

IDIOMATIC EXPRESSIONS USING *HIGH*

- high and dry (alone; stranded)

  George was left *high and dry* after his failed run for class president.
- to be in high spirits (to feel good)

  MaryBeth *was in high spirits* after receiving an *A* on the midterm.

IDIOMATIC EXPRESSIONS USING *LINE*

- to draw the line (to set a limit)

  The Japanese government supported the West financially during the Persian Gulf War, but it *drew the line* at military involvement.
- to read between the lines (to understand what is being implied in spoken or written word)

  The company's announcement does not mention layoffs, but if you *read between the lines*, it is clear layoffs will occur.
- in line with (in agreement or consistent with)

  The results were not at all *in line with* the government's optimistic projection.

IDIOMATIC EXPRESSIONS USING *MIND*

- to make up one's mind (to decide)

  John *made up his mind;* he bought the mountain bike rather than the racing bike.
- to be out of one's mind (to act in a crazy way)

  You would have to be *out of your mind* to go all the way to New Orleans and not walk down Bourbon Street.
- to pass through one's mind (to be a sudden thought; to occur)

  Though I thought the performance dull, the thought of leaving never *passed through my mind.*
- to have something on one's mind (to have something in one's thoughts)

  I *had lunch on my mind* during the lecture.
- to speak one's mind (to say what one thinks)

  The senate let Dr. Reiser *speak her mind* at the hearing.
- to read someone's mind (to know what someone is thinking)

  How did you know I wanted pizza for dinner? You *read my mind.*

IDIOMATIC EXPRESSIONS USING *SHORT*

- to be short of (to not have enough of)

  We *are short of* money this month, so our payment will be late.

(continued)

- to be short with (to be impatient)

  Rich complained to the manager because the sales clerk *was short with* him.
- to run short of (to not have enough)

  Because Madeline expected fewer people at the rally, she *ran short of* pamphlets.
- to fall short of (to fail to reach a goal)

  The blood drive *fell short of* its goal of 1,000 pints of blood.

IDIOMATIC EXPRESSIONS USING *WAY*

- to go out of one's way (to make an extra effort)

  Deborah *went out of her way* to see that our stay at her house was comfortable.
- to make one's way (to overcome a difficulty or to make a path for one's self)

  Tommy *made his way through* the underbrush to get to the swimming hole.
- to rub the wrong way (to annoy or bother someone)

  Kelly's boasting about her new car *rubbed her friends the wrong way.*

IDIOMATIC EXPRESSIONS USING *WORD*

- by word of mouth (orally)

  Clay learned of the free kittens *by word of mouth.*
- to get a word in (to get a chance to say something)

  With everyone talking at the same time, Mary found it difficult *to get a word in* to the conversation.
- play on words (to use words playfully)

  Shakespeare's comedies are known for their *play on words.*
- take at one's word (to believe what someone says)

  I *took you at your word* when you said you wanted to go to Anchorage in February; here are the plane tickets.

IDIOMATIC EXPRESSIONS USING *WORLD*

- to be dead to the world (to be fast asleep)

  You would have *to be dead to the world* not to hear my alarm ring in the morning.
- to be out of this world (to be excellent)

  David's chocolate fudge swirl cake *is out of this world.*

MISCELLANEOUS IDIOMATIC EXPRESSIONS

- to burn the midnight oil (to stay up late working or studying)

  Roger had *to burn the midnight oil* to get his research paper written on time.
- to call the shots (to be in charge)

  Doctors *call the shots* in the operating room.

(continued)

- to clear the air (to dispel tensions)

  We had a long meeting *to clear the air* about disagreements in the workplace.
- to cut corners (to do in the quickest or least expensive way)

  To get his paper written on time, Roger had *to cut corners* in his research.
- to hold the line (to maintain one's position)

  Because the faculty *held the line* on its demand for a two percent raise, the strike began yesterday.

You should learn as many idioms as possible, since they can help your speech and writing become easy and natural. Read through the accompanying chart to familiarize yourself with some common idiomatic expressions. You should also build your own list of idioms from conversation, reading, class lectures and discussions, and the media. Practice using the idioms in your speech and, when appropriate, in your writing.

EXERCISE 16–19   Using Idiomatic Expressions with Nouns

Write a paragraph using three idiomatic expressions that include nouns. Ask your teacher or a native speaker to check your use of idioms.

Grammar and Writing

English as a Second Language

If your first language is a language other than English, you will need to be careful in revising and editing your writing. This chapter highlights many elements of written English that ESL learners find troublesome. Use its many charts and boxes to review your written work.

One thing you can do right away, however, is to identify the three or four features of English that cause you the most difficulty. When you revise your writing, review it carefully for these troublesome difficulties, focusing on them one at a time as you go through your draft.

EXAMPLE

Much   was   Much

[Many] information[s] [were] included in the orientation packet. [Several]

of the information was helpful.

Remember that you already have a good deal of experience using grammar in your first language. Some of that experience and knowledge can be transferred to your study of English. However, not all rules and principles can be applied directly from your native language to English. Learning to control grammar in written English takes time, effort, and attentiveness. Progress comes with practice.

PART 5

Clear and Effective Sentences

Writing Grammatically Correct Sentences

*S*entences are the fundamental units of expression in English as well as in other languages. Sentences convey thoughts and feelings: *The film ended too abruptly. Did you have that sense as well?* Sentences provide the framework through which we express our opinions, explain our ideas, and provide evidence for our judgments. Grammatically, a sentence must contain a *subject* (a noun or pronoun identifying what the sentence is about) and a *predicate* (a verb that says something about the subject). Although people do not always speak in grammatically complete sentences, most college writing requires complete sentences.

The chapters in Part Five will help you write clear sentences that effectively express your meaning. Chapter 17 explains how to avoid sentence fragments, groups of words that are grammatically or logically incomplete. Chapter 18 identifies comma splices and fused sentences and how to avoid and correct these sentence errors.

The remaining chapters of Part Five discuss other ways to recognize and correct confusing sentences. Chapter 19 examines modifiers, especially how their proper placement contributes to clear writing. Chapter 20 describes methods for dealing with confusing shifts in verb tense and pronoun use. Chapter 21 identifies procedures for correcting problems with pronoun reference. Finally, Chapter 22 illustrates how mixing incompatible grammatical structures and omitting sentence elements lead to awkward writing and shows how to correct such problems.

CHAPTER 17

Sentence Fragments

A **sentence fragment** is a group of words that is punctuated as a sentence (beginning with a capital letter and ending with end punctuation) but is not grammatically complete. A sentence fragment may lack a subject or a finite verb, or both. A **finite verb** is the main, complete verb of a clause; it changes form to indicate tense, person, number, voice, and mood. A **nonfinite verb** (a verbal) does not change form or show tense; it needs an auxiliary verb to change form and act as the main verb of a sentence.

FINITE VERB	Drew *works* on his paper.
NONFINITE VERB	Jennifer was *working* on her paper.

A sentence fragment might also be a dependent clause that is not joined to an independent clause. (See 10d for more on identifying dependent and independent clauses.)

17a Correcting sentence fragments

Fragments can be corrected simply by supplying the missing sentence part: the subject, verb, or independent clause.

FRAGMENT	Gave the band the support it had been hoping for. [Subject is missing: Who or what gave the band that support?]
REVISED	*Two well-attended performances* gave the band the support it had been hoping for.
FRAGMENT	Two well-attended performances. [Verb is missing: What is being said about those performances?]
REVISED	Two well-attended performances *gave the band the support it had been hoping for.*
FRAGMENT	The performances giving the band support. [Complete verb is missing: The *-ing* form requires an auxiliary verb to function as the main verb in a sentence (see 11b).]

REVISED   The performances *are* giving the band support.

FRAGMENT   Because the two performances were well attended. [An independent clause to complete the idea initiated by *because* is missing: What happened as a result of those performances?]

REVISED   Because the two performances were well attended, *the band got the support it had been hoping for.*

As you can see from the following example, there are several ways to correct a sentence fragment.

FRAGMENT   The wind shrieking through the hills.

REVISED   The wind *was shrieking* through the hills. [auxiliary verb added to verbal]

REVISED   The wind *shrieked* through the hills. [verbal changed to finite verb]

REVISED   *We listened to* the wind shrieking through the hills. [independent clause added to dependent clause]

REVISED   The wind, shrieking through the hills, *frightened the animals.* [verb, *frightened,* and direct object, *the animals,* added]

Sometimes the best way to correct a sentence fragment is to combine the fragment with the sentence preceding or following it.

FRAGMENTS   Jimmy Santiago Baca was born in 1952 in Santa Fe, New Mexico. And has lived as well in North Carolina, California, and Arizona. He makes his home on a small farm. Where he lives with his wife and children. Outside Albuquerque.

REVISED   Jimmy Santiago Baca was born in 1952 in Santa Fe, New Mexico, and has lived as well in North Carolina, California, and Arizona. He makes his home on a small farm, where he lives with his wife and children outside Albuquerque.

Always check your drafts for fragments and rewrite them as complete sentences. You can spot fragments by checking to see if each sentence has a subject, a verb, and subordinating words. Use the accompanying chart to help you find fragments.

EXERCISE 17–1   Identifying and Correcting Sentence Fragments

Identify the sentence fragments in the following list and explain how you can correct each one. (Some entries may be correct as is.) Example:

To the lighthouse.

Add an independent clause: *They planned a trip* to the lighthouse.

1. With only the funds from last year's collection.
2. Who lost the car keys?
3. Learning a foreign language.
4. Because he could only hope to go.
5. The children who left school early.
6. Cruising the streets late at night in a new sports car.
7. Who was promoted during the company's days of expansion.
8. Something to do with the graduation ceremony.
9. Since she was a little girl.
10. Throughout Africa and perhaps throughout Asia as well.

Checking for Sentence Fragments

- **Locate the subject.** If a sentence has neither an explicit nor an implied subject, it is a fragment (see 10a).

- **Locate the verb.** If a sentence does not have a verb, or if it has a verbal without an auxiliary verb, it is a fragment (see 10c-2).

- **Look for subordinate conjunctions at the beginning of clauses.** A sentence must have at least one independent clause, a clause that has a subject and a main verb and that does not begin with a subordinating conjunction (see 14c-3).

- **Look for relative pronouns at the beginning of clauses.** If a relative pronoun introduces a clause, it is not a sentence. (Questions may begin with interrogative pronouns [12b], some of which are the same as relative pronouns, but those questions are still complete sentences: *Who won the game? Which team did you root for?*)

17b   Revising phrase fragments

Phrases (groups of related words that lack a subject or a finite verb) function as verbs, prepositions, nouns, or appositives. Sometimes verbal phrases, prepositional phrases, noun phrases, or appositive phrases are used, incorrectly, as complete sentences. A phrase misused as a sentence is called a phrase fragment.

1   Verbal phrase fragments

A *verbal phrase* consists of a verbal (an infinitive, a present or past participle, or a gerund) and any related objects or modifiers (see 10c-2). A verbal phrase fragment lacks a finite verb and sometimes a subject. Fragments consisting of verbal phrases can either be combined with a related independent clause or be converted to independent clauses.

FRAGMENT   The Clinton welfare plan was designed to accomplish a number of goals. Including putting more people to work.

REVISED   The Clinton welfare plan was designed to accomplish a number of goals, *including putting more people to work.* [The fragment is combined with a related independent clause.]

REVISED   The Clinton welfare plan was designed to accomplish a number of goals. *Its goals included a reduction of the deficit.* [The fragment is converted to an independent clause.]

2   Prepositional phrase fragments

A *prepositional phrase* consists of a preposition, its object, and any object modifiers. Prepositional phrase fragments have neither subjects nor finite verbs. Revise a prepositional phrase by combining it with a related independent clause.

FRAGMENT   The Clinton welfare plan required an increase in taxes. For the middle class.

REVISED   The Clinton welfare plan required an increase in taxes *for the middle class.*

3   Noun phrase fragments

A *noun phrase* consists of a noun and its modifiers (see 10c-1). Noun phrase fragments do not have finite verbs. Revise a noun phrase fragment by combining it with a related independent clause.

FRAGMENT   Various new therapies for the common cold. They created hope that a cure was likely to be found soon.

REVISED   *Various new therapies for the common cold created* hope that a cure was likely to be found soon.

4   Appositive phrase fragments

Appositives are nouns, pronouns, or noun phrases that rename other nouns (see 10c-2). An appositive cannot stand alone as a sentence and is best revised by combining it into the independent clause it refers to.

FRAGMENT   One of the people I remember fondly from high school is the baseball coach, John Ramos. A gentle man who knew the game well.

REVISED   One of the people I remember fondly from high school is the baseball coach, John Ramos, *a gentle man who knew the game well.*

EXERCISE 17–2 Working with Phrase Fragments

Change the following phrase fragments into independent clauses. Then add whatever elements are necessary to make the sentences complete. Example:

> Jane owns a convertible. One of the fastest cars in town.
> Jane owns one of the fastest cars in town, a convertible.

1. We used to have fun in that convertible. Cruising up and down Lincoln Avenue.
2. Jane would drive us all over town. Without a care in the world.
3. The other day she drove her convertible into another car. A dark blue sedan with a broken headlight.
4. The black and white patrol car at the curb. The officer approached her.
5. I left the scene of the accident. To find the driver of the abandoned car.

17c Revising compound predicate fragments

Compound predicates consist of two or more verbs and their objects (see 10a-2). A compound predicate fragment results when one predicate is set off in a separate sentence without its subject. Correct a compound predicate fragment by combining it with the related independent clause.

FRAGMENT They put the difficult year behind them. And looked to the future.

REVISED They put the difficult year behind them *and looked to the future.*

EXERCISE 17–3 Revising Phrase Fragments and Compound Predicate Fragments

Revise each of the following fragments by combining it with an independent clause or by rewriting it as a separate sentence. Example:

> He heard the ice breaking. All around the lake.
> All around the lake he heard the ice breaking.

1. The president proposed numerous changes. In the tax laws.
2. The painters scraped the house all day in preparation for painting. And then painted the next day.
3. She forgot her glasses. A fancy pair with red and silver rims.
4. His argument in favor of abolishing grades. It persuaded the administration to agree to a trial term.

5. They presented the proposal without fanfare. Assuming that it would not spur much debate.

6. The fire raging through the San Gabriel mountains. It was a terrifying sight.

7. Hoping to restructure the curriculum. A few faculty members began meeting. To draft a proposal for curricular reform.

8. Every weekend the most popular movies are rented. And then returned and rented again.

9. Searching through the mountains for the lost campers. The rescue team refused to give up hope.

10. They looked forward to seeing their friends. Happy energetic people.

17d   Revising dependent clause fragments

Dependent clauses begin with either a subordinating conjunction (such as *if, when, after, unless*) or a relative pronoun (*who, which, that*). Although dependent clauses have both a subject and a verb, they cannot stand alone as sentences. A dependent clause requires an independent clause to complete its meaning (see 10d); otherwise, it is a dependent clause fragment.

Revise a dependent clause fragment by combining it with an independent clause either before or after the fragment. Or convert the dependent clause fragment into an independent clause.

FRAGMENT	Much of the country watched. As the Dallas Cowboys won the Super Bowl.
REVISED	Much of the country watched *as the Dallas Cowboys won the Super Bowl.*
REVISED	Much of the country watched. *The Dallas Cowboys won the Super Bowl.*

(See 10d for more on distinguishing between dependent and independent clauses.)

Certain writing choices such as beginning a sentence with a subordinating conjunction occasionally lead to sentence fragments. You should not refrain from using such constructions in your writing, but you should be aware of the constructions in which fragments tend to occur. Use the cues in the accompanying chart, which will help you assess your writing for sentence fragments.

EXERCISE 17–4   Revising Dependent Clause Fragments

For each of the following items, identify the dependent clause fragment as (DC) and the complete sentence as (C). Then revise each fragment to make it part of the complete sentence.

1. They hoped to win the lottery. Which would solve their financial problems.
2. David Hicks is a teacher. Whose approach best suits the needs of his students.
3. When Kate was just three years old. Her parents enrolled her in a special nursery school.
4. I really did not know what to think. Whether to believe them or not.
5. Anita studies for six hours each night. Even though she works at the store five hours a day.
6. The executive left for the airport. As soon as the meeting was over.
7. Whoever hoped to complete the program requirements with distinction. Would have to do it within the allotted time.
8. Whenever I have a long stretch of work ahead of me. I make sure to take regular breaks.
9. Dad would reward me with a night at the movies. If I cleaned my room once every two months.
10. The birds flew from the cherry tree to the oak in the rock garden. Then over to their nest in a plant hanging on our porch.

Situations that Can Lead to Sentence Fragments

- When you begin a sentence with a subordinating word, be sure the sentence contains an independent clause. The following are the most commonly used subordinating words.

after	before	since	where
although	even if	so that	whether
as	even though	that	which
as if	how	though	while
as soon as	if	unless	who
as though	in order that	until	whose
because	now that	when	why

FRAGMENT	Although they were tired. They decided to go out to a movie.
REVISED	*Although they were tired,* they decided to go out to a movie.
FRAGMENT	They wanted to see a new film. That they had read about.
REVISED	They wanted to see a new film *that they had read about.*

- When using a transitional word or phrase to introduce examples or a list, check that the word or phrase is attached to an independent clause. The following are some commonly used transitional expressions.

also	especially	in addition	namely
and	for example	like	that is
as well as	for instance	mainly	such as
but			

(continued)

FRAGMENT	Everyone seemed interested. Especially the children.
REVISED	Everyone seemed interested, *especially the children.*

- When you begin a sentence with an infinitive, check to see that the sentence also includes a finite verb.

FRAGMENT	To win the approval of the judges. The young gymnasts performed energetically and enthusiastically.
REVISED	*To win the approval of the judges,* the young gymnasts performed energetically and enthusiastically.

- When you begin a sentence with a participle (*-ing* form of the verb used as a modifier), check to see that the sentence also contains an independent clause.

FRAGMENT	Finishing first in league play. The basketball team should make it to the tournament finals.
REVISED	*Finishing first in league play,* the basketball team should make it to the tournament finals.

17e   Using acceptable fragments

Although sentence fragments are rarely used in formal writing, experienced writers sometimes use them to achieve special effects, particularly for emphasis. Sentence fragments are more likely to appear in informal writing than in academic writing. Articles in popular magazines such as *Newsweek* and *People* use sentence fragments for emphasis and to effect a breezy style. Advertisements also often use sentence fragments.

The Esquire Watch. It has your name on it.

American Playhouse. The film festival in your living room. Only on PBS.

Unless you are striving for an informal style or are trying an occasional fragment for emphasis, you should generally avoid sentence fragments.

EXERCISE 17–5   Using Fragments in Writing

Rewrite the following paragraph to eliminate all sentence fragments. Compare the two versions, and explain which version you prefer and why.

It's a health spa. The place you come to when you want to get in shape. Of course, no one defines what "in shape" means. It's assumed. Inherent in the culture. Western societies of the 1990s define "in shape" to mean lean, trim, taut. And the ability to breathe normally after a six-mile run. A steady pitch is heard across America: "Take care of your body, it's a precious commodity."

Tiny Tim knew it when he said "You are what you eat." And out came a generation of tofu-eating, beansprout-picking, exercise-addicted people striving for bodily perfection. No longer do we need Socrates to explain the absolutes of beauty and truth. We have Arnold Schwarzenegger. And health spas.

—Mary Fitzgerald, student

EXERCISE 17–6   Collaboration: Observing Fragments in Advertisements

Select two advertisements from a newspaper or magazine and examine their uses of sentence fragments. Discuss the effects of the sentence fragments with a small group of your classmates.

EXERCISE 17–7   Considering Intentional Fragments

Identify the fragments in the following passage. Explain why you think the writer intentionally used fragments instead of a complete sentence. Then, assuming you want to avoid the fragments, explain how you would revise the passage and how your revision would affect the piece.

People in Stamps used to say that the whites in our town were so prejudiced that a Negro couldn't buy vanilla ice cream. Except on July Fourth. Other days he had to be satisfied with chocolate.

—Maya Angelou

Grammar and Writing

Sentence Fragments

You can apply what you have learned about sentence fragments to your own writing. In checking your drafts of papers and reports, look to see that you have written grammatically complete sentences. Identify the subject and verb in each sentence. Check to see whether any -*ing* verb forms lack auxiliary verbs. Check for other situations that can lead to sentence fragments by using the chart on p. 370 for guidance.

As an aid to writing grammatically complete sentences, try reading your drafts aloud. Listen for places your voice drops, indicating a stopping place between sentences. Check each time to see if what you read before you drop your voice makes sense by itself. Try to develop an ear for hearing the difference between a grammatically complete sentence and a sentence fragment.

CHAPTER 18

Comma Splices
and Fused Sentences

A complete sentence consists of at least one independent clause. When other clauses are added to that independent clause, certain punctuation rules must be followed to avoid comma splices and fused sentences. A **comma splice** is a sentence error in which two independent clauses are incorrectly separated by a comma instead of a period. A **fused sentence** is an error in which two sentences are run together without a punctuation mark between them. Comma splices and fused sentences are types of **run-on sentences** because they run together sentences that should be separated. With comma splice and fused sentence errors, the logical stopping point of an idea is ignored, creating confusing run-on sentences.

COMMA SPLICE	Beethoven was not born deaf, he lost his hearing gradually.
REVISED	Beethoven was not born *deaf. He* lost his hearing gradually.
FUSED SENTENCE	Beethoven was not born deaf he lost his hearing gradually.
REVISED	Beethoven was not born *deaf; he* lost his hearing gradually.

The accompanying chart outlines the various ways to correct comma splices and fused sentences. The method you choose to fix your comma splices and fused sentences will depend on where the errors appear in your writing and on what you wish to emphasize.

Ways to Eliminate Comma Splices and Fused Sentences

- Divide independent clauses into separate sentences (18a).
- Join clauses with a semicolon (18b).
- Join clauses with a semicolon and a conjunctive adverb (18c).
- Join clauses with a comma and coordinating conjunction (18d).
- Combine clauses into a single independent clause (18e).
- Convert one of the two clauses into a dependent clause (18f).

Dividing clauses into separate sentences

Often the most convenient way to revise comma splices and fused sentences is to put a period after each independent clause.

COMMA SPLICE	Mickey Mouse is among the most popular American cartoon characters, he is often accompanied by his companion Goofy.
FUSED SENTENCE	Mickey Mouse is among the most popular American cartoon characters he is often accompanied by his companion Goofy.
REVISED	Mickey Mouse is among the most popular American cartoon *characters. He* is often accompanied by his companion Goofy.

18b   Joining clauses with a semicolon

When the ideas in two independent clauses are closely related and equally important, join them with a semicolon (see 34a).

COMMA SPLICE	Supermarket tomatoes often taste bland, homegrown garden tomatoes are juicier and sweeter.
FUSED SENTENCE	Supermarket tomatoes often taste bland homegrown garden tomatoes are juicier and sweeter.
REVISED	Supermarket tomatoes often taste bland; homegrown garden tomatoes are juicier and sweeter.

In this example, the second independent clause elaborates on the first statement by providing a contrast. Use a semicolon when an idea developed in one clause is expanded in another.

USAGE NOTE   Separate independent clauses with a colon instead of a semicolon or a period when the second clause explains or summarizes the first one (see 34f).

There are two ways to lose weight: you can eat less or exercise more.

The Fifth Amendment is, of course, a wise section of the Constitution: you cannot be forced to incriminate yourself.

—Lillian Hellman

Separate independent clauses with a semicolon rather than a period when the second clause is closely related to the first, especially when the latter clause contrasts or shares the form of the first.

Excess of sorrow laughs; excess of joy weeps.

—William Blake

Before 8000 BC wheat was not the luxuriant plant it is today; it was merely one of many wild grasses that spread throughout the Middle East.

—Jacob Bronowski

EXERCISE 18–1   **Identifying Comma Splices and Fused Sentences**

In the following sentences, circle where any comma splices begin and underline the points at which two sentences are fused. Then revise the sentence. Example:

The plums were delicious, they were sweet and cold.

The plums were delicious: they were sweet and cold.

1. The art of photography developed in the nineteenth century it is continually being perfected.
2. Some states have passed laws banning smoking in public places, soon others will follow.
3. The store ran a special on dairy items butter, milk, and cheese were being sold at bargain prices.
4. Whenever I feel overwhelmed with work, I stop for a while I try to relax and collect myself to return to the task at hand.
5. Some say that youth is wasted on the young, I cannot agree, however.

18c   Joining clauses with a semicolon and a conjunctive adverb

When two independent clauses are linked with a conjunctive adverb such as *however, therefore,* or *furthermore* (see 14c-4), you need to punctuate the sentence carefully. Although conjunctive adverbs indicate the same types of relationships of addition, contrast, alternative, negation, explanation, and result, as coordinating conjunctions (*and, but, yet, or, nor, for, so*), they are punctuated differently than coordinating conjunctions because one clause is usually more important than the other. A clause that includes a conjunctive adverb must always follow a period or a semicolon. Consider the following examples.

COMMA SPLICE	The project will take a long time to complete, therefore, we should should begin work on it now.
FUSED SENTENCE	The project will take a long time to complete therefore we should begin work on it now.
REVISED	The project will take a long time to *complete; therefore,* we should begin work on it now.

Here the conjunctive adverb *therefore* follows immediately after the semicolon. The conjunctive adverb is usually followed by a comma.

In the following example, the word *lately* begins the independent clause with the conjunctive adverb *however. Lately* follows immediately after the semicolon. When that happens, the conjunctive adverb is set off from the clause with two commas.

COMMA SPLICE	The ideas of cultural anthropologists were neglected for years, lately however their ideas have become increasingly influential.
FUSED SENTENCE	The ideas of cultural anthropologists were neglected for years lately however their ideas have become increasingly influential.
REVISED	The ideas of cultural anthropologists were neglected for *years; lately, however,* their ideas have become increasingly influential.

Conjunctive adverbs can be placed in different positions in a sentence. (See 14c-4 for a list of common conjunctive adverbs and 34b for additional advice about using them in your writing.)

WRITING HINT   Conjunctive adverbs tend to increase the formality of writing. Conjunctive adverbs create a less conversational tone than that achieved by using coordinating conjunctions. Remember also that using too many conjunctive adverbs can slow your sentences down because the semicolons signal longer pauses than commas. (See Chapter 34 for more on semicolons.)

The flowers *fell, but* the fruit remained.

The flowers *fell; however,* the fruit remained.

18d   Joining clauses with a comma and a coordinating conjunction

To link closely related independent clauses of equal importance, use a comma followed by a coordinating conjunction (*and, but, or, nor, for, so, yet*). Make sure you place the comma before the coordinating conjunction.

He wanted to go, *but* she wanted to stay.

Also make sure to choose the coordinating conjunction that logically expresses the link you wish to express between the two independent clauses.

Use *but* or *yet* to indicate contrast or opposition.

He wanted to go, *but* he could not.

She wanted to stay, *yet* she did not.

- Use *so* or *for* to introduce an explanation.

  They were only a few miles from their destination, *so* they kept on walking.

  They were undecided about whether to continue, *for* they had lost their sense of direction.

- Use *and* to indicate the addition of two or more things.

  They went out to dinner, *and* they went to a movie.

- Use *or* to indicate alternatives.

  They could go to the concert, *or* they could stay home and listen to it on the radio.

In the following examples, note that the comma splice and fused sentence errors are corrected by adding a comma and a coordinating conjunction.

COMMA SPLICE	We could have ordered pasta and garlic bread, we could have selected something from the budget menu.
REVISED	We could have ordered pasta and garlic *bread, or* we could have selected something from the budget menu.
FUSED SENTENCE	I finally found the book it was not what I expected.
REVISED	I finally found the *book, but* it was not what I expected.

EXERCISE 18–2   Revising Comma Splices and Fused Sentences

Using a semicolon, conjunctive adverb, or coordinating conjunction, correct the following comma splices and fused sentences. Revise each sentence error in two different ways. Example:

His was the most moving speech hers was the least.
His was the most moving *speech, and* hers was the least.
His was the most moving *speech; hers* was the least.

1. It was one of the team's best games of the season they played with conviction and authority.
2. The truth sometimes may be hard to acknowledge, it is necessary if improvement is to follow.
3. I usually love pizza for dinner, I had it for lunch.
4. The hummingbird may be hardly bigger than a bumblebee it is really a bird, not an insect.
5. Ask not what your country can do for you ask what you can do for your country.

18e Converting two clauses into a single independent clause

Sometimes the two clauses of a comma splice or fused sentence are best revised by combining them into a single independent clause.

COMMA SPLICE	Medical knowledge was in its infancy during the Civil War, little was known about the causes of infection.
FUSED SENTENCE	Medical knowledge was in its infancy during the Civil War little was known about the causes of infection.
REVISED	*Medical knowledge about the causes of infection* was in its infancy during the Civil War.

The revised version combines the beginning and concluding words of the two preceding run-together sentences. The revision is more precise; it identifies exactly what kind of medical knowledge was in its infancy. The revised sentence is also more succinct because it eliminates unnecessary repetition.

18f Converting one of two independent clauses into a dependent clause

When the idea in one independent clause is more important than the idea in the other independent clause, the less important clause can be made dependent by introducing it with a subordinating conjunction (such as *because* or *although*). (See 14c-3 for a list of common subordinating conjunctions.)

COMMA SPLICE	Television news shows are largely entertainment, they should be clearly identified as such.
FUSED SENTENCE	Television news shows are largely entertainment they should be clearly identified as such.
REVISED	*Because* television news shows are largely entertainment, they should be clearly identified as such.

The revised sentence clarifies the relationship between the clauses; the emphasis falls on what should be done.

EXERCISE 18–3 Rewriting Comma Splices and Fused Sentences

Correct the following comma splices and fused sentences by combining the two independent clauses into a single sentence. Example:

People are often willing to give advice, they are less inclined to take it.
People are often willing to give advice *but are* less inclined to take it.

1. Jerome circled the block several times, he was searching for a parking space.
2. We left right after the game, we went to get a pizza.
3. You have no basis for a lawsuit you have no witnesses.

Correct the following comma splices and fused sentences by changing one of the two independent clauses into a dependent clause. Example:

We had to stop finally, we were so exhausted.
We were *so exhausted that* we finally had to stop.

4. I had a good record my first season I never had another one as good.
5. We went home there was nothing else to do.
6. She was crossing the street, she lost the heel of her right shoe.

18g Using comma splices and fused sentences appropriately

Some writers use comma splices deliberately, though sparingly, for effect. In the following passage, for example, the writer, a correspondent during the Vietnam War, splices sentences together to convey his sense of confusion.

> I'd just missed the biggest battle of the war so far, I was telling myself that I was sorry, but it was right there all around me and I didn't even know it. I couldn't look at anyone for more than a second, I didn't want to be caught listening, some war correspondent, I didn't know what to say or do, I didn't like it [the war] already.
>
> —Michael Herr, *Dispatches*

The effect of the deliberate use of a comma splice is to keep the lines moving quickly as they bunch together related comments. Punctuating the lines conventionally would deliberately separate the clauses into distinct ideas.

WRITING HINT In your own writing, use comma splices and fused sentences even more sparingly than you would use sentence fragments. Avoid comma splices and fused sentences in academic and professional writing, and use them in more creative writing only when they enable you to achieve effects you could not otherwise achieve.

Use the guidelines in the accompanying chart to correct comma splices and fused sentences.

Checking for Comma Splices and Fused Sentences

- Put brackets around each independent clause in your drafts.
- Underline the words that link the independent clauses.
- Circle the punctuation marks that separate the independent clauses.
- If you identify independent clauses with only a comma between them, you have found a comma splice.
- If you identify independent clauses with no punctuation and no words between them, you have found a fused sentence.
- If you identify independent clauses linked by a conjunctive adverb (such as *however* or *therefore*), check for appropriate punctuation: a semicolon between the independent clauses or a comma following the conjunctive adverb.

EXERCISE 18–4 **Correcting Comma Splices and Fused Sentences**

Correct each of the following comma splices and fused sentences two different ways, using a coordinating conjunction, a conjunctive adverb, or a subordinating conjunction. Note the logical relationship between the two clauses you are joining, and choose a connector that clarifies that relationship. Example:

Ralph is always bragging, no one seems to mind. [comma splice]

Ralph is always *bragging, but* no one seems to mind. [add a coordinating conjunction]

Ralph is always *bragging; however,* no one seems to mind. [add a conjunctive adverb]

Even though Ralph is always bragging, no one seems to mind. [add a subordinating conjunction]

1. Ralph has a good friend, Ed Norton, he does not always appreciate Ed.
2. Ralph's wife, Alice, is patient with his far-fetched schemes, she loses her temper from time to time.
3. Ralph is a very large man he is basically gentle and sweet.
4. Ralph is a bus driver he has been a bus driver for quite a few years he will more than likely remain a bus driver all his working days.

Comma Splices and Fused Sentences

Comma splices and fused sentences are sometimes referred to as *run-on sentences* because both run sentences together without the full stop of a period to separate them. Comma splices and fused sentences are also considered sentence boundary errors because they indicate a lack of certainty about where sentences begin and end.

Put your knowledge of comma splices and fused sentences to work as you check a recent paper or report that you have written.

EXAMPLE

It's important to create [appropriate] sentence boundaries readers can understand [better with them] replacing commas with periods and inserting periods where punctuation is missing aids understanding.

(editing marks: "⊙ With them ⌃ more easily"; "what you write ⊙"; "needed"; "readers'")

Read your writing aloud to listen for places where you should end sentences. When you read aloud, listen for places where you pause and drop your voice. Check those places to see if you have used periods. If you have not, check your grammar. One way you can test whether you have observed the rules of grammar on sentence boundaries is to use the chart on p. 380.

CHAPTER 19

Misplaced, Interrupting, and Dangling Modifiers

A **modifier** is a word or a phrase that functions as an adjective or adverb to limit or to qualify the meaning of another word, phrase, or clause in a sentence. For modifiers to be effective, you must make sure that they point clearly to the words, phrases, or clauses they modify. If the connection between a modifier and the word or words they modify is unclear, your readers will be confused. There are three types of mistakes that can be made with modifiers; see the guidelines in the accompanying chart to help you revise misplaced, interrupting, or dangling modifiers.

Revising Misplaced, Interrupting, and Dangling Modifiers

- Connect misplaced modifying words, phrases, or clauses with the word(s) they modify (19a–c).
- Recast squinting modifiers so they refer to only one word or group of words (19d).
- Bring together interrupting modifiers that are split off from the word(s) they modify (19e–h).
- Correct dangling modifiers by making sure they logically modify some word or sentence element (19i–j).

Misplaced Modifiers

A **misplaced modifier** is a modifier that is positioned in a sentence so that it is unclear which word, clause, or phrase is modified. Often, a modifier is misplaced when it can modify more than one word, clause, or phrase in a sentence.

19a   Revising misplaced words

One type of misplaced modifier is the awkward placement of a single word, usually an adverb (see 13a).

CONFUSING   Andrew watched the snow fall excitedly.

As written, *excitedly* modifies *fall* in this sentence—implying that the snow drifted with excitement. More likely, however, *excitedly* should modify *watched*. Because the adverb could modify both verbs, it is misplaced. The sentence needs to be revised to eliminate the confusion.

REVISED   Andrew excitedly watched the snow fall.

You also need to be especially careful about where you place limiting modifiers in a sentence. **Limiting modifiers,** such as *almost, even, hardly, just, merely, nearly, only, scarcely,* and *simply,* restrict the meaning of the word or phrase that immediately follows it. Make certain that the modifier is placed correctly.

CONFUSING   The office only is open in the afternoon. [Does *only* modify the noun *office,* or the prepositional phrase *in the afternoon?*]

CLEAR   *Only* the office is open in the afternoon. [Everything else is closed in the afternoon.]

CLEAR   The office is open *only* in the afternoon. [The office is never open in the morning.]

With limiting modifiers, you need to be sure to convey your intended meaning. Notice how changing the placement of *nearly* in the following sentences changes the meaning.

Nearly all of the one hundred people who attended the lecture were from the neighborhood.

All of the *nearly* one hundred people who attended the lecture were from the neighborhood.

EXERCISE 19–1   **Placing Limiting Modifiers**

For each of the following limiting modifiers, write two sentences, placing the modifier in a different position in each sentence to change its meaning. Example:

     only   You can *only* look at the car.
              Only you can look at the car.

1. almost   3. hardly   5. simply
2. even   4. just

19b   Revising misplaced phrases

The guidelines for revising misplaced words also apply to misplaced phrases. Place phrases as close as possible to the words they modify. This guideline is especially important for placing prepositional phrases in sentences (see 10c-1).

1   Misplaced prepositional phrases

Prepositional phrases should be placed directly before or immediately after the words they modify. Notice how misplaced prepositional phrases cause confusion in the following examples.

CONFUSING   Sixty doctors play golf in the hospital. [It is unlikely that the doctors play golf inside the hospital.]

REVISED   Sixty doctors *in the hospital* play golf.

CONFUSING   Ann was unhappy that she failed to win first place by a large margin. [Did Ann win first place by a small margin, or did she fail to win first place?]

REVISED   Ann was unhappy that she failed *by a large margin* to win first place.

2   Misplaced participial phrases

Similarly, misplaced participial phrases (see 10c-2) can cause confusion. The solution is to place participial phrases directly before or immediately after the words they modify.

CONFUSING   Stretching across the yard, I saw a clothesline. [It is unlikely that the speaker was stretching across the yard.]

REVISED   I saw a clothesline *stretching across the yard*.

CONFUSING   We showed the untrained puppy to our friends blocked off in the kitchen. [Are the friends blocked off in the kitchen?]

REVISED   We showed the untrained puppy *blocked off in the kitchen* to our friends.

WRITING HINT   If possible, place phrases that modify nouns immediately after the words they modify.

MISPLACED   The castles are breathtaking in Wales.

IMPROVED   The castles *in Wales* are breathtaking.

> MISPLACED   He needed a car for his trip with automatic transmission.
>
> IMPROVED   He needed a car *with automatic transmission* for his trip.

USAGE NOTE   Although phrases that modify nouns should immediately follow the words they modify, phrases used as adverbs can often be placed at different points within a sentence. An adverb phrase can be placed within a sentence near the word it modifies (usually the verb).

The Bulldogs lost in the first round to their cross-town rivals.

But the same phrase can also be placed at the beginning or the end of the sentence:

In the first round, the Bulldogs lost to their cross-town rivals.

The Bulldogs lost to their cross-town rivals *in the first round.*

Revising misplaced clauses

The guidelines for revising misplaced words and phrases also apply to misplaced clauses. Remember to keep dependent clause modifiers as near as possible to the words they modify.

> CONFUSING   Professor Ricks taught a seminar on contemporary American films that the students enjoyed. [What did the students enjoy, the seminar or the films?]
>
> REVISED   *The students enjoyed* Professor Ricks's seminar on contemporary American films.
>
> CONFUSING   Grisham decided his son would be a lawyer before the boy was ten years old. [The clause modifies *decided*, not *would be*.]
>
> REVISED   *Before the boy was ten years old,* Grisham decided his son would be a lawyer.

EXERCISE 19–2   Revising Misplaced Word, Phrase, and Clause Modifiers

Revise the following sentences to eliminate the awkwardness and confusion caused by misplaced modifiers. Example:

Strung along the path through the park, the people saw brightly colored Japanese lanterns.

The people saw brightly colored Japanese lanterns *strung along the path through the park.*

1. The president of the Czech Republic was comfortably able to speak in front of his political opponents.

2. The shirt was torn to pieces that he was throwing away.
3. John and Annie jogged through the winding streets past the old courthouse in their new sneakers.
4. Laurie bought a miniature tape recorder from the electronics store that uses microcassettes.
5. Rolling dangerously near the edge of the cliff, the driver stopped the car.
6. The swimmers crouched ignoring the cheers on their blocks.
7. My parents showed the new car to me sitting in the garage.
8. There are many autographs of athletes on the walls who have eaten at Malcolm's diner.
9. The suspect was described as a big man with curly red hair weighing two hundred pounds.
10. Jay and Charlene almost ate the entire giant sandwich.

19d   Revising squinting modifiers

A modifier should refer to only one word, clause, or phrase. A **squinting modifier** is a type of misplaced modifier that confuses the meaning of a sentence because it appears to modify the words that come both before and after it. Revise squinting modifiers by moving them to their correct position, where they refer clearly to only one word or sentence element.

SQUINTING	The man who spoke quickly ran out of breath. [Did the man speak quickly, or did that man quickly run out of breath?]
REVISED	The man who *quickly* spoke ran out of breath.
REVISED	The man who spoke ran *quickly* out of breath.

EXERCISE 19–3   Revising Squinting Modifiers

Rewrite each sentence two times to eliminate the squinting modifiers. Example:

SQUINTING	Going for a long walk often relaxes her.
REVISED	A long walk *often* relaxes her.
REVISED	To relax, she *often* goes for a long walk.

1. The position he expected to get finally was eliminated.
2. The mayor announced when he completed his trip he would schedule a news conference.
3. Students who cheat on exams often escape detection.

4. Writing teachers tell students when they are older they will appreciate the course.
5. She awoke suddenly getting out from beneath the covers.

Interrupting Modifiers

Like misplaced modifiers, **interrupting modifiers** are modifiers whose placement causes confusion in sentences. Unlike other types of misplaced modifiers, however, interrupting modifiers disrupt the continuity of thought in a sentence and can make it difficult to understand the meaning of a sentence. Avoid letting modifiers separate verbs and subjects, separate verbs and direct objects, split infinitives, or parts of a verb phrase.

19e   Revising lengthy modifiers that separate a verb from its subject

Phrases and clauses that come between a subject and verb can be awkward or confusing.

AWKWARD   The concert, because it snowed heavily all day, was canceled.

REVISED   Because it snowed heavily all day, *the concert was canceled.*

AWKWARD   The toys, long forgotten and collecting dust in the attic, were eventually given to charity.

REVISED   Long forgotten and collecting dust in the attic, *the toys were eventually given* to charity.

19f   Revising modifiers that separate a verb from its direct object or a subject complement

Sentences in which direct objects and subject complements follow immediately after the verb are clear and easy to read. Avoid using modifiers to separate a verb from its object.

AWKWARD   Dan Marino threw, during his best season as the Miami Dolphins quarterback, forty-eight touchdown passes. [The verb is separated from the object.]

REVISED   During his best season as the Miami Dolphins quarterback, Dan Marino *threw forty-eight touchdown passes*. [The object directly follows the verb.]

AWKWARD   The repulsive caterpillar became, after fourteen days in a chrysalis, a beautiful monarch butterfly. [The verb is separated from the subject complement.]

REVISED   After fourteen days in a chrysalis, the repulsive caterpillar *became a beautiful monarch butterfly*. [The subject complement directly follows the verb.]

19g   Revising modifiers that split an infinitive

Because the infinitive form of a verb is a two-word unit, splitting that unit with words or phrases can create a confusing sentence. Avoid placing an adverbial modifier between *to* and the verb of an infinitive.

AWKWARD   President Lincoln expected the North to quickly and decisively win the war.

REVISED   President Lincoln expected the North *to win* the war quickly and decisively.

Occasionally, however, splitting an infinitive is less awkward than not splitting it. In such cases, you should probably choose to rewrite the sentence so that it does not include an infinitive.

AWKWARD   Community college enrollment is expected to more than double in the next decade.

REVISED   More than double the current community college enrollment is expected in the next decade.

But sometimes the split infinitive is the best choice for effectively conveying a meaning.

We need *to carefully weigh* expected benefits against unexpected losses.

19h   Revising modifiers that separate parts of a verb phrase

A verb phrase consists of a main verb along with one or more auxiliary verbs: *will go, were being seen* (see 10c-1). A single adverb or two consecutive adverbs can usually be inserted into a verb phrase without causing confusion or awkwardness. But in all other cases avoid splitting parts of a verb phrase.

ACCEPTABLE   They *had* only rarely *eaten* vegetarian dishes. [Two one-word adverbs break up the verb phrase *had eaten*.]

AWKWARD   Many television viewers will, when it is time for a commercial, change channels or get something to eat.

REVISED   When it is time for a commercial, many television viewers *will change* channels or get something to eat.

WRITING HINT Experienced writers sometimes separate sentence parts intentionally to create suspense or add emphasis.

The old writer, like all of the people in the world, had got, during his long life, a great many notions in his head.

—Sherwood Anderson

You may decide to use a disrupting modifier for effect—to delay the verb or to save an important word for the end of a sentence. (See 26a for more on achieving emphasis in the sentence.)

The culprit looked around quickly and, realizing we were watching, jumped out the window.

When you experiment with separating sentence parts, be careful to ensure that your meaning remains clear.

EXERCISE 19–4   Revising Interrupting Modifiers

Revise each of the following sentences to eliminate the interrupting modifiers. Example:

The recent graduate wanted to eventually attend graduate school.
The recent graduate wanted *eventually to attend* graduate school.

1. Political protests began to, among youth, be popular during the Vietnam War.
2. Most adolescents have by the time they are eighteen years old become physically mature.
3. The school senate finally passed, in response to pressure from administrative lobbyists, a resolution banning smoking on campus.
4. The organizers of the carnival expect to if they can recoup their investment.
5. Many great composers were by the time some of their best works were performed no longer alive.

Dangling Modifiers

A **dangling modifier** is a word, phrase, or clause that does not modify any element in a sentence. A dangling modifier often seems to refer to something that is implied in the sentence. Readers try to correct a dangling modifier, often to humorous effect, by having it modify the closest word in the sentence. *Singing sweetly, the baby stopped crying.*

To correct dangling modifiers, you will want to add a word or words to the sentence for the modifier to modify. *Singing sweetly, he got the baby to stop crying.* You could also change the dangling modifier into a phrase or a clause that clearly modifies another part of the sentence. *When he began singing sweetly, the baby stopped crying.*

19i   Revising dangling word and phrase modifiers

Dangling word modifiers are often adverbs. To revise a dangling word modifier, add the word or words for the modifier to modify.

DANGLING   Courageously, the suspect was apprehended. [It is unlikely that the suspect is courageous.]

REVISED   *Courageously,* the officer apprehended the suspect.

Dangling participial phrases and prepositional phrases are best revised either by adding the word or words for the modifier to modify, or by changing the modifier into a phrase or a clause that clearly modifies another part of the sentence.

DANGLING   Singing for his supper, Mark and Heidi giggled. [Did Mark and Heidi sing for his supper?]

REVISED   Singing for his supper, *Fred made* Mark and Heidi giggle.

REVISED   *As he sang for his supper,* Fred made Mark and Heidi giggle.

DANGLING   After a long run, a cold shower is enjoyable and refreshing. [Did the shower go on a long run?]

REVISED   After a long run, *I enjoy* a refreshing cold shower.

DANGLING   As a small child, Sally's mother used to tell her bedtime stories. [Did the child-mother tell Sally bedtime stories?]

REVISED   When *Sally* was a small child, *her mother* used to tell her bedtime stories.

19j Revising dangling elliptical clauses

An **elliptical clause** is a dependent clause that lacks all or part of the subject or predicate. To revise a dangling elliptical clause, include the words implied by the clause.

DANGLING	While brewing, Kristie can determine how fresh the coffee is.
REVISED	*While the coffee is brewing,* Kristie can determine how fresh it is.
DANGLING	When sunny, Colin's spirits are as bright as the day is.
REVISED	*When the day is sunny,* Colin's spirits are bright.

EXERCISE 19–5 Revising Dangling Modifiers

Revise each of the following sentences to correct the dangling modifiers. Example:

> Having missed classes for a month, my grades were in jeopardy.
> *Because I missed classes for a month,* my grades were in jeopardy.

1. Flying over Detroit, the Canadian border appeared part of the city.
2. Thinking about the day's events, the ringing phone startled her.
3. When driving along Lake Shore Drive, the sun shone brightly on the lake.
4. To protest the increase in tuition, administrative offices were occupied by student groups.
5. To become a doctor, four years of postgraduate study must be completed, medical boards must be passed, and a residency completed.

EXERCISE 19–6 Revising Misplaced, Interrupting, and Dangling Modifiers

Revise the following sentences to eliminate the misplaced, interrupting, and dangling modifiers. Example:

> Soaring high in the sky, they saw two eagles.
> They saw two eagles soaring high in the sky.

1. Instead of going to the movies with friends, exams kept me home studying.
2. After studying the entire afternoon, it was too late to go to the museum.
3. Eating less often makes a difference.
4. Deer tick bites have been increasing in many northeastern states, which can lead to Lyme disease.

5. The woman held the baby in high heels.
6. To be successful in college, the system must be understood by students.
7. Reaching into the air, the ball dropped into his glove.
8. With a long list of written requirements, I was not sure I would be able to do the work for the course.
9. Before attending the lecture, dinner would have to be eaten.
10. They agreed when the game was over they would meet for burgers at the diner.

Grammar and Writing

Placing Modifiers

Placing modifiers appropriately makes your writing clear and easy to understand. Placing modifiers carelessly can create confusion for your readers and embarrassment for you.

EXAMPLE

Rolling rapidly down the hill, I slammed on the brakes.

[*Who* or *what* was rolling rapidly down the hill?]

As the car rolled rapidly down the hill, I slammed on the brakes.

You can put your knowledge of modifier placement to work by checking how you positioned modifiers in a recent paper or report that you wrote. Check to see that each modifier is close to the word or phrase it modifies. Check also for squinting modifiers—those that appear to modify more than one word or phrase. And check finally for dangling modifiers, usually adverbs that do not actually modify any part of a sentence.

EXAMPLE

After finishing a heavy meal, a nap is just the thing.

[*Who* is finishing a heavy meal?]

After finishing a heavy meal, I am ready for a nap.

You can use the chart on p. 382 for guidance.

CHAPTER 20

Avoiding Shifts and Maintaining Consistency

A shift is an abrupt change from one verb tense, mood, or voice to another, or from one pronoun person or number to another, that results in confusing writing. Generally, when you write, you should maintain consistency in the *tense, mood,* and *voice* of verbs and the person and number of pronouns. Furthermore, you should maintain consistency in your *diction* (selection of words) and *tone* (attitude toward your subject). The accompanying chart identifies the types of unnecessary shifts that can cause confusion. The guidelines in this chapter will help you identify and eliminate unnecessary and confusing shifts.

Unnecessary Shifts

- Shifts in pronoun person and number (20a)
- Shifts in verb tenses (20b)
- Shifts in mood (20c)
- Shifts in voice (20d)
- Shifts between direct and indirect quotations (20e)
- Shifts in diction and tone (20f)

20a Maintaining consistency of person and number

When you write with pronouns, avoid unnecessary shifts among first-person pronouns (*I, we*), second-person pronouns (*you*), and third-person pronouns (*he, she, it, one, they*). (For more on pronoun person, see the chart in 12c.)

INCONSISTENT   When *one* travels abroad, *you* should take traveler's checks instead of cash. [shift from third-person pronoun to second person]

REVISED   When *you* travel abroad, *you* should take traveler's checks instead of cash.

REVISED   When *one* travels abroad, *one* should take traveler's checks instead of cash.

Also avoid shifts between singular and plural nouns and pronouns (shifts in number).

INCONSISTENT   Mary thought *a dog* a more active pet than *cats*.

REVISED   Mary thought *dogs* more active pets than *cats*.

INCONSISTENT   *Jen and Lily* drank *her* iced teas.

REVISED   *Jen and Lily* drank *their* iced teas.

Sometimes, however, your meaning will clearly warrant such a shift.

Jen and Lily swam in *his* Olympic-size pool.

Shifts in number often involve inaccurate agreement between pronouns and their antecedents.

INCONSISTENT   When teachers assign *a reading*, they should discuss *them*.

REVISED   When teachers assign *a reading*, they should discuss *it*.

EXERCISE 20–1   Avoiding Shifts in Pronoun Person and Number

Underline the unnecessary shifts in person and number in the following sentences. Then rewrite each sentence to eliminate the shift. Example:

Studies have shown that <u>one</u> is subject to increased risk for heart attack if <u>you</u> lead a sedentary life.

Studies have shown that *people* are subject to increased risk for heart attack if *they* lead sedentary *lives*.

1. When one visits Gettysburg, you should be sure to walk over to Cemetery Ridge and look for Little Round Top.
2. A person likes to feel that they are appreciated.
3. All the speakers invited to the conference had a good reputation in the field.
4. If a person travels abroad they will encounter different customs.
5. Many secretaries are poorly paid, even though a secretary does important work.

 20b   Maintaining consistency in verb tenses

A verb tense establishes the time of the action of a piece of writing. A change in tense indicates a change in time. Shifting between different tenses unnecessarily or illogically can confuse and distract readers.

INCONSISTENT	The committee meeting *began* when the chair *calls* the members to order. [confusing shift from past tense to present tense]
REVISED	The committee meeting *begins* when the chair *calls* the members to order. [present tense]
REVISED	The committee meeting *began* when the chair *called* the members to order. [past tense]

Sometimes more than one verb tense is used in a sentence, paragraph, or essay when the meaning calls for such a shift. Combining tenses may be necessary to explain changes or continuities among different periods of time. In the following example, the tense of verbs changes to describe the phenomenon.

Inflation *persists* as a problem in the world economy. It has been an insurmountable problem in many developing countries. Moreover, it will probably continue to be a difficult problem both in this country and abroad. [The tenses are logical: the present (*persists*) describes the current economic problem; the present perfect (*has been*) indicates the problem began in the past and is still going on; and the future (*will continue*) says the problem will persist.]

Use the present tense (also called *the literary present*) to describe action in works of literature and in films.

INCONSISTENT	I have heard about a production of Shakespeare's play *The Taming of the Shrew* in which the "shrew" *was* a man whom a woman *tamed.*
REVISED	I have heard about a production of Shakespeare's play *The Taming of the Shrew* in which the "shrew" *is* a man whom a woman *tames.*

Also use the present tense when describing general truths.

Researchers now *know* that passive smoking *causes* cancer.

(See 11f–i for more on verb tenses.)

EXERCISE 20–2 Avoiding Shifts in Verb Tenses

Underline the unnecessary or illogical verb tense shifts in the following sentences. Then rewrite each sentence to eliminate the shift. (Some sentences may be correct as written.) Example:

The authority of the president <u>is being</u> questioned. A good example <u>was</u> the committee's vote to censure him.

The authority of the president *is being* questioned. A good example *is* the committee's vote to censure him.

1. Smoke billowed from the windows as people run in every direction.
2. If I find the money, I will return it.

3. Once upon a time, there is a family of bears that lived in the forest.
4. The requirements for graduation will be changed next year. The change will have affected only next year's first-year college students; it does not affect students already matriculated.
5. Given the strength and amount of the evidence, it was hard to believe that it takes the jury members so long to have made up their minds.

EXERCISE 20–3   **Shifting Tenses Logically**

Think of something important in your life that has changed—a situation, an opinion, or a relationship, for example. What caused the change? Was it for the better? Write a paragraph in which you explain what changed. Use the past tense to describe how things were before the change and the present tense to describe how things are today.

20c   Maintaining consistency in mood

Always avoid shifts from one verb mood to another. Verbs in the indicative mood make statements and ask questions (*She swims well. Are they home?*). Verbs in the imperative mood give commands and offer advice (*Close the window. Try this on for size.*). Verbs in the subjunctive mood express wishes, conditions, or statements contrary to fact (*If only they were here.*).

INCONSISTENT	*Drive* slowly on snowy roads and you *should keep* the car in lower gears than usual. [shift from imperative to indicative]
REVISED	*Drive* slowly on snowy roads and *keep* the car in lower gears than usual.
INCONSISTENT	If she *is* available for the job, she *could take* it. [shift from indicative to subjunctive]
REVISED	If she *were* available for the job, she *would take* it.

(See Chapter 11 for more on the mood of verbs.)

20d   Maintaining consistency in voice

Avoid shifting unnecessarily between the active voice (*They bought their tickets early*) and the passive voice (*Their tickets were bought early*). Subjects with active voice verbs initiate action; subjects with passive voice verbs receive action.

INCONSISTENT	The Japanese army *was being fought* in the Pacific Ocean while the Allies *defeated* the German army at Normandy.
REVISED	The Japanese army *fought* in the Pacific Ocean while the Allies *defeated* the German army at Normandy.
INCONSISTENT	While we *waited* in the park, birds *could be heard* singing their distinctive songs. [shift from active to passive voice]
REVISED	While we *waited* in the park, we *could hear* birds singing their distinctive songs.

However, a shift between the active and passive voice is occasionally both logical and necessary to maintain focus on a subject.

The campaign workers *labored* tirelessly for their candidate and *were rewarded* with her election. [The shift from the active to passive voice keeps the focus on the original subject—*campaign workers*.]

(See 11j–k for more on the voice of verbs.)

EXERCISE 20–4   Avoiding Shifts in Mood and Voice

Underline the unnecessary mood and voice shifts in the following sentences. Then rewrite each sentence to eliminate the shift. Example:

Jodie <u>requested</u> a raise and asked <u>that she be</u> transferred.
Jodie *requested* a raise and asked for a transfer.

1. Even though I enjoy seafood, a steak is enjoyed even more.
2. The coach demanded an explanation and that she was given an apology.
3. If the test were too easy, it is not a challenge.
4. Remember to proofread your paper and you should submit it on time as well.
5. Although concert violinists often play violins made by Antonio Stradivari, those instruments are rarely owned by the musicians.

20e   Avoiding shifts between direct and indirect quotations

Direct quotations, also called direct discourse, reproduce someone else's exact words. When you use direct discourse, place the quoted words within quotation marks.

When Ernest Hemingway was asked why he rewrote the ending to *A Farewell to Arms* more than forty times, he responded, "To get the words right."

Indirect quotations, or indirect discourse, report or summarize what someone else has said or written without repeating the same words.

Ernest Hemingway once explained that he rewrote the ending to *A Farewell to Arms* more than forty times so that he could get the words just the way he wanted them.

Shifting between direct and indirect discourse within the same sentence can result in confusing sentences. Avoid such shifts in your essays, especially in research essays, where you are most likely to incorporate quotations from secondary sources.

INCONSISTENT	Stephen Jay Gould has said that "evolution is a theory" and he has also argued that it is a fact. [shift from direct to indirect discourse]
REVISED	Stephen Jay Gould has argued that evolution is both a fact and a theory. [indirect discourse]

(See 36a and 44d-2–3 for more on quoting and paraphrasing.)

WRITING HINT　The differences between direct and indirect discourse usually involve tense and person. Ordinarily, the verbs in an indirect quotation are in the same tense as the main verb (MV).

　　　　　┌MV┐

Charmaine *asked* us where Allen *was.*

In a direct quotation the verbs are in the tense that the speaker actually used.

Charmaine *asked* us, "Where *is* Allen?"

Notice, too, that the pronouns in an indirect quotation refer to the speaker in the third person (as someone being talked *about,* not talked *to*). In contrast, the pronouns in a direct quotation are the ones that the speaker actually used.

INDIRECT	President Clinton said that *he* wanted Congress to support *his* tax cut.
DIRECT	President Clinton said, "*I* want Congress to support *my* tax cut."

EXERCISE 20–5　Maintaining Consistency in Direct and Indirect Discourse

Write two sentences for each of the following quotations, one using direct discourse and the other indirect discourse. Maintain consistency in verb tense in each sentence. Example:

"I regret I have only one life to lose for my country."　　—*Nathan Hale*

DIRECT   Nathan Hale once announced: "I regret I have only one life to lose for my country."

INDIRECT   Historians have described Nathan Hale as a quintessential patriot because he once said he regretted he had only one life to lose for his country.

1. "Societies need to have one illness which becomes identified with evil, and attaches blame to its 'victims.' "   —*Susan Sontag*

2. "It is a mark of many famous people that they cannot part with their brightest hour."   —*Lillian Hellman*

3. "Those who are ignorant of history are condemned to repeat it."   —*George Santayana*

4. "It is a complex fate to be an American."   —*Henry James*

5. "War will pass when intellectual culture and activity have made possible to the female an equal share in the control and governance of modern national life."   —*Olive Schreiner*

6. "The prejudice against color, of which we hear so much, is no stronger than that against sex."   —*Elizabeth Cady Stanton*

7. "What we see in the mind is as real to us as what we see by the eye."   —*Wallace Stevens*

8. "Fondly do we hope—fervently do we pray—that this mighty scourge of war may speedily pass away."   —*Abraham Lincoln*

9. "Nothing in life is to be feared. It is only to be understood."   —*Marie Curie*

10. "Science without religion is lame; religion without science is blind."   —*Albert Einstein*

20f   Maintaining consistency in diction and tone

Diction refers to a writer's word choice. Strive for consistency in diction by using the same level of language throughout a piece of writing. If you are using formal language, for example, you should avoid contractions (*you're, it's*), colloquialisms, and slang expressions (see 28c).

INCONSISTENT   The significance of Columbus's voyages continues to be debated, sparked by recent celebrations of the five hundredth anniversary of the discovery of America. *Some scholars are out to trash Columbus's cultural contribution.* They see him as more of a villain than a hero. [The italicized sentence should be made consistent with the level of diction of the other sentences.]

REVISED   The significance of Columbus's voyages continues to be debated, sparked by recent celebrations of the five hundredth anniversary of the discovery of America. *Some scholars argue for a revisionist interpretation of Columbus's cultural contribution.* They see him as more of a villain than a hero.

Tone refers to the writer's attitude toward the subject. It is conveyed by a writer's choice of words, by the length and complexity of sentences, and by the selection of details. Tone, like diction, can be technical, formal, informal, or colloquial. (For examples of varied tones, see 1d-3.)

Unless you want to vary your tone or to achieve some intentional effect or purpose (e.g., for comic effect or to shock readers), avoid shifting your tone in a piece of writing. In the following passage, note how the writer's unintentional shift in tone sounds odd and inappropriate.

The Catcher in the Rye captures the dissatisfaction of mid-century youth with adult society. The narrator, Holden Caulfield, tells his story in an extended monologue. He describes the phoniness of his surroundings at a boarding school, Pencey Prep, and recounts his running away for two aimless, adventurous days in New York, where he meets a prostitute, flees from the homosexual advances of his former English teacher, and visits his sister Phoebe. All in all, Holden's an unusual kind of guy—for the narrator of a book. Funny . . . bright . . . observant. Tells it like it is. In the end, getting his act together (finally), he decides he'll "go home next month maybe."

WRITING HINT   Occasionally, you may choose to shift tone for special effect. This type of intentional shift in tone is not easy to do well, but when successful it can be extremely effective in conveying emphasis or humor. Consider how the following passage employs shifts of tone to create humor.

The third week of September has always been a grisly time for schoolchildren. It is then that the romance of education, sparked by the back-to-school excitement of fresh books, new teachers, virginal fountain pens and notebooks unstained by ink blots and baffling mathematical formulas, begins to yield to reality.

And what is that reality? It is knowledge. Knowledge that it will be nine long months before summer vacation rolls around again. Knowledge that the geography teacher dislikes you. Knowledge that the gym instructor finds your physique absurd.

—Russell Baker, "The Cruelest Month"

EXERCISE 20–6   Avoiding Shifts in Diction and Tone

Revise the following paragraphs to achieve consistency in diction and tone.

Why has the guitar become so popular an instrument? There are a number of reasons. First, perhaps, is its simplicity and economy of design. A guitar, in its most basic form, is simply a box with a sound hole across which six strings are strung along a neck. The instrument is light and portable. One can carry it anywhere, and you can play it without the need for anything other than your two hands. Second is its playability. You can learn a few chords in a matter of minutes. And with just a bit of practice you can sound really great strumming and accompanying yourself on simple tunes.

Mastery of the instrument, however, is another matter altogether. Performers such as Andrés Segovia and Julian Bream have spent a lifetime learning the intricacies of the instrument. These masters of the classical guitar are complemented by jazz masters such as Charlie Christian, folk guitar experts such as Paul Simon, and rock players such as Eric Clapton, all of whom spent years learning to coax their different style guitars to yield the sounds they wanted.

EXERCISE 20–7 Avoiding Unnecessary Shifts and Inconsistencies

Revise the following paragraph to eliminate unnecessary shifts and inconsistencies—in pronoun person and number, in verb tense, in voice and mood, in direct and indirect discourse, and in diction and tone.

The conventional definition of a classic is a work that has withstood the test of time. One proponent of this definition is the eighteenth-century writer Samuel Johnson, who in his *Preface to Shakespeare,* suggested that regarding works of genius, "of which the excellence is not absolute and definite, but gradual and comparative . . . no other test can be applied than length of duration and continuance of esteem." Johnson's definition is really great because it suggests that a work that continues to engage readers in different times can be considered somehow extra special. They have that extra kick that grabs your attention. But you should be able to tell if a work were to become a classic long before it is judged to have become one.

Grammar and Writing

Maintaining Consistency

One of the simplest but hardest of writing guidelines to follow is to be consistent. To write clearly and well you should strive for consistency in your use of verbs and pronouns, in diction and tone, and in using direct and indirect discourse. You can apply what you have learned about these grammatical issues by analyzing a recent paper or report you wrote. Use the chart on p. 393 and the advice in the corresponding chapter sections to check your work for grammatical consistency and for clarity of meaning.

(continued)

You can use the following checklist of questions as a guide:

- Are your pronouns consistent in person and number?
- Are your verb tenses consistent?
- Are your verbs consistent in mood and voice?
- Is your level of diction consistent?
- Have you maintained a consistent tone?

EXAMPLE

Many more college students work today than ever before. [One] needs a job ^They^ ^s^
to pay tuition. Working many hours makes it difficult for [a] students to
keep abreast of coursework. [This makes it really tough for them.] Though
sympathetic to [their] economic realities, [they] must continue to set high ^students'^ ^teachers^
standards and [they should] require regular attendance.

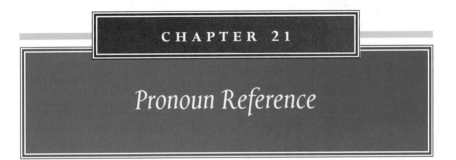

CHAPTER 21

Pronoun Reference

A **pronoun** replaces a noun in a sentence. Substituting pronouns in place of nouns enables writers to avoid using the same word repeatedly and to add variety to a sentence. For example, instead of writing *Carl rejoined the team when Carl recovered from Carl's injury,* you would write *Carl rejoined the team when he recovered from his injury.*

When you write with pronouns, you need to make certain that the pronoun's **antecedent,** the noun that the pronoun refers to, is clear. A pronoun that can refer to two antecedents makes for a confusing sentence: *Emily told Beth she won the prize.* (Did Emily or Beth win the prize?) *The family agreed on the distribution of the inheritance, but it would take time.* (Does *it* refer to the family, the distribution, or the inheritance?) The accompanying chart provides advice for revising unclear pronoun reference.

Revising Ambiguous Pronoun Reference

- Make each pronoun refer to a single antecedent (21a).
- Keep pronouns and antecedents close together (21b).
- Check uses of *this, that, which,* and *it* for clarity (21c-1).
- Avoid the indefinite use of *it, they,* and *you* (21c-2).
- Use *who, which,* and *that* with appropriate antecedents (21c-3).
- Avoid using adjectives or possessives as antecedents (21c-4).

21a   Making sure a pronoun refers to a single antecedent

Make sure that pronouns in your writing clearly refer to only one antecedent. For example, the sentence *Grace told Diane she was not going* is not clear because the pronoun *she* could refer to either Grace or Diane. The sentence should be revised so that the pronoun refers to only one antecedent—either Grace or Diane. If the reference cannot be made clear, the sentence should be rewritten without the pronoun.

REVISIONS   Grace told Diane to forget about going.

Grace said that Diane was not going.

Grace said to Diane, "I am not going."

WRITING HINT   When you write sentences that report what someone has said, and especially sentences using such verbs as *said* and *told,* use direct rather than indirect quotation (see 20e).

CONFUSING   Ozzie told Izzie that he was upset.

CLEAR   Ozzie told Izzie, "I am upset."

CLEAR   Ozzie said, "I am upset."

21b   Keeping pronouns and antecedents close together

Placing a pronoun too far from its antecedent can confuse readers. Most problems with remote pronoun antecedents occur in paragraphs when a pronoun in a later sentence refers to a noun in an earlier one. In such cases readers may forget what the pronoun refers to or other nouns may intervene between the antecedent and the pronoun, making the connection unclear.

CONFUSING   I. M. Pei is a world-renowned architect who designed *the pyramid addition* to the Louvre Museum. The John Fitzgerald Kennedy Library in Boston, the John Hancock Building also in Boston, and the Johnson Museum of Art at Cornell University are other buildings designed by Pei. Many critics call *it* a controversial yet aesthetically pleasing sight. [The antecedent of the pronoun *it* is *the pyramid addition,* but several nouns appear between the antecedent and the pronoun, making that connection unclear.]

To avoid confusion caused by remote pronoun reference, keep pronouns and antecedents as close together as possible. Sometimes you may have to repeat the noun or use a synonym for the noun to make the reference clear.

REVISED   I. M. Pei is a world-renowned architect who designed *the pyramid addition* to the Louvre Museum. The John Fitzgerald Kennedy Library in Boston, the John Hancock Building also in Boston, and the Johnson Museum of Art at Cornell University are other buildings designed by Pei. Many critics call *the pyramid addition* a controversial yet aesthetically pleasing sight.

REVISED   I. M. Pei is a world-renowned architect who designed *the pyramid addition* to the Louvre Museum. Many critics call *it* a controversial yet aesthetically pleasing sight. The John Fitzgerald Kennedy Library in Boston, the John Hancock Building also in Boston, and the Johnson Museum of Art at Cornell University are other buildings designed by Pei.

EXERCISE 21–1   **Clarifying Ambiguous and Remote Pronoun Reference**

Revise the following sentences to eliminate all unclear pronoun references. Make sure that all pronouns refer to only a single antecedent and are placed close to their antecedent. Example:

> When you meet the officials at the Olympic games, you will be impressed by them.

> You will be impressed by the officials at the Olympic games.

1. While Jeff was at work, Matthew found the books he had misplaced.
2. Tina told Cathy her children would be having dinner at her house.
3. My grandparents grew up in different parts of Italy. My grandmother came from Parma, a city in northern Italy, near the French border. My grandfather was born and raised in Palermo, in Sicily. They could not have been more different.
4. The British shaped many aspects of the culture of the Indian subcontinent, including education and governmental institutions. They had little effect on their religion, however.
5. There is a difference between the athletes of today and those of a generation ago. Most of them are bigger, stronger, and faster.
6. Halley's comet, which is due to appear again in 2061, is named after Edmund Halley, the astronomer who first plotted its orbit. Although extensive records document the existence of other comets, his is the most famous.
7. When Joan set the Chinese vase on the glass table, it cracked.
8. A few years after American Express bought the Shearson investment company, it was sold.
9. When abstract ideas are illustrated with concrete everyday examples, students understand them better.
10. They hoped to spend their summer learning a foreign language and traveling abroad, though they were not sure they could do it.

21c   Clarifying confusing references with particular pronouns

Even though you may strive to keep pronouns near their antecedents and to avoid ambiguous pronoun reference, a few pronouns may still cause special problems: *this, that, which, it; it, you, they;* and *who, which, that.* When you revise and edit your work, always check to make sure you have used these words clearly.

1   Using *this, that, which,* and *it*

Sometimes writers use *this, that, which,* or *it* to refer to an idea or circumstance described in a previous clause, sentence, or paragraph. If you do this, however, be sure your pronoun reference is clear. For example, in the preceding sentence, the pronoun *this* clearly refers to the description of what writers do that is set up in the first sentence. But using the words *this, that, which,* and *it* in writing to refer to ideas or circumstances can more often than not be vague and confuse readers. Restrict such broad use of these words to informal conversation: *At least I was on time, which is more than I can say for you.*

The following examples illustrate ways to revise these pronouns so that they refer to specific nouns rather than a sweeping idea. Notice how the revised sentences are more precise than the original.

CONFUSING   Light can be explained as either a series of particles or a series of waves. The particle theory envisions light as composed of discrete, individual bits of light. The wave theory describes light as larger units, whose behavior differs from that of particles. *This* was not understood before the early twentieth century. [What was not understood? The particle theory? The wave theory? Both points?]

REVISED   Light can be explained as either a series of particles or a series of waves. The particle theory envisions light as composed of discrete, individual bits of light. The wave theory describes light as larger units, whose behavior differs from that of particles. *The differences between these theories* were not well understood before the early twentieth century.

CONFUSING   Contrary to the beliefs of his contemporaries, Galileo theorized that the earth revolved around the sun. *That* earned him a severe reprimand from the Catholic Church. [There is no explicit antecedent for *that*.]

REVISED   Contrary to the beliefs of his contemporaries, Galileo theorized that the earth revolved around the sun. *Galileo's refusal to alter this belief* earned him a severe reprimand from the Catholic Church.

CONFUSING The students read three analyses of the economic indicators, *which* they found encouraging. [Did the students find the indicators or the analyses encouraging?]

REVISED The students read three analyses of the economic indicators and found *the explanations* encouraging.

REVISED The students read three analyses of the economic indicators, *analyses* they found encouraging.

WRITING HINT   One way to avoid vague usage of *this* is to develop the habit of following *this* with a noun. Ask yourself the question: This *what?* Your answer—this *theory*, this *refusal*, this *change*, this *analysis*, and so on—will help you choose an appropriate noun. (Of course, you could also use plural forms where appropriate: these *theories*, these *changes*, these *analyses*.)

2   Avoiding indefinite use of *it, they,* and *you*

In everyday conversation, people use *it, they,* and *you* indefinitely.

It said in the news that the refugee situation is worsening.

They say that New York City is a great place for the wealthy to live.

You know who your real friends are when adversity strikes.

These uses, however, are too informal for academic writing. To avoid ambiguity in your writing, use *you* to refer only to "you, the reader," and use *it* and *they* to refer only to clear antecedents.

INFORMAL   In the introduction, *it* explains the author's thesis.

FORMAL   The introduction explains the author's thesis.

INFORMAL   In England *they* serve tea in the mid-afternoon.

FORMAL   Many people in England serve tea in the mid-afternoon.

INFORMAL   Automobile advertisements often try to make *you* associate cars with power.

FORMAL   Automobile advertisements often suggestively associate cars with power.

EXERCISE 21–2   Avoiding Broad and Indefinite Pronoun Reference

Revise the following paragraph to eliminate broad use of *this, that, which,* and *it,* and to clarify indefinite pronoun references of *it, they,* and *you.*

In Jane Austen's *Emma,* the title character is an intelligent young woman who thinks she knows more about men than she actually does. This gets her into trouble because she makes mistakes and misjudgments about a number of different men. One of them is critical, which almost leads her to turn bitterly against a very good and kindhearted man. That is what the novel emphasizes, and this is what later helps her to see it, which you understand before she does.

3　Using *who, which,* and *that* with appropriate antecedents

Always be sure to use the relative pronouns *who, which,* and *that* appropriately. Use *who* to refer to people or animals with names.

Bill Moyers, *who* was once Lyndon B. Johnson's press secretary, now is a regular political commentator for PBS.

You would enjoy our cat, Dolce, *who* entertains us regularly.

Use *which* or *that* to refer to things, ideas, unnamed animals, and anonymous or collective references to people.

The Appalachians, *which* are among the most accessible of mountains, are also among the most beautiful.

We need to do something about the raccoons, *which* have been raiding our dumpster and strewing garbage all over.

The novel *that* received the National Book Award was relatively unknown.

This world is a comedy to those *that* think, a tragedy to those *that* feel.

　　　　　　　　　　　　　　　　　　　　　　　—Horace Walpole

4　Avoiding pronouns with adjectives and possessives as antecedents

Pronouns cannot refer to adjectives and possessives as antecedents. Since a pronoun can only stand in for a noun, only nouns can function as the antecedents of pronouns.

CONFUSING　Throughout Walt Whitman's work, *he* celebrates the American land and its people. [There is no noun antecedent to which *he* can refer.]

REVISED　*Throughout his work, Walt Whitman* celebrates the American land and its people.

REVISED　*Walt Whitman's work* consistently celebrates the American land and its people.

The accompanying chart suggests ways to check your use of pronouns for accuracy.

Checking Pronoun Reference

- Does each pronoun clearly refer to only one antecedent? Are the antecedents nouns, not adjectives or possessives?
- Do intervening nouns make the references unclear? Do you need to repeat a noun or use a synonym?
- Are the antecedents of *this, that, which,* and *it* clear and precise? Do you follow every *this* with a noun?
- Do the pronouns *it, they,* and *you* have definite antecedents? If *you* is used, does it clearly refer to the reader?
- Are the antecedents for *who, which,* and *that* appropriate?

EXERCISE 21–3   Establishing Clear and Appropriate Pronoun Reference

Revise the following sentences to correct unclear or inappropriate pronoun references. (Some sentences may be correct as written.) Example:

In the Swiss Alps they use carefully trained St. Bernards for rescue missions.
Skiers in the Swiss Alps use carefully trained St. Bernards for rescue missions.

1. They announced on television that the ecosystem of the Grand Canyon is in jeopardy.
2. They had room in their car for three additional riders, which would have to sit in the backseat.
3. In television comedies, it almost always happens that things work out in the end.
4. My cousin has a tarantula who lives in the basement.
5. Recent research suggests that the damaging effects of multiple sclerosis can be dramatically reduced.
6. In the U.S. senatorial races of 1992, six women were elected, which is three times as many female senators as served before the election.
7. University policy disallows reimbursements of even partial tuition after the start of the term, which angers many students and their parents.
8. After Matthew and Andrea discussed the value of a college degree with their teachers, they saw the educational system differently.
9. Attila the Hun was a warrior that terrorized many people.

10. Not enough jurors are skeptical of expert witnesses, the testimony of which is sometimes not reliable.

EXERCISE 21–4   Revising for Clear Pronoun Reference

Revise the following paragraph to eliminate vague and unclear pronoun references.

In the seventeenth century they used punctuation far more casually than we do today. The abundance of punctuation marks and their sometimes strange placement have been blamed on the printers, who were often illiterate and served by apprentices, which knew even less about it. Scholars have surmised that they tossed in punctuation simply to fill in spaces in the lines of print they set. But could they have randomly placed it in a text and have it still appear readable? They may have left them out now and then because of laziness, but you should not blame them for the lack of consistency in Elizabethan punctuation.

EXERCISE 21–5   Checking Pronoun Reference in Your Writing

Examine one of the papers you wrote recently for a course. Check it for unclear, confusing, or inappropriate pronoun references. Use the guidelines in this chapter to revise any problems with pronoun reference.

Grammar and Writing

Controlling Pronoun Reference

Like prepositions and conjunctions, pronouns are little words that can cause big problems for writers. By using common sense and by checking a few grammatical guidelines, you can control your use of pronouns to clarify rather than confuse the meaning of your writing.

The chart at the beginning of the chapter can serve as a handy checklist for double-checking your pronouns. For a fuller set of guidelines for checking pronoun reference, use the chart on p. 409. Answer each of the bulleted questions for all the types of pronouns your writing includes.

Often pronouns are incorrectly used in a piece of writing because a writer was careless, perhaps even lazy. Checking each pronoun's reference for clarity and accuracy is a way to avoid embarrassing or confusing mistakes.

(continued)

EXAMPLE:

In the 19th century [they] ^{people} had more space for themselves than they do today. When the immigrants [that] ^{who} came from Europe settled in the Midwest they found a vast expanses of land and water. [This] ^{The size of the country} profoundly affected them.

CHAPTER 22

Mixed and Incomplete Sentences

*T*o keep your meaning clear, you should avoid mixed and incomplete sentences in your writing. You can avoid these sentence faults by ensuring that the parts of your sentences fit together logically and grammatically, and that they include complete, rather than partial, grammatical structures. This chapter provides guidelines for recognizing mixed and incomplete sentences along with remedies for correcting them. Refer to the accompanying chart, which identifies the most common causes of mixed and incomplete sentences.

Causes of Mixed and Incomplete Sentences

- Incompatible grammatical patterns (22a)
- Faulty predication (22b)
- Confusing elliptical constructions (22c)
- Missing words (22d)
- Incomplete comparisons (22e)

Mixed Sentences

A **mixed sentence** results when incompatible grammatical structures are combined or when an illogical relationship between subject and predicate creates confusion in meaning. Mixed sentences with incompatible grammatical patterns are often garbled and awkward. Mixed sentences with illogical subject–predicate relationships are said to suffer from *faulty predication* (see 22b).

22a   Revising mixed sentences with incompatible grammatical patterns

A mixed sentence will often begin with one grammatical pattern and switch to another, incompatible one. Consider this example.

MIXED   After hearing so many conflicting views was the reason we became confused.

This sentence begins with an introductory prepositional phrase (*After hearing so many conflicting views*), which the reader expects to be followed by an independent clause. Instead, the prepositional phrase is followed by a verb (*was*) and a subject complement (*the reason*). There is no subject for *was* because the gerund *hearing* is the object of the preposition *after* and cannot also function as the subject of an independent clause. These grammatical parts (prepositional phrase + verb + subject complement) do not fit together to form one of the basic patterns for a complete sentence. (See 10e for more on sentence patterns.)

This particular mixed sentence can be revised in a number of ways. Often no single type of revision of a mixed sentence is better than any other. Thus, you need to revise mixed sentences in ways that fit the context of your writing. However, all of the following revisions share a clear and logical relationship between subject and predicate. Creating a clear subject–predicate relationship should be your primary objective when revising mixed sentences. Note how the mixed sentence can be revised.

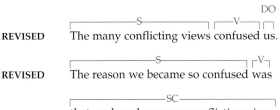

REVISED   After hearing so many conflicting views, we became confused. [Eliminating *was the reason* establishes an independent clause, now modified logically by the introductory phrase.]

REVISED   Hearing so many conflicting views confused us.   [Eliminating the preposition *after* allows the gerund phrase *hearing so many conflicting views* to function as subject.]

REVISED   The many conflicting views confused us.

REVISED   The reason we became so confused was

that we heard so many conflicting views.

WRITING HINT   Mixed sentences sometimes result from the careless use of an introductory phrase or clause. Remember that adverb clauses and prepositional phrases are modifiers; they cannot function as the subject of a sentence.

MIXED   In walking briskly for twenty minutes is an effective aerobic exercise. [*Walking* is the object of *in,* not the subject of *is.*]

REVISED   In walking briskly for twenty minutes, you perform an effective aerobic exercise.

REVISED   Walking briskly for twenty minutes is an effective aerobic exercise.

MIXED   Because of his courage and honesty made Arthur Ashe an important spokesperson for AIDS awareness. [The dependent clause *Because of his courage and honesty* cannot function as the subject of *made.*]

REVISED   His courage and honesty made Arthur Ashe an important spokesperson for AIDS awareness.

REVISED   Because of his courage and honesty, Arthur Ashe became an important spokesperson for AIDS awareness.

22b   Revising mixed sentences with faulty predication

When the subject and predicate do not make sense together, the result is an illogical relationship known as **faulty predication.** In a mixed sentence with faulty predication, the subject is described as being or doing something it logically cannot be or do. Faulty predication often occurs with the verb *be.* When using forms of *be,* make sure that the subject of your sentence is logically related to the complete predicate (see 10a). Consider the following example.

FAULTY   The *purpose* of the presidential debates *was intended* to give the public a better understanding of the issues. [The subject, *purpose,* is illogically linked with the predicate, *was intended.* Since *purpose* suggests an intention, the predicate, *was intended,* is redundant.]

REVISED   The purpose of the presidential debates *was* to give the public a better understanding of the issues.

REVISED   The presidential debates *were intended* to give the public a better understanding of the issues.

1   *When* and *where* used with *be*

One common type of faulty predication results from using the adverbs *when* or *where* after the verb *be.* Avoid using *is when* or *is where* to define or explain a term or an idea.

FAULTY	A debate *is when* opposing viewpoints are presented. [*When* indicates a time; it cannot be used to define or modify *debate*.]
REVISED	In a debate, opposing viewpoints are presented.
REVISED	A debate involves the presentation of opposing viewpoints.
FAULTY	A strike *is where* you knock down all ten pins with a single roll of the bowling ball. [*Where* indicates a place; it cannot be used meaningfully to define a strike in bowling.]
REVISED	In bowling, a strike involves knocking down all ten pins with a single roll of the ball.

2   The reason . . . is because

Faulty predication also results from using the construction *the reason . . . is because*. Use either *reason* or *because* in providing explanations, but not both words together. Using *reason* and *because* together is redundant.

FAULTY	*The reason* Tim whistles during exams *is because* he is nervous.
REVISED	*The reason Tim whistles during exams is that he is nervous.*
REVISED	Tim whistles during exams *because* he is nervous.

USAGE NOTE   Although you often hear or use *is when, is where,* and *the reason . . . is because* in everyday conversation, this phrasing is not acceptable in standard written English. And *be* is not the only verb that can lead to clumsy and inconsistent predication. You should check all of your sentences for faulty predication.

FAULTY	The history of preventive dentistry reduced the dental treatment costs. [*Preventive dentistry,* not its history, reduced treatment costs.]
REVISED	*Preventive dentistry reduced* the cost of dental treatment.
FAULTY	The invention of the computer symbolizes the postmodern era. [The computer, not its invention, symbolizes the postmodern era.]
REVISED	*The computer symbolizes* the postmodern era.

EXERCISE 22–1   Revising Mixed Sentences

Revise the following sentences to eliminate mixed grammatical constructions and faulty predication. (More than one revision is possible.) Example:

A sentence fragment is leaving out a subject or a verb.
A sentence fragment is a group of words that lacks a subject or a verb.

1. When the Berlin Wall was torn down was a turning point in the demise of communism in Eastern Europe.

2. Racial discrimination is when a person is treated unfairly based on the color of his or her skin.

3. Jean knew studying the map can help keep her from getting lost on the hike.

4. By following up on his interview with a letter will improve Jeff's chances for getting the job.

5. One ingredient of a good friendship is when two people have mutual respect.

6. To see if Suzy needed glasses waited for the results of her eye exam.

7. When Michael realized he was going to college on a full scholarship caused him to be overjoyed.

8. The reason cattle ranchers are concerned is because of the drought.

9. In Cooperstown, New York, is where they have the Baseball Hall of Fame.

10. Because typhoons destroy so much so fast is why they are dangerous.

EXERCISE 22–2 **Working with Predication**

Complete each of the following sentences in a clear and logical way. Example:

By working two jobs _____ .

By working two jobs *she hoped to pay off her student loans* _____ .

1. When children are punished for no reason _____ .
2. Maturity is _____ .
3. By registering early _____ .
4. The use of sun blockers is _____ .
5. The reason we left early _____ .

Incomplete Sentences

An **incomplete sentence** results from leaving out essential words, phrases, or clauses. Sentence fragments, the most serious kind of incomplete sentence, have no subject or predicate (see Chapter 17). But a sentence can also be incomplete because the writer has omitted a word or a phrase that is needed for the meaning of the sentence to be clear.

22c Revising confusing elliptical constructions

An **elliptical construction** is a compound structure in which words are left out or implied rather than directly stated. Writers and speakers use elliptical constructions to streamline their discourse, to avoid repetition, and to emphasize points.

In the following example, four words (*of a book should*) have been omitted from the sentence. Their appearance in brackets indicates that they are implied and need not be included for the sentence to make sense. This elliptical construction, which does not cause confusion, results in a more streamlined sentence.

> The beginning of a book should capture the reader's interest and the ending [*of a book should*] leave the reader with something to think about.

When you write with elliptical constructions, be sure that the omitted words match the words that have not been omitted (that is, that they are parallel). For example, if you leave out a phrase in the second part of a compound structure, it should be the same as the phrase that you used in the first part. Similarly, a verb or an auxiliary omitted in the second part of a compound should be parallel to the verb in the first part.

> The Russian skaters finished first and the Americans [*finished*] second.

> In the accident the driver was killed but the passenger [*was*] only injured.

(See 12g for using pronouns in elliptical constructions. For more on using parallel structures, see 24a–c.)

Notice the confusion that results when the elliptical structure does not maintain a parallel structure.

FAULTY   The first part of the test *requires* quick thinking and fast writing, the other two more sustained analysis and interpretation. [The first subject, *first part,* is singular and takes a singular verb; the second subject, *the other two,* is plural and should take a plural verb.]

REVISED   The first part of the test *requires* quick thinking and fast writing; the last two sections *require* more sustained analysis and interpretation.

REVISED   The first part of the test requires quick thinking and fast writing, the last [*requires*] more sustained analysis and interpretation.

22d Revising sentences to include missing words

It is not uncommon for writers to leave out words by mistake (especially articles, pronouns, and prepositions) in the haste of composition. Such omissions may result in confusion. You should proofread your writing carefully to look for these unintended omissions.

Some omissions, however, are acceptable—those that do not obscure your meaning.

> We believed [*that*] they would come.

In this instance the omission of *that* creates no problem with understanding the meaning of the sentence.

In the following example, however, the meaning is obscured by omitting *that*. The incomplete sentence requires revision to clarify the ambiguities.

> FAULTY   Max and Al heard many songs from the 1960s had become familiar to the next generation. [The sentence is unclear about whether 1960s songs became familiar to the next generation or whether Max and Al listened to 1960s songs that had become familiar to the next generation.]
>
> REVISED   Max and Al heard *that* many songs from the 1960s had become familiar to the next generation.
>
> REVISED   Max and Al heard many songs from the 1960s *that* had become familiar to the next generation.

Many English idioms involve phrasal verbs whose meaning changes with the addition of different prepositions. The phrasal *give in*, for example, means something different from *give out, give up,* or *give away.* Often, prepositions that function as part of an idiomatic phrase are omitted in elliptical constructions. Be especially careful when using this kind of elliptical construction that the prepositions are identical.

> Ellen both believed and participated *in* the seance. [The phrasals in the elliptical construction are *believed in* and *participated in.*]

If the prepositions are not identical, both must appear in the sentence so that each idiomatic phrase maintains its meaning.

> FAULTY   The tribe not only believed but also lived *by* these traditions.
>
> REVISED   The tribe not only believed *in* but also lived *by* these traditions.

(See 10c for more on phrasal verbs. For a list of common idiomatic expressions, consult the chart in 16r.)

If English is not your native language, you may also want to check for omitted articles (*a, an, the*). See 16c on using articles and other determiners.

22e   Revising incomplete comparisons

When you use comparisons in your writing, be sure that they are complete, clear, and logically consistent. Comparisons are statements that express a relation between two or more things, as in *Bicycles are a more suitable form of transportation than cars around campus,* or *Her motorcycle is a more expensive model than his.* (See 13e on comparative forms of adjectives and adverbs.)

1   Complete comparisons

To be complete, a comparison must express the relation or connection between the items compared with sufficient precision and fullness to ensure clarity.

INCOMPLETE   Peg's dedication was greater. [Greater than whose or what?]

REVISED   Peg's dedication was greater *than ours.*

REVISED   Peg's dedication was greater *now than ever before.*

2   Clear comparisons

A clear comparison avoids ambiguity and cannot be understood in more than one way. If a comparison is ambiguous, it must be revised to convey only one meaning.

UNCLEAR   The study session helped Rose more than her roommate. [Did the session help her more than it helped her roommate or more than her roommate helped her?]

CLEAR   The study session helped Rose more than her roommate *did.*

CLEAR   The study session helped Rose more than *it helped* her roommate.

3   Logically consistent comparisons

To be logically consistent, a comparison must make sense. The words in one part of the comparison must not contradict those in the other part.

ILLOGICAL   Harold is taller than any student in the class. [Harold cannot be taller than himself.]

LOGICAL   Harold is taller than any *other* student in the class.

ILLOGICAL   Oliver Stone's films are as timely as Spike Lee. [It is illogical to compare a person's work with a person.]

LOGICAL   Oliver Stone's films are as timely as *Spike Lee's.*

EXERCISE 22–3   Revising Incomplete Sentences

Revise the following sentences to eliminate confusing elliptical constructions or unclear, inconsistent, or incomplete comparisons. Some sentences may be correct as written. Example:

The employees feared their boss would reject their request.
The employees *feared that* their boss would reject their request.

1. The entertainers' salaries are higher than teachers.
2. Bureaucrats are often more concerned with filling out forms than problems.
3. The French drink more wine than people in Italy.
4. Bryant's property is closer to the pond than the woods.
5. Most Americans might believe that pizza and pasta are better.
6. Sandy and Drew had a special interest and feeling for Renaissance architecture.
7. Their cakes are made with butter but their pie with shortening instead.
8. Modern scientists have a better understanding of the medical value of leeches than before.
9. Victoria likes classical music better than Joan.
10. Few people stop to consider the word *woman* derives from *man*.

Grammar and Writing

Writing Clear and Complete Sentences

Most often, a writer's primary goal is to communicate an idea or fact clearly. Two problems that undermine an attempt at clear communication are mixed sentences and incomplete sentences. Now that you know how these types of sentences can occur, you can apply what you have learned to your own writing.

One place to start is the checklist on p. 412 of this chapter. It is unlikely that all of the problems listed there will plague your writing. Identify the one or two that cause you the most trouble, even if it is only occasional. Then consult the relevant chapter section and discussion as you review your writing.

There are no shortcuts to clear, communicable writing. The wide variety of faults discussed in this chapter suggests an array of ways that sentences can go awry. Many of these faults occur when writers work quickly or carelessly. These faults can be caught and corrected by reviewing your writing slowly, carefully, and deliberately. Reading your drafts aloud is one way to slow yourself down sufficiently so you can better see and hear what you have written. Your ear will often catch confusing glitches and patches of writing that do not make sense.

Sentence Style

Writing with Style

Style refers to the distinctiveness with which something is said or done. You can dress with style, act with style, speak with style, live with style, and write with style. Writing with style involves using language not merely correctly but clearly, fluently, even gracefully. Chapters 23 and 24 demonstrate how controlling structure can add clarity and forcefulness to your sentences. Chapter 25 illustrates how varying the length, form, and openings of sentences can enhance their effectiveness. Finally, Chapter 26 identifies techniques that will help you write succinctly and vigorously.

A writing style reflects a particular way of experiencing the world. Your writing style conveys your unique perceptions of the world through your unique way of using language.

In writing about Charles Dickens, a nineteenth-century novelist known for his realistic yet sentimental style, the American critic J. Hillis Miller offered the following observations:

> The pervasive stylistic traits of a writer, his recurrent words and images, his special cadence and tone, are as personal to him as his face or his way of walking. His style is his own way of living in the world given a verbal form.

The following chapters will help you develop that kind of distinctiveness of verbal form. One of the goals of Part Six of the *Handbook,* thus, is to provide you with resources for developing your own writing style. Another is to enable you to write sentences that are readable, interesting, and memorable.

CHAPTER 23

Writing Coordinate and Subordinate Sentences

*U*se **coordination** to emphasize that certain ideas and actions are equally important.

WORDS   They walked and *talked*.

PHRASES   The movie's violent scenes occurred *in the beginning* and *at the end*.

CLAUSES   *They considered going to a movie,* but *they went to the mall* instead.

Notice that the coordinate structure in each example is linked by a coordinating conjunction (*and, but, or, nor, for, so, yet*).

Use **subordination** to distinguish a main idea or action from less important ones. Usually the main idea or action appears in an independent clause, and the less important idea or action in a phrase and a dependent clause. (See 10d on dependent and independent clauses.)

As they walked, they talked. [Their talking is emphasized.]

Although the movie's violent scenes occurred in the beginning and at the end, the violence was neither excessive nor protracted. [When the violence occurs is less important than its intensity and duration.]

After considering going to a movie, they went to the mall instead. [Going to the mall is emphasized over going to the movies.]

23a   Using coordination to relate equal ideas

1   Writing sentences with coordination

When you want to express a relationship between ideas of equal importance, you could write two separate sentences: *The Civil War began in 1861. It ended in 1865.* You could also combine the two sentences into one using a coordinating conjunction—*and, but, or, nor, for, so, yet* (see 14c-1).

The Civil War began in 1861, *and* it ended in 1865.

Coordinated structures can be used to indicate a variety of relationships. When using coordinate structures, be sure the coordinating conjunctions you use are logically appropriate. Notice how the following sentences use coordinate conjunctions to express different kinds of relationships between independent clauses.

EQUIVALENCE   They found jobs, *and* they acquired independence.

CONTRAST   There is authority in the classroom, *but* it does not belong to the teacher.

ALTERNATIVES   Economic conditions must improve quickly, *or* political chaos will ensue.

EXPLANATION   We wanted to visit the museum, *for* we had heard it was full of marvelous relics.

CONSEQUENCE   It was a dreary, rainy day, *so* we remained indoors.

DISTINCTION   He wanted to ask her to the concert, *yet* he feared rejection.

WRITING HINT   When you join two independent clauses with a coordinating conjunction, be sure to use a comma before the conjunction. However, when the independent clauses are short, you may choose to omit the comma.

It was dark *and* it was cold.

You do not need a comma between two coordinate words, phrases, or dependent clauses.

He enjoys apple pie *but* not cherry pie.

They have traveled in Europe *and* in Asia.

If the air is heavy *or* when the wind is still, the heat can become unbearable.

You might also write coordinate structures without a conjunction. Coordination is indicated by a semicolon between two independent clauses, especially those parallel in structure (see 24c and 34a).

She liked lasagne and garlic bread; he preferred lighter fare.

Physics majors spend many hours doing problems; history majors devote a lot of time to reading books.

When you use a semicolon to join coordinate clauses, you will sometimes want to use a conjunctive adverb, such as *however, therefore,* or *moreover,* along with appropriate punctuation (see 34b).

Thoreau grew the food he ate at Walden Pond; *however,* on Sundays he went to a friend's house for dinner.

The basketball players' brawl was the worst in the league's history; the league president, *therefore,* imposed heavy fines on the players involved.

You can also create coordinate structures by using the correlative conjunctions *either . . . or, neither . . . nor, both . . . and,* and *not only . . . but also* in the sentence (see 14c-2).

You will need to sell *either* your car *or* your motorcycle.

Human behavior can be *neither* predicted *nor* controlled.

We *both* anticipated *and* feared the news.

USAGE NOTE   When you use *not only . . . but also,* be certain that the correlative conjunction coordinates grammatically related elements within the sentence.

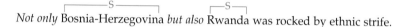

Not only Bosnia-Herzegovina *but also* Rwanda was rocked by ethnic strife.

The school administrators *not only* underestimated the drop in enrollment,

but also failed to plan for the expected drop in funding.

Both . . . and is not used to coordinate independent clauses; it is used only to connect elements within a sentence.

Both coffee *and* tea contain a lot of caffeine.

Coordination is especially useful in revising your writing. If you find that a draft sounds choppy and disconnected, using coordinate conjunctions and conjunctive adverbs to link related ideas can clarify your writing and enhance its fluency. Consider how coordination improves the following passage.

WITHOUT COORDINATION

I know very little about laboratory science. I have the impression that conclusions are supposed to be logical. From a given set of circumstances a predictable result should follow. The trouble is that in human behavior it is impossible to isolate a given set of circumstances. It is also impossible to repeat the circumstances. This is true in history, too. Complex human acts cannot be reproduced. They cannot be deliberately initiated. They cannot be counted upon like the phenomena of nature.

WITH COORDINATION

I know very little about laboratory science, *but* I have the impression that conclusions are supposed to be logical; *that is,* from a given set of circumstances a predictable result should follow. The trouble is that in human behavior *and* history it is impossible to isolate *or* repeat a given set of circumstances. Complex human acts cannot be *either* reproduced *or* deliberately initiated—*or* counted upon like the phenomena of nature.

—Barbara Tuchman, "Is History a Guide to the Future?"

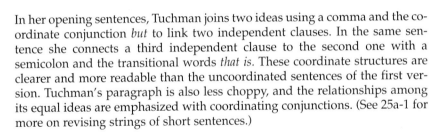

In her opening sentences, Tuchman joins two ideas using a comma and the coordinate conjunction *but* to link two independent clauses. In the same sentence she connects a third independent clause to the second one with a semicolon and the transitional words *that is*. These coordinate structures are clearer and more readable than the uncoordinated sentences of the first version. Tuchman's paragraph is also less choppy, and the relationships among its equal ideas are emphasized with coordinating conjunctions. (See 25a-1 for more on revising strings of short sentences.)

2   Avoiding excessive coordination

Coordination can be overused. If you are using coordination as the only or primary way to link independent clauses, then you are probably relying too heavily on it. Notice how, in the following example, excessive coordination results in monotonous and stilted writing.

EXCESSIVE COORDINATION

Eating fast food is now a common experience for many people, *and* this is the case in many countries around the world. People frequent fast-food eateries such as Burger King and McDonald's, *and* they take food out *and* eat it at home *or* in their cars. The food is not especially good, *but* it isn't too bad either, *and* you get used to it. The food is not especially tasty *nor* is it healthy. Some people defend the taste, however.

REVISED

Eating fast food is now a common experience for many people *not only* in the United States *but also* in other countries. People throughout North America, Europe, *and* Asia frequent such fast-food eateries as Burger King and McDonald's. Although many people eat inside the restaurants, many others take their fast food home *or* eat it in their cars. Though *neither* particularly tasty *nor* especially healthy, the fast food served at such places has its defenders.

The revised version uses coordination more effectively than the excessively coordinated version. In addition, the revised version more accurately expresses the relationship among its ideas. The revision, moreover, offers relief from the monotony of the first version's repeated coordinate structures.

3   Avoiding illogical coordination

Illogical coordination occurs when the ideas in two connected clauses are unrelated or when the coordinating word expresses an inaccurate relationship between the ideas.

ILLOGICAL	Mozart was a brilliant composer, *and* he was a crass man. [The two ideas may be true, but they are not logically connected or equally important and therefore should not coordinate.]
REVISED	Mozart, though a crass man, was a brilliant composer.
ILLOGICAL	Prices for air travel increased for the summer, *and* they are sure to decrease in the fall. [Using *and* is illogical since the two clauses suggest contrast.]
REVISED	Prices for air travel increased for the summer, *but* they are sure to decrease in the fall.

The accompanying chart offers advice for analyzing the coordinate structures in your writing.

Checking Coordination in Your Writing

- Locate coordinate conjunctions: *and, but, or, nor, for, so,* and *yet.* Check to see that the conjunction linking independent clauses is appropriate and logical.
- Check for excessive coordination. Consider revising to subordinate some of your coordinate structures (see 23b). Or consider replacing some coordinate conjunctions with conjunctive adverbs. You may want to rewrite the independent clauses as complete sentences.
- Check for independent clauses joined only by a semicolon. Consider whether the ideas on both sides of the semicolon are equally important.

EXERCISE 23–1 Combining Sentences to Coordinate Related Ideas

Combine the following short sentences into longer ones that better coordinate related ideas. Supply a logically appropriate coordinating conjunction, correlative conjunction, or conjunctive adverb. Or simply link the clauses with a semicolon. Write two versions for each combination. Example:

Why Houdini made his escapes can be explained. How he made some of them remains a mystery.

Why Houdini made his escapes can be explained, *but* how he made some of them remains a mystery.

1. Humans have highly developed senses of touch and taste. They cannot rival dogs for hearing and smell.
2. It was the best of vacations. It was the worst of vacations.
3. It was not what the ravens did that intrigued the researcher. It was the way they did it that amazed him.

4. The pitcher looks in to the batter. The pitcher receives a signal from the catcher. The pitcher winds up. The pitcher delivers the ball. It is hit hard into the outfield.

5. When the day is done, we will go to the gym. We will have dinner. We will read. We will go to bed around midnight.

EXERCISE 23–2 Revising to Eliminate Excessive or Illogical Coordination

---

Revise the following sentences to eliminate excessive or illogical coordination. Example:

> He was losing his hair and his eyesight remained good.
> He was losing his hair, *but* his eyesight remained good.

1. The snow was only an inch deep, and it was melting quickly, and there was a lot more snow in the forecast, but it could create rush-hour traffic problems.

2. They never did get to go on a honeymoon. And they decided to take a special trip on their fifth anniversary.

3. Jack bought tea for himself, so he forgot to buy coffee for Lynda.

4. They received applause for their outstanding performance, so they accepted it gracefully.

5. The pond was filled with fish, and they were jumping to the surface at the food thrown to them by the campers, and then the children ran out of food, but the fish continued to jump, and then finally they stopped, and the surface of the pond was calm.

23b Using subordination to distinguish main ideas

1 Writing sentences with subordination

Subordination is a writing technique that distinguishes the main idea in a sentence from qualifying or expanding ideas. Typically, the main idea appears in an independent clause, and related ideas and details fall in phrases or dependent clauses (see 10d). Although all information in a sentence is valuable, you can convey the relative importance of related ideas by using subordinate constructions. Consider the following example.

> Mr. Kaspar was a gifted master carpenter who loved to grow vegetables, especially squash, peppers, and tomatoes.

This sentence emphasizes Mr. Kaspar's carpentry ability while relegating the less important information about his gardening hobby to a dependent clause.

To emphasize Mr. Kaspar's gardening talents, the sentence could be rewritten to subordinate his ability as a carpenter.

> Mr. Kaspar, *who was a gifted master carpenter,* loved to grow vegetables, especially squash, peppers, and tomatoes.

> *Although he was a gifted master carpenter,* Mr. Kaspar loved to grow vegetables, especially squash, peppers, and tomatoes.

The technique of subordination offers you options. You choose how to use it to add detail. You decide what to emphasize in your sentences.

One choice you make is deciding where to place a subordinate construction in relation to the main idea of a sentence. Consider this example.

> If they can make their argument carefully, they should win the debate.

> They should win the debate, if they make their argument carefully.

Although these two sentences use identical words, they have slightly different meanings. In the first sentence the independent clause falls in the final, emphatic position of the sentence and the focus is on their winning the debate. The second sentence puts the dependent clause at the end and therefore focuses on their argument.

WRITING HINT   Usually, the independent clause in a sentence receives the greatest emphasis. But in short sentences and in those in which the dependent and independent clauses are similar in length, either clause may appear more emphatic.

> No one will race unless there is another entry.

In many cases, the placement of the clauses is as important for emphasis as the kind of clause. In the following sentence, notice how the *if* clause is the most emphatic because it comes at the end of the sentence.

> Advertising is a valuable economic factor because it is the cheapest way of selling goods, especially if the goods are worthless.

> —Sinclair Lewis

Subordination has other uses as well. Use subordination to combine short sentences that have implied relationships. It signals logical relationships among facts and details, typically with the subordinating conjunctions *unless, if, after,* and *because* (see 14c-3).

> *When* the first simple flower bloomed on some raw upland late in the Dinosaur Age, it was wind pollinated, just like its early pine-cone relatives. It was a very inconspicuous flower *because* it had not yet evolved the idea of using the surer attraction of birds and insects to achieve the transportation of pollen. It sowed its own pollen and received the pollen of other flowers by the simple vagaries of the wind. Many plants in regions *where* insect life is scant still follow this principle today.

> —Loren Eiseley, "How Flowers Changed the World"

Subordination is a good technique to use when developing details of cause, concession, condition, time, location, choice, and purpose.

- To show **cause** or to explain why, use *because* or *since.*

  Because snow was forecast, they decided not to hike up the mountain that day.

- To express a **concession,** use *although, as if, though,* or *even though.*

  Although Thomas was attracted to the arts, he studied biology and eventually went to medical school.

- To indicate a **condition,** use *even if, provided, since,* or *unless.*

  Unless the Bosnians and the Serbs can learn to live together peacefully, they are in for a stormy future.

- To establish **time,** use *as soon as, after, before, since, when, whenever, while,* or *until.*

  LeeAnn did not choose a graduate program *until* she received several acceptances.

- To indicate **location,** use *where* or *wherever.*

  President Clinton attracts a crowd *wherever* he goes.

- To indicate **choice,** use *rather than* or *whether.*

  Whether I go on the foreign exchange trip or not, I will have enjoyed dreaming about it.

- To show **purpose,** use *that, in order that,* or *so that.*

  His friends helped him finish the yard work *so that* he could join them for a card game.

WRITING HINT Another way to subordinate involves introducing adjective clauses with a relative pronoun, such as *that, when, where, which,* or *who.*

He admired the dress *that she was wearing.*

She remembered the times *when her whole family got together.*

They vacationed on a remote island *where no one lived.*

They are a couple *who seems to have everything.*

EXERCISE 23–3   **Combining Sentences to Subordinate Related Ideas**

Combine each of the following sets of short sentences into a longer sentence. Use subordinate structures to signal the relationship among details or ideas. Example:

We opened the front door. A bird flew from the nest. It had built a nest in a plant that hung from our porch roof.

When we opened the front door, a bird flew from the nest it had built in a plant that hung from our porch roof.

1. I was reaching over the counter for a chocolate layer cake. I noticed a banana chocolate cream pie. I decided to buy both.

2. *In Country* is a novel by Bobbie Ann Mason. It is about a young American girl coming to terms with the Vietnam War. It is a moving book.

3. The tennis team had performed well all season. The team members were invited to a postseason tournament. They performed well in the tournament. They made it to the semifinals.

4. Bill's car needs new brakes. The brakes squeal when he steps on the brake pedal. The repair will cost a few hundred dollars. The car is dangerous to drive.

5. *Cheers* is one of the great television sitcoms. It was on television for eleven seasons. It takes place in a Boston bar. Both critics and general viewers enjoyed it.

---

2 Avoiding excessive subordination

In an effort to avoid excessive coordination or to keep from writing too many short, choppy sentences, writers sometimes use too many dependent clauses. The result is excessive subordination. Sentences with excessive subordination tend to run on and lose emphasis, and the relationships between ideas become confused. Revise them by writing shorter, clearer, and more emphatic sentences.

EXCESSIVE SUBORDINATION

Because the owners of Ben and Jerry's, which is located in Vermont, were concerned that small dairy farms that were family run were going out of business, they made a commitment to buying only dairy products from Vermont rather than dairy products from large western dairy farms even though buying products from the family-run farms was more expensive.

REVISED

The owners of Ben and Jerry's, which is located in Vermont, were concerned that small, family-run dairy farms were going out of business. They therefore made a commitment to buying only local dairy products rather than less expensive dairy products from large western dairy farms. [Note that the revision is two sentences long and that several subordinating phrases have been changed to one- or two-word adjectives.]

3 Avoiding illogical subordination

Illogical subordination occurs when the most important idea or information is placed in a dependent clause, or when the subordinating conjunction inaccurately identifies the relationship between the clauses.

ILLOGICAL   Isadora Duncan died in 1927, *even though* she greatly influenced modern dance.

The idea in the subordinating clause is more important than that in the independent clause.

REVISED   *Even though* she died in 1927, Isadora Duncan greatly influenced modern dance.

ILLOGICAL   *Because* Isadora Duncan died in 1927, she founded dancing schools in Berlin, Paris, and Moscow.

Duncan's founding of the schools was not a direct result of her death as the subordinating clause suggests.

REVISED   *Before* Isadora Duncan died in 1927, she founded dancing schools in Berlin, Paris, and Moscow.

WRITING HINT   To avoid both excessive subordination and excessive coordination, strive for a blend of coordinate and subordinate structures. Take note of this kind of blending in the following example.

> I was never much of an athlete, but I was once the member of a team. Indeed, I was its star, and we were champions. During high school I belonged to a squad of speed readers in Ohio, although I was never awarded a letter for it. Still, we took on the top 10 in our territory and read as rapidly as possible every time we were challenged to a match, hoping to finish in front of that towheaded punk from Canton, the tomato-cheeked girl from Marietta, or that silent pair of sisters, all spectacles and squints, who looked tough as German script and who hailed from Shaker Heights or some other rough neighborhood full of swift, mean raveners of texts.
>
> —William H. Gass, "Of Speed Readers and Lip Movers"

The accompanying chart provides guidance for using subordinate structures.

Checking Subordination in Your Writing

- Underline the subordinate structures in each of your sentences.
- Check to see that the most important idea appears in the main or independent clause and that related details appear in the subordinate structures.
- For clauses introduced by subordinating conjunctions, consider alternative placement in the sentence—with corresponding shifts of emphasis.
- Check for sentences that include strings of subordinate clauses. Consider whether the main idea of the sentence is sufficiently clear and emphatic.
- Check for logical relationships between clauses by examining the meaning of the subordinating conjunctions you use.

EXERCISE 23–4 Eliminating Illogical and Excessive Subordination

Revise the following sentences to eliminate illogical or excessive subordination. Example:

> The president's budget would not be passed although a compromise could be reached.
>
> The president's budget would not be passed *unless* a compromise could be reached.

1. Beethoven lost his hearing even though he continued to compose music.
2. Under the circumstances, since the teacher will not reconsider my grade, and if the department chair is unyielding, I may have to take my complaint to the dean, unless that route is closed to me.
3. Old homes are common in New England even though they are often painted white.
4. She wanted to forget the entire matter and he would not let her.
5. When the results are finally tabulated, each side is convinced that its candidate will be victorious, though there are some skeptics on each side who believe no such thing, for they expect defeat not victory, but they are prepared for that disappointment.

EXERCISE 23–5 Revising with Coordination and Subordination

The following passage consists of simple sentences. Use coordination and subordination to emphasize main ideas and express logical relationships.

> Photographs furnish evidence. An event seems proven when a photograph of it exists. A photograph passes for proof that a particular event occurred. The picture may distort the reality. It may approximate what occurred. It may capture only a small part of it. It does capture something like what actually happened, what was. A photograph is selective. What it selects is a slice of the actual. Photographs certify experience.

EXERCISE 23–6 Using Coordination and Subordination in Writing

Write a paragraph in which you blend at least two coordinate and two subordinate structures. Possible topics include why you are attending college; why you chose your college; a favorite leisure activity; a memorable meal; a recent news event.

Grammar and Writing

Coordination and Subordination

You can apply what you know about coordination and subordination to your writing when you draft and revise your essays, papers, and reports. When you compose a draft, use coordinate and subordinate structures to clarify your expression of ideas and your presentation of information.

Use the charts on p. 426 and p. 431 to check for excessive use of either coordination or subordination in your writing when you revise. Too much of either grammatical form may create monotonous or unemphatic writing. Try for a blending of coordinate and subordinate grammatical structures.

The most important aspect of coordination and subordination for writers is also the most complex and challenging: using these grammatical structures logically. As you write and revise, check to see that your uses of *and* and *but*, of *if* and *because* (and other coordinate and subordinate conjunctions) link clearly expressed and logically thought-out relations among the parts of your sentences.

EXAMPLE:

but

She was never much of a musician, [and] she did briefly study piano and

violin.

Because

Her playing lacked musicality, [and] her teachers discouraged her from con-

tinuing her musical study.

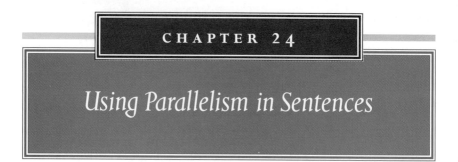

CHAPTER 24

Using Parallelism in Sentences

*P*arallelism in writing involves using a similar grammatical form for two or more coordinate elements. Parallel structure expresses a close connection or contrast between sentence elements, whether they are words, phrases, or clauses. Using parallelism will tighten your writing by making it balanced and rhythmical. Note how the parallel structures in the following sentences, which have been aligned for visual clarity, emphasize symmetry and balance.

> The oak tree provided shelter for *birds,*
> > *squirrels,*
> and *children.*

> On coming to a new place, my father would *take a pinch of dirt,*
> > *sprinkle it in his palm,*
> > *sniff it,*
> > *stir it with a blunt finger,*
> then *rake it on his tongue,* tasting.

> —Scott Russell Sanders

The accompanying chart identifies how parallelism can help you improve your writing.

Uses of Parallelism

- To coordinate elements in a series (24a)
- To pair ideas (24b)
- To enhance coherence (24c)
- To organize lists and outlines (24d)

24a Using parallelism to coordinate elements in a series

All items listed in a series—whether single words, phrases, or clauses—need to be written in parallel grammatical structures.

NOUNS   Among the necessities of life are *food, clothing,* and *shelter.*

VERBS   The boat *yawed, jibed,* and *veered* perilously close to the rocks.

PHRASES   Aaron and Elaine could not decide whether to spend their vacation *at the shore* or *in the mountains.*

CLAUSES   Tell me *where you went, what you saw,* and *why you returned* early.

Presenting parallel elements in nonparallel grammatical form upsets the reader's expectations, frequently creating awkwardness and confusion.

NONPARALLEL   The vacation package included *food, lodging, recreation,* and *having entrance fees paid for.* [The first three items included in the series are nouns, the last is a participial phrase.]

REVISED   The vacation package included *food, lodging, recreation,* and *entrance fees.* [All four items are nouns.]

NONPARALLEL   Some college graduates attend law school because *they hope to get high-paying jobs, not being ready to work,* or because *they are not sure what else to do.* [The first and third items in the series are clauses, the second is a participial phrase.]

REVISED   Some college graduates attend law school because *they hope to get high-paying jobs,* because *they are not yet ready to work,* and because *they are not sure what else to do.* [All three elements in the series are now subordinate clauses.]

Each revision makes its point with clarity, with balance, and with rhythm.

24b Using parallelism with pairs

One of the more common uses of parallelism in writing is to pair two ideas. When you want to compare or contrast ideas, use a coordinate conjunction, a correlative conjunction, or the subordinate conjunction *as* or *than,* to connect the ideas, and state the ideas in parallel grammatical form.

A sentence that includes two clauses in a grammatically parallel structure is called a **balanced sentence.** In a balanced sentence, the two clauses are closely paired so that the meaning of each clause is reflected off the other.

Buddies seek approval but friends seek acceptance.

—Ellen Goodman

There is a time for joy; there is a time for sorrow.

Balanced sentences create a memorable pairing and can be emphatic, memorable, and humorous, as the following example illustrates.

This man, I thought had been a Lord among wits; but, I find, he is only a wit among Lords!

—Samuel Johnson

1   Parallelism with coordinate conjunctions

Use similar grammatical structures when connecting sentence elements with a coordinating conjunction—*and, but, or, nor, for, so, yet.*

Buddies bond *but* friends love.

—Ellen Goodman

Life is ten percent what you make it and ninety percent how you take it.

—Irving Berlin

When sentence elements joined by a coordinating conjunction are not parallel, the relationship between them may not be evident.

NONPARALLEL	The film was *terrifying* and *with a lot of suspense.*
REVISED	The film was *terrifying* and *suspenseful.*
NONPARALLEL	Three things to consider when buying a stereo system are *the amount of power you need, your budget,* and *where you intend to use the stereo equipment.*
REVISED	Three things to consider when buying a stereo system are *the amount of power you need, the amount of money you have,* and *the place you intend to use it.*

2   Parallelism with correlative conjunctions

Use parallel forms with correlative conjunctions, such as *either . . . or, neither . . . nor, both . . . and,* and *not only . . . but also.* The grammatical structure following the first part of the correlative conjunction should be identical to that following the second part (see 14c-2).

Deborah Tannen's book not only *states* that men and women have different ways of communicating, but also *explains* these differences.

NONPARALLEL   He writes neither *checks* nor *uses a credit card.* [A noun follows *neither,* but a verb phrase follows *nor.*]

REVISED   He neither *writes checks* nor *uses a credit card.*

NONPARALLEL   They go to Florida in not only *the spring* but also *in the fall.* [Preposition *in* comes before *not only* and after *but also.*]

REVISED   They go to Florida not only *in the spring* but also *in the fall.* [Prepositional phrases follow each part of the correlative conjunction.]

3 Parallelism with the subordinate conjunctions *than* and *as*

In using *than* and *as* when connecting ideas, be sure to use a similar grammatical structure in both parts of your comparison or contrast.

As my spirits declined, my opponent's score rose.

It is not greedy to enjoy a good dinner, any more than it is greedy to enjoy a good concert.

—G. K. Chesterton

NONPARALLEL   Many recent college graduates have chosen *to become doctors* rather than *studying law or business.*

REVISED   Many recent college graduates have chosen to become *doctors* rather than *lawyers or business executives.*

REVISED   Many recent college graduates have chosen to study *medicine* rather than *law or business.*

USAGE NOTE   In short sentences, you can sometimes omit prepositions, articles, and subordinating conjunctions that are repeated in a parallel series. But sometimes including these elements may make the parallelism clearer and more effective.

You can lease this office by the week, [*by the*] month, or [*by the*] year.

Olga told me that I had insulted Kit, [*that*] he was angry, and [*that*] he expected an apology.

(See 26a-3 for more on deliberate repetition.)

EXERCISE 24–1   **Identifying Parallelism**

Underline the parallel elements in the following sentences. Example:

He neither <u>confirmed</u> nor <u>denied</u> the allegation.

1. "It was the arrival of this fly that convinced me beyond any doubt that everything was as it always had been, that the years were a mirage, and that there had been no years." —*E. B. White*

2. "Some books are to be tasted, others to be swallowed, and some few to be chewed and digested." —*Francis Bacon*

3. "Read not to contradict and confute; nor to believe and take for granted; nor to find talk and discourse; but to weigh and consider." —*Francis Bacon*

4. "This freedom, like all freedoms, has its dangers and its responsibilities." —*James Baldwin*

5. "One must be something to be able to do something." —*Johann Wolfgang von Goethe*

6. "In some ways writing is the act of saying *I*, of imposing oneself upon other people, of saying listen to me, see it my way, change your mind." —*Joan Didion*

7. "In my imagination I was always there for just another few months, just until Christmas or Easter or the first warm day in May." —*Joan Didion*

8. "I want to talk to you today about privilege and about tokenism and about power." —*Adrienne Rich*

9. "To collect photographs is to collect the world. Movies and television programs light up walls, flicker, and go out; but with still photographs the image is also an object, lightweight, cheap to produce, easy to carry about, accumulate, store." —*Susan Sontag*

10. "Persons attempting to find a motive in this narrative will be prosecuted; persons attempting to find a moral in it will be banished; persons attempting to find a plot in it will be shot." —*Mark Twain*

EXERCISE 24–2 Imitating Parallelism

Select any five sentences from Exercise 24–1 and write new sentences that imitate the parallel structures. Example:

"This freedom, like all freedoms, has its dangers and its responsibilities." —*James Baldwin*

This political idea, like all political ideas, has its advocates and its critics.

24c Using parallelism to enhance coherence

Parallelism emphasizes the connections among related elements in sentences and paragraphs. This emphasis on connections results in coherence because readers can readily see how sentence elements are related.

Write about winter in the summer. Describe Norway as Ibsen did, from a desk in Italy; describe Dublin as James Joyce did, from a desk in Paris. Willa Cather wrote her prairie novels in New York City; Mark Twain wrote "Huckleberry Finn" in Hartford. Recently scholars learned that Walt Whitman rarely left his room.

Annie Dillard uses parallel structures to enhance connections both within and between sentences and to emphasize her point that writing relies, in part, on imagination.

1 Parallelism within sentences

The following example illustrates how parallelism works within sentences. As you read the paragraph, identify mentally how the parallel elements structure and clarify the writers' point.

> Like cultural literacy, scientific literacy does not refer to detailed, specialized knowledge—the sort of things an expert would know. When you come across a term like "superconductor" in a newspaper article, it is enough to know that it refers to a material that conducts electricity without loss, that the main impediment to the widespread use of superconductors is that they operate only at very low temperatures, and that finding ways to remove this impediment is a major research goal in materials science today. You can be scientifically literate without knowing how a superconductor works at the atomic level, what the various species of superconductor are, or how one could go about fabricating a superconducting material.

> —Robert M. Hazen and James Trefil, *Science Matters*

Hazen and Trefil include two long sentences in this paragraph, but by using parallelism they make their ideas easy to follow. Notice how the second sentence contains three parallel clauses beginning with the word *that:* "that it refers . . . that the main impediment . . . that finding ways to remove. . . ." Each of these clauses explains one of the things you need to know about superconductors. Similarly, the paragraph's last sentence uses parallel clauses to identify three things you do not need to know: "how a superconductor works . . . what the various species of superconductor are . . . how one could go about fabricating a superconducting material."

WRITING HINT   To use parallelism to enhance the coherence of your writing, you do not have to use word-for-word, identical grammatical structures, especially in long sentences (as in the paragraph by Hazen and Trefil). Briefer uses of parallelism do not have to match exactly, either. But do remember to keep the grammatical structures—words, phrases, or clauses—identical.

The pilot flew *over the clouds* and *into the clear, thin air of the stratosphere.*

They were less interested *in achievement itself* than *in the careful steps by which it could be approached.*

2   Parallelism among sentences within a paragraph

You can also use parallelism to enhance the connections among related sentences or ideas within a paragraph. Consider how parallel structure connects related ideas in the first three sentences of the following example.

> The Middle Ages of Europe were a continuation and a formation. They were a continuation of old Rome in race, language, institutions, law, literature, and the arts. They were also a continuation of cultures independent of Rome. The Franks and the Saxons, the Greeks and the Arabs, contributed their own civilizations to western Europe to help make the new civilization that we inherit. The English language, formed in the Middle Ages and drawn from every source, from Sanskrit to Icelandic, is a symbol of our blended culture.

Each of the first three sentences uses a similar grammatical structure, which emphasizes the relationship among them. The first states the general idea that the Middle Ages were a continuation; the second indicates how they continued Roman traditions; the third suggests that they continued other traditions as well. The remainder of the paragraph then identifies some of those other traditions. (See 8c-2 and 8c-5 for more on how parallelism and repetition contribute to coherence.)

The accompanying chart will help you check for parallelism in your writing.

Checking for Parallelism

- Check places where you list items in a series. Be sure you use a parallel grammatical structure for all items.
- Check places where you use coordinate and correlative conjunctions. Consider whether your grammatical structures are similar before and after each conjunction.
- Check places where you use *than* and *as*. Look to see that you have used similar grammatical structures for both parts of any comparisons or contrasts.
- Check elements of an outline to ensure that you have used parallel grammatical form for equivalent outline elements.

WRITING HINT   You can use parallelism to emphasize an idea or to build a sentence or paragraph toward a climax. Consider the following example.

> I lived it over and over again, the way one relives an automobile accident after it has happened and one finds oneself alone and safe. I could not get over two facts, both equally difficult for the imagination to grasp, and one was that I could have been murdered. But the other was that I had been ready to com-

mit murder. I saw nothing very clearly but I did see this: that my life, my *real* life, was in danger, and not from anything other people might do but from the hatred I carried in my own heart.

—James Baldwin, "Notes of a Native Son"

EXERCISE 24–3   Revising for Parallelism

Revise the following paragraph to express coordinate ideas in parallel form.

Many word processors will work together with other programs that check your spelling and they find typographical errors. These programs read through your essay and pointing out every word they do not recognize. Each program has a dictionary, or word list, and when a word in your essay is flagged, that means it is not in the program's dictionary. You have a choice of moving on or you can correct the error. Some programs will even suggest a spelling: if you wrote *spagetti,* the program will display the word *spaghetti,* ask if that is what you mean, and you can substitute the correct form. Although spelling checkers may make your writing process easier, you still have to do some of the proofreading yourself. For instance, the program recognizes *their, there,* and *they're* as correct, but you may have written the wrong one for your context. The program will not catch mechanical problems either, like capitalization, spacing errors, and if you left a word out or repeated one. Careful proofreading of the final copy by the writer is still a necessity.

24d   Using parallelism to organize lists and outlines

Lists are useful memory aids, and outlines provide a convenient way to sketch out a plan for action or writing. Lists and outlines are clearest and most effective when their elements appear in parallel grammatical form. Nonparallel lists and outlines can be confusing and difficult to remember. Consider the following list.

NONPARALLEL   The grievance committee's letter to the editor focused on

1. the need for more parking facilities

2. decreasing quality of campus food

3. increased tuition

Each of these issues is listed in a different grammatical structure. For a clearer, logical, and elegant presentation, make all elements in a list grammatically equivalent.

PARALLEL   The grievance committee's letter to the editor focused on

1. parking facilities

2. campus food

3. increased tuition

While creating sketchy outlines, like mapping and researching, will help you develop an idea for a paper, when you prepare a final outline for a paper or a report, check to see that the elements that make up your outline are grammatically consistent. This exercise will help you evaluate the structure of your paper. (See 1f-1 for more on outlining.)

EXERCISE 24–4   Writing with Parallel Structures

Write a paragraph in which you include at least three parallel sentences. (You may create your own paragraph or model one of the paragraphs in 24c.) Underline the parallel structures in your paragraph to make them easier to locate.

Grammar and Writing

Parallelism

One way to improve your writing is to use parallel grammatical structures consistently for clarity and emphasis. When you draft essays, papers, and reports, keep this principle in mind. When you revise, check for opportunities to use parallelism. You can refer to the "Checking for Parallelism" chart in 24c for guidance.

Be alert for small-scale occasions to use parallel structures—joining items in a series, for example, or linking comparative or contrastive phrases.

EXAMPLE:

                              or they would lose their opportunity for choice.

They would have to decide quickly [or their opportunity for choice would

be lost].

Look also for opportunities to employ parallelism in your longer and more complex sentences. Parallel structures help readers follow your meaning more easily, even when that meaning is complex and your sentences are long.

Don't overlook possibilities to write sentences parallel with one another. In drafting and revising your writing, make your paragraphs coherent by using the same grammatical structures in different sentences, thus binding them more closely. Finally, look for opportunities to use parallelism to achieve emphasis as well as clarity and coherence.

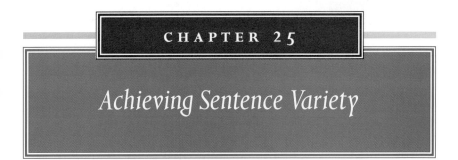

CHAPTER 25

Achieving Sentence Variety

Sentence variety involves using different kinds of sentence structures throughout a piece of writing for stylistic effect. A lack of variety in writing by beginning too many sentences the same way or using sentences of a similar type or length makes for monotonous writing and tedious reading. Varying your sentences in the ways outlined in the accompanying chart can make your writing interesting by being unpredictable.

Ways to Achieve Sentence Variety

- Mix long, short, and medium-length sentences (25a).
- Begin sentences in different ways: with transitions, with phrases and clauses, with subjects (25b).
- Vary sentence types by including occasional questions, commands, and exclamations (25c).
- Vary sentence structure by blending simple, compound, and complex sentences. Use both periodic and cumulative sentences (25c).

 Varying sentence length

Varying sentence length makes for better writing, partly because sentences of different lengths do different jobs. Short sentences emphasize ideas. Long sentences tend to elaborate, to explain, or to define ideas. Sentence variety also contributes to the movement or flow of prose, partly through the emphasis created with short sentences, partly through the rhythms created in longer, more complex ones.

1   Avoiding strings of short sentences

Using too many short sentences in succession can create a jarring uniformity and a choppy rhythm. A series of short sentences also fails to highlight the relative level of importance among major and minor points.

UNVARIED SHORT SENTENCES

Once Thoreau had to spend a night in jail. He did not pay his poll tax. He wanted to protest against a U.S. government policy. The government had a policy toward Mexico that Thoreau disapproved of. His friend Emerson came to the jail. He bailed Thoreau out. Before he did he asked Thoreau why he was behind bars. Thoreau responded by asking Emerson why he was not.

REVISED

Thoreau once had to spend a night in jail for refusing to pay his poll tax. Thoreau objected to the tax on the grounds that it supported U.S. policy toward Mexico, a policy Thoreau strongly disapproved of. When his friend Emerson came to bail him out of jail and asked Thoreau why he was in jail, Thoreau responded by asking Emerson why he was not.

The revised version eliminates the choppiness of the string of short sentences, creating a smoother flowing prose. Notice, too, that the revised paragraph uses fewer repeated words. Also, the ideas in the first sentence are emphasized because it is the shortest.

2   Avoiding strings of long sentences

A succession of long sentences lacks focus. Although long sentences are necessary to explain complex relationships among ideas, too many long sentences make it difficult to find the important points, which often are embedded within strings of clauses. The following rewritten version of a passage by Francine du Plessix Gray illustrates this problem.

UNVARIED LONG SENTENCES

In the notebooks in which I recorded my months of Soviet research, I listed several dozen basic categories of human experience with which to organize my themes: friendship, family, childhood, heroism, education, sex, marriage, religion. I realized upon finishing my list that one fundamental category, love, was missing from it, and this was not an oversight, [for] throughout my time in the Soviet Union, I barely, if ever, heard one mention of the word *lyubov*—"love" in its romantic sense. It confirmed my suspicion that love in the Soviet Union is a luxury, an accessory, but hardly the prerequisite for marriage or happiness that it is in Western Europe or the United States.

DU PLESSIX GRAY'S VERSION

In the notebooks in which I recorded my months of Soviet research, I listed several dozen basic categories of human experience with which to organize my themes: friendship, family, childhood, heroism, education, sex, marriage, religion. I realized upon finishing my list that one fundamental category was missing from it: love.

It was not an oversight. Throughout my time in the Soviet Union, I barely, if ever, heard one mention of the word *lyubov*—"love" in its romantic sense. It confirmed my suspicion that love in the Soviet Union is a luxury, an accessory, but hardly the prerequisite for marriage or happiness that it is in Western Europe or the United States.

—Francine du Plessix Gray, Soviet Women

Notice how the long sentences explain the relationship among du Plessix Gray's ideas, while the shorter ones signal which points she is emphasizing, and contribute to a pleasing rhythm.

3   Mixing long and short sentences

Alternating between short and long sentences will enable you to use the short sentences to emphasize important points, while retaining longer ones to express more complex relations among ideas. Notice how the following paragraph mixes sentences of varying lengths.

I still shy away from nightclubs, from bars, from parties where the solvent is alcohol. My friends puzzle over this, but it is no more peculiar than for a man to shy away from the lions' den after seeing his father torn apart. I took my own first drink at the age of twenty-one, half a glass of burgundy. I knew the odds of my becoming an alcoholic were four times higher than for the children of nonalcoholic fathers. So I sipped warily.

—Scott Russell Sanders, "Under the Influence"

As you can see, Sanders's first and third sentences are of nearly identical length (fifteen and sixteen words, respectively), while his second and fourth sentences are a little longer (twenty-five and twenty words, respectively). His last sentence—a mere four words—stands out in stark comparison to the longer preceding sentences and thus concludes his paragraph emphatically.

Placing a short sentence at the end of a paragraph is one way to achieve sentence variety and emphasis. But you can also achieve emphasis by placing a short sentence first. Sanders uses this technique at the beginning of "Under the Influence."

My father drank. He drank as a gut-punched boxer gasps for breath, as a starving dog gobbles food—compulsively, secretly, in pain and trembling.

A short sentence can also be effective in the middle of a paragraph, especially as a transition between main ideas. The following paragraph from "Under the Influence" illustrates this effect.

> The secret bores under the skin, gets in the blood, into the bone, and stays there. Long after you have supposedly been cured of malaria, the fever can flare up, the tremors can shake you. So it is with the fevers of shame. You swallow the bitter quinine of knowledge, and you learn to feel pity and compassion toward the drinker. Yet the shame lingers and, because of it, anger.

Use the accompanying checklist to help you avoid the tedium of too many sentences of similar length.

Checking for Varied Sentence Length

- Count the words in each sentence.
- If many sentences are the same length (within five words), rewrite some to vary their lengths.
- Look at strings of short sentences to see if they should be combined to express more clearly the relationship between their ideas.
- Look at your longest sentences to see if any contain more than a single idea. Consider splitting such sentences to better emphasize their different ideas.

EXERCISE 25–1   Varying Sentence Length

Revise the following passage to vary sentence length.

> Alice Walker's "Everyday Use" is about two sisters who are raised together in the South. Their mother is a poor, uneducated black woman who has worked hard to support her daughters. Each daughter has developed a different idea of what her future will be. Dee is the older and is determined to break away from her life of poverty and traditionalism. Her sister, Maggie, chooses to remain with their mother and follow a more traditional lifestyle.

EXERCISE 25–2   Revising Your Writing to Vary Sentence Length

Examine one of the papers you recently wrote for a course. Revise it to achieve better variety in sentence length.

25b   Varying sentence openings

Varying the types of sentence openings you use is as important as varying the length of your sentences in terms of creating emphasis and interesting rhythms. Notice how each sentence in the following passage begins with the subject.

UNVARIED SENTENCE OPENING

> Spring is a welcome season in regions with varying climates. It is most appreciated after long cold winters when the ice and snow have lingered. The arrival of spring brings hope and joy. Spring is a time for trees to bud and flowers to bloom, for ice and snow to melt away in the warmth of the sun. It is the season of sport and activity.

The paragraph could be revised by varying the sentence openings by introducing transitions, dependent clauses, or introductory prepositional or verbal phrases. Here is one possible revision that includes each of these types of sentence openings.

VARIED SENTENCE OPENING

> Spring is a welcome season in regions with varying climates. Most appreciated after long cold winters when ice and snow have lingered, the arrival of spring brings hope and joy. In spring, trees bud and flowers bloom. Ice and snow melt away in the warmth of the sun. In addition, spring is the season of sport and activity.

1   Using transitions to create sentence variety

Transitions, whether words or phrases, explicitly link one sentence or paragraph with another. Words indicating time, such as *now*, *then*, and *later*, serve as transitional links, or bridges, between sentences describing a series of events.

> The students were playing catch, tossing frisbees, or just sitting in the quad, soaking up the April sun. *Later*, they said, they would do their homework.

Phrases such as *on the other hand*, *in spite of*, and *on the contrary* explicitly indicate a contrast between what has come before and what comes after.

> On the one hand, the arrival of April means warmer temperatures and more sunshine. *On the other hand*, it also means tax day and tornado watches.

(For more on transitional words and phrases see 8c-3.)

WRITING HINT Adverbs sometimes make effective sentence openers. Using them occasionally can make your sentence openings more interesting.

Eventually the snow melted and the plants began to emerge.

Rarely did we come close to resolving our differences.

2   Using dependent clauses to create sentence variety

To avoid beginning all sentences with a simple subject or a transition, begin some sentences with dependent clauses (see 10d). For example, the paragraph about spring could begin like this.

Although spring is a welcome season in regions with varying climates, it is most appreciated following a long cold winter, one accompanied by abundant ice and snow.

Begin your sentences with dependent clauses when doing so helps clarify the relationship among the ideas in your sentence or achieves a desired emphasis of the independent clause.

Because the weather was unpredictable, we decided to hold the party indoors.

While the lecturer droned on, students in the back row slept soundly.

3   Using phrases to create sentence variety

Beginning some sentences with phrases is another way to achieve sentence variety. Use prepositional phrases (10c-1) and verbal phrases—including participial, infinitive, and absolute phrases (10c-2)—as introductory phrases.

PREPOSITIONAL PHRASES

In spring crowds fill the streets and the parks.

During warm spring afternoons, offices empty as workers find places to sit in the sun and enjoy their lunch.

VERBAL PHRASES

Caught up in the general optimism brought on by the arrival of spring, people tend to be friendlier and happier. [participial phrase]

To take advantage of the warm sun and the cool breeze, we took our papers and moved out to the deck to finish our work. [infinitive phrase]

Equipment cleaned and oiled for the start of the season, anglers are among the many sports enthusiasts who take to the outdoors. [absolute phrase]

WRITING HINT   One of the quickest ways to check sentence openings for variety is to circle the first two or three words of each of your sentences. You will see quickly whether you repeatedly begin sentences with the same part of speech. You may find that you begin every sentence with a noun, pronoun, or adjective, or that you repeatedly begin sentences with coordinating conjunctions (14c-1), subordinating conjunctions (14c-3), or conjunctive adverbs (14c-4). Whatever pattern you find, use the techniques described in this chapter as guides for revision.

EXERCISE 25–3   **Practicing Ways to Vary Sentence Openings**

Combine each of the following pairs of sentences into a single sentence using different kinds of openings. Omit and change words as needed. Experiment with different versions to come up with the most effective opener. Example:

> I finally learned to operate my VCR. It was quite a difficult process.
> *With some difficulty,* I finally learned to operate my VCR.

1. I read the instruction manual carefully. I hoped to learn how to program the timer on my VCR.
2. A friend who knows about computers came to my rescue. She did so just before I gave up entirely.
3. Learning to record was still not easy. It was not easy even with help.
4. I can set the machine to record a day in advance. This is a great convenience.
5. I seldom go out to the movies anymore. I have now learned to use my VCR.

EXERCISE 25–4   **Writing to Ensure Varied Sentence Openings**

Write a paragraph of six to ten sentences in length about the highlights of spring, summer, winter, or fall. Be sure to vary your sentence openings.

 25c   **Varying sentence types**

Another way you can achieve sentence variety is to use different sentence types. Sentences are classified grammatically as simple, compound, complex, or compound-complex (see 10f-2). Mixing these different kinds of sentences will contribute to a varied and interesting writing style.

You can also vary sentences according to function. You can use declarative sentences to assert, interrogative sentences to question, imperative sentences to command, or exclamatory sentences to express strong feelings (see 10f-1).

Notice how the following passage mixes mild commands and an exclamation with its declarative statements and uses all sentence types to great effect.

> I wish that I could jump up (a move that, in reality, would probably result in the loss of the rest of my teeth) and hug my daughter and all her classmates in a gargantuan embrace and shout to them, "Listen! No matter how happy you think you are today, you will be happier, I promise you. You can't imagine the women you will grow into, how large those women's spirits will become, stretching and stretching to encompass the challenges their lives will proffer. Take all these challenges as gifts, no matter how dubious their value seems at the time. They'll come in handy one day, you'll see. They'll open you up for joy."
>
> —Nancy Mairs, "Happiness"

You can also vary sentences within paragraphs according to their rhetorical effects. Rhetorical variety can, in fact, be one of the most effective ways to add variety to a sentence. Rhetorically, sentences can be classified as cumulative or periodic.

1   Cumulative sentences

A **cumulative sentence** states the main idea in the independent clause first and includes any modifying phrases later. Cumulative sentences get longer by accumulating details, adding modifying phrases and clauses to follow the main idea. These sentences are useful when you want to identify the main point of a sentence right away. They are also effective when you have a lot of detail to include and you want to emphasize a concrete image at the end of a sentence.

The following paragraph contains four consecutive cumulative sentences. Notice how the final sentence, introduced by the conjunction *but*, offers a refreshing change to the series of sentences that seem to emphasize information rather than synthesizing information.

> I have grown fond of semicolons in recent years. The semicolon tells you that there is still some question about the preceding full sentence; something needs to be added; it reminds you sometimes of the Greek usage. It is almost always a greater pleasure to come across a semicolon than a period. The period tells you that that is that; if you didn't get all the meaning you wanted or expected, anyway you got all the writer intended to parcel out and now you have to move along. But with a semicolon there you get a pleasant little feeling of expectancy; there is more to come; read on; it will get clearer.
>
> —Lewis Thomas, "Notes on Punctuation"

2   Periodic sentences

A **periodic sentence** delays the main idea of the sentence to the end of the sentence, in part to build suspense. Notice how the following sentence uses this strategy of the periodic sentence to build to a climactic end.

> Where justice is denied, where poverty is enforced, where ignorance prevails and where any one class is made to feel that society is in an organized conspiracy to oppress, rob and degrade them, neither persons nor property will be safe.
>
> —Frederick Douglass

EXERCISE 25–5   **Writing Cumulative and Periodic Sentences**

Rewrite the following paragraph first with cumulative sentences and then with periodic sentences.

> These men work with animals, not machines or numbers. They live outside in landscapes of torrential beauty. They are confined to a place and a routine embellished with awesome variables. They go to the mountains as if on a pilgrimage to find out what makes a herd of elk tick. Their strength is also a softness. Their toughness is a rare delicacy.

EXERCISE 25–6   **Revising for Sentence Variety**

Revise the following paragraph to vary the lengths, openings, and types of its sentences.

> Norma Jean wants to change her life or at least her lifestyle. She has become an avid weight lifter and health nut. She is now taking an English class at the community college. Leroy gets defensive about this, feeling his English may not be up to par for her. Leroy had been working, and he was constantly on the road. He never really knew what his wife was doing. He did know that she was there when he came home, and she had a wonderful meal prepared. Leroy is home all the time now. He sees less and less of Norma Jean. She may be trying to avoid him. She is also trying to improve herself physically and mentally. This seems admirable.

Grammar and Writing

Sentence Variety

Using sentence grammar effectively involves more than simply writing grammatically correct and complete sentences. Even while you increase your knowledge of basic sentence grammar, you can begin using that knowledge to improve your writing style. One area you can focus on is sentence variety.

Without varied sentences, writing can become monotonous and tedious. Every writer can apply a few basic principles during the drafting and revising process to increase sentence variety.

- Vary sentence lengths.
- Vary sentence beginnings.
- Vary sentence types.

The first principle is easy enough to apply. Simply use the guidelines provided in the checklist in 25a. To apply the second principle, circle the first few words of your sentences from one of your essays or papers. Unless you are using similar grammatically structured openings for a specific and clearly defined purpose (as, for example, in the list above), revise to vary the ways your sentences begin. You can use the guidelines in this chapter for assistance.

To vary the types of sentences in your writing, consider using an occasional question to season your declarative sentences. Why? Because questions engage readers. They also invite answers and thus provide a one-two writing punch that is often emphatic. Also blend simple sentences with compound-complex ones, using the methods shown in 25c for guidance.

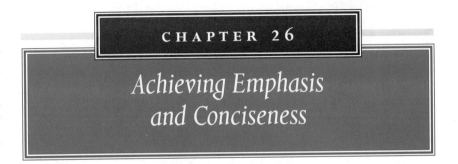

CHAPTER 26

Achieving Emphasis and Conciseness

*T*wo aspects of effective writing reinforce one another: emphasis and conciseness. Emphasis involves stressing key words and ideas, conciseness
expressing ideas directly and succinctly. Conciseness leads to emphasis;
emphasis results from conciseness.

 26a Writing with emphasis

Good writing is emphatic writing. When you write with **emphasis,** your
sentences stress your most important words, phrases, and ideas. You can write
emphatic sentences by following the advice in the accompanying chart.

Ways to Write with Emphasis

- Use parallel structures (26a-1).
- Use short sentences with longer ones (26a-2).
- Repeat important words, phrases, and clauses (26a-3).
- Place the most important words and ideas last or first in sentences (26a-4).
- Invert, or reverse, normal word order (26a-5).
- Use an occasional short paragraph (26a-6).

---

1 Achieving emphasis with parallel structures

Parallelism is a writing strategy that uses similar grammatical structures
to coordinate words, phrases, or clauses both within and between sentences.
(See Chapter 24.)

PARALLEL WORDS   They were *tired, cold,* and *hungry.*

PARALLEL PHRASES   *With laughter, with tears,* and *with unease,* the mother was reunited with her estranged daughter.

PARALLEL CLAUSES   *Until the day of justice dawns, until the moment our bonds are cut,* we shall not be free.

You can use parallel structures emphatically by placing them in order of least to most important, as the following passage illustrates.

> It was a feeling of closeness. It was something strange. It was as though there were only we two in the world. It was as though I had been jerked suddenly out of myself, out of my world of the schoolboy, out of a world in which I was ashamed of my father.

—Sherwood Anderson, "Discovery of a Father"

Anderson uses parallel clauses (*It was . . . It was as though . . .*) and parallel phrases (*out of myself . . . out of my world . . . out of a world . . .*) to coordinate within and between sentences. The last sentence is the most important sentence in the passage, and the last phrase of that sentence is the most important phrase. This final position is emphatic not only because the passage builds up to it, but also because it is the point that the reader sees last and is most likely to remember. By using parallelism and selective placement of important thoughts, Anderson successfully emphasizes his key points.

When you include items in a series, whether words, phrases, or clauses, save the most important one for last.

UNEMPHATIC   To be successful they would have to invest their money, their energy, their very lives, and their time.

EMPHATIC   To be successful they would have to invest *their time, their money, their energy, and their very lives.*

WRITING HINT   The most emphatic place of a sentence or paragraph is the end because it is the final word the reader is left with. The next most emphatic place is the beginning because it introduces an idea. The least emphatic is the middle.

2   Achieving emphasis with short sentences

Short sentences can be emphatic when they are used in contrast to a series of longer sentences. Short sentences can also carry emphasis related to their placement.

Ralph Waldo Emerson begins a long paragraph on self-reliance with this two-word sentence: "Trust thyself." Similarly, Henry David Thoreau in *Walden* follows a series of longer sentences with this one-word sentence: "Simplify!" Both brief sentences command reader attention.

In the following passage, a short sentence follows two longer ones. Note how the final sentence is emphatic because it stands in contrast to the preceding sentences.

Victory would mean peace forced upon the loser, a victor's terms imposed upon the vanquished. It would be accepted in humiliation, under duress, at an intolerable sacrifice, and would leave a sting, a resentment, a bitter memory upon which terms of peace would rest, not permanently, but only as upon quicksand. Only a peace between equals can last.

—Woodrow Wilson

3   Achieving emphasis with repetition

Words repeated within a sentence can have an emphatic effect.

It had something to do with his blackness, I think—he was very black—with his blackness and his beauty, and with the fact that he knew that he was black but did not know that he was beautiful.

—James Baldwin, "Notes of a Native Son"

Writers sometimes repeat phrases and clauses from one sentence to another for emphasis. Note how Alice Walker uses repetition in the following passage.

But add to all of these things the one thing that seems to me second to none in importance: He gave us back our heritage. He gave us back our homeland; the bones and dust of our ancestors, who may now sleep within our caring and our hearing. He gave us the blueness of the Georgia sky in autumn as in summer. . . . He gave us continuity of place, without which community is ephemeral. He gave us home.

—Alice Walker, "Choice: A Tribute
to Dr. Martin Luther King, Jr."

In this passage, Walker uses not only repetition of the phrase *He gave us*, but also parallelism and word placement to achieve emphasis. Notice, too, how the ideas in the shortest sentence are emphasized, in part because it is the last sentence of the passage.

WRITING HINT   Although purposeful repetition of important words can add emphasis and coherence to your writing, careless repetition is clumsy and distracting. Avoid putting words near each other that sound the same or almost the same. The disparity between sense and sound can be confusing.

CLUMSY   Employers are *finding* it increasingly difficult to *find* people who can write well.

REVISED   Employers are finding it increasingly difficult to *hire* [or *recruit*] people who can write well.

CLUMSY   Congress rejected the president's *plan* to establish a national service *plan.*

REVISED   Congress rejected the president's *national service plan.*

(See 26b-4 for more on avoiding unnecessary repetition.)

4   Achieving emphasis by placing important elements in key positions

Alice Walker's passage from "Choice: A Tribute to Dr. Martin Luther King, Jr." in the preceding section ends with a short sentence that sums up her most important observation about King's legacy for African Americans: "He gave us home." By reserving her most important idea for the end of the paragraph, Walker leaves that idea ringing in readers' minds.

Placing the most important words of a sentence last achieves a similar emphatic effect.

> To become finalists the gymnasts need strength, grace, and discipline.

Placing *discipline* last in this sentence implicitly suggests that it is the most important quality in the list. Reordering that list can change the emphasis so that a different item seems more important.

> To become finalists the gymnasts need strength, discipline, and grace.

Another way to emphasize an idea is to place it at the beginning of a sentence or paragraph. This arrangement is a bit less emphatic than the end-of-sentence (or paragraph) placement.

EMPHATIC	"License and registration, please," said the police officer to the motorist.
MORE EMPHATIC	The police officer said to the motorist, "License and registration, please."
EMPHATIC	Discipline and desire are the qualities that make good athletes great.
MORE EMPHATIC	The qualities that make good athletes great are discipline and desire.

EXERCISE 26–1   Recognizing Techniques of Emphasis

Identify the techniques of emphasis used in the following passage.

> People have been reading the Bible for nearly two thousand years. They have taken it literally, figuratively, or symbolically. They have regarded it as divinely dictated, revealed, or inspired, or as a human creation. They have acquired more copies of it than of any other book. It is quoted (and misquoted) more often than other books. It is called a great work of literature, the first work of history. It is at the heart of Christianity and Judaism. Ministers, priests, and rabbis preach it. Scholars spend their lives studying and teaching it in universities and seminaries. People read it, study it, admire it, disdain it,

write about it, argue about it, and love it. People have lived by it and died by it. And we do not know who wrote it.

—Richard Elliott Friedman, *Who Wrote the Bible?*

EXERCISE 26–2   Writing with Emphasis

Write two sentences for each phrase listed here. In the first sentence, place the phrase in an emphatic position; in the second, put it in a less emphatic position. Example:

> every day
> Every day we went swimming at the lake. [emphatic]
> We went swimming every day at the lake. [less emphatic]

1. in a few days
2. without hesitation
3. as soon as you can
4. carelessly
5. grinning from ear to ear

---

5   Achieving emphasis with inversion

Inverting a sentence involves reversing the normal sentence pattern by putting some part of the predicate before the subject. The inverted sentence pattern looks like this.

object (or complement) → verb → subject

Readers are accustomed to the usual order of a grammatical sentence: a subject followed by its predicate and any objects or complements. Since inversion reverses the expected order of sentence elements, it should be used sparingly. Used occasionally, however, inverted sentences can effectively emphasize a word, a phrase, or the entire sentence.

> **STANDARD**   A fox occasionally appeared in the far corner of the yard.

> **INVERTED**   In the far corner of the yard, there occasionally appeared a fox.

The inverted sentence keeps the reader waiting to find out what will happen in that corner of the yard and thereby creates suspense which, in turn, creates emphasis.

In the following sentence, E. B. White makes his point about the paradoxes of the circus in inverted clauses.

Out of its wild disorder comes order; from its rank smell rises the good aroma of courage and daring; out of its preliminary shabbiness comes the final splendor.

—E. B. White, "The Ring of Time"

White's triple inversion also illustrates the sentence's climactic order; that is, the elements appear in order of increasing importance. The overall effect emphasizes the three words *order, daring,* and *splendor,* but the greatest emphasis is on *splendor,* because White places it last in the sentence.

6 Achieving emphasis with short paragraphs

Just as using an occasional short sentence within a paragraph can emphasize an idea, so too can a short paragraph. In the following example, a student begins with a paragraph of average length and then sets off a short paragraph for emphasis.

> As the older class lines up in front of the younger, one of the fourth graders catches sight of the first-grade Asian-American girl sitting with her classmates. He begins to pick on her, bowing deeply at the waist with his hands clasped together as if in prayer. He is singsonging, "Ah-so, Ah-so." An expression of sheer pleasure illuminates his face, and a smile spreads across his mouth. He continues his revelry until he gets his food and sits down with his friends.
>
> And what of the girl? What becomes of her?
>
> She is digesting what she will later recognize as the first racial slur she has ever experienced. Presently she does not know this. . . .

—Suyin So, "Grotesques"

The short paragraph in this example also uses interrogative sentences to achieve emphasis (see 25c). Like inverted sentences and short paragraphs, however, interrogative sentences are emphatic only when they are used sparingly and skillfully. The same is true of sentence fragments used intentionally for emphasis (see 17e).

EXERCISE 26–3 Recognizing the Techniques of Emphasis

Identify the various techniques of emphasis used in the following passage: label inverted sentences (I), circle repeated words, underline repeated phrases and clauses, and put brackets around short sentences.

"What is honor?" asked Falstaff and answered "a word." With such an understanding of the way the name, look, and gesture of honor were becoming more important than the thing itself, he would hardly be surprised by our own preoccupation with the democratic descendant of honor, fame. What is honor? What is fame? A name? A face? The *it* in *making it*? Every day, from every corner of the world, faces and names pour into our eyes and ears. If we read, if we see, if we hear, we cannot escape the flood of human images that, desired or not, forces itself upon us. Some few last for a lifetime and beyond, most for no longer than it takes to scratch their initials on the walls of our attention. And yet all this effort, substantial as much as trivial, is done in the name of what is called fame.

—Leo Braudy, *The Frenzy of Renown*

EXERCISE 26–4   **Writing with Emphasis**

Write a paragraph in which you use at least four of the six techniques for achieving emphasis discussed in 26a. You may choose a topic of your own or one of these: a family member, a friend, a valued possession, an experience, an ambition, a newsworthy event.

26b   Writing with conciseness

Readers expect writers to get to the point directly and succinctly, to write with **conciseness.** Yet concise writing involves much more than banging out one short sentence after another; it involves avoiding unnecessary words and using precise grammatical constructions. Consider the following wordy passage and its more concise revision.

WORDY   In order to reach a fair decision for the issue at hand, it would be necessary for the members of the committee involved with the decision to hear the testimony of a number of different people.

CONCISE   To decide the issue fairly, the committee needs to interview a number of people.

To write concisely, avoid using words and phrases that could be expressed in fewer words. Follow the guidelines in the accompanying chart to write sentences concisely.

1   Eliminate unnecessary intensifiers

An **intensifier** is a word (typically an adjective or adverb) that emphasizes the word it modifies. Some intensifiers, such as *very* and *really*, are usually unnecessary or could be more precisely worded. For example, to say that an eventuality is *very likely possible* is to say that it is *probable*. To say that you are *very, very tired* is to say that you are *exhausted*. If something makes you *really happy,* it may make you *ecstatic* or *excited* or simply *happy.* Intensifiers in such cases often add nothing but verbiage. They also keep you from writing exactly and with vividness (see 28b).

In addition, overused intensifiers defeat their purpose; that is, too many uses of *very* and *really* diminish the power of the words they modify. If your words are too weak or ambiguous to stand alone with no intensifiers, perhaps you should choose other, more precise words instead.

Ways to Write More Concisely

- Eliminate unnecessary intensifiers (26b-1).
- Replace wordy phrases (26b-2).
- Avoid negations (26b-3).
- Eliminate redundancy (26b-4).
- Avoid overuse of the verb *be* (26b-5).
- Prefer verbs to nouns (26b-6).
- Prefer the active to the passive voice (26b-7).
- Avoid the overuse of prepositions and prepositional phrases (26b-8).

---

2   Replace wordy phrases

Wordy phrases use more words than necessary to convey meaning or to make a point. To streamline your writing, replace wordy phrases with precise words where possible. Here is a list of wordy phrases and their more concise alternatives.

WORDY	CONCISE
at the present moment	now
due to the fact that	because
at this point in time	now
at all times	always
in this day and age	today
by means of	by
for the most part	mostly
in order to	to
give consideration to	consider
I am of the opinion that	I think
in view of the fact that	since
a large number of	many
few in number	few
lend assistance to	assist

WORDY	CONCISE
make contact with	contact
past experience	experience
persons of the Catholic faith	Catholics
sufficient amount of	enough
ideas of a serious nature	serious ideas
until such time as	until
in light of the fact that	since
regardless of the fact that	although
for the purpose of	to
in close proximity to	near
aware of the fact that	know
in the event that	if
in the nature of	like
in the final analysis	finally
has the capacity for	can
disappear from view	disappear
destroy by fire	burn

Wordy phrases often contain buzzwords—words that sound important but that express little real meaning. Buzzwords can be nouns (e.g., *area, factor, sort, thing*), adjectives (*interesting, significant, weird*), or adverbs (*absolutely, awfully, basically, quite*). The following wordy sentence with buzzwords can be revised in several ways to become more concise.

WORDY   Those types of basically complicated questions are the sort of ones that most often appear on the final.

CONCISE   *Complicated questions* often appear on the final.

CONCISE   *That type of complicated question* often appears on the final.

3   Avoid negating words

To reduce wordiness, you may want to eliminate negating words (i.e., words that negate a positive word or phrase), such as *no* and *not*.

WORDY   I *do not approve* of the administration's response to the student protests.

CONCISE   I *disapprove* of the administration's response to the student protests.

WORDY   He is *not feeling well*.

CONCISE   He is *ill*.

But remember that sometimes you may want to maintain that emphasis on the negative that this structure offers.

4   Eliminate redundancy

Redundancy is the needless repetition of words, phrases, sentences, paragraphs, or ideas. Redundant expressions add nothing to what has already been said in a sentence. Redundancy comes in three forms: redundant word pairs, redundant modifiers, and redundant categories.

Redundant word pairs

REDUNDANT   *Each and every* one of us won a prize.

REVISED   *Each* of us won a prize.

REDUNDANT   *If and when* the packages arrive, please sign for them.

REVISED   *When* the packages arrive, please sign for them.

Redundant modifiers

REDUNDANT   Our *future hope* was for a chance to travel around the world.

REVISED   Our *hope* was for a chance to travel around the world.

REDUNDANT   The *true facts* were exposed in the courtroom.

REVISED   The *facts* were exposed in the courtroom.

Redundant categories

REDUNDANT   A book *blue in color* was left on the desk.

REVISED   A *blue* book was left on the desk.

REDUNDANT   He had an *arrogant manner.*

REVISED   He was *arrogant.*

Redundancies are easy to overlook in writing because they are used so often on television, at the movies, in advertisements, in newspapers, in magazines, and in books. Advertisers offer "free gifts," and they boast of "billions and billions sold." Weather reporters describe the temperature as "minus five degrees below zero." Sportscasters describe a college athlete as having a "fine future ahead of her." Journalists report that a pair of convicts "successfully escaped" and that "foreign imports" threaten "our country's internal economy." Here is a list of some additional redundancies to avoid.

REDUNDANCIES

basic fundamentals	important essentials
circle around	join together
component parts	past history

continue on	positive benefits
cooperate together	refer back
crisis situation	repeat again
expensive in price	

Make sure you look for redundancy in your writing and rewrite those passages more concisely.

EXERCISE 26–5   **Recognizing Redundancies**

The following exercises can help you become more aware of the types of redundancies to avoid in your writing.

1. Watch a television news broadcast from beginning to end. List the redundancies you hear.
2. Watch a television comedy or drama. List the redundancies you hear.
3. Choose five advertisements from a popular magazine. List the redundancies you find.

---

5   Avoid excessive use of the verb *be*

The verb *be* is an important one. It is used to express relations between things and as both a linking verb and an auxiliary verb (see 11b). But excessive use of *be* in its most common forms—*is* and *was*, *are* and *were*—often makes writing static, bland, and flat. Consider the following sentence.

EXCESSIVE USE OF *BE*
> It *is* sometimes the case that students *are* absent from class when an assignment *is* due.

REVISED   Students sometimes miss class when assignments are due.

USAGE NOTE   The forms of the verb *be* are useful and necessary, especially as auxiliaries (see 11b). You will need to use varying forms of *be* often. Notice any opportunities to substitute active verbs when forms of *be* proliferate in your prose.

Using too many sentences that begin with the expletive *It is*, *There is*, or *There are* can weaken your writing. These introductory words delay the real subject to the middle of the sentence, both making the reader wait to know the subject and putting the subject in a less emphatic position than at the beginning of the sentence. If you intend to delay the subject to create suspense or emphasis (see 25c), keep the expletive. If not, revise to eliminate it.

WEAK   *It is* essential for news anchors today to have a full head of hair.

REVISED   News anchors today must have a full head of hair.

WEAK   *There is* a new Whoopi Goldberg movie *that* is much better than her last one.

REVISED   The new Whoopi Goldberg movie is much better than her last one.

USAGE NOTE   Although expletives can be wordy and roundabout, sometimes they are the best way to express a thought or provide emphasis.

There is no excuse for missing the appointment.

It was the worst mistake *that* I ever made.

6   Prefer verbs to nouns

The tendency to use nouns rather than verbs to carry a sentence's meaning is called **nominalization.** It results when a verb form is changed to a noun: the verb *instruct* becomes the noun *instruction.* Nominalization tends to make writing abstract. It also reduces the energy and liveliness of writing. Consider these examples.

NOMINALIZATION   Universities around the country are currently involved in an *examination* of their curriculums, which is part of a *reevaluation* of their goals.

REVISED   Universities around the country are *examining* their curriculums and *reevaluating* their goals.

NOMINALIZATION   It is our *expectation* that we will receive an answer soon.

REVISED   We *expect* to receive an answer soon.

WRITING HINT   Check your writing for words that end with the suffixes *-ment, -tion,* and *-ance* (or, the less common *-ity, -ize,* and *-ness*). To invigorate your writing, change those words to verbs when possible. Be aware, however, that there is nothing inherently wrong with nouns ending in the suffixes listed here. Simply be conscious of using them when their corresponding verb forms would work better in a sentence.

WRITING HINT   Another way to eliminate nominalizations is to be aware of the weak verbs that typically accompany them. The verbs *make, take,* and *give,* for example, frequently lead to nominalization.

We will *make a recommendation.* [We will *recommend.*]

She will *give a ruling* on the issue. [She will *rule* on the issue.]

EXERCISE 26–6   Revising Nominalizations

Rewrite the following sentences to eliminate nominalization. Example:

> The board's *discussion* concerned a tuition increase.
> The board *discussed* a tuition increase.

1. The intention is to increase support staff salaries.
2. The senators have no expectation that the governor will consider their request.
3. The governor's refusal of the request is a certainty.
4. The appearance of the union representative before the board was on July 30.
5. The union's assessment of the salary problem was correct.

---

7   **Use the active rather than the passive voice**

Using too many passive-voice verbs contributes to wordiness. As a general guideline, use the active voice most of the time and the passive voice only when you do not want the agent of the verb to be the subject of the sentence. Remember when a verb is in the passive voice, its subject is the recipient of the action, not the doer of the action. (See Chapter 11 for more on the active and passive voices.)

> **PASSIVE**   The boy *was bitten* by the dog. [The subject, *boy,* does not act but is acted on.]

> **ACTIVE**   The dog *bit* the boy. [The subject, *dog*, acts.]

The revised sentence is not only easier to follow but also uses fewer words.

Passive constructions can be more than just wordy. Sometimes they are used by writers and speakers to conceal important information from audiences. As a writer, you should avoid the evasiveness of the passive voice.

> **EVASIVE**   It has been decided that a decision about increasing tuition will be postponed until all relevant data have been reviewed.

This sentence leaves readers asking, "*Who* is doing the deciding?"

> **REVISED**   The Board of Trustees decided to postpone its decision about increasing tuition until it has reviewed all relevant data.

USAGE NOTE   Do not avoid the passive altogether. At times it is necessary and effective, as the following examples illustrate.

The streets of Paris *are laid out* in a circular pattern.

Walt Whitman's brother *was wounded* during the Civil War.

EXERCISE 26–7   **Evaluating Your Writing for Wordiness**

Go through one of the papers you recently wrote and edit it for passive voice constructions, excessive use of *be*, and excessive nominalization.

8   Avoid the excessive use of prepositional phrases

Prepositions indicate the position, location, and relations of words used in sentences (see 14a–b). Used skillfully, prepositions clarify meaning and enhance the beauty and power of writing. Used excessively, however, prepositions contribute to wordiness.

WORDY   In the presence of so many temptations in such alluring guises, it is no wonder that people without strong convictions of morality and a confident sense of their own self-worth find themselves responding in a highly engaged manner to the promises of gratification, happiness, and pleasure that temptations of such power hold out to them.

REVISED   Given so many alluring temptations, people without strong moral convictions and a sense of self-worth readily respond to the powerfully attractive rewards such temptations promise.

EXERCISE 26–8   **Revising for Conciseness**

Revise the following wordy paragraph to make it more concise. Pay particular attention to unnecessary words, passive voice constructions, and excessive use of expletives, prepositions, and forms of *be*.

There are many reasons why it is dangerous for college students to accept the barrage of credit-card offers that will be made available to them, beginning as early as their first year in college. The most obvious reason, of course, is that most students will be tempted to use the cards to purchase things that they need, perhaps including their books and clothes, even food—although many will not be in a very good position for the money to be paid when due to the credit-card company or bank that was the primary issuer of the card. Although it is certainly very important that young adult males and females learn to make good use of credit that is made available to them, it is simply unwise for many to try to learn the use of credit while they are students and not members of the workforce.

EXERCISE 26–9   Revising Wordy Sentences

Revise the following wordy sentences, eliminating unnecessary words and phrases and making them more concise. Example:

> It was necessary that he explain the range of options available for the solution of the problem.

> He needed to explain the options to solve the problem.

1. There are many factors to be considered when one is attempting to decide whether or not to change majors.
2. Once she began to pay even closer attention to how she looked in appearance, many people made positive-sounding comments in praise of her appearance.
3. At this point in time, it is not that we are not able to make up our minds but only that certain elements of the situation are making it less than easy to come to a conclusion about the matter.
4. Due to the fact that the budget deficit was already very high, many legislators were of the opinion that additional spending on newly added social programs would not be the most desirable of investments.
5. At the present moment, one of the most pervasive and wide-ranging dangers is that resulting from the excessive use of force by some members of the police force of Los Angeles.

EXERCISE 26–10   Reducing Wordiness in Your Writing

Go through one of the papers you wrote recently and eliminate the various types of wordiness discussed in 26b. Use the strategies described in this chapter to guide your revision.

Grammar and Writing

Emphasis and Conciseness

Emphasis and conciseness go hand in hand. Conciseness leads to emphasis; striving for emphasis invites conciseness. Emphasis and conciseness enhance each other.

Writing emphatically does not simply involve employing strategies for emphasis as often as possible. Techniques of emphasis, like seasonings for food, are best used sparingly. In trying to emphasize everything, you emphasize nothing. Less, sometimes, is more.

Writing concisely does not mean using only short sentences and nothing else. An occasional short sentence will make it stand out from longer ones. A few short sentences in succession will slow readers down, enabling them to focus on a series of briefly stated emphatic points.

You can use your knowledge of grammar and style to achieve emphasis and conciseness. Follow the guidelines in the charts in 26a–b for help. Your readers will appreciate it.

Words

Thinking about Diction

What do you speak my Lord?
Words. Words. Words.

—William Shakespeare, *Hamlet*

You have been using words to communicate for most of your life. Words name your experiences, express your feelings, and explain your thoughts. As you know, words have different degrees of formality as well as varying levels of social acceptability. *Ain't*, for example, is not acceptable in academic settings. And contractions, such as *I'm* and *you're*, are acceptable in informal conversation but not in academic writing.

Moreover, some words—*set*, for instance—have multiple meanings. Other words such as *love* and *mother* have a wide range of connotations, or associations. You also learn propriety of words as determined by audience and occasion. Consider, for example, the kinds of words you would hesitate to use in conversation with your parents or teachers.

How, then, do you decide which words are best? Since individual words are not "right" or "best" in themselves, you need to choose words that suit your audience, occasion, and purpose. You need to make your **diction,** or choice of words, appropriate to these contexts. The discussion of words in Part Seven will help you do that with confidence.

Chapter 27 explains how to use dictionaries to find more than the meanings of words. Chapter 28 presents different ways of classifying words and shows how to use different types of words in your writing. Chapter 29 focuses on biased language and eliminating it from your writing. Chapters 30 and 31 explain how to develop your vocabulary and improve your spelling. All five chapters in Part Seven will help you develop your skills in using language effectively.

CHAPTER 27

Using a Dictionary

*H*ow many times have you heard someone say (or said yourself), "Look it up in the dictionary" or "The dictionary says . . ."? The assumption behind these comments is that the dictionary contains the last word about word usage.

This assumption, however, exaggerates the dictionary's authority to establish usage rules. Although it is true that dictionaries record agreed-upon spellings, meanings, and pronunciations of words (along with other information), they do not tell you how to use words in sentences. Dictionaries are not prescriptive. Like the meanings of the words they catalog, dictionaries change to reflect the times in which they are written. So when you consult a dictionary, be aware that you are consulting a reference work that reflects how language is used today, not how someone thought it should be used for all time.

Finally, be aware that many dictionaries exist. This chapter provides an overview of the different types of dictionaries and discusses the one type of dictionary essential for college work—an abridged college dictionary. As you read the chapter and complete the exercises, you will become ready to take advantage of this valuable resource.

27a Exploring a dictionary

Although you probably consult your dictionary most often to find the meanings of words, dictionaries also contain other useful information. They include the proper spelling and pronunciation of a word, its syllable divisions, and other details about its origins, usage, and grammatical functions.

Consider, for example, the sample entry for *cordial* from *The American Heritage Dictionary of the English Language*, Third Edition. As you can see, a dictionary entry contains much information in a small space. In fact, the labels in the example do not exhaust all that a dictionary may indicate about a word. Generally, a dictionary will include the highlighted information about a word.

Spelling: Dictionary entries begin with a word's spelling. If more than one spelling is provided, the first spelling listed is preferred but the others provided are also acceptable.

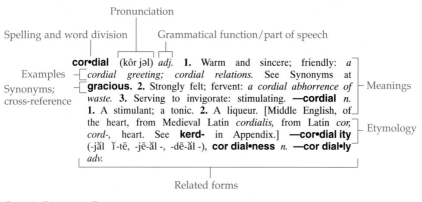

Sample Dictionary Entry

Word division: Dictionaries use dots, bars, or spaces to separate a word's syllables, indicating where the word can be divided at the end of a line with a hyphen. *Cordial,* for example, can only be divided *cor-dial* (neither *co-rdial* nor *cord-ial* is correct).

Pronunciation: Dictionaries indicate which syllable to stress by placing an accent mark over or immediately after the stressed syllable. The entry for *cordial* shows that the accent goes on the first syllable: *cor´dial.* Dictionaries also indicate, by various markings, how to pronounce a word's vowels and consonants. The ˆ over the *o* in *côrdial,* for example, indicates that the *o* is pronounced *aw.* You can find a key explaining these pronunciation marks at the front or back of your dictionary. You will also find a brief version of the pronunciation key at the top or bottom of your dictionary's pages.

Part of speech: Dictionaries identify words by indicating their grammatical functions. *Cordial,* for example, is listed and defined as both an adjective (abbreviated *adj.*) and a noun (abbreviated *n.*). Typically, verbs are listed as transitive or intransitive, and adjectives and adverbs are shown with comparative and superlative forms.

Etymology or origin: A word's derivation or history (see 30a) appears. This entry explains that *cordial* derives from the Latin *cor,* meaning "heart." Sometimes the languages from which a word derives are abbreviated. These and all abbreviations are explained in the front or back of every dictionary.

Meanings: A word's meanings appear numbered according to either their historical order (with the oldest meaning given first), or in order of frequency of use. The entry for *cordial* is arranged according to frequency of use, with the most common meaning placed first. Your dictionary explains how it lists meanings.

In addition to these typical features, dictionaries may include other information about entries.

dic•tion (dik shən) *n.* **1.** Choice and use of words in speech or writing. **2.** Degree of clarity and distinctness of pronunciation in speech or singing; enunciation. [Middle English *diccion,* a saying, word, from Old French, from Latin *dictiō, diction-,* rhetorical delivery, from *dictus,* past participle of *dīcere,* to say, speak. See **deik-** in Appendix.] —**dic tion•al** *adj.* —**dic tion•al•ly** *adv.*

SYNONYMS: *diction, wording, vocabulary, phraseology, phrasing.* These nouns denote choice of words and the way in which they are used. *Diction* is the selection and arrangement of words in relation to effective expression: *very poor diction in the essay; a new poetic diction. Wording* stresses style or manner of expression: *writing in which the wording takes on a regional flavor. Vocabulary* is the aggregate of words a person understands or uses: *the general vocabulary of an educated native speaker of English. Phraseology* and *phrasing* include vocabulary, characteristic style, and the way in which words are grouped: *the abstruse phraseology of physics; a composition marked by elegant phrasing.*

Sample Dictionary Entry

Related words or varied forms of a word: Related to the adjective *cordial* are the nouns *cordiality* and *cordialness* and the adverb *cordially.* All three words (called *cognates*) are expansions on *cordial* and are commonly included with its entry. You should also realize that if you look up *cordiality, cordialness,* and *cordially,* you may not find separate entries for them, since they will appear in the entry for *cordial.* Dictionaries are set up this way to conserve space and to avoid redundancy.

Examples: Many dictionaries include examples of a word's use in the context of a phrase or a sentence. The entry for *cordial* includes three examples, two for the primary meaning and one for the secondary meaning.

Usage labels: Some words carry labels indicating the contexts in which a word is or is not acceptable. The following are common usage labels: *obsolete* (indicates words no longer used—e.g., *coxcomb,* meaning "a jester's cap"); *archaic* (signals words rarely used—e.g., *whilom,* meaning "formerly"); *colloquial* (indicates informal words—e.g., *irregardless*); *slang* (refers to extremely informal words—e.g., *cool*); and *dialect* (indicates how words are used or pronounced in a particular geographical region—*vaquero* and *buckaroo,* meaning a "ranch hand" or "cowboy" in Texas and California, respectively).

Field labels: Most dictionaries indicate when a word has a specific meaning in a particular field or discipline. The word *depression,* for example, means different things in the fields of astronomy, economics, meteorology, and psychology. Such field-specific meanings are sometimes indicated with abbreviated labels (e.g., *astron., econ., meteorol., psychol.*).

Synonyms and antonyms: Some dictionaries include brief discussions of words related to an entry, either by being similar or opposite in meaning. As the sample entry for *diction* shows, *The American Heritage Dictionary of the English Language* lists and compares meanings of the synonyms *wording, vocabulary, phraseology,* and *phrasing.*

Idioms: Dictionaries also occasionally list idiomatic uses of words. Many of these are listed in verb entries with multiple meanings as phrasal verbs. The entry for *hand,* for example, typically begins with a definition of the word as a noun and then follows with various phrasal verbs, such as *hand down, hand on, hand over, hand out,* and with idiomatic uses, such as *by hand* and *in hand.*

Your dictionary likely includes still other resources, depending on its size, scope, and organization. It may contain some or all of the following: an extensive preface on how to use the dictionary, with explanations of abbreviations and symbols; a history of the English language; tables of weights and measures; geographical and biographical information (when such information has not been included with the alphabetized list of words and their definitions); printer's symbols used in editing; rules of punctuation and grammar; keys to pronunciation and spelling; and an index to the dictionary's special features and coverage.

Dictionaries also contain information about **morphemes,** the smallest meaningful elements according to which words can be analyzed. Although dictionaries provide meanings of words, you should be aware that the dictionary also breaks words down into their component parts. Consider, for example, the word *prefabricated.* It is composed of three parts—a prefix, or beginning part (*pre-*), which means "before"; a suffix, or end part (*-ed*), which signals a past tense verb; and a root, or main part (*fabricate*), which means "to make or build." Each part tells you something different about the word; you learn not only what it means ("something constructed or made beforehand") but also why it means what it does. (See 30b–c for a discussion of prefixes, suffixes, and roots.)

EXERCISE 27–1   Checking Spelling

Find the preferred spellings for the following words in your dictionary.

1. dextrous   *or*   dexterous
2. fondue   *or*   fondu
3. marshal   *or*   marshall
4. marvelous   *or*   marvellous
5. license   *or*   licence

EXERCISE 27–2   Determining Correct Pronunciation

Use your dictionary to identify the pronunciation of the following words.
1. mnemonic
2. epitome
3. inchoate
4. chauvinism
5. colonel

EXERCISE 27–3   Investigating Word Origins

Use your dictionary to explain the etymologies of the following words.

1. assassin	6. hamburger
2. breakfast	7. euthanasia
3. impediment	8. transgression
4. monologue	9. spirit
5. ambidextrous	10. salary

EXERCISE 27–4   Identifying Usage Labels

Identify any usage labels your dictionary gives for its definitions of these words.

1. reckon	6. joint
2. odd	7. circle
3. quark	8. horse
4. career	9. hoagie
5. goof	10. ain't

27b   Using different types of dictionaries

1   Abridged dictionaries

Abridged dictionaries, sometimes called **desk dictionaries,** are the kind most regularly consulted by students, teachers, and writers. Though they lack the completeness of the unabridged dictionaries from which they derive, abridged dictionaries are easy to use because they are smaller. The reduced size and scope of abridged dictionaries are manageable and sufficient for most writing situations.

The following are all reliable abridged dictionaries for writers.

Random House Webster's College Dictionary (1996). This dictionary is based on the unabridged *Random House Dictionary.* Two special features of this dictionary deserve note: an appendix on avoiding sexist language and dates that indicate when words first entered the language.

Webster's New World Dictionary of the American Language, Fourth College Edition (1996). This dictionary includes biographical and geographical entries among its entries for words, rather than in separate sections as some other dictionaries do. It lists meanings chronologically in the order they entered the language, and it emphasizes simplified definitions, even of technical and scientific terms.

The American Heritage Dictionary of the English Language, Third Edition (1992). One of the hallmarks of this dictionary is its extensive use of illustrations. It also includes usage notes that explain the contexts in which words are likely to be used acceptably. This dictionary includes sets of synonyms, current scientific and technical terms, and an appendix on Indo-European roots.

2   Unabridged dictionaries

Unabridged, or **unabbreviated, dictionaries** are the most comprehensive and scholarly of all dictionaries. Aside from their completeness, they typically emphasize the history of words and their various uses. They also often contain extensive quotations illustrating the different meanings of words throughout history. In fact, they are the most historically minded of dictionaries. The best known and most highly respected of unabridged dictionaries are *Webster's Third New International Dictionary of the English Language* (1986) and the *Oxford English Dictionary,* Second Edition (20 volumes, 1989). Both are now available on CD-ROM.

Webster's Third New International Dictionary caused some controversy upon its publication because, instead of prescribing which usages are correct or incorrect for its more than 450,000 entries, this dictionary describes how a broad spectrum of speakers and writers actually use the words. Numerous quotations illustrate meanings of words with few labels about their correctness or acceptability.

The monumental *Oxford English Dictionary* (known as the *OED*), begun in the 1880s, took until well into the twentieth century for its first complete edition to be published. Its twenty volumes define more than 500,000 words. Entries record the varying spellings, pronunciations, and meanings of words over the centuries, largely through illustrative quotations drawn from writers from 1300 to the present, more than two million quotations in all. An abridged version of the *OED* is available in two-volume and one-volume formats. The entire dictionary is available on CD-ROM.

3 Specialized dictionaries

Specialized dictionaries define a particular category of word (slang, idioms), a single type of information (etymology), or a single subject (art, engineering). Such dictionaries provide extensive and detailed coverage of their topics. (For a list of specialized dictionaries see 43d-2.) Writers may find specialized dictionaries of usage, synonyms, and thesauruses especially useful.

When you have a usage question your unabridged dictionary does not answer, you can consult a dictionary of usage. Two possibilities are Wilson Follett's *Modern American Usage* and Jacques Barzun's book of the same title.

When you need a synonym for a word, consult a book such as *Webster's New Dictionary of Synonyms*. You can also use a thesaurus, which often includes antonyms as well as synonyms. In using either of these references, take care when substituting synonyms for other words because their connotations may differ. (See 28a for more on connotation.)

WRITING HINT   Use a dictionary to look up the synonyms you find in a thesaurus or synonym dictionary before actually using the words. Check for differences among their meanings. Then select the synonym most appropriate to the purpose and context of your writing.

A number of dictionaries are devoted to specific categories of words. Among them are the following, the titles of which suggest their contents.

The Oxford Dictionary of English Etymology. Ed. C. T. Onions. New York: Oxford UP, 1966.

Fowler, H. W. *A Dictionary of Modern English Usage*, 2nd ed. Revised and edited by Sir Ernest Gowers. New York: Oxford UP, 1965.

Dictionary of American Regional English. Ed. Frederick G. Cassidy. Cambridge: Harvard UP, 1985.

New Dictionary of American Slang. Ed. Robert L. Chapman. New York: Harper, 1986.

NTC's English Idioms Dictionary. Ed. Richard A. Spears and Betty Kirkpatrick. Lincolnwood, IL: National Textbook, 1993.

EXERCISE 27–5   Using the Dictionary as a Biographical and Geographical Reference

Look up in your dictionary five historical figures and five geographical locations. What does your dictionary reveal about them? Where is this information included? Some possibilities include (people) Winston Churchill, Marie Curie, Joe DiMaggio, Indira Gandhi, Florence Nightingale; and (places) Lascaux, Las Cruces, Olympia, Revere, and Salzburg.

EXERCISE 27–6   **Working with Synonyms**

Look up the word *dictionary*. Explain its etymology. Identify three or four cognates. Then look up *cognate*. Explain its etymology and identify three or four of its cognates.

CHAPTER 28

Using Appropriate Words

*T*o communicate effectively as a writer, you need to understand the connotative, or associative, meanings of words as well as their denotative, or dictionary, meanings. You also need to distinguish among abstract words and concrete words, among general words and specific words, and among formal words and informal words. This chapter discusses these and other distinctions between words as well as various ways you can use words to suit your purpose and audience. The accompanying chart identifies key characteristics of words that all writers need to understand in order to choose words appropriately.

Characteristics of Words

- Denotation and connotation (28a)
- General and specific words (28b)
- Abstract and concrete words (28b)
- Formal and informal language (28c)
- Jargon (28d)
- Archaisms, neologisms, and acronyms (28e)
- Regionalisms and dialect expressions (28f)
- Euphemisms (28g)
- Clichés (28h)
- Similes and metaphors (28i)

28a Understanding denotation and connotation

Denotation is a word's literal meaning; **connotation** is a word's associations along with its literal meaning. Denotations tend to be neutral and objective. Connotations are subjective and personal, frequently involving feelings and suggesting concrete images.

Consider the word *dictator*. The denotative meaning of *dictator* is "a person exercising absolute power, especially one who assumes absolute control without the free consent of the people." In reading or hearing that word, however, you may conjure up connotative images of a specific individual as well as the purges, executions, and oppression that dictator engaged in. More than likely these connotations are negative because dictators, historically, have been ruthless tyrants. The images you associate with the word *dictator* will be influenced partly by your previous knowledge and by your personal experience.

As a writer, it is important to know the connotations of the words you use. Although you cannot know how different readers may react to particular words, you do need to understand the positive and negative connotations certain words convey. For example, although *mother* means "female parent," to limit the word's meaning to that objective definition is to ignore its emotional power. For a writer, remembering the connotations of words is essential because a word's connotation can, at times, affect readers more deeply than a word's denotation.

Words such as *dictator* and *mother* have strong connotations, whereas words such as *metaphalanges* and *sodium bicarbonate* typically have weak connotations, largely because the meanings of such scientific terms are limited almost exclusively to their denotations. These technical words lack the personal response and emotional power of more connotatively charged words. The technical terms convey more precise information than does the familiar term; the familiar term conjures up immediate images and feelings that the technical terms do not. Though the words are equally useful, they serve different purposes. As a writer, you will choose words depending upon your audience, occasion, and purpose. Knowing both the denotations and connotations of words will enable you to communicate effectively.

EXERCISE 28–1   **Determining a Word's Connotations**

Identify as many connotations as possible for each of the following words. Which words have the fewest connotations for you? Why?

1. skeleton
2. eagle
3. silk
4. hydrogen sulfate
5. green
6. bed
7. black hole
8. lottery
9. food
10. electromagnetic field

EXERCISE 28–2 **Determining Positive and Negative Connotations**

Put each of the following sets of words on a continuum, showing how they range from negative to positive connotations. Example:

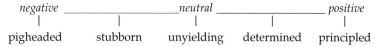

negative _____ *neutral* _____ *positive*

pigheaded   stubborn   unyielding   determined   principled

1. shy, bashful, reticent, timid, reserved, withdrawn
2. famous, renowned, celebrated, well-known, notorious, infamous
3. miserly, stingy, parsimonious, frugal, economical, mercenary, cheap
4. difficult, arduous, challenging, demanding, exacting
5. courage, bravery, fearlessness, valor, fortitude

EXERCISE 28–3 **Using Historical Perspective to Determine Connotations**

The war fought in the United States between 1861 and 1865 is typically referred to as the Civil War, but it has been identified in other ways. Which of the following terms favor the North, which favor the South, and which seem neutral?

1. The American Civil War
2. The War between the States
3. The War of the Rebellion
4. The War for the Union
5. The War for Southern Independence
6. The War of Secession
7. The Yankee Invasion
8. The War of the North and South
9. The War of Northern Aggression
10. The Second American Revolution

EXERCISE 28–4 **Finding Connotations in Advertisements**

Select an advertisement from a newspaper or magazine. Examine the words it uses and discuss their connotations. Then do the same with an editorial from your campus newspaper or a local or national newspaper.

EXERCISE 28–5 **Using Denotative and Connotative Language**

Using the following list of details, write a paragraph in which you invent a scenario using words with neutral connotations. Then use the same details to write a paragraph in which you include words with either positive or negative connotations.

a woman wearing a coat, hat, and gloves
moves along a street at night

a dog is close by
she is about five foot six and 120 pounds
she is carrying a package
she appears about thirty years old

28b   Using general and specific, abstract and concrete words

General words identify broad categories (*country, president, books*); **specific words** identify individual people or objects (*Thailand, president of the AFL-CIO, dictionaries*). **Abstract words** identify ideas and ideals that cannot be perceived by the senses (*education, generosity, fatherhood*); **concrete words** identify something tangible to the senses (*rose, stone, tomato*). Good writing uses words from both ends of the spectrum, from abstract and general words to concrete and specific ones. Abstract and general terms represent ideas, explain attitudes, and explore relationships such as contingency (if something will happen), causality (why it occurs), and priority (what is first in time or importance). Concrete and specific words clarify and illustrate general ideas and abstract concepts. Successful writers typically alternate between abstract and concrete words and general and specific language, blending them naturally.

To achieve this mix, use abstract and general words to state your ideas. Use specific and concrete words to illustrate and support them.

GENERAL/ABSTRACT

Technology revolutionized communication in the 1990s.

SPECIFIC/CONCRETE

The invention of cellular phones made mobile phone conversations possible.

Notice how the language used in the second sentence creates a more focused image than does that of the first sentence. The following examples, which build on the first two sentences, focus the idea more because the language becomes more and more specific and concrete.

SPECIFIC/CONCRETE

Industrialists with cellular phones have meetings from their cars.

SPECIFIC/CONCRETE

Donald Trump has probably made business deals from the back seat of his limousine.

Although no rule dictates when to use general and abstract words or when to use concrete and specific ones, concrete images and specific details can help make your writing clear and more vivid. Notice how the following example becomes clearer when concrete, specific words replace more general ones. Notice, too, that the revised passage is longer because more images, more details, more words are added.

GENERAL   The storm caused serious damage throughout the region. It was one of the worst ever to hit the area.

SPECIFIC   The hurricane caused extensive destruction in three northern counties. Hundred-mile-an-hour winds toppled trees, blew roofs off houses, and upended cars, trucks, even small planes. Torrential rains swept across the state, swelling creeks and rivers until they flooded homes and offices, washing away coastline houses, creating rivers in what had been walkable streets.

The revised passage is effective because it offers readers detailed information. That information is described in concrete language, providing a comprehensive picture of what happened.

EXERCISE 28–6   Expanding General Statements with Concrete Details

---

Expand each of the following sentences with specific and concrete words. Example:

Transportation in Holland is excellent.

Holland has the densest rail network in the world. Trains link all major cities and nearly all towns and villages. The trains consistently run on time, and they run so frequently that thirty minutes is the average span between trains departing for any particular destination.

1. Social policy must be a top priority of the administration.
2. The show included many different types of cars.
3. After being accused of a crime he did not commit, he began to wonder about his future.
4. The food was abundant and delicious.
5. Standards of permissible violence in the films of the 1990s differ from the standards of the past.

EXERCISE 28–7   Revising for Concreteness and Specificity

Rewrite the following sentences to make them more concrete and specific. Example:

Our cat's behavior amused us.
Our cat's habit of nibbling at our toes made us giggle.

1. Protect yourself and your passengers while you are driving.
2. A mosquito's feeding habits are repulsive.
3. Avoid certain foods to keep your weight down.
4. For dessert we had pie, fruit, and ice cream.
5. The visitors' conduct displeased their hosts.

28c Using formal and informal language

Formal language represents the standard or level of discourse suitable for academic and business writing. The tone of formal language is usually serious without being stuffy or pretentious. It is also not especially intimate or personal. In addition, the sentences adhere to the conventions of standard English, including rules of grammar, sentence structure, and punctuation. **Informal language,** by contrast, is more conversational; it establishes a closer relationship between writer and audience. In using informal language, you may address the reader personally as *you*. And you can refer to yourself as *I*, something you usually avoid in more formal writing. You might also begin a sentence with an informal transition such as *And* rather than with a more formal transition such as *Moreover* or *In addition*.

The formality or informality of language is relative, a matter of degree. Much writing, for example, is neither exclusively formal nor completely informal. This book blends a formal and informal style, as the preceding paragraph illustrates. However, the *Handbook* does not use the extreme informality of colloquialism and slang that is more typical of speech than of academic writing. Nor does this book use contractions (e.g., *let's* for *let us*, or *here's* for *here is*), another feature of informal usage. You, too, should avoid extreme informality in your academic and professional writing, striving for a tone appropriate to your subject and audience.

Keep in mind that highly formal language is traditionally reserved for ceremonial occasions, such as the inauguration of a president or a traditional wedding. Highly informal language is used within small groups, among family and friends, for example, who may even invent their own words, especially slang and jargon.

Be aware, however, that the level of formality in writing or speech is more than a matter of word choice. Level of formality also involves the length and complexity of sentences (see 23a, 24b, 25a, and 25c) and the ways that figurative language (see 28i) and rhetorical devices (e.g., repetition and emphasis) are employed.

1 Colloquialisms

Colloquialisms are informal expressions appropriate to ordinary spoken language but not to written language. The expressions *hang out with* and *get* *even with* are considered colloquial. These expressions may be appropriate for casual conversation but should be avoided in academic writing. To raise the level of formality suitable for professional and academic writing, you would instead use the standard English words *spend time with* or *retaliate*.

Colloquialisms also include clipped forms of words, such as *dorm* for *dormitory*, *prof* for *professor*, or *vet* for *veterinarian*. Clipped word forms are appropriate only when you want to create a conversational tone. Notice the difference in level of formality in the following examples.

STANDARD	Students who live in the *dormitories* have more opportunities to meet with their *professors* than students who commute.
CONVERSATIONAL	Students who live in the *dorms* have more opportunities to meet with their *profs* than students who commute.
INFORMAL	*Dorm* students have more chances than commuters to meet with their *profs*.

2   Slang

Informal language also includes **slang**, a vocabulary of playful but typically short-lived words and phrases that deliberately displace standard language, sometimes with vividness and irreverence. Most slang words go out of fashion in a few years, though some become part of the commonly used vocabulary of English. Slang words like *far out* and *grind* are no longer current, having been displaced by *awesome* and *geek,* respectively. Whereas a previous generation of students *cut* classes, the current generation *blows them off*. Most likely, current slang terms will, before long, be replaced with others invented by a new generation of speakers and writers.

Slang identifies its users as part of a group different from established authority. It is used as much as a badge of social solidarity as to communicate information. Although you should avoid slang in academic writing, you might want to use it in creative pieces in which you deliberately imitate the voice of a person speaking informally.

WRITING HINT   Avoid mixing slang or colloquial language with more formal discourse. Check your academic writing for any excessively informal words or phrases. Similarly, check for excessive formality in your informal writing. Strive to keep the level of formality consistent in each piece of writing.

EXERCISE 28–8   **Revising for Different Levels of Formality**

Write five sentences that use slang terms you are familiar with. Then rewrite the sentences using standard words and phrases that convey the same meaning.

28d   Avoiding jargon

Jargon is the specialized or technical language of a trade, profession, or other group. For those who understand it, jargon is a kind of shorthand that makes lengthy explanations unnecessary. At its best, jargon is precise and efficient. Lawyers, for example, use the word *tort* to refer to any wrongful act, other than a breach of contract, for which the wronged party is entitled to seek compensation. Doctors use the term *cholecystitis* to indicate an inflammation of the gallbladder.

Among members of specialized groups, jargon is an effective and useful communication tool. For communicating with those outside the group, however, jargon can confuse and needlessly complicate a subject. While doctors easily understand *viral rhinorrhea* (the common cold) and may prescribe a *salicylate* (aspirin) to alleviate its symptoms, most patients would not know those terms. Using jargon with an audience unfamiliar with its meanings can result in confusion and misunderstanding.

Jargon is also sometimes used to make an idea or fact sound more important or more impressive than it is. The scientist, for example, who writes "Although solitary under ordinary circumstances, squirrels may collocate in situations of artificially enhanced nutrient resource availability" would, on the surface, appear to be making a more complicated and a more important point than "Though squirrels live alone, if you put some food out they will gather in a group." Avoid inflating your writing with jargon to make your ideas appear more complex than they are.

JARGON   Energy consumption of a hummingbird is greater than a comparable measurement of a bovine quadruped.

FAMILIAR   Ounce for ounce, a hummingbird consumes more energy than a cow.

You should be aware that technical words sometimes carry both a standard and a specialized meaning. Computer language, for example, has absorbed a number of words from standard English and given them specialized meanings within the jargon of computerspeak. Here are just a few of them: *bit, boot, crash, disk, hacker, memory, mouse,* and *virus.* Using such computer jargon with a specialized audience can enhance communication as well as identify you as someone with knowledge of computers. But using these words with their specialized meanings in noncomputer contexts and with those outside a group of computer users can result in confusion. If you need to use technical terms in writing about a specialized subject for a general audience, be sure to define the terms for your readers.

WRITING HINT   In your academic and professional writing, use standard English and avoid extreme formality or informality. Also avoid pretentious use of jargon and casual use of slang and colloquialisms.

EXERCISE 28–9 Using Jargon and Slang

1. Think of some group or team you belong to or a hobby or leisure activity you pursue. Make a list of its specialized words and meanings (whether or not they can be found in a dictionary).

2. Create a dialogue in which two people are speaking the special language of their shared interest.

28e Using archaisms, neologisms, and acronyms

Archaisms are words or expressions that were once common but are no longer current. Archaisms such as *beweep* ("weep"), *quoth* ("said"), and *bethink* ("to think upon") are listed in dictionaries because they are found in older literary works and historical documents. It is useful to know such words because as a reader you will better understand literature that includes them. However, you should avoid them in your own academic writing.

Neologisms are newly created words that have not come into common usage and are not recorded in dictionaries. The word *brunch* was once a neologism but has now come into established usage, as have the words *gridlock, telemarketing, makeover,* and *surrogate mother.* Other recent additions include *infomercial, bullet train, liposuction,* and *slam dunk.* Until newly minted words make repeated appearances in print, however, avoid using them in academic writing.

One form of neologism you can use in all types of writing is the **acronym**. An acronym is an abbreviation that comes to have the familiarity and currency of an ordinary word. Examples of acronyms include NAFTA (North American Free Trade Agreement), MADD (Mothers against Drunk Driving), RAM (random access memory). Remember not to use periods following the letters of an acronym. (For more on using acronyms, see 40b.)

There are two issues to keep in mind when you use acronyms. The first occurs with former acronyms, such as *radar.* Although *radar* was originally an acronym for the sequence of words *radio detection and ranging,* it is now a word that is written in lowercase letters, unlike *NATO* and *AIDS.* Be sure to check your dictionary if you are uncertain about how to spell or use an acronym or initialism. The second complication occurs with clipped forms, such as *sitcom* for *situation comedy.* In such cases, the acronym is composed of shortened forms of words rather than of the first letters of the words in sequence. Notice that these abbreviated words combine to form a new word, a kind of neologism, and as such are written in lowercase letters. (See also Chapter 40 on these and other types of abbreviations.)

WRITING HINT   In using acronyms in writing, you can either spell out the words the acronym represents when you first use it and then use the acronym for each subsequent appearance, or you can use the acronym from the start and include at its first appearance a parenthetical explanation—as with "ROM (read only memory)."

EXERCISE 28–10   Discovering Archaisms, Creating Neologisms

1. Read the first act of any play by Shakespeare, and find three archaisms.
2. Create three neologisms for a sport, discipline, or area you know well.

EXERCISE 28–11   Understanding Acronyms

Find out what the following acronyms mean. See if your dictionary can help.

1. NOW
2. snafu
3. UNESCO (or Unesco)
4. laser
5. OPEC

28f   Understanding regionalisms and dialect expressions

Pronunciation and accents vary in different parts of the United States and in different parts of the world where English is used. Differences also occur in diction, or word choice. As a reader, you will find that understanding the meaning of regional variations in language and dialect expressions can aid your comprehension. As a writer, you can use your awareness of the regional and dialect expressions in your geographic region to select appropriate language for different audiences and occasions.

1   Regionalisms

Regionalisms are expressions distinctive to a particular area or region. The northerner's *pail* is the southerner's *bucket;* a Northeast *bag* is a Midwest *sack.* In Chicago *pop* is something to drink rather than something to eat (an ice cream or ice pop), as a New Yorker would have it. In Appalachia, a Ph.D. is a *teacher-doctor* and a cemetery is a *burial ground.* In certain parts of the South you will hear *reckon* in place of *guess* (*I reckon I'll get on my way*) and *right* for *very* (*I'm right sorry about that*). Although they occur unconsciously in conversation, such regional expressions should be used in writing only when you wish to achieve a particular rhetorical purpose, such as to establish a regional identity or to convey the temper of a place.

The same is true of regional expressions that extend beyond national borders. In reading you would understand that a Scottish *loch* is a lake, a South African *dorp* is a village, Jamaican *dunny* is money, and European *football* is American soccer. In writing or speaking to a British audience about cars and driving, you would use their terms (*boot* for trunk, *bonnet* for hood, *lorry* for truck, *roundabout* for traffic circle). You would make such linguistic choices primarily to be understood. But you might also do so out of courtesy, or to demonstrate your familiarity with the local or national idiom, or to establish common ground with your audience.

2   Dialect expressions

Dialect is language that uses regional variations in grammar, vocabulary, and spelling. The study of regional dialects, *dialectology*, democratizes linguistic differences, acknowledging all dialects as inherently valuable. Every dialect of English is an authentic and legitimate subsystem of the language with an inherent logic governing it. Dialects of English, such as Black English and Appalachian English, are systematic with grammatical rules governing syntax and standards of usage relating to word choice. These and other subsystems of English have changed in various ways throughout history, sometimes accommodating themselves to the standard, other times remaining distinctively different from it.

Each of us speaks or writes a particular dialect of English, one that expresses our racial and ethnic identity as well as our regional identity. The varieties of English spoken throughout the United States and around the world testify to the richness of the language and to its diversity. Moreover, some dialects, such as Black English and Appalachian English, are of great antiquity and of significant cultural value in conveying shared beliefs and ways of perceiving the world among its users. Each dialect is a systematic form of the language governed by a grammar and by standards informing its choices of words and expressions. Like other language systems, dialects of English change over time with old expressions dropping out and new ones added.

The following examples illustrate a few of the many dialects of spoken and written English.

BLACK ENGLISH

Verb Forms

He walk home.   She have car.

She work late.   She be workin' late.

Possessive forms

John coat.

They look across the room at they friends.

Adverb forms

We ate quick.

APPALACHIAN (MOUNTAIN) ENGLISH

Verb forms

John was a-eatin' his lunch.

He go soon.

Plural forms

feets   peoples

childrens (or chillerns)

Possessive forms

hisn   yourn

hisself

HISPANIC ENGLISH

Verb forms

The things she ask me I bring.

The woman and the girl is home.

Possessives

They're brush the hair.

Responses

What are they doing? Washing his teeth.

Dialects of different population groups show consistent patterns of usage in speech and writing. Within the context of their dialect systems, these language variations can be logically and rhetorically effective. Dialect expressions, however, may create problems in communication when the audience extends beyond the specific dialect language community. In those instances, writers and speakers need to consider the efficacy of various linguistic choices. When dialect expressions impede communication, they should be omitted. When they enhance group cohesion or establish group identity, they may be freely used.

We use our dialect in communicating through speech and writing in various social contexts. When we communicate with the larger world, as when we write a letter of application for a job opening or an application essay for university admission, we may choose to emphasize or mute features of our regional, ethnic, or racial identity. Such linguistic choices are open to writers and speakers in many communicative situations. Your decision to highlight linguistic identity through the use of regionalisms and dialect expressions should be made carefully and consciously according to your aims and goals in speaking and writing.

In most public situations, including professional and academic contexts, it is usually best to observe the grammatical patterns of standard English in your speech and writing. Follow the suggestions on grammar, spelling, usage, and mechanics provided in the *Handbook* when you communicate in most academic and professional settings.

EXERCISE 28–12   Considering the Social Acceptability of Words

Look up five of the following words. Explain what your dictionary reveals about their social acceptability. Identify contexts in which you would use or avoid each word.

1. scram	6. menfolk
2. honky	7. hoagie
3. soul food	8. reckon
4. lingo	9. howdy
5. hillbilly	10. fink

28g   Avoiding euphemisms

A **euphemism** is an inoffensive term used as a substitute for a more direct and possibly offensive one. Funeral directors, for example, use the euphemism *slumber room* to describe the place where a corpse has been laid out. Because the word *corpse* strongly connotes death, *the deceased* often replaces it. Euphemisms are often used to spare people's feelings and to be polite. You will rely on euphemisms from time to time in your everyday experience when you judge that circumstances warrant avoiding harsh or overly direct words. In academic writing, however, you should avoid euphemisms and instead express yourself as directly and honestly as you can.

EUPHEMISM   Downsizing the employee base became necessary to maintain the profitability of the organization.

REVISED   Laying off employees became necessary to maintain the profitability of the organization.

Euphemisms are common in political discourse, where they typically result in evasiveness. George Orwell perhaps put it best when he suggested that political language consists "largely of euphemism, question-begging and sheer cloudy vagueness." Orwell's examples are compelling and relevant.

Defenceless villages are bombarded from the air, the inhabitants driven out into the countryside, the cattle machine-gunned, the huts set on fire with incendiary bullets: this is called *pacification*. Millions of peasants are robbed of their farms and sent trudging along the roads with no more than they can carry: this is called *transfer of population* or *rectification of frontiers*. People are imprisoned for years without trial, or shot in the back of the neck or sent to die of scurvy in Arctic lumber camps: this is called *elimination of unreliable elements*. Such phraseology is needed if one wants to name things without calling up mental pictures of them.

—George Orwell, "Politics and the English Language"

EXERCISE 28–13   **Playing with Euphemism**

1. Euphemize the following words and phrases.

    a. garbage collector   c. hung over   e. pain   g. riot

    b. to get fired   d. pregnancy   f. toilet   h. steal

2. De-euphemize the following words and phrases.

    a. relocation center   d. adult entertainment

    b. underachiever   e. intelligence gathering

    c. supervisory personnel   f. ethnic cleansing

28h   Avoiding clichés

Clichés are expressions that have been overused and have become trite. If you hear someone say that a situation is "sad but . . ." you know that the next word will be *true*, as in the cliché "sad but true." You can probably fill in the blanks on many of the following: *cut and* _____ ; *beck and* _____ ; *a new lease on* _____ ; *between a rock and a* _____ . *You get the* _____ . Clichés are so familiar that in hearing or reading them you can easily predict what is to come, and nearly always accurately. As a result, the freshness and surprise that characterize effective writing are lost.

If you use figurative language in your writing (see 28i), you may find yourself using clichés. Many common clichés, in fact, are also similes (comparisons using *like* or *as*): *steady as a rock; quick as lightning; free as a bird; white as a sheet; easy as pie.* Remember that clichés are too predictable and too familiar to be interesting.

EXERCISE 28–14 **Rewriting Stale Clichés**

Choose three clichés from the following list and write either comic variations or fresh versions. You can change a word, phrase, or the entire expression to bring the cliché back to life. Examples:

> sadder but wiser
> sadder but kinder
>
> hit below the belt
> hit below the belly button

1. absence makes the heart grow fonder
2. thrown off the track
3. tried and true
4. the not-too-distant future
5. add insult to injury
6. know the score
7. sell like hotcakes
8. green with envy
9. hot and heavy
10. dressed to kill

28i Using figurative language

Language can be classified as either literal or figurative. When we speak or write *literally,* we mean exactly what each word conveys; when we use **figurative language,** however, we mean something other than the literal meaning of the words. Literally, telling someone "go jump in a lake" means telling that person to go for a swim. Figuratively, the expression means something closer to "Go away" or "I do not want to consider what you have to say."

Rhetoricians have cataloged more than 250 figures of speech. These include *hyperbole* (pronounced "hi per' buh lee"), a statement that exaggerates (*My parents will kill me if I don't get an* A); *litotes* (pronounced "lie toe' tees") or understatement (*Having your fingernails torn out is somewhat uncomfortable*); and *personification,* endowing inanimate objects or abstract concepts with human qualities (*The trees bled syrup last winter*). Two frequently used figures of speech are especially important for reading and writing: metaphor and simile.

1 Metaphor

A **metaphor** is an expression that compares two seemingly dissimilar things. The heart of metaphor is resemblance, in which one thing is described in terms of another. Metaphors make connections between apparently unrelated things, often with the power of surprise.

More than 2,300 years ago Aristotle defined metaphor as "an intuitive perception of the similarity in dissimilars." He also suggested that to be a "master of metaphor" is the greatest of a writer's achievements. In our own century, Robert Frost has echoed Aristotle by suggesting that metaphor is central to poetry. Frost was a master of metaphor in his poetry and prose as well as in his conversation, which he seasoned liberally with metaphor. For example, Frost was fond of saying that writing free verse (poetry without a strict pattern of rhythm or rhyme) is like playing tennis without a net.

Metaphor is not used only by poets. You use metaphor in your daily conversation, especially when you describe your feelings or explain events and circumstances to people who did not experience them. Using metaphor is natural, even inescapable. It is so common, in fact, that some comparisons (called *dead metaphors*) have become so familiar we hardly notice them as metaphors at all. We refer, for example, to the *legs* of a table, the *eye* of a needle, the *arms* of a chair, the *head* of an organization. We describe people who are tense as *on edge*, people who are detached as *distant*. With metaphor, *it was very painful* can become *it was the lash of a whip upon my flesh.*

In writing with metaphors, be careful not to create a **mixed metaphor,** a metaphor involving an inconsistent comparison. Mixed metaphors can often lead to unintentional humor.

MIXED   Paul and Mary's argument was a battle that blazed with anger. [The metaphors of war and light are mixed.]

REVISED   Paul and Mary's argument was a fight with well-defined battle lines.

As readers, we can better understand what writers mean when we interpret their metaphors. As writers, we can more richly convey our meaning through the use of metaphor because we can create unexpected, interesting connections. Much of the sample writing that appears throughout the *Handbook* is richly metaphorical. Look, for example, at E. B. White's paragraphs on the moon walk (see 4b). Notice how White's metaphors reveal his idea and his attitude toward it.

2   Simile

When a metaphorical connection is made explicitly by means of the words *like, as,* or *as though,* the comparison is called a **simile.** *Karen dances like an angel* is a simile; *Karen is an angel* is a metaphor. The difference between the two types of figurative language involves more than the word *like:* the comparison in the simile is more restrictive than it is in the metaphor. That is, Karen's angelic qualities are extensive in the metaphor—she has many angelic qualities. In the simile, however, she only dances like an angel.

WRITING HINT   Do not be afraid to use similes and metaphors in your writing. But be careful about mixing metaphors and lapsing into cliché or trite comparisons (see 28h). To improve your ability to use metaphor and simile, attend to how good writers use them.

Checking Your Diction

Use the following questions to check your choice of words.

- Consider the positive and negative connotations of your words.
- Clarify and illustrate generalities and abstractions with specific examples and concrete details.
- Suit your level of formality to your audience and purpose. Eliminate slang or colloquialisms.
- Eliminate or define jargon, unless you are writing for an audience of specialists.
- Be sure the meanings of neologisms or acronyms are clear to your audience.
- Revise to eliminate euphemisms or archaisms.
- Unless they are appropriate for the audience and occasion, revise regional or dialect expressions.
- Rephrase to eliminate clichés.
- Check for mixed metaphors, and revise any that you find.

EXERCISE 28–15   **Identifying and Evaluating Similes and Metaphors**

Underline the metaphors and similes in the following passages. Explain what is being compared and comment on the effectiveness of each comparison.

1. What happens to a dream deferred?
    Does it dry up like a raisin in the sun?

    —Langston Hughes

2. Life's but a walking shadow, a poor player
    That struts and frets his hour upon the stage
    And then is heard no more. It is a tale
    Told by an idiot, full of sound and fury,
    Signifying nothing.

    —William Shakespeare

EXERCISE 28–16   **Revising Mixed Metaphors**

Revise any mixed metaphors you find in the following sentences to make the metaphors and similes consistent. Example:

> His actions sowed the seeds of confusion, resulting in a rising tide of criticism. His actions resulted in a rising tide of criticism.

1. Difficulties emerged like mosquitoes from a stagnant pool, creating thorny problems for all involved.
2. The howling wind bent the branches, which tilted gracefully like dancers swaying to a tune.
3. The book was filled with brilliant insights that continued to buzz in her mind.
4. His ideas, rooted in a strong belief in tolerance and understanding, left a trail of believers in their wake.
5. He had to get off the fence and take the plunge.

CHAPTER 29

Avoiding Biased Language

One aim of writing is to communicate clearly so your readers will understand your ideas. Another is to write persuasively so they will accept and perhaps come to share your views. A form of language that interferes with both of these aims is **biased language,** which disparages, stereotypes, or patronizes others. Biased language almost always reflects negative assumptions about race, ethnicity, sex, age, social class, religion, physical or mental characteristics, geographical area, or sexual orientation. Biased language should be avoided because it almost always offends people. This chapter describes ways to use language so it remains sensitive to people's differences.

29a Avoiding racially and ethnically biased language

The language of racial and ethnic prejudice reflects generalizations that unfairly stereotype all members of a particular racial or ethnic group. Not all African-American males want to be professional basketball players, nor do all white Anglo-Saxon Protestant youths attend prep schools. Not all Japanese are expert in the martial arts, and not all Asian Americans are mathematical whizzes. When these **stereotypes,** or assumptions about members of a group, persist, they perpetuate the idea that all members of a group share qualities or behaviors that may or may not apply to a few.

One adverse consequence of racially and ethnically biased language, then, is its stereotypical straitjacketing. (See 7f-2 on stereotyping.) Stereotyping is inaccurate, simplistic, and unfair. It suggests notions that do not accurately reflect the diverse beliefs, attitudes, and behaviors of the many people it lumps together. In its excessive generalization, biased or prejudiced language is simpleminded. It is also unfair toward the many who do not exhibit the characteristics presumed by the stereotype.

Biased language insults the person or group to which it is applied. In denegrating others, biased language creates division and separation. In using biased language about races and ethnic or cultural groups, speakers and writers risk alienating members of those groups, thus undermining the communication and shared understanding language should promote, but which biased language inhibits.

In referring to race and ethnicity, you need to take pains to choose your language carefully, so as not to offend those you might hope to persuade. You need to use the term preferred by particular groups for identifying themselves. It is a speaker's or writer's responsibility to know these preferences and to respect them. If you are unsure how to refer to a group or to any of your acquaintances, you should ask—if you can. As you read newspapers and magazines and watch films and television, notice changes in preferred terminology for racial and ethnic groups. Currently, the following terms are usually preferred.

INSTEAD OF	USE
Negro	African American or Black
white	Caucasian
Indian	Native American
Eskimo	Inuit
Oriental	Asian American

However, you should also realize that most people prefer to be thought of and spoken about as individuals rather than as members of groups. Resentments about being arbitrarily grouped with others may underlie many of today's protests about titles and terminology.

29b   Avoiding sexually biased language

Sexually biased language, or **sexist language,** ignores or minimizes the contributions of one gender, while emphasizing and giving credit to those of the other. Historically, the roles played by men are more likely to be glorified than those played by women. Writers who wish to avoid perpetuating sexist ideas must consciously use inclusive language. For example, when referring to an unknown person or to people in general, you should avoid using such words as *man* and *mankind*, which exclude half the human race; use instead more inclusive terms such as *human being(s), humanity, people, persons* and *individual(s).*

You should also avoid using language that patronizes either gender. For example, do not refer to a man's wife as his "little woman," or make statements such as "He is a good teacher, for a man." Also avoid describing women with reference to their looks, age, or style of dress unless those descriptions are necessary to the context or you do the same for men. And, finally, avoid calling attention to gender in circumstances where gender is irrelevant, such as in referring to female students as *coeds.*

Since sexual bias pervades our language, you need to be vigilant to catch and revise instances of it in writing. When Neil Armstrong first walked on the moon, he was referred to as the first *man* on the moon (not the first *human, individual,* or *person* there). Armstrong's carefully chosen words uttered as he walked on the moon were: "That's one small step for [a] man, one giant leap for mankind." This was acceptable usage in 1969, and most people did not take offense at Armstrong's use of *mankind* instead of *humankind* or *the human race*. A quarter-century later, however, people have become far more sensitive to the gender exclusion implicit in such a choice of words.

1   Sexist pronouns

Perhaps the most challenging problem for writers using inclusive language occurs with pronouns (see 12b–c). To avoid sexist writing, do not use masculine pronouns when referring to someone who might be either male or female. And avoid using the generic *he*—letting *he* refer to a person of either sex. Revise the sentences using plural forms to be more inclusive.

SEXIST   A professor knows *he* is responsible for keeping *his* office hours.

REVISED   Professors know *they* are responsible for keeping *their* office hours.

SEXIST   Every kindergarten teacher has *her* own techniques for motivating young children.

REVISED   Kindergarten teachers have different techniques for motivating young children.

Especially troublesome are indefinite pronouns, such as *everybody, anyone,* and *everyone*. Consider the sentence *Everyone has his own ideas about the issue*. Grammatically, indefinite pronouns are singular and thus must take singular pronouns (see 15d). However, in the previous example, the singular pronoun *he* excludes women. To be more inclusive, you can write *his or her*: *Everyone has his or her own ideas about the issue*. Although more inclusive, this solution can become cumbersome when you need many references to *she and he, him and her*, and *his and her* in a piece of writing. A better solution is to revise indefinite pronouns to make them plural: *People have their own ideas about the issue*. Or you can eliminate the pronoun altogether: *People have different ideas about the issue*.

2   Occupational stereotypes

Another area to look out for sexist language is that of occupational stereotypes. Do not assume, for example, that all grade school teachers are women, that all surgeons are men, or that secretaries and nurses are always women. And be careful to avoid using such words as *fireman* and *policeman* when *fire fighters* and *police officers* are more inclusive and equally effective terms. As in other instances of gender-specific language, only mention an individual's gender when it is relevant.

Use the following list to help you avoid words that may reflect gender bias and to choose appropriate alternatives.

INSTEAD OF	CONSIDER USING
anchorman	anchor
businessman	business executive; manager
chairman	chair
cleaning lady	housecleaner
clergyman	priest; rabbi; minister
congressman	legislator; member of Congress
fireman	fire fighter
foreman	supervisor
insurance man	insurance agent
mailman	letter carrier; mail carrier; postal worker
policeman	police officer
salesman	sales representative
stewardess	flight attendant
weatherman	weather reporter; meteorologist
workman	worker

Sexually biased language is fairly easy to revise. Use the accompanying guidelines to keep your language free of sexist bias.

Ways to Avoid Sexist Language

- Avoid using the word *man* or *men* to refer to both women and men. Also avoid words containing those terms, such as *congressman* and *man-made* (use *legislator* and *synthetic* instead).

  SEXIST   It is time for all good *men* to stand up and be counted.

  REVISED   It is time for all good *people* to stand up and be counted.

  SEXIST   The *congressmen* should vote against the proposal.

  REVISED   The *legislators* should vote against the proposal.

- Avoid "feminine" suffixes such as *-ess* and *-ette.*

  SEXIST   Rita Dove is a prominent American *poetess.*

  REVISED   Rita Dove is a prominent American *poet.*

- Use parallel terms when referring to members of both sexes. Do not always put the male term first as if it were the more important.

  SEXIST   Dr. Noel Rogers and Linda Rogers have been *man and wife* for ten years.

  REVISED   Noel and Linda Rogers have been *husband and wife* for ten years.

  Instead of *men and ladies,* say *ladies and gentlemen* or *men and women.*

(continued)

- Use plural forms instead of singular masculine forms.

  SEXIST   *A doctor* must work as an intern and resident before *he* can be licensed to practice medicine independently.

  REVISED   *Doctors* must work as interns and residents before *they* can be licensed to practice medicine independently.

- Eliminate the pronouns entirely.

  REVISED   *A doctor* must work as an intern and resident before *being* licensed to practice medicine independently.

- Avoid using gender terms unnecessarily, as with *male nurse* or *female lawyer*.

  SEXIST   The *male nurse* was represented by three *women lawyers*.

  REVISED   The *nurse* was represented by three *lawyers*.

- Avoid using language that patronizes either sex.

  SEXIST   His response to a crisis is *womanish*.

  REVISED   His response to a crisis is *ineffectual*.

EXERCISE 29–1   Eliminating Sexist Language

Consider how the following sentences may reveal gender bias. Revise to eliminate the bias.

1. Take the car to your mechanic and ask him to check the gas manifold.
2. The material in that shirt is completely man-made.
3. I was surprised at how compassionate the male nurse was.
4. A secretary should always be ready to do her boss's bidding, even if she finds him pushy and arrogant.
5. The girls in the class outnumbered the men.
6. We will need all the manpower we can get.
7. The proprietress was an old lady.
8. My aunt was the first of the daring lady stuntmen.
9. If you have a complaint about the food, make sure to tell your waitress.
10. The common man may be unaffected by the power struggle in Russia.

EXERCISE 29–2   Thinking about Stereotypes in Advertisements

Look at advertisements in a popular magazine. Identify words, phrases, and situations that seem stereotypically feminine or masculine. Consider whether the illustrations convey these stereotypes as well.

29c   Avoiding other kinds of biased language

Racial, ethnic, and gender bias are not the only biases language can convey. Other forms include expressions that show insensitivity toward age, social class, religion, geographical location, physical and mental qualities, and sexual orientation. In using any of these characterizing terms, be careful that your language does not offend.

1   Age

Certain words referring to a person's age may be taken as disparaging, even when you have no intention of being so. A young person may resent being called an *adolescent*, a *kid*, or even a *teenager*, while an older person may prefer not to be described as *a senior* or *elderly*. Moreover, referring to an individual as an *old woman* or *a man who looks good for his age* may seem simply descriptive, but may be taken as unflattering and, indeed, unnecessary to the context. *Old woman* carries with it suggestions of wrinkles and sagging skin. A man who *looks good for his age* implies that the man looks physically fit only if his age is considered. Take care to use age descriptors carefully, with sensitivity, and only as necessary.

2   Social class

When describing social class, take care not to use terms that patronize or demean a group of people, and do not use social class to build an argument or pigeonhole members of a group. Because they express prejudice and stereotypical attitudes about class, avoid disparaging terms such as *redneck, white trash,* and *wealthy snob.* Remember that your readers may come from across the social spectrum and you should therefore take care to avoid negative and unfairly biased class terms in all your writing.

3   Religion

Although most words used to designate religious groups do not convey bias (Protestant, Muslim, Christian, Jew, Buddhist), make sure you refer to religion reasonably and fairly, regardless of your own beliefs. Avoid assuming that your religious preferences or beliefs are the norm. Be careful to avoid generalizing about the religious beliefs of others. When referring to religious figures, beliefs, or events, keep your language free of judgmental words. Take care to avoid overgeneralization by implying, for example, that all Catholics have big families, that all Protestants can quote Scripture, or that all Muslims wear turbans and speak Arabic.

4   Geographical area

People from one region or section of a country sometimes consider those from other parts of the country less sophisticated, less advanced, or less capable than they are. For example, some city dwellers think of their rural counterparts as naive country *hicks*. The insult is reversed with the country dweller's view of the urban inhabitant as a *city slicker*, someone not to be trusted.

Even when geographical references are not directly patronizing or denigrating, they may convey ignorance in their simplistic or overly general ideas. Not all New Yorkers are rude, for example, nor do they all live fast-paced lives. Southerners do not all speak with a drawl, nor are they all hospitable. Californians are not all sun worshipers and surf lovers, nor are all Midwesterners untutored farmhands. Always avoid such generalizations.

5   Physical and mental characteristics

Avoid language that calls unnecessary attention to an individual's or a group's physical or mental characteristics. When such references are necessary, as when a group prefers not to have a disability minimized, be careful to use language that does not offend. For example, when referring to people who are hearing impaired, avoid calling them *deaf mutes* or *deaf and dumb*. The word *dumb* originally meant "unable to speak" and was not derogatory. Over time, however, it acquired the secondary meaning of "stupid." To avoid both negative (and inaccurate) meanings, simply refer to deaf people as "deaf." Note, too, that the preferred terms for disabilities are constantly changing. It is your responsibility to know these preferences and to respect them.

In referring to people with a developmental disability such as mental retardation or autism, be equally sensitive to the words you choose, always avoiding cruel, denigrating terms. Also, refrain from mentioning a mental condition when it is not relevant to your discussion. In a moving article about his son Jon, who was born with Down's syndrome, columnist George Will reminds his readers that they must choose language carefully when speaking of people like his son. George Will's son does not "suffer from" Down's syndrome. He lives with that disorder the way other people live with other imperfections. Nor is Jon abnormal or in any way incomplete. His son, Will notes, "is a complete Jon and that is that."

Take care, then, to write about other people with sensitivity. Avoid stereotyping them, and show respect for their preferences.

WRITING HINT   In general, avoid labeling people as *victims*—as *AIDS victims, cancer victims,* or *victims of Down's syndrome,* for example. Instead refer to them as people—people with AIDS, individuals with cancer, or people with Down's syndrome. Give the person priority over the illness or physical or mental condition.

6   Sexual orientation

In the same way you avoid denigrating language in referring to people's race, ethnicity, age, social class, or other characteristics, be careful when making references to sexual orientation. Do not assume that your readers share your sexual orientation any more than they may share your political views or religious beliefs. Be as unbiased toward different sexual orientations as you are toward behaviors resulting from different social backgrounds or cultural traditions. Avoid referring to a person's sexual orientation if such a reference would be gratuitous and irrelevant. In discussing the acting career of Rock Hudson, for example, you would avoid mentioning his homosexuality— unless it was directly relevant to your point.

EXERCISE 29–3   **Becoming Aware of Biased Language**

Find a newspaper or magazine article or advertisement that exhibits sexist bias. Find another that exhibits one of the other biases discussed in this chapter. Explain which words and phrases may be considered offensive and why.

EXERCISE 29–4   **Revising Biased Language**

Revise the language of the item you located for Exercise 29–3 to eliminate the bias.

CHAPTER 30

Enriching Your Vocabulary

A vocabulary is the complete stock of words in a language. Your *reading vocabulary* consists of the words you recognize and understand. Your *writing vocabulary* consists of the words you use in communication. This chapter is designed to help you increase your reading and writing vocabularies.

To add to your vocabulary, you need to do more than simply look up the meanings of unfamiliar words in a dictionary. You increase your chances of remembering and using those words by relating them to what you already know: to other words or parts of words, to stories associated with their meanings, and to their origins. The strategies outlined in the accompanying chart will help you learn about new words and retain that knowledge. These strategies are covered in detail in this chapter.

Strategies for Developing Your Vocabulary

- Learn about the history of the English language (30a).
- Recognize the roots of words (30b).
- Understand the meanings of prefixes and suffixes (30c).
- Learn the stories behind words (30d).
- Use context clues (30e).

30a Learning about the history of the English language

Many English words derive from other languages. Learning where English came from will help you better understand the language, enhance your appreciation of it, and increase your ability to use it.

English descends from a 5,000-year-old language that scholars have designated as *Indo-European* (a name given both to the ancestor of European languages and to the ancestor of languages spoken on the Indian subcontinent). Some of the people who originally used this language migrated throughout what is now Europe. The languages of Armenian, Greek, French, Polish, Swedish, and English, to name a few, can be traced to this common root.

The earliest form of English, called Old English or Anglo-Saxon, was brought to England by invaders around A.D. 400. Old English was changed by several exterior forces. Christianity was reintroduced to England around 600, which affected not only the Anglo-Saxon religion, but also its language. With the accommodation of Christianity into everyday life came the accommodation of Christianity's linguistic influences, Latin and Greek. Words such as *abbot, altar, angel, apostle, candle, chalice, disciple, litany, martyr,* and *mass* originated in this era of the development of the language. The Viking invasions of England, beginning in the 700s, further changed Old English. With the invasions came words such as *bank, die, fellow, harbor, keg, knife, sky, spear, steak,* and *trust.*

It was the Norman Conquest of England in 1066, however, that transformed the English language most dramatically. The Normans, who spoke Old French, introduced many French words into English. With the invasion came changes in political and linguistic life, and the English language evolved into what we now refer to as Middle English. Since the Normans controlled the political and legal systems, French became the language of politics and law, though English continued to thrive as the everyday language. Words that entered the language in this period include *court, duke, majesty, noble, royal, sovereign,* and *traitor; abbey, cathedral, mercy, miracle, prayer, saint,* and *sermon; jury* and *verdict; siege* and *lieutenant; pearl* and *robe; romance, art,* and *beauty.*

The differences between Old English (400–1100) and Middle English (1100–1500) are astonishing. Compare the vocabulary and spelling in the following Old English and Middle English passages.

OLD ENGLISH

Sum monn him plantode wingeard and betynde hine ond dealf anne seath and getimbrode anne stiepel and gesette hine mid eorthtilium and ferde on eltheodignesse.

TRANSLATION

A certain man planted a vineyard for himself and enclosed it [him] and dug a pit and built a tower [steeple] and peopled [set] it [him] with farmers [earth-tillers] and went into a foreign country.

—New Testament

MIDDLE ENGLISH

Ther was also a Nonne, a Prioresse,
That of hir smylyng was ful symple and coy;
Hir gretteste ooth was but by Seinte Loy;

And she was cleped [called] madame Eglentyne.
Ful weel she soong the service dyvyne.

—Geoffrey Chaucer, *Canterbury Tales*

Modern English, the language used throughout much of the world today, was established by about 1600, the time Shakespeare was writing his poems and plays. Although Shakespeare's language may at times seem anything but modern, its vocabulary and word order are essentially the same as those we use today. Compare the following excerpt written in 1600 with those written in the Old English and Middle English periods.

If to do were as easy as to know what were good to do, chapels had been churches, and poor men's cottages princes' palaces. It is a good divine that follows his own instructions; I can easier teach twenty what were good to be done than to be one of the twenty to follow mine own teaching.

—William Shakespeare, *The Merchant of Venice*

Words from other languages also pervade English: from Italian *(cameo, macaroni, volcano)*; Spanish and Portuguese *(alligator, cannibal, cocoa, guitar)*; Persian *(bazaar* and *caravan)*; Turkish *(coffee)*; Dutch *(easel, landscape, cruise)*; Arabic *(harem, alcohol)*; Algonquin *(wampum)*—and many other words from a wide variety of languages. English words are sometimes difficult to spell because many words have been adopted from other languages and follow spelling rules of those languages. But from being influenced by other languages English has become a rich language with a varied *vocabulary* (Latin), or *lexicon* (Greek), or *word-hoard* (Anglo-Saxon).

EXERCISE 30–1 Identifying Word Origins

Look up the following words in your dictionary and note their origin. If your dictionary does not provide this information, consult an unabridged dictionary in your college library.

1. voodoo
2. zucchini
3. chowder
4. cookie
5. plaza
6. shawl
7. ghoul
8. ketchup
9. sauna
10. rainbow

EXERCISE 30–2 Determining the Derivations of Synonyms

English speakers and writers can often choose between two or more ways of expressing the same idea (though there are differences in level of formality and connotation). Identify which of the following words you think derived from French, which from Latin, and which from Old English or other languages.

1. initiate, commence, start
2. end, terminate, finish
3. smart, intelligent, bright
4. wind, turbulence, airflow
5. moon, lunar, sun, solar

30b Recognizing the roots of words

A word's **root** is the unchanging part that is related to other words. The root of the word *pedal*, for example, is *ped*, a Latin root meaning "foot." This root is evident in such words as *quadruped* (four-footed) and *pedestrian* (a person traveling on foot). Other words that use the same root include *centipede*, *pedometer*, and *pedestal*. One of the benefits of learning roots is that once you learn a single root, you can determine the meanings of many related words.

But learning related words using roots has its limitations. The following words seem to include the root *ped: pediatrician, pedantry, pedigree, pediment, pedicure*. Of these five words, however, only one has a connection with feet: *pedicure* (cosmetic care of feet and toenails).

You should observe the following cautions in learning word roots.

1. Learn the meaning and etymology of words from the dictionary (see 27a).
2. Be aware that words that look similar may derive from different roots.

Once you understand these guidelines, you can have some fun in thinking of how words with similar roots relate to each other. For example, the Greek-derived *podiatrist* (a foot specialist) is related to the words *tripod* (a three-legged stand) and *arthropod* (a type of animal having jointed appendages). And a bit further in sound but from the same Greek root, *pous* (meaning "foot"), are *Oedipus* (the Greek tragic hero whose name means "swollen foot") and *octopus* (a creature with eight tentacles).

The accompanying chart lists Greek and Latin roots that are commonly used in English and notes their meanings. As you look over the words and roots in the chart, try to think of other related English words. Becoming familiar with word roots will help you enhance your vocabulary.

EXERCISE 30–3 Identifying Word Roots

Identify the roots and determine the meanings of the following words. List five other words that contain the same roots. Consult your dictionary to check your work.

1. inference	6. interlocutor
2. audible	7. translucent
3. disaster	8. bibliophile
4. geometry	9. intermittent
5. primogeniture	10. compassion

Common Roots and Their Meanings

ROOT (ORIGIN)	MEANING	EXAMPLE
-aster-, -astr- (Greek)	star	astronomy, astrology
-audi- (Latin)	to hear	audiology, audience
-auto- (Greek)	self	automobile, autoimmune
-bene- (Latin)	good, well	benefactor, benefit
-bio- (Greek)	life	biology, biosphere
-chrono- (Greek)	time	chronology, chronometer
-dict- (Latin)	speak	dictation, dictaphone
-fer- (Greek)	bear, carry	ferry, infer, conifer
-gen- (Greek)	give birth, race	genealogy, genesis
-geo- (Greek)	earth	geography, geology
-graph- (Greek)	write	graphic, pictograph
-greg- (Latin)	herd, flock	gregarious, segregate
-jur-, -jus- (Latin)	law	justice, jury
-log-, -logue- (Greek)	thought, word	monologue, loquacious
-luc- (Latin)	light	lucid, elucidate
-manu- (Latin)	hand	manufacture, manual
-meter-, -metr- (Greek)	measure	thermometer, metrical
-mit-, -mis- (Latin)	send	missile, transmit
-omni- (Latin)	all	omnipotent, omnivorous
-op-, -oper- (Latin)	work	opera, inoperable
-path- (Greek)	feel, suffer	pathetic, sympathy
-phil- (Greek)	love	philosophy, sophistry
-phon- (Greek)	sound	phonograph, telephone
-photo- (Greek)	light	photosynthesis, photon
-port- (Latin)	carry, bear	portable, transport
-psych- (Greek)	soul	psychic, psychology
-scrib-, -script- (Latin)	write	transcript, scripture
-sent-, -sens- (Latin)	feel	sensation, insensate
-tele- (Greek)	far off	telegraph, telepathy
-ter-, -terr- (Latin)	earth	terrestrial, terrain
-therm- (Greek)	heat	thermal, thermometer
-vac- (Latin)	empty	vacation, vacate
-verb- (Latin)	word	verbose, verbal
-vic-, -vin- (Latin)	conquer	victor, invincible
-vid-, -vis- (Latin)	see	invisible, vista

30c   Understanding the meanings of prefixes and suffixes

Prefixes and suffixes are groups of letters added to words or to word roots to make new words. (See also 27a on morphemes.) A **prefix** is a letter or group of letters attached to the beginning of a word. A **suffix** is a letter or group of letters attached to the end of a word. Both prefixes and suffixes are known as *affixes,* or attachments.

1   Prefixes

Prefixes offer a handy way to determine the meanings of words. By looking at a word's prefix, its root, and its suffix, you have a reasonably good chance of figuring out its meaning.

Use the accompanying chart to help you learn prefixes. Learning the meanings of these common prefixes can help you decipher the meanings of unfamiliar words.

Common Prefixes and Their Meanings

Prefixes of number and quantity

PREFIX	MEANING	EXAMPLE
uni-, mono-	one	unicycle, monopoly
du-, bi-, dis-, dy-, di-	two	dual, bipolar, disparate
tri-	three	trilogy, triangular
quadr-, tetra-	four	quadrangle, tetrameter
quint-, penta-	five	quintet, pentagon
sex-, hexa-	six	sextuplets, hexagonal
sept-, hepta-	seven	septet, heptagon
oct-, octo-, octa-	eight	octet, octopus, octagon
nov-, non-, ena-	nine	novena, nonagenarian
decim-, deca-	ten	decimal, decathlon

Prefixes of negation

PREFIX	MEANING	EXAMPLE
a-	without, not	asexual, amoral
anti-	against	antipathetic
contra-	against	contradict
de-	from, remove, take away	detoxify, devalue

(continued)

dis-	apart, away	disappear, disconnect
il-, im-, in-, ir-	not	illegal, immoral, innocuous
mal-	bad, wrong	malevolent, malnutrition
mis-	wrong, bad	mistake, miscue
non-	not	noncompliant
un-	not	unbearable

Prefixes of time

PREFIX	MEANING	EXAMPLE
ante-	before	antecedent, anterior
fore-	before	foretell
pre-, pro-	before	precede, project
post-	after	posterior
re-	again	rewrite
syn-	the same time	synchronize

Prefixes of space, direction, position

PREFIX	MEANING	EXAMPLE
ad-	to, for	adverb, adhere
circum-	around	circumstantial
co-, col-	with	coequal, collude
com-, con-, cor-	with	communicate, contact

PREFIX	MEANING	EXAMPLE
e-, ex-	out of	eject, extract
hetero-	other	heterodox
homo-	same	homonym
hypo-	under, less	hypoallergenic
hyper-	over, more	hyperkinetic
inter-	between	interview, internecine
intra-	within	intramural
sub-	under	subterranean
super-	above	supersonic
trans-	across	transcontinental

Note: The spelling of some prefixes varies, usually to make pronunciation easier: *ad-* becomes *ac-* in *accuse* and *ag-* in *aggregate*. This is analogous to the prefix *in-* changing to *im-* in *immovable*, to *ir-* in *irreverent*, and to *il-* in *illegible*. (See 31c-6.)

EXERCISE 30–4   Identifying the Prefixes of Number and Quantity

---

Find the number prefixes in the following words, determine what the words mean, and then explain why the words mean what they do, given their prefixes.

1. duplicity	4. October	7. quatrain	10. decalogue
2. pentathlon	5. bilateral	8. dichotomy	
3. trivial	6. univocal	9. sextet	

EXERCISE 30–5   Working with Prefixes

For each of the following words, find one word with an opposite meaning by working with prefixes. Include the meaning of each word. Example:

malevolent (wishing or doing evil)

benevolent (wishing or doing good)

1. benign	6. interoffice
2. dissident	7. reactive
3. inhibit	8. progressive
4. extroverted	9. heterogeneous
5. postnatal	10. hyposensitivity

EXERCISE 30–6   Working with Prefixes of Negation

Write an antonym using prefixes for each of the following words. Example:

functional—dysfunctional

1. movable	6. accelerate
2. visible	7. compose
3. passive	8. classify
4. rational	9. increase
5. significant	10. please

---

2   Suffixes

Suffixes—letter attachments that follow word roots—not only provide clues to the meanings of words, but also change the grammatical function of words. Attaching the suffixes *-ful* and *-less* to the noun *use* converts it to the adjectives *useful* and *useless*. The verb *use* can be transformed into the adjective *usable*. The adjective *white* can be made into the verb *whiten*. And the verb *contemplate* can be made a noun *(contemplation)*, an adjective *(contemplative)*, or an adverb *(contemplatively)*. The only suffix that consistently creates adverbs is *-ly*. (See 13a on adverb suffixes.)

You can often rely on your knowledge of word meanings and of familiar suffixes to help you decipher the meanings of unfamiliar words. For example, you may be familiar with the suffixes *-cide* (kill), *-cracy* (rule), and *-ologist* (specialist). If you come across the unfamiliar words *regicide, plutocracy,* and *oncologist,* you can make an educated guess about a part of their meanings by recognizing the suffix. Use the accompanying chart of common suffixes to help you work with suffixes.

Common Suffixes and Their Meanings

Verb suffixes

SUFFIX	MEANING	EXAMPLE
-ate	cause to become	eradicate, regulate
-en	cause to become	lengthen, enlighten
-ify	cause to become	deify, codify
-ize	cause to become	synthesize, organize

Noun suffixes

SUFFIX	MEANING	EXAMPLE
-acy	state or quality	democracy
-al	process of	portrayal
-ant	one who	participant
-ion	process of	addition
-er, -or	one who	trainer, protector
-ism	doctrine, belief	Confucianism
-ist	one who	chemist
-ity, -ty	quality	capacity, cruelty
-ment	condition of	deportment
-ness	state of being	heaviness
-sion, -tion	state of being	concession, perdition

Adjective suffixes

SUFFIX	MEANING	EXAMPLE
-able, -ible	capable of being	presentable, edible
-al	pertaining	consequential
-esque	reminiscent of	statuesque, grotesque
-ful	notable for	fanciful, wonderful
-ic, ical	pertaining to	poetic, gigantic, musical
-ish	the quality of	fiendish, standoffish
-ous, -ious	characterized by	portentous, surreptitious
-ive	having the nature of	festive, restive
-less	without	regardless, helpless
-y	characterized by	dirty, sleazy

EXERCISE 30–7   Working with Verb Suffixes

Think of five words for each verb suffix listed in the accompanying chart.

EXERCISE 30–8   Working with Adjective Suffixes

Think of two words for each adjective suffix listed in the accompanying chart. Use five of these words in sentences.

EXERCISE 30–9   Working with Suffixes to Change Grammatical Function

By adding and altering suffixes, change the following verbs to nouns and the nouns to verbs. Example:

> reservation—reserve
> portray—portrayal

1. **Verbs:** initiate, fluctuate, betray, describe, teach, prohibit, develop
2. **Nouns:** analysis, synthesis, complication, hesitation, beauty, validity

EXERCISE 30–10   Working from Suffixes to Roots

Think of two words for each of the following suffixes: *-cide, -ologist, -phobia, -phil,* and *-cracy*. Think of two other words that use the roots you wrote in the first step of the exercise.

> ***-cide:** fratricide, matricide   fraternity, fraternal, matriarchy, maternal*

30d   Learning the stories behind words

Learning the roots of words and learning something about their etymology are important ways of developing your vocabulary. Another way is to learn the stories associated with some words. Many words have interesting stories connected with people, places, and myths. Most dictionaries include at least some information about words derived from mythology as well as those associated with people and places. Knowing the stories connected with words will help you remember their meanings and develop your vocabulary. Two words that derive from actual people are *Machiavellian* and *mesmerize*.

Machiavellian means "suggestive of or characterized by the principles of expedience, deceit, and cunning." In his book *The Prince,* Niccolo Machiavelli (1469–1527) advocated such qualities as the way for political leaders to acquire and retain power.

Mesmerize means "to hypnotize or enthrall." F. A. Mesmer (1734–1815) first described and demonstrated the techniques of mesmerism, or hypnosis.

The names of some fictional characters have also become function words. The word *gargantuan,* for example, derives from the character Gargantua in François Rabelais's (1494–1553) book *Gargantua and Pantagruel,* in which Gargantua is a huge king with an enormous appetite. Thus the word has come to mean anything of immense size or large scale.

Words that take their meaning from places are not as common as those that derive from historical figures and fictional characters. Two examples of place-associated words are *mecca* and *meander.* Mecca, a city in Saudi Arabia, was the birthplace of Muhammad. As such, it is a holy place that attracts many pilgrims. The word *mecca* means "a place with a special aura" and "a goal of pilgrimage." *Meander,* which means "to wander aimlessly," comes from the name of a river in Turkey or Asia Minor (Meander or Maiandros) known for its winding course.

A number of English words such as *saturnine, Apollonian,* and *mercurial* derive from Greek mythology. If you know that the Greek hero Achilles was invulnerable except for one weak spot (his heel), you will know that an *Achilles heel* is an expression meaning a small but significant weakness. If you know that Prometheus was a Greek character who braved the wrath of the gods by stealing fire from them and giving it to humans, you will know that a *Promethean* task is one that is boldly creative and original.

EXERCISE 30–11   Learning Words Based on People and Places

Look up the following words in a dictionary and identify the people, places, or literary characters from which they derive. Then use each word in a sentence.

1. bowdlerize
2. chauvinism
3. sadistic
4. billingsgate
5. masochism
6. maverick
7. utopian
8. samaritan

EXERCISE 30–12   Learning the Stories behind Words

Look up three of the following words in your dictionary. Learn the stories connected with them so that you can explain why they mean what they do. Use each word in a sentence.

1. erotic	5. odyssey
2. narcissism	6. protean
3. procrustean	7. Olympian
4. jovial	8. bacchanalian

30e   Using context clues

One of the best ways to develop your vocabulary is to use the context in which a word appears to determine its meaning. The familiar words appearing before and after an unfamiliar one provide clues that can help you decipher the new word's meaning. These clues are called *context clues.* You often use context clues instinctively, whenever you read or hear unfamiliar words.

Writers occasionally define words, especially unusual ones, in the sentences in which those words appear. And even when a word unfamiliar to you is not defined, you can often get a general sense of its meaning by recognizing its grammatical function (e.g., as a noun or adjective), by considering the writer's topic, or by discerning the writer's tone. Using your general experience with language and your particular vocabulary knowledge to guide you, you can increase your chances of understanding unfamiliar words.

For example, although you may not fully understand every word in the sentence *Looking directly at an annular eclipse can damage the eye's cornea and retina,* you can infer the meaning of each word from those around it. You would know that *annular* is a word describing a kind of eclipse and that *cornea* and *retina* are parts of an eye. Since the context does not implicitly define these words, look them up in a dictionary if you feel that you need a more precise meaning.

The accompanying chart identifies common types of context clues that can help you develop your vocabulary.

READING HINT   As you read, keep a record of unfamiliar words. You need not stop reading to find these words in a dictionary. Instead, jot them down, or underline them. Try to determine their meanings from their roots, prefixes, and suffixes, as well as from context clues. Later, look the words up in your dictionary and record the definitions in a notebook. Most importantly, however, read regularly to build your vocabulary and improve your understanding of words.

EXERCISE 30–13   **Using Context Clues**

Read the following passage. Using context clues, determine the meanings of the italicized words.

One morning in Stockholm, after rain and just before November, a mysteriously *translucent* shadow began to paint itself across the top of the city. It skimmed high over people's heads, a *gauzy* brass net, keeping well above the streets, *skirting* everything *fabricated* by human arts—though one or two steeples were allowed to dip into it, like pens filling their nibs with palest ink. It made a sort of watermark over Stockholm, as if a faintly *luminous* river ran overhead, yet with no more weight or *gravity* than a vapor.

—Cynthia Ozick, "Enchantments at First Encounter"

Common Types of Context Clues

1. **Restatement:** Sometimes familiar words repeat or define unfamiliar words.

   Igneous rock, formed under intense heat and pressure, constitutes the earth's core.

2. **Contrast:** Sometimes familiar words will be set in opposition to unfamiliar words.

   We hoped that the new provost would be a *boon* to the faculty, but we soon found him to be a *detriment*.

3. **Exemplification:** Sometimes unfamiliar words will be explicitly illustrated.

   The Renaissance was a time of renewed interest in *antiquity*. Renaissance artists, for example, studied the statues made by Greek and Roman sculptors.

CHAPTER 31

Improving Your Spelling

*E*nglish spelling can be troublesome, mostly because English is a complex language that derives from a variety of other languages, including Old German, Old Norse, Danish, Norman French, Latin, and Greek (see 30a). English words taken from these languages can be tricky to spell because they are based on different sound systems. This is so whether a word is pronounced in English as it is in the host language (e.g., *cello*, from Italian) or whether its pronunciation and spelling have been modified in English (e.g., *beef*, from French *boeuf*).

In addition, spelling certain English words correctly is challenging because words with similar sounds may be spelled differently. The *ee* sound in *beef*, for example, appears in words with many varied spellings: *be, sea, key, esprit, belief, conceit, people, eon, these.* The following poem records some of the different sounds that similar letter patterns convey.

> Dearest **crea**ture in **crea**tion,
> Studying English pronunciation,
> I will teach you in my verse
> Sounds like **corpse**, **corps**, **hor**se and **wor**se . . .
> Just compare **heart**, **hear** and **heard**,
> **Die**s and **die**t, **lor**d and **word**,
> **Sword** and **sward**, re**tain** and Bri**tain**,
> (Mind the latter, how it's wri**tten**) . . .
>
> —Gerard Nolst Trenité, "The Chaos"

Even though numerous inconsistencies plague English spelling, most English words are spelled the way they sound. The exceptions do not diminish the usefulness of rules for spelling. This chapter covers both the rules and practical hints that will help you improve your spelling.

31a Using word meanings to aid spelling

English spelling depends heavily on the connection between words and their meanings. You should consider spelling, then, in relation to vocabulary

517

and *etymology,* or word origins (see Chapter 30). To improve your spelling while increasing your vocabulary, learn the meanings of words in clusters to discover the relationships among words and to connect the spelling of words with their meanings.

If you know, for example, that the word *copyright* has something to do with the right of legal protection for creative work, you will not misspell it as *copywrite,* even though you may also know that a person who works for an advertising agency writing copy for ads is a *copywriter.* The difference in spelling reflects a very real difference in meaning. The similar sound of the words is not nearly as important as their significant difference in sense.

One way to learn spelling is the way you learn anything else—by making connections between what you are learning and what you already know. But sometimes you cannot determine a word's spelling from its etymology. In these cases, you will have to rely on some of the other suggestions in this chapter.

31b Recognizing homonyms

Homonyms are words that sound alike but are spelled differently and have different meanings: *bored/board; horse/hoarse; cite/sight/site; plane/plain; night/knight; rain/rein/reign.* For these and many other words identical or similar in sound (*advice/advise; allusion/illusion*) you cannot use pronunciation as a guide to spelling.

The two accompanying charts identify homonyms that can create spelling confusion. The first chart lists words that appear frequently in writing; the other lists common homonyms. Always check your use of these words carefully. Although not especially difficult to spell, they are easy to confuse.

Although it is possible to list hundreds of word groups for you to memorize, to distinguish among homonyms you need to learn their etymologies and cognates, or related words. Refer to the accompanying charts, the Glossary of Usage, or your dictionary for any homonyms that give you trouble.

Frequently Confused Homonyms

its	(possessive form of *it*)	to	(toward)
it's	(contraction of *it is*)	too	(also; very)
their	(possessive form of *they*)	two	(number after one)
they're	(contraction of *they are*)	whose	(possessive form of *who*)
there	(in that place)	who's	(contraction of *who is*)
than	(as compared with)	your	(possessive form of *you*)
then	(at that time; therefore)	you're	(contraction of *you are*)

Other Commonly Confused Homonyms

accept	(to receive)	eminent	(distinguished)
except	(to leave out)	immanent	(inherent)
		imminent	(impending)
advice	(a recommendation)		
advise	(to recommend)	fair	(just; light complexioned)
affect	(verb: to influence; noun: an emotion)	fare	(a charge for transportation)
effect	(verb: to make happen; noun: a result)	gorilla	(an ape)
		guerrilla	(a soldier)
all ready	(prepared)		
already	(by this time)	hear	(to perceive by ear)
		here	(in this place)
allude	(to refer)		
elude	(to avoid)	heard	(past tense of *hear*)
		herd	(group of animals)
allusion	(indirect reference)		
illusion	(false idea or appearance)	hole	(an opening)
		whole	(entire)
ascent	(movement up)	lead	(noun: a metal; verb: to go before)
assent	(agreement)		
		led	(past tense of *lead*)
bare	(naked, uncovered)		
bear	(verb: to carry, endure; noun: an animal)	loose	(not tight)
		lose	(fail to win; misplace)
board	(piece of lumber)	passed	(past tense of *pass*)
bored	(uninterested)	past	(after, beyond)
brake	(to stop)	patience	(forbearance)
break	(to smash)	patients	(persons under medical care)
capital	(seat of government)		
capitol	(government building)	peace	(absence of war)
		piece	(a part of something)
complement	(to make complete)		
compliment	(to praise)	presence	(attendance)
		presents	(gifts)
conscience	(feeling of right and wrong)	principal	(school administrator)
conscious	(aware)	principle	(a basic truth or law)
council	(an assembly)	scene	(setting, part of a play)
counsel	(to advise)		
		seen	(past tense of *see*)
desert	(noun: dry sandy terrain; verb: to abandon)	stationary	(standing still)
		stationery	(writing paper)
dessert	(last part of a meal)		
		threw	(past tense of *throw*)
elicit	(to draw out)	through	(finished; by means of)
illicit	(illegal)		

(continued)

waist	(part of the body)	weather	(climatic conditions)
waste	(to squander)	whether	(which of two)
weak	(feeble, not strong)	which	(what; that)
week	(seven-day period)	witch	(sorcerer)

1   Recognizing homonyms with more than one form

Homonyms sometimes appear as a single word and sometimes as more than one word. Be sure to choose the homonym form that conveys your meaning. If you are unsure what a particular form of a homonym means, check your dictionary. Here are some homonyms whose different forms occasionally cause confusion.

They *always* [invariably] approach problems in *all ways* [every way] before deciding which solution is the best.

Every day [each day] you go to class, you wear *everyday* [usual] clothes.

I *may be* [might be] late, but then *maybe* [perhaps] I will be early.

They were not *altogether* [entirely] sure that gathering people *all together* [in a group] was the best way to discuss the issue.

By the time I had my paper *all ready* [completely finished], the deadline had *already* [before] passed.

Other variable-form homonyms include the following.

anybody [anyone]; *any body* [any single person]

anymore [ever]; *any more* [more of something]

sometimes [occasionally]; *some times* [certain times]

somebody [someone]; *some body* [some individual person]

SPELLING HINT   Keep in mind the following words that may also cause you occasional trouble: *cannot,* which is always spelled as one word, and *a lot* and *all right,* which are always spelled as two words.

2   Distinguishing between American and British/Canadian spellings

Some English words are spelled differently in other English-speaking countries. In Britain and Canada, for example, the endings of words sometimes vary from American spellings.

AMERICAN	BRITISH/CANADIAN
honor; color	honour; colour
judgment	judgement
connection	connexion
center; theater	centre; theatre
criticize; realize	criticise; realise
traveled	travelled

If you are unsure how to spell such a word, refer to your dictionary.

EXERCISE 31–1   Choosing the Appropriate Homonym

For each of the following sentences, underline the appropriate homonym. Example:

Never _lose_/loose _sight_/cite of your goal.

1. When _your_/you're finished, put _your_/you're papers over there/their/they're.
2. Please accept/except our advice/advise.
3. This is the principal/principle affect/effect of the scene/seen.
4. Who's/Whose to say weather/whether it was a better film then/than her last?
5. My patience/patients should have long passed/past.

31c   Applying common spelling rules

1   Distinguishing between *ie* and *ei*

You probably know the *ie/ei* rule: "*i* before *e* except after *c*, or when sounded like 'ay,' as in *neighbor* or *weigh*." This rule yields the following spellings.

i **before** *e*: belief, field, grief, hygiene, pier, relieve

but *e* **before** *i* **after** *c*: ceiling, conceit, conceive, deceive, receive, perceive

ei **pronounced "ay"**: beige, eight, freight, sleigh, vein, weight

But the *ie/ei* rule does not always hold true. **Some exceptions to the *ie/ei* rule:** *caffeine, conscience, either, financier, foreign, forfeit, leisure, seize, sovereign, species, their, weird.* Also notice that adding a *t* to the word *sleigh*, for example, yields the word *sleight*, which looks similar to *sleigh* but is pronounced differently. (*Sleight* rhymes with *right*, not with *hate*.)

2   Dropping or retaining the final *e*

In adding suffixes to words ending in a silent *e*, drop the *e* when the suffix begins with a vowel.

explor[e] + ation = exploration   requir[e] + ing = requiring
forc[e] + ible   = forcible

Exceptions: To avoid homonym confusion, use *dyeing* (staining with a color) and *singeing* (to burn slightly).

dye + ing   = dyeing [not *dying*, present participle of *die*]
singe + ing = singeing [not *singing*, present participle of *sing*]

To keep the sound of *c* or *g* soft in certain words, note the following.

notice + able = noticeable
courage + ous = courageous

Retain the silent *e* if the suffix begins with a consonant.

require + ment = requirement   care + ful = careful
state + ly   = stately

EXCEPTIONS   argu[e] + ment   = argument
               judg[e] + ment   = judgment
               acknowledg[e] + ment = acknowledgment
               aw[e] + ful   = awful
               tru[e] + ly   = truly
               whol[e] + ly   = wholly
               nin[e] + th   = ninth

3   Spelling words ending in *-cede*, *-ceed*, *-sede*

With the exception of *supersede*, all words ending in a suffix pronounced "seed" end either in *-cede* or in *-ceed*. Only three words end in *-ceed*: *exceed*, *proceed*, and *succeed*. All others end in *-cede*: such as *intercede*, *precede*, *secede*, *concede*, *recede*.

4   Distinguishing *-ally* from *-ly*

Use the suffix *-ally* for words ending in *-ic*.

logic + ally   = logically
magic + ally   = magically

EXCEPTION   *publicly* (not *publically*)

Use the suffix *-ly* instead of *-ally* for words that do not end in *-ic*.

slow + ly   = slowly
haphazard + ly = haphazardly

EXERCISE 31–2   **Spelling by the Rules**

Identify the correctly spelled words and use each one in a sentence.

1. fatally/fataly
2. tragicly/tragically
3. uncharacteristicly/uncharacteristically
4. initially/initialally
5. wholely/wholly/wholy
6. adviseable/advisable
7. deceitful/decietful
8. heinous/hienous
9. grievous/greivous
10. hygeine/hygiene

5   Retaining the final *y* or changing it to *i*

To add a suffix to words that end in *y*, change the *y* to *i* when the letter before the *y* is a consonant.

beauty + ful = beautiful   defy + ance = defiance
merry + ly = merrily   forty + eth   = fortieth
spy + ed   = spied   happy + ness = happiness

Exceptions: Keep the *y* before the suffix *-ing*.

hurry + ing = hurrying   bully + ing   = bullying
cry + ing   = crying   purify + ing = purifying

Retain the *y* in some one-syllable words.

wry + ly   = wryly   fry + er = fryer
dry + ness = dryness

When a word ends in *y* preceded by a vowel, keep the *y* when adding a suffix.

employ + er   = employer   deploy + ment = deployment
disobey + ed = disobeyed

Also, proper names retain the *y* and simply add the suffix.

June and James P. Grundy = the Grundys
Candy + esque   = Candyesque

EXERCISE 31–3   **Spelling Words with *y* or *i***

Identify the correctly spelled word in each of the following pairs.

1. gayly/gaily
2. dayly/daily
3. lonelyer/lonelier
4. fancyful/fanciful

5. supplyed/supplied
6. hurryed/hurried
7. dressyer/dressier

8. dryness/driness
9. complyance/compliance
10. fussyly/fussily

6 Doubling consonants

Adding a prefix or a suffix to an existing word sometimes results in a doubled consonant. The following guidelines will help you know when to double a consonant and when not to.

Doubling consonants when adding prefixes

In adding a prefix that ends in a consonant to a word that begins with one, combine the two consonants.

mis + spell = misspell
under + rated = underrated

If the word begins with a vowel, combine the prefix and the word.

mis + appropriate = misappropriate
de + emphasize = deemphasize

Sometimes, you need to make a slight adjustment in the prefix when you combine it with words that begin with a consonant. For example, if you combine the prefix *in* (meaning "not") with the following words, you need to adjust the prefix to double the initial consonant of the root word.

(in) im + mobile = immobile
(in) il + legible = illegible
(in) ir + relevant = irrelevant

The technical term for this prefix change is *assimilation*. This same process occurs with other prefixes, such as *con* (meaning "with"): *collect, correlate, commiserate.* Other examples include *accept (ad + cept)* and *eccentric (ex + centric).* (See 30c-1 for more on prefixes.)

Doubling the final consonant when adding suffixes

For one-syllable words that end in a consonant, double the final consonant when you add a suffix.

hop + ing = hopping
flop + y = floppy
scar + ed = scarred

For two-syllable words, double the consonant when the accent falls on the second syllable.

control' + able = controllable   concur' + ed = concurred
begin' + ing   = beginning

Exceptions: Words ending in *d* and *y* never double the consonant.

reward + ed = rewarded   dismay + ing = dismaying
rotund + ity = rotundity   decay + ed   = decayed

When not to double the final consonant when adding suffixes

Do not double the consonant when the accent falls on the first syllable of a multisyllable word.

pro'fit + able = profitable   tar'get + ed   = targeted
hap'pen + ing = happening   con'fident + ly = confidently
ben'efit + ed   = benefited

Do not double the consonant when the suffix begins with a consonant.

equip + ment = equipment
adroit + ness = adroitness

Do not double the consonant when the final consonant is preceded by more than one vowel or by another consonant.

sweep + ing = sweeping   light + ly = lightly
blurt + ed   = blurted

Do not double the consonant when a word's accent changes with the addition of the suffix.

refer' + ence = ref'erence

SPELLING HINT   In spelling words with *long vowel sounds,* include an *e* at the end.

pine   cone   scare   cure   hope

An *e* at the end of each of these words makes its internal vowel long. Without the *e* at the end, the words are pronounced with a *short vowel sound.*

pin   con   scar   cur   hop

Be careful to select the word and spelling appropriate to your meaning. Be alert especially for certain multiple-syllable words such as *envelop* (a verb, which should be distinguished from *envelope,* a noun).

EXERCISE 31–4   **Deciding When to Double Consonants**

Add suffixes and prefixes to the following words, and decide whether or not to double the consonant.

1. merit + orious	6. dis + qualified
2. worship + ing	7. mis + spent
3. confer + ing	8. re + apportioned
4. toboggan + ing	9. pre + programmed
5. noncommit + al	10. re + entry

31d Forming plurals

1 Regular plurals

The most common way to form the plural of nouns is to add *-s*.

boy/boys   marble/marbles   auction/auctions

However, words ending in *s*, *sh*, *z*, *x*, or *ch* form their plurals by adding *-es*.

pass/passes	wish/wishes	buzz/buzzes
ax/axes	church/churches	fax/faxes

For words ending in *o*, add either *-s* or *-es*. If the final *o* is preceded by a vowel, add *-s*. If the final *o* is preceded by a consonant, add *-es*.

patio/patios   tomato/tomatoes

EXCEPTIONS
piano/pianos   pro/pros
memo/memos   solo/solos

For words ending in *y*, change the *y* to *i* and add *-es*—but only when the *y* is preceded by a consonant.

history/histories   eulogy/eulogies   ally/allies

When the *y* is preceded by a vowel, retain the *y* and add *-s*.

attorney/attorneys   toy/toys   alley/alleys

EXCEPTION
Proper names: There are three *Harrys* in the class.

For most words that end in *-f* or *-fe*, change the *-f* or *-fe* to *v* and add *-es*.

shelf/shelves   yourself/yourselves   wife/wives

EXCEPTIONS
roof/roofs   dwarf/dwarfs *or* dwarves
safe/safes   hoof/hoofs *or* hooves
                    scarf/scarfs *or* scarves

2   Irregular plurals

For irregular plurals and words that use the same form in both the singular and the plural, become familiar with the appropriate forms.

man/men	locus/loci	deer/deer
woman/women	alga/algae	sheep/sheep
child/children	basis/bases	moose/moose
foot/feet	alumna/alumnae	series/series
tooth/teeth	alumnus/alumni	species/species

3   Plurals of compound nouns

Form the plural of compound nouns written as one word by making the last part of the word plural.

streetcar/streetcars	bloodhound/bloodhounds
briefcase/briefcases	bookshelf/bookshelves

Compound words that are separated or hyphenated form plurals by making the most important part of the compound plural.

sister-in-law/sisters-in-law
lieutenant governor/lieutenant governors
leap year/leap years

EXERCISE 31–5   **Spelling Plural Nouns**

Form the plural of each of the following nouns.

1. mother-in-law
2. bride-to-be
3. cash
4. fish
5. speech
6. criterion
7. cupful
8. fox
9. crutch
10. turkey

31e   Spelling words with unstressed vowels and consonants

Although it is not a letter of the alphabet, the **schwa** is the most common sound in the English language. This sound is considered an unstressed vowel—an "uh" sound we make in many of the words we speak. Pronounce the following words and listen for the unstressed vowel.

acad[e]my	emph[a]sis	mir[a]cle
hist[o]ry	wom[a]n	sent[e]nce
hum[a]n	comp[e]tent	

The schwa is designated by an upside-down *e* (ə). You can find the schwa in the pronunciation key of your dictionary.

It is not always easy to remember whether *definate* or *definite* is the correct spelling; whether *grammer* should be spelled *grammar* or which of *demacratic, demecratic,* or *democratic* is correct. To spell these words and others with an unstressed vowel or schwa, think of a related word in which the vowel is stressed. Let us take *deml]cratic* as an example. How do you know that the unstressed vowel should be *o* rather than *i* or *e*? Because in all likelihood you know that a related word, *democracy,* is spelled with an *o.* Likewise, you know that the word *hist[ ]ry* is spelled *history* and not *histery* because you know the related words *historian* and *historical,* in which the vowel *o* is stressed and easy to hear.

The four-step process outlined in the accompanying chart is also useful in helping determine how to spell words with a silent consonant: *condemn, malign, muscle,* and *sign.* Related to *condemn* is the word *condemnation;* related to *malign* is *malignant;* related to *muscle* is *muscular;* related to *sign, signal.*

A Strategy for Spelling Words with Unstressed Vowels

1. Isolate the unstressed vowel (the schwa) of the word you are trying to spell:
   cons[ ]lation
2. Think of a related word of a similar form:
   console
3. Isolate the stressed vowel that matches the schwa:
   cons[o]le
4. Substitute the stressed vowel in the related word(s) for the unstressed vowel of the word you are trying to spell:
   consolation

Here is a brief list of words with silent consonants.

aisle	indict	pneumonia
climb	knee	surprise
column	knight	thumb
foreign	paradigm	Wednesday

EXERCISE 31–6   Spelling Using the Schwa

For each of the following words, supply the missing vowel without checking the dictionary. Then compare your guess with the dictionary.

1. affirm_tive	6. rep_tition	11. auth_r	16. pres_dent
2. exist_nce	7. sed_tive	12. conserv_tory	17. narr_tive
3. friv_lous	8. gramm_r	13. med_cine	18. comp_rable
4. prec_dent	9. defin_te	14. hyp_crisy	19. not_riety
5. nutr_tive	10. ill_strate	15. monot_nous	20. des_lation

31f   Spelling words with the hyphen

Some compound words are spelled as single words *(birdsong)*, some are written as two words *(ice cream)*, and some are joined with a hyphen *(walk-on)*. When you are unsure of how to spell compound words, consult an up-to-date dictionary. Words such as *figurehead* and *benchmark*, now single words, were formerly hyphenated. The accompanying chart offers guidelines as to when you should use a hyphen to join compound words.

EXERCISE 31–7   Spelling Compound Words

Add hyphens only when appropriate in the following compound words. Use a dictionary to check your work.

1. home run hitter
2. dust buster
3. fifty five
4. U turn
5. governor elect

31g   Six steps to better spelling

Remember that the spellings and meanings of English words are always related, even though pronunciation may vary. Use meaning to guide your spelling efforts, but also follow these practical spelling tips.

1   Keep a list of your misspelled words

Compile a list of all the misspelled words you find when you edit or proofread your writing. You can set up a three-column list, with misspellings

---

When to Hyphenate Compound Words

- When two or more words serve as a single modifier before a noun:
  He is a *well-respected* dancer.
  We filed an *out-of-state* tax return.
- But not when the modifier occurs after the noun:
  As a dancer, he is *well respected*.
- When a compound adjective appears as part of a series:
  They were due in at either *eight-* or *nine-o'clock*.
- With fractions:
  one-fourth
- With whole numbers between *twenty-one* and *ninety-nine*.
- With coined compounds (words not ordinarily linked):
  She gave me an *over-the-shoulder* smile.
- When attaching prefixes to words beginning with a capital letter:
  They were accused of being *un-American*.
  It was to be a conference on *non-Eurocentric* issues.
- When attaching suffixes to capital letters:
  the *A*-train

---

in the first column, correct spellings in the second, and notes about how you can remember to spell the words correctly in the third.

MISSPELLED	CORRECT	NOTES
recieve	receive	*ie/ei* rule (31c-1)
offerring	offering	no double consonant (31c-6)
enterance	entrance	pronunciation problem (check dictionary)
allusion	illusion	homonyms confused (31b)

Analyze your list to see if patterns of misspelling occur. Try to discover why those words give you trouble. It may be because you are mispronouncing a word—for example, *Febuary* instead of *February* or *nucular* instead of *nuclear*. It may be that you associate one word with another that is spelled differently—for example, *affect* instead of *effect*.

2 Develop the habit of observing words

Develop your visual memory of how words look as well as your aural memory of how words sound. Try to create a mental picture of the word. Also try to use some memory aids or mnemonic devices, and write the words out for practice. Writing and speaking the words correctly will help you remember how to spell them.

WORDS	VISUAL AND MEMORY CUES
discernment	*Discern* contains an *n;* so does *discernment.*
separate	Two *e*'s surround two *a*'s.
metropolis	*Metropolis* is composed of two *o* words: metro and polis.

The more you read, the more opportunities you will have to see how words are spelled. Reading is a key not only to better spelling, but also to an enriched vocabulary (see Chapter 30), and a mind stocked with ideas and information (see Chapters 2, 3, and 4).

3   Use your dictionary

Keep your dictionary handy when you are studying and writing. Rather than looking up every word as you write, jot down, circle, or underline words whose spellings you want to check. Look them up at a designated time—at the end of your writing period or on the hour, for example.

You can also keep a list of words you misspell in the front of your dictionary. This will help you determine if you continue to have trouble with certain words.

4   Edit and proofread your writing carefully

Sometimes misspellings occur because of carelessness. Give yourself enough time to edit your writing and additional time to proofread it for typographical errors, omitted letters, and other mistakes.

Avoid doing your final proofreading on a computer screen. Ideally, you should do a preliminary editing and proofreading job while you are working on the computer. After printing out a copy, edit and proofread once more, before making final corrections on the computer and printing out your final copy. (See 1i on editing and proofreading and Chapter 50 on writing with the computer.)

5   Use a spell checker with caution

If your word processor has a spell checker that you use regularly, remember that the spell checker will not catch all misspelled words. A spell checker can certainly help, but it cannot find incorrectly chosen words. If you type *their* when you mean *there,* for example, your spell checker will not indicate that mistake. Nor will it be able to recognize most misspelled proper names or foreign words—unless you add such words to the spell checker's dictionary.

But do use your spell checker; take advantage of the misspellings it can help you catch and correct. However, always proofread your spelling carefully on your own. Also, get in the habit of looking up in your dictionary not only the spelling, but also the meanings of words.

6   Study lists of spelling words

Make a list of your own special spelling demons and familiarize yourself with the charts in this chapter. Put a check mark next to each word you often misspell, and then use the advice and techniques presented in this chapter to master the spellings of those words.

Frequently Misspelled Words

absence	entirely	manageable	sergeant
accessible	especially	miniature	similar
accommodate	exceed	mirror	sophomore
acknowledge	existence	morale	strict
address	extremely	necessary	supersede
aggravate	fascinate	niece	surely
amateur	foreign	nuisance	suspicious
angel	friend	occasion	technical
ascend	gauge	opportunity	thorough
athlete	ghost	parallel	tragedy
bargain	grief	perceive	tyranny
believe	harass	persistence	unanimous
bureaucracy	humorous	pleasant	undoubtedly
cemetery	hypocrite	prairie	usually
column	immediately	preferred	variety
committee	incidentally	prejudice	vegetable
conceive	independence	privilege	verbal
controversial	initiate	prominent	versus
courteous	intelligence	quiet	villain
deceive	irrelevant	receipt	visible
descendant	island	relief	vulnerable
develop	jeopardy	reminisce	warrant
disastrous	knowledge	repetition	whale
discipline	leisure	resistance	wholly
doctor	library	ridiculous	woman
efficient	lightning	sacrifice	wreak
embarrass	magazine	schedule	writing

Punctuation and Mechanics

Conventions of Punctuation and Mechanics

Punctuation and mechanics contribute to the clarity of good writing. Just as we use pauses, gestures, stress, and pitch to "punctuate" our speech, we use spaces and symbols to help our readers understand our written communication. Punctuation involves a system of rules and conventions that writers need to know and that readers expect to be observed. Although these rules and conventions have changed over the centuries, we need to learn the conventions that apply in the academic and professional worlds of our own day.

Punctuation, however, involves more than rules and conventions. Punctuation helps us communicate clearly. It also helps us express our thoughts in cadenced or rhythmical prose. Commas slow sentences down, as in this sentence; semicolons break into them; and periods stop sentences completely. Other marks—dashes and parentheses among them—perform still other functions, such as interrupting the movement of a sentence. These punctuation marks and their functions are described in Chapters 32–37.

Mechanics, in theory, includes matters such as usage and spelling, as well as hyphenation and the use of italics. Essentially, mechanics refers to a set of conventions—how to abbreviate and when to capitalize, for example. Chapters 38–42 describe and illustrate when and how to use capital letters, italics, abbreviations, numbers, and hyphens.

Observing the conventions of punctuation and mechanics makes your writing correct. Using them accurately is also a courtesy to your readers.

CHAPTER 32

End Punctuation

The period, question mark, and exclamation point indicate where one sentence ends and another begins. All three marks are thus considered **end punctuation** (or terminal punctuation) marks. More often than not you will punctuate the end of a sentence with a period, but you have some choice between using a period, a question mark, or an exclamation point.

32a Using the period

Use a period (.) to end a sentence that makes a statement or gives a mild command.

STATEMENTS	The day was unlike any she had ever experienced.
	These are the times that try our souls.
MILD COMMANDS	Let your imagination soar.
	Give me my arrows of desire.

Use a period for an indirect question, which implies a question rather than asks it directly.

INDIRECT QUESTION	I have often wondered why some people learn languages easily.
INDIRECT QUESTION	Students often ask what it takes to earn an *A*.

Most abbreviations take periods. Note, however, that the abbreviations in the last two columns of the following list may be written with or without periods. Whichever style you adopt, make sure you use it consistently. If you are not sure how to punctuate an abbreviation, look it up in your dictionary.

Mr.	i.e.	B.A. (or BA)	A.D. (or AD)
Mrs.	e.g.	M.A. (or MA)	B.C.E. (or BCE)
Ms.	etc.	Ph.D. (or PhD)	U.S.S.R. (or USSR)
Rev.	a.m.	M.D. (or MD)	U.K. (or UK)
Dr.	p.m.	J.D. (or JD)	U.S.A. (or USA)

USAGE NOTE   Strictly speaking, *Ms.* is not an abbreviation. Some authorities, therefore, advocate that *Ms* be written without a period. However, we use a period for the following reasons: (1) *Ms.* is modeled on the abbreviations *Mr.* and *Mrs.*; (2) the name of an influential magazine carries the title *Ms.* Readers will expect a period after the abbreviation *Ms.* (Do not confuse this abbreviation with the lowercased one for a manuscript—*ms.*)

Do not include periods when using the postal abbreviations for states.

    FL   TN   CA

However, you can write either Washington, DC or Washington, D.C.

Do not use a period when abbreviating names of organizations, companies, and agencies: *NAACP* (National Association for the Advancement of Colored People), *EPA* (Environmental Protection Agency), *CNN* (Cable News Network). **Acronyms**—abbreviations that are also pronounced as words—omit the period: *AIDS* (acquired immune deficiency syndrome), *NASA* (National Aeronautics and Space Administration), *NOW* (National Organization for Women). (See Chapter 40 for more on abbreviations.)

EXERCISE 32–1   **Using Periods in Abbreviations**

In each of the following sentences, insert periods in the abbreviations only where appropriate. Some sentences may be correct. Example:

> Mr Julio Rodriguez received an MBA.
> Mr. Julio Rodriguez received an M.B.A. (or MBA.)

1. OU has many students studying for their MA.
2. Some 1990 graduates earned both an Ed.D and a PhD.
3. Senator Smith has an L.LD.
4. The APA held its annual meeting in Brooklyn, NY.
5. I.B.M. is the familiar abbreviation for International Business Machines.

32b   Using the question mark

The question mark (?) is used most often after direct questions. Direct questions often begin with an interrogative word (*who, what, when, why, how*); they usually involve inverted word order.

> When is the question mark used?
> Where have all the flowers gone?

It is drizzling, is it not?

Do you understand this rule?

Indirect questions are followed by a period rather than a question mark: *I often wondered when a question mark should be used.* The word order in an indirect quotation is not inverted.

We never did find out where all the flowers went.

Question marks may be used within sentences to indicate questions in a series.

I had trouble resolving a number of questions: who would come on the trip? what would our itinerary be? how long would we remain abroad?

You can also punctuate such questions as complete independent sentences.

I had trouble resolving a number of questions. Who would come on the trip? What would our itinerary be? How long would we remain abroad?

Both methods are grammatically correct. Notice, however, that the single-sentence version creates a more swiftly moving sentence. Using capital letters to begin new sentences slows down the pace. Use the method that best serves your purpose.

The question mark can also be used to express uncertainty about a date, number, or word.

Geoffrey Chaucer, 1343(?)–1400, author of the *Canterbury Tales,* held a number of court appointments, including collector of taxes.

Do not use a question mark to indicate uncertainty about an event.

INCORRECT   It will snow (?) over the weekend.

CORRECT   It might snow over the weekend.

In punctuating questions that include quotations, place the question mark before the closing quotation marks when the question is part of the quotation. Do not use a comma or period after a question mark.

FAULTY   The most frequently asked question is "When are we paid?".

REVISED   The most frequently asked question is "When are we paid?"

When the question is not part of the quotation, however, place the question mark after the closing quotation marks.

Who was it that said, "Cut these words and they bleed"?

Do you agree that "it takes a thief to catch a thief"?

(For more on punctuating questions with quotation marks, see 36i-3.)

EXERCISE 32–2 Using the Question Mark

Revise the following sentences by adding or deleting question marks, or by substituting other punctuation marks as appropriate. Example:

> He asked his sister, "Why do you spend so long in the bathroom."
> He asked his sister, "Why do you spend so long in the bathroom?"

1. The coach asked, "Who missed the practice."
2. Is it true that the proposal will save the company money.
3. "May I use this?," asked Priscilla.
4. They all looked at me and asked me why I had come.
5. Some questions remained: Who would go, when would they leave, and how long would they be gone.

32c Using the exclamation point

Use the exclamation point (!) to indicate surprise or strong emotion. You can also use the exclamation point to give a command.

Help!   What a gifted comedian she is!

Oh no!   On your marks! Get set! Go!

Do not use a period or a comma after an exclamation point in direct quotation.

FAULTY   He exclaimed, "I can't believe what I'm hearing!".

REVISED   He exclaimed, "I can't believe what I'm hearing!"

Exclamations are more likely to occur in speech, where we can use our voices to indicate the emotion. They usually do not work as well in writing. Use exclamation points sparingly in academic writing, for they can be distracting. They also tend to exaggerate the importance of a point by calling too much attention to it. (Exclamation points shout!)

Overreliance on the exclamation point results, ironically, in a lack of emphasis. To create emphasis, choose your words carefully (see Chapter 28) and construct your sentences to highlight important points (see 26a). As Lewis Thomas once noted, "If a sentence really has something of importance to say, something quite remarkable, it doesn't need a mark to point it out."

EXERCISE 32–3   **Revising Direct and Indirect Questions**

Convert the following direction questions to indirect questions and the indirect questions to direct ones. Example:

> He asked whether we had a good time.
> He asked, "Did we have a good time?"

1. They asked whether justice had been done.
2. Is it always necessary to end a sentence with a mark of end punctuation?
3. Was it a good idea or a bad one?
4. What an extraordinary acrobat!
5. Will you please hurry up!

EXERCISE 32–4   **Deciding on Terminal Punctuation**

Insert the correct end punctuation mark in each of the following statements.

1. You were the only one to receive a perfect score
2. Will you please, please, please, please stop talking
3. The answer to the question is not easily found
4. Do you agree that "It's not over till it's over"
5. Was it U. S. Grant or W. T. Sherman who said "War is hell"

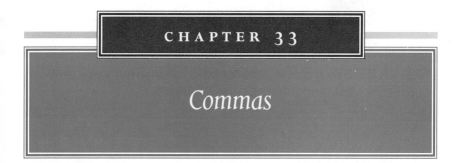

CHAPTER 33

Commas

Unlike end punctuation (see Chapter 32), commas (,) slow down a sentence rather than end it. One function of the comma, then, is to direct the rhythm of the sentence. Writers use commas to pace their writing, to enable readers to feel its pulse, to suggest when they can pause. In fact, commas can be heard as slight pauses in a sentence.

Commas also help writers make their meaning clear. To some extent commas help guide a reader's understanding, in part by separating the grammatical parts of sentences from each other. Clauses or phrases, for example, can be set off from the rest of a sentence with commas. The accompanying chart identifies the uses of the comma covered in this chapter.

Uses of the Comma

- To separate main clauses linked by a coordinating conjunction (33a)
- To separate introductory words and phrases from the main clause of a sentence (33b)
- To set off nonrestrictive elements (33c)
- To separate items in a series (33d)
- To separate coordinate adjectives (33e)
- To set off transitional and parenthetical elements (33f)
- To set off absolute phrases (33g)
- To set off contrasting elements, *yes* and *no,* tag questions, and mild interjections (33h)
- To set off dates, addresses, places, titles, and numbers (33i)
- To set off quotations (33j)
- To aid comprehension (33k)

33a   Use a comma before a coordinating conjunction that links independent clauses

Use a comma to separate two independent clauses when the second clause is preceded by a coordinating conjunction (*and, but, or, nor, for, so, yet*). An independent clause includes a subject and predicate but no introductory subordinating conjunction (see 10d). The comma signals the end of one independent thought and the beginning of the next.

She encouraged him, *and* her support gave him the impetus to continue.

It was not the best of possible outcomes, *but* it was not the worst.

The flowers must be watered this weekend, *or* they will die.

The forces of repression have reasserted themselves, *yet* the people's thirst for freedom has not been quenched.

USAGE NOTE   Although a comma usually precedes a coordinating conjunction that joins independent clauses, use a semicolon to join long clauses that contain internal commas. (See Chapter 34.)

People around the country, though generally satisfied with the verdict, were disappointed with the punishment the judge meted out; *yet* they did not erupt into violence, remaining calm and orderly instead, throughout the long holiday weekend.

You can omit the comma before the coordinating conjunction when the clauses are short and closely related in meaning.

My heart leapt up and I ran to her.

I played well but I could not win.

Always use a comma if a sentence would be confusing without it.

CONFUSING   Watson had to be prepared for Holmes had many questions.

REVISED   Watson had to be prepared, for Holmes had many questions.

Always use a comma and a coordinating conjunction between independent clauses. Using only a comma results in a comma splice, a type of run-on sentence error (see 18d).

EXERCISE 33–1   Punctuating Linked Independent Clauses

Add commas and/or coordinating conjunctions where necessary in the following sentences. Example:

We would have gone home for the reunion but we had to work.
We would have gone home for the reunion, but we had to work.

1. They circled the arena three times and they ran as if possessed.
2. I found the videocassette of the concert and I also found a good audiotape.
3. Changes would have to be made in the way the vote was to be recorded or the results of the balloting could not be considered reliable.
4. Some say that college athletic scholarships should be abolished but others argue for continuing to provide them.
5. Skiers should use only reliable equipment and they should be sure to keep it in good condition.

33b Use a comma to set off introductory elements

Use a comma to follow an introductory word, expression, phrase, or clause. Introductory elements include adverbs (13a); conjunctive adverbs (14c-4); transitional expressions (33f); adverb clauses (10d); and participles, infinitives, and various kinds of phrases (10c).

Fortunately, the rain stopped and the tennis match began. [adverb]

Moreover, it was a very lucrative offer. [conjunctive adverb]

On the other hand, you may be right. [transitional expression]

After suffering through an uneventful opening week, the play became the most popular of the season. [adverb clause]

Overjoyed, he leaped into the air. [participle]

In a reversal of opinion, the chair voted for the plan. [prepositional phrase]

Her decision made, Joy dropped the letter in the mailbox. [absolute phrase]

Carrying his new fishing rod, Juan headed for the lake. [participial phrase]

To justify his decisions, the president went on national TV. [infinitive phrase]

The participial and infinitive phrases in the preceding examples are used as modifiers. When they are used as subjects, however, these and other verbals are not followed by a comma.

Carrying his new fishing rod was a proud moment for Juan.

To justify his decisions is the president's first responsibility.

You may omit the comma after short introductory elements if doing so does not cause confusion.

CLEAR	By the end of the term you should have written six essays.
CLEAR	After class we should meet for lunch.
CONFUSING	By thirty-five careers of professional ballplayers are often over.
REVISED	By thirty-five, careers of professional ballplayers are often over.

EXERCISE 33–2   **Punctuating Introductory Elements**

Insert commas after the introductory elements where necessary in the following sentences. Example:

> After the Oscars had been awarded ticket sales of the winning films increased dramatically.

> After the Oscars had been awarded, ticket sales of the winning films increased dramatically.

1. Clearly this would not be an easy task.
2. Bodies tensed for the jolt the wrestlers collided.
3. As with other college applications this one required a personal statement.
4. Unless you have decided on a career you should consider majoring in liberal arts or in one of the sciences.
5. To prepare for an exam you should devise a series of study strategies.

 33c   Use commas to set off nonrestrictive elements

Words, phrases, and clauses that constitute **restrictive elements** of a sentence limit the meaning of the words they modify and are not set off from the main clause of the sentence with commas. **Nonrestrictive elements,** which do not limit the meaning of the words they modify, are set off from the main clause of a sentence with commas.

| RESTRICTIVE | Professional athletes *who perform exceptionally* deserve their high salaries. |
| NONRESTRICTIVE | Bobby Bonds, *who led the league in home runs and batting average*, deserves his high salary. |

In the first example, the clause *who perform exceptionally* is essential to the meaning of the sentence since it modifies, or restricts, *professional athletes*. The modifying clause is thus not set off by commas. In the second example, the clause *who led the league in home runs and batting average* does not limit the noun it modifies, *Bobby Bonds*. Instead, it provides additional information about him. It is therefore nonrestrictive and is set off with commas. Restrictive elements, especially clauses and participial phrases, usually identify the noun they modify: *who perform exceptionally* identifies which athletes deserve high salaries. The clause modifying the noun *Bobby Bonds* does not identify or restrict the noun to a greater degree.

Sometimes a modifying element can be interpreted as either restrictive or nonrestrictive. Your use of commas, or no commas, will tell the reader what you intend. Consider how the punctuation changes the meaning of the following sentence.

The houses, needing a coat of paint, were given one.

The houses needing a coat of paint were given one.

The first sentence suggests that all the houses needed a coat of paint. The second sentence implies that only some houses needed a coat of paint.

WRITING HINT   You can decide whether to set off an element with commas by imagining your sentence without the words in question. If the words can be deleted without altering the meaning of the sentence or without confusing its meaning, they are nonrestrictive and should be set off with commas. If they cannot be deleted without altering sentence meaning, they are restrictive and should not be set off with commas.

> The major computer manufacturers, which have been battling for control of the U.S. market, have begun a series of joint ventures. [The clause *which have been battling for control of the U.S. market* adds incidental information about the major computer manufacturers but does not identify them. Removing the clause would not change the basic meaning of the sentence; the clause is nonrestrictive.]

> The companies that stand to lose the most are manufacturers of software. [The clause *that stand to lose the most* defines which companies are being talked about. Removing the clause would make the sentence almost meaningless; the clause is therefore restrictive and should not be separated by commas.]

1   Nonrestrictive adjective and adverb clauses

A clause that functions as an adjective or an adverb in a sentence can be either restrictive or nonrestrictive. Only nonrestrictive clauses are set off with commas.

NONRESTRICTIVE CLAUSES

The American political system, *although it has faults,* remains one of the finest in the world. [The clause is not necessary to the meaning of the independent clause and is therefore nonrestrictive.]

I borrow books from my local public library, *which has a splendid collection of material on animals.* [The clause is not essential to the meaning of the independent clause and is thus set off with a comma.]

RESTRICTIVE CLAUSES

They visited a place *where their ancestors first settled in America*. [The clause restricts the meaning of *a place*. Without the clause the reader does not know which place was visited.]

Every approach *that the group thought reasonable* was tried. [The clause restricts the meaning of *Every approach*. Dropping the clause would change the meaning of the sentence.]

WRITING HINT   When you write sentences that include relative clauses, use *that* only for restrictive clauses. Some writers use *which* for both restrictive and nonrestrictive clauses, although many prefer to use *which* only for nonrestrictive clauses.

2   Nonrestrictive phrases

Both participial and prepositional phrases can be either restrictive or nonrestrictive, though prepositional phrases are usually used restrictively.

NONRESTRICTIVE PHRASES

Nicole and Pierre, *pleased with their first game,* decided to play another.

Marilyn Monroe, *even with all the adulation she received,* was unhappy.

RESTRICTIVE PHRASES

Money received *as a gift* is not as special as money earned.

The tray *for the dessert* is on the top shelf.

3   Nonrestrictive appositives

An **appositive** is a noun or noun substitute that replaces another noun or noun substitute by renaming it. Those appositives that are nonessential to the meaning of what they rename are set off with commas.

NONRESTRICTIVE APPOSITIVES

Raymond Carver, *one of contemporary America's best short-story writers,* never published a novel.

Michelangelo's *David, a sculpture carved from an enormous block of Carrera marble,* is approximately eighteen feet high.

Restrictive appositives are usually proper nouns of one or two words. A restrictive appositive usually comes right after a common noun and identifies which person, place, or thing is being described.

RESTRICTIVE APPOSITIVES

The American writer *Ernest Hemingway* once remarked that all of modern American literature derived from Mark Twain's *The Adventures of Huckleberry Finn*. [*Ernest Hemingway* identifies which American writer made the remark.]

Michael Jackson's album *Thriller* remains his best seller. [*Thriller* identifies which album.]

EXERCISE 33–3 Punctuating with Nonrestrictive Elements

Identify the restrictive and nonrestrictive clauses, phrases, and appositives in the following sentences. Add commas to set off the nonrestrictive elements where necessary. Example:

Marie Curie a French scientist discovered radium.
Marie Curie, a French scientist, discovered radium.

1. The enormous oak with the diseased branch was scheduled for surgery.
2. Fileting is a technique that eliminates the bones from meat and fish.
3. Rudy is looking forward to the day when he can retire.
4. The finest American red wines are made from the cabernet grape which grows well in California.
5. The Colorado Rockies a Denver franchise are a recent addition to baseball's National League.

33d Use commas between items in a series

Use commas to separate items in a series of three or more words, phrases, or clauses.

He didn't know whether the car was a Ford, a Buick, or a Chevrolet.

To read, to write, to think—all are necessary for academic success.

In a moment, without haste, but against his better judgment, he made the desperate leap.

If the time is right, if the place seems suitable, and if the occasion warrants it, make your move.

USAGE NOTE Some writers, particularly journalists, omit the comma before the next-to-last item in a series (the one before the coordinating conjunction).

Gertie ordered tomato juice, pancakes and coffee with cream.

However, in academic and other writing, the final comma in a series helps keep the meaning clear.

UNCLEAR Gertie ordered tomato juice, pancakes, bacon and eggs and coffee with cream. [Did she order four or five items?]

CLEAR Gertie ordered tomato juice, pancakes, bacon and eggs, and coffee with cream.

When one or more items in a series contains commas, separate the items with semicolons rather than with commas (see 34c).

We brought an apple pie; lemonade; and red, white, and blue streamers to the party.

33e Use commas to separate coordinate adjectives

In using **coordinate adjectives** (two adjectives that modify the same noun or pronoun) separate them with a coordinating conjunction or with commas.

Beds of colorful and long-stemmed flowers adorned the yard.

Beds of colorful, long-stemmed flowers adorned the yard.

Do not, however, use both a comma and a coordinate conjunction to separate coordinate adjectives.

INCORRECT Beds of colorful, and long-stemmed flowers adorned the yard.

In cases where the adjectives are *cumulative* rather than coordinate, do not use commas. Adjectives are *cumulative* when the one nearer the noun is more closely related to the noun in meaning.

COORDINATE The job required careful, patient, methodical work. [Each adjective individually modifies the noun *work*.]

COORDINATE The warm, quiet, fragrant evening put me to sleep. [Each adjective independently modifies the noun *evening*.]

CUMULATIVE The dark blue fabric appealed to them. [No comma is needed because *dark* modifies *blue* and *blue* modifies *fabric*.]

CUMULATIVE When she travels, she likes to read fast-paced science fiction novels. [The compound adjective *fast-paced* modifies *science fiction*, and *science fiction* modifies *novels*.]

To check whether you should use commas between adjectives, try putting the word *and* between them or rearranging the order of the adjectives. If you can do either of these things, you need commas between the adjectives.

Consider the previous examples and apply these tests.

EXAMPLE	The dark blue fabric appealed to them.
TEST I	The dark and blue fabric appealed to them. [Adding *and* confuses the meaning; the adjectives are cumulative.]
TEST II	The blue dark fabric appealed to them. [Putting *blue* before *dark* is confusing; *dark blue* makes more sense.]

These tests are not always reliable. (See Chapter 13 for more on adjectives.)

EXERCISE 33–4 **Punctuating Items in a Series**

Add or delete commas as necessary in the following sentences. Example:

Their favorite pastimes were reading exercising and eating out.
Their favorite pastimes were reading, exercising, and eating out.

1. The party was long loud and enjoyable.
2. Their goals were modest: to win a few games and to have some fun.
3. He was fashionably dressed in a double-breasted pin-striped suit, a starched pure white shirt with a colorful paisley tie and elegant black calfskin loafers.
4. The teachers assigned read and graded the many required papers.
5. We went to the hardware store for paint spackle rollers tray liners and brushes.

33f Use commas to set off transitional and parenthetical expressions

Transitional expressions include conjunctive adverbs (such as *therefore* and *however*) and other words and expressions used to join sentence elements. **Parenthetical expressions** add supplementary information or digressions and are not essential to the grammatical structure of the sentence. Both transitional and parenthetical expressions are set off from the main clause of the sentence with commas.

It was, in fact, an amazing discovery.

On the other hand, it should not have been so surprising.

Recent studies have suggested that diets that include red wine, surprisingly, and cheese, even more surprisingly, lower one's risk of heart disease.

33g Use commas to set off absolute phrases

An **absolute phrase** modifies an entire independent clause, rather than a particular word or group of words in the clause. An absolute phrase usually consists of a participle and its subject. Absolute phrases may occur anywhere in a sentence. Wherever they occur, they are always set off by commas.

The game being over, the fans headed for the exit ramps.

Her boyfriend, his ardor cooled by her icy demeanor, sat meekly in the rear.

EXERCISE 33–5 Punctuating Transitional and Parenthetical Expressions and Absolute Phrases

Insert commas where necessary in the following sentences. Example:

We went along though with some reservations with the plan.
We went along, though with some reservations, with the plan.

1. Stocks having plunged sharply investors waited cautiously before buying.
2. In the meantime preparations were being made for an offensive.
3. It was furthermore a time of great hope.
4. Their work done it was time to relax.
5. This period of change however also remained a time of continuity.

33h Use commas to set off contrasting elements, *yes* and *no*, direct address, and tag questions

Commas are used to set off contrasting elements, the words *yes* and *no*, expressions of direct address, and tag questions (short questions "tagged on" to statements you make in expressions of direct address).

CONTRASTING ELEMENTS

The boys were willing to work, though not all day long.

The children, not the adults, had the best roles.

YES AND *NO*

Yes, I do want to go to Martha's Vineyard.

No, that will not be an acceptable form of payment.

DIRECT ADDRESS

Friends, Romans, countrymen, lend me your ears.

Please hear me out, Howard.

TAG QUESTIONS

It was not a good movie, was it?

You don't have any aspirin, do you?

EXERCISE 33–6 **Punctuating Contrasting Elements, *yes* and *no*, Direct Address, and Tag Questions**

Insert commas where necessary in the following sentences. Example:

No it was not the best solution was it Bill?
No, it was not the best solution, was it, Bill?

1. We have to consider the long-range consequences not just the immediate payoff.
2. We were never really in the game were we?
3. Yes indeed this is the way a trip should go.
4. The world has become on the other hand a global village.
5. Do you really think Kim that this is the right decision?

Use commas with dates, addresses, place names, numbers, and titles

Use commas with dates, addresses, place names, and numbers. Use commas to separate personal and professional titles from the name before them.

DATES

Use a comma to separate the day of the month from the year. Also put a comma after the year, unless the year ends the sentence.

The book was published on August 30, 1994, though not released until January 1, 1995.

When dates appear in inverted order, as they often do in British usage, commas are unnecessary. Commas are not needed when a date contains only a month and year.

The book was published on 30 August 1994 and released four months later.

The United States entered the war in December 1941.

ADDRESSES AND PLACE NAMES

Use a comma after each part of a place name when written out in a sentence, but do not use a comma directly before or immediately after a ZIP code.

Dover, New Jersey, bears little resemblance to Dover, Delaware.

The address is Mr. D's Music Store, 14 Main Street, Columbus, Ohio 12345.

NUMBERS

Use commas in numbers of four or more digits.

The book has 3,662 pages.

More than 50,000 fans attended last night's free concert in the park.

Do not use a comma in a date, within street numbers, in telephone numbers, in Social Security numbers, or in ZIP codes.

We are fast approaching the year 2000.

Our previous address was 3119 Poe St., Berkeley, California 90123.

Please call me at 329-555-6572.

TITLES

Use a comma between a name and a title that follows the name. Also use a comma to separate a title from whatever follows it in a sentence. Note that the final period in a title is included before the comma.

Lucia Hernandez, Ph.D., is the youngest economist on the faculty.

Richard Kim, Jr., has been elected mayor.

EXERCISE 33–7 **Punctuating Dates, Addresses, Place Names, Titles, and Numbers**

Insert commas where needed in the following sentences. Example:

It is difficult to find a new car that costs less than $10000.
It is difficult to find a new car that costs less than *$10,000.*

1. Philip Weber M.D. is a graduate of Brown Medical School.
2. The town's population has gone over the 25000 mark.
3. Please send your remittance to 23875 Kissena Boulevard Flushing New York 01234.
4. The referendum was held in April 1994 and new elections were to follow on January 15 1995.
5. Participants are expected from Brussels Belgium and Anchorage Alaska.

33j   Use commas with quotations

Use commas to set off quotations from introductory words and from words that identify the source of the quotation. Always place commas before the quotation marks (see 36i-1).

Of Montaigne's essays Emerson said, "Cut these words and they bleed."

"Much madness is divinest sense," wrote Emily Dickinson in one of her best-known poems.

Do not use commas when explanatory words follow a quotation that ends in a question mark or an exclamation point (see 36i-3).

"How could this have happened?" she wondered.

"What an outrageous idea!" he exclaimed.

Commas are also unnecessary following a verb or when quotations are introduced by *that.*

Leo Tolstoy's novel *Anna Karenina* begins "All happy families are alike, but each unhappy family is unhappy in its own way."

John Donne wrote that "no man is an island."

When using an indirect quotation, one that does not repeat a speaker's exact words, do not use a comma.

Olive Schreiner declared that if women ran governments, wars would be eliminated.

Montaigne says that he knows no one as well as he knows himself.

EXERCISE 33–8   Using Commas with Quotations

Insert or delete commas as needed in the following sentences. Example:

Who said "Boredom is the root of all evil"?
Who said, "Boredom is the root of all evil"?

1. Einstein once remarked "God does not play dice with the universe."
2. What do you think Portia means when she says that "The quality of mercy is not strained?"
3. "The world will little note, nor long remember, what we say here" said Abraham Lincoln in his Gettysburg Address.
4. "Where can I find the registrar's office?", she inquired.
5. Jason asked if we wanted to go to the lake with him.

33k Use commas to aid comprehension

You may need to use a comma for no other reason than to prevent confusion or misunderstanding.

CONFUSING   Before the game finished the players were celebrating.

REVISED   Before the game finished, the players were celebrating.

CONFUSING   Of twenty five experienced difficulty solving the problem.

REVISED   Of twenty, five experienced difficulty solving the problem.

EXERCISE 33–9   Using Commas to Avoid Confusion

Insert commas where needed in the following sentences. Example:

For Gloria Joan was a role model.
For Gloria, Joan was a role model.

1. Unlike Harvard Yale requires no expository writing course.
2. For many flowers are nothing more than pollen sources.
3. Even when they are tired bus drivers need to remain alert and courteous.
4. Those who can do.
5. In grade school subjects are required.

EXERCISE 33–10   Using Commas to Alter Meaning

Explain how the meaning of the following sentences is changed when the commas are deleted.

1. Harold saw Tanya when he arrived, and blushed.
2. The book includes comments from writers Al Hart and Jim Seal, bartenders, and former alcoholics.
3. No, stopping is advised.
4. The Browns' daughter, Janice, majored in engineering.
5. The film was shown in places such as Phoenix and Sacramento, little towns, and villages.

331   Avoid using unnecessary commas

Commas used unnecessarily can distract or confuse readers. They can also inhibit fluency in writing.

1   Omit commas between subjects and verbs, verbs and objects or complements, and prepositions and their objects

Needless commas cause confusion and disrupt the flow of the sentence.

UNNECESSARY	The jubilant crowd, welcomed the victorious home team. [comma separates subject and verb]
REVISED	The jubilant crowd welcomed the victorious home team.
UNNECESSARY	We had decided, to agree on the plan despite our reservations about, one of its major objectives. [comma separates verb and object; comma separates preposition and object]
REVISED	We had decided to agree on the plan despite our reservations about one of its major objectives.

2   Omit commas around restrictive elements

Do not use commas to set off elements that restrict or limit the meaning of the words they refer to (see 33c).

UNNECESSARY	Jane Austen's novel, *Pride and Prejudice*, is a classic. [The commas suggest, incorrectly, that Austen wrote only one novel.]
REVISED	Jane Austen's novel *Pride and Prejudice* is a classic.
UNNECESSARY	The props, that the director used, were clever.
REVISED	The props that the director used were clever.
UNNECESSARY	The prohibition, against smoking, is strictly enforced.
REVISED	The prohibition against smoking is strictly enforced.

3   Omit commas in compound constructions

Do not use a comma before or after a coordinating conjunction that joins two words, phrases, or clauses of a compound construction.

UNNECESSARY	We should eat quickly, and get ready to leave.
REVISED	We should eat quickly and get ready to leave. [compound verb]
UNNECESSARY	We saw the bikers race down the hill, and around the pond.
REVISED	We saw the bikers race down the hill and around the pond. [compound prepositional phrases]
UNNECESSARY	They want an increase in course offerings, and a decrease in class size.
REVISED	They want an increase in course offerings and a decrease in class size. [compound direct objects]

4   Omit commas before the first and last items in a series

Although you need commas between the items in a series, you do not need them before the first and last items.

UNNECESSARY	The film included, action, sentiment, and humor.
REVISED	The film included action, sentiment, and humor.
UNNECESSARY	Swimming, tennis, and cycling, were their favorite sports.
REVISED	Swimming, tennis, and cycling were their favorite sports.

Always check your sentences for missing or unnecessary commas. You can use the accompanying checklist to familiarize yourself with the most frequent uses of the comma.

EXERCISE 33–11   Omitting Needless Commas

Eliminate unnecessary commas from the following sentences. Example:

The quilt, that lay on the antique bed, was made by her grandmother.
The quilt that lay on the antique bed was made by her grandmother.

1. At the beginning, and the end of the race a gong is sounded.
2. They said, that there would be plenty of opportunity for advancement.
3. Shakespeare's play, *Hamlet,* is his most famous.
4. The study showed, that some diets can be harmful to one's health.
5. The cross-country skier took long, smooth, strides over the snow.

Using Commas

- Use commas to separate independent clauses in compound sentences (33a).
  We may be too tired to study, but we are not too tired to go dancing.
- Place commas after introductory elements (33b).
  In fact, there was no rain that summer.
- Place commas before and after nonrestrictive elements (33c).
  The entire cast, including the children, performed magnificently.
- Use commas between items in a series (33d).
  He spoke of blood, sweat, and tears.
- Use commas with transitions and parenthetical expressions (33f).
  However, the Romans excelled equally in civil engineering.
  The winner, as some expected, was Bill Clinton.
- Use commas to separate quotations from their identifying phrases (33j).
  "No one," he advised, "should underestimate the power of an opponent."

EXERCISE 33–12　Using Commas

Insert commas where appropriate in the following passage.

> The commas are the most useful and usable of all the stops. It is highly important to put them in place as you go along. If you try to come back after doing a paragraph and stick them in the various spots that tempt you you will discover that they tend to swarm like minnows into all sorts of crevices whose existence you hadn't realized and before you know it the whole long sentence becomes immobilized and lashed up squirming in commas. Better to use them sparingly and with affection precisely when the need for each one arises nicely by itself.
>
> —Lewis Thomas, "Notes on Punctuation"

EXERCISE 33–13　Checking for Commas

Review one of your papers for its use of commas. Use the charts at the beginning and end of this chapter for guidance. Be alert for both missing commas and for unnecessary commas.

CHAPTER 34

Semicolons and Colons

*I*t is important to learn to distinguish between the semicolon and the colon. Use the *semicolon* to indicate a stop; use the *colon* to signal an addition or to create a sense of expectation.

In some cases both marks of punctuation may be grammatically correct or rhetorically effective. It will be up to you to choose the effect you wish to create with a colon or semicolon.

> We wanted to visit our friends; bad weather, however, forced us to postpone our plans.

> We hoped to see our friends soon: our plans were to visit them the very next day.

Refer to the accompanying chart for a summary of when to use a semicolon and colon.

Using the Semicolon and the Colon

SEMICOLON
- To signal a close link between the ideas in independent clauses (34a–b)
- To separate clauses linked by a conjunctive adverb (34b)
- To separate independent clauses that contain commas (34c)
- To separate long items in a series (34d)

COLON
- To introduce a statement that summarizes, amplifies, or explains a statement made in an independent clause (34f)
- To introduce a list (34g)
- To introduce a long or a formal quotation (34h)
- To introduce appositives (34i)

(continued)

- To separate a book's title from its subtitle (34j)
- To follow the salutation of a letter (34j)
- To follow the headings in a memo (34j)
- To separate hours from minutes (34j)
- To separate chapter from verse in Bible references (34j)

Semicolons

Semicolons (;) are used to separate sentence elements, usually independent clauses; they are also used to separate items in a series when those items contain commas; and they are used between clauses linked with a conjunctive adverb. The pause indicated by a semicolon is shorter than a period's full stop but longer than the breathing space of a comma.

34a   Use semicolons to signal a close relationship between independent clauses

When you write sentences with closely related independent clauses, use a semicolon between them to signal that relationship. In the following example, the relationship is close because the second clause explains the first.

I refused the prize; I thought the contest rules were unfair.

You may write sentences in which one clause restates another or in which an independent clause expands upon or contrasts another. You may use a semicolon instead of a comma and conjunction when the phrasing in the clauses is balanced.

RESTATEMENT	The semicolon indicates something more is coming; the sentence is not yet finished.
EXPANSION	To earn an *A* in a lab science course, you have to pay the price; that price typically includes many hours performing laboratory experiments.
CONTRAST	The Red Sox have strong pitching and weak hitting; the Mariners have strong hitting and weak pitching.

BALANCE   If you can begin to work on a difficult project, you can build momentum to continue it; if you can sustain your momentum, you will be likely to complete it.

The following example includes two additional clauses that expand the initial independent clause.

She had come in steerage; she knew not a word of English when she stepped off the horsecar into Madison Street; she was one of the innumerable unsleeping aliens.

—Cynthia Ozick, "The Question of Our Speech"

USAGE NOTE   A comma can be used between short independent clauses not joined by a coordinating conjunction. But a semicolon is also correct.

His round face was mournful, his shoulders slumped, his belly sagged.

—Tom Wicker, *A Time to Die*

The train gathered speed; the brakes squeaked; it lurched and stopped.

—Paul Theroux, *The Great Railway Bazaar*

A comma is used between balanced clauses that make a comparison.

The more they earned, the less they saved.

The sooner we start, the better we will feel.

34b   Use semicolons between independent clauses linked with a conjunctive adverb or a transitional phrase

Independent clauses joined by conjunctive adverbs (see 14c-4), such as *however, therefore,* or *moreover,* require a semicolon between them.

They expected the concert to be boring; *however,* they found it completely engaging.

I have been overcharged for these items; *therefore,* I am entitled to a refund.

They will be here on time; *moreover,* they will arrive ready to work.

A semicolon is also required between independent clauses that are linked by a transitional phrase, such as *after all, as a result, at any rate, even so, for example, in fact,* or *on the other hand.*

The president's approval rating dropped ten points; *as a result,* the White House stepped up its media blitz.

The birthrate on soap operas is eight times higher than the U.S. birthrate; *in fact,* it's higher than the birthrate of any developing nation in the world.

USAGE NOTE   Be careful not to punctuate conjunctive adverbs and transitional phrases that come at the beginning of independent clauses with a comma before and after. Use commas before and after conjunctive adverbs and transitional phrases only when they occur later in the clause.

They expected the concert to be boring; they found it, *however,* completely engaging.

I have been overcharged for these items; I am entitled, *therefore,* to a refund.

As you can see, conjunctive adverbs and transitional expressions are movable and thus do not carry the full impact of a connector—which is why you need a semicolon between the independent clauses.

34c   Use semicolons to separate long and complex independent clauses and those that contain commas

The use of semicolons makes the long sentence in the following example easy to follow. The ideas are closely related and therefore belong in one sentence; however, the clauses are long and somewhat complicated.

He was not a young man when we were growing up and he had already suffered many kinds of ruin; in his outrageously demanding and protective way he loved his children, who were black like him, and menaced like him; and all these things sometimes showed in his face when he tried, never to my knowledge with much success, to establish contact with any of us.

—James Baldwin, "Notes of a Native Son"

34d   Use semicolons to separate items in a series

You most often separate items in a series with commas (see 33d). However, when the items contain commas or other punctuation, using semicolons to separate them will make your sentences clearer to readers.

The course objectives included understanding the beliefs of Confucianism, Buddhism, Islam, Judaism, and Christianity; appreciating the cultural values, attitudes, and assumptions associated with those beliefs; and recognizing the diverse ways the world's peoples acknowledge the divine.

Notice that all elements of the series are separated by semicolons even though the last one contains no commas. If any element of a series includes commas within it, all elements of that series must be separated by semicolons.

As an English major you can expect to read works of many different genres; to write different kinds of papers, including critical analyses and research essays based on your reading; and to present oral reports.

34e Avoid semicolon errors

1 Do not use semicolons to separate an independent clause from a phrase or from a dependent clause

INCORRECT The birds built a nest; which was protected by the roof.

REVISED The birds built a *nest, which* was protected by the roof.

INCORRECT In a corner of the yard, far from the house; grew an oak sapling the children planted.

REVISED In a corner of the yard, far from the *house, grew* an oak sapling the children planted.

2 Do not use semicolons to introduce a list or a series

Use a colon to introduce a series (see 34g).

INCORRECT The documentary described five kinds of intelligence; analytical, social, physical, verbal, and mathematical.

REVISED The documentary described five kinds of intelligence: analytical, social, physical, verbal, and mathematical.

3 Do not overuse semicolons

Too many semicolons can distract and confuse readers by contributing to choppy and unclear writing.

OVERUSED Their trip to Europe included visits to Paris, France; Rome, Italy; Madrid, Spain; and Berlin, Germany; their trip gave them a chance to make many new acquaintances and experience different customs; it also stimulated their interest in learning more about the countries they visited; in fact, upon returning they enrolled in courses in European languages and history.

REVISED Their trip to Europe included visits to Paris, Rome, Madrid, and Berlin. The trip gave them a chance to make many new acquaintances and experience different customs. It stimulated their interest in learning more about the countries they visited; in fact, upon returning they enrolled in courses in European languages and history.

Notice how the revised version replaces some semicolons with periods, thus creating separate sentences. You should revise overuse of the semicolon in this way.

EXERCISE 34–1   **Punctuating Independent Clauses with the Semicolon**

Insert semicolons where necessary in the following sentences. Example:

> A few companies did well most others did not.
> A few companies did well; most others did not.

1. Many small computer companies have been going out of business they are simply unable to survive the drastic price wars.
2. The companies that have survived so far make a superior product they also offer outstanding service.
3. Some of these companies, such as Dell and Compaq, have grown considerably since they started they offer an array of products and services that surpasses those of former industry giants such as IBM.
4. What is happening in the computer industry is similar to what happened in the airline industry a few powerful companies are driving out competition from smaller and less financially secure operations.
5. The short-term consequence is lower prices for consumers the long-term consequence will almost certainly be a price escalation.

EXERCISE 34–2   **Using the Semicolon to Separate Clauses Linked with Conjunctive Adverbs**

Insert a semicolon where needed in the following sentences. Also insert appropriate commas to set off the conjunctive adverbs. Example:

> I did not buy the car instead I leased it.
> I did not buy the *car; instead,* I leased it.

1. We knew the lines for the free meals would be long therefore we arrived hours before the food was distributed.
2. The excursion fare was well below the normal price it was not as low as the special weekend fare however.
3. Preparing for the Olympics brought residents of Atlanta together moreover their preparations helped them appreciate their city.

4. They had no desire to go out in the heavy rainstorm nevertheless they felt obliged to fulfill their promise to attend a party with friends.

5. It was a splendid meal indeed it was perhaps the best I have ever had.

EXERCISE 34–3 Punctuating Correctly with Semicolons

Revise the following sentences to correct any misuses of the semicolon. Example:

> As far as we could see; nothing would be done now.
> As far as we could *see, nothing* would be done now.

1. There were two matters to consider; the cost of the program and its likelihood of success.

2. From among the many suggestions made by workers; management selected two for immediate implementation.

3. Throughout its history; Poland has had to resist aggressors.

4. Four automakers were involved in deliberations; regarding import quotas.

5. Political relations between the United States and Vietnam have a long history; the administrations of FDR, Truman, Eisenhower, JFK, and LBJ had dealings with Vietnam; moreover, the legacy of Vietnam has involved intricate negotiations for subsequent administrations, especially those of Richard Nixon and Jimmy Carter; however, the Reagan, Bush, and Clinton administrations have not been exempt.

Colons

The **colon** (:) is used to introduce statements that recapitulate, summarize, or explain an independent clause. Colons are also used to introduce a list, a quotation, or an appositive. In addition, writers use colons between the titles and subtitles of books; between numbers indicating minutes, hours, and seconds; and in the salutation of a business letter (see 49a).

34f Use colons to introduce a statement that qualifies a statement in an independent clause

Use colons to introduce summary, amplifying, and explanatory material in a sentence.

She was certain she would win: the stars had indicated it, and she had dreamt about it every night for a week.

It had been a typical day on the job: he set up his waiter station, served throngs of customers, and cleaned up before heading home, exhausted, at midnight.

When an independent clause follows a colon, it is generally not capitalized (see 38a). However, you may use a capital letter to emphasize the importance of the second statement.

The Economy has only one credo: Anyone can play who's willing to play.

—Fanny Howe, "The Plot Sickens"

 Use colons to introduce a list

Use a colon to introduce a list only when the words before the colon make up an independent clause.

These are the requirements for the course: faithful attendance, active participation, and timely submission of assignments.

When we cleaned the attic we accumulated a collection of forgotten goods: a prewar sewing machine, broken toys, a bag of marbles, a pile of bottle caps, and a shoe box full of baseball cards.

 Use colons to introduce long or formal quotations

To introduce a long or formal quotation, or to introduce a quotation formally, use a colon before the quotation.

This is the opening sentence of the story: "It was lunchtime and they were all sitting under the dining tent pretending that nothing had happened."

Whenever a colon follows quoted material, place the colon after the closing quotation marks.

These are the opening words of Sylvia Plath's poem "Mirror": "I am silver and exact. I have no preconceptions."

34i **Use colons to introduce delayed appositives**

You can achieve a dramatic stylized effect by using the colon to introduce a delayed appositive.

He wanted only one thing from her: money.

She wanted only one thing before she left: her mother's forgiveness.

 34j **Use colons in salutations, memo headings, hours/minutes, titles/subtitles**

Use the colon to follow the salutation of a formal letter, to follow the headings in a memo, to separate hours from minutes, and to separate the title of a book from its subtitle.

FORMAL LETTER	Dear Professor Funk:
MEMO HEADINGS	To: Madalyn Stone From: Tony English Re: Sales Estimates
HOURS/MINUTES	6:45 p.m.
TITLE/SUBTITLE	*Emily Dickinson: A Critical Introduction*

USAGE NOTE   When you refer to chapters and verses from the Bible, use a colon between chapter and verse. *Genesis 3:4*, for example, indicates the book of Genesis, chapter 3, verse 4.

 34k **Avoid misuse of the colon**

Be careful not to misuse the colon. A colon can only follow an independent clause in the situation described in 34i. Do not use a colon after an incomplete sentence or partial statement.

INCORRECT	We bought: milk, bread, cheese, and ice cream.
REVISED	We bought milk, bread, cheese, and ice cream.

A colon is not used after words such as *including* and *such as*.

INCORRECT	This *Handbook* discusses punctuation marks such as: the comma, the colon, and the semicolon.
REVISED	This *Handbook* discusses punctuation marks such as the comma, the colon, and the semicolon.

Do not use a colon after a verb.

INCORRECT	The most important statistic for a pitcher in baseball is: earned run average.

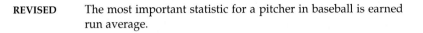

REVISED   The most important statistic for a pitcher in baseball is earned run average.

EXERCISE 34–4   Using the Colon

Insert colons where necessary or delete them where unnecessary. Example:

Remember one thing above all, look ahead, not back.
Remember one thing above all: look ahead, not back.

1. The title of this important book is *Foods; Their History and Uses.*
2. Dear Senator Inouye,
3. Three things were necessary for survival food, water, and shelter.
4. We will always remember our first date. We got a flat tire and ran out of gas.
5. The opening words of the poem are: "Once upon a midnight dreary."

EXERCISE 34–5   Writing with the Colon

Write three sentences using colons. Imitate sentences in this chapter, if you wish.

EXERCISE 34–6   Using Colons and Semicolons

Punctuate the following sentence pairs by replacing the period after the first sentence with a colon or semicolon. Explain your choices. Example:

We felt exhilarated. Our proposal had been entirely accepted.

We felt exhilarated: our proposal had been entirely accepted.
[replace period with colon, since second clause explains first]

1. The sight held awesome wonders. Power, beauty, grace, and violence.
2. We won first prize in the drawing. The new red Miata was ours.
3. Some were satisfied. Others were not.
4. In Rome and Florence, Italians lunch on McDonald's hamburgers. In Boston and New York, Americans often lunch on pasta.
5. Faulkner's prose is copious, sensuous, and sonorous. Hemingway's writing is spare, taut, and generally stripped of ornamentation.

CHAPTER 35

The Apostrophe

*T*he apostrophe's (') primary use is to indicate possession. In nouns, possession is shown either by a phrase beginning with the word *of* (*the sins of the father*) or with an apostrophe and an *-s* ending (*the Smith's house, the day's work*).

The apostrophe is also used to form the plurals of letters (*dot your i's*), numbers (two 5's for a 10), and symbols (&'s). And the apostrophe is used in contractions to show the omission of a letter or number (*it's* for it is; *a '91 Chevy*).

 35a Use apostrophes to form the possessive case of nouns and indefinite pronouns

The possessive case indicates ownership or possession (see 12c).

1 **Singular nouns or indefinite pronouns**

Add an apostrophe and *-s* to form the possessive case of singular nouns or indefinite pronouns.

Georgia O'Keeffe's paintings of flowers are among her most beautiful.

It was really *nobody's* fault.

2 **Singular nouns ending in -s**

For a singular noun ending in *-s,* most writers add *-'s* to show possession.

The expert *witness's* testimony seemed convincing.

Yeats's book *Collected Poems* was first published by Macmillan in 1939.

For singular nouns ending in *-s,* it is also acceptable to form the possessive by adding only an apostrophe, if this spelling better represents your own pronunciation: *the witness' testimony, Yeats' poems.* Be consistent throughout a piece of writing in the way you show possession for such singular nouns.

3 Plural nouns

Indicate the possessive case of plural nouns by adding an apostrophe and -*s* for words not ending in -*s*.

The *children's* books of E. B. White have become classics of our literature.

The Feminine Mystique by Betty Friedan helped launch the *women's* movement.

For plural nouns ending in -*s*, add only the apostrophe.

The three defense *witnesses'* testimony held up well under cross-examination.

The *girls'* clothing section is on the second floor.

4 Compound words and phrases

Add an apostrophe and -*s* to the last word in compound words and phrases.

My *father-in-law's* trips to Italy, France, and Ireland have provided some of his most memorable dining experiences.

William Carpenter II's office is at 50 Ridge Street.

It was *nobody else's* affair.

5 Joint possession for two or more nouns

Add an apostrophe and -*s* to the last noun when two or more nouns are joined by *and* to show joint possession.

David and Hilda's new condominium has been tastefully furnished. [David and Hilda own the condominium jointly.]

Laurel and Hardy's comedy routines illustrate classic slapstick. [Laurel and Hardy perform as a team.]

6 Individual possession for two or more nouns

Add an apostrophe and -*s* to each noun when two or more nouns are joined by *and* to show individual possession.

Lee's and Kai's offices are equipped with computers and telephones. [Lee and Kai have separate offices similarly equipped.]

The administration's and the faculty's positions on the issue began to coalesce. [The two different positions started to come together.]

EXERCISE 35–1   Using Apostrophes with Singular and Plural Noun Possessives

Insert an apostrophe or an *-s* where necessary to form the correct possessive case of the words in parentheses. Example:

It had to be (somebody) coat.
It had to be somebody's coat.

1. The (president) proposals were modified by Congress.
2. It was one of (Vince Gill) best vocal performances.
3. Students sometimes disregard their (teachers) advice.
4. (Andrew and Miguel) grades were the two highest in the class.
5. We could not decide whether to eat at (D.J. or Sabatino).

35b   **Do not use an apostrophe to form the possessives of personal pronouns and adjectives**

Possessive pronouns (see 12c-3) and possessive adjectives (see 13h) do not use apostrophes. Be careful not to confuse possessive pronouns and possessive adjectives with contractions (see 35c).

PRONOUN	POSSESSIVE FORMS	
he	his	[*not* his']
she	her, hers	[*not* her's, hers']
it	its	[*not* it's, its']
we	our, ours	[*not* our's, ours']
you	your, yours	[*not* your's, yours']
they	their, theirs	[*not* their's, theirs']
who	whose	[*not* who's, whos']

Be especially careful to distinguish between *its*, the possessive form, and *it's*, a contraction meaning *it is* or *it has*. Similarly, distinguish between *whose*, the possessive form, and *who's*, a contraction for *who is*.

FAULTY   The bank is currently reviewing *it's* mortgage lending policy.

REVISED   The bank is currently reviewing *its* mortgage lending policy.

FAULTY   The team, *who's* owner is out of town, won three straight games.

REVISED   The team, *whose* owner is out of town, won three straight games.

EXERCISE 35–2 **Selecting the Correct Form of Possessive Pronouns and Possessive Adjectives**

Underline the appropriate possessive form in each of the following sentences. Example:

The book was his, not (*hers/her's*).

1. The fault was (*yours/yours'*) entirely.
2. I could not decide (*whose/who's*) argument was more persuasive.
3. (*Its/It's*) owner will turn up eventually.
4. (*Theirs'/Theirs*) was not the only valuable suggestion.
5. (*His'/His*) time will come.

 35c **Use the apostrophe in contractions and to indicate missing letters, numbers, or words**

A **contraction** is a shortened form of a word or a group of words. Contractions are two-word combinations that use apostrophes to signal that letters have been omitted from one of the words. Although contractions are common in speaking and informal writing, you should avoid them in academic writing—except in cases when you wish to establish a less formal tone. Consider your audience, your purpose, and your writing occasion before deciding whether to use contractions.

The accompanying chart lists the most frequently used contractions.

Common Contractions			
ORIGINAL	CONTRACTION	ORIGINAL	CONTRACTION
cannot	can't	let us	let's
could not	couldn't	she is, she has	she's
did not	didn't	should not	shouldn't
do not	don't	they are	they're
he is, he has	he's	was not	wasn't
has not	hasn't	we are	we're
have not	haven't	who is, who has	who's
I am	I'm	will not	won't
I would	I'd	would not	wouldn't
it is	it's	you are	you're

Contractions are also used to indicate omissions of letters and numbers in some common phrases.

five of the clock   five o'clock

class of 1999   class of '99

Writers use the apostrophe to reflect dialect speech patterns in fiction, poetry, essays, and drama. Notice how the apostrophes in the following poem convey the way the speaker, a mother, talks to her son.

> Life for me ain't been no crystal stair. . . .
> But . . . I'se been a-climbin' on,
> And reachin' landin's,
> And turnin' corners,
> And sometimes goin' in the dark.
> Where there ain't been no light.
> So boy, don't you turn back.
> Don't you set down on the steps
> 'Cause you finds it's kinder hard.

—Langston Hughes, "Mother to Son"

EXERCISE 35–3   **Using the Apostrophe with Contractions**

Spell out the words for each contraction in the following sentences. Example:

> I would've come if only I'd known.
> I would *have* come if only I *had* known.

1. It's only one of many topics we need to discuss.
2. There wasn't a single example to illustrate their idea.
3. Do you really believe she doesn't care?
4. If they won't come, then we'll have to go without them.
5. Let's see what we can do about it tomorrow.

35d   Use the apostrophe to form the plural of letters, numbers, symbols, and words used as words

My handwriting is hard to decipher because I rarely cross my *t*'s, and my *a*'s sometimes look like *o*'s.

The *1590's* can be designated the decade of the English sonnet, the *1950's* the decade of the folk song.

There were many *'s scattered throughout the document.

There are no *if's, and's,* or *but's* about it.

Be aware that you can form the plural of years and symbols with or without the apostrophe: 1990's, 1990s; #'s, #s. However, use whichever style you choose consistently.

35e Avoid using the apostrophe incorrectly

Be careful not to insert apostrophes where they do not belong. The accompanying list details the common apostrophe errors and how to correct them.

Revising Apostrophe Errors

Do not use an apostrophe with present-tense verbs.

> **INCORRECT** Stress increases' a person's susceptibility to illness.
>
> **REVISED** Stress increases a person's susceptibility to illness.

Do not use an apostrophe to make a nonpossessive noun plural.

> **INCORRECT** Research studies' have repeatedly demonstrated a link between stress and the onset of illness.
>
> **REVISED** Research studies have repeatedly demonstrated a link between stress and the onset of illness.

Do not use an apostrophe before -s when indicating the plural possessive of a noun. Use an -s followed by an apostrophe for plural possessives.

> **INCORRECT** The general public continues to follow researcher's efforts to further investigate this link.
>
> **REVISED** The general public continues to follow researchers' efforts to further investigate this link.

EXERCISE 35–4 **Using Apostrophes in Plurals**

Use the plural of each of the following in a complete sentence.

1. i
2. z
3. if
4. but
5. 1980 (the decade)

EXERCISE 35–5   Using the Apostrophe to Indicate Possession

Change each phrase in parentheses to a possessive noun. Example:

> The films (of Peter Greenaway) are bizarre.
> Peter Greenaway's films are bizarre.

1. The attitude (of the participants) bordered on hostility.
2. The goal (of the team) was to win 75 percent of its games.
3. The causes (of the war) should be considered in light of the previous political and economic circumstances (of the century).
4. The power (of the god) was believed to be such that neither sun nor stars would shine without his assistance.
5. The vacations (of the Webers and the Hammonds) were both disrupted by the political instability in Greece.

EXERCISE 35–6   Revising Apostrophe Errors

Supply all missing apostrophes in the following passage.

> Shoppings function as a form of therapy is widely appreciated. You dont really need, lets say, another sweater. You need the feeling of power that comes with buying or not buying it. You need the feeling that someone wants something you have—even if its just your money. To get the benefit of shopping, you neednt actually purchase the sweater, any more than you have to marry every man you flirt with. . . .
>
> But even shopping for blue jeans at Bobs Surplus on Main Street—no frills, bare bones shopping—is an event in the life of the spirit. Once again I have to come to terms with the fact that I will never look good in Levis. Much as I want to be mainstream, I never will be.
>
> —Phyllis Rose, "Shopping and Other Spiritual Adventures in America Today"

CHAPTER 36

Quotation Marks

Quotation marks, used in pairs (" ") at the beginning and end of a quotation, and used singly (' ') in quotes within quotes, tell your audience that certain words have been borrowed from another source. For example, *Abraham Lincoln once said that "a house divided against itself cannot stand."* Quotation marks also set off titles, definitions, and words used in certain ways (e.g., to indicate irony). For advice on how to use quotation marks with other punctuation, refer to the section listed in the accompanying chart. See also 44i on using quotations in research writing.

Directory for Using Quotation Marks with Other Punctuation

- With commas (33j and 33j)
- With brackets (37c-2)
- With ellipses (37d)
- With capital letters (38b)
- With semicolons and colons (36i-2)
- With question marks, exclamation points, and dashes (36i-3)

36a Use quotation marks for direct quotations

Direct quotations record the exact words of a source, whether those words are spoken or written. It is important to record the quotation verbatim, exactly as it appears in the original source.

Do not use quotation marks for indirect quotations, those that do not record the exact words of a source.

INDIRECT The coach said that she would accept no excuse for sloppy play.

DIRECT The coach said, "I will accept no excuse for sloppy play."

36b Use single quotation marks for quotes within quotes

When quoting a source directly, place the quotation inside double quotation marks.

Albert Einstein once said, "Imagination is more important than knowledge."

Single quotation marks are used when you enclose one quotation within another. Double quotation marks appear at the opening and closing of a quotation, but any quotes within quotes take single quotation marks.

In one of his essays, Russell Baker humorously remarks, "I know what 'the price has been adjusted' means in New Age Babble. It means 'price is going up.' "

USAGE NOTE   British practice in handling quotation marks is the opposite of the American convention. Single quotes are used for normally quoted material and double quotation marks for quotes within quotes.

36c Set off lengthy quoted passages

For quoted passages that exceed four typed lines in your paper, begin a new line and indent ten spaces from the left margin for each line of the quotation. This format, called block quotation, does not require quotation marks because the blocked passage is set off visually from the rest of your text.

In <u>Culture and Truth</u>, Renato Rosaldo explains why the topic of culture is so important to Americans today:

> These days questions of culture seem to touch a nerve because they quite quickly become anguished questions of identity. Academic debates about multicultural education similarly slip effortlessly into the animating ideological conflicts of this multicultural nation. How can the United States both respect diversity and find unity?

(For more on using block quotations, see Chapter 44 on research.)

36d Use quotation marks with poetry

Quote poetry as you would prose. Separate the lines of poetry with slashes. Include a space before and after each slash.

The dramatist Lorraine Hansberry derived the title of her best-known play, *A Raisin in the Sun,* from a poem by Langston Hughes. In "Dream Deferred" Hughes asks, "What happens to a dream deferred? / Does it dry up / like a raisin in the sun?"

When your poetry quotation exceeds three lines, indent the lines of the poem ten spaces from the left margin of your text. Reproduce the formatting of the poem as closely as possible. Do not use quotation marks around the block quotation.

In one of his most engaging poems, "Waiting Table," Kraft Rompf describes how waiters will do whatever is necessary for a tip from their customers.

> But for a
> tip--for a tip, for a tip
> I would work so very, very
> hard, and so gladly let
> them shine into my soul,
> and bow to them and laugh
> with them and sing. I would
> gladly give them everything.

36e Use quotation marks for dialogue

When you quote conversations or dialogue, enclose the words of each speaker in double quotation marks. Indicate changes in speaker by beginning a new paragraph. This will make it easier for your readers to follow the dialogue.

"Will you have lime juice or lemon squash?" Macomber asked.
"I'll have a gimlet," Robert Wilson told him.
"I'll have a gimlet too. I need something," Macomber's wife said.

—Ernest Hemingway, "The Short Happy Life
of Francis Macomber"

36f Use quotation marks to enclose titles and definitions

When referring to titles of short poems, short stories, articles, essays, songs, sections or chapters of books, or episodes of television and radio programs, enclose the titles in quotation marks.

At nineteen Adrienne Rich wrote the poem "Aunt Jennifer's Tigers."

Katherine Anne Porter's short story "Rope" describes a married couple's escalating argument and its eventual resolution.

Both *Business Week* and *Time* once ran articles entitled "The Mommy Track."

George Orwell's "Politics and the English Language" is one of the most frequently reprinted twentieth-century essays.

"Mrs. Robinson" was one of Simon and Garfunkel's most popular songs.

The best-known chapter in Loren Eiseley's *The Immense Journey* is entitled "How Flowers Changed the World."

For the titles of longer works, such as long poems, plays, and novels, use italics (or underlining) rather than quotation marks (see 39a on italics).

Definitions can be set off with quotation marks, though underlining or italicizing them is more common. Italicize the original language and use quotation marks for the translation.

The Italian words *la dolce vita* can be translated *"the sweet life."*

36g Use quotation marks for words used in special ways

Use quotation marks for words used ironically.

My growing brother's "little lunch" consisted of an eight-ounce steak, two baked potatoes, a half-gallon of milk, and a quart of ice cream.

Use quotation marks around any invented words.

Nobody can apply for a job these days—or interface with a personnel recruiter in the hopes of impacting on his bottom line—without a degree in "bizbuzz," the jargon that prioritizes the career path of the rising young ballpark figurer.

—William Safire, "Bizbuzz"

Words referred to as words can be italicized (underlined) or placed within quotation marks. Whichever method you choose, use it consistently.

INCONSISTENT   The words *imply* and *infer* are frequently confused. So are "affect" and "effect."

CONSISTENT   The words "imply" and "infer" are frequently confused. So are "affect" and "effect."

36h Avoid common misuses of quotation marks

Avoid using quotation marks merely to emphasize particular words or phrases. Also, do not use quotation marks around slang or other forms of colloquial language (see 28c). In both cases the quotation marks call undue attention to words, which can be better emphasized by careful word choice and effective word order.

MISUSED Theirs was not the most "exciting" of relationships, but at least it was "stable."

REVISED Theirs was not the most exciting of relationships, but at least it was stable.

MISUSED Every October I go to Vermont to see the "totally awesome" foliage.

REVISED Every October I go to Vermont to see the spectacular foliage.

36i Follow established conventions for using quotation marks with other punctuation

You will often need to use quotation marks with other punctuation marks. The following guidelines explain how to use quotation marks with periods, commas, semicolons, colons, question marks, exclamation points, and dashes.

1 Periods and commas

Periods and commas usually appear immediately before closing quotation marks.

"It was not the first time this happened," she said. "Nor will it be the last."

For sentences that end with a parenthetical citation of a source (e.g., a page number or an author and page number), place the period after the citation. (For more information on punctuating parenthetical citations, bibliographies, and Works Cited lists, see Chapters 45 and 46 on research writing.)

INCORRECT In his book *The Great War and Modern Memory,* Paul Fussell describes the German trenches as "efficient, clean, pedantic, and permanent." (45)

INCORRECT	In his book *The Great War and Modern Memory*, Paul Fussell describes the German trenches as "efficient, clean, pedantic, and permanent." (45).
REVISED	In his book *The Great War and Modern Memory*, Paul Fussell describes the German trenches as "efficient, clean, pedantic, and permanent" (45).

2   Semicolons and colons

Semicolons and colons appear immediately after closing quotation marks.

Some thought it necessary to engage in what George Orwell describes as "doublespeak"; most, however, saw no reason for it.

George Orwell coined the term "doublespeak": language used hypocritically to give a false impression, usually an opposite impression of what is true.

USAGE NOTE   Unlike American conventions, British publications place colons and semicolons before the closing quotation marks rather than after.

3   Question marks, exclamation points, and dashes

If a question mark, exclamation point, or dash is part of the quotation, place it before closing quotation marks. If a mark of punctuation is not part of the quotation, place it after closing quotation marks.

PART OF QUOTATION

"Did you call?" he asked.

"Leave him alone!" we shouted.

"If you do, I'll—" she warned.

NOT PART OF QUOTATION

Do you remember the story "The Most Dangerous Game"?

I loved the *Seinfeld* episode called "The Raincoat"!

"Get with it"—that's an expression I just can't stand.

EXERCISE 36–1   **Using Quotation Marks**

Supply quotation marks where they are needed in the following sentences. Example:

Willa Cather's short story Paul's Case is one of her finest works.
Willa Cather's short story "Paul's Case" is one of her finest works.

1. The last lines of Shakespeare's Sonnet 29 are For thy sweet love rememb'red such wealth brings, / That then I scorn to change my state with kings.
2. Franz Schubert's song The Trout is based on a poem by Heinrich Heine.
3. Smith and Moore acknowledged that a cure for cancer may never be found.
4. Suarez and O'Rourke write, even under the best of circumstances a relatively high rate of recidivism exists.
5. The words amount and number are sometimes confused with each other.

EXERCISE 36–2   Revising Use of Quotation Marks

Revise each of the following sentences to supply missing quotation marks, eliminate unnecessary ones, or move those incorrectly placed. Example:

"In the last episode of *Dallas*", the instructor remarked, "we can see the major themes of the show reflected".

"In the last episode of *Dallas*," the instructor remarked, "we can see the major themes of the show reflected."

1. You could hear the fear in his voice when he asked, How is she?
2. What is the final word in Walt Whitman's "When I Heard the Learn'd Astronomer?"
3. How many times have you been told to "stop and smell the roses?"
4. The title of the popular '60s "hit" song is "Where Have All the Flowers Gone?".
5. In her article The End of Reading, Melinda Melendez argues that "visual" and "oral" literacy have already replaced the "printed" word.

EXERCISE 36–3   Supplying Marks of Punctuation

Revise the following sentences by inserting commas, periods, question marks, exclamation points, colons, and semicolons where they belong. Example:

"It was not the time for it" he said.
"It was not the time for it," he said.

1. "Please be ready on cue with your lines" said the director.
2. Who has the line "If that's how you feel, it's time I left"
3. It was Annie Dillard, not Joan Didion, who wrote "Living Like Weasels"

4. What year did Robert Frost write "The Road Not Taken"
5. Did Lewis Thomas write an essay called "On Punctuation"

The accompanying chart summarizes the rules for using quotation marks in writing.

Using Quotation Marks

Use quotation marks
- For direct quotations and for quotes within quotes
- For titles of short works
- For dialogue and definitions
- For words used ironically

Do *not* use quotation marks
- For indirect quotations
- For titles of long works
- For words you want to emphasize
- For long block quotations (five or more prose lines; four or more poetry lines)

Place quotation marks
- After periods and commas
- Before semicolons and colons
- After question marks, exclamation points, and dashes that are part of the quotation
- Before question marks, exclamation points, and dashes that are not part of the quotation

---

Note: For guidance on using quotations in your writing, see the following sections of the *Handbook:*

- Quotations versus summaries and paraphrases (44d1–3)
- Introducing quotations into your writing (44d-5 and 44i-1)
- Citing sources for quotations (44j and 45a)
- Avoiding plagiarism when you include quotations (44j)

CHAPTER 37

Other Punctuation Marks

*L*ike the punctuation marks discussed in Chapters 32–36, those explained in this chapter—dashes, parentheses, brackets, ellipses, and slashes—help writers express their meaning clearly and emphatically. Using these punctuation marks effectively will also help you vary the tone of your writing.

 **37a** Using the dash

The **dash** (—), whether used singly or in pairs, allows you to interrupt a sentence to insert nonessential information. Although dashes can appear anywhere in a sentence, pairs of dashes often occur near the middle and single dashes at the end of sentences.

> **PAIR OF DASHES** Television brought the Vietnam War—mostly its daily battles and body counts—into our living rooms.
>
> **SINGLE DASH** I was enthralled with the skeletal models of the two biggest dinosaurs—the brontosaurus and the diplodocus.

With most typewriters and word processors you make a dash by combining two unspaced hyphens (--). Do not put a space before, between, or after the hyphens.

1 Use dashes to insert an interrupting comment

Use dashes to insert an interrupting comment, whether for illustration, explanation, or emphasis.

ILLUSTRATION

I remember a day in class when he leaned far forward in his characteristic pose—the pose of a man about to impart a secret—and croaked, "If you don't know how to pronounce a word, say it loud!"

—E. B. White, "Will Strunk"

EXPLANATION

It is a serious matter to shoot a working elephant—it is comparable to destroying a huge and costly piece of machinery—and obviously one ought not to do it if it can possibly be avoided.

—George Orwell, "Shooting an Elephant"

EMPHASIS

During the "working" day, she labored beside—not behind—my father in the fields.

—Alice Walker, *In Search of Our Mothers' Gardens*

2 Use dashes to indicate a shift in tone, a hesitation in speech, or a break in thought

SHIFT IN TONE

The engaged girls—how many of them there seem to be!—flash their rings and tangle their ankles in their long New Look skirts.

—Cynthia Ozick, "Washington Square, 1946"

HESITATION IN SPEECH

"Don't—don't go," he pleaded.

BREAK IN THOUGHT

She began to see a way out, but then—nothing.

3 Use dashes to introduce or comment on a list

INTRODUCING A LIST

He loved everything about his room—the quiet space, the way light filtered through its tiny windows, the memorabilia on the walls.

COMMENTING ON A LIST

Honesty, decency, integrity, generosity—these were the ideals by which she desired to live.

4 Use dashes to set off parenthetical expressions within parenthetical expressions

The architecture of Versailles, Louis XIV's resplendent "country" palace—originally a hunting lodge—and primary seat of the royal court, provided every luxury except plumbing.

A colon can also be used to insert an explanation or introduce a list. But the dash is less formal than the colon (see 34g). The dash marks a sharp, pronounced break in the continuity of a sentence. Use dashes sparingly in academic writing, since heavy use of dashes can create fragmented writing that is difficult to read.

EXERCISE 37–1   Using Dashes

Put dashes where they belong in the following sentences. Some sentences may be correct as written. Example:

> I will arrive at least I will try to arrive before noon.
> I will arrive—*at least I will try to arrive*—before noon.

1. My attendance at meals may be somewhat haphazard for six months or so I will not adhere to any kind of schedule.
2. Though the emphasis was on exercise hiking, swimming, running we had plenty of time to relax.
3. The army doctors would put a strap around your head, clamp some sort of instrument over your eyes, and then stick a hose into your ear and pump cold water into your ear canal.
4. I took to calling at Clay's every few days it is simply a pleasant place to be.
5. It was to be honest a complete fiasco.

EXERCISE 37–2   Writing with Dashes

Use dashes to combine each pair of sentences into a single, concise sentence. You may need to add, drop, or change some words. Example:

> Reena decided to quit her job and look for a better one. It was a brave decision.
> Reena decided to quit her job—*a brave decision*—and look for a better one.

1. It rained all night at Seven Islands but the rain tapered off in the early morning to drizzle and mist. It rained heavily and steadily.
2. Darwin was far from being an atheist, but he was deeply puzzled by this enormous multiplicity of forms. He had, after all, taken a degree in divinity from Cambridge.
3. All of the committees went to work immediately on the project. The committees were finance, program, and local arrangements.
4. The faculty, the students, the staff were all opposed. They were opposed to the provost's decision to curtail library hours.
5. Both the streets and the lanes were paved with the same material. They were paved with tough black mud in wet times, deep dust in dry.

Write five sentences of your own that contain dashes. Include at least two sentences with pairs of dashes. You can, if you wish, use example sentences from 37a as models for your sentences.

37b   Using parentheses

Parentheses (   ) typically enclose words, phrases, and clauses of secondary importance to a sentence. They are also used to enclose numbers and letters used in lists. Parentheses are often used with other punctuation, including periods, commas, question marks, and exclamation points.

1   Use parentheses to enclose nonessential explanatory information

Nonessential explanatory information may amplify, specify, exemplify, or otherwise expand what precedes it.

AMPLIFY

The author's first novel (written on a summer fishing trip in Vermont) was excessively self-indulgent and almost entirely autobiographical.

SPECIFY

Beethoven's middle period (1800–15) is the source of many of his most famous and most moving works, including the Razumovsky Quartets (opus 59) and the fifth and sixth symphonies (opus 67 and opus 68, respectively).

EXEMPLIFY

Although other books had occasioned court battles (*Ulysses*, for example), Lawrence's *Lady Chatterly's Lover* achieved the greatest notoriety.

2   Use parentheses to enclose numbers and letters within lists

We can isolate four major areas for investigation: (1) social; (2) economic; (3) political; (4) environmental.

Parentheses can also be used to restate a spelled-out number, as is often done in business and legal writing; to enclose a date, especially when identifying the year of a work's publication or first performance; and to enclose a parenthetical citation (see Chapters 45 and 46).

The bill is due in nineteen (19) days.

Kate Chopin's *The Awakening* (1904) was one of the first feminist novels.

Socrates has been considered both Plato's teacher and his nemesis (Vlastos 24).

3   Use parentheses carefully with other punctuation

Periods

Place a period inside a closing parenthesis when the material inside the parentheses is a complete sentence and when the parenthetical sentence is not enclosed within another complete sentence. (When a complete sentence is enclosed within another complete sentence, do not use a period.) When the material inside the parentheses is not a complete sentence, place the period outside the closing parenthesis. For additional information on end punctuation (including punctuating with periods), see Chapter 32.

Commas

A comma may come after the closing parenthesis, but not before the opening parenthesis.

Even though it did not attain television's highest ratings for a sitcom's final episode (*M*A*S*H* achieved that distinction), the final episode of *Cheers* was watched by millions.

Question marks and exclamation points

Place question marks and exclamation points before the closing parenthesis if the material in parentheses is a question or an exclamation.

We tried to recall the mathematical formulas (but how could we possibly remember them all?) as we prepared to answer the test questions.

Our laughter (so deep was our joy!) turned to tears.

Quotation marks

If all of the words requiring quotation marks occur within parentheses, place the quotation marks within the parentheses as well.

Richard Selzer wrote an essay ("The Masked Marvel") about a famous wrestler who later became one of Selzer's medical patients.

Be careful not to overuse parentheses because, like dashes, parentheses can break up the continuity of your writing.

WRITING HINT   The choice of commas, dashes, or parentheses depends on how you want to be understood. Prefer commas most of the time, use dashes to signal a striking interruption, and use parentheses to enclose information that is more a helpful courtesy than an essential part of your message. But in many instances, commas, dashes, and parentheses are interchangeable. The choice of one or the other necessarily will change the emphasis of a statement, but no one choice will be more correct than another.

Choosing Dashes, Parentheses, or Commas

Dashes, parentheses, and commas can all be used to set off nonessential information, including parenthetical expressions. Ordinarily, dashes are the most emphatic way to set off such expressions and parentheses the least emphatic. Consider the following sentence from Alice Walker's "In Search of Our Mothers' Gardens," first as she wrote it—with dashes—then with parentheses and commas in their place.

- **Dashes** initially create a strong pause and heavy emphasis (37a).

    They dreamed dreams that no one knew—not even themselves, in any coherent fashion—and saw visions no one could understand.

- **Parentheses** downplay the interrupting effect of the parenthetical information, giving it the character of an aside (37b).

    They dreamed dreams that no one knew (not even themselves, in any coherent fashion) and saw visions no one could understand.

- **Commas** simply include the parenthetical information. Commas are the least interruptive way to include parenthetical information (33f).

    They dreamed dreams that no one knew, not even themselves, in any coherent fashion, and saw visions no one could understand.

Avoid using more than one set of dashes or parentheses in a single sentence—though you may try including one set of each (along with a set of commas) in a single sentence.

For lunch try a fruit salad—say, cottage cheese, grapes, bananas, orange sections, and strawberries (you can substitute melon balls if you're prone to hives)—and see how satisfying it can be.

—Claire Cook, *Line by Line*

EXERCISE 37–4   **Practice with Parentheses**

Add any parentheses that would be either helpful or necessary in the following sentences. Example:

Clearly not a historic occasion or even an event of much significance, it was fun, nonetheless.

Clearly not a historic occasion *(or even an event of much significance)*, it was fun, nonetheless.

1. They learned that many creative artists, directors and choreographers, for example, had been invited to participate in the conference.

2. An astonishing variety of items, power tools, underwear, office furniture, buttons, even bicycles, could be ordered from the Sears catalog.

3. Some of the possibilities included: 1 a sales tax, 2 a sin tax, 3 a value-added tax, and 4 an increased income tax.

4. Claude Raines once starred in an unusual film *The Invisible Man,* based on the H. G. Wells novel.

5. The most vocal of the protesters were those from Mothers against Drunk Driving MADD.

EXERCISE 37–5   **Selecting Dashes or Parentheses**

Replace commas in the following sentences with dashes or parentheses where appropriate.

1. The Reagan proposal was, not surprisingly, extremely favorable to business.

2. He had long suspected that the three candidates, LaRue, Johnson, and Hirsch, might split the vote and imperil a woman's chance to win the election.

3. The Central Park concert, already interrupted twice by rain, was postponed indefinitely.

4. Many instructors believe in the efficacy of freewriting, a kind of informal, exploratory writing, as a way to help students discover what they think.

5. Some outstanding actors, Robert Redford and Paul Newman among them, have shared star billing in at least one film.

37c   **Using brackets**

Brackets [**]** enclose parenthetical elements already within parentheses—they are parentheses within parentheses. Brackets are also used around words inserted within a quotation.

1 Use brackets to enclose parenthetical material within parentheses

The overwhelming concern (at least according to EPA [Environmental Protection Agency] officials) was that the oil spill be contained.

As an introduction to the subject (Freud's psychological theories [especially his dream theory] and other influential ideas), Calvin Hall's *A Primer of Freudian Psychology* is compact and useful.

2 Use brackets to enclose words inserted into quotations

To have a direct quote make logical or grammatical sense, you sometimes need to replace words in the quote. Indicate this replacement by putting brackets around the new word.

According to Ortega, "[Suarez] possessed [charisma] to an extraordinary degree."

As Allen Waters has noted, "Without question, the most valuable player in the history of the franchise [the New York Yankees] has been Babe Ruth."

Use the word *sic* (which means "thus") in brackets generally to indicate an error in punctuation, spelling, grammar, or usage in the quoted passage. *Sic* tells the reader that the error is in the original and is not your mistake.

E. T. Smith writes, "Only two American families have contributed more than one U.S. President: the Adams and Rosevelt [sic] families."

EXERCISE 37–6 **Using Brackets**

Insert into the parenthetical passages you created in Exercise 37–4 an occasional clarifying word or detail. Put the words or details in brackets.

EXERCISE 37–7 **Using Brackets for Clarification**

Assume you are quoting the following statement and want to clarify the scientific terms for your readers. Use brackets to add the information that the Mesozoic era occurred about 180 million years ago, the Miocene epoch about 25 million years ago.

Dinosaurs lived during the Mesozoic era. Dinotheres lived during the Miocene epoch and, like the dinosaurs, are now extinct.

37d   Using ellipses

Ellipses, three equally spaced periods (. . .), usually signify that words have been omitted from a direct quotation. They may also indicate a pause or hesitation the same way a dash does (see 37a).

1   Use ellipses with quotations

When you need to incorporate directly quoted material into an essay, you may occasionally want to use only a portion of a passage. If the part you want to quote includes words from different sections of the passage, but not the entire passage, you must indicate the omitted words with ellipses.

ORIGINAL TEXT

Literacy is not merely the capacity to understand the conceptual content of writings and utterances, but the ability to participate fully in a set of social and intellectual practices. It is not passive but active, not imitative but creative, for participation in the speaking and writing of language is participation in the activities it makes possible.

—James Boyd White, "Literacy and the Law"

OMISSION OF WORDS IN THE MIDDLE OF A SENTENCE

As James Boyd White suggests, "Literacy is . . . the ability to participate fully in a set of social and intellectual practices."

When an ellipsis falls within a sentence, each of the three periods is preceded and followed by a space. You can use more than a single ellipsis in a passage.

OMISSION OF WORDS FROM DIFFERENT SENTENCES

"Literacy," writes James Boyd White, "is . . . the ability to participate fully in a set of social and intellectual practices. . . . It is . . . active . . . [and] creative . . . participation in the speaking and writing of language."

When an ellipsis coincides with the end of your sentence, use the ellipses followed by the end of sentence punctuation.

OMISSION OF WORDS AT THE END OF A SENTENCE

James Boyd White writes, "Literacy is not merely the capacity to understand the conceptual content of writings and utterances. . . ."

Whenever ellipsis marks occur after a grammatically complete sentence, include this fourth period without any space before it. The closing quotation marks come after the end punctuation (see 36h).

But if your quotation includes a parenthetical reference to a source, you must place the end punctuation after the parenthetical source citation.

James Boyd White writes, "Literacy is not merely the capacity to understand the conceptual content of writings and utterances . . ." (23).

(See 36h–i for more on punctuating quotations, and Chapter 45 for more on punctuating source citations.)

2   Use ellipses to indicate pause or hesitation

PAUSE   What I'm looking for is . . . another chance.

HESITATION   And the winner of this year's award for best picture . . . is . . . *Schindler's List.*

37e   Using slashes

The **slash** is a diagonal line also called a *virgule* or *solidus* (/). Slashes are used to indicate line divisions in poems quoted within a text (see 36d), to separate terms, to separate the parts of a fraction, and to separate parts of shorthand dates.

INDICATING LINE DIVISIONS IN POETRY

The last lines of the poem convey the speaker's sense of regret: "What did I know, what did I know / Of love's austere and lonely offices?" (See also 36d on quoting poetry.)

There is a space before and after the slash only in quotations of poetry.

SEPARATING ALTERNATIVES

It was one of those either/or situations.

He took the course with a pass/fail option.

SEPARATING PARTS OF FRACTIONS

They began swimming when they were only 2-1/2 years old.

(See 41a–b for advice on spelling out numbers.)

SEPARATING MONTH, YEAR, AND DAY IN SHORTHAND DATES

May 27, 1997

5/27/97

EXERCISE 37–8 Using Brackets, Slashes, Ellipses, Parentheses, and Dashes

Use the punctuation marks discussed in this chapter as needed in the following sentences. Example:

> The night of April 20, 1995, was if I remember correctly the night of a severe storm.

> The night of April 20, 1995, was *(if I remember correctly)* the night of a severe storm.

1. Consider the last two lines of Shakespeare's Sonnet 138: "Therefore I lie with her, and she with me, And in our faults by lies we flattered be."

2. According to one source, "John Fitgerald Kenedy sic was groomed for politics from the day he was born."

3. In 1861 a quick succession of events sparked by the attack on Fort Sumter a military stronghold in South Carolina led to the outbreak of civil war in the United States.

4. Those who market books not just those who write them argue that publicity is crucial to a book's success if it is to have any success at all.

5. Our many hours spent cleaning the attic or should I say the oven nearly sent us to the hospital.

EXERCISE 37–9 Using Varied Punctuation Marks in Writing

Write an eight- to twelve-sentence paragraph in which you use the following punctuation marks at least once: dash (or dashes), parentheses, brackets, ellipses, and slashes.

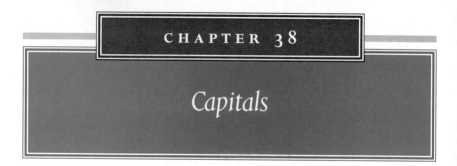

CHAPTER 38

Capitals

*T*he most important function of capital (or uppercase) letters in writing is to signal the beginning of a sentence. Without capital letters as indicators of sentence boundaries, you would have a difficult time making sense of what you read because sentences would run into one another. Capital letters are also used for the first letter in quotations and lines of poetry, for proper nouns and adjectives, for certain words in titles, and for the letters *I* and *O*. However, because the conventions of using capitals are changing, you should consult a new or recently revised dictionary when you are unsure about an accepted form.

38a Capitalizing the first word of a sentence

Capitalize the first word of a sentence.

This is the most rigorous course I have ever taken. Can you help me?

A number of capitalizing situations require the writer to choose a particular style and then stick with it.

Capitals with a series of questions

When you write a series of questions, you may or may not use capitals for the first word of each question. But be consistent with the style you choose.

Which problem should the administration tackle first? The budget deficit? Education? Health care?

Which problem should the administration tackle first? the budget deficit? education? health care?

Capitals with sentences following colons

When using colons in writing, you may or may not use capitals for the first letter that follows the colon. But be consistent with the style you choose.

She welcomed the opportunity to perform: It meant a lot to her.

She welcomed the opportunity to perform: it meant a lot to her.

Capitals with parentheses and dashes

A complete, separate sentence within parentheses should begin with a capital letter.

Cause of death has an important effect: degenerative disease often entails a substantial diminution of brain size. (This effect is separate from the decrease attributed to age alone.)

Do not use capitals when incorporating a parenthetical independent clause within a sentence—whether you set it off with parentheses or with dashes.

The true beauty of nature is her amplitude; she exists neither for nor because of us, and possesses a staying power that all our nuclear arsenals cannot threaten (much as we can easily destroy our puny selves).

—Stephen Jay Gould, *Bully for Brontosaurus*

They assume—this is the orthodox assumption of the industrial economy—that the only help worth giving is not given at all, but sold.

—Wendell Berry, "Feminism, the Body and the Machine"

38b   Capitalizing the first word of a quotation

In using quotations, capitalize the first word of full-sentence quotations, except when the quote is introduced by the word "that."

The motto "Live free or die" appears on New Hampshire license plates.

Kwame said to Abdullah, "The next time you need help, ask for it."

Is it true that "it's better to be a live dog than a dead lion"?

You may need to adjust sentences with quotations to indicate any capitalization changes you make. See also 32b.

Embedded quotations

Do not capitalize quotations incorporated into the body of one of your sentences, even if the original quotation begins with a capital. Instead, use brackets to indicate how the quotation's first letter has been altered.

ORIGINAL QUOTATION

"Only a mediocre person is always at his best."

EMBEDDED QUOTATION

W. Somerset Maugham once remarked that "[o]nly a mediocre person is always at his best."

Interrupted quotations

When you break up a sentence from a quotation with words of your own, do not capitalize the word that begins the second part of the quotation sentence. Capitalize the first part if it is capitalized in the original.

ORIGINAL QUOTATION

"I have nothing to declare but my genius."

INTERRUPTED QUOTATION

"I have nothing to declare," Oscar Wilde told U.S. custom officials, "but my genius."

38c   Capitalizing the first letter in a line of poetry

Traditionally, poets capitalize the first letter of each line of a poem. Some poets, however, do not observe this convention. If you write poetry, you have the option of capitalizing or not capitalizing the first word of each line. In quoting poetry, capitalize the lines exactly as the poet does.

Between my finger and my thumb,
The squat pen rests.
I'll dig with it.

—Seamus Heaney, "Digging"

If when my wife is sleeping
and the baby and Kathleen
are sleeping

—William Carlos Williams, "Danse Russe"

38d   Capitalizing proper nouns and adjectives

Use capitals for **proper nouns** (names of specific people, places, and things [see 12a]): *Lisette, Paris,* the *Eiffel Tower.* Use capitals for **proper adjectives** (adjectives formed from proper nouns): a *Parisian* cafe. Do not capitalize articles (*a, an, the*) accompanying proper nouns or proper adjectives. (Also note that some people such as poet e. e. cummings and musician k. d. lang do not use capital letters in their names.)

When proper nouns are used in a common or everyday context, they are not capitalized.

Please *xerox* the report.

Would you like ketchup with your *french* fries?

Be aware that writers may capitalize nouns and pronouns unconventionally. Emily Dickinson did so routinely, mostly for emphasis.

We grow accustomed to the Dark—
When Light is put away—

Advertisers often capitalize unconventionally: "Narcisse for the Bath and Body"; "Visit our Infiniti showroom for a Guest Drive." Similarly, corporations refer to the *Board of Trustees* and university administrations to the *Faculty,* the *College,* or the *University.*

When you use a common noun as an integral part of a proper name—*college,* for example, as in *Boston College*—capitalize the common noun. Words such as *street, river, county, prize,* and *award* are capitalized only when they become part of a specific (proper) term: *Basin Street,* the *Mississippi River, Dade County, Pulitzer Prize, Academy Award.* The accompanying chart provides additional guidance on capitalization.

Commonly Capitalized Words

NAMES OF PEOPLE

Booker T. Washington	Helen Keller
Pythagorean theorem	Shakespearean sonnet
Steffi Graf	Arthur Ashe

NAMES OF PLACES AND GEOGRAPHICAL REGIONS

Africa	Indian Ocean
Tibet	Mount Rainier
Indianapolis	Connecticut Avenue

NAMES OF STRUCTURES AND MONUMENTS

the Washington Monument	the Golden Gate Bridge
the Sears Tower	the Lincoln Tunnel

DAYS OF THE WEEK, MONTHS, AND HOLIDAYS

Monday night football	Sunday brunch
an October day	April showers
Canada Day celebrations	Memorial Day parade

(continued)

HISTORICAL EVENTS, PERIODS, MOVEMENTS

the Boer War	the Inquisition
Modernist writers	the Stone Age
the Fabulous Fifties	the Baroque Era

NAMES OF ORGANIZATIONS, INSTITUTIONS, AND BUSINESSES

International Business Systems	the Democratic Party (*or* party)
the Boy Scouts of America	Daughters of the American Revolution
Dell Computer Corporation	the Colorado State Legislature

ABBREVIATIONS AND ACRONYMS

SAT	NATO	NBC	TV
AFL-CIO	NAACP	YWCA	VCR

RELIGIONS AND RELIGIOUS TERMS

Muslims; Islam	Allah; Muhammad; the Koran
Christians; Christianity	Jesus; the Christ; the New Testament
Buddhists; Buddhism	Buddha; the Enlightened One
Jews; Judaism	Moses; the Bible; the Hebrew Scriptures

ETHNIC GROUPS, NATIONALITIES, AND LANGUAGES

Latino/Latina	Arabic
Italian American	Chinese philosophy
African American	Thai cuisine

TRADE NAMES

Nike	Wrangler's
Sony	Kleenex
Wheaties	Jeep

COMPOUND WORDS

Native-American artifacts
Mexican-Indian foods
Asian-American communities

ACADEMIC INSTITUTIONS AND COURSES

Pace University	Spelman College
Anthropology 200	our History 101 teacher

---

1   Capitalize titles of individuals

Capitalize titles when used before a proper name. Do not capitalize titles that follow a proper name or titles used alone.

Justice Scalia	Antonin Scalia, a Supreme Court justice
Governor Christine Todd Whitman	Christine Todd Whitman, governor of New Jersey

Professor Howard Livingston   Howard Livingston, an English professor
Doctor Maria Velásquez   Maria Velásquez, a local doctor

2 Capitalize academic institutions and courses

Capitalize the names of specific schools, departments, and courses. Do not capitalize common nouns for institutions or areas of study.

University of Michigan   a Michigan university
Economics Department   an economics major
Biology 101   an introductory biology course

38e Capitalizing the titles and subtitles of works

Capitalize the first word, the last word, and all words in between (except articles, prepositions, and conjunctions) for titles and subtitles of works.

In Search of Our Mothers' Gardens (book)
Across the River and into the Trees (book)
Landscape with the Fall of Icarus (painting)
The Marriage of Figaro (opera)
The Day after the Bomb (movie)
Poe's Narrators: A Study (report)
"Living Like Weasels" (essay)
"I Stand Here Ironing" (short story)
"To Helen" (poem)
"The River Merchant's Wife: A Letter" (poem)

38f Capitalizing *I* and *O*

Capitalize the personal pronoun *I* (except in quoting literary works that use the lowercase form). Capitalize the interjection *O* (an old form for the more modern, "oh"). Capitalize *oh* only when it begins a sentence.

Do you realize that I have been studying for three hours straight?

Hear our prayer, O Lord.

"Oh, we are in for it now," we said.

There were oh, so many books to read.

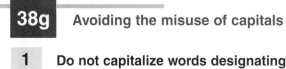

38g   Avoiding the misuse of capitals

1   Do not capitalize words designating family relationships

Use capitals with words designating family relationships only when they are used as names or titles, or in combination with proper names. However, when you substitute a word indicating a family relationship for a name, or use such a word as part of a name, capitalize it.

When he was a boy, *Father* became a good auto mechanic.

When he was a boy, *my father* became a good auto mechanic.

It was a pleasure to visit *Uncle Andy* and *Aunt Marge*.

It was a pleasure to visit *our uncle* and *aunt*.

2   Do not capitalize words denoting seasons or parts of the year

summer vacation	fall term
winter quarters	spring weather
autumn leaves	sophomore year

3   Do not capitalize words for compass directions except when designating a specific geographic area

We headed south first, then west.

The Northeast was hard hit by the economic slump of the 1990s.

EXERCISE 38–1 Supplying Capital Letters

Restore the following passage to its original form by inserting capitalization where it is needed. Also eliminate any unnecessary use of capital letters.

to be married in las vegas, clark county, nevada, a bride must swear that she is eighteen or has parental permission and a bridegroom that he is twenty-one or has parental permission. someone must put up five dollars for the license (on sundays and holidays, fifteen dollars. the clark county courthouse issues marriage licenses at any time of the day or night except between noon and one in the afternoon, between eight and nine in the evening, and between four and five in the morning.) nothing else is required. the state of nevada, alone among these united states, demands neither a premarital blood test nor a waiting period before or after the issuance of a marriage license. driving across the mojave from los angeles, one sees the signs way out on the desert, looming up from that moonscape of rattlesnakes and mesquite, even before the las vegas lights appear like a mirage on the horizon: "getting married? free license information first strip exit." perhaps the las vegas wedding industry achieved its peak operational efficiency between 9:00 p.m. and midnight of august 26, 1965, an otherwise unremarkable thursday which happened to be, by presidential order, the last day on which anyone could improve his draft status merely by getting married. one hundred and seventy-one couples were pronounced Man and Wife in the name of clark county and the state of nevada that night, sixty-seven of them by a single justice of the peace, mr. james a. brennan. mr. brennan did one wedding at the dunes and the other sixty-six in his office, and charged each couple eight dollars. one bride lent her veil to six others. "I got it down from five to three minutes," mr. brennan said later of his feat. "I could've married them *en masse*, but they're people, not cattle. people expect more when they get married."

—Joan Didion, "Marrying Absurd"

EXERCISE 38–2   **Observing Unconventional Capitals**

Collect samples of unconventional uses of capitalization from a newspaper, a magazine, and a literary work. Bring the samples to class and be prepared to explain the effects of any unusual capitalization you find.

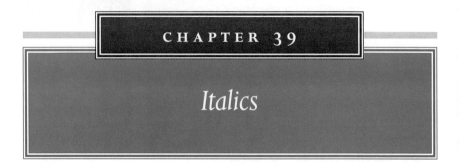

CHAPTER 39

Italics

*I*talic type is a style of printing *in which the letters are slanted to the right.* Italic type is used for certain kinds of material such as book titles, for words requiring special distinction, and for emphasis. Many computers and printers can reproduce italic type. If you do not have printer capability for italics, use <u>underlining</u> in its place.

  Using italics for titles

Use italics to indicate the titles of long or complete works such as novels (see the accompanying chart). Note that the Modern Language Association suggests neither capitalizing nor italicizing any articles that precede the names of magazines or newspapers (the *Atlantic Monthly,* the *New York Times*). Titles of shorter works, such as poems and essays, and titles of sections of works, such as chapters, are set off with quotation marks (see 36f).

Titles to Italicize (or Underline)	
BOOKS	
Pride and Prejudice	*Plagues and Peoples*
FILMS	
Casablanca	*Aladdin*
PLAYS	
A Doll House	*The Glass Menagerie*
LONG POEMS	
The Prelude	*Paradise Lost*

(continued)

NEWSPAPERS

the *Atlanta Constitution*   the *Los Angeles Times*

MAGAZINES

Newsweek   *Science News*

PAMPHLETS

Dangerous Drugs   *Wines of California*

WORKS OF VISUAL ART

van Gogh's *Starry Night*   Kahlo's *Self-Portrait with Monkeys*

MUSICAL WORKS

Tchaikovsky's *Nutcracker*   Mozart's *Don Giovanni*

TELEVISION AND RADIO PROGRAMS

Prime Time Live   *All Things Considered*

RECORDINGS

Bruce Springsteen's *Born to Run*   Whitney Houston's *Bodyguard*

JOURNALS

Nursing Review   *Journal of Economics*

PUBLISHED SPEECHES

Lincoln's *Gettysburg Address*   King's *I Have a Dream* speech

EXCEPTIONS

Titles of sacred works and their parts as well as public documents do not take italics.

the Bible	the Bill of Rights
the New Testament	the U.S. Constitution
the Koran	the Magna Carta

39b   Using italics for words, letters, numbers, and phrases used as words

The word *groovy* has dropped out of current usage.

The letter *y* is not part of the Italian alphabet.

Robert Parish wore the number *00* when he played for the Boston Celtics.

Who coined the phrase *over the hill*?

You may use quotation marks instead of italics in these situations (see 36g). Whichever style you choose, be sure to use it consistently.

Italics may also be used to highlight words being defined.

> The researchers were looking for *microcytes*, abnormally small red blood cells, often associated with anemia.

39c Using italics for foreign words and phrases

English has acquired many words from foreign languages (see 30a). Many of these words are now part of the English language and should not be italicized: spaghetti (Italian), chef (French), kindergarten (German), mesa (Spanish). To find out whether a word or expression is considered foreign, look it up in a dictionary.

> The famous opening movement of Beethoven's Fifth Symphony is marked *allegro non ma troppo* (fast, but not too fast).

> The common sunflower, *Helianthus annuus*, has a tall coarse stem and large, yellow-rayed flower heads that produce edible seeds rich in oil.

39d Using italics for the names of trains, ships, aircraft, and spacecraft

Although you should italicize the names of specific trains, ships, aircraft, and spacecraft, do not italicize general types and classes of these vehicles.

> We took Amtrak's *Empire Builder* to Seattle.

> We rode the Metroliner between Boston and Washington.

TRAINS

the *Orient Express*   the *Silver Streak*

SHIPS

the *Nina*   *U.S.S. Constitution*

AIRCRAFT AND SPACECRAFT

the *Spirit of St. Louis*   the space shuttle *Endeavor*

39e Using italics for emphasis

Although you can use italics for emphasis, do so only sparingly to avoid a tone of insistent exaggeration. Writing becomes more effective when emphasis is created through conciseness, careful word choice, and well-constructed sentences (see 26a and 28b).

> I wanted to find out in what way the *specialness* of my experience could be made to connect me with other people instead of dividing me from them.
>
> —James Baldwin

> "Mommy, there's a *world* in your eye."
>
> —Alice Walker

> And above all I did not wish to be *trivial*; I did not wish to be embarrassing.
>
> —Mary Gordon

EXERCISE 39–1 Using Italics

In the following sentences, add italics where necessary by underlining. Indicate unnecessary italics by circling the incorrectly italicized words. Example:

> *The New Yorker* has a long tradition of distinguished writing.
> (The) *New Yorker* has a long tradition of distinguished writing.

1. The Apollo launch was successful; the spacecraft began its ascent.
2. You can order à la carte if you like, but the special prix fixe dinner is a wonderful value.
3. Although one of Mary Cassatt's most consistent subjects in her art was family life, paintings like The Bath and The Family avoid sentimentality.
4. Brancusi and Rodin, among other sculptors, have rendered people *kissing.*
5. Among the *ships* that made the *voyage* was the Cristofero Colombo.
6. Thor Heyerdahl's book Kon-Tiki describes his sailing adventures on a raft he built and sailed in the South Seas to Easter Island, in Polynesia.
7. The Memoirs of Ulysses S. Grant is one of the finest autobiographical commentaries on the Civil War. Another outstanding memoir in the form of a diary, Mary Chesnut's Civil War, has been recently edited.
8. The film Glory depicts the contributions of an all-black regiment, the Massachusetts 54th, led by Colonel Robert Gould Shaw.
9. Bonnie Raitt's breakthrough recording was Nick of Time.
10. Disparate accounts of the event were presented in *the New York Times*, the San Francisco *Chronicle*, and the Minneapolis *Star*.

CHAPTER 40

Abbreviations

*A*bbreviations serve as a form of shorthand. They enable writers to replace long names and titles with simple, brief sets of letters. A convenience, abbreviations can help writing and reading become more efficient.

The guidelines for using abbreviations outlined in this chapter pertain to nontechnical academic writing and most other writing geared toward a general audience. Technical writing typically includes more numerous and varied abbreviations. (For information concerning abbreviations in documenting source citations in the humanities and sciences, see Chapters 45 and 46.)

40a Abbreviating personal and professional titles and academic degrees

Some personal and professional titles and some academic degrees are abbreviated when placed before or after a name.

Mr. Magnus Larsen	Mrs. Bizet
Ms. Anne Fujiyoshi	Dr. Weber *or* Kaare Weber, M.D.
St. Joan of Arc	Carolyn Smith, Ph.D.
Robert M. Chang, Jr.	Archangelo Narazitti, LL.D.

USAGE NOTE   In sentences, the abbreviations for junior (Jr.) and senior (Sr.) are set off with commas.

Like his son Martin Luther King, Jr., Martin Luther King, Sr., was a distinguished preacher.

Other titles, including religious, military, academic, and governmental titles, should not be abbreviated in academic writing (*President Nelson Mandela,* not Pres. Nelson Mandela). In nonacademic writing you may abbreviate titles before a full name, but you should spell them out when they appear before a surname only.

Rev. John Kauta	Reverend Kauta
Gen. Andrew Jackson	General Jackson

Prof. Elaine Showalter   Professor Showalter
Sen. William Bradley   Senator Bradley

Abbreviate academic degrees when used alone. Do not, however, abbreviate personal or professional titles used alone.

ACCEPTABLE   He received his Ed.D. the same year his sister received her Ph.D.

UNACCEPTABLE   She had a reputation as a tough prof.

REVISED   She had a reputation as a tough professor.

Be careful not to abbreviate a single title twice with a person's name. Use an abbreviated title before *or* after the name, but not in both places.

UNACCEPTABLE   Dr. Amelia Sternheim, M.D.

ACCEPTABLE   Dr. Amelia Sternheim

ACCEPTABLE   Amelia Sternheim, M.D.

However, you can use two abbreviations for two different titles.

Prof. Peter Edelson, Esq.

40b   Using familiar acronyms and abbreviations

Acronyms are abbreviations that are pronounced as words, such as *NATO* (North Atlantic Treaty Organization) and *MADD* (Mothers against Drunk Driving). Abbreviations not pronounced as words are sometimes called **initial abbreviations** or **initialisms** (to emphasize that each letter is sounded). Examples include *IBM* (International Business Machines) and *NBC* (National Broadcasting Company). Usually, initial abbreviations use all capital letters. Sometimes, however, they may be written with only the first letter capitalized: *Unesco, Nabisco,* and *Nimby,* for example. (See 32a for information on punctuating acronyms and abbreviations.)

If you use a term that has an abbreviated form only once in an essay or a report, spell it out. However, when a term appears often in a report, or when you write for an informed audience, use the abbreviation. Spell out the full term on first use, note the abbreviation in parentheses, and use the abbreviation thereafter.

The Modern Language Association (MLA) has published a guide for writers that contains detailed guidelines on issues of manuscript style for papers in the humanities. The MLA has entitled the book *MLA Handbook for Writers of Research Papers,* Third Edition. Writers of papers and articles in the social sciences should consult the publication of the American Psychological Association

(APA). The APA guide, which can be found in most libraries, is entitled *Publication Manual of the American Psychological Association,* Fourth Edition.

40c Using the abbreviations *a.m.*, *p.m.*, *B.C. (BC)*, *A.D. (AD)*, and symbols

Using *a.m.* and *p.m.*

The abbreviations *a.m.* and *p.m.* should be used only with exact times.

Class begins at *11:15 a.m.* and ends at *1:15 p.m.*, exactly two hours later.

The notation *a.m.* abbreviates the Latin *ante meridiem,* meaning "before noon"; *p.m.* abbreviates the Latin *post meridiem,* meaning "after noon."

USAGE NOTE   The abbreviations *a.m.* and *p.m.* should be used only with numbers, never with the words *morning, evening,* and *night.*

INCORRECT	We met at 7:30 p.m. in the evening.
REVISED	We met at 7:30 p.m.
REVISED	We met at seven-thirty in the evening.

Using *B.C. (BC)* and *A.D. (AD)*

In abbreviations for years, place *B.C.* ("before Christ") or *B.C.E.* (before the common era") after the year: *500 B.C.; 5000 B.C.E.* Place *A.D.* (*anno Domini*—"the year of the Lord") or *C.E.* ("common era") before the year: *A.D. 1066; C.E. 1995.* Note that you should use these abbreviations only when your readers may be confused about the time period you are referring to: *The Hopewell culture flourished in what is now the Midwest of the United States from 100 B.C. to A.D. 550.*

Using symbols ($, %, @, #, &, +, −, =)

Symbols, such as $, %, @, #, &, +, −, and =, are spelled out except in technical discussions that refer to numbers and symbols frequently. As a general rule, avoid using symbols in academic papers, except in graphs and tables.

| INAPPROPRIATE | Nearly 100% of those applying are accepted. |
| REVISED | Nearly 100 percent of those applying are accepted. |

It is acceptable, however, to use the dollar sign before certain figures: *$10 million.*

The university's fund-raising goal is $10 million.

In writing scientific and business reports that require many numbers and symbols, using the symbols (rather than words) will make your writing easier to understand. Let the nature of your writing task, your audience, and your purpose influence your decision about using such symbols. And remember to use the style you choose consistently.

40d Using Latin abbreviations for documentation

In general, avoid using the following Latin abbreviations except when citing sources in a research paper or when making a parenthetical point.

ABBREVIATION	MEANING
i.e.	that is (*id est*)
e.g.	for example (*exempli gratia*)
etc.	and so forth (*et cetera*)
cf.	compare (*confer*)
et al.	and others (*et alia*)
N.B.	note well (*nota bene*)

INAPPROPRIATE   Some companies provide extensive benefits for their employees; e.g., they offer health and dental plans, vacation time, stock options, etc.

REVISED   Some companies provide extensive benefits for their employees; for example, they offer health and dental plans, vacation time, stock options, and the like.

WRITING HINT   Avoid ending a sentence with an abbreviation. A sentence that ends with *etc.*, for example, gives readers the impression that you ran out of examples or did not bother to provide specifics.

40e Using other types of abbreviations

Given names and academic courses

INCORRECT   Chas. is taking Robt. Mitchell's advanced chem. course.

REVISED   *Charles* is taking *Robert* Mitchell's advanced *chemistry* course.

Months, days, and holidays

INCORRECT   Did Jan. 17, 1993, fall on a Tues.?

REVISED   Did *January* 17, 1993, fall on a *Tuesday*?

INCORRECT   New Yr's Eve is my favorite holiday.

REVISED   New *Year's* Eve is my favorite holiday.

Geographical designations

INCORRECT   They drove from Nashville, TN to Miami, FL.

REVISED   They drove from Nashville, *Tennessee,* to Miami, *Florida.*

Exceptions include *Washington, D.C.,* and *U.S.* (the latter can serve as an adjective but not as a noun.)

U.S. involvement in Vietnam was a hotly contested issue in the 1960s.

Many immigrants who visit Washington, *D.C.,* come away with a sense of pride in the United States. [*United States* as noun]

State Abbreviations

Use the U.S. Postal Code abbreviations for states only in full addresses on mail or in text, and in documentation. In all other cases, spell out the name of the state.

STATE	ABBREVIATION	STATE	ABBREVIATION
Alabama	AL	Montana	MT
Alaska	AK	Nebraska	NB
Arizona	AZ	Nevada	NV
Arkansas	AR	New Hampshire	NH
California	CA	New Jersey	NJ
Colorado	CO	New Mexico	NM
Connecticut	CT	New York	NY
Delaware	DE	North Carolina	NC
Florida	FL	North Dakota	ND
Georgia	GA	Ohio	OH
Hawaii	HI	Oklahoma	OK
Idaho	ID	Oregon	OR
Illinois	IL	Pennsylvania	PA
Indiana	IN	Rhode Island	RI
Iowa	IA	South Carolina	SC
Kansas	KS	South Dakota	SD
Kentucky	KY	Tennessee	TN
Louisiana	LA	Texas	TX
Maine	ME	Utah	UT
Maryland	MD	Vermont	VT
Massachusetts	MA	Virginia	VA
Michigan	MI	Washington	WA
Minnesota	MN	West Virginia	WV
Mississippi	MS	Wisconsin	WI
Missouri	MO	Wyoming	WY

Units of measurement

Avoid abbreviating units of measurement, except in technical writing.

INCORRECT   Mary is five ft., two in. tall.

REVISED   Mary is five *feet*, two *inches* tall.

Exceptions include *mph* (miles per hour), *rpm* (revolutions per minute), and *cps* (cycles per second).

We were traveling at 70 mph when the police pulled us over.

Do not abbreviate parts of a company's name (e.g., *Inc.*, *Bros.*, or *Co.*) unless the abbreviation is part of the actual name. Use the ampersand (&) only when it is part of the company's name.

Company names

INCORRECT   Sears, Roebuck and Co. opened a store next to the A and P.

REVISED   Sears, Roebuck & *Company* opened a store next to the *A&P*.

 ## Using abbreviations for reference information

Although it is conventional to abbreviate such words as *editor* (*ed.*), *page* and *pages* (*p.* and *pp.*), *chapter* (*ch.*), and *volume* (*vol.*) in citing sources, do not use such abbreviations in the body of a paper.

INCORRECT   The preface to the 1855 ed. of Whitman's *Leaves of Grass* is often reprinted with the last edition (the 1892 or deathbed ed.) of this revolutionary book of poems.

REVISED   The preface to the 1855 edition of Whitman's *Leaves of Grass* is often reprinted with the last edition (the 1892 or deathbed edition) of this revolutionary book of poems.

For information about abbreviating when citing sources, see Part Nine on research writing and the accompanying checklist.

Abbreviations Checklist

Check your writing for incorrect or inappropriate use of abbreviations. Consult the appropriate sections in this chapter for advice about using the following types of abbreviations.

- Personal and professional titles such as *Ms.* and *Dr.* (40a)
- Academic degrees such as *B.S. [or BS]*, *M.A. [or MA]*, and *Ph.D. [or PhD]* (40a)

(continued)

- Acronyms such as *OPEC* and *NATO* (40b)
- Times, years, and symbols such as *7:15 a.m., 500 B.C.,* and *$1,500* (40c)
- Latin abbreviations such as *etc.* and *e.g.* (40d)
- Given names and academic courses (40e)
- Months, days, and holidays (40e)
- Geographical designations such as *NJ* and *Calif.* (40e)
- Units of measurement such as *mph* and *rpm* (40e)
- Company names such as *A&P* (40e)
- Reference information such as *p., vol.,* and *ed.* (40f)

EXERCISE 40–1   Using Abbreviations

Revise the following sentences to provide abbreviations where they are acceptable in academic writing. Also eliminate any inappropriate abbreviations. Example:

> The pres. vetoed the bill, even though it had been approved by 75% of the senators who voted.

> The president vetoed the bill, even though it had been approved by 75 *percent* of the senators who voted.

1. When you order cold cuts, you can ask for them by the kg or by the lb.
2. Of the many summer courses offered, Expository Writing and Economics were among the most heavily subscribed. Expos and Econ have long been popular with visiting students.
3. Of the many titles she could have used, Eliz. Bennet, Esq., opted for the one that meant the most to her: Dr.
4. It was on a cold and dark Dec. night, a Sat., I believe, around 11:59 p.m., that I was first visited by that infernal raven. The willful creature stayed past my normal bedtime of one a.m. in the morning.
5. To get the best possible mpg, try to keep the engine at around 2,200 rpm when you are doing fifty-five mph.
6. Anthony Perotsky, junior, did not want to work in the lingerie business established by Mr. Perotsky, sr. Instead, he wanted to earn a BA, an MA, and a PhD in anthropology.
7. Sanibel Isl. is a beautiful spot just SW of Fort Myers, FL.
8. The ball soared sixty yds before sailing through the uprights for a three-pt. field goal.
9. Although more than seventy % of the students at OU are female, only one-third of the faculty and none of the sr. administrators are women.
10. The morning bio and chem sections are already fully enrolled.

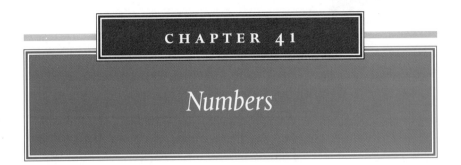

CHAPTER 41

Numbers

When you use numbers in writing, you will sometimes spell them out and other times write them as numerals. In scientific and technical writing, numbers are usually written as figures. However, in non-technical writing geared toward a general audience, numbers are usually spelled out according to the conventions outlined in this chapter.

41a Spelling out numbers of one or two words

In a nontechnical piece of writing that uses numbers, if you can spell out a number in one or two words, do so.

The twenty-five members of the class were all present for the party.

A hyphenated number, as in the preceding example, is considered one word. (See 42b-3 for more on using hyphens with compound numbers.)
Use figures for numbers that cannot be spelled out in one or two words.

She needed another 122 votes to win the election.

When a sentence contains some numbers that should be spelled out and others that should be written as figures, make sure to use one convention consistently.

INCONSISTENT   Our cruise was a short one hundred miles; other vacation-ers elected longer trips—up to 475 miles.

CONSISTENT   Our cruise was a short 100 miles; other vacationers elected longer trips—up to 475 miles.

41b Spelling out numbers at the beginning of a sentence

Always spell out numbers that begin a sentence. However, sentences that begin with spelled-out numbers of more than two words can be awkward and difficult to read. In that case, revise the sentence to begin with another word.

INCORRECT   100,000 or more marchers demonstrated at the rally.

REVISED   More than 100,000 marchers demonstrated at the rally.

AWKWARD   One hundred fifty-seven million dollars was the selling price of the two companies combined.

REVISED   The selling price of the two companies combined was $157 million.

USAGE NOTE When you use more than one number to modify a noun, spell out the first number or the shorter of the two numbers to avoid confusion: *six 8-inch slats, 300 one-gallon containers.*

41c Using figures according to convention

Although convention generally requires that most numbers of one or two words be spelled out, there are many exceptions. As the accompanying chart shows, figures are always used for days and years; pages, chapters, and volume numbers of books; acts, scenes, and lines of plays; decimals, fractions, ratios, and percentages; temperatures; addresses; scores and statistics; exact amounts of money; and the time of day.

Guidelines for Using Figures

DAYS AND YEARS

February 15, 1945	February 1945	A.D. [*or* AD] 700	the 1990s
15 February 1945	June 3rd	406 B.C. [*or* BC]	1980–88

Note: Reserve the use of ordinal numbers expressed as figures (*1st, 2nd, 3rd*) for dates without the year. In other instances, spell out ordinal numbers (*first, second, third*).

Exception: The day of a month may be expressed in words when the year does not follow: *October first.*

PAGES, CHAPTERS, VOLUMES

page 49	chapter 15
pages 135–47	volume 2

ACTS, SCENES, LINES

Othello, act 5, scene 1, lines 1–12 [*or Othello*, 5.1.1–12]

(continued)

DECIMALS, FRACTIONS, RATIOS, AND PERCENTAGES

    37.5   3/4   4:1 [*or* four to one]   [51% *or* 52 percent]

TEMPERATURES

    721 °F   10 °C

ADDRESSES

    244 Orchard St., Apt. 3K
    Aberdeen, NJ 07654

SCORES AND STATISTICS

    a combined SAT score of 1200
    a margin of 2 to 1

AMOUNTS OF MONEY

    $3.75 $2.16 million   75¢

    Exceptions: Round dollar or cent amounts of two or three words may be
    spelled out: *twenty-five dollars, fifty cents.*

TIME OF DAY

    7 a.m.   2:45 p.m.   1640 hours

    Exceptions: When expressing time without *a.m.* or *p.m.*, spell out the num-
    bers: *seven in the morning, seven-thirty in the evening* (not *7 in the morn-
    ing* or *7:30 in the evening*). When using *o'clock* to indicate time, express
    the number in words: *three o'clock* (not *3 o'clock*).

EXERCISE 41–1   **Using Numbers**

Revise the following sentences so that the numbers are expressed as numerals or
words according to the conventions outlined in this chapter. Example:

> The Battle of Gettysburg began on July 1st, 1863.
> The Battle of Gettysburg began on *July 1,* 1863.

1. Not long ago a subway ride cost 50 cents.

2. Hamlet's famous soliloquy that begins "To be or not to be" can be found near
   the beginning of the third act. To be precise, it occurs at lines 55–89 of the first
   scene of act three.

3. Our biology text was published in nineteen seventy-five.

4. His birthday, April first, is often cause for practical jokes as well as for cele-
   bration. His brother, born on January 1, considers himself luckier since he can
   be considered a New Year's baby rather than an April fool.

5. One hundred billion dollars is a staggering sum.

6. On December 5th, 1985, a cold snowy day that registered zero °F, J. D. Spencer, a halfback for the Los Angeles Raiders, carried the ball for two hundred sixty-nine and a half yards. This impressive record of running yardage was complemented by a 3:2 ratio of yards from pass receptions.

7. Spencer began the game at 4 o'clock in the afternoon and finished 3 hours later, at 7:09 in the evening, to be exact. His feat was broadcast over channel seven on television and on the radio station six hundred sixty AM, WFAN. You can find these statistics in the imaginary volume of *Great Sports Stats for the Nineteen Eighties* on page one thousand two hundred and fifty-nine.

8. Read all of act two, scene three for tomorrow, and look ahead to act two, scene four, lines one through two hundred fifty-seven.

9. The board measured ten ft. three and one-half in. by one ft. one in.

10. 200 people attended the meeting.

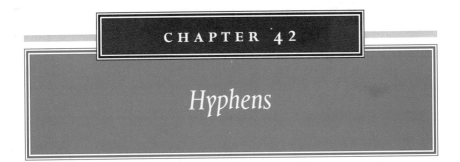

CHAPTER 42

Hyphens

Hyphenation occurs most often for the simple reason that a word is too long to fit at the end of a line of type. In such cases the writer divides the word, putting part of the word at the end of one line and the remainder of the word at the beginning of the next line. Writers also use hyphens to join words or parts of words, as in *go-between* and *knick-knack.* Do not confuse a **hyphen** (-) with a dash (—), which is made by combining two hyphens (see 37a).

42a Use hyphens to divide words at the end of a line

When you must divide a word at the end of a typewritten line, be sure to divide it between syllables and to place the hyphen immediately after the first part of the divided word. The word *intricate,* for example, which contains three syllables (*in•tri•cate*), can be divided after *in-* or after *intri-.* Dictionaries indicate syllabication for all words; to be sure your word divisions are correct, check a reliable dictionary (see 27a).

In addition, follow the conventions described in the accompanying chart on dividing words at the end of a typewritten line.

Conventions for Dividing Words at the End of a Line

- Do not divide one-syllable words, even long ones such as *thought* and *health.*
- Although the first letter of a word may comprise a syllable, do not leave one letter on a line. Leave at least two letters on each line when dividing a word.

INCORRECT	Guard against infection by applying an i-odine ointment to the wound.
REVISED	Guard against infection by applying an io-dine ointment to the wound.

- Do not divide abbreviations, contractions, or numbers. *U.S.A., couldn't,* and *50,000* should not be hyphenated.

(continued)

615

- Do not hyphenate names of people and places. Neither *Thomas Jefferson* nor his home, *Monticello,* can be hyphenated.
- Only divide words between syllables. You cannot hyphenate the word *recess,* for example, as *rec-ess* but only as *re-cess.*
- Divide compound words only between the words that form the compound. Split the word *homecoming,* for example, across two lines as *home-coming,* not as *ho-mecoming* or *homecom-ing.*
- Divide words according to their prefixes and suffixes. Divide *subordinate* after the prefix (*sub-ordinate*) and the word *fairly* before the suffix (*fair-ly*).
- Remember to attach the hyphen to the part of the word on the first line and not to the part of the word that begins the next line.

EXERCISE 42–1   **Deciding Where to Hyphenate Words**

Divide each of the following words into syllables. Then place a hyphen after each syllable that can be left at the end of a line.

1. contract
2. burped
3. laudable
4. introverted
5. swimming
6. certitude
7. didn't
8. synonymous
9. hardworking
10. meaty

42b   Use hyphens with compound words

Compound words consist of two or more words joined together as a single word. Some are written as one word, others as hyphenated words, and still others as separate words without hyphens.

ONE WORD   skyline, scarecrow, outlaw

HYPHENATED   brother-in-law, cross-examination, nation-state

SEPARATE   junior high, energy guide, ice cream

It is sometimes difficult to determine when to hyphenate a compound word. Conventions shift rapidly and are unpredictable. Even compound words that begin with the same word are treated differently: *breakthrough, break dance, break-in.* And although many words pass through successive stages—from two words (*base ball*) to a hyphenated form (*base-ball*) to a single word (*baseball*)—some remain at the first or second stage. Consult your dictionary for help with hyphenating compound words. (See also 31f on spelling hyphenated words.)

1   Hyphens with compound adjectives

Use a hyphen for **compound adjectives**—two or more adjectives that function as a unit to modify a noun or pronoun—when the adjective precedes the noun or pronoun. When the compound adjective follows the noun or pronoun, however, do not hyphenate.

Steffi Graff is a world-renowned tennis star.

Steffi Graff is world renowned as a tennis star.

Do not use a hyphen when part of the compound adjective ends in *-ly*.

The surprisingly short concert disappointed the audience.

2   Hyphens with coined compounds

A **coined compound** connects words not ordinarily linked or hyphenated. Use coined compounds sparingly in formal and academic writing; reserve them to create an informal tone.

They were in a let-it-all-hang-out frame of mind.

3   Hyphens with fractions and compound numbers

Use a hyphen when spelling out fractions to connect the numerator and denominator.

The cake was one-quarter finished before dinner even began.

The strip of wood was three-eighths of an inch wide.

Also use a hyphen to spell out whole numbers from twenty-one through ninety-nine, even when those numbers are part of larger numbers.

one thousand thirty-five

eighty thousand six hundred fifty-two

Usually compound numbers are expressed as figures (see 41a).

4   Hyphens in a series

Use a hyphen for a series of compound words built on the same base. Be sure to leave a space after the first word.

First- and second-generation immigrants composed the class.

42c   Using hyphens with prefixes and suffixes

Prefixes are generally combined with word stems without hyphens: *prefatory*, *interview*, *disbelief*, *non*compliant, *re*elect. In cases where the prefix precedes a capital letter or when a capital letter is combined with a word, separate the two with a hyphen: anti-American, pre-Columbian, H-bomb.

Certain prefixes, such as *all-*, *self-*, *quasi-*, and *ex-* (to mean "formerly"), normally take a hyphen when combined with words: *all*-encompassing, *self*-denial, *ex*-player, *quasi*-convincing.

Very few suffixes take a hyphen. Two of these are *-elect* and *-some*, as in governor-*elect* and twenty-*some*.

Using Hyphens with Prefixes

- Use hyphens when using the prefixes *all-*, *ex-*, *quasi-*, and *self-*.

    all-important, ex-wife, quasi-independent, self-reliant

- Use a hyphen when the base word is a proper noun, a number, or a capitalized word.

    pro-European, post-1990, mid-August

- Use a hyphen when the base word is a compound.

    anti-abortion rally, ex-governor

- Use a hyphen with two or more prefixes for a base word.

    pro- and anti-war demonstrations

- Use a hyphen to prevent confusion in meaning between two similar words. Distinguish *recall* (a recollection), for example, from *re-call* (to call back).

- Use a hyphen to prevent confusion that could result from combinations of vowels and consonants (e.g., double *i*'s or consonants) in such words as *anti-intellectual* and *non-native*. But note that some prefixes, especially those with double vowels, do not use the hyphen: *reentry*, *cooperation*, *coordination*, *nonexistent*. Check your dictionary when in doubt.

WRITING HINT   Do not capitalize words containing the prefix *ex-* and the suffix *-elect*, even in titles with proper names.

INCORRECT	Ex-Mayor Bradley
REVISED	ex-Mayor Bradley
INCORRECT	Governor-Elect Ramirez
REVISED	Governor-elect Ramirez

EXERCISE 42-2   Using the Dictionary to Check Hyphenation

Consult your dictionary to see how to hyphenate the following words.

1. scofflaw
2. ringmaster
3. oil slick
4. head start
5. interdependent
6. reevaluate
7. aftermath
8. preprogrammed
9. retrograde
10. profeminist

EXERCISE 42-3   Using Hyphens

Add hyphens where appropriate in the following sentences. (Some sentences may be correct as written.)

1. The summer of 1994 marks the twenty fifth anniversary of Woodstock.
2. Four fifths of the class selected the take home examination option.
3. The team had completed one half of its schedule, with a three fourths to one fourth ratio of victories to defeats.
4. Her ex spouse refused to pay the child support directly to her.
5. Intra uterine devices are not as prevalent now as they were a generation ago.

Research

An Essential Truth about Research

There is nothing mysterious about the research process. It is fundamental to much that you do, whether you are developing an interesting idea for one of your courses or solving a problem. Even the simplest decisions—what to wear, what movie to see, whether to study now or later—involve calling experience from memory and weighing it before acting. This decision-making process forms the basis for the more structured research you will do when you develop an idea about a selected or assigned topic for your research essay.

Part Nine will teach you essential skills for writing that essay.

- How to use the library's resources efficiently to become more knowledgeable about your topic (Chapter 43)

- How to do field research (43g)

- How to develop an idea about a topic, take notes, use and integrate sources, and write a research essay that presents your idea about a topic to an audience (Chapter 44)

- How to credit sources in MLA, APA, and other documentation styles (Chapter 45)

You will also see how one student, Ericka Kostka, worked her way through this entire research process as she decided whether the gray wolf, an endangered species, should be reintroduced into Yellowstone National Park. Ericka's essay—her defense of her thesis about the gray wolf—appears in Chapter 46.

CHAPTER 43

Understanding Research

*D*oing research is not some new experience that you have to learn from scratch. You have been researching most of your life. Every time you solve a problem, you follow a familiar process of doing research in your head. The research you will need to do to write a research essay is more structured, and it relies on more than the evidence you cull from memory. But that structured research has much in common with the problem-solving process that has become second nature to you.

Directed research is the formal research you will do to accumulate evidence and develop a thesis on an assigned or selected research topic. Eventually, you will present and defend that thesis—your reasoned conclusion about the accumulated evidence—in a research essay.

Directed research often begins as you read your required course materials and come upon a topic that intrigues you. Your quest to find out more about this topic can involve such diverse activities as conducting experiments, administering surveys, and undertaking field research; but most often, your search takes you into the library. It may also lead you to the Internet and to the World Wide Web. These information systems connect you to a wide array of computer networks and resources that give you immediate access to information that can supplement your library's collection. Once in the library or on the Internet, you can locate books, journals, magazines, newspapers, and other sources that contain additional information on the subject you have chosen or been assigned. This process that begins with your interest in a particular topic leads to your acquiring more knowledge about it, forming a thesis about it, and finally writing a research essay on it. The process can also lead to discovery and excitement.

To look upon research as a tedious or boring trip to the library where you do no more than select sources, go back to your room to read, fill out index cards, organize evidence, and write a report of your findings is to overlook the potential for excitement at discovering your own idea about a topic and communicating that idea to your audience. As a researcher, you seek out and find answers to questions. You experience the pleasure of learning new things and enrich your understanding of your topic. Along the way, you should acquire a sense of what it is like to be a productive scholar and an accomplished problem solver.

The research process includes both directed research and writing the research essay (see Chapter 44). Like the writing process we explored earlier in the *Handbook* (see Chapter 1), the research process follows a recursive path that moves back and forth from researching to writing and from writing to researching. You may do some preliminary research after finding a topic that interests you, draft a bit, and then discover that you need to revise your topic or completely start anew. You will then do additional research and more writing as you learn more about your topic and start to develop an idea.

This chapter will help you make sense of your research assignment and will show you how to select an appropriate topic. You will also learn how to use library and Internet resources and do field research to compile a collection of sources on your topic for use in a research essay. In addition, this chapter, as well as Chapters 44 and 46, will follow Ericka Kostka's research process so that you can see how research is done.

1   Understand the assignment

Whatever research assignment you are given, carefully consider any written guidelines or your instructor's advice about the assignment. Analyze the assignment by breaking down and sorting the individual tasks. Consider the purpose and audience, length requirements, and the due date and any interim deadlines (e.g., for completing preliminary research, for submitting a tentative thesis, and for handing in drafts).

The assignment given to Ericka Kostka, whose research essay appears in Chapter 46, specified the following requirements.

> Investigate an issue that has far-reaching social and ethical consequences, and write an essay of six to twelve pages for a general audience, using primarily secondary sources. Your research essay should present and defend your point of view about the issue. You have four weeks to complete the assignment.

2   Think about purpose and audience

Your overarching purpose for doing research will always be to become knowledgeable about a given topic so that you can develop a thesis about it and write a research essay. And, within your essay, your purpose may be to provide information or to persuade readers of your point of view. But when you read your assignment, look carefully for other implied purposes so that you know what your instructor expects in response to the assignment. Make sure, for example, that you understand the key terms that specify your assignment: *analyze, explain, argue, survey, compare or contrast, explore, persuade.* Each of those terms indicates a particular way of approaching your topic. If you have any doubts about what you are being asked to do, discuss the assignment with your instructor.

Once you have established your purpose, consider your potential audience. Your audience will likely be your instructor, but the assignment or the topic itself may specify or suggest a wider audience. You need to know whether you will be writing for a general audience of interested readers or whether you will be addressing an audience of specialists. You should think about whether your audience will be friendly or hostile and what opinions and attitudes that audience might hold. In addition, give some thought to the response you hope to elicit from your audience. (See 1d for more details on audience and purpose.)

3   Devise a schedule and pace yourself

It is often difficult to know at the outset how long it will take to complete your research and your writing. The recursive process of going back and forth from research to writing should continue until you can develop and defend your thesis. Often, your instructor will help you limit the scope of your research by specifying a deadline, a required length for the final essay, and the approximate number of sources that you should consult. You may also be told the types of sources to consult; generally you will have to consult a mix of primary and secondary sources (43c).

The amount of time you spend on research and writing will depend on your efficiency in locating sources in the library and on the Internet, as well as on your effectiveness as a critical reader and as a writer.

This chapter and the others in Part Nine will help you learn the essential skills that make an effective research writer. A useful beginning step is to develop a workable schedule for your research project. The accompanying overview chart will give you a sense of what is involved in a research project (see the sections cited in parentheses for detailed information on each task). Use this overview to plan a strategy for researching and writing that will enable you to complete your project within the allotted time frame. You can make notations about your schedule as well as about your topic and your reading in a *reading* or *research journal* (see 1e-1–2).

Scheduling your research project will be much easier after your first visit to the library. Once you begin to assemble your working bibliography (see 43h), start reading, and restrict your topic, you will have a clearer sense of your topic, and you will be able to judge better your own speed for performing these various tasks. You will be able to pace yourself.

If you are required to conduct field research—surveys, interviews, experiments (see 43g)—be aware that your project can take more time because you may need to supplement the field research with directed library research. In addition, field research can be time consuming. You may need to mail away surveys and wait for the replies; you will then have to factor in time for sorting the data that are returned to you. You may also need to schedule interviews in advance or repeat experiments over time. Consider these variables, plan carefully, and structure your schedule accordingly.

Schedule and Overview of the Research Process

DUE   **DO PRELIMINARY RESEARCH**

_____   1. Understand the nature of the assignment (43a-1), consider purpose and audience (43a-2), and devise a schedule (43a-3).

_____   2. Select a topic that interests you (43b).

_____   3. Do preliminary research to get background information (43d).

_____   4. Compile a working bibliography containing each useful source you encounter (43h).

_____   5. Based on what you learned from your initial foray in the library, restrict your topic (44a).

EXTEND THE RESEARCH

_____   6. Do more research on your restricted topic and evaluate the sources in your working bibliography (44a–c).

_____   7. Read your sources critically and evaluate their effectiveness in light of your topic and purpose (44c).

_____   8. Take accurate notes on helpful sources. Use summaries, paraphrases, and quotations, as appropriate (44d). Be careful to avoid plagiarism (44j).

_____   9. Devise a focusing question to help guide your research. That focusing question will develop into your thesis (44e).

_____ 10. Reflect on your sources and notes to help spark your creativity, make connections, and generate ideas (44d-4).

_____ 11. Consider whether to do field research (43g).

PLAN, WRITE, RESEARCH SOME MORE, AND REVISE

_____ 12. Begin developing an informal outline of your essay indicating how you might organize and present the defense of your thesis. Revise this plan as you do additional research (44g).

_____ 13. Consider your audience and purpose (44f).

_____ 14. Draft your essay (44h).

_____ 15. Incorporate evidence from your note cards to support and develop your thesis (44i).

_____ 16. Determine the required documentation style and be sure to document all of your sources properly (Chapter 45) both in the text (45a and 45d) and at the end of the paper in a list of Works Cited (45c) or a reference list (45f).

_____ 17. Revise the essay. Consult with your instructor and collaborate with your classmates to help with your revisions. Do additional research if necessary (44k).

_____ 18. Prepare the final manuscript (44l).

_____ 19. Submit the final essay.

43b Selecting your topic

Whether you are choosing from a list provided by your instructor or se-lecting your own, you should try to work with a topic that interests you and that you care about. It makes little difference whether you know a great deal about the topic; at the outset, interest is paramount.

Try thinking about what you have been studying in the course to get ideas. Go back to your reading journal or your personal journal and see what questions you recorded about the course, looking for the material that really sparked your interest. Do some reading; skim, preview, or reread your text-books for the course; look at magazines, journals, encyclopedias, or other ref-erence books (see 43d-2). Try various techniques for generating ideas, such as freewriting (2b-2), annotating (2b-1), questioning (4a and 47a-3), and listing details and observations (47b-1) to get your creative juices flowing. Also con-sider what you would like to know more about, and make a list of two or three topics for investigation. Let those topics be the subject of your initial search in the library (43d).

Ericka Kostka, for example, selected the gray wolf as a topic for research in her Social and Ethical Issues writing course in 1993. When her instructor asked students to select a topic that had far-reaching social consequences, Er-icka recalled her interest in the gray wolf that had arisen a few years earlier during a visit to Yellowstone National Park. What she learned there sparked her interest in unnatural ecological imbalances. She wanted to pursue the topic and the gray wolf in a research essay. The following statement reflects Ericka's early interest in the demise of the gray wolf and her concern about the feasibility of bringing wolves back to the park.

During the summer of 1985, I was one of the 215,000 people who trooped through the "Wolves and Humans" informational slide show at Yellowstone. It was here that I heard the chilling howl of the gray wolf that communicates some-thing about which humans can only speculate. I saw the wolf as the hunted when I heard of its systematic decimation at the beginning of the century. I saw the wolf as the hunter when I heard of its place as the premier predator of the park's hooved animals. Having confirmed this faithful representation of the duality of the gray wolf's history in Yellowstone, I wanted to come to my own conclusions about the restoration proposal that would try to reestablish the gray wolf population in the park.

As you can see, Ericka had a personal interest in her research. She had been affected by what she saw and heard earlier on that trip to the park. When she began her research, that personal interest propelled but did not limit her. She knew that she had to move beyond her personal experience to *investigate* the problem so that she could think more rigorously about it. In addition, she had to reach her own conclusion about how to solve the gray wolf problem. These two tasks, investigating the topic thoroughly and reaching a conclusion about it, are fundamental in the research process. The tasks will likely lead you, as they led Ericka, to the library.

Try to get feedback from your instructor before becoming too involved in researching and writing about a topic. You will want to determine whether your topic will interest others, whether there are adequate resources in your library or in your community to enable you to proceed, and whether the topic can be completed in the allotted time. Your instructor may have helpful hints on these matters. Often, as a starting point for discussion, instructors will require a brief statement about your planned topic.

43c Using primary and secondary sources

In your research, you will likely be consulting both primary and secondary sources. *Primary sources* are firsthand accounts: historical documents, interviews, surveys, experiments, diaries, journals, letters, books, articles, eyewitness accounts of an event, or a writer's original work (a novel, poem, short story, or essay)—any source that you can examine directly as raw evidence, as if you are the first to look at it.

Secondary sources are materials written about primary sources. Secondary sources include analyses of raw evidence by scholars, experts in a field, or other researchers. Secondary sources also include critical writing that expresses an opinion, draws conclusions, or explains an issue or circumstance. You can find secondary sources in the form of books, pamphlets, reviews, articles, and essays.

When you read or examine primary sources, you do all of the analytical work. Yours will be a fresh look at the source, free of the bias of other researchers. That freedom to interpret can be exciting, but it can also be a bit intimidating. Secondary sources can help you analyze the primary sources because in them you will find interpretations, ways of looking at the raw evidence. But be aware that secondary sources can bias the way you look at raw material. When you turn to secondary sources, look for insight but not for an answer. Only you can come up with the thesis or the solution to the problem you are investigating.

Most of your research will involve consulting both primary and secondary sources. Let your purpose and assignment determine the types of sources you consult in your research. On occasion, you may use only primary evidence collected from your own interviews, experiments, or surveys (see 43g). In that case, your research effort will involve evaluating the primary evidence.

At other times, you will use only secondary sources. When you do, you should be reading those sources for insight, not only to learn more about your topic, but also to find out what other researchers and writers may have overlooked; read critically (see Chapter 2) even as you read to accumulate knowledge. In her research, Ericka consulted secondary sources because she was not able to conduct field research.

43d Discovering the library's resources

The library contains a wealth of information that will be a great help to you as a researcher. Whether you are beginning to do background reading to find a topic, looking for information to help you focus your topic, or preparing to investigate your topic in depth, the library is the place to go.

Before Ericka went to the library, she considered limiting her investigation to the wolf problem in Yellowstone. But because she did not yet know enough about the problem to decide how to restrict her topic (see 44a), she decided instead to keep an open mind. She needed more information. Once in the library, Ericka had a more immediate problem than the gray wolf controversy; she had to find her way around and learn to use the library's resources efficiently.

To be an efficient researcher, it helps to have some kind of research strategy. Begin by learning the physical layout of the library and the organization of the book stacks; familiarize yourself with the available reference guides and the library's card and online catalogs. Your research will go smoother if you identify key words related to your topic (see 43e-2 on key word searches). *Key words* consist of synonyms or other words that capture a part of what the topic is about. They will help you as you search through the library's catalogs. Ericka's list of key words included *wolf, wolf restoration, animal repopulation,* and *endangered species.*

Once you are oriented in the library, devise a plan of action. Where will you start? How will you proceed? Try to be systematic in your research (e.g., find all the sources you can about one particular key word at a time), but also realize that research is a process of discovery. Allow yourself to find the unexpected and to pursue interesting sidetracks up to a point; but try to stay organized and focused on your topic. Ericka probably found many intriguing subjects listed when she searched for her key word *wolf.* But had she become too involved in tracing interesting topics such as the importance of wolves in the folklore of many cultures, she would have lost valuable time and shifted her focus.

1 Getting oriented in the library

Your first stop in the library should be the circulation or information desk. The library staff will answer your questions and provide information about the library's floor plan, its resources, and its computers. The floor plan shows you where the books are shelved. A map also shows you the location of the reference room, where you can begin your general research; the periodical room, where you can find the most recent copies of magazines, newspapers, and journals; and the storage area for other periodicals, including those on microfilm and microfiche. Larger libraries may have a computer resource room and many other specialized areas where you can find collections of books, journals, and indexes related to specific academic disciplines; your library may also have different reference centers for science, humanities, social sciences, and government documents. Once you know what resources the library contains and where to find them, you are ready to start your preliminary research.

If you feel overwhelmed or confused while doing research, or if you just have a simple question, take advantage of one of the most helpful resources a library has to offer: its staff and, in particular, the reference librarian. Reference librarians are familiar with all of the library's holdings and are experts in retrieving information. They are especially good at helping you find and use reference material that will lead you to other sources. And they can help you figure out where periodicals are stored—whether they are bound in hard copy, stored on some kind of microform, or accessible on the library's computer files.

2　Using reference books

The library's reference room is perhaps the most important room in the library for a researcher. There you will find encyclopedias, dictionaries, indexes, abstracts, bibliographies, and so forth. These reference books do not circulate. They are always in the reference room, and a librarian is usually there to offer assistance. But remember that these reference materials merely point you toward other sources—books, periodicals, other indexes, other bibliographies— that will help with your research. You cannot finish your research in the reference room.

You can use reference materials to decide if a particular topic interests you or to get a general sense of the issues and controversies that surround your topic. Thus, the reference room is a good starting point for preliminary research. These references are not difficult to use, but they differ slightly from each other. Always look in the front of each reference work for information about how to use it.

All of the printed indexes and guides in the following discussion should be in the reference room. Many reference works are also available on CD-ROM (compact disk, read-only memory); these disks give you immediate access to computer-based sources ranging from dictionaries to periodical indexes. You will have to consult the floor plan to locate your library's card catalog, online catalog, CD-ROM, and other computer resources.

Guides to reference books

Two important general guides organize and list reference books by fields and provide useful summaries.

Balay, Robert, ed. *Guide to Reference Books.* 11th ed. Chicago: ALA, 1996.

Walford's Guide to Reference Material. 7th ed. London: Library Association, 1996.

These general guides lead you quickly to other reference books that can help you locate sources for your essay. Sheehy covers specialized references as well as general references.

General and specialized encyclopedias

General encyclopedias provide good background information on a wide range of topics. Short articles can help you identify areas of scholarly debate associated with your subject. A short bibliography of related sources often appears at the end of these articles.

Specialized encyclopedias provide longer and more detailed articles about topics, often by specialists in a particular field. They may also provide more bibliographic information than you find in general encyclopedias.

Remember, encyclopedias, like all reference materials, enable you to familiarize yourself with your topic. They cannot be your main source of information. They are just a starting point.

GENERAL ENCYCLOPEDIAS

Collier's Encyclopedia. 24 volumes. General coverage of a wide range of topics. Designed for high school and college use.

Encyclopaedia Britannica. 30 volumes. Consists of three parts: the *Micropaedia,* containing short factual articles; the *Macropaedia,* containing longer entries with depth of coverage; and the *Propaedia,* outlining the information contained in the other volumes—and serving as an index to the other two parts of the encyclopedia.

Encyclopedia Americana. 30 volumes. Strong in science and technology.

The New Columbia Encyclopedia. 1 volume. General encyclopedia.

Random House Encyclopedia. 1 volume. General encyclopedia.

SPECIALIZED ENCYCLOPEDIAS

Encyclopedia of Anthropology
Encyclopedia of Asian History
Encyclopedia of Banking and Finance
Encyclopedia of Bioethics
Encyclopedia of Biological Sciences
Encyclopedia of Chemistry
Encyclopedia of Computer Science and Technology
Encyclopedia of Crime and Justice
Encyclopedia of Earth Sciences

Encyclopedia of Economics
Encyclopedia of Education
Encyclopedia of Educational Research
Encyclopedia of Management
Encyclopedia of Philosophy
Encyclopedia of Physical Education, Fitness and Sports
Encyclopedia of Physics
Encyclopedia of Psychology
Encyclopedia of Religion and Ethics
Encyclopedia of Social Work
Encyclopedia of Sociology
Encyclopedia of Southern Culture
Encyclopedia of World Art
International Encyclopedia of the Social Sciences
McGraw-Hill Encyclopedia of Environmental Science
McGraw-Hill Encyclopedia of Science and Technology
McGraw-Hill Encyclopedia of World Drama

For additional specialized encyclopedias on your topic or in your discipline, consult a reference librarian.

For her preliminary research, Ericka consulted both the *Encyclopedia Americana* and the *Encyclopaedia Britannica;* each helped her get a better sense of the gray wolf problem. In the *Americana* Ericka found not only general information about the wolf's physical characteristics, she also found information about the wolf's eating habits. They reminded her of what she had learned at Yellowstone about the wolf as hunter and as hunted. Ericka also found this short bibliography at the end of the encyclopedia article.

Bibliography

Davidson, Max, *The Wolf* (Merrimack 1984).
Fox, Michael W., *Behavior of Wolves, Dogs, and Related Canids* (1971; reprint, Krieger 1984).
Klinghammer, Erich, *The Behavior and Ecology of Wolves* (Garland 1979).
Mech, L. David, *The Wolf: The Ecology and Behavior of an Endangered Species* (Univ. of Minn. Press 1981).
Pimlott, Douglas H., ed., *Wolves* (Unipub 1975).
Simon, Noel, *Wolves* (Biblio. Dist. 1985).

Because the *Britannica* contains both short, factual articles and long, narrative articles, Ericka decided to look first in the index for an overview of the topical coverage. She looked under *wolves* and found nothing; under *wolf,* she found the following entries.

wolf 12:726:2b
  major ref. in Mammals **23:**414:1a
  ancestry of dog **4:**149:2a; **17:**444:1b
  effect of predators on biosphere
    14:1032:1b
  for a list of related subjects see
    PROPAEDIA: Section 313

She checked each entry listed. In the first article, she read that the gray wolf "performs an important natural function in controlling the number of large herbivores and in weeding out those less fit for survival." The article—on the effect of predators on the biosphere—also provided additional information about the natural selection problem.

Because Ericka was doing general reading and was not yet ready to restrict her topic, she was writing informal notes in her reading journal about the ideas that came to her. She made a note about the wolf as the hunter and the hunted and began to wonder who—conservationists or the landowners— might be right about the wolf. She knew that it would take more research to find out, and she had other sources to consult in the reference room.

Biographical reference books

Biographical sources provide information about the lives of famous people. They often include pictures, bibliographies, and historical information associated with the people whose lives are highlighted.

American Men and Women of Science
American Women Writers
Contemporary Authors
Contemporary Dramatists
Contemporary Novelists
Contemporary Poets
Current Biography
Dictionary of American Biography, plus supplements
Dictionary of American Scholars
Dictionary of National Biography, 1882–1900 plus supplements
International Who's Who
Notable American Women
Who's Who in America
Who's Who of American Women
Who's Who in Government
World Authors

Specialized bibliographies

It is standard practice in scholarly writing to include at the end of books or chapters and at the end of articles a list of the sources that the writer consulted or cited. Those lists, or bibliographies, often include sources that you will also want to consult. You saw such a listing for the encyclopedia article that Ericka read.

But other more specialized and comprehensive bibliographies are available. These bibliographies list important articles and books related to specific fields of study. They are excellent starting points for focused research because they are more detailed and technical than the bibliographies you will find in general reference books.

Annual Bibliography of English Language and Literature
Bibliographic Index
Bibliographical Guide to the History of Indian-White Relations in the United States
Bibliographies in American History
Bibliography of North America
Essay and General Literature Index
Foreign Affairs Bibliography
Goldentree Bibliographies in Language and Literature
International Bibliography of the Social Sciences
International Bibliography of Sociology
MLA International Bibliography of Books and Articles on the Modern Languages and Literatures
New Cambridge Bibliography of English Literature
Science and Engineering Literature
Social Work Education: A Bibliography
The Year's Work in English Studies

Dictionaries

Unabridged and specialized dictionaries offer authoritative information on language beyond what you can find in a standard college or abridged dictionary. Unabridged dictionaries provide a wide range of meanings for words, some historical information about the derivation of words, and information about usage, among other things. (For a more detailed discussion of the different types of dictionaries and how to use them, refer to Chapter 27.)

UNABRIDGED DICTIONARIES

Funk and Wagnall's New Standard Dictionary of the English Language
Oxford English Dictionary
Random House Dictionary of the English Language
Webster's Third New International Dictionary of the English Language

SPECIALIZED DICTIONARIES

Follett, Wilson. *Modern American Usage.* Ed. Jacques Barzun.
Fowler, H. W. *Dictionary of Modern English Usage.*
Onions, Charles T., et al., eds. *The Oxford Dictionary of English Etymology.*
Partridge, Eric. *A Dictionary of Slang and Unconventional English.* 8th ed. Ed. Paul Beale.
Webster's New Dictionary of Synonyms.

Atlases and gazetteers

An atlas is a collection of maps; a gazetteer is a dictionary of places. Look to these sources for geographical data.

Columbia Lippincott Gazetteer of the World
Cosmopolitan World Atlas
Encyclopaedia Britannica World Atlas International
Goode's World Atlas
National Atlas of the United States
National Geographic Atlas of the World
The New York Times Atlas of the World
Webster's New Geographical Dictionary

Almanacs and yearbooks

Almanacs and yearbooks provide statistics and other factual information, often on current events. These reference sources are compiled annually.

Americana Annual
Annual Register of World Events
Facts on File
Guinness Book of World Records
The World Almanac and Book of Facts

Book indexes

Book indexes can help you locate books when you do not have complete bibliographic information about a book or when you have an author's name and want to know if that author has published relevant books on your topic. The indexes are listed by author, subject, and title and are available online (O) or on CD-ROM, as indicated.

Books in Print (O, CD-ROM)
Cumulative Book Index (CD-ROM)
Paperbound Books in Print (CD-ROM)

3 Using periodicals

Periodicals include magazines (published weekly or monthly), journals (usually published quarterly), and newspapers. In magazines and newspapers you will find general information to help with your research. Occasionally you will also find highly specialized articles on a subject. Rely on magazines and newspapers as important sources for your preliminary research.

They will contain current events and up-to-date information that you may not be able to find in books.

Journals almost always pertain to a particular academic field and contain specialized information and critical articles related to that field. Journals not only provide important information but also offer critical analyses of that information. Thus, journal articles help you attain perspective on your topic. To find articles in magazines, journals, and newspapers, you need to search the periodical indexes and computer databases in your library (see 43d–e).

During your research, you are likely to find periodicals stored on one of three types of *microform*: *microfilm* (film on a reel—usually 35mm), *microfiche* (a flat sheet of film), and *microprint* (a reduced image printed on an opaque white card). Microform condenses printed material and saves valuable storage space in libraries. Because you cannot read microform with the naked eye, you will have to use one of the library's reading machines; they magnify the material and often allow you to print copies of selected pages. Fees for copying vary. Remember that the periodical you need is most likely on microform. When you do not find it in the periodical reading room or on the shelves with other bound periodicals, always check microform.

Periodical indexes

Periodical indexes will direct you to articles in periodicals. These indexes are not difficult to use, but they do vary widely in content, format, and organization. Look in the front of the index for a list of the abbreviations used as well as guidelines for using the index. A number of different indexes are available, each covering a select group of periodicals. Check the beginning of the index or volume to determine which periodicals it lists.

Also be sure to check whether your library has the periodicals you want to consult. The *serials catalog,* which you can find in the periodical reading room, or the online catalog will inform you of your library's periodical holdings; these catalogs should also tell you whether the periodicals can be found on microform or in their original printed form. You will likely find current issues in the library's periodical room, but back issues may be stored elsewhere. When looking for periodicals, you can save time by asking the librarians for assistance.

Printed indexes are being replaced by the library's online catalog of holdings. Even if your library has printed indexes or a serials catalog, try the online catalog first. Check the printed indexes, usually located in the periodical reading room, if you do not find what you want on the online catalog.

Many libraries offer CD-ROM computer database versions of periodical indexes. Check with your reference librarian for information about what systems are available in your library and how to use them. (For more on using databases, see 43e-3.)

General periodical indexes

General indexes for periodicals list articles from newspapers and general-interest magazines. These periodicals can provide current sources on your topic. However, these general-interest sources may not provide sufficient coverage.

InfoTrac. A computerized index to more than one thousand periodicals, available on CD-ROM. A single disk covers three years, and coverage—including law, business management, technology, social sciences, and humanities—begins in 1982 or later. InfoTrac includes the *General Periodicals Index, Magazine Index Plus, National Newspaper Index,* and *Academic Index.*

Magazine Index. This monthly index covers more than one thousand magazines. Available on microfilm, online through DIALOG and Bibliographic Retrieval Service (BRS), and InfoTrac.

National Newspaper Index. Indexes major newspapers, including the *Christian Science Monitor,* the *Los Angeles Times,* the *New York Times,* the *Wall Street Journal,* and the *Washington Post.* Available in print, on microfilm, and online through DIALOG and BRS.

New York Times Index. Indexes the most complete national newspaper and provides important summaries of longer news items. Useful for dating events. Arranges stories chronologically under subject heading. Published every two weeks, with annual consolidations. Available online and on CD-ROM.

Poole's Index to Periodical Literature. Indexes periodicals from 1802–1906.

Popular Periodicals Index. A subject index for popular periodicals not listed in other indexes, especially the *Reader's Guide.*

Reader's Guide to Periodical Literature. Indexes general-interest periodicals from 1900 to the present. This indispensable guide for over 200 publications—appearing semimonthly with quarterly and annual consolidations—helps you investigate political trends, current social issues, recent scientific discoveries, and important cultural events. Entries are arranged by author and subject. It is also available online and on CD-ROM.

Wall Street Journal Index. Indexes the newspaper and *Barrons.* Available on CD-ROM.

Ericka went to the *New York Times Index* for more information on how to approach the gray wolf problem. In the consolidated index for 1985–89, she found numerous entries under *wolves,* including the following, which seemed important to her.

> **WOLVES. See also**
> Hunting and Trapping, **1985:** F 20, Mr 26, **1989:** D 5
> Oil (Petroleum) and Gasoline, **1988:** My 11
> Parks and Other Recreation Areas, **1985:** F 18
>   US Fish and Wildlife Service reviews National Park
> Service proposal to reintroduce 30 breeding pairs of timber

wolves to Yellowstone National Park, move opposed by
Wyoming Congressional delegation and Idaho Cattleman's
Association (S), Je 3,III,4:6 (1986)
    Twelve wolves from the Rocky Mountains in the
Canadian province of Alberta settled in Glacier National
Park, Montana, where they spent the winter hunting deer
and elk; map (M), Je 29,I,22:1 (1986)
    William E Schmidt article on plan by US Fish and Wildlife
Service to repopulate Alligator River National Wildlife
Refuge in North Carolina with red wolves; illustration; map
(M), N 13,I,22:3 (1986)
    British Columbia campaign to kill wolves, which includes
shooting of wolves from helicopters, stirs opposition, most of
it from Project Wolf, headed by Paul Watson; opponents
fear extinction of wolf and charge that scientific rationale
for kill program is flawed; proponents argue that failure to
thin out wolves will exacerbate decline in prey population;
photo (M), Mr 3,III,3:1 (1987)
    Federal Fish and Wildlife Service plan to reintroduce grey
wolves in Yellowstone National Park is thwarted by
resistance of sheep and cattle ranchers; service is
proceeding with plans to release red wolves, which are even
scarcer, in Alligator River National Wildlife Refuge in
North Carolina (S), My 17,I,53:2 (1987)

Ericka then consulted four entries from the 1985 *Reader's Guide:* one on
Yellowstone; three on problems related to wolves elsewhere.

Wolves
>   *See also*
>   Coyotes
>   Crying wolf in Yellowstone. S. Begley. *Newsweek* 106:74
>   D 16 '85
>   FCC stops Alaska's aerial wolf hunt [use of radio telemetry]
>   *Sci News* 127:57 Ja 26 '85
>   How delicate is the balance of nature? [study of wolf
>   control in Minnesota] L. D. Mech. il *Natl Wildl* 23:54–9
>   F/Mr '85
>   Revered and reviled. Minnesota's wolves are in trouble
>   again. D. Nevin. il *Smithsonian* 15:78–87 Ja '85

Specialized periodical indexes

Specialized periodical indexes list articles from scholarly journals, usually
related to a particular academic discipline; these indexes help you research
your topic in depth. Ask a reference librarian for help in using these indexes,
many of which are available online (O) or on CD-ROM, as indicated.

Applied Science and Technology Index (O, CD-ROM)

Art Index (O, CD-ROM)

Biography Index (O, CD-ROM)

Biological and Agricultural Index (CD-ROM)

Business Periodicals Index (O, CD-ROM)

Computer Literature Index

Current Index to Journals in Education (O, CD-ROM)

ERIC (Education Resources Information Center)

Essay and General Literature Index

General Science Index (O, CD-ROM) A cumulative subject index for periodicals, arranged in alphabetical order, that contains a separate listing of citations to book reviews. Subject fields include astronomy, atmospheric science, biology, chemistry, mathematics, microbiology, and zoology.

Humanities Index (O, CD-ROM)

Index to U.S. Government Periodicals (O, CD-ROM)

Music Index (CD-ROM)

Philosopher's Index (O, CD-ROM)

PsycLIT (O, CD-ROM) Compiled by the American Psychological Association and made available online and through several CD-ROM vendors, this database contains citations and abstracts to over 1,300 periodicals in psychology and the behavioral sciences as well as to book chapters and book records.

Public Affairs Information Service (O, CD-ROM)

Social Sciences Index (O, CD-ROM)

Technical Book Review Index

Vertical File Index (O)

Ericka consulted the *General Science Index* and found twelve entries under *wolves*, including the following.

Waiting for wolves to howl in Yellowstone. T. Williams.
   il *Audubon* 92:32-4+ N '90
Who's afraid of the big bad wolf? L. D. Mech. il *Audubon*
   92:82-5 Mr '90
Wolves from the north. F. Hoke. *Environment* 32:23-4
   Je '90
Wolves vs. dogs. F. Graham, Jr. *Audubon* 92:18+ N
   '90
Yellowstone lets the wolf through the door. C. Joyce.
   New Sci 126:21 Je 2 '90
                    Food and feeding
Validation of estimating food intake in gray wolves
   by ^{22}Na turnover. G. D. Delgiudice and others. bibl
   il *J Wildl Manage* 55:59–71 Ja '91

Ericka then found thirty-one entries listed under *wolves* in the *PsycLIT* index, including the following.

TI   DOCUMENT TITLE: The public and the timber wolf in Minnesota.
AU   AUTHOR(S): Kellert, -Stephen-R.
IN   INSTITUTIONAL AFFILIATION OF FIRST AUTHOR: Yale U, School of Forestry &
Environmental Studies, New Haven, CT, US
JN   JOURNAL NAME: Anthrozoos; 1987 Fal Vol 1(2) 100–109
IS   ISSN: 08927936
LA   LANGUAGE: English
PY   PUBLICATION YEAR: 1987
AB   ABSTRACT: Reviews the results of a study of public attitudes, knowledge,
behaviors, and symbolic perceptions of the timber wolf in Minnesota. Data were
obtained from telephone interviews with urban and northern counties residents in

Minnesota, including deer hunters, livestock farmers, and trappers. Limited factual knowledge of the timber wolf was found among the general public, although considerably greater knowledge was found among trappers and, to a lesser degree, hunters. Most Ss, except farmers, viewed the wolf in favorable and positive terms. (PsycLIT Database Copyright 1989 American Psychological Assn, all rights reserved)

```
KP   KEY PHRASE: public attitudes & knowledge & behaviors & perceptions of timber wolf;
     farmers & hunters & trappers & general public
DE   DESCRIPTORS: PUBLIC-OPINION; KNOWLEDGE-LEVEL; BEHAVIOR-; SOCIAL-PERCEPTION;
     ANIMAL-ETHOLOGY; ADULTHOOD-; WOLVES-
CC   CLASSIFICATION CODE(S): 3120; 2440; 31; 24
PO   POPULATION: Animal
UC   UPDATE CODE: 8904
AN   PSYC ABS. VOL. AND ABS. NO.: 76-11819
JC   JOURNAL CODE: 3155
```

Ericka's use of periodical indexes

The *New York Times Index* gave Ericka a clear sense that the wolf problem was not confined to Yellowstone National Park, and it became clear to her that she would eventually have to limit her research to a particular area. From these index entries about Yellowstone, she could also see that there was vigorous opposition to bringing wolves back into the park. This information contrasted with what she had read earlier in the encyclopedia article, which described how wolves stabilize populations in some herds and thereby help balance the ecosystem. She noted these facts in her reading journal and photocopied the page from the *New York Times Index* so that when she was ready, she could locate and read these articles to provide background information. Ericka was already compiling a working bibliography (see 43h)—a preliminary list of books and articles that she might use in her essay and that she would read to help her limit her topic (see 44a).

Ericka also checked the *Reader's Guide to Periodical Literature* and the *General Science Index*. Her instructor advised her to look at several of the yearly volumes in the *Reader's Guide* to get a sense of whether there was continuing interest in her topic. She consulted each of the annual indexes from 1985 to 1991 and found numerous entries under *wolves* for each of those years.

Because Ericka found so many articles on her topic in the *Reader's Guide* and the *General Science Index*, she began to feel confident, even before consulting the sources themselves, that she could find enough information about the wolf problem in Yellowstone to write a good research essay. Nevertheless, she still kept an open mind about whether to limit her research and just how to limit it.

Abstracts and citation indexes

Abstracts provide summaries of articles or books in designated fields of study that can help you gauge the usefulness of particular sources. The title of the abstract suggests the nature and extent of the coverage. Many journals print an abstract with each article, and collections of abstracts are published regularly. *Citation indexes* allow you to track what has been written about an article or book so that you can see how articles comment on one another. Some citation indexes and abstracts are available online (O) or on CD-ROM, as indicated.

ABSTRACTS

Biological Abstracts (CD-ROM)
Chemical Abstracts (O)
Communications Abstracts
Dissertation Abstracts International (O; CD-ROM)
Ecology Abstracts (O: DIALOG; CD-ROM)
Historical Abstracts (O)
Physics Abstracts (O: INSPECT)
Psychological Abstracts (O; CD-ROM: PsycLIT)
Science Citation Index (O; CD-ROM: SciSearch)
Sociological Abstracts (O; CD-ROM: Sociofile)
Social Sciences Citation Index (O; CD-ROM: Social SciSearch)

CITATION INDEXES

Arts and Humanities Citation Index (O: BRS; CD-ROM)
Science Citation Index (O: DIALOG; CD-ROM)
Social Sciences Citation Index (O: BRS, DIALOG; CD-ROM)

4   Using the library's special resources

In addition to books, journals, magazines, and newspapers, libraries often have other resources that can support your research and provide important information. Usually a librarian will be available to help you with these resources.

- **Art collections.** Drawings, engravings, paintings, photographs, and 35-mm slides.

- **Audio collections and listening areas.** Music, readings, speeches, radio dramas, and documentaries recorded on audiocassettes, compact disks, and records—as well as listening areas equipped with cassette decks, turntables, and compact disk players.

- **Government documents.** U.S. government reports, catalogs, pamphlets, hearings, newsletters, and other documents. The *United States Government Publications Index* and *Monthly Catalogue of United States Government Publications*, available online and on CD-ROM, will help you identify sources.

- **Interlibrary loans.** Librarians can often borrow books for you through interlibrary loans. Such loans take time to arrange, but they can bring you books and periodicals that your library does not have in its collection.

- **Microcomputer center.** Usually contains software for a wide range of applications including word processing, spreadsheet, and database management packages, as well as microcomputers for students and faculty to use.
- **Special collections.** Manuscripts, memorabilia, rare books, and other archival materials.
- **Video collections.** Filmstrips, slides, and videocassettes.

43e Searching for sources in the library and on computers

The arrival of the computer in most institutions and many homes has transformed the process of searching for sources. A search that in recent times was conducted from print indexes or card catalogs is now done almost entirely from a keyboard.

1 Using the library catalog

The *library catalog* lists all of a library's holdings, including books, periodicals, cassettes, films, and microforms. In the past, all libraries used a card catalog system to record their holdings. Recently, however, most libraries have transferred the record of their holdings to an online catalog or a microfiche catalog. The online system enables researchers to use public computer terminals to search quickly and efficiently for information.

All library catalogs list holdings alphabetically three ways: by author, by title, and by subject. In addition, all catalog entries include a call number that will help you locate books on the shelves. The call numbers appear in the library catalogs and on the spine of the books. Be sure to copy the correct numbers before going to get the books. The books are shelved according to these call numbers. The librarian can recall books that have been checked out or retrieve a book from the special storage area. Recalling a book that has been checked out takes time, so plan accordingly. If your library has closed stacks and you cannot take the books from the shelves, you must fill out a slip with the call number, present it at the circulation desk, and wait for the book to be brought to you.

The call number system used by most academic libraries is the Library of Congress System. Its call numbers begin with letters: *A* for general works, *B* for philosophy, *C* and *D* for history, and so forth. Some libraries use the older Dewey Decimal System. Its call numbers begin with three digits, 000 to 999. Each number indicates a category of information: 300–399 for social sciences, 500–599 for natural science, 800–899 for literature, and so forth. Some libraries use both systems to classify books.

When you do a library search, consult the *Library of Congress Subject Headings* (LCSH), a three-volume reference book that lists all of the subject headings used to classify books. You can find the LCSH in the reference room or near the catalog in libraries that use the Library of Congress call number system. LCSH will help you locate books by subject. It will also help you select key words for use in your other computer searches.

Using key words that are closely related to your subject will help make you a more efficient researcher. A precise subject heading or key word will clearly identify your topic and direct you to relevant sources. Broad subject headings may lead you to thousands of entries that will overwhelm you and may not be relevant to your search. The LCSH, in fact, can help you find key words that might not occur to you on your own. Ericka, for example, found these other subject headings under the entry *wolves: Canis lupus, Gray Wolves, Timber Wolves, Canis, Wolves—extermination, Wolves—Control,* and *Folklore.* She also found the Library of Congress call numbers associated with these general categories: *wolves, control,* and *folklore.*

You are likely to have better luck with subject searches using the online catalog or CD-ROMs because the computer can search quickly and extensively.

Using the online catalog

The online catalog gives you rapid access to the same kind of information that you find in the card catalog. But note that the two catalogs do not necessarily contain the same listings. Sometimes only part of a library's holdings are online. Also, books and other materials acquired before the switch to a computerized system may not be listed in the online catalog, and more current books may not appear in the card catalog. It is a good idea to check both catalogs when you are looking for a particular book or are doing extensive searches. A librarian can tell you how the two catalogs differ at your library.

Many libraries are connected through nationwide computer networks to other libraries' catalogs and to the Online Computer Library Center (OCLC) that links libraries across the country. Smaller, local networks connect affiliated colleges, universities, museums, and institutes that have agreed to pool their research resources. These computer networks are particularly useful for verifying bibliographic citations and for helping you find books that are not in your school's library. You can request materials from other libraries through the interlibrary loan service provided by your reference librarian.

The first time you use an online catalog, ask a librarian for assistance, or read the library's printed instructions for using the online system. When you walk up to one of the computer terminals, usually located in the reference room near the card catalog, press the *enter* key to receive instructions about what to do. The commands will vary from system to system, but you will be able to locate books by title, author, and subject.

You may also be able to search for sources online by call number and by various combinations of words (partial titles, incomplete names, and key words). See the next section on performing key word searches.

If you search for a book in the computer catalog by author or title, you will get individual entries such as the following, which Ericka found.

Location: BOB-Stacks QL737.C22M4
Author: Mech, L. David.
Title: The wolf: the ecology and behavior of an endangered species,
                 by L. David Mech.
Publisher: Garden City, N.Y., Published for the American Museum of
                 Natural History by the Natural History Press [1970]
                 xx, 384 p. illus., maps. 24 cm.

Sample Online Catalog Entry, Author

If you search the online system for books by subject, you will see a list such as the following one on the screen. When you type one of the numbers from this list and press the *Enter* key, the computer will give you a full citation for the book.

This subject: Wolves.   has   11 citations
                                              in entire catalog

Ref#	Author	Title	Date
1	Barry, Scott.	The kingdom of wolves /	1979
2	Eckels, Richard Preston, 1909–	Greek wolf-lore . . .	1937
3	Fiennes, Richard.	The order of wolves /	1976
4	Fox, Michael W., 1937–	The soul of the wolf /	1980
5	Gesell, Arnold Lucius, 1880–196>	Wolf child and human child; being a>	1941
6	Lopez, Barry Holstun, 1945–	Of wolves and men /	1978
7	Mech, L. David.	The wolf: the ecology and behavior >	1970
8	Miller, Gerrit Smith, 1869–1923>	The names of the large wolves of no>	1912
9	Peters, Roger.	Dance of the wolves /	1985
10	Rutter, Russell J.	The world of the wolf ,	1968
11	Zimen, Erik, 1941–	The wolf : his place in the natural>	1981

Type a number to see associated information.

Sample Online Catalog Entry, Subject

2   Performing key word searches

Key word searches, which take advantage of the computer's speed and its ability to search across the entire catalog, are especially useful when you are searching by subject rather than by title or author. The key word search matches words or terms that you select with words or terms in the catalog or another database. Instructions for doing key word searches will be available on the computer's screen when you select a search function or in printed handouts available at the computer terminals.

You should do a key word search when you do not know exact titles, subject headings, or the author's full name; the search will help you locate a particular source when you do not have enough information to call it directly to the screen. But you can also use a key word search to control the way the computer scans the catalog. In essence, you can modify the search to meet your own needs by combining key words with special symbols that are explained in the instructions. The process is simple. Key word searches of this kind are especially helpful when you are beginning to narrow your topic or when you want to search for a particular subtopic; you can instruct the computer to locate only the sources in the catalog that connect the subtopic with your main topic.

When Ericka did her computer search, she decided to see what she could find by doing a key word search using the words *gray wolf*. She had no success. Then she tried the word *wolves* and found twenty-five items, many of them very general and irrelevant.

To narrow the search, Ericka decided to use the special search function that allowed her to combine key words and special symbols to find more specific references. She chose the words *wolves* and *Yellowstone* as her key words and then used a designated connecting symbol (/) between the words (*wolves/Yellowstone*), thereby limiting the search to only those sources that contained both of her key words. Her search yielded no titles. After scanning the twenty-five titles that she had obtained with the word *wolves*, Ericka realized that she would have to do most of her research from periodicals, rather than from books.

Ericka's instructor had no objection to the types of sources she used in her research. However, you should always check with your instructor to ensure that you are using the required balance of primary and secondary source materials, books, and periodicals.

3   Using computerized databases

Many libraries now have access to large online database networks. These databases store vast amounts of specialized information about books and periodicals, and their listings give you more information than you can get from single library catalogs. Specifically, databases can provide (1) a list of sources related to your topic, (2) abstracts or brief summaries of sources, and (3) the full text of a source that may not be available in your library.

The most widely used database services in academic libraries are the Bibliographic Retrieval Service (BRS) and DIALOG, systems that provide access to hundreds of databases and over a million sources of information. The Research Libraries Information Network (RLIN) also provides a bibliographic database (BIB) and access to Anthropological Literature, Avery Index to Architectural Periodicals, Hispanic American Periodicals Index, Handbook of Latin American Studies, History of Science & Technology database, Inside

Information (from the ten thousand most requested journals at the British Library's Document Supplement Centre), Public Affairs Information Service, and Periodical Abstracts. RLIN is an online database with millions of bibliographic records for books, journals, archival materials, and videos. These items are owned and cataloged by over 100 major research libraries that are members of the Research Libraries Group (RLG). Ask a librarian for help with these online database networks; the librarian will advise you about the feasibility of doing a database search for your particular topic.

You can also access many of these databases from your computer at home if it is equipped with the proper software and a modem, a device for connecting your computer through a phone to other computer networks. Often you have to pay a fee to subscribe to these networks, but more and more colleges and universities are giving students access to their mainframe computer systems and to the Internet (see 43f for more on the Internet and the World Wide Web). Check with your academic computing facilities and with the reference librarians for information about accessing these services.

Databases on CD-ROM are often more accessible than those online, and you can use them free of charge in your library. Many databases that were only available online have been transferred to CD-ROM and can be used at special computer terminals in the reference room. InfoTrac is one such database; it provides information about more than one thousand business, technical, government, and general-interest periodicals. The business, psychology, and scientific databases from DIALOG have been transferred to CD-ROM. ERIC (Educational Resources Information Center) indexes both published articles and unpublished papers and reports and is available through DIALOG and InfoTrac. Access to many of these services is usually controlled by software programs such as ProQuest (offering a broad spectrum of information in formats ranging from abstracts and indexes to image disks that contain facsimiles of original articles) and SilverPlatter (providing information on nursing, psychology, and sociology).

A few minutes spent reading the user guidelines for the databases will save you hours of searching through printed indexes and will likely give you access to information that you might not find in published reference materials. These online services give you immediate access to *Newspaper Abstracts, Periodical Abstracts,* the *New York Times Index,* and the *MLA International Bibliography,* among others. For recent additions to online databases and CD-ROM, check *Ulrich's International Periodicals Directory.*

As helpful as database searches can be, they sometimes yield an overwhelming amount of information. Thus, the key words you select for conducting a database search, whether authors, titles, or words related to your subject, should be very specific so that the database does not give you too many sources. Specificity will help make your search manageable. Try consulting the thesaurus of *descriptors* (key words) found in most databases to help you limit your search, or brainstorm with your reference librarian for terms most likely to yield useful sources.

Ericka consulted Periodical Abstracts—Research II on ProQuest (providing abstracts and indexing to articles from over 1,600 general reference publications as well as the most recent six months of the *New York Times* and *Wall Street Journal*) for January 1989–90. Her search using the key word *wolves* yielded ninety-three possible sources; eight of those looked promising because they were about problems associated with the wolf as an endangered species.

When Ericka wrote her research paper on the gray wolf controversy in 1993, her online computer search had yielded very few sources. Three years later, if she had returned to update her work, she would have found much more. The search on the Research Libraries Information Network (RLIN) located more than thirty important sources that focused on the wolf controversy at Yellowstone. The success of that search can be attributed to at least two factors: the popularity of the wolf recovery project since Ericka completed her original research project and the rapid advances being made in online storage and retrieval procedures.

Ericka could use the same key words, *wolves* and *Yellowstone,* to discover much new and old material through advanced search techniques that are now built into most search programs. These advanced techniques (often called *Boolean search techniques*) allow you to choose whether to search for each of your key words separately (*wolves* OR *Yellowstone*) or to combine them as a way of limiting your search so that you find only sources containing both terms (*wolves* AND *Yellowstone*), or to combine some terms and exclude others (*wolves* AND *Yellowstone* NOT *Idaho*). The precise techniques for initiating these combinations vary from program to program. Follow the on-screen instructions (see 43e-2).

43f　Researching on the Internet and the World Wide Web

There is yet another computer network that can give you access to current events and national news; world news; ongoing research in almost every field; topics of cultural, scientific, and educational interest; library holdings; bibliographies; and even conversations among researchers and special interest groups. This vast network of computers, known as the *Internet,* is what allows you to send **e-mail,** electronic mail, to one another. The Internet also connects you to the *World Wide Web* (abbreviated as **WWW,** or the **Web**), a system of linked documents placed on the network. These documents, each of which is called a *Web page,* contain information that can supplement and enhance your research. Individual Web pages may be linked to other pages at a given *site*—locations where information is stored—on the WWW, or they may be linked to other pages at different sites.

1   Accessing the Internet

You normally gain access to the Internet through a *modem* (a device for connecting your computer to a telephone) or an *internal interface card* for your computer that gives you direct access to a mainframe computer system and a pathway to the Internet. You must have software installed in your computer that will allow it to interface with the Internet or the connecting computer system, and you will also need an account with an Internet service provider. That provider can be a commercial one, such as America Online, Prodigy, the Microsoft Network, or a commercial Internet provider. Access can also be provided through your college, university, or corporate computer facility. These providers usually supply software for your computer so that you can communicate through their system, while you may supply necessary hardware—the modem or the internal interface card.

Sometimes there will be terminals in dorms to provide direct access to your school's computer system. Check with the academic computing facilities at your college or university to find out what you need to do to open your own account and gain access to the system.

If you do not have a computer, check with your library's staff. Often the library will have computers that will give you direct access to the Internet. All you have to do is sit in front of the computer, follow either the printed instructions or those onscreen, and begin searching. Librarians should be able to direct you to these computers and to those members of the staff who can help you use them.

2   Navigating the Web

The distinctive navigating features of the World Wide Web are tied to *hypertext links,* electronic pathways within a Web page, from page to page, or from Web site to Web site. These links often appear underlined in color or as a "button" device on your computer screen. When you point to these hypertext links with your mouse, the pointer on the screen indicates that you have pointed to a link that can take you to another location with more information. To move from one link to another location or another Web site, you only need to point and click. Moving from link to link is called *browsing the Web.*

The first screen you see at any WWW site is usually the home page. *Home page* can also refer to the first page you see when you start your *browser*—software, such as Netscape or Internet Explorer, that allows you to search the Internet. The browser uses other software devices, called *search engines,* to go out on the Web and find information. Among the most common and most powerful of these search engines are Webcrawler, Yahoo, AltaVista, InfoSeek, and Eureka. New engines appear frequently.

Internet formats that predate the WWW, such as FTP (File Transfer Protocol, a direct computer-to-computer process for delivering files), and also older network media of the late 80s and early 90s, used their own search engines to locate and transfer files. These include Gopher, a non-graphic file network popular in the early 90s, and WAIS—Wide Area Information Server, which combined many local networks and archive sources. Although new web-based search engines make use of older tools and searching systems, they also have more advanced search tools of their own.

Today's browsers do most of the searching automatically when you ask for information; they make use of the search engines and the older formats. These browsers read the key words that you enter on the home page, select a search engine, call up other tools and protocols that locate and transfer files, and give you, almost instantaneously, a list of promising sites related to the key words that you selected. From this list of sites, you can click and choose as you wish, moving from one site of information to another, gaining access to thousands of documents while you sit at your personal computer or one of your school's terminals.

As you do your searches, follow the procedures in the accompanying chart. Remember that the browser and the search engine will select sites on the basis of prearranged parameters. You can find more about these parameters by clicking information buttons on the home page for the browser or the search engine. You can modify the search parameters (including the way key words are combined) by following onscreen instructions. You can also change search engines.

If you want to designate a different search engine when the home page has no button, you will have to enter a complete Internet address in the address box. Addresses must follow a convention known as the *Domain Name System* that allows each computer on the Internet to have a named location.

Benefits of the Web and some limitations and pitfalls

The biggest problem you face as you confront this vast array of information on the Web is how to value it, how to judge its reliability. Because the information is often new and has not been processed and subjected to the scrutiny of rigorous review procedures, you must be careful about relying on it uncritically; it is often not as reliable as the information you find in printed sources in the library. Remember this: *Anyone can post information on the Internet.* This means researchers on the Web must be especially concerned with reliability and evaluation of sources (see section 43f-3 on evaluating Internet sources).

The second problem with the WWW is its inherent seductiveness; it can eat away your time. The ease with which you can move from site to site around the country and around the world (and the slow loading time on some equipment) can draw you into hours of browsing when your time could be better spent elsewhere—conducting research in the library or writing your research essay. You must be a strict manager of your time when you search the Web, or searching will steal your time. When conducting research, go to the Web for specific purposes; find your sources; and either download them onto your computer (store them on your hard disk or on a floppy) or print them. Do some serious evaluating before you decide to copy, and pay particular attention to document length. You can often find book-length documents on the Web.

Guidelines for Internet Searches

- Link your computer to the Internet and open your browser.
- From the browser's home page, go to the search box (or follow the browser's procedure for selecting a particular search engine).
- Enter the key words needed for your search. (See 43e-2–3.)
- When the search engine shows a list of its "top" 10 to 25 sites, survey the list to identify the most promising of them and click on these. The engine may also give you more lists (lower in its hierarchy) that are often worth pursuing.
- When a site you visit gives you links or references to others that are related, click on the hyperlinks provided (or make an exact copy of addresses if there are no direct links).
- After skimming the site you visit, you may decide to print or download its pages for later examination. Note the size and downloading time of the document to be sure it is worthwhile. Also record or store the address and references from the source for later documentation or a return access (see 45).
- If you are not satisfied with the first search results, you can (a) try new search words (see 43e-2–3); (b) try a different search engine on your browser; (c) in the browser's address box, enter an exact copy of any related addresses that seemed promising in an earlier search.
- Do not be afraid to experiment. Retracing your steps on the browser's *back* button or its *home* button may let you pursue another line of inquiry.

What are the biggest benefits of the Internet?

Just thinking about what is out there on the Web and not being able to visualize exactly where all that information is and how it is organized might make you wonder why you should bother searching the Web. You might well imagine that the information is in the library anyway. But the fact is, much of the information on the Web is *not* in your library.

The Internet gives you access to a great deal of information that is more current than that available in printed texts. For example, the Web can give you access to conversations that researchers in almost every field of knowledge are having with one another. Often, these researchers communicate through Usenet Discussion Groups (called **newsgroups**) or Discussion Lists (called **Listservs**). Sharing common interests, researchers of all kinds establish these electronic bulletin boards so that they can exchange information. You can often visit these sites through hypertext links, browsing as the links appear on your screen during your searches, or you can direct the search engines to go to designated sites when you know their names.

Using the Domain Name System

- To access a domain on the Internet, follow this convention:

  Type the technical designation by which the domain is to be accessed (usually *http*, or *hypertext transfer protocol*), followed by the characters :// followed by the domain name. Example: http://webcrawler.com. This entire string is known as the URL (*universal resource locator* or the Internet address).

- Consult directories on the Internet, a list provided by search engines from a key word search, or a printed directory for Internet addresses.

Access to newsgroups

Newsgroups are available to anyone. If you want to participate in a Listserv, you must subscribe by sending to the Listserv an e-mail message that contains three elements: the word *subscribe*, the name of the Listserv, and your name. Here is an example of a message to a group for information on Oceanography:

   subscribe usfia.ac.be Michael Johns

Do not type the commas, and use care not to add space around periods (called *dots* in address descriptions).

   Consult *http://www.liszt.com* on the Web for a listing of current academic Listservs. Follow the instructions on this site's home page for additional information.

3   Evaluating electronic sources

The reliability of the information you find on the Web will vary from document to document, so you must apply sound judgment as you evaluate each of your electronic sources just as you would the print sources you find in the library. But you can be fairly confident that the print sources have gone through review processes, that they have been judged by other scholars, and that the editorial and production process that resulted in the published book contributed to its reliability. This is especially true of books published by university presses and articles in scholarly journals where there has usually been a rigorous review and evaluation process.

A good rule of thumb to apply when you are evaluating documents involves *reliability*. A source can be considered reliable when you and your audience are sufficiently convinced of its truth or value to act on it. Because we know that truth or value can be relative (different people looking at the same piece of information may see its value quite differently), you must be very careful to consider viewpoints other than your own when judging a document's reliability. Never assume that the information is reliable just because it convinces you at the moment you read it. Check it against other information that you find in your research; check it, too, against the demands of special-interest groups who have a vested interest in your topic but may not agree with your point of view (see 1d and 44e–f for more on special-interest groups). Finally, consider what your collective audience might think of the reliability of that information if you use it as evidence in your research essay; would that audience be likely to act on (or assent to) that information?

Keep in mind our earlier note of caution: anyone can enter information on the Web. Pay attention to the site where the information is posted. Is it a Listserv whose members have academic credentials and who seem to be conducting scientific investigations with as little bias as possible, or are the members part of a discussion group bound together by a passionate interest in the subject that could bias their discussion and their selection and presentation of information? You many need to eavesdrop on discussions over a period of time (often called *lurking*) to be able to discern what you need to know about credentials and biases. Always try to consult more than one source. Whenever possible, always check electronic sources against print sources in your library.

Do not hesitate to enter into discussions with the participants of discussion groups or Listservs via e-mail. Ask probing questions; keep track of those conversations. You might want to save and document the conversations as well as the posted information. Such conversations could be conducted just like an interview. (See 43g-1 for more on interviewing techniques.) Conversations could take place over several weeks as you are conducting research. As you begin to know more and more about your subject, you can return to an earlier conversation with someone in a discussion group or on a Listserv and ask more informed questions about what you need to know.

Be extremely wary of anonymous documents on the Web, especially if they are posted indiscriminately. When you can return to a particular Web site that is well established and that continues to post relevant information about your topic, you can begin to have confidence that the information you find there is more reliable than information that has been posted on a new discussion site. But all information needs to be reevaluated continually against what you are learning from other sources, both electronic and print. Be rigorous in your scrutiny, and question what you read. (See 4a for more on questioning.) Guidelines for determining the reliability of online sources are summarized in the accompanying chart.

Questioning and Evaluating Electronic Sources

- Always be concerned about the document's *reliability.*
- What would various special-interest groups think about the reliability of the information from the Web?
- Does the discussion group or the Listserv seem reliable? What do conversations with members reveal about their seriousness, their credentials, and their biases?
- How do the electronic sources measure up to the print sources in terms of reliability and currency?
- Is the electronic source anonymous, or did it come from a specific person at an established, reliable site?
- Am I sufficiently convinced of the value of the source to cite it in my research essay?

Updating and supplementing Ericka's sources from the Internet

If Ericka were conducting research today on the World Wide Web to update her research, she would find abundant electronic information about what has happened to the gray wolf project at Yellowstone since she completed her research essay in 1993 that recommended gray wolves be reintroduced into Yellowstone. The first wolves were brought to Yellowstone on January 12, 1995; the fourteen wolves, comprising three family groups, were placed in enclosures to accustom them to their homes. Since that date, wolves have been released into the wilderness, wolf cubs have been born, and a few wolves straying out of the park's boundaries have killed stock. On the Internet, at numerous Web sites, you can read about all of these events and the disputes that continue between ecologists and ranchers over the reintroduction of wolves. You have already read that a new search of RLIN yielded more than thirty print sources related to the Yellowstone project (43e-3). The Internet yielded even more. What you can find on the Web now serves as a concise reminder of the value of doing electronic searches to supplement your research project.

On pages 653–655 are excerpts from key word searches that were conducted at the same time using two different search engines (key words: gray wolf Yellowstone). You can see that the results from Webcrawler differ considerably in form and content from those obtained from a Yahoo search powered by AltaVista. Each of these entries serves as a link to various sites.

A quick evaluation of these lists suggests that far more entries represent ecologists' special interests than ranchers' and stockgrowers'. But if you read the entries and sources with an open, questioning mind, they suggest a great deal about the many sides of the gray wolf controversy. Look particularly at the name

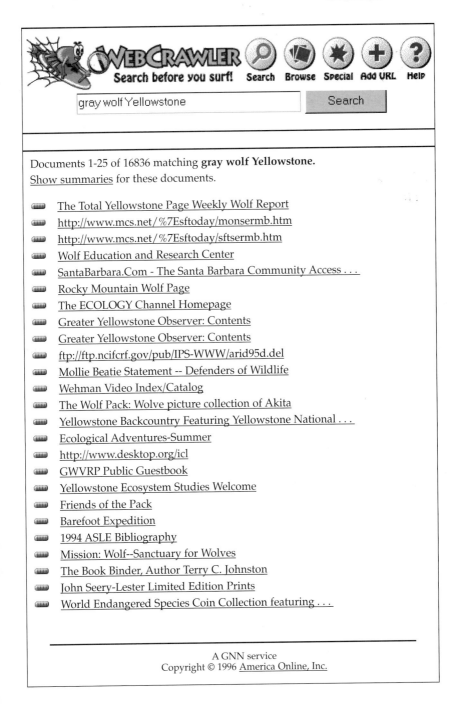

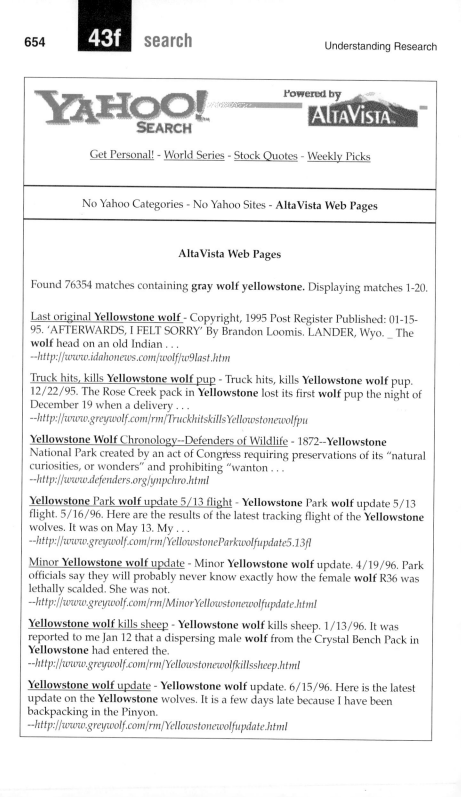

YAHOO! SEARCH

Powered by **ALTAVISTA**

Get Personal! - World Series - Stock Quotes - Weekly Picks

No Yahoo Categories - No Yahoo Sites - **AltaVista Web Pages**

AltaVista Web Pages

Found 76354 matches containing **gray wolf yellowstone**. Displaying matches 1-20.

Last original **Yellowstone wolf** - Copyright, 1995 Post Register Published: 01-15-95. 'AFTERWARDS, I FELT SORRY' By Brandon Loomis. LANDER, Wyo. _ The **wolf** head on an old Indian . . .
--http://www.idahonews.com/wolf/w9last.htm

Truck hits, kills **Yellowstone wolf** pup - Truck hits, kills **Yellowstone wolf** pup. 12/22/95. The Rose Creek pack in **Yellowstone** lost its first **wolf** pup the night of December 19 when a delivery . . .
--http://www.greywolf.com/rm/TruckhitskillsYellowstonewolfpu

Yellowstone Wolf Chronology--Defenders of Wildlife - 1872--**Yellowstone** National Park created by an act of Congress requiring preservations of its "natural curiosities, or wonders" and prohibiting "wanton . . .
--http://www.defenders.org/ynpchro.html

Yellowstone Park **wolf** update 5/13 flight - **Yellowstone** Park **wolf** update 5/13 flight. 5/16/96. Here are the results of the latest tracking flight of the **Yellowstone** wolves. It was on May 13. My . . .
--http://www.greywolf.com/rm/YellowstoneParkwolfupdate5.13fl

Minor **Yellowstone wolf** update - Minor **Yellowstone wolf** update. 4/19/96. Park officials say they will probably never know exactly how the female **wolf** R36 was lethally scalded. She was not.
--http://www.greywolf.com/rm/MinorYellowstonewolfupdate.html

Yellowstone wolf kills sheep - **Yellowstone wolf** kills sheep. 1/13/96. It was reported to me Jan 12 that a dispersing male **wolf** from the Crystal Bench Pack in **Yellowstone** had entered the.
--http://www.greywolf.com/rm/Yellowstonewolfkillssheep.html

Yellowstone wolf update - **Yellowstone wolf** update. 6/15/96. Here is the latest update on the **Yellowstone** wolves. It is a few days late because I have been backpacking in the Pinyon.
--http://www.greywolf.com/rm/Yellowstonewolfupdate.html

Crying "**Wolf**" In **Yellowstone** - Crying "**Wolf**" In **Yellowstone**. Predator Project Note: This is a slightly expanded version of an opinion editorial by Tom Skeele, which was printed in the . . .
--*http://www.wildrockies.org/WildRock/ActivOrg/PredProj/PPnews/Wintr_96/CryWolf.html*

Yellowstone wolf 12 heads south - **Yellowstone wolf** 12 heads south. 1/20/96. In a surprise dispersal, the largest **wolf** in the Soda Butte Pack split from the pack in December and headed . . .
--*http://www.greywolf.com/rm/Yellowstonewolf12headssouth.htm*

Yellowstone Wolf Recovery Plan is Blocked - Vol. XXII, No. 4 -- September 1991. **Yellowstone Wolf** Recovery Plan is Blocked. There are no known wolves in **Yellowstone** and only occasional reports of . . .
--*http://www.edf.org/pubs/EDF-Letter/1991/Sep/c_wolf.html*

Wildlife Agency Offers Reward for Information on Dead **Yellowstone Wolf** - NEWS RELEASE. U.S. FISH AND WILDLIFE SERVICE 134 UNION BOULEVARD LAKEWOOD, COLORADO 80228. February 23, 1996. Michael Smith 303-236-7905 Sharon Rose . . .
--*http://r6alph.irm.r6.fws.gov/www/fws/pressrel/96-16.html*

The Total **Yellowstone** Page Weekly **Wolf** Report - The Total **Yellowstone** Page Weekly **Wolf** Report. Furnished by Call of the Wild Foundation. This page contains a rundown of what is happening with the . . .
--*http://www.issnet.com/pagemakers/yellowstone/wolf.htm*

First **Wolf** Pups of 1996 for **Yellowstone** - May 6, 1996. First pups of year for **Yellowstone**. They're here! After weeks of waiting, the first verified **Yellowstone** pups of 1996 were spotted this week . . .
--*http://www.defenders.org/tl050696.html*

Another **Wolf** Found Dead at **Yellowstone** - April 16, 1996. Another **wolf** was found dead during Sunday's **wolf** overflight in **Yellowstone**. The **wolf**, part of the pair known as the Lone Star pack, was . . .
--*http://www.defenders.org/tl041696.html*

of the Web sites under the AltaVista search: idahonews.com, greywolf.com, defenders.org, wildrockies.org, edf.org. There is a newspaper site, a site devoted to the gray wolf, a site for the Defenders of Wildlife, a site that is hard to figure out without visiting it, and a site for the Environmental Defense Fund. There are apparently no sites in that list representing other interests.

The Webcrawler list is harder to decipher without visiting the sites, but the FTP site looks most promising as an unbiased source—ftp://ftp.ncifcrf.gov/pub/IPS-WWW/arid95d.del. But checking it yields nothing. The least promising, Yellowstone Wolf chronology on the AltaVista list, yields the most information. This site gives a detailed chronology of wolves and Yellowstone from 1872 to May 22, 1996. These excerpts from the 1995 and 1996 entries highlight conflicts between stockgrowers and ecologists, and they also suggest how the wolves are faring:

1995

January, 3—U.S. District Judge William Downes in Cheyenne, Wyoming, denies preliminary injunction sought by Wyoming Farm Bureau Federation. On January 9, government begins shipment of wild wolves from Alberta, Canada, but Farm Bureau wins temporary stay order from federal appellate court in Denver.

January 12—First wolves arrive in Yellowstone National Park after capture in Alberta, Canada. Fourteen wolves, comprising three family groups, are placed in enclosures to accustom them to their new home. . . .

March 21—Doors to Yellowstone acclimation pens are opened.

April 26—Discovery of the radio-collar of an adult male wolf in the vicinity of Red Lodge, Montana, indicates first illegal mortality in Yellowstone. Defenders of Wildlife immediately offers a $5,000 award for information leading to the arrest of the wolf killer. An informant comes forward, and the wolf's head and hide are soon discovered in a cabin. The shooter claims he thought the animal was a dog. . . .

1996

January 12—Yearling wolf #3 kills two sheep near Yellowstone Park. The wolf is relocated to the park and the landowner is reimbursed by Defenders of Wildlife. . . .

February 5—Male wolf #3 from Yellowstone park is shot by federal agents after it returns to a sheep ranch near Emigrant, Montana.

February 26—Chad McKittrick is sentenced for the April 1995 killing of the Red Lodge, Montana, wolf in violation of the Endangered Species Act. . . .

March 30—Female wolf #11 of the Soda Butte pack was found shot to death near Meeteetse, Wyoming. A federal judge denies the request of the Montana Stockgrowers' Association and a Montana rancher to stop the release of wolves from their acclimation pens. . . .

May 8—The alpha female of the Nez Perce pack was spotted at her den site in the Custer National Forest in the Stillwater drainage. Five pups were counted. . . .

The entries about deaths and court activity could be followed up with library research. Government documents, newspapers, reports of the Montana Stockgrowers' Association could round out the picture of what has happened since the wolves were reintroduced. This single site suggests focused, directed work to be done in the library.

Even a cursory glace at the sources available on the Web suggests several important features: that you can find important information quickly; that the search engines limit the parameters of the search and give you information that is likely to yield useful information; and that you can conduct these preliminary searches and evaluate the source either from the annotated lists provided by the search engines or by quick visits to the sites. Even during these initial searches, it would be wise to download or copy these lists; they are relatively short, contain a great deal of useful information about links, and change often. Having the list will save valuable time should you decide to return to the Web later (see 44d for more on note taking). Remember that you will have to document the sources that you use from the Internet; keep track of those sources.

Tips about Downloading and Printing

- Download and store material on your computer to save time and money; you generally pay for the time on the Internet.
- Download electronic documents as plain text (rather than storing them with various Internet codes). Your computer should give you choices about the way you want to save the information when you click *Save as* under *Edit*.
- Store electronic documents in a designated folder in your computer or on a floppy disk so that you can find them easily. Evaluate the documents later.
- After evaluating the documents, print only portions that you need for future reference.
- Always keep up with where you found the material on the Internet because you will have to document electronic sources if you use them in your research essay. You may not be able to go back to the Internet at a later date and find the documents. (See 45c-4 and 45f-4 for more on documenting electronic sources.)

43g Doing field research

Based on your audience, purpose, and course requirements, you may find it necessary to gather your evidence for your research paper outside the library by doing *field research*—conducting interviews, collecting information through surveys, and making direct observations. Field research is a fairly common part of research projects in the social sciences, the natural sciences, and business (see Chapter 48 on writing in the social and natural sciences).

As a field researcher seeking raw evidence, you are responsible for determining where to find the information, how to gather it, and from whom to get it. (See also 48a and 48e on research methodology in the sciences.)

1 Conducting interviews

Interviewing involves asking questions of people so that you can collect information about your topic. When you find it necessary to conduct interviews, think about who can help you. Do you need to question experts or a sample of people in your community? You must also devise your questions in advance and prepare a realistic schedule for your interviews. Whether you are talking to a leading scientist or a randomly chosen motorist at a congested intersection, you are taking busy, committed people away from their lives and work; you owe them the courtesy of being efficient and considerate. Most of what you do in interviews is dictated by common sense, but the accompanying chart lists practical tips that will help you plan and conduct your work.

2 Conducting surveys

Conducting surveys requires the same kind of careful planning that interviews do. In fact, a series of interviews could be the basis for your survey. But surveys can also take the form of questionnaires distributed through the mail or handed out in one of your classes, at your dormitory, or in your community.

Tips for Conducting Successful Interviews

- Generate your questions carefully (see 4a on questioning); be precise and thorough. You are not likely to be granted follow-up interviews. Keep in mind three important principles as you draw up your questions.

  1. Ask for facts. "How many wolves have you observed in the park over the last decade?" "How many wolves have wandered out of the park's boundaries and attacked sheep?" Such questions lead to straightforward and informative answers, but they also lead to other questions, to interpretations, and to important digressions.

  2. Ask for an interpretation of the facts. "What do you think about the current debate over reintroducing the wolf into wilderness preserves?" "You said there have been four wolf attacks on sheep in the last decade. What do you make of those attacks?" Interpretative or open-ended questions take longer to answer. Factor in time for such answers.

  3. Ask for an expert opinion, as appropriate. Expert witnesses know a great deal about the topic and can give you considerable information, perhaps far more than you need. Be prepared to keep your questions and the interview focused.

- Establish a set time frame for the interviews. You will probably have no more than an hour to conduct the complete interview; plan accordingly.

- Set up your interviews in advance. It is always a good idea to make an appointment and to ask for permission if you expect to use a tape recorder or a video camera.

(continued)

- Practice your interviewing technique with a friend. Develop the art of listening. Learn to ask your questions as the opportunity arises. Be flexible. Take a minute near the end of your practice interview to review your list of questions to see that you have asked them all.

- On the day before the interview, call to confirm the appointment. Check all of your equipment. If you are using audiovisual equipment, purchase extra batteries and tapes, and gather together pencils and pens, a notebook, and your final list of questions.

- Dress appropriately, considering where the interview will be conducted.

- Arrive a few minutes early; respect the time limits of the interview; enjoy the occasion to talk with an expert or eyewitness; take adequate notes to ensure that you have a record of the interview; and at the end of the interview thank the person. A follow-up thank-you note is also a good idea.

Whatever your purpose, whether you are trying to find out about corporate decision-making procedures or the voting patterns of college students, you will have to make a special effort to design an appropriate questionnaire. Because you are not likely to have the opportunity to talk with questionnaire respondents, you should create a questionnaire that is carefully tailored to your needs.

Drawing up an effective questionnaire is demanding work, requiring not only knowledge of the commonsense guidelines associated with interviewing, but also special planning and a good deal of legwork. The accompanying chart outlines guidelines for designing and administering questionnaires.

How to Design and Administer Questionnaires

- Devise questions that are easy to tabulate. Fact questions and questions that ask for responses on a scale from 1 to 5 will make your analysis of the data easier. If you ask open-ended questions, make them precise and limit the amount of space for answers.

- Consider using a computer to help you tabulate the results of your questionnaire. Ask your instructor for guidance or check with your computer center about programs that tally data.

- Think about your respondents. Settle on a representative sample that will provide reliable and adequate coverage of the population you are surveying. Consider how many questionnaires you can expect to have returned to you.

(continued)

- Get expert advice. After you know what you are looking for and who your target audience will be, consult someone who does research for a living (such as a mathematics, social science, or psychology professor on your campus). Ask for advice about sample size. Before you interview the expert, consult the interviewing guidelines in this chapter. Also do some background reading on sampling techniques.

- Ask a friend to help you test your questions. Or let your instructor review your draft questionnaire. Based on the input you receive, revise the questions. Always aim for objective questions.

- Make your questionnaire easy to use. Type it up, leaving adequate space for responses. Be sure your questions are easy to understand. Deliver or mail the questionnaire directly to the respondents. Designate a convenient collection point or provide a stamped, addressed envelope. Specify a desired return time. Decide whether you will follow up with those who do not return the survey (of course, follow-up is impossible if the survey is anonymous).

3 Observing

Collecting data, or evidence, through observation can lead you to a neighborhood mall, where you might sit in the optical shop observing customer behavior, or into the wilderness, where you might track wolves. Whatever your project, you will be observing for the primary purpose of collecting evidence that will help you solve your research problem or confirm or refute your hypotheses.

Before heading out into the field to observe, devise an observation plan. Careful planning is just as important to successful observing as it is for effective interviewing and surveying. Think about what your assignment and goals are. What do you want to know? If you are trying to find out what hours an optical shop should remain open to maximize profits and customer satisfaction, you might have to experiment with observing during different hours of operation to get a better sense of customer needs. You might also benefit from combining observation with interviews and questionnaires to get a more comprehensive picture of customer needs. You will also need to think about observing customers long enough to find out whether there are consistent patterns. However basic or complicated your means of observation, it is necessary to plan carefully and well in advance.

Also realize that you need to keep some distance from what you are observing; it is important to be objective and to avoid introducing bias into your findings. Just as you avoid devising survey questionnaires that lead respondents to a particular, preferred reply, as an observer you need to keep professional distance and avoid either projecting your own ideas onto what you are seeing or altering your surroundings in any way.

You also need a system for recording what you observe. You might have to rely on special equipment such as a video camera or tape recorder. When observing, you should always take notes and make sketches in field notebooks, recording details of what happened, what did not happen, and what mistakes and discoveries you made. Question your evidence and make connections (see 4a on questioning, and 4c on connecting). Consider working with a partner so you can compare observations. Review the accompanying observation checklist before you get started.

Checklist for Observing

- Prepare well in advance and plan carefully. Decide how and when to observe in light of your purpose.
- Record what you observe as you observe it. Use a field notebook to take notes or make sketches, but also use electronic equipment, such as a video camera and tape recorder, when useful and feasible.
- Keep your observations and your reflections separate so that you will be able to distinguish the evidence from what you thought about it.
- Be objective. Avoid introducing bias into your results.
- Try to work with a partner to compare results and thereby minimize error.

43h   Compiling a working bibliography

A *working bibliography* is the list of books, articles, and all other sources that you compile as you do your research. As you do preliminary research with reference books, periodical indexes, library catalogs, and databases, prepare source cards for any and all sources that look worthwhile. The sources you put in the working bibliography are there tentatively, however. After you consult the listed sources and evaluate them, you may discover they are not helpful (see 44b–c on evaluating and reading sources); if so, you can then remove the source from your list. (Although, if your instructor requests a list of *works consulted*—all of the sources you consulted as opposed to those you actually cite in your essay—you may need to keep all of your source cards.)

Eventually, after you have evaluated and selected sources and started writing your essay, what remains in your working bibliography will become your Works Cited list (if MLA style), or your References list (if APA style) (see 45c and 45f).

Ericka Kostka began her research by reading from encyclopedias; one of those encyclopedia articles included a brief but promising bibliography at its

end, so Ericka photocopied it for her working bibliography. But when Ericka consulted the *New York Times Index* and then the *Readers' Guide to Periodical Literature,* she found so many promising sources that listing and photocopying became inefficient. At that point, she began to prepare source cards (also called bibliography cards) for each of the useful-looking sources she encountered. Examples of her source cards follow.

Begley, Sharon. "Crying Wolf in Yellowstone." <u>Newsweek</u>
    16 Dec. 1985: 74.

A Source Card for a Periodical Article

After Ericka finished preparing her source cards from the *Readers' Guide,* and before she located the sources, she consulted the library's card and online catalogs to make sure she had not overlooked obvious sources associated with the gray wolf problem. She also consulted abstracts and citations. She drew up source cards for all of the sources that looked promising, including this source card for a book.

Lopez, Barry H. <u>Of Wolves and Men</u>. New York: QL
    Scribner's, 1987.   737.C22
                                         L66

A Source Card for a Book

Ericka was careful to include on each source card the information she would need both to locate the source in the library and to prepare her Works Cited list.

Ericka's instructor asked students to use the Modern Language Association (MLA) documentation style, commonly used in humanities courses. Be sure to check with your instructor about the required documentation style for your project before proceeding with your research or devising source cards. (See Chapter 45 on documentation styles, including MLA.) Familiarize yourself with the various citation formats in your documentation style and use them as you compile your working bibliography. That way you will have all the information you need to help you find the sources and the information will be in the appropriate format for preparing your Works Cited list.

The accompanying chart outlines the information you should include on source cards. Carefully recording this information as you go along will save you time in the long run and will keep you from having to retrace your steps later.

Information to Record in a Working Bibliography

BOOKS

> Library call number
> Author's name
> Editor's name (if any)
> Translator's name (if any)
> Full title, including subtitle
> Place of publication
> Publisher
> Date of publication
> Other: volume number, edition, page numbers for relevant sections or chapters

PERIODICAL ARTICLES

> Author's name
> Full title of article, including subtitle
> Full title of periodical
> Volume number and issue number (if any)
> Date of issue
> Page numbers for the entire article

SOURCES FROM INDEXES

> Name of the index so you can return to it if necessary
> Call number
> Any other information to help identify and locate the source in the library

(continued)

ELECTRONIC SOURCES—CD-ROM, COMPUTER SERVICES, INTERNET

Author's name
Title
Print source (if this is an electronic equivalent of a print source)
Date of original printing
Page numbers, volume, etc., if available
Database name (if any)
Electronic source (CD-ROM, Computer Services—Online, Prodigy, etc., or Internet)
Internet or network path or address for reaching the source
Date of electronic posting and electronic address

NONPRINT SOURCES

Note where you found the information
List it in the specified documentation style and format on your source card

---

When you begin consulting the sources themselves, always check the accuracy of the data you have recorded from indexes, database searches, the World Wide Web, and nonprint sources against the information on the title page and copyright page of a book, the table of contents of a periodical article, or the Web site.

To prepare your working bibliography, use 3 × 5-inch index cards, one for each source. Using cards gives you great flexibility for arranging the cards either alphabetically by author or by type of source. If you would prefer not to work with index cards, use notebook paper or a computer. If you do work on a computer, look into the various functions of your software that can help you compile lists or format your sources.

Directed research in the library and field research are necessary parts of the research process. In Chapter 44 you will learn how to evaluate the sources and evidence you accumulated in your research. You will also learn how to take notes and write the research essay. Inevitably, writing the essay will bring you back to the library; as you write your essay, you will discover the need for additional research.

Writing the Research Essay

*I*n this chapter you will see how the evidence collected from research can be used to develop an essay. You will learn how to restrict a topic, evaluate sources, take notes, and then how to plan, organize, draft, and revise a research essay. To illustrate the research process, we will continue to follow the work of one student, Ericka Kostka, to see how she researched her topic (the fate of the gray wolf) and wrote an essay to defend a thesis. (Ericka's full essay appears in Chapter 46.)

44a Restricting your topic

Once you settle on a topic that interests you and compile a working bibliography (see 43b and 43h), you are ready to start thinking about the potential sources you have compiled. You are also ready to begin reading those sources to expand your knowledge of your topic. As you consider the sources in your working bibliography and as you begin to locate those sources and read them, your aim should be to restrict your topic as soon as possible. Restricting a topic involves narrowing from the broad and general to the more specific and manageable. Essentially, you restrict or limit a topic to help focus your research effort. Instead of locating and reading all the sources you can find on a very general or broad topic, you rein yourself in and do thorough research on a specific topic. Topic restriction will save you valuable research time; it will also give you the opportunity to delve into a particular area and become an expert on it.

To restrict your topic adequately, follow the advice in the accompanying guidelines. Admittedly, restricting a topic is not always easy. At the outset, when you consider a topic like Ericka's, the possibilities may seem endless: "Should I try to account for the extermination of wolves all across North America? Should I try to focus on stockgrowers' opposition to wolves in Wyoming and Minnesota, or should I try to figure out why Alaska is allowing hunters to kill wolves at a time when the park service in Wyoming is thinking about reintroducing wolves into Yellowstone?" Reaching a decision about just where to focus your research depends on your being knowledgeable

Guidelines for Topic Restriction

- Become knowledgeable about your unrestricted topic by doing preliminary research. You might read encyclopedia articles or other reference books and consult representative sources from your working bibliography. Always avoid restricting when you have too little information.

- As you gather background information about your topic, try to identify a problem or controversial issue about which experts or special-interest groups disagree. When you find controversy, you can be sure you are on to a topic worth pursuing. Where there is controversy, there is a problem to solve and an opportunity to interpret—for you to make your own sense of an issue, to explain or find a solution (see 4d and 2d on controversies and interpretation).

- Limit the scope of your investigation. For example, you might focus on only one geographical area, such as gray wolves in Yellowstone National Park. Or you could study only one aspect of the topic, such as tracking wolves with radio-transmitter collars as opposed to the broader topic of tracking wolves. Perhaps you could limit the time frame of your research, considering only the efforts made during the last five years to introduce wolves into sanctuaries, for example. Or you might use a combination of these methods.

- Be sure that your research can provide sufficient sources on the topic and that all the material you need will be accessible. Also consider whether you will have adequate time to work with the materials and complete the assignment. Be sure, too, that your evidence is sufficient for you to develop a reasonable and objective thesis (see 44e).

about your topic and the availability of sources. Consult with your instructor if you have difficulty restricting your topic.

Let's look at how Ericka restricted her topic. As outlined in Chapter 43, Ericka was interested in wolves when she began her research. She had first been introduced to wolf recovery during a visit to Yellowstone, but she had no specific knowledge of the issue. By doing some preliminary research, Ericka found ample background information on wolves in two encyclopedia articles and from the listing of periodical articles that she found in the *New York Times Index*, the *Readers' Guide to Periodical Literature*, and the *General Science Index* (see 43d). She discovered a long-standing debate between environmentalists who wish to protect wolves and stockgrowers who view protected wolves as an inevitable threat to their livestock.

Ericka's first visit to the library had taken less than two hours. She spent most of the time in the reference room consulting periodical indexes, abstracts, and the online catalog. She found more than twenty sources for her working bibliography; each of these sources looked promising.

As she scanned her working bibliography and thought about the potential sources listed there, Ericka saw that the issue extended far beyond the boundaries of Yellowstone. The presence of the gray wolf was a problem in several states including Wisconsin, Minnesota, and Wyoming. But she could see from the titles of recent articles that a great deal of attention was being given to the wolf problem at Yellowstone. Restricting her topic to that particular area seemed reasonable, and, based on her preliminary research, she was sure she would be able to find sufficient information about wolves in Yellowstone.

But Ericka's instructor had cautioned the class against restricting the topic based on too little information, so before settling on her topic, Ericka decided to read two of the periodical articles from her working bibliography—a general article on wolves in North America by Diane Edwards in *Science News*, and a specific article on wolves at Yellowstone by Ted Williams in *Audubon*—to get a clearer sense of the controversy between environmentalists and stockgrowers. These articles gave Ericka much more detailed information than did the encyclopedias and confirmed the wisdom of restricting her research to the wolf problem at Yellowstone. In particular, Diane Edwards gave Ericka a clear sense that the problem in North America was too broad to deal with in a six- to twelve-page research essay.

44b   Evaluating the usefulness of sources

Evaluating sources involves a preliminary assessment or scanning of the sources in your working bibliography and then a more thorough and critical reading of the sources themselves (see 44c). Both steps will help you determine the usefulness of sources.

As soon as you restrict your topic, you should evaluate the usefulness of the sources in your working bibliography. Begin by scanning the bibliography for sources that seem to have nothing to do with the newly restricted topic and weed them out. Check the titles of sources to determine their relevance, but be aware that titles can be misleading. Place any pulled source cards in a separate "dead" file; do not throw them away because you may need to go back to them later to consult a source you initially deemed unusable. If you have doubts about eliminating a source, leave the card in your working bibliography until you can check the source or read an abstract.

Ericka started weeding sources as soon as she restricted her topic to the wolf problem in Yellowstone. All the sources that dealt with the wolf in other geographical areas, with the selected killing of wolves in Alaska, or with the introduction of wolves into Minnesota and North Carolina, were pulled out and the source cards relegated to a separate file.

After you have scanned the source cards, go to the library, locate the sources remaining in your working bibliography, and scan them. You should not be reading the sources closely or taking detailed notes at this point, but browsing, skimming, investigating research possibilities. Read the table of contents, preface, first few paragraphs, abstract, or headings within a source.

The accompanying guidelines will help you with this initial assessment of sources. Once you have done this preliminary evaluation, you can start reading whatever sources remain to evaluate them more closely.

Guidelines for Evaluating the Usefulness of Sources

- Consider the relevance of the source to your restricted topic. Ask yourself whether the source will help you learn more about the topic.
- Consider whether the source is too general or specific for your research needs.
- Check the date of publication. Is the source current? Will current sources serve your purpose, or would older sources be more appropriate? Do you want a combination of older and current sources?
- Look at the author's credentials to establish whether he or she is an authority on the topic. Does the author's name turn up in other sources? If so, that person is probably a reliable expert. You can also check to see what other experts have written about the author. Consult a biographical reference book or index for more information on a particular author.
- Ascertain the author's point of view on the topic and whether that point of view seems reasonable. Consider the author's tone and intended audience.
- Do a preliminary source evaluation; scan rather than read the sources in your working bibliography. Scan the table of contents, the preface, the index, the title, notes about the author, subheadings, available abstracts, the afterword, and the listed sources. Once you have eliminated sources that are obviously irrelevant, do a more thorough evaluation of the remaining sources.
- Be sure to record connections you make while scanning or reading. Note these connections and any other ideas about your sources in a reading journal (1e-1), in a double-column notebook (2b-3), or on note cards (44d). For any notes you take, keep track of your sources to avoid unintentional plagiarism (44j).
- Scan electronic sources that you have downloaded and deemed reliable. (See 43f-3 for more on evaluation of electronic sources.) After you judge electronic sources reliable, evaluate their usefulness as you would for any other sources.

44c   Reading sources critically

Once you have done a preliminary assessment of sources, you can begin a more thorough evaluation that involves reading the sources that remain in your working bibliography. You will want to read those sources carefully and critically.

To read critically, keep the guidelines in the accompanying chart in mind. (Also see Chapter 2 on critical reading.) You will also find that as you read your sources and become more knowledgeable about your topic, you will be able to focus your research and restrict your topic even more.

As you read and evaluate your sources, you will get a clear sense of the different points of view on your topic and of the arguments offered in support of those viewpoints. You will also start to evaluate the substance of the arguments you encounter—identifying strengths, weaknesses, and gaps in each. Begin to think about audience and purpose. (See 3d on logical thinking and Chapter 2 on critical reading.)

To help keep yourself on track, it is a good idea to develop a focusing question from your restricted topic. You will seek to answer that focusing question as you read and do subsequent research. In addition, the question will give direction to your research; it will help you know just what to look for as you continue reading and evaluating sources.

As Ericka read her sources, she pinpointed five special-interest groups, each with its own perspective on the wolf population controversy: (1) the National Park Service; (2) environmentalists and wolf experts; (3) the Wyoming Stockgrowers' Association; (4) the National Wool Growers Association; and (5) politicians from bordering states. As she learned more, Ericka was able to develop a focusing question about her restricted topic, the wolf population problem in Yellowstone. This focusing question directed her inquiry.

> To what extent does it seem reasonable, given all of those conflicting interests, to make an effort to restore the wolf population in Yellowstone?

How to Read Sources Critically

- Read with an open mind to expand your knowledge of your restricted topic. Be receptive to different points of view and do not take sides—read objectively. Try to distinguish facts from emotional appeals or theories about those facts.

- Question what you are reading. Ask yourself many questions. (See the questioning guidelines in 4a.)

  What do I notice as I read? What patterns do I see emerging? How do I feel about what I am reading? What is the writer's main idea? How well does the evidence (facts, anecdotes, examples) support the idea?

- Let your reading lead you to other sources. The reference lists at the end of books and articles can alert you to other sources.

- Write as you read. Take notes (see 44d), that can be incorporated into your essay. These notes can also include your comments and reflections about that evidence.

- Think about the relevance and reliability of your sources using the evaluation guidelines in 44b. Continue to weed out unusable sources.

The best focusing questions are like Ericka's: specific, straightforward, and manageable. They require more than a simple *yes* or *no* in response; they encourage thinking about what you are reading and researching. They also require you to be analytical, reasonable, and objective—to weigh various points of view against one another so you can decide where you stand on your topic or issue.

Once you have settled on a focusing question, you will also be able to consider your sources objectively—to look carefully at the facts and distinguish facts from emotional appeals. For example, Ericka had no doubt that stockgrowers who lose cattle and sheep to wolves would be emotional about their losses and that their arguments would reflect their emotions. She knew, too, that some environmentalists might overstate their case in favor of the wolf. But with her focusing question in mind, she was able to consider those emotionally charged defenses without being swayed or biased. She focused on weighing what she read against the real threat to the wolf population.

A good focusing question should also lead you to more questions and eventually to a reasonable and objective thesis (see 44e) that explains the accumulated evidence. Ericka's focusing question spurred her to ask herself these questions as she read each source. You can ask yourself these or similar questions as you read and evaluate your sources and work your way to a reasonable thesis.

- What does this source reveal about the special-interest group's argument—its main points, its evidence, its underlying concerns?
- In what ways does this information about a particular group contribute to my understanding of the larger problem?
- Does the evidence in the source seem logical and convincing?
- What has the source failed to consider?
- Can I detect any bias in the source?
- Is the writer aligned exclusively with a special-interest group, or are other points of view considered?
- Do I find myself resisting the information in the source? How exactly do my findings differ from those of this writer?

44d Taking notes

As you critically read sources and determine their usefulness, you will want to take notes. Thorough and accurate note taking during research will help you once you start writing the research essay and when you need to acknowledge your sources.

The notes you take will serve two purposes. They will help you learn about your topic; the writing you do will clarify what you are reading and will help you organize your thoughts about it. In addition, the notes you take as you read and evaluate sources may eventually become the evidence you incorporate into your essay to help readers understand your thesis. You will eventually have to decide what to include and what to leave out of your essay based on audience considerations and your purpose (see 44f and 44i).

As you take notes, always try to distill your sources into a form you can use later in your essay, such as a summary (44d-1), a paraphrase (44d-2), a direct quotation (44d-3), reflections on what you are reading (44d-4), or a combination of these (44d-5). Your notes should always be carefully and accurately recorded. If your notes include accurate and complete information, you will not have to waste valuable time later going back to the original sources to clarify confusing entries or to fill in gaps. In addition, it is crucial that you clearly distinguish your reflections from the ideas and words of the sources themselves. Taking careful notes will help you avoid accidental plagiarism (see 44j).

Note taking is not a mechanical process of copying from your sources to your note cards. You should be doing a great deal of thinking and reflecting (44d-4) as you read and take notes. As you read and think about your sources, try to make connections between ideas. When you come across a word, a phrase, or an idea in one source that reminds you of something in another, record that connection; it could turn out to be important when you start organizing your notes and writing your essay. Develop a system of cross-referencing that will permit you to keep track of the connections you make as you proceed with your research.

Although there is no single, correct way to take notes, most researchers find that 4 × 6-inch index cards provide enough space for detailed notes and complement the system of using 3 × 5-inch index cards for your working bibliography (making it easy to distinguish source cards from note cards). Some researchers, however, prefer using a notebook or computer when taking notes. The accompanying guidelines will help you as you take notes, no matter what system you use.

Guidelines for Note Taking

- At the top of each 4 × 6-inch index card, notebook page, or computerized note entry, include the author's last name, an abbreviated form of the title, and inclusive page numbers for the material you include from the source. There is no need to include full bibliographic information, such as publication date, since you will have recorded that in your working bibliography (see 43h).

- Provide a subject or category heading at the top of each card, identifying in two or three words the main subject or idea of the notes. This heading will help you later when you organize your notes.

(continued)

- Use a separate card for each fact or idea that you take from a source. If you put several ideas or notes on a single card, it will be difficult to arrange your notes when you organize them in preparation for writing the essay.
- Clearly identify the type of note on the card. If you quote verbatim from a source, use quotation marks at the beginning and at the end of the quotation. If you summarize, label the notes as a summary or signal the summary with an S at the beginning and at the end; if you paraphrase, label the notes as a paraphrase or signal the paraphrase with a P at the beginning and the end. Use double slash marks (//), a different color ink, or some other signal to distinguish clearly your own comments from source material.
- Cross-reference connections that occur to you as you read your sources.
- Check the accuracy of your notes before you put the source aside. Have you quoted accurately? Are all of your facts, numbers, and other data correct? Did you include the correct page numbers for the material in your notes? If your note includes material that extends for more than one page in a source, indicate the page break in your notes by putting the page number in brackets: *[223]*. Then record inclusive page numbers at the end of the note: 222–23. This way, if you decide to use only part of the note in your essay, you will know the exact page for the material without having to consult the original source again.
- Be careful not to plagiarize—to take someone else's words or ideas, organizational patterns, or computer programs without giving proper credit.

1 Summarizing

When you write a **summary,** you condense a fairly lengthy passage of text into a few sentences of your own words. A summary is always shorter than the original source. It captures the essence of the source, the writer's main idea(s); it also enables a reader unfamiliar with the source to understand the idea.

As you summarize, remember three things: (1) You may eventually use the summarized material in your own essay, so begin to think of what your reader needs to know to understand your summary. Let the reader's needs guide you as you decide how much detail to include. (2) Even though you are summarizing someone else's work in your own words, the idea and the information belong to the other writer, not to you. If you use that summarized material in your essay, you must give the author credit for it (see 44j and Chapter 45). (3) Remain true to the author's intended meaning. When you select a passage from a source that you want to summarize, or when you choose to summarize a complete source (such as an article or an essay), follow the Guidelines for Summarizing.

Ericka Kostka relied a great deal on summary as she read, evaluated, and took notes from her sources. Three paragraphs from a journal article gave her important information about the way political influence caused the Park Service at Yellowstone to curtail its educational program on wolves.

ORIGINAL SOURCE

The message from "the environmental President" to the Park Service was clear. And it encouraged other messages: "I demand that the department disavow itself of this lobbying effort," brayed Wyoming Senator Malcolm Wallop to Interior Secretary Manuel Lunjan when he discovered that the Park Service was sending out educational wolf packets containing natural history of the sort that Wallop doesn't believe. Montana Representative Pat Williams went further, still, questioning "the appropriateness of providing the public with *information* [my emphasis], about wolf reintroduction." Similar complaints were voiced by Senator Burns and Congressman Marlenee.

Patiently, the Park Service noted that the Endangered Species Act requires it to use "all methods and procedures necessary" to restore the wolf—in this case, dispelling precisely the sort of mythology that western ranchers and politicians clutch to their breasts. And it noted that its own management policies require it to "identify and promote" the conservation of endangered species.

At the same time, however, the Park Service backed off. It agreed not to mail out its educational packets (which had run out anyway). It temporarily canceled an immensely popular wolf-restoration slide show. It stopped writing about wolf reintroduction in the park newspaper. And it prohibited Defenders of Wildlife from selling pro-wolf-restoration posters at park visitor centers.

—Ted Williams, "Waiting for Wolves to Howl in Yellowstone"

Guidelines for Summarizing

- Read the source, looking for the writer's main idea.
- As you read, note key words, striking images, and important sentences.
- In your own words, write down the main idea of the passage.
- Test your summary of the main idea during a second reading. Carefully check the summary against the passage itself. Make sure you have captured the essence of the passage.
- A summary is a substantially shortened version of the source but includes sufficient information so that your reader can understand the source.
- If you decide to incorporate a few of the writer's key words or phrases into your summary, be sure to enclose them in quotation marks and record the page numbers in parentheses right after the closing quotation marks.
- Be sure you have an entry in your working bibliography for the source.
- Follow the Guidelines for Note Taking on pp. 671–72 as you prepare your summary.

Ericka completed several note cards as she read Williams's article. The accompanying card contains her summary of the three paragraphs and her reflections.

Williams 38   Politics

   S / According to Williams, political pressure has hindered the park's educational programs on the issue of wolf recovery. / S
   // Williams does a good job in this fairly long section on politics. Besides the three paragraphs on p. 38, he also lets us see in an earlier section how political pressure leads to commissioned studies that slow down decision making. S / Williams argues that these studies take time, relieve pressure on the Park Service to get the job done, and also satisfy scientists who get paid to do them. Everyone benefits from not getting the job done. (p. 36) / S. In this other section of the essay, Williams shows how complicated and messy this political business can get. // See Diane Edwards for more on wolf politics.

Note Card with Summary, Reflection, and Connection

Notice how Ericka summarizes the essence of Williams's argument and reduces three paragraphs to one sentence, in her own words (see the first sentence identified by the S/). On that same note card, Ericka chooses to reflect and refer to an earlier, related section in Williams's article. Within her reflections, she summarizes the earlier section. Because she clearly distinguishes between her notes and reflections and labels her note cards properly, Ericka will be able to work with these notes easily.

2   Paraphrasing

When you **paraphrase,** you aim to convey in your own words the essence of the source and a sense of its structure—the ordered way in which the writer reaches a conclusion, develops an idea, or creates emphasis. A paraphrase follows the structure of the original source closer and may include more details than a summary. Paraphrases may be as long as or longer than the original source. If the writer's structure is as important as the idea itself, paraphrase the selection rather than summarize. If the development of the idea is more important than the author's wording, paraphrase rather than quote.

Because you follow the original source closely in a paraphrase and may include considerable detail from it, you must be especially careful not to use key words and phrases from the source unless you enclose them in quotation marks. As a general rule, write the entire paraphrase in your own words, quoting only when the words of the source are essential to preserve meaning. As you paraphrase, follow the accompanying guidelines.

Guidelines for Paraphrasing

- Read the source, looking for the writer's main idea.
- Write down, in your own words and using your own sentence structure, what you think the main idea is. Order your paraphrase just as the original source is ordered; include appropriate details.
- Check your paraphrase against the source. Make sure that you have captured the essence of the source and that your wording differs significantly from the wording in the original source.
- Include sufficient information in your paraphrase so that your reader can understand the source.
- Avoid plagiarism (see 44j) by giving credit to the author of the paraphrased material. Note source page numbers. If you include important terms and phrases from the source, put those words in quotation marks.
- Reflect on the source but be sure to separate your reflections and paraphrase.
- Be sure you have an entry in your working bibliography for the source.
- Follow the Guidelines for Note Taking (see pp. 671–72) as you prepare your paraphrase.

Ericka was especially interested in the last of Williams's three paragraphs about the effects of politics on the Park Service's information program (see 44d-1). She believed the order in Williams's paragraph created emphasis, so she decided to paraphrase that paragraph. Notice how Ericka's wording and sentence structure differ from the original but retain the same order of information.

Williams 38   Effects of Politics

P / As a result of political opposition, the Park Service stopped mailing educational material about wolves, canceled its slide show on the wolf, stopped writing about restoring the wolf population, and prohibited selling wolf posters in the park. / P

// This is the essence of Williams's case about the effects of politics on the educational program. He makes this case convincingly, citing considerable details. No hesitation on my part to accept these conclusions. //

Note Card with Paraphrase and Reflection

3 Quoting

When you use a **quotation,** you record the writer's words verbatim and enclose them in quotation marks. When you quote, record a writer's exact words, being careful to preserve the punctuation marks, capitalization, and spelling in the original. If you make any alterations to the quoted passage do so carefully and sparingly. To add words, substitute words, or provide explanations within the quoted passage, put those additions in brackets (see 37c-2). If you delete words or phrases, indicate these deletions with an ellipsis (see 37d). If the writer has made a mistake within the quoted material, you can, if you choose, indicate that mistake by placing the Latin word *sic* (meaning "thus") within brackets immediately after the error. As with paraphrases and summaries, when quoting, always give credit to the writer by documenting what you quote (see Chapter 45 on documentation). (Also see Chapter 36 on quotation marks.)

Several reasons to quote rather than summarize or paraphrase are outlined in the accompanying chart. Always quote sparingly and in the situations described in the chart. (Also see 44i-1.)

As Ericka evaluated Williams's article about the gray wolf in Yellowstone, she was struck by the politicians' language as they voiced opposition to the reintroduction of wolves into the park. She saw immediately that their own words undercut the effectiveness of their arguments. She decided to record some of those voices from Williams's article in note cards, anticipating that she could use the quotations later in her essay.

Williams (36)   Politicians
                                                       against Wolves

"Wyoming Senator Alan Simpson has asserted that wolves eat people. Montana Senator Conrad Burns predicts that if wolves are returned to Yellowstone, 'there'll be a dead child within a year.' . . . Simpson's office now claims he really didn't say 'wolves eat things human and alive' (although he did)" (36).

// 2d Simpson response came after he was questioned about his earlier statement. Williams has summarized Simpson in the first sentence and quoted him in the third. //

Note Card with Quotations and Reflection

To see how Ericka used these quotations, see 44i.

When to Quote

- When the writer's words are so cogent and memorable that summarizing or paraphrasing would undercut their effectiveness or alter their meaning
- When you believe the writer's words will lend authority to what you have to say and will be more persuasive than your summary or paraphrase of those words
- When you want to take exception to what a writer has said
- When you want to comment on a writer's words as a way of expressing your own position or idea (44d-4)
- When you want to let a speaker's own words expose the weakness of his or her argument
- When you want to cite statistical information from the source

---

4   Reflecting

Reflecting on your sources is an important part of the process of taking useful notes. When you reflect, you enter into a conversation with the source you are reading; you think carefully about the source, trying to make connections with other sources, to relate ideas that come to mind, to clarify and gain insight. Learn to listen to these thoughts. In doing so you become an active, critical reader who hears a text and your mind's reaction to it. (See also Chapter 2 on reading.)

Noting your reflections on sources will prove beneficial when the time comes to organize and write your research essay. From those reflections in your notes or in your reading journal, you can find ideas and discover patterns and additional connections. Your research essay will not merely be a compilation of the ideas of other writers and researchers; it will contain what you think about your sources. Maintaining a record of your reflections as you take notes will help you make sense of your research; it will help you make the leap from the ideas and words of others to your own ideas on your topic.

When you record your reflections in your notes, be sure always to distinguish them from the information you take directly from the sources in the form of summaries, paraphrases, or quotations. Always take care to avoid plagiarism.

5   Combining summary, paraphrase, quotation, and reflection

Often, you will combine summary, paraphrase, quotation, and reflection on the same note card. Combining gives you the flexibility to adapt the source material to your own needs and to make it easier to maintain your own style and voice in your essay. Ensure that combining does not become the occasion for carelessness. Be exact when you use a source verbatim; enclose the borrowed words in quotation marks. When you summarize and paraphrase, make sure you do not inadvertently borrow key words and phrases from the source without enclosing them in quotation marks.

Ericka uses a combination of summary, quotation, and reflection on a note card that captures the essence of the continuing debate between stockgrowers and biologists over the reintroduction of wolves into Yellowstone.

ORIGINAL SOURCE

The Montana Stock Growers Association, for example, predicts that the wolves will wander outside the parks and, in Montana alone, would kill up to 1,000 livestock a year.

Biologists with the National Park Service disagree. In a study delivered last week, they found no scientific grounds for refusing to bring the wolves back. The study argues that wolves will kill few livestock and will thin herds of elk that have grown too large to be sustained in protected areas.

—Christopher Joyce, "Yellowstone Lets the Wolf through the Door"

Joyce 21   Debate

S / In a recent article in the <u>New Scientist</u>, Christopher Joyce reports on the continuing debate between stockgrowers and biologists over the reintroduction of wolves into Yellowstone. Biologists claim there are "no scientific grounds" for stockgrowers' prediction that stray wolves will "kill up to 1,000 livestock a year" in Montana. / S

// This is yet another variation on the debate between stockgrowers and environmentalists. Here, the biologists' claims are based on a study; the stockgrowers' are not. // Cross-reference: see note cards for Diane Edwards and Ted Williams for more on the debate.

Note Card Combining Summary, Quotation, and Reflection

Researchers often photocopy source material when time is limited. Coin-operated photocopy machines are usually available in the library's reference room. If you make photocopies, be careful not to consider the copies your own notes or your own thinking about a source. Be sure to record all of the information you will need to prepare note cards and your list of sources (see 45c and 45f).

44e Developing a reasonable thesis

You read and evaluate sources and take notes from them in order to collect enough information about your topic so that you can develop a reasonable thesis about it. As you develop that thesis, you will use the information recorded in your notes or in your reading journal to help you support, illustrate, and account for your thesis. Your notes—whether summary, paraphrase, quotation, or reflection—will become the evidence you incorporate and cite in your essay. (See also 44i for more on incorporating evidence.)

An effective thesis is a reasonable one. It emerges from a careful consideration of your focusing question and the conflicting points of view on your topic. As your own position within a controversy begins to emerge, always test the reasonableness of your thesis by asking yourself how other researchers and writers might react to your thesis. Use the questions in the accompanying chart to test the reasonableness of your thesis.

If you have read or listened to those who have entered the debate about your subject, you will likely have the knowledge and background to anticipate objections and counter them. Ignoring other points of view can only weaken your argument. That kind of single-mindedness makes your thesis seem unreasonable. (See 7b for more on developing a reasonable thesis.)

Gauging the Reasonableness of Your Thesis

- Is my thesis based on the investigative work I have done?
- Is my thesis focused?
- Is my thesis objective, fair, and deliberate, taking into consideration all sides of the issue?
- Have I avoided a heated, two-sided debate or a simple declaration that invites resistance?
- Have I let my readers know that I have considered and anticipated the responses of those who might disagree with me?
- Have I been thorough in my research or do I need to do more research on my topic to get a fuller picture of other points of view?

When Ericka Kostka finished evaluating all of her sources and began to think about writing her essay, she saw quite clearly that the five special interest groups she had been considering fell into two general categories: the stockgrowers (and their constituents) and the environmentalists (and theirs). After researching, taking notes, and then writing in her journal about these two groups and their various arguments for and against the wolf, Ericka began to see that there might be a way for the wolf population to be restored to Yellowstone and for the stockgrowers to be protected. She wanted to offer reasonable alternatives to the stockgrowers; otherwise, she knew she would be unable to convince them to reintroduce the wolf into the park.

Rarely will you settle on a thesis on your first attempt at devising one. As you write, think, and do additional research, you make discoveries about your topic that will inevitably lead you to modify your thesis. Many writers, in fact, begin by devising a working thesis to guide the organization and writing of their first draft. Ericka devised a working thesis that was modified as she started writing and discovered gaps in her argument.

ERICKA'S WORKING THESIS

Because evidence strongly indicates that wolf populations are important to the predator-prey balance in Yellowstone and because that repopulation can be viable for both the gray wolf and its opponents, I believe we should reverse the one-sided concessions forced upon a now endangered population and restore the wolves in the park.

This working thesis was not an idea Ericka brought to the assignment. It evolved through learning and writing, as she considered conflicting points of view, reflected about them, and questioned them. For a clear sense of this evolutionary process, reread the sections on Ericka's selection of a topic (43b), her restriction of the topic (44a), and her focusing question. (Also see Chapter 4 on arriving at a thesis.)

44f Considering your audience

Once you have developed a working thesis, you will have to figure out how to communicate that thesis to your readers. To do that, try to answer the following three questions.

1. What evidence should I include in my essay?
2. How do I present the evidence to my readers so that they will understand it?
3. How do I order the evidence for my readers?

The following general advice should help you as you try to answer these questions with regard to your particular essay.

1. Select the evidence that will, in your mind, help your audience see what it is you want them to see.
2. Present your evidence with adequate explanation—provide enough background information, draw inferences, form conclusions about the connections you jotted down in your notes or journal, clarify the relationship between

your evidence and your ideas. Do not throw raw evidence at your readers; interpret it for them. And be sure to be clear and objective.

3. Order or arrange your evidence in a way that will make it easy for your audience to follow your reasoning (see 44g).

Research essays that are also arguments require an especially keen attentiveness to audience because your goal is to convince that audience of your conclusion without inviting opposition or hostility. To be persuasive, you must show a real concern for what your readers might think about a given subject and how they might react to the way you think about that subject (refer to 1d for more on considering audience). Most audiences—whether hostile or friendly, whether you know them well or have no idea how to persuade them to adopt your point of view—will respond to logic and reasonableness. The rules of formal logic will help you ensure that your argument is fair and reasonable rather than unbalanced, hotheaded, or fallacious (see Chapter 3 on logical thinking).

44g Organizing your essay

Once you have compiled notes and reflections on your sources, you are ready to start writing. But because writing research essays tends to be a fairly long and complicated process, it is a good idea to organize your notes and your thoughts first.

There is no single right way to order your research; always work with your audience in mind, thinking of what readers need to know to understand your thesis. Grouping your notes by subject headings and outlining are two useful strategies for organizing.

1 Organizing your notes

If you are careful to label each note with a subject heading in the upper right-hand corner (see 44d), you will have an easier time organizing your notes. Those subject headings can also lead you to ideas about how to structure your essay and to make connections that you missed while reading your sources. You might also notice gaps in your research. Essentially, these subject headings—whether on note cards, pieces of paper, or a computer file—will help you analyze your notes, group related information together, and see how all your information might be ordered within the essay.

The following general subject headings helped Ericka organize her note cards and ultimately revealed the key to her essay's organization: politicians' concerns, legal background for extermination, bad wolf folklore, environmentalists' concerns, radio tracking, stockgrowers' concerns, public concerns, and Park Service's concerns. As Ericka evaluated her notes, she saw that they fell logically into categories that represented the special-interest groups.

Ericka had also cross-referenced her sources as she read and evaluated them (see 44d), and those cross-references helped her get organized, kept her thinking about the interrelationships of her sources, and made her mindful about the way special-interest groups responded to one another. She could see the weaknesses in the arguments of some sources—what the various groups failed to say as they responded to the wolf population problem.

2 Outlining

Outlines are useful organizational devices. As explained in Chapter 1, an outline is a visual representation of how you expect to organize your essay. You will find that an outline will help you map out in your mind just how you will present your argument to convince your audience of the reasonableness of your thesis.

Your outline will also help you assess the effectiveness of your organization. It can show you whether you need to reorganize, provide more details, offer more explanation, or do more research. Be prepared to revise your outline as you learn and write and perhaps shift your focus.

Ericka's informal outline guided her as she began to draft her essay and incorporate information from her note cards.

ERICKA'S INFORMAL OUTLINE

1--Background on Extermination of Wolves
    Legal Basis--the Law
    Bad Wolf Folklore
    Real Threats
2--The Wolf as Endangered Species
    Yellowstone, Prime Territory for Wolves
    Restoring Ecological Balance, Starvation versus Predation
3--Stockgrowers' Continuing Opposition
4--Concessions and Restitution for Damage
    Radio Tracking
    Monetary Compensation
5--Mounting Political Opposition
6--Public Support

Notice how the subject headings from Ericka's notes have been ordered in her outline. Ericka is beginning to use her notes to build an argument that will support her working thesis favoring the reintroduction of the wolf into Yellowstone. She does not yet know how reasonable that argument will sound once she writes it down and tries to defend it. Much will depend on her ability to offer sound, reasonable explanations of the evidence she found during her research.

Ericka constructed a formal sentence outline after she wrote her first draft. She used that formal outline to check the logical relationships among the various sections of her essay and to reveal any gaps that required further research or explanation. Ericka's final outline appears in Chapter 46.

44h   Drafting your essay

Beginning a research essay can be easier if you organize your note cards and prepare an informal outline before you start drafting the essay. Organizing will help you see how your evidence and your supporting ideas work together and whether you have gathered enough evidence to make your ideas clear and compelling to your reader. Organizing will also help you determine what you want to say and where you might want to begin writing.

Begin writing wherever you feel most comfortable. It might seem logical to begin at the beginning, but doing so is not always advantageous. The beginning—or introduction—should interest your readers in your topic, give them a clear sense of your entire argument, and suggest how you will present your case. But you may not have all of that worked out as you begin drafting, so it might be wise to start writing the middle of your essay—the argument itself. You can write your beginning (and your ending) after you have worked out the details of the argument. (See Chapter 7 for more on writing an argumentative essay.)

Let your notes, your outline, your working thesis, and your sense of audience help direct you as you draft. Be aware that drafting can often reveal gaps in your knowledge and a need for more research about a particular supporting idea. When you discover such gaps, you need not stop writing altogether. You can skip over the troubling section of your essay until you have time to return to the library and consult additional sources.

Keep in mind that you will be writing multiple drafts of your essay. Rarely do writers get the words right the first time. Allow yourself the freedom to draft and to discover ideas as you write. Be open to new ideas that may emerge and to new research you may encounter as you write.

Also, provide citations for your sources (see Chapter 45) as you incorporate them into your draft. Providing citations as you write will ensure accuracy and help you avoid inadvertent plagiarism. It will also save you time when you prepare the final draft because you will not have to go back and sort through your notes to locate sources.

Ericka had a fairly clear sense of how she wanted to develop her argument. At the outset, she wanted to work out some of the more difficult sections in the middle of the essay. She began by following her informal outline. After drafting the first section on the extermination of wolves in Yellowstone, she decided to skip the next main section on the wolf as an endangered species (she anticipated this to be a relatively straightforward section) and turn to the stockgrowers' opposition. Understanding her major opponents would help her develop what she considered the most crucial part of her argument: that the stockgrowers should receive specific concessions and restitution when wolves wandered out of the park and killed stock. There was no doubt that wolves would cross boundaries; the question was what to do about it. With the opposition from stockgrowers and politicians in mind, Ericka thought she could do a better job of presenting the ecological claims that favored reintroduction of the wolf into Yellowstone. As she drafted the paragraphs in the middle of her essay, Ericka also incorporated information from her note cards into those paragraphs and documented that information using her working bibliography. (See Chapter 7 for more on drafting. See also the accompanying annotations to Ericka's complete essay in Chapter 46 to see how she developed her essay.)

44i   Incorporating evidence

As you begin incorporating evidence from your note cards into draft paragraphs, remember that your task is to use your evidence to develop your thesis and supporting ideas. Work at showing your readers how the evidence is related to the idea you are developing.

Incorporating evidence involves integrating or weaving your summaries, paraphrases, quotations, and reflections into the essay while maintaining your own authority and voice. You will want to interpret your evidence, analyze it, make connections from it, and draw inferences from it for your audience. Subject headings and cross-references on your note cards will help you remain organized during this process. When incorporating evidence, be sure that your words and ideas, rather than those of your sources, dominate the essay. Use your sources to explain, justify, and support your own ideas.

One way to maintain your own authority and voice as you incorporate evidence into the essay is to mine your research journal and reflections in your notes for your own ideas about the evidence. Let your ideas guide you. Be especially careful to separate your own thoughts from those of your sources. Doing so will also help ensure that you do not plagiarize. The tips in the accompanying chart will keep you on track as you incorporate evidence into your essay.

1   Integrating source material

When you put information from your notes into your paragraphs, introduce that material by identifying the author or title of the source. You can also identify the author's special credentials if you are appealing to his or her authority to help you establish your claim.

At the end of each summary, paraphrase, or quotation, cite information about the source in parentheses. Parenthetical information normally includes the author's last name (unless you have already cited the name in your paragraph) and relevant page numbers. The title (or a shortened version of it) can

---

Tips for Incorporating Evidence

- Clearly introduce and conclude each summary, paraphrase, or quotation in such a way that readers know where it begins and ends.

- Ensure that the incorporated material blends smoothly into your sentences and paragraphs (see 44i-1). Avoid shifts in verb tense or awkward phrasing that would contrast sharply with the incorporated evidence, making your sentences difficult to read and understand.

- Provide a parenthetical citation within the essay to document the source of your evidence and avoid plagiarism. That in-text citation will correspond to the source list at the end of the essay (see Chapter 45).

- Explain the incorporated evidence so that readers can understand how the evidence relates to a paragraph's main idea and, when appropriate, to your thesis (see 44i-2).

---

also appear as a part of the parenthetical citation when more than one work by that author appears in your list of sources, or when you do not know the author. This parenthetical information signals for your readers the end of the incorporated material. (See Chapter 45 for more precise information on citing references.)

You will also want to integrate your sources so they blend smoothly into your paragraphs. Avoid awkward phrasing or indiscriminate shifts in verb tense that might distract the reader from your idea. To avoid such problems, be sure the tense of your verbs matches or is compatible with the tense of the verbs in the borrowed passage.

AWKWARD

Wildlife biologist John Weaver has made the observation that wolves would be released in Yellowstone wearing radio collars that "may be equipped with remote-controlled tranquilizing darts, a new device that could greatly facilitate the capture of problem animals" (qtd. in Cauble 29).

REVISED

Wildlife biologist John Weaver observed that wolves will be released in Yellowstone wearing radio collars that "may be equipped with remote-controlled tranquilizing darts, a new device that could greatly facilitate the capture of problem animals" (qtd. in Cauble 29).

Always consider reducing quoted material to the words you consider most essential. The fewer quoted words, the less difficult the integration.

When you introduce quotations, pay particular attention to your selection of verbs. Write in the active voice. Your verb choice can convey directly and clearly your attitude about the subject. Verb choice can also suggest your own evaluation of the writer and the source material. In Ericka's revised opening sentences, she chooses the neutral verb *observed*. Had she chosen the disparaging verb *belittle*, she would have conveyed Weaver in a different sense: "Wildlife biologist John Weaver belittled the fact that wolves will be released in Yellowstone wearing radio collars. . . ." These are some of the effective verbs that you can use to introduce quotations: *comments, explains, observes, says, suggests, alleges, claims, grants, condemns, deplores.* The verbs in this list move from neutrality toward judgment. Choose a verb that accurately represents both the writer's attitude and your evaluation.

Integrating a paraphrase or summary

You will often use a paraphrase or a summary in your essays to help illustrate or substantiate your idea. In the following example you can see how Ericka paraphrased one of her sources and used it in a draft paragraph. She paraphrased in this case because she wanted to present the information in the same order she found it in the source, and she wanted to include more detail than she could in a summary. Notice how she uses her own words throughout the paraphrase.

ORIGINAL SOURCE

At the same time, however, the Park Service backed off. It agreed not to mail out its educational packets (which had run out anyway). It temporarily canceled an immensely popular wolf-restoration slide show. It stopped writing about wolf reintroduction in the park newspaper. And it prohibited Defenders of Wildlife from selling pro-wolf-restoration posters at park visitor centers.

—Ted Williams, "Waiting for Wolves to Howl in Yellowstone"

ERICKA'S PARAGRAPH

Yellowstone should uphold the interests of the wild, not those of the prevailing political view. But the park buckled under pressure. According to Ted Williams, the park not only stopped mailing educational material, it also canceled its slide show on the wolf, stopped writing about restoring the wolf population, and prohibited the sale of wolf posters at the park (38).

Integrating parts of quotations

Brief quotations—words or phrases—can be incorporated into your sentences by enclosing the words in quotation marks and ensuring that you blend in the quotation so that your sentence is easy to read and understand.

In the following paragraph, Ericka decided to quote only the factual information she found in Diane Edwards's article on reintroducing wolves to Yellowstone. Notice how Ericka introduced the quoted material by including Edwards's name and the title of the periodical in her paragraph.

ORIGINAL SOURCE

Biologists, who seek an "ecological wholeness" in the natural preserve by reintroducing the missing wolf, say they have set a goal of 10 breeding pairs (only one pair of wolves in a pack of 3 to 25 produces offspring).

—Diane D. Edwards, "Recall the Wild Wolf"

ERICKA'S PARAGRAPH

I believe that a compensation program similar to that used in Minnesota is a more direct and consistent way to deal with the slight economic loss that may affect western sheep and cattle growers as a result of wolf recovery than allowing ranchers to kill an endangered species. Diane Edwards, writing for <u>Science News</u>, reports that biologists "have set a goal of 10 breeding pairs" producing offspring for three consecutive years (379). Declassification must only be allowed after the recovery goal has been reached and the gray wolf is no longer considered to be on the verge of extinction.

Integrating long quotations

Occasionally you will want to incorporate a lengthy quotation into your essay. Formatting these *block quotations* is determined by the conventions set forth in the documentation style you are using. Set off quotations of more than four typed lines (according to MLA) or forty words (according to APA) from the rest of your paragraph by indenting each line of the block quotation ten spaces (MLA) or five spaces (APA). (See Chapter 45 on documentation as well as Chapter 36 on the mechanics of using quotation marks, especially 36c on block quotations.)

Here is an example of one of Ericka's block quotations integrated into a paragraph of her essay and documented according to MLA requirements.

Collaring wolves will allow that this federal control over nuisance animals can be effectively exercised. Wildlife biologist John Weaver made this observation:

> Each wolf released in Yellowstone would be wearing a radio collar, enabling researchers to keep tabs on its wanderings. The collars may be equipped with remote-controlled tranquilizing darts, a new device that could greatly facilitate the capture of problem animals. (qtd. in Cauble 29)

Under this proposal, wolves would be subject to reasonable federal control, rather than to the vengeance of ranchers whose hatred for them tends to be deeply rooted.

Like other incorporated material, block quotations should be introduced to ensure that they fit in with the rest of the paragraph and should include parenthetical documentation. Notice that Ericka's block quotation does not include quotation marks and that the parenthetical citation falls after the concluding punctuation—according to MLA style.

Use block quotations sparingly. Too many of them interrupt the rhythm of your paragraphs and suggest that you are doing little thinking. If you find yourself relying on too many block quotations, try to glean the essence of those long quotations; either summarize or paraphrase the essential information and quote only the words or phrases that you need to make your point.

If you are in any way altering a quotation—adding, deleting, or noting an error in the original—as you integrate it, be sure to use brackets, ellipses, and the Latin word *sic* properly. (See 44d-3, as well as 37c on brackets and 37d on ellipses.)

2 Reflecting on integrated source material

Remember that you incorporate information from sources to help clarify and substantiate your ideas. In addition to introducing source material so that it flows well, documenting it, and making sure that your reader knows where it begins and ends, you should also offer your reflections on it as a way of linking the source material with your ideas. Ericka links her sources—in this case, two quotations—with her argument that wolves should be reintroduced to Yellowstone in the following paragraph from her essay. The underscored sentences highlight her reflections.

> Political figures opposing park education programs find them to be biased because accurate information and evidence on the subject support repopulation. These officials, with an eye to special interest groups, would prefer the public to be exposed to the unsupported rhetoric that they offer as testimony on the wolf, testimony such as Montana Representative Ron Marlenee's declaration that wolves are "cockroaches" (qtd. in Williams 36). Despite a lack of any evidence to support his claim, Wyoming Senator Alan Simpson "has asserted that wolves eat people" (Williams 36). Given the prevalence of misinformation about the wolf, even among elected officials, it is especially critical that the National Park Service adhere to its educational efforts so that the public can make informed judgments on the issue.

Ericka's reflections will help her readers understand the idea in the paragraph as well as the idea behind the essay itself (her thesis). In addition, Ericka cites the source of the two quotations, keeping her reflections separate from the source material.

44j Avoiding plagiarism and acknowledging sources

Plagiarism is the act of using someone else's words, ideas, or organizational patterns without giving credit to the source. It is a serious offense that can result from careless note-taking or deliberate misuse of someone else's material. Whether unintentional or deliberate, plagiarism is stealing. To avoid plagiarism, you need to know what sources to acknowledge within your essay and to make sure your reader can tell the difference between the material you have borrowed and your own ideas. (Also see 44d for guidelines on note-taking techniques that will help you avoid plagiarism, and 44i on incorporating evidence.)

The most common kind of plagiarism results from carelessness. For example, when writers try to build their entire essay from a patchwork of passages selected from sources, piling summary, paraphrase, and quotation on top of one another, doing little if any of their own thinking, there is a good chance that the ideas and words of others will make their way into the final essay without proper acknowledgment. Sometimes writers plagiarize because they are not careful while taking notes; they might accidentally omit quotation marks when quoting from a source, reproduce the structure of ideas from a source, or summarize or paraphrase without signaling the beginning and ending of the borrowed material. Less frequent, but prevalent, is deliberate plagiarism such as when writers knowingly leave off the quotation marks, purchase a completed paper or use a paper written by a friend, or leave out the source to mislead readers into thinking that the incorporated material actually belongs to the writer rather than to someone else.

The consequences of plagiarism are serious because plagiarism is a form of theft, whether intentional or not. It amounts to scholarly dishonesty and usually results in course failure and sometimes dismissal from college, depending on the seriousness of the particular offense.

1   Knowing what sources to acknowledge

To avoid plagiarizing material, it helps to know what sources require acknowledgment and what sources do not. As a general rule, always acknowledge someone else's words, ideas, or organizational patterns. However, you do not need to acknowledge source material that you generate. Nor do you need to acknowledge source material that is commonly known. The following specific guidelines will help direct you.

Source materials requiring acknowledgment

The following materials must always be properly acknowledged if you are to avoid plagiarism.

- **Someone else's words.** When you use someone else's words verbatim, you must enclose those words in quotation marks and acknowledge the source from which they were taken. Someone else's words can take the form of complete sentences or paragraphs, or they can be individual key words or phrases integrated into one of your own sentences, paraphrases, or summaries.

- **Someone else's ideas, organizational patterns, or facts.** When you use someone else's ideas—whether unsubstantiated opinions or well-developed assertions—you must acknowledge the source. Someone else's ideas can take a number of forms: for example, if you incorporate the words or ideas of an interviewee or if you develop your entire essay in response to someone else's thesis, you must acknowledge that the material is not yours. If you develop or order your ideas in the same way that your source did, even if you use your own words, you must acknowledge the source. In addition, when you use facts—whether statistics, graphs, illustrations, or tables—that constitute the work or findings of a particular individual rather than the widely known data in a field, you must acknowledge the source.

- **Help provided by others.** Credit anyone who helps you develop an idea, conduct a survey, or organize your essay. An acknowledgment page can follow the title page, or acknowledgments can be given in explanatory or content notes (see 45b and 45e).

Source materials not requiring acknowledgment

The following types of source materials need not be acknowledged.

- **Results of your own field research.** If you conduct surveys, use questionnaires, conduct laboratory experiments, or record personal observations in your journal, you can explain and claim credit for that work in your essay (see the sample student essays in Chapter 46, for example). However, always acknowledge anyone else who may have contributed to the research.

- **Common knowledge.** Information that is widely known or circulated in a field is known as common knowledge. Consider historical dates, the standard definitions of words, and information that is known to everyone who has basic knowledge about a given field of study or a particular problem as common knowledge. That Sigmund Freud and Carl Jung advanced early theories about the analysis of dreams need not be acknowledged; nor need knowledge that on January 27, 1973, the peace accord ending the conflict in Vietnam was signed. A good test for common knowledge is whether you find information repeated from article to article (especially in encyclopedias and other general information sources) without acknowledgment. If you are in doubt about whether material from a source constitutes common knowledge, acknowledge the source to be safe.

2   Being alert for plagiarism in your writing

The most important thing you can do to avoid plagiarism is to exercise care when you take notes and then again when you incorporate source material from your notes into your essay. The techniques outlined in sections 44d and 44i will help you by keeping you mindful of the difference between your own thoughts and the source material.

A more general and more important way to avoid plagiarism is to have ideas of your own. Interpret the evidence, make inferences from it, and analyze it to discover your own ideas. Then, when you write your essay, use the evidence to support your ideas, acknowledging it properly, as you move beyond the analysis found in your sources to your own thinking.

As you conduct research, take notes, and write your essay, always distinguish your ideas from the ideas you find in your sources; separate the evidence you produce through independent field research from the evidence you borrow from sources. Acknowledge whatever is not yours.

The difference between plagiarism and being honest is also a practical matter that comes down to mechanics, to the way you incorporate borrowed evidence into your essay. The most obvious kind of plagiarism results from failure to cite the source of borrowed information either in the text of your paragraph or in parentheses, at the appropriate place in your paragraph.

Tips for Avoiding Plagiarism

- Develop ideas of your own, always keeping them distinct from the ideas you find in sources. Also, distinguish between the evidence you create through your own field research and the findings of others that you encounter in sources.

- You do not need to acknowledge your own ideas, facts, or findings, but always acknowledge material taken from sources unless that material is common knowledge.

- If you quote verbatim from a source, use quotation marks. Be sure your summaries and paraphrases are in your own words. Careful note-taking will help. (See the Guidelines for Note Taking on p. 671–72.)

- Integrate source material carefully. (Follow the Tips for Incorporating Evidence on p. 685.)

- Be sure that your voice predominates in your essay. Remember, you are the thinker and writer. You use sources to help clarify and substantiate your ideas and thesis and to lend authority to your argument. Never simply compile a report about someone else's research and ideas unless you have been specifically instructed to do only that.

- Be sure that you have adequate parenthetical citations and that each citation corresponds to the list of sources at the end of the essay (see Chapter 45).

Plagiarism that does not seem deliberate is nevertheless serious. It results from using phrases from a source without giving credit for those borrowed forms of expression, even though the writer gives credit for the ideas.

ORIGINAL SOURCE

At the same time, however, the Park Service backed off. It agreed not to mail out its educational packets (which had run out anyway). It temporarily canceled an immensely popular wolf-restoration slide show. It stopped writing about wolf reintroduction in the park newspaper. And it prohibited Defenders of Wildlife from selling pro-wolf-restoration posters at park visitor centers.

—Ted Williams, "Waiting for Wolves to Howl in Yellowstone"

PLAGIARISM

Yellowstone should uphold the interests of the wild, not those of the prevailing political view. But the park buckled under pressure. According to Ted Williams, the park stopped mailing its educational packets, canceled a popular wolf-restoration slide show, stopped writing about wolf reintroduction, and prohibited selling pro-wolf-restoration posters at park visitor centers (38).

In this paragraph, acknowledgment is given to Williams for the information, but not for the borrowed language. Such plagiarism usually results from sloppy note taking or from rushing through research. To correct this plagiarized paragraph, the writer should revise by summarizing or paraphrasing all of the borrowed material or by putting borrowed phrasing in quotation marks.

44k Revising your research essay and collaborating

Writers inevitably go through several drafts of a research essay. As you draft and reread your work, you revise. **Revising** is re-seeing what you have written, considering it with an eye to whether you have done what you set out to do and whether your audience will understand you. As you revise, you will also want to consider how you have used your evidence and whether all parts of the essay—beginning, middle, and ending—come together and work toward communicating your thesis. Based on your assessment of your accomplishments, you rewrite and revise. The basic guidelines for revising covered in 1g will serve you well as you reread the draft of your research essay looking for ways to improve it. The strategies of distancing yourself from your work, reading and rereading, and seeking objective opinions and advice are especially valuable.

Try to find a collaborator to help you spot problems and confirm your accomplishments. If you give your draft to a fellow student or talk about it with your instructor, you are likely to get additional insight about the effectiveness of your essay along with ideas for revision. (See 1h and 4e on collaboration.)

Ericka went through numerous drafts and revised often as she reread and reevaluated her work. She filled in the gaps that she and her collaborators identified in the first draft and improved the way she incorporated evidence into her paragraphs. She also added a final section to her essay that gave her readers a sense of public opinion about the wolf reintroduction problem at Yellowstone to complement the perspectives of politicians and experts addressed elsewhere in her essay. The suggestion to do that came from a classmate during a collaborative workshop, and it strengthened her argument and essay.

You may be wondering how, then, do you know when to stop drafting and revising? There is no conclusive answer to that question, but when you can say "yes" to the following questions, you have likely reached a final draft that is ready to be edited, proofed, and prepared for submission (44l).

1. Can my readers follow my train of thought?
2. Have I made my point clearly and convincingly?
3. Have I included sufficient evidence to illustrate what I mean and to be convincing?
4. Have I acknowledged my sources properly?
5. Am I satisfied with what I have written?

In addition, reconsider your draft in light of the accompanying checklist on rethinking and revising the research essay.

Rethinking and Revising Your Research Essay

- **Reconsider what you set out to do.** Have you solved the problem you set out to solve; namely, have you resolved the controversy to your satisfaction? If your purpose was to inform or explain, have you done so? Have you interpreted the evidence, formulated a thesis, and presented an explanation and defense of that thesis that seems reasonable to you?

- **Consider your accomplishments in light of what others have said about your essay.** Take all of the feedback that you may have received during collaborative workshops and private consultations with friends, classmates, and your instructor. Consider all of their suggestions in light of what you are trying to do. Revise your essay and your thesis if necessary.

- **Fill in the gaps.** After you have considered your own assessment of the draft and input from your collaborators, do additional research if you need more evidence. Perhaps consult discarded working bibliography cards. You might also just resume drafting, adding more reflections to clarify the relationship between your evidence and ideas.

(continued)

- **Consider the structure of your draft by writing a formal outline.** After you fill in the gaps and complete other revisions, develop a formal sentence outline as a way of verifying for yourself the logical relationships among the sections of your essay (see 1f-1 on outlining). Consider moving parts of your essay around to make the essay more convincing; refine your explanations of the evidence.

- **Check the accuracy of all incorporated evidence.** Check summaries, paraphrases, and quotations against your note cards. Make sure that the source material you are using is accurate and that you have documented each citation. Return to the original source if you are in doubt—never be sloppy.

- **Create a title.** Devise a title that will catch the reader's interest and convey a sense of your essay and your point of view.

- **Consider the way the beginning, middle, and ending work together to make your essay more effective.** Read through the entire essay to see how beginning, middle, and ending complement one another. If you spot problems, revise and then reread the essay.

44l   Preparing the final manuscript

After you have completed drafting and revising your essay, prepare an alphabetical list of all of the sources you cited in your essay. This list will be entitled "Works Cited" in MLA style (see 45c) or "References" in APA style (see 45f).

You also must prepare a final copy of the manuscript, making it as clean, neat, and near perfect as possible. As you prepare this final copy, check for errors in grammar, usage, spelling, punctuation, and mechanics as well as the physical layout of the essay. Edit and proofread carefully using the guidelines in 1i. Consult Appendix A on preparing a final manuscript and Chapter 50 if you are working on a computer. You can see two complete student research essays, one formatted in MLA style and one in APA style, in Chapter 46.

Attention to detail and presentation will pay off. Your readers will find your essay pleasurable and will not be distracted from the essay by careless mistakes. You can be confident that you will benefit from what Roy Reed, a distinguished journalist, calls "putting the final shine on the piece."

CHAPTER 45

Documenting Sources

*I*n writing a research essay you use facts and opinions from outside sources as evidence to support your ideas. You have an obligation to document the source of this cited material, whether you use the actual language of the source or restate it in your own words.

Established conventions for documenting sources vary from one academic discipline to another. The Modern Language Association (MLA) style of documentation is preferred in literature and languages. For papers in the social sciences the American Psychological Association (APA) style is preferred, whereas papers in history, philosophy, economics, political science, and business disciplines are formatted in the Chicago Manual of Style (CMS) system. The Council of Biology Editors (CBE) recommends varying documentation styles for different natural sciences. This chapter covers MLA and APA styles of documentation and briefly illustrates the CMS and other CBE documentation systems. If you are in doubt about which style to use, check with your instructor.

Whatever style of documentation you use, be certain to format your citations consistently within that style. You will need to acknowledge your sources in two ways: (1) with in-text, parenthetical citations (see 45a and 45d); (2) with a list of sources at the end of your paper (see 45c and 45f). In-text, or parenthetical, citations identify the specific page of a source for a quotation, an idea, a fact, an interpretation, or another type of reference. Parenthetical citations provide readers with an immediate indication of what material you borrowed. For more detailed information about a paper's sources, readers can consult the list of sources at the end of the paper. There they will find complete bibliographical data about the source.

MLA Documentation Style

The method of documentation described and illustrated in this section is recommended by the Modern Language Association in its *MLA Handbook for Writers of Research Papers* (4th ed. New York: MLA, 1995). MLA documentation style is used both in student papers and in scholarly articles in literature and languages. Consult the accompanying chart that lists MLA forms for an overview of the types of citations described in this section. But do not be intimidated by the number of citation samples. Mastering the basic citation forms for books and periodicals will give you the formula from which any citation can be derived.

Directory of MLA Sample Entries

In-text, Parenthetical Citations (see 45a)
1. Author not named in text, 698
2. Author named in text, 698
3. Entire work, 698
4. Work with two or three authors, 698
5. Work with more than three authors, 699
6. Multivolume work, 699
7. Anonymous work, 699
8. Corporate author, 699
9. Indirect citation, 700
10. Literary work, 700
11. Author of two or more cited works, 700
12. Authors with the same last name, 700
13. Two or more sources in a single citation, 701
14. Nonprint source, 701

Works Cited Sample Entries (see 45c)
BOOKS
1. Book with one author, 704
2. Book with two or three authors, 704
3. Book with more than three authors, 704
4. Book with an anonymous author, 705
5. Book with an author and an editor, 705
6. Book with an editor, 705
7. Selection from an anthology, 705
8. Two or more selections from an anthology, 705
9. Book with a corporate author, 706
10. Book in a series, 706
11. Book with a title within the title, 706
12. Two or more books by the same author, 706
13. Multivolume book, 707
14. Translation, 707
15. Revised edition, 707
16. Republished book, 707
17. Printed conference proceedings, 708
18. Book published before 1900, 708

(continued)

19. Preface, foreword, introduction, or afterword, 708
20. Article in a reference book, 708
21. Pamphlet, 708
22. Government publication, 709

PERIODICALS

23. Article in a journal paginated by volume, 710
24. Article in a journal paginated by issue, 710
25. Article in a magazine, 710
26. Article with multiple authors, 710
27. Article with a title within the title, 710
28. Article in a newspaper, 711
29. Article with an anonymous author, 711
30. Editorial, 711
31. Letter to the editor, 711
32. Review, 711

OTHER SOURCES

33. Interview, 712
34. Letter, 712
35. Lecture or speech, 712
36. Dissertation, 713
37. Performance, 713
38. Musical composition, 714
39. Work of art, 714
40. Film, 714
41. Television or radio program, 714
42. Recording, 715
43. Videotape or videocassette, 715
44. Map or chart, 715
45. Cartoon, 715
46. Sources on CD-ROM, tape, or diskette, including computer software, 716
47. Online sources, 717

45a   MLA style for in-text, parenthetical citations

MLA style uses two methods for citing borrowed material within the text: (1) The author and page number of the source are identified immediately following the borrowed material. (2) The author is identified in the text and the page reference is given immediately following the borrowed material. In-text citations guide readers to the appropriate source in the Works Cited list where readers can get the bibliographic information they need to locate the material within a particular source.

Use the following guidelines when writing with parenthetical citations.

- Keep the citations concise, but provide all necessary information.
- Use an author's last name in the first and subsequent in-text citations. Use an author's first initial and last name if two authors in the Works Cited list share the same last name.
- Punctuate and format the parenthetical citations in the following manner.
  1. Place the parenthetical citation either at the end of the sentence or at a natural pause within the sentence. In either case, the citation should follow, as closely as possible, the material it refers to.
  2. If the citation is placed immediately following a quotation, place the citation after the closing quotation marks.
  3. Place any punctuation marks in the text immediately following the closing parenthesis of the citation.
  4. In block quotations, place the parenthetical citation two spaces following the final punctuation mark of the quotation.
  5. Include a page reference for the borrowed material.

1.   Author not named in text

When the author is not named in the text, place that author's last name and the page reference in parentheses, at a point where the citation does not interrupt the flow of your writing. Do not use a comma or the abbreviations *p.* or *pp.* within the parentheses.

Hawthorne's son Julian recalled that his father read novels for relaxation, but that he seriously <u>studied</u> popular newspapers and magazines (Reynolds 114).

2.   Author named in text

If the author is identified in the text, cite only the page number in parentheses.

Herzog notes that there are more protests against experiments on domestic animals like dogs and cats than against research involving animals like snakes (349).

3.   Entire work

When citing an entire work such as a complete article or book rather than a particular passage within the work, do not refer to the work within a parenthetical citation. The source must be cited in the Works Cited list.

Bennett and Ames survey the use and abuse of alcohol in various cultures.

4.   Work with two or three authors

Include the last name of each author in the text or in a citation.

Lichtenstein and Danker have noted that beginning in 1974, the New Orleans Center for the Creative Arts (NOCCA) has produced successful performers such as Wynton Marsalis and Harry Connick, Jr. (284).

Classroom research can be done most effectively when one becomes a "participant observer" (Cohn, Kottkamp, and Provenzo 89-91).

5. Work with more than three authors

When citing a work with four or more authors, either list the last name of each author or list the author whose name appears first on the title page, followed by *et al.* (meaning "and others").

A pregnant adolescent "experiences restricted social relationships and less positive interactions with both friends and family" and so is subject to severe emotional stress (Passino et al. 118).

6. Multivolume work

Cite the author, volume number, and page reference (Hamilton 26: 293). Separate the volume number and the page reference by a colon followed by one space. Do not use the words *volume* or *pages* or the abbreviations *vol.* or *p.* when referring to passages within a volume. An arabic number to the left of the colon identifies the volume and a number to the right of the colon indicates the page number(s).

Alexander Hamilton may have foreseen the fatal result of his duel with Aaron Burr because on 4 July 1804 he wrote to his wife: "Fly to the bosom of your God and be comforted" (26: 293).

To refer to an entire volume of a multivolume work, follow the author's name with a comma and the abbreviation *vol.* (Hamilton, vol. 3). Do not abbreviate *volume* when using the word in text: "In volume 3, Hamilton mentions. . . ."

7. Anonymous work

Cite an anonymous work by its title, which may be shortened to a key defining word or phrase (as is the article "Democracy and Mega-Scandal" in the following example).

The truth about the Contras, Iran, Star Wars, and other controversies will probably never be known ("Democracy" 6-8).

8. Corporate author

It is best to cite the name of a corporate, or collective, author in the text rather than in a long parenthetical reference.

A 1990 report by the State Board of Education of New York urges curricular revisions that emphasize multiculturalism (2-4).

9. Indirect citation

When quoting from an indirect or secondary source (such as an author's report of someone else's statement), use the abbreviation *qtd. in* (meaning "quoted in") and then cite the source. Always identify the original writer or speaker in the text or citation.

Robert Coughlan wrote that Faulkner "acts like a farmer who had studied Plato and looks like a river gambler" (qtd. in Blotner 2: 1468).

10. Literary work

Give the page number(s) from the edition of the work that is being cited. Because some literary works exist in many different editions, it is helpful to follow the page numbers with a semicolon and appropriate abbreviations for major divisions of the work (210; ch. 15) or (5; act 1). For a poem, cite line number(s) and in your first reference use the word *line(s)*.

For verse plays, do not use page numbers. Give the act, scene, and line numbers separated by periods.

Hamlet's last words are "the rest is silence" (5.2.247).

11. Author of two or more cited works

To distinguish among multiple works by an author, include the title or a shortened title in an in-text phrase or in a parenthetical citation.

Kingston describes how she had to learn the appropriate cultural behavior for a Chinese-American female (Woman 35-40).

In this example, *Woman* is an abbreviated form of Maxine Hong Kingston's book entitled *The Woman Warrior*.

12. Authors with the same last name

When two or more authors cited in a paper have the same last name, include the author's first name in a brief in-text phrase or in a parenthetical citation. To distinguish Larry L. King from Martin Luther King, Jr., for example, do the following.

In his essay "American Redneck," Larry L. King describes his early manhood.

Do the same for parenthetical citations.

"American Redneck" (L. King) describes a young writer's experiences.

13. Two or more sources in a single citation

In referring to more than one source in parentheses, include information for both sources, separated by semicolons.

Recent interpretations of Shakespeare's The Tempest consider the play's racist implications (Takaki 52; Greenblatt 121).

14. Nonprint source

Provide enough information for readers to locate the source in the Works Cited list.

The TV series The Civil War includes a moving letter written by Sullivan Ballou to his wife shortly before his death.

45b MLA style for explanatory and reference notes

1 Explanatory notes

Explanatory notes are used for incidental comments or for information that does not relate directly to an essay's thesis or idea and that would be disruptive if placed in the body of the paper. Explanatory notes can be used to clarify, illustrate, or further explain an idea; to provide definitions; or to identify individuals and events. Avoid overusing explanatory notes because they can distract from the main text of the essay.

Use a superscript arabic number immediately after the term or passage to be expanded upon. That number corresponds to a list of notes placed at the end of the paper (endnotes). Head this separate page "Notes" and place it immediately before the Works Cited list. (The corresponding list of notes could be placed at the bottom of the typewritten page and called footnotes.)

To format the notes, indent five spaces and place the superscript number followed by one space and the explanatory note. Double-space the notes and arrange them in numerical order.

TEXT WITH SUPERSCRIPT

The Volstead Act provided for enforcement of the Eighteenth Amendment by empowering federal agents to prosecute bootleggers and other violators.[1]

EXPLANATORY NOTE

[1]The law, passed in 1919, was named for its sponsor, Andrew Joseph Volstead, congressman from Minnesota.

2   Reference notes

Reference notes direct readers to additional sources and often to another section of an essay. References that support an essay's ideas usually include the word *see,* and those that contradict an essay's ideas include the word *compare.* A source named in a reference note should be included in the Works Cited list. These notes are formatted like explanatory notes.

TEXT WITH SUPERSCRIPT

Mark Twain was convinced that the novels of Sir Walter Scott had infected the South with false romantic notions.[2]

REFERENCE NOTE: BOOK

[2]For a full account of Twain's opinion of Scott, see Sydney J. Krause, <u>Mark Twain as Critic</u> (Baltimore: Johns Hopkins UP, 1967) 145-49.

The format for reference notes in MLA style differs from the format for items in a Works Cited list. There is no brief introductory phrase introducing a citation in a Works Cited list, and the publication information is organized slightly differently.

A reference note that refers to a book should follow these formatting conventions.

- Indent the first line of the reference note five spaces. Any subsequent lines of the note do not indent.
- Include the author's name exactly as it appears on the book's title page.
- Separate the author from the title with a comma.
- Place the publication information after the title and in parentheses. Begin with the city of publication followed by a colon and one space before listing the publisher and the year of publication separated by a comma.
- Place the page number(s) outside the closing parenthesis and do not put a comma or period between them.

To format a reference note for an article in a scholarly journal, follow these guidelines.

- Indent the first line of the reference note five spaces. Any subsequent lines of the note do not indent.
- Include the author's name exactly as it appears in the article, followed by a comma and a space.
- Place the full title of the article within quotation marks. Place a comma before the closing quotation mark.
- List the full name of the publication (without including initial articles).
- Provide the volume and date of publication and page number(s) as necessary.

REFERENCE NOTE: PERIODICAL

[3]A contrasting view is provided by Dana Jonelson, "Mark Twain's Debt to Sir Walter Scott," <u>American Quarterly</u> 42 (1989): 54.

45c   MLA style for the Works Cited list

All the sources cited in a paper should be listed at the end of the paper. This separate listing is called the "Works Cited" list. A concluding list of sources that were examined but not cited in a paper is called a "Works Consulted" list. In a typical research paper a single listing of Works Cited is all that is required.

Following the last page of the paper and any concluding notes, begin the list with the title "Works Cited" without quotation marks or underlining, centered, and an inch from the top of the page. The Works Cited list is paginated as the rest of the paper. Double-space between the title and the first entry.

Arrange the citation entries in alphabetical order by authors' last names. If a source is anonymous, alphabetize it by the first major word in its title (not *a, an,* or *the*). Begin each entry flush with the left margin, but indent all subsequent lines of the entry one-half inch. Double-space within and between entries. Sample Works Cited entries for books, periodicals, and other sources follow.

1   Books

A standard MLA entry for a book consists of three elements: author, title, and publication information. These three elements are separated from one another by a period and two spaces. The entry concludes with a period.

Keep the following guidelines in mind when preparing book entries for the Works Cited list.

1. **Author:** An author's name (exactly as it appears on the title page) should appear last name first, followed by a comma, then by the first and middle names or initials. Put a period after the author's name followed by two spaces.

2. **Title:** Copy the title and subtitle (if any) from the title page, not from the cover or spine of the book. Underline the title and capitalize all major words (see 38e on capitalizing titles). Separate the main title from the subtitle with a colon. Put a period and two spaces after the title and subtitle.

3. **Publication information:** Copy the publication information (the city of publication, the publisher, and the year of publication) from the title and copyright pages. If more than one city is listed on the title page, cite the first one only. If the name of the city is not well known or if it is confusing, include a state or country abbreviation following a comma. Put a colon and one space after the city of publication before the publisher's name. Abbreviate or shorten names of publishers by dropping articles and words such as *Press* and abbreviations such as *Co.* ("Bantam Books, Inc." becomes "Bantam"), using only the last names of persons ("Charles Scribner's Sons" becomes "Scribner's"), and by using only the first in a string of last names ("Harcourt Brace Jovanovich, Inc." becomes "Harcourt"). Abbreviate "University Press" so that it reads "UP." If the publisher is an imprint of another publisher (as Belknap Press is an imprint of Harvard University Press), include both publisher names separated by a hyphen ("Belknap-Harvard UP") in the Works Cited list. The publisher's name is followed by a comma, one space, and the most recent year of publication.

COMPUTER WRITING HINT   If you use a word processor to prepare your Works Cited list, turn off the right-side justification to avoid disrupting your spacing and your placement of punctuation marks. In fact, it is a good idea to avoid using right-side justification throughout your research papers since your text will include citations within parentheses and other documentation details, all of which must follow precise spacing requirements.

1.   Book with one author

Benton, Janetta Rebold. <u>The Medieval Menagerie: Animals in the Art of the Middle Ages</u>. New York: Abbeville, 1992.

2.   Book with two or three authors

List the authors' names as they appear on the title page. Invert the name of the first author only. Separate the authors' names from one another with commas.

Lichtenstein, Grace, and Laura Danker. <u>Musical Gumbo: The Music of New Orleans</u>. New York: Norton, 1993.

McCrum, William, William Cran, and Robert MacNeil. <u>The Story of English</u>. New York: Viking, 1986.

3.   Book with more than three authors

List only the first author (last name first) followed by a comma and the Latin abbreviation *et al.* ("and others").

Bendure, Glenda, et al. <u>Scandinavian and Baltic Europe on a Shoestring</u>. Berkeley: Lonely Planet, 1993.

4. Book with an anonymous author

Begin the entry with the title. Alphabetize the entry using the first main word in the title (not *a, an,* or *the*). Do not use the word *anonymous* in the entry.

The World Almanac and Book of Facts. New York: NEA, 1983.

5. Book with an author and an editor

Begin the entry with the author's name. Place the editor's name after the title, introducing it with *Ed.* ("edited by").

Orwell, George. Orwell: The War Commentaries. Ed. W. J. West. New York: Pantheon, 1985.

If, however, the in-text citations generally refer to the editor, begin the entry with the editor's name.

West, W. J., ed. Orwell: The War Commentaries. By George Orwell. New York: Pantheon, 1985.

6. Book with an editor

In general, treat the editor(s) as you would an author.

Bennett, Linda A., and Genevieve M. Ames, eds. The American Experience with Alcohol: Contrasting Cultural Perspectives. New York: Plenum, 1985.

7. Selection from an anthology

Include the author and the title of the selection, followed by the title of the anthology, its editor, the publication information, and inclusive page numbers. Put the selection title within quotation marks, but underline it if the work was originally published as a book.

Chrisman, Noel J. "Alcoholism: Illness or Disease?" The American Experience with Alcohol: Contrasting Cultural Perspectives. Ed. Linda A. Bennett and Genevieve M. Ames. New York: Plenum, 1985. 7-21.

8. Two or more selections from an anthology

Cite each selection by cross-referencing it to the anthology within the Works Cited list. Be sure to include the editor(s) and inclusive page numbers in the selection citations.

Bennett, Linda A., and Genevieve M. Ames, eds. The American Experience with Alcohol: Contrasting Cultural Perspectives. New York: Plenum, 1985.

Freund, Paul J. "Polish-American Drinking: Continuity and Change." Bennett and
    Ames 77-92.

Stivers, Richard. "Historical Meanings of Irish-American Drinking." Bennett and
    Ames 109-29.

9.   Book with a corporate author

When a corporation, committee, or other group is listed as the author on
the title page, cite it as you would a person. If the same group published the
book, abbreviate words in the publisher listing.

National Geographic Society. <u>Discovering Britain and Ireland</u>. Washington:
    Natl. Geog. Soc., 1985.

10.   Book in a series

Provide the name of the series and the series number (if there is one),
immediately after the title. The name of the series is neither in quotation marks nor underlined. The publication information follows the series
information.

Gannon, Susan R., and Ruth Anne Thompson. <u>Mary Mapes Dodge</u>. Twayne's
    United States Authors Ser. 604. New York: Twayne-Macmillan, 1993.

11.   Book with a title within the title

If a book title contains a title normally enclosed in quotation marks, keep
the quotation marks. If a book title contains a title normally underlined, the
shorter title is not underlined.

Renza, Louis A. <u>"A White Heron" and the Question of Minor Literature</u>. Madison:
    U of Wisconsin P, 1984.

McCarthy, Patrick A., ed. <u>Critical Essays on James Joyce's</u> Finnegan's Wake. New
    York: Hall, 1992.

12.   Two or more books by the same author

Cite the name of the author in the first entry only. In subsequent entries
by that same individual author or group of authors, use three hyphens followed with a period and two spaces in place of the author's name. List the
works alphabetically by the first major word in the title (not *a, an,* or *the*).

Woodward, C. Vann. <u>The Future of the Past</u>. New York: Oxford UP, 1989.

---. <u>Origins of the New South</u>. 1951. Baton Rouge: Louisiana State UP, 1971.

---. <u>Reunion and Reaction</u>. Boston: Little, 1966.

13. Multivolume book

If two or more volumes of a multivolume book are used, list the total number of volumes immediately after the title.

Malone, Dumas. <u>Jefferson and His Time</u>. 6 vols. Boston: Little, 1943-77.

When only one volume of a multivolume work is used, give the volume number after the title and include the total number of volumes in the work at the end of the entry. When the volume has its own title, include that title after the author's name and before the publication information. Follow with the volume number and the title of the complete work. Conclude with the total number of volumes followed by the inclusive publication dates for the work.

Blotner, Joseph. <u>Faulkner: A Biography</u>. Vol. 1. New York: Random, 1974. 2 vols.

Malone, Dumas. <u>The Sage of Monticello</u>. Boston: Little, 1977. Vol. 6 of <u>Jefferson and His Time</u>. 6 vols. 1943-77.

14. Translation

Begin the entry with the author's name followed by the title; then give the translator's name, introduced by *Trans.* ("translated by"). If the translated work also has an editor, give the names in the order they appear on the title page.

Wilhelm, Richard. <u>Confucius and Confucianism</u>. Trans. George H. Danton and Annina Periam Danton. New York: Harcourt, 1931.

If the in-text citations generally refer to the translator's work or commentary, place the translator's name first.

Danton, George H., and Annina Periam Danton, trans. <u>Confucius and Confucianism</u>. By Richard Wilhelm. New York: Harcourt, 1931.

15. Revised edition

If an edition other than the first is specified on the title page of a book, include that information in the Works Cited entry. Use the abbreviation *Rev. ed.* if the title page lists the book as a "Revised edition."

Holloway, Mark. <u>Heavens on Earth: Utopian Communities in America, 1660-1880</u>. 2nd ed. New York: Dover, 1966.

16. Republished book

When a book is republished (e.g., by a different publisher or in a different binding), give the year of original publication immediately after the title, followed by a period. Then give the publication information for the book.

Austen, Jane. <u>Emma</u>. 1816. New York: Penguin, 1986.

17. Printed conference proceedings

Cite printed proceedings as a book.

Jackson, Janice, ed. <u>Proceedings of the Dyson College Society of Fellows</u>. New York: Pace UP, 1994.

18. Book published before 1900

Omit the publisher from the citation. The city and the year of publication are separated by a comma.

Kennedy, J. P. <u>Horse-Shoe Robinson: A Tale of the Tory Ascendancy</u>. Rev. ed. Philadelphia, 1865.

19. Preface, foreword, introduction, or afterword

First identify the author and then identify the name of the item being cited (Preface, Foreword, Introduction, or Afterword). Follow with the title of the book and the book's author preceded by the word *By*. Inclusive page numbers are included at the end of the publication information.

Monette, Paul. Foreword. <u>A Rock and a Hard Place: One Boy's Triumphant Story</u>. By Anthony Godby Johnson. New York: Crown-Random, 1993. xiii-xvii.

20. Article in a reference book

Treat an encyclopedia article or a dictionary entry as an entry from an anthology. Do not, however, cite the editor of the reference work. Begin an entry for a signed article with the author; begin an entry for an unsigned article with its title. (If the article is initialed, consult the list of names that correspond to the initials, printed elsewhere in the work.)

"Cochise." <u>Encyclopedia of Indians of the Americas</u>. St. Clair Shores, MI: Scholarly, 1974.

For familiar reference books it is not necessary to cite full publication information. List instead the edition (*ed.*) and the year of publication.

Fosco, Mariani. "Marco Polo." <u>Encyclopaedia Britannica: Micropaedia</u>. 1993 ed.

21. Pamphlet

Cite a pamphlet as a book. Be aware, however, that some publication information may be missing, as in the following example in which *N.p.* means "no place of publication" and *n.p.* following the colon means "no publisher."

Hastings, Gerald. <u>To Your Good Health</u>. N.p.: n.p., 1987.

22. Government publication

Because government publications differ widely from one another, documenting them can be confusing. If no author is given, begin the entry with the government agency issuing the document. For a congressional publication, include the number, session, and house of Congress as well as the type of document. Use recognizable abbreviations such as *HR* for House of Representatives and *GPO* for Government Printing Office for the publisher information.

United States. Dept. of Commerce. <u>U.S. Industrial Outlook '92: Business Forecasts for 350 Industries</u>. Washington: GPO, 1992.

United States. Cong. House. Committee on Ways and Means. <u>Hearings on Comprehensive Tax Reform</u>. 106th Cong., 1st sess. 9 vols. Washington: GPO, 1986.

2   Periodicals

Periodicals such as scholarly journals, magazines, and newspapers supply useful, up-to-date information for research essays. Like the listing for a book, a basic Works Cited entry for a periodical consists of three elements: author, title, and publication information. These three elements are separated from one another by a period and two spaces. The entry ends with a period.

Keep the following guidelines in mind when preparing periodical entries for the Works Cited list.

1. **Author:** An author's name should appear last name first, followed by a comma, then by the first and middle names or initials. Put a period after the author's name followed by two spaces.

2. **Title:** Enclose the article title (and subtitle, if any) within quotation marks, and capitalize all major words (see 38e on capitalizing titles). Put a period at the end of the title, inside the closing quotation mark, followed by two spaces to the publication information.

3. **Publication information:** Include the periodical title (copied from its cover), underlined, with introductory articles deleted (*New York Times*, not *The New York Times*); follow with one space. If appropriate, give the volume and issue numbers, followed by one space. Give the year of publication, in parentheses, followed by a colon and one space. For magazines and newspapers, list the

day and month (abbreviated except for May, June, and July) of publication, with the day before the month, the month before the year (19 Dec. 1967). End the entry with inclusive page numbers of the entire article; do not use the abbreviations *p.* or *pp.*

23. Article in a journal paginated by volume

If a journal's pages are numbered consecutively from issue to issue, do not specify an issue number. Follow the journal title with the volume number in arabic numerals, but do not use the abbreviation *vol.*

Williams, Adelia. "Jean Tardieu: The Painterly Poem." Foreign Language Studies
    18 (1991): 114-25.

24. Article in a journal paginated by issue

If pagination begins with "1" in each issue of a journal, identify the number of the issue immediately after the volume number. Separate the two numbers with a period, but do not add any space. Look for the issue number on the spine, the front cover, or the contents page.

Bender, Daniel. "Diversity Revisited, or Composition's Alien History." Rhetoric
    Review 12.1 (1987): 108-24.

25. Article in a magazine

Give the date of the issue (day, month, and year) immediately after the name of the magazine. Do not include a volume or issue number. Follow the date with a colon and the inclusive page number(s).

Howard, Bill. "Portable Computing: Power without the Pounds." PC Magazine
    Aug. 1993: 125-269.

Use the symbol "+" to indicate discontinuous paging when an article is interrupted and continues later in the magazine.

Jennings, Andrew. "Old Money and Murder in Chechina." Nation 20 Sept. 1993: 265+.

26. Article with multiple authors

Treat an article with multiple authors as a book with more than one author. The article cited in the following example has seven authors.

Passino, Anne Wurtz, et al. "Personal Adjustment during Pregnancy and
    Adolescent Parenting." Adolescence 28 (1993): 97-122.

27. Article with a title within the title

If an article title contains an underlined or italicized title, keep the underlining or italics for that title. If an article title contains a quotation or a title within quotation marks, use single quotation marks around the quotation or the shorter title.

Hicks, David. "'Seeker for He Knows Not What': Hawthorne's Criticism of Emerson in the Summer of 1842." <u>Nathaniel Hawthorne Review</u> 17.1 (1991): 1-4.

28.   Article in a newspaper

Follow the author and title of the article with the name of the newspaper (without the articles *a, an,* or *the*). Provide the date of publication, the section letter, and page numbers. Use a plus sign to indicate discontinuous paging if necessary. Provide the city of publication only if the newspaper is a regional and only if the city of publication is not evident from the paper's title.

Claiborne, William. "Boxes Full of Conspiracy? Researchers Dig into JFK Assassination Papers." <u>Washington Post</u> 24 Aug. 1993: A1+.

29.   Article with an anonymous author

An unsigned article is alphabetized by the first major word in the article title (not *a, an,* or *the*).

"Democracy and Mega-Scandal." <u>New Yorker</u> 27 Sept. 1993: 6-8.

"Nissan Motors May Sell Some Stockholdings." <u>Wall Street Journal</u> 10 Sept. 1993: B4.

30.   Editorial

Follow the title with the word *Editorial*, but do not underline it or place it within quotation marks. Begin the citation with the author's name if it is known.

"Another Tug-of-War over a Child." Editorial. <u>Chicago Tribune</u> 7 Sept. 1993: 20.

31.   Letter to the editor

Follow the title (or the author if no title is given) with the word *Letter*, but do not underline it or place it within quotation marks.

Weber, Carl. "In Health Care, U.S. Is Best." Letter. <u>New York Times</u> 30 May 1990: A25.

32.   Review

Begin with the name of the reviewer and the title of the review, if provided. Follow with *Rev. of* (meaning "review of") and the title of the work reviewed. Include all relevant publication information. If neither the reviewer nor the title of the review is identified, begin the entry with the abbreviation *Rev. of* followed by the title of the work reviewed; alphabetize such an entry according to the reviewed work's title. For reviews of performances, provide any relevant information about the production.

Jefferson, Margo. "The Department Store and the Culture It Created." Rev. of <u>Land of Desire: Merchants, Power and the Rise of a New American Culture</u>, by William Leach. <u>New York Times</u> 1 Dec. 1993: C24.

Rothstein, Edward. "Blood and Thunder from the Young Verdi." Rev. of <u>I Lombardi</u>. Metropolitan Opera House, New York. <u>New York Times</u> 4 Dec. 1993: C11.

3 Other sources

33. Interview

Begin by identifying the person interviewed. Follow with the title of the interview (if there is one) in quotation marks. If there is no title, include the word *Interview* without underlining or quotation marks. Follow with a period and then give the necessary publication information. If the interview has not been published, provide relevant information—such as whether it was a personal interview, a telephone interview, or a televised interview.

Salter, James. "James Salter: The Art of Fiction XCCCIII." Interview. <u>Paris Review</u> 127 (1993): 54-100.

Selzer, Richard. Telephone interview. 7 Jan. 1992.

34. Letter

Cite a published letter as a selection from an anthology. Identify the date of the letter after the title. If the letter is numbered, provide that number.

Keats, John. "To Benjamin Bailey." 22 Nov. 1817. Letter 31 of <u>The Letters of John Keats</u>. Ed. Maurice Buxton Forman. 4th ed. London: Oxford UP, 1952. 66-69.

For personal letters, follow this form.

Dillard, Annie. Letter to the author. 10 Apr. 1988.

For unpublished letters in archives, identify the name of the collection and the city and institution that houses it.

Kurowsky, Agnes von. Letter to Ernest Hemingway. 15 Feb. 1919. Hemingway Collection. John F. Kennedy Lib., Boston.

35. Lecture or speech

Begin with the speaker's name and follow with the title of the lecture or speech (if there is one) in quotation marks. If there is no title, use a descriptive word such as *Lecture* or *Keynote speech* (without underlining or quotation marks). Identify the meeting and sponsoring organization, if relevant. End the entry with the location (city) and date of the lecture or speech.

Anstendig, Linda. "Curriculum Design for the '90s: Developing Personal Growth
    and Social Consciousness." Conference on College Composition and
    Communication. Boston. 19 Mar. 1991.

36. Dissertation

Enclose the title of an unpublished dissertation in quotation marks. After
the title, add *Diss.* (meaning "Dissertation") without quotation marks or underlining, the name of the university granting the degree in shortened form, and
the year of acceptance.

Martin, Rebecca E. "The Spectacle of Suffering: Repetition and Closure in the
    Eighteenth-Century Gothic Novel." Diss. CUNY, 1994.

Cite a published dissertation as a book, but add relevant dissertation information. If the dissertation was published by University Microfilms International (UMI), include the UMI number after the publication information.

Kauta, John B. Analysis and Assessment of the Concept of Revelation in Karl
    Rahner's Theology: Its Application and Relationship to African Traditional
    Religions. Diss. Fordham U, 1992. Ann Arbor: UMI, 1993. 9300240.

When citing an abstract from *Dissertation Abstracts International (DAI)*, include the *DAI* volume number, publication year, and page number after the
abstract title. The name of the university granting the degree follows the *DAI*
information.

Jenkins, Douglas Joseph. "Soldier Theatricals: 1940-1945." Diss. Bowling Green
    State U. DAI 53 (1993): 4133A.

37. Performance

List the title (if any) underlined, followed by the names of the key people
involved in the performance. Also include the theater or concert hall, the city,
and the date of the performance. If the performance does not have a title, use
a word such as *Concert* or *Recital*. The organization of that information within
the citation will depend on the aspect of the performance the paper refers to.
For example, when the work of an individual is the focus of the text discussion, begin the entry with that person's name.

In the Summer House. By Jane Bowles. Dir. JoAnne Akalaitis. Perf. Dianne Wiest,
    Alina Arenal, and Jaime Tirelli. Vivian Beaumont Theatre, New York. 1 Aug.
    1993.

Slatkin, Leonard, cond. St. Louis Symphony Orchestra. Concert. Carnegie Hall, New
    York. 23 Oct. 1994.

38.   Musical composition

Begin the citation with the composer's name. The title of a musical composition, ballet, or opera is underlined, but a composition identified only by form, number, and key is neither underlined nor placed in quotation marks. Cite a published musical score as a book, including relevant publication information.

Beethoven, Ludwig van. Symphony no. 5 in C minor, op. 67.

Mozart, Wolfgang Amadeus. Don Giovanni.

39.   Work of art

Include the artist's name, the title, and the museum or other repository and its city. To cite a reproduction of the work in a book, include the book's publication information at the end of the entry.

Bernini, Gianlorenzo. Apollo and Daphne. Galleria Borghese, Rome.

Moses, Grandma. The Barn Dance. Hammer Galleries, New York. Grandma
    Moses. By Otto Kallir. New York: Abrams, 1973. Illustration 940.

40.   Film

Begin with the film's title followed by the director, producer, major performers, distributor, and year. But if citing an individual's work within that film, begin your entry with that person's name and title.

The Age of Innocence. Dir. Martin Scorsese. Prod. Barbara DeFina. Perf. Daniel
    Day-Lewis, Michelle Pfeiffer, and Winona Ryder. Columbia, 1993.

Scorsese, Martin, dir. The Age of Innocence. Prod. Barbara DeFina. Perf. Daniel
    Day-Lewis, Michelle Pfeiffer, and Winona Ryder. Columbia, 1993.

41.   Television or radio program

Begin with the program's title, underlined. Follow with the network, the local station that broadcast the program, that station's location, and the date of broadcast. Add information such as director, producer, and performers as appropriate. If citing an individual's work, begin the entry with that person's name.

Chantilly Lace. Dir. Linda Yellen. Prod. Steven Hewitt. Perf. Lindsay Crouse, Jill
    Eikenberry, and Martha Plimpton. Showtime. New York. 18 July 1993.

Friedson, Michael, and Felice Friedson. Jewish Horizons. WWNN-AM, Fort
    Lauderdale. 19 Sept. 1993.

48 Hours: State of Fear. Narr. Dan Rather. CBS. WHDH, Boston. 8 Dec. 1993.

42. Recording

An entry for a recording can begin with the name of the composer, the conductor, or the performer, depending on the emphasis of the research. Follow the name with the title of the recording, underlined unless the recording is a composition identified by form, number, and key (see sample entry 38). If relevant, identify the recording medium after the title. Conclude the entry with the manufacturer, any catalog number, and the year of issue, all separated by commas.

Bartoli, Cecilia. The Impatient Lover: Italian Songs by Beethoven, Schubert, Haydn, and Mozart. Compact disc. London, 440 297-2, 1993.

Gaines, Ernest. A Gathering of Old Men. American Audio Prose Library, 6051, 1986.

43. Videotape or videocassette

Identify the medium after the title. The rest of the citation resembles the form for a film (see sample entry 40).

The Dakota Conflict. Narr. Garrison Keillor. Videocassette. Filmic Archives, 1992.

44. Map or chart

Cite a map or chart as a book with an anonymous author. Add the word *Map* or *Chart* (without underlining or quotation marks) after identifying what the map or chart describes. Conclude with the publication information.

France. Map. Chicago: Rand, 1988.

45. Cartoon

Begin the entry with the cartoonist's name, followed with the title of the cartoon (if any) in quotation marks, and the label *Cartoon* (without underlining or quotation marks). Conclude with the appropriate publication information for a periodical.

Trudeau, Garry. "Doonesbury." Cartoon. Boston Globe 19 Sept. 1994: 23.

4   Electronic sources

The MLA "Works Cited" system (as described in the *MLA Handbook for Writers,* 4th ed.) distinguishes electronic citation forms according to whether the material is available on a CD-ROM or diskette or whether it is available through various channels online.

Because electronic media are continually changing, the details of citations may evolve even as the basic needs for citing references stay the same. Whatever the medium, researchers using electronic material need to provide complete data to identify a source and give clear and consistent directions for locating it wherever it has been found. A complete treatment of electronic references in MLA format is given in Xia Li and Nancy Crane (1996), *Electronic Styles: An Expanded Guide to Citing Electronic Information.* This reference work also has a Web page address at http://www.uvm.edu/~xli/reference/estyles.html.

46. Source on CD-ROM, tape, or diskette, including computer software

Citations for sources—including software programs—on electronic storage devices are distinguished according to whether the material was published once, like a book; whether it is published in periodical or regularly updated form, like a magazine; and whether it has a print equivalent or not.

CD, tape, or diskette produced as a single publication (like a book)

Begin with the author's name, a chapter or section title (if any) enclosed in quotation marks, and main title underlined—as with a book. Then give the product or series title (if any) underlined, followed by data on the release or version, and identify the source as CD-ROM, diskette, or tape. For software application programs, any appropriate technical details that identify the program (such as operating system) may be added. Finally, give the publication information: city, publisher, and date (as for a book).

DeLorme Mapping. "Vestfirdhir [Iceland]." Global Explorer. CD-ROM. Freeport, ME: DeLorme, 1993.

CD, tape, or diskette updated periodically, which also has a print equivalent

Begin with the author's name, followed by complete information for the print equivalent in the same format, as for any periodical (using quotation marks around the article title and underlining for the journal). Follow this with the database name (if any), underlined; then identify the source as CD-ROM, diskette, or tape. Finally, give the database provider or vendor if available, and the date of the publication.

Lacayo, Richard. "This Land Is Whose Land?" Time 23 Oct. 1995: 68-71. Academic ASAP. CD-ROM. Infotrac. Dec. 1995.

CD, tape, or diskette updated periodically, which has no print equivalent

List the author or institution's name followed by a period. Then, depending on the information available, give the article's title and its original date or inclusive dates, enclosed in quotation marks. Follow this with the database name, underlined, and identify the source as CD-ROM, diskette, or tape. For software application programs, any appropriate technical details that identify the program (such as operating system) may be added. Finally, give the location and provider or vendor of the database if available, and the date of the publication.

Levi Strauss. "The Levi Strauss Co.: Balance Sheet, 1/l/95-12/31/95." Compact
     Disclosure. CD-ROM. New York: Digital Library Systems. Jan. 1996.

47. Online sources

Online sources are cited somewhat differently according to whether their material has a print equivalent or not. Also, citation requirements for Internet sources are somewhat different from those for commercial or subscription online services—consumer services like America Online, Compuserve, or Prodigy, or subscription services like LEXIS-NEXIS, DIALOG, and WILSONLINE.

Online source with a print equivalent

Give the author's name followed by all the basic information for the print-equivalent publication: article title enclosed by quotes; name of the paper or periodical underlined; the date of its original print publication. Then, depending on the information available, list the name of the database (or category), underlined, and identify it as *Online*. Finally, name the computer service (Compuserve, DIALOG, etc.), or follow Internet requirements (following). In any case, give the date of your electronic access to that file.

O'Brien, John. "Chicago at Heart of Heroin Case." Chicago Tribune 15 Oct. 1996:
     A1. Chicago Tribune Online. Online. America Online. 29 Oct. 1996.

Online source with no print equivalent

Begin with the author's name. Then give available data about the electronic posting, including the article's title enclosed in quotes, followed by any date given for its electronic posting. Next, list the name of the database (or data category), underlined, and identify it as *Online*. Finally, name the computer service (Compuserve, DIALOG, etc.), or follow Internet requirements (following). In any case, give the date of your electronic access to that file.

Shimabukuro, Jim, ed. "Internet in 10 Years--Essays." <u>Electronic Journal on Virtual Culture</u> 3.1 (1995): 62 pars. Online. BITNET. 20 Oct. 1996.

Online source from the Internet

Because researchers using the Internet seek complete and precise source citations from this rapidly evolving resource, significant modifications or adaptations have been proposed in the conventions for Internet citations as outlined in *The MLA Handbook for Writers of Research Papers,* fourth edition (1995). The Internet citation forms presented here are based on modifications that are widely accepted (by the Alliance for Computers and Writing and Other groups) as compiled by Janice R. Walker and Todd Taylor in *The Columbia Guide to Online Style* (Columbia UP, 1998). The wide variety of materials and reference cues available on the Internet require that research citations use whatever information is given, presented in the following sequence:

a. If the Internet posts material that does have a print equivalent, start the citation with the author's name followed by the basic information for the print-equivalent publication: article title enclosed in quotation marks; name of the paper or periodical underlined; the date of its original print publication. Add any reference numbers further indentifying the piece—such as volume, issue, installment number, etc. Depending on the information available, identify the number of pages, paragraphs, or sections according to any visible divisions (using standard abbreviations).

b. If the Internet posting has no apparent print equivalent, identify the name of the article or piece, enclosed in quotation marks; then identify and underline the name of any larger complete work or institutional association sponsoring the piece cited—such as a journal, newsletter, conference, or sponsor.

c. Give any other identifying file number or version number that is available.

d. Give any available date for the origin or the posting of the document, without parentheses.

e. Give an exact citation of the Internet address or the URL locators for the World Wide Web sites, with protocol identifications (see Internet name systems, p. 650) and path locators used to gain access. Preserve slashes, mechanics, and spaces within the address, without adding any final period.

f. Follow this immediately with the date of your access to the posting, enclosed within parentheses, to separate it from other unpunctuated data.

gopher site

Caplan, R. "General Agreement on a New Economy: A New Website on Sustainable Economics." <u>Economics Working Group/Project of the Tides Foundation.</u> 17 pars. 10:19 PM Mar. 19, 1996. gopher://gopher.igc.apc.org/00/ environment/forests/western.lands/current (29 Oct. 1996).

FTP site (searched via archie, veronica, or WAIS)

Deutsch, Peter. "archie--An Electronic Directory Service for the Internet." Mar. 1993.
ftp://ftp.sura.net/pub/archie/docs/whatis.archie (15 July 1996).

Telnet site (reached via Web or direct access to local networks)

Gomes, Lee. "Xerox's On-Line Neighborhood: A Great Place to Visit." <u>Mercury
News</u> 3 May 1992. telnet lambda.parc.xerox.com 8888,@go #50827, press 13
(5 Dec. 1996).

Web site

Trudeau, Garry. "Getting over Getting Stoned." <u>Time Magazine</u> 16 Sept. 1996:
13. 148. <u>Time Magazine Online</u> 24 Oct. 1996. http://pathfinder.com/
@@2AaRwUA5je6...zine/domestic/960916/essay.html (1 Nov. 1996).

Newsgroup/Usenet posting

Kostka, Ericka. Online newsgroup discussion posting. Usenet:rec.animals.wildlife
(28 Oct. 1996).

Listserv discussion message

Bruckman, Amy S. "MOOSE Crossing Proposal." mediamoo@media.mit.edu
(4 Jan. 1997).

Personal e-mail

Williams, Ted. "Educating the Public about Restoring Wolves to Yellowstone."
Personal e-mail. (15 Oct. 1996).

Synchronous communication (MOOs, MUDs, IRC)

Guest. Personal Interview. telnet://purple-crayon.media.mit.edu 8888 (9 Jan. 1996).

APA Documentation Style

The documentation style described in this section is that recommended in
the *Publication Manual of the American Psychological Association* (4th ed. Washington: APA, 1994). This system, usually referred to as APA style, is used in
psychology and in other social science disciplines, such as anthropology and

sociology. But because variations exist among the documentation styles in the social sciences, you should check with your instructor about his or her preferred documentation style before beginning your paper.

Like the MLA style, the APA style includes brief in-text, parenthetical citations of borrowed material and lists at the end of the paper the sources cited . APA style, however, uses fewer abbreviations than does the MLA style. In addition, some publication data are included in APA parenthetical citations. Dates are important for readers and researchers in the social sciences since so much of the research in psychology and related disciplines updates, builds upon, and corrects previous research.

The end-of-paper citations in APA style follow a pattern that, once learned, can be adapted easily to fit just about any desired work. Consult the accompanying chart of APA forms for an overview of the types of citations described in this section.

Directory of APA Sample Entries

In-Text, Parenthetical Citations (see 45d)

1. Author not named in text, 722
2. Author named in text, 722
3. Work with two authors, 722
4. Work with three to five authors, 723
5. Work with six or more authors, 723
6. Anonymous work, 723
7. Corporate author, 723
8. Author of two or more cited works, 724
9. Authors with the same last name, 724
10. Two or more sources in a single citation, 724
11. Portions of a source, 724
12. Personal communication, 724

References List Entries (see 45f)

BOOKS

1. Book with one author, 726
2. Book with two or more authors, 726
3. Book with an anonymous author, 727
4. Book with an editor, 727
5. Selection from an anthology, 727
6. Book with a corporate author, 727
7. Multivolume book, 728
8. Translation, 728
9. Revised edition, 728

(continued)

10. Republished book, 728
11. Two or more books by the same author, 728
12. Government publication, 729

PERIODICALS

13. Article in a journal paginated by volume, 730
14. Article in a journal paginated by issue, 730
15. Article in a magazine, 730
16. Article with an anonymous author, 730
17. Article in a newspaper, 730
18. Editorial, 731
19. Letter to the editor, 731
20. Review, 731

OTHER SOURCES

21. Abstract, 731
22. Published interview, 731
23. Dissertation, 732
24. Report, 732
25. Film, 732
26. Videotape or videocassette, 732
27. Television or radio program, 732
28. Map or chart, 733
29. Source on CD-ROM, tape, or diskette, including computer software, 733
30. Online source, 733

45d   APA style for in-text, parenthetical citations

APA style uses two methods for citing borrowed material within the text:
(1) Author and date are identified immediately following the borrowed
material. (2) Author is identified in the text of the paper; the date is given immediately following the borrowed material. In-text, parenthetical citations
provide readers with information needed to locate the source of borrowed information in the list of references at the end of the paper. In APA style, parenthetical citations identify what was borrowed from a source and when that
source was published. Use the following guidelines when preparing parenthetical citations.

- Keep the citations concise, but provide all necessary information.
- Use an author's last name either in the text of the paper or in parentheses immediately after the borrowed material. Use an author's first initial and last
  name if two authors in the References share the same last name.
- Punctuate and format the parenthetical citations in the following manner.

1. Place the parenthetical citation either at the end of the sentence or at a natural pause within the sentence. In either case, the citation should follow, as closely as possible, the material it refers to.

2. If the citation is placed immediately following a quotation, place the citation after the closing quotation marks.

3. Place any punctuation marks in the text immediately following the closing parenthesis of the citation.

4. In block quotations, place the parenthetical citation two spaces following the final punctuation mark of the quotation.

- Include a page reference for the borrowed material.

1. Author not named in text

When an author is not identified in the text, place the author's last name and the year of publication in parentheses at a point where the citation does not interrupt the flow of your writing. Separate the author and date with a comma. Be sure that there is no confusion between what you are documenting and your own text.

During the Civil War, Thomas Carlyle supported the South, but after the war he admitted that he might have been wrong (Kaplan, 1983).

2. Author named in text

When an author is identified in the text, cite only the date within parentheses. If the same source is cited more than once in the same paragraph, you need not repeat the year in that and subsequent citations.

Kaplan (1983) analyzes Thomas Carlyle's admiration for strong leaders like Cromwell and Frederick the Great.

In citing a direct quotation, include a parenthetical reference to the page number(s). The abbreviation *p.* or *pp.* is included.

"We are never innocent travelers; we arrive with ideas about the place in our minds. These ideas may be more vivid than the place can sustain when we see it; they may be more resistant to change than the place itself" (Howe, 1993, p. 62).

Howe (1993) has observed that "we are never innocent travelers; we arrive with ideas about the place in our minds" (p. 62).

3. Work with two authors

Always cite the surnames of both authors in all text citations. Use an ampersand (&) to separate the authors' names in a parenthetical citation, but use the word *and* to separate their names in the text of the paper.

The New Orleans Center for the Creative Arts has produced successful performers such as Wynton Marsalis and Harry Connick, Jr. (Lichtenstein & Danker, 1993).

Lichtenstein and Danker (1993) demonstrate how the New Orleans Center for the Creative Arts has produced successful performers such as Wynton Marsalis and Harry Connick, Jr.

4. Work with three to five authors

If a work has more than two but fewer than six authors, cite them all in the first reference.

The Tivoli in Copenhagen, one of the world's best-known amusement parks, offers rides, games, fireworks, and other attractions (Bendure, Friary, Noble, Swarey, & Videon, 1993).

In subsequent references, however, cite only the first author followed by *et al.* (meaning "and others") neither italicized nor underlined.

According to Bendure et al. (1993), the Tivoli has no peers.

5. Work with six or more authors

When a work has six or more authors, cite the surname of the first author followed by *et al.* in all in-text citations. Include the names of all the authors in the end-of-paper list of references. The following example shows a sample citation for a work by Rorschbach, Aker, Zorn, Flugel, Erskine, and Zieffer.

As Rorschbach et al. (1993) have suggested, the consequences of radical demographic and cultural change on midsize cities of the American heartland have yet to be fully felt.

6. Anonymous work

Cite an anonymous work by using the first two or three words of the title in the in-text citation or parenthetically in place of the author's name. (See 39a on punctuating titles.)

While many questions about the Iran-Contra affair persist, it seems unlikely any answers will be found ("Democracy," 1993).

7. Corporate author

Usually cite the full name of the corporate author in each in-text reference. If, however, the corporation's name is long or if an abbreviation for the company is easily recognized, abbreviate the corporate name in second and subsequent entries.

Recently published statistics show a decline in the incidence of cerebral palsy (United Cerebral Palsy Association [UCPA], 1994).

Governmental support for those with the disease cannot be curtailed (UCPA, 1994).

8. Author of two or more cited works

In referring to two or more of the same author's works published in the same year, distinguish between them in the parenthetical citations by alphabetizing the works in the reference list and providing each work with a lowercase letter. Thus, Annette Kolodny's "Dancing through the Minefield" would be labeled *Kolodny, 1981a,* while her "A Map for Rereading" would be designated *Kolodny, 1981b.*

9. Authors with the same last name

To distinguish works by authors with the same last name, use each author's first initial(s) in each citation.

E. Jones (1930) wrote a pioneering study of psychology and literature.

10. Two or more sources in a single citation

Cite two or more different authors in a single citation in alphabetical order and separated by a semicolon (Fetterley, 1978; Kolodny, 1975). Cite two or more works by the same author in a single citation in chronological order, separated by a comma (Flynn 1980, 1983).

11. Portions of a source

If you refer to a large portion of a source, identify it in the parenthetical citation by an abbreviation: *chap.* (chapter), *Vol.* (Volume), *Pt.* (Part).

A recent writer argues that religions are politically intermediate institutions, which should influence government and affect the political process but which should be little influenced by government (Carter, 1993, chap. 2).

12. Personal communication

Material such as letters, telephone conversations, messages from electronic bulletin boards, and personal interviews should be acknowledged in the text with the person's name, the identification *personal communication,* and the date. These sources are not included in the list of references because readers cannot retrieve them.

J. Holmes, president of Mayfair Fashions, predicts that formal evening gowns will become more popular next year (personal communication, December 29, 1993).

45e APA style for content notes

Content notes (or footnotes) expand upon or supplement information in a paper. Use APA-style content notes to clarify, illustrate, or explain an idea or to provide definitions and identify individuals and events. Make these notes as brief as possible so that they do not distract the reader from the text.

Use a superscript arabic number in the text immediately after the term or passage to be footnoted. Number any content note superscripts consecutively throughout the paper so they correspond to the notes themselves, which are typed on a separate page and placed at the end of the paper immediately before the list of references. Head this page "Footnotes."

To format content notes, indent five spaces and place the superscript number followed by the note. Double-space within and between the notes and place them in numerical order.

TEXT WITH SUPERSCRIPT

The age of the women involved, their marital status, and their economic well-being were important elements considered in designing the follow-up questionnaire.[1]

CONTENT NOTE

[1]Susan Crawford and Priscilla Denby, both of whom have extensive involvement with women's issues and social programs, provided helpful input and feedback throughout the study.

45f APA style for the References list

APA style requires that all the sources of borrowed material in a paper be listed on a separate page at the end of the paper. This separate listing is called the "References." The References list should include only material that was used in the research and preparation of the paper.

Following the last page of the paper (but before any concluding notes or appendices) begin the list with the title "References" without quotation marks or underlining, centered, and an inch from the top of the page. The References list is paginated as the rest of the paper. Double-space between the title and the first entry on the list.

Arrange the citation entries in alphabetical order by authors' last names. If a source is anonymous, alphabetize it by using the first major word in its title (not *a*, *an*, or *the*). Begin each entry flush with the left margin, but indent all subsequent lines three spaces. Double-space within and between entries.

1   Books

A standard APA entry for a book consists of four elements: author, date of publication, title, and publication information. These four elements are separated from one another by a period. The entry concludes with a period. (Note that these formatting instructions are for preparing student papers. If you are submitting a paper to a journal for publication, refer to the *APA Publication Manual* for formatting guidelines.)

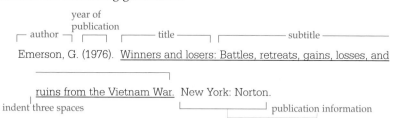

Keep the following guidelines in mind when preparing book entries for the References list.

1. **Author:** An author's name should appear last name first, followed by a comma and first and middle initials. Put a period after the author's name.

2. **Year of publication:** Enclose the year of publication in parentheses and follow with a period.

3. **Title:** Underline the title and capitalize the first word of the title, the first word of the subtitle, and any proper nouns. Separate the main title from the subtitle with a colon. Put a period after the complete title.

4. **Publication information:** Include the city of publication and the publisher, separated from one another with a colon. If two or more locations are given for the publisher, either give the location that is listed first on the title page or give the site of the publisher's home office. If the name of the city is not well known or if it is confusing, include a state or country abbreviation following a comma. Omit the word *Publisher* and abbreviations such as *Inc.* and *Co.* from the publisher name. However, include the complete names of university presses and associations. Put a period after the publication information.

1.   Book with one author

Emerson, G. (1976). <u>Winners and losers: Battles, retreats, gains, losses, and ruins from the Vietnam War.</u> New York: Norton.

2.   Book with two or more authors

List all of the book's authors last name first followed by initials. Commas separate authors' names. An ampersand connects the final two names.

Lichtenstein, G., & Danker, L. (1993). <u>Musical gumbo: The music of New Orleans.</u> New York: Norton.

Bellah, R. N., Madsen, R., Sullivan, W., Swidler, A., & Tipton, S. M. (1985). <u>Habits of the heart: Individualism and commitment in American life.</u> Berkeley: University of California Press.

3. Book with an anonymous author

Begin the entry with the title. Alphabetize the entry using the first main word in the title (not *a, an,* or *the*). If "Anonymous" appears on the title page, then begin the entry with the word *Anonymous* and alphabetize the entry as if "Anonymous" were the author's name.

<u>The world almanac and book of facts.</u> (1983). New York: Newspaper Enterprise Association.

4. Book with an editor

Place the editor's name where an author's name would be placed. Note that the number of the cited volume is placed in parentheses after the title.

Syrett, H. C. (Ed.). (1986). <u>The papers of Alexander Hamilton</u> (Vol. 26). New York: Columbia University Press.

5. Selection from an anthology

Begin with the name of the author(s), the year of publication, and the title of the article or chapter neither underlined nor in quotation marks. Follow with the editor(s) listed in normal order with the abbreviation *Ed.* or *Eds.* in parentheses. Conclude the entry with the title of the book, the page numbers for the article or chapter, and the publication information.

Chrisman, N. J. (1985). Alcoholism: Illness or disease? In L. A. Bennett & G. M. Ames (Eds.), <u>The American experience with alcohol: Contrasting cultural perspectives</u> (pp. 7-21). New York: Plenum.

6. Book with a corporate author

Begin the entry with the corporate or group name and alphabetize the entry by the first major word in the name. When the same group is listed as both author and publisher, use the word *Author* at the end of the entry in place of the publisher's name.

National Geographic Society. (1988). <u>Discovering Britain and Ireland.</u> Washington, DC: Author.

7. Multivolume book

Include the abbreviation *Vol.* or *Vols.* and the number of volumes used in the paper. Place this information after the title, enclosed within parentheses, and place a period after the closing parenthesis. The following example indicates that both volumes were used in the paper.

Cohen, J., & Chiu, H. (1974). People's China and international law: A documentary
　　study (Vols. 1-2). Princeton: Princeton University Press.

8. Translation

Include the names of the translator(s) in parentheses immediately following the title.

Le Goff, J. (1980). Time, work, and culture in the Middle Ages (A. Goldhammer,
　　Trans.). Chicago: University of Chicago Press.

9. Revised edition

Indicate the appropriate edition in parentheses immediately after the title. Use the abbreviation *Rev. ed.* if the title page lists the book as a "Revised edition."

Pauk, W. (1993). How to study in college (5th ed.). Boston: Houghton Mifflin.

10. Republished book

Cite the date of original publication in parentheses at the close of the entry. The in-text citation should include both publication dates (*Veblen, 1899/1953*).

Veblen, T. (1953). The theory of the leisure class: An economic study of institutions.
　　New York: New American Library. (Original work published 1899)

11. Two or more books by the same author

Begin each entry with the author's name followed by the year of publication. Arrange the entries chronologically, the earliest first.

Takaki, R. (1989). Strangers from a different shore: A history of Asian Americans.
　　Boston: Little, Brown.

Takaki, R. (1993). A different mirror: A history of multicultural America. Boston:
　　Little, Brown.

For two or more works by the same author published in the same year, arrange the entries alphabetically by the first main word in the title. Add lowercase letters (starting with *a*) to the entries (after the dates) to distinguish them from one another.

Gardner, H. (1982a). <u>Art, mind, and brain: A cognitive approach to creativity.</u> New York: Basic Books.

Gardner, H. (1982b). <u>Developmental psychology</u> (2nd ed.). Boston: Little, Brown.

12. Government publication

Begin the entry with the name of the government agency issuing the publication (unless an author's name is provided). If the publication appears in multiple volumes, indicate that, as in the second entry that follows.

U.S. Department of Commerce. (1992). <u>U.S. industrial outlook '92: Business forecasts for 350 industries.</u> Washington, DC: U.S. Government Printing Office.

U.S. House of Representatives. Committee on Ways and Means. (1986). <u>Hearings on comprehensive tax reform</u> (Vols. 1-9). Washington, DC: U.S. Government Printing Office.

2   Periodicals

A standard periodical entry in APA style includes the same information as an APA standard book entry: author, date of publication, title, and publication information. These elements are separated from one another by a period. The entry ends with a period. (Note that these formatting instructions are for preparing student papers. If you are submitting a paper to a journal for publication, refer to the *APA Publication Manual* for formatting guidelines.)

```
                    year of
                    publication
  ┌ author ┐     ┌─┐  ┌──────── title ────────┐   ┌──────────── subtitle ──────────────┐
Geertz, C. (1968).  Thinking as a moral act: Dimensions of anthropological field-
```

```
  ┌─────────────────────┐
  │ work in the new states.  Antioch Review, 28, 139-158.
  │
indent three spaces        └──── publication information ────┘
```

Keep the following guidelines in mind when preparing periodical entries for the References list.

1. **Author:** An author's name should appear last name first, followed by a comma, then by the first and middle initials.

2. **Year of publication:** Give the year of publication. For magazines and newspapers, include the month and date of publication. Enclose the year of publication information in parentheses and follow with a period.

3. **Title:** The article title and subtitle are neither underlined nor set in quotation marks. Capitalize the first word of the title, the first word of the subtitle, and any proper nouns. Separate the main title from the subtitle with a colon. Put a period after the title.

4. **Publication information:** Begin with the complete title of the publication, with all the major words capitalized. Underline the title. Provide the volume number (underlined and not preceded by the abbreviation *vol.*). End with the inclusive page numbers for the article. (APA includes the full sequence of page numbers.) Use the abbreviation *p.* or *pp.* for articles in newspapers but not journals or magazines. Put a period at the end of the publication information.

13. Article in a journal paginated by volume

Herzog, H. (1993). Human morality and animal research. American Scholar, 62, 337-349.

14. Article in a journal paginated by issue

If each issue in a volume begins with page 1, enclose the number of the issue in parentheses immediately after the volume number. Underline the volume number but not the issue number.

Livingston, H. (1980). Hamlet, Ernest Jones, and the critics. Hamlet Studies, 2(1), 25-33.

15. Article in a magazine

In citing the date, give the year first, followed by the month and day of publication, separated by a comma. For an article with discontinuous pages, use a comma to separate page numbers.

Klaeger, R. (1986, November). Hiring the recent college grad. Video Manager, pp. 14, 20.

16. Article with an anonymous author

When no author is identified, begin with the title of the article. Alphabetize the entry by the first significant word in the title (in this example, by the word *talk*).

The talk of the town: Fanciers. (1990, December 31). The New Yorker, pp. 28-29.

17. Article in a newspaper

Include the complete name of the publication after the article title. List all discontinuous page numbers.

Claiborne, W. (1993, August 24). Boxes full of conspiracy? Researchers dig into JFK assassination papers. The Washington Post, pp. 1A, 7A.

18. Editorial

Place the identifying label *Editorial* in brackets after the title of the piece. Note that no period follows the last word of the article title.

Another tug-of-war over a child [Editorial]. (1993, September 7). The Chicago Tribune, p. 20.

19. Letter to the editor

Place the words *Letter to the Editor* in brackets after the title of the piece. Note that no period follows the last word of the article title.

Deonarine, B. (1993, August). Basketball as a way out [Letter to the editor]. Harper's, pp. 77-78.

20. Review

Begin the entry with the reviewer and/or the title of the review, if provided. Follow with the date of publication. In brackets, include the identifying label *Review of* and the title of the piece that was reviewed. If neither the reviewer nor the title of the review is identified, begin the entry with the bracketed information; alphabetize such an entry according to the reviewed work's title.

Daynard, R. A. (1979). [Review of the book Watergate and the Constitution]. American Journal of Legal History, 23, 368-370.

3   Other sources

21. Abstract

If only the abstract of a work is used, identify the author, year of publication, title, and full, original publication information for that work. Include the citation for the collection of abstracts parenthetically at the end of the entry.

Parked, K. R. (1992). Mental health in the oil industry: A comparative study of onshore and offshore employees. Psychological Medicine, 22, 997-1009. (From Psychological Abstracts, 1993, 80, Abstract No. 27688)

22. Published interview

Begin with the interviewer's name followed by the date. Place the identifying label *Interview with* in brackets, then name the person interviewed.

Zunes, S. (1993, October). [Interview with George McGovern]. The Progressive, pp. 34-37.

23.   Dissertation

Underline the title of an unpublished dissertation, and follow with the words *Unpublished doctoral dissertation* and the university granting the degree.

Etiegni, L. W. (1990). Wood ash recycling and land disposal. Unpublished doctoral dissertation, University of Idaho, Moscow.

When citing an abstract from *Dissertation Abstracts International (DAI),* do not underline the dissertation title. The words *Doctoral dissertation* and the name of the university granting the degree parenthetically follow the abstract title. Include the *DAI* volume number, publication year, and page number.

Jenkins, D. J. (1993). Soldier theatricals: 1940-1945 (Doctoral dissertation, Bowling Green State University, 1992). Dissertation Abstracts International, 53, 4133A.

24.   Report

Cite a report as you would a book, but include after the title any identifying number the report may have.

Jones, S. (1991). Traffic flow and safety in mid-size urban communities (Report No. TR-11). Albany: New York State Transportation Authority.

25.   Film

Begin the citation with the name or names of those responsible for the production, followed by their titles in parentheses. Identify the medium in brackets after the title. Provide the city and name of the distributor.

Scorsese, M. (Director), & DeFina, B. (Producer). (1993). The age of innocence [Film]. Hollywood: Columbia Pictures.

26.   Videotape or videocassette

Begin the citation with the name of the major contributor and that individual's title. State the medium after the title of the work enclosed in brackets, but use parentheses if an identifying number is given. End with publication information.

Keillor, G. (Narrator). (1992). The Dakota conflict (Videocassette No. 5790A). Botsford, CT: Filmic Archives.

27.   Television or radio program

Begin the citation by identifying those responsible for creating the program and their titles.

Shapiro, E. (Director), Clifford, T. (Producer), & Rather, D. (Anchor and Reporter). (1993, December 8). <u>48 hours: State of fear.</u> Boston: WHDH, CBS.

28. Map or chart

Cite maps and charts as anonymous works. Use the words *Map* or *Chart* (without underlining or quotation marks) after the title, enclosed in brackets.

<u>Hearing, language, social skills, motor skills</u> [Chart]. (1981). Duluth: University of Minnesota, Department of Communicative Disorders.

4 Electronic sources

APA format requires relatively minor variations from standard citation in describing electronic sources but requires a description of the path or address needed to retrieve online material.

29. Source on CD-ROM, tape, or diskette

List information on author, date, and title of article or larger work as for print sources. Following the title, label the medium CD-ROM, tape, or diskette, enclosed by brackets. Then, for software, list technical information (e.g., operating system). Complete the citation with publication information for the city and the publisher.

Investment Tax Analyst. (1994). [Computer Software]. DOS 6.0, 128K. New York: Wiley.

30. Online source

List information on author, date, and title of article or larger work title, as for print sources. For online sources other than the Internet, follow the title with the label *Online* enclosed by brackets. Then give page or section information if available. Insert the word "Available:" (not underlined, with colon) and the complete description of the path or location, with information about the service or database. A date of access is not included.

Unlike MLA, APA does not include transient or unrecorded sources , such as e-mail, among the retrievable "References." In more recent research practice, these sources are often listed among the References.

Commercial subscription service

O'Brien, J. (1996, October 15). Chicago at heart of heroin case. <u>Chicago Tribune</u> [Online], p. A1. Available: America Online/Newstand/Chicago Tribune Online/search/local news

Internet sources

The rapid evolution of research on the Internet has produced a demand for modifications or adaptations in the Internet citations as outlined in *The Publication Manual of the APA,* fourth edition (1994). The Internet citation forms presented below are based on modifications as compiled by Janice R. Walker and Todd Taylor in *The Columbia Guide to Online Style* (NY: Columbia UP, 1998).

Citations for Internet sources in APA format should (a) list complete information on author, date, and title of article or larger work title, in the same format as for print sources. Then (b) give a complete citation of the Internet address or the URL site, with protocol identifications (see Internet name systems, p. 650). Preserve slashes, mechanics, and spaces within the address, without adding any final period. Finally (c) add the date of access.

gopher site

Caplan, R. (1996, March 19). "General agreement on a new economy: A new web site on sustainable economics." Economics Working Group/Project of the Tides Foundation. gopher://gopher.igc.apc.org/00/environment/forests/ western.lands/current/55 (29 Oct. 1996).

Web site

Trudeau, G. (1996, September 16). "Getting over getting stoned." Time Magazine Online 24 Oct. 1996. http://pathfinder.com/@@2AaRwUA5je6...zine/ domestic/960916/essay.html (1 Nov. 1996).

Newsgroup/Usenet posting

Kostka, E. Online newsgroup discussion posting. Usenet:rec.animals.wildlife (28 Oct. 1996).

Synchronous communication (MOOs, MUDs, IRC)

Guest. Personal interview. telnet://purple-crayon.media.mit.edu 8888 (9 Jan. 1996).

CMS Documentation Style

45g   CMS style for footnotes (or endnotes) and bibliography

Many disciplines, including history, philosophy, political science, economics, and business, use the citation system established by *The Chicago Man-*

ual of Style, 14th edition (Chicago: University of Chicago Press, 1993), which features in-text numbered note references linked to endnotes describing the works cited, plus a bibliography for full reference details. Some instructors in other disciplines may prefer this system as well. You will likely encounter note and bibliography style in your research.

1 Bibliography entries

Format the bibliography as you would an MLA-style Works Cited list (see 45c). If you use footnotes, place your bibliography in the same place as you would a Works Cited list—after the last page of your paper. If you use endnotes rather than footnotes, place the bibliography after the page(s) of notes.

2 Notes—endnotes or footnotes

Endnotes, which are placed together at the end of a paper, or **footnotes** at the bottom (or foot) of a page, provide publication information about sources you quote, paraphrase, summarize, or otherwise refer to in the text of a paper. When using the note system of documentation, place superscript numbers (raised slightly above the line—[1]) in the text of the paper. Place the number at the end of the sentence, clause, or phrase containing the material that you are documenting. Superscript numbers should be typed with no space between the letter or punctuation mark that precedes it. Number the citations sequentially throughout the paper. Each number will correspond to an entry in your footnotes or list of endnotes.

TEXT

As Janetta Benton has noted, gargoyles are usually located in "visually inaccessible locations,"[1] peripheral to the medieval cathedral. She also speculates that gargoyle sculptors can be compared with medieval manuscript illuminators in their artistic freedom and imaginativeness.[2]

NOTES

[1]Janetta Rebold Benton, The Medieval Menagerie: Animals in the Art of the Middle Ages (New York: Abbeville, 1992) 57.

[2]Benton 58-59.

Use the following guidelines when writing with endnotes or footnotes.

- Place all endnotes at the end of the paper. Start a new page with the heading "Notes" (without underlining or quotation marks), centered and one inch from the top margin of the page. Double-space to the first note entry and between entries. This system is recommended by CMS and is widely preferred to footnotes. Often endnote numbers are shown online with periods before the note rather than with superscript numerals.

- Place footnotes at the base of the page where the superscript number appears. The first line of the footnote begins four line spaces from the last line of text on the page. Single-space within a footnote, but double-space between footnotes.
- Indent each note five spaces from the left margin to the superscript number. Follow the superscript number with one space. (Subsequent lines in an entry do not indent.)
- For the first occurrence of the standard note, begin the entry with the author's name in normal word order followed by a comma, the title of the source, the publication information in parentheses, and the page number(s).
- For the second and subsequent references to a source, use a shortened form of the entry consisting of the author's last name and the page number(s) separated by a space. When you use the shortened form of the entry for multiple citations to more than one work by the same author, include an abbreviated title in the entry.

BOOKS

Book with one author

[1]Janetta Rebold Benton, <u>The Medieval Menagerie: Animals in the Art of the Middle Ages</u> (New York: Abbeville, 1992) 57.

Book with two or three authors

[2]Grace Lichtenstein and Laura Danker, <u>Musical Gumbo: The Music of New Orleans</u> (New York: Norton, 1993) 124.

Book with more than three authors

[3]Glenda Bendure et al., <u>Scandinavian and Baltic Europe on a Shoestring</u> (Berkeley: Lonely Planet, 1993) 26.

Book with an anonymous author

[4]<u>The World Almanac and Book of Facts</u> (New York: NEA, 1983) 264-68.

Book with an author and an editor

[5]George Orwell, <u>Orwell: The War Commentaries</u>, ed. W. J. West (New York: Pantheon, 1985) 210.

Book with an editor

[6]Linda A. Bennett and Genevieve M. Ames, eds., <u>The American Experience with Alcohol: Contrasting Cultural Perspectives</u> (New York: Plenum, 1985) 15.

Selection from an anthology

[7]Noel J. Chrisman, "Alcoholism: Illness or Disease?" <u>The American Experience with Alcohol: Contrasting Cultural Perspectives</u>, ed. Linda A. Bennett and Genevieve M. Ames (New York: Plenum, 1985) 7-21.

Multivolume work

[8]Joseph Blotner, <u>Faulkner: A Biography</u>, vol. 1 (New York: Random, 1974) 257.

PERIODICALS

Article in a journal paginated by volume

[9]Adelia Williams, "Jean Tardieu: The Painterly Poem," <u>Foreign Language Studies</u> 18 (1991): 119.

Article in a journal paginated by issue

[10]Daniel Bender, "Diversity Revisited, or Composition's Alien History," <u>Rhetoric Review</u> 12.1 (1987): 115.

Article in a magazine

[11]Bill Howard, "Portable Computing: Power without the Pounds," <u>PC Magazine</u> Aug. 1993: 254.

Article in a newspaper

[12]William Claiborne, "Boxes Full of Conspiracy? Researchers Dig into JFK Assassination Papers," <u>Washington Post</u> 24 Aug. 1993: A1+.

SHORTENED FORMS

Second and subsequent notes to the same source appear in a shortened form that lists the author's last name and page number only. Note that entries 14 and 15 show two works by the same author.

[13]Howard 254.

[14]Benton, <u>Menagerie</u> 145.

[15]Benton, "Perspective" 34.

```
╔══════════════════════════════════════════════════════╗
║                CBE Documentation Style                 ║
╚══════════════════════════════════════════════════════╝
```

The CBE styles of writing and documentation are described in the *CBE Style Manual: A Guide for Authors, Editors, and Publishers in the Biological Sciences,* 5th ed., revised and expanded (Chicago: CBE, 1983). Just as with MLA and APA styles of documentation, the CBE system includes both in-text, parenthetical citations and a list of end-of-paper references that contains more detailed bibliographic information about the sources cited. The CBE styles of in-text citation include the name-and-year system, which closely resembles APA style, and the number system, which is similar to the MLA note style. This section explains and illustrates CBE in-text forms for both the name-and-year-system and the number system. The section also includes guidelines for preparing the CBE end-of-paper reference list.

45h   CBE style for in-text, parenthetical citations

1   The name-and-year system

To use the name-and-year system for in-text, parenthetical citations, provide the author's name and the publication year in parentheses. Do not separate author and date with a comma.

Edwin Hubble confirmed Heber Curtis's hypothesis that spiral nebulae are galaxies of stars (Ferris 1988).

If the author's name is mentioned in the text, use only the date in parentheses.

Ferris explains that Edwin Hubble confirmed Heber Curtis's hypothesis that spiral nebulae are galaxies of stars (1988).

To cite a work by an organization or agency when no author is listed, use the corporate or group name as the author.

The Child Health Encyclopedia notes that one infant in a hundred is born with some type of heart defect (Boston Children's Medical Center 1975).

To distinguish between one of two or more works published by the same author in a single year, assign letters to the books according to the alphabetical order of the titles' first major word (excluding *a, an,* or *the*). For example, to differentiate between I. Bernard Cohen's *The Birth of the New Physics* and his *Revolution in Science,* both published in 1985, cite the first book as *Cohen 1985a* and the second as *Cohen 1985b*.

2   The number system

The number system for in-text, parenthetical citations involves using parenthetical arabic numerals to identify the sources. This system has two variations. The *order-of-first-mention* variation provides reference numbers for each work in the order in which they appear in the paper and lists the full citations in that order in the reference list. Alternatively, the *alphabetized* variation allocates in-text reference numbers for works as they appear in the alphabetized list of references at the end of the paper.

ORDER OF FIRST MENTION

According to Gregory, Einstein drew on Planck's formula as it was then used to describe oscillations of matter (1). Once Einstein applied Planck's work to light, the age of relativity, as Ferris (2) suggests, was born.

ALPHABETICAL ORDER

According to Gregory, Einstein drew on Planck's formula as it was then used to describe oscillations in matter (2). Once Einstein applied Planck's work to light, the age of relativity, as Ferris (1) suggests, was born.

Whichever method you use, use it consistently and make sure the in-text citations correspond in number to the references listed at the end of the paper.

45i   CBE style for the References list

The separate list of references that appears at the end of the paper is the reference list. This list can be titled *Literature Cited, References Cited,* or *References* and should be formatted much the same way as the reference list described in the APA documentation style (see 45f).

The arrangement of the entries in the reference list depends upon the system of in-text citation used in the paper. If the name-and-year system is used in the paper, arrange the entries in the reference list alphabetically. Take care to double-space within and between items in the reference list and begin each entry at the left margin (any subsequent lines should indent three spaces). If either of the number systems is used in the paper, each citation in the reference list will begin with the number used in the text. Follow the number with a period and two spaces to the entry (any subsequent lines should align on the first letter of the entry). (See 45f for how to organize the reference lists.)

Keep the following guidelines in mind when preparing book entries for the reference list.

1. **Number:** Assign a number to each entry only if a numbered in-text citation system is used.

2. **Author:** An author's name should appear last name first, followed by a comma and middle initials. Put a period after the author's name. (Alphabetize the reference list by the author's last name if you are using the name-and-year system of in-text citation.)

3. **Title:** Capitalize the first word of the title and any proper nouns. Separate the main title from the subtitle with a colon. Put a period after the title.

4. **Publication information:** For a book, include the city of publication and the full name of the publisher, separated from one another with a colon. Put a semicolon after the publisher's name and provide the year of publication. Put a period after the publication year.

1   Books

Book with one author

1. Ferris, T. Coming of age in the Milky Way. New York: Doubleday, Inc.; 1988.

2. Gregory, B. Inventing reality: physics as language. New York: John Wiley & Sons; 1988.

Book with two authors

3. Hazen, R. M.; Trefil, J. Science matters: achieving scientific literacy. New York: Doubleday, Inc.; 1991.

Book with a corporate author

4. Boston Children's Medical Center. Child health encyclopedia. New York: Dell Publishing Co., Inc.; 1975.

Book with an editor

5. Held, A., editor. General relativity and gravitation. New York: Plenum Press; 1977.

Two or more books by the same author published in the same year

6. Cohen, I. B. The birth of the new physics. New York: W. W. Norton and Co., Inc.; 1985a.

7. Cohen, I. B. Revolution in science. Cambridge, MA: Harvard University Press; 1985b.

2   Periodicals

When citing periodical articles, keep the following in mind.

1. **Journal titles:** Abbreviate the title of the journal unless it is one word. Do not underline it. For example, the *Journal of Molecular Biology* would be abbreviated *J. Mol. Biol.*

2. **Publication information:** Provide the volume number (in arabic numerals) followed by a colon and the inclusive page numbers (without the abbreviations *p.* or *pp.*). For journal articles, conclude with a semicolon followed by the year of publication and a final period.

Article in journal paginated by volume

8. Rickey, V. F. Isaac Newton: man, myth, and mathematics. Coll. Math. J. 18:362-389; 1987.

Article in journal paginated by issue

9. Eisenkraft, A.; Kirkpatrick, L. Atwood's marvelous machines. Quantum 3(1):42-45; 1993.

Article in a newspaper

10. Stevens, W. M. In new data on climate changes, decades, not centuries, count. The New York Times. 1993 Dec. 7:C4 (col. 1).

Other sources

Media sources

11. Kroopnick S. Treasures of the Titanic [Videocassette]. New York: Cabin Fever; 1988. VHS.

Computer disk

12. The New Grolier multimedia encyclopedia [CD-ROM program]. Danbury, CT: Electronic Publishing; 1993. 2 MB RAM, 1 MB hard drive space, Microsoft Windows 3.1 with Multimedia Extensions 2.21.

Chart

13. Department of Communicative Disorders. Duluth: University of Minnesota. Hearing, language, social skills, motor skills [chart]; 1981.

For information about variations of these formats, consult the *CBE Style Manual.* Also, see the accompanying chart that lists style manuals you can refer to for additional information on documenting sources in various disciplines.

Style Manuals in the Disciplines

Biology	CBE Style Manual Committee. *CBE Style Manual: A Guide for Authors, Editors, and Publishers in the Biological Sciences.* 5th ed., revised and expanded. Chicago: Council of Biology Editors, 1983.
Chemistry	Dodd, Janet S., ed. *The American Chemical Society Style Guide: A Manual for Authors and Editors.* Washington: ACS, 1985.
Education	National Education Association. *NEA Style Manual for Writers and Editors.* Rev. ed. Washington, DC: NEA, 1974.
General	Turabian, Kate L. *A Manual for Writers of Term Papers, Theses, and Dissertations.* 5th ed. Chicago: U of Chicago P, 1987.
	University of Chicago Press Editorial Staff. *The Chicago Manual of Style.* 14th ed. Chicago: U of Chicago P, 1993.
Law	Garner, Diane L., and Diane H. Smith. *The Complete Guide to Citing Government Information Resources: A Manual for Writers and Librarians.* Bethesda, MD: Cong. Info. Serv., 1993.
Languages and Literature	Gibaldi, Joseph. *MLA Handbook for Writers of Research Papers.* 4th ed. New York: MLA, 1995.
Mathematics	American Mathematical Society. *A Manual for Authors of Mathematical Papers.* Rev. 8th ed. Providence: AMS, 1990.
Physics	American Institute of Physics. *AIP Style Manual.* 4th ed. New York: AIP, 1990.
Psychology	*Publication Manual of the American Psychological Association.* 4th ed. Washington: APA, 1994.
Political Science	Kelley, Jean P., et al., eds. *Style Manual for Political Science.* Rev. ed. Washington: American Political Science Association, 1985.

RESEARCH HINT   Whenever you are assigned a research paper, make certain you know the documentation style your instructor expects you to use. If you have questions, ask.

If a style manual is unavailable and you are uncertain about documentation practices, ask a faculty member or a librarian for the name of a reputable journal in the field in which you are working. Follow the citation style used in the articles in that journal as a model, but do not hesitate to ask your instructor for assistance.

CHAPTER 46

Reading Two Research Essays

This chapter presents two student research essays. One is an argumentative essay by Ericka Kostka using the documentation style recommended in the *MLA Handbook for Writers of Research Papers* (MLA style). The other is an excerpt from a literature review and analytical essay by Rosette Schleifer using the documentation style recommended in the *Publication Manual of the American Psychological Association* (APA style).

Reading and analyzing these essays will help you see how writers move from their research, notes, and drafts to a properly formatted final version of the essay that is ready for an audience. Annotations accompanying the sample essays point out important features and offer advice that you can use in your essays.

See Chapter 45 for more information on MLA and APA documentation styles. See Appendix A for additional guidance on preparing the final manuscript of your essay for submission.

46a Sample research essay in MLA style

You saw in Chapters 43 and 44 how Ericka Kostka researched and started writing an essay on the gray wolf. Her complete essay follows, accompanied by detailed explanatory annotations on facing pages. Within the annotations are "WRITING NOTES" and "WRITING HINTS." The NOTES have been included to help you understand how Ericka made key decisions about organization, revision, and other matters as she composed her essay and incorporated evidence. The HINTS offer practical advice that you can apply when writing your own essays.

1

Preserving the Wild:

The Gray Wolf in Yellowstone

by

Ericka Kostka

Expos 16, Section 10

Professor Ed Miller

December 20, 1993

1. Cover page format. Provide a separate cover sheet if your instructor requests it and if you are including an outline of the paper (as Ericka does). About one-third of the way down on her cover page, Ericka gives the title of her essay, her own name (preceded by "by"), and information about the course (course number, section, instructor's name, and the date)—all centered and double spaced.

If your instructor does not require a cover sheet, place your name, course information, and date on the first page of your essay, double spaced as shown here. If you do use a cover page, you do not need to repeat all of this information on the first essay page. Instead, use the first-page format of page 1 of Ericka's essay.

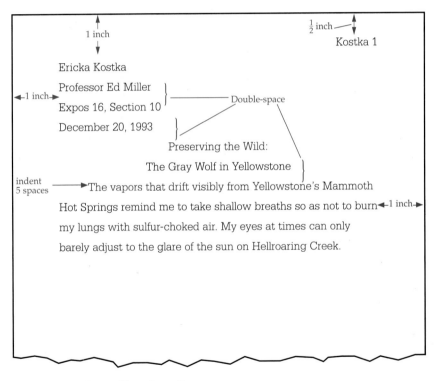

Format for First Page without Cover Page

1 inch $\frac{1}{2}$ inch

Kostka i

Outline

<u>Thesis Statement:</u> Given that the evidence strongly indicates   2

that wolf populations are important to the predator-prey balance

of nature and that repopulation can be viable for both the gray

wolf and its opponents, we should reverse the one-sided con-

cessions that were forced upon a now-endangered population

and restore wolves in the park.

  I. Wolves wandered freely throughout the Yellowstone area for   3

     two million years until the government launched an intense

     extermination effort.

    A. Because of the wolves' predatory nature, the park con-

       sidered wolves a danger to animal herds within the

       park.

    B. Folklore about bad wolves being a threat to humans

       intensified opposition to the wolf.

    C. Considerable opposition came from stockgrowers who

       blamed the wolf for all of their losses.

 II. As a result of the assault on the gray wolf over the last

     seventy-five years, the species is now classified as

     endangered.

III. Yellowstone is considered to be the prime location for the

     repopulation effort.

    A. Environmentalists estimate that the park's wildlife popu-

       lation can support several packs totaling a population of

       about one hundred wolves.

    B. The wolf's presence in the park would restore the

       predator-prey balance that was destroyed with the

       elimination of the wolf.

2. Outline format.   If your instructor asks for a final, formal outline, place it after the cover page but before the first page of your essay. Number the outline pages with lowercase roman numerals in the upper right-hand corner, placing your last name just before each page number. Center the heading "Outline" 1 inch from the top of the page.

WRITING NOTE   Ericka wrote an informal topic outline when she began organizing and drafting her essay (see 44g-2); that outline guided her as she wrote to clarify her ideas and eventually evolved into the formal sentence outline required as part of the assignment.

3. Outline content.   Ericka includes her thesis statement in her outline so that readers can recognize the logical relationships among the parts of her essay. Each main division of her outline (identified by roman numerals) relates to the thesis statement; subdivisions (identified by capital letters and arabic numerals) relate to the main divisions. The thesis also appears in the second paragraph of Ericka's essay (see p. 1 of her essay). (For more on constructing outlines, see 1f-1.)

Kostka ii

IV. Concerned that the return of the predator will bring economic disaster upon them, sheep and cattle ranchers have
lobbied to gain political support from officials in the states
surrounding the park.

   A. Opponents to repopulation fear having no recourse
against wolves that might stray from the park and
threaten their livestock.

   B. Opponents seek to remove the wolf from the endangered species list.

      1. Wolves that wander out of the park could be shot if
no longer classified as endangered.

      2. Some biologists regard declassification as an accept-
able compromise to get past a political stalemate on
the issue of wolf repopulation.

V. Removing the gray wolf from federal protection could only
be a hindrance to recovery.

   A. It could grease the political gears, but at the expense of
an open season on still-endangered animals.

   B. Only under federal protection will wolves have a chance
of surviving in the inevitable event that their pioneering
instincts lead them into the outer zone of recovery.

VI. Reintroducing wolves as an experimental population, as
permitted under a 1986 amendment to the Endangered
Species Act, is more acceptable than taking wolves off the
endangered species list.

   A. Wolves would remain under federal protection from the
public, while allowing federal agents to remove or destroy wolves that become a problem for ranchers.

     B. Collaring wolves with radio transmitters will allow federal control over animals that wander outside the park's boundaries.

     C. Stockgrowers can be reimbursed for livestock damage.

          1. Compensation can be paid from a $100,000 fund established by the Defenders of Wildlife.

          2. Based on losses in Minnesota under a similar wolf-recovery program, losses and costs will be minimal.

VII. Political opposition runs counter to popular support for wolf repopulation.

     A. The effectiveness of the park's educational program is being undercut by uninformed political opponents.

     B. The public strongly favors wolf repopulation.

1 inch

$\frac{1}{2}$ inch

Kostka 1

Double-space

Preserving the Wild:

The Gray Wolf in Yellowstone   4

1   The vapors that drift visibly from Yellowstone's Mammoth   5

◄—1 inch—► Hot Springs remind me to take shallow breaths so as not to burn

my lungs with sulfur-choked air. My eyes at times can only

barely adjust to the glare of the sun on Hellroaring Creek. A sin-

gle stroke of blue crayon on paper was my childhood represen-

tation of the flat plane above what was to me Massachusetts

sky. I never was able to make accommodations in my sketch-

book for the western sky arching overhead, encasing its land in

a dome more brilliant than crystal.

indent
5 letter   **2**   Adjustments are invariably in order when people and na-   6
spaces
ture come into contact. My purpose for venturing to Yellowstone

was to experience its wild beauty, so I adapted myself to it. But

when we hold our own intentions primary, the concessions can

tilt harshly the other way. The elimination of the gray wolf from   7

Yellowstone National Park during the early part of this century

marked a major ecological concession to the interests of stock-

growers. Over the past decade, a controversial proposal to re-

populate Yellowstone with wolves in accordance with the

Endangered Species Act has met with objections similar to the

justifications originally given for eradicating wolves from the

Rocky Mountains. These objections range from lingering unsup-

ported superstitions about the wolf to economic concerns that

an effective recovery plan should address. Given that the evi-   8

dence strongly indicates that wolf populations are important to

nature's predator-prey balance and that repopulation can be

viable for both the gray wolf and its opponents, we should re-

verse the one-sided concessions that were forced upon a now-

endangered population and restore wolves in the park.

4. **Title.** Select a title that gives readers a clear sense of your topic and that sparks their curiosity. Ericka combines a general sense of her topic ("Preserving the Wild") with a more specific reference to the problem she explores in her essay in a subtitle ("The Gray Wolf in Yellowstone"). Readers can infer from her title that preserving the wolf is important to Ericka and to her argument.

5. **Paper format.** The margins of the paper are 1 inch all around. Because Ericka includes a title page, she begins the first page of her paper with the title typed 1 inch from the top of the page (always double-space a title of more than one line) and double spaced to the first line of text. The title is not enclosed in quotation marks or underlined. The entire essay is double spaced. All paragraphs indent five letter spaces. Pages are numbered consecutively beginning with the first page of the essay; place page numbers in the upper right-hand corner, following your last name, one-half inch from the top of the page.

6. **Beginning the essay.** A good beginning or introduction for an essay entices readers to keep reading, foreshadows the development of the rest of the essay, and states the thesis (see 9a on beginning paragraphs).

WRITING NOTE   Ericka's beginning consists of two paragraphs. She starts on a personal note in the first paragraph, but in the third sentence of the second paragraph, she shifts to a more objective presentation of the topic she will address in her essay: reintroducing wolves into Yellowstone.

WRITING HINT   Research essays need not include personal experience as evidence, but they can when such experience establishes the writer's commitment to the subject. However, all research essays need to be grounded in evidence derived from other, more objective sources (books, articles, and so forth). Ericka's shift to a more objective stance suggests the thoroughness of her research and gives readers a preview of what follows in the middle of her essay. (To see how Ericka selected a topic of interest to her, see 43b.)

7. **Audience considerations.** When Ericka started writing, she thought about what her audience needed to know in order to understand her essay. Because she was writing for an audience of generalists who may have only passing knowledge of the debate over wolves in Yellowstone, she knew she needed to provide some explanation. Had she been writing for an audience of specialists, she might have omitted this brief overview. Ericka also considered how to persuade her audience of the reasonableness of her thesis. She shows an awareness of the various interest groups involved in the debate over reintroducing wolves. (See 1d and 44f for more on considering audience.)

8. **Thesis placement.** Ericka strategically places her thesis at the end of her introduction for two reasons: her thesis has the most impact in that position, and it helps prepare her readers for the argument that immediately follows. (To see how Ericka arrived at her thesis, see 44e.)

WRITING HINT   The thesis need not always fall at the end of the introduction, but that terminal position is the place of greatest emphasis.

Kostka 2

3   Wolves wandered freely throughout Yellowstone for two **9**
million years until the government launched an intensive exter- **10**
mination effort. Because of their predatory nature, wolves were
regarded as "a decided menace to the herds of elk, deer, mountain sheep, and antelope" (McNamee 12). Government hunters
used guns, traps, and poisons during their war on Yellowstone **11**
wolves between 1915 and 1926. The campaign ended in 1926
when the National Park Service, established in 1916, succeeded
in eliminating the gray wolf from Yellowstone. The charter called
for the Park Service "to conserve the scenery and the natural
historic objects and wildlife . . . and to provide the enjoyment of **12**
the same in such manner and by such means as will leave them
unimpaired for the enjoyment of future generations" (qtd. in
Williams 32). Although there have been a few sightings of a lone
wolf over the past sixty years in the area, it is widely held by
park officials and biologists that a viable population of wolves no
longer exists in the park. Candace Savage, who has for years **13**
been studying the demise of the wolf in North America, points
out the irony inherent in the loss: "Although the wolf has the **14**
greatest natural range of any mammal except ourselves, it is
now extinct over much of its former range" (29).

4   Centuries of folklore made a powerful case against the wolf
and fed a lack of sympathy for its plight. Wolves have been depicted as vicious from Brothers Grimm tales to old-timers' yarns.
These accounts wrongly paint the wolf as a danger to humans.
Ted Williams argues that organizations such as the Common
Man Institute provide inflammatory information to hunters and **15**
ranchers "which they, their elected officials, and their lobby
groups trustingly quote in public" (41). Dick Mader, founder of
the institute, has compared the wolf to mass murderer

9. From outline to essay.   Paragraphs 3–5 constitute the first section of the middle of Ericka's essay and correspond to part I of her outline (see p. i).

WRITING NOTE   In paragraphs 3–5, Ericka provides important background information about how the wolf became an endangered species, but she also renders judgments and prepares readers for the argument that she will offer in support of her thesis.

10. Quoting sources.   In paragraph 3, Ericka uses three quotations from sources to provide historical background and lend authority to her argument.

WRITING NOTE   Ericka uses the first two quotations because they highlight an interesting contradiction between the park's presumed mission of preserving wildlife and its official stance regarding the wolf as a "menace." Notice how smoothly Ericka blends the quoted words into her own sentences.

11. Parenthetical citation, author not named in text.   Because Ericka does not introduce the quotation by naming the author, she places the author's name and the page number in parentheses immediately after the quotation.

12. Altered quotations.   The ellipses used in the quotation indicate that Williams omitted words from the park's mission statement when he quoted it. (See 44d-3 on quoting with ellipses.)

13. Common knowledge.   The information about the "viable population of wolves" is common knowledge (see 44j-1). Almost every article Ericka cites about wolves at Yellowstone confirms the demise of the wolf in the park. She does not have to document what is generally known in the field.

14. Parenthetical citation, author named in text.   Because Ericka introduces the quotation by naming the author, she gives only the page number in the parenthetical citation.

15. Quoting effectively and for impact.   Ericka effectively uses Ted Williams's assessment of those who oppose wolves. She also makes good use of Dick Mader's words to expose his bias and undercut his claims. Ericka had to work through a few drafts to integrate the source material and eliminate the awkward blending of the words of her two sources. Compare this early draft with the final version in paragraph 4 of her essay.

EARLY DRAFT

These accounts wrongly paint the wolf as a danger to humans. Dick Mader, founder of the Common Man Institute "think tank that funnels information to western hunters and ranchers and which they, their elected officials, and their lobby groups trustingly quote in public," has compared the wolf to mass murderer Ted Bundy (Williams 41). Tales Dick Mader heard as a child helped to form his fearful perceptions of wolves. "As a kid," Mader recalls, "I had heard them old-timers tell

Kostka 3

Ted Bundy. "As a kid," Mader recalls, "I had heard them old-
timers tell about these wolf kills. . . . When I was a kid, the older
people were absolutely one thousand percent agin' the wolf"
(qtd. in Williams 41). In spite of this image that the wolf is a
threat to humans, experts agree that there has never been an attack by a nonrabid wolf on a human in North America (Gallagher   **16**
38). The same cannot be said of many popular dog breeds.

5   More divisive than the imagined threats to humans are   **17**
the threats that predatory wolves pose to cattle and sheep that
ranchers rely on for their livelihood. It was for this reason that
wolves were systematically hunted down and eliminated from
many western regions. Though some of the perceived threat has
been exaggerated, wolves proved an easy target for human frustration. Journalist John Skow relates that ranchers who lost their   **18**
entire herds to harsh winters irrationally spent large amounts of
money and energy to take vengeance on wolves. Skow reminds
us that "Barry Lopez, in his haunting book Of Wolves and Men,
tells of wolves drenched with gasoline and set afire, wolves
pulled apart by horses." Notes Skow, "You can't dismember an
April blizzard" (13).

6   As a result of the assault on the gray wolf over the last   **19**
seventy-five years, the species is now classified as endangered.
Given that there are but 1,200 wolves in Minnesota and 50 in
Wisconsin and Michigan, "if a new disease hit these populations, it could spell the end of the species in the continental
United States" (Begley 74). The Endangered Species Act of 1973
mandates that federal agencies, such as the Park Service, take
"all methods and procedures necessary" to restore species that
have been driven to virtual extinction (qtd. in Williams 32). In
accordance with this act, a plan for wolf repopulation has been

about these wolf kills. . . . When I was a kid, the older people were absolutely one thousand percent agin' the wolf" (qtd. in Williams 41).

Ericka's revised paragraph clarifies Williams's argument and makes it easier to see how she uses both Williams and Mader to support her claims.

WRITING HINT   Introducing quotations properly not only helps clarify the meaning of borrowed material but also makes your paragraphs easier to read and understand. (See When to Quote in 44d-3 and 44i for more on integrating source material.)

16. **Engaging readers by using understatement.**   In the last sentence in paragraph 4, Ericka implies that some dogs are more vicious than wolves. She seems to be asking, "Why all the fuss about the threat of wolves?" The sentence undercuts the reliability of the folklore about wolves.

WRITING HINT   Sometimes it is more effective to imply something than to say it straight out, thereby inviting readers to infer and become involved in figuring out the writer's judgment.

17. **The topic sentence.**   Each of Ericka's paragraphs is tight and well constructed. She includes a topic sentence that states the paragraph's main idea so her readers know where the paragraph is going and how it relates to her thesis. The paragraph develops this main idea.

WRITING NOTE   Ericka often places her topic sentences at or near the beginning of paragraphs, as she does in paragraph 5.

18. **Summarizing and quoting.**   Citing authorities can strengthen your case and convince readers of your point. Here Ericka makes good use of two authorities on wolves in order to undercut the claims of the stockgrowers.

WRITING NOTE   Ericka first summarizes John Skow to capture the essence of his remarks. She then follows with Skow's exact words (on a second wolf authority, Barry Lopez) because these ironic and compelling quotations reinforce her idea about wolves being used as scapegoats.

19. **From outline to essay.**   Paragraph 6 constitutes part II of Ericka's outline. It is also a **transitional paragraph** that points back to previous paragraphs and prepares readers for the argument that follows.

WRITING NOTE   Ericka wants to alert readers to a shift from earlier paragraphs on history and background to the upcoming paragraphs about the Park Service's mandate.

Kostka 4

proposed by the Northern Rocky Mountain Wolf Recovery Team
established by the U.S. Fish and Wildlife Service. Wolf recovery is
strongly supported by the Environmental Defense Fund (EDF-Letter).

7   Yellowstone is considered to be the prime location for the   **20**
repopulation effort. American's leading wolf expert, L. David   **21**
Mech, explains that Yellowstone "is a place that literally begs to
have wolves. It's teeming with prey" (qtd. in Williams 32). Mech
believes that wolves would help rebalance the park's ecosystem.   **22**
With its vast terrain and abundant populations of elk, deer,
bighorn sheep, and bison, Yellowstone is definitely ideal wolf
country. Environmentalists estimate that the park's wildlife
population can support several packs totaling a population of
about one hundred wolves (Satchell 29).

8   More appropriate than focusing on the park's ability to   **23**
support the wolves is considering the critical role that the wolf
will play for the area's ecosystem. The wolf's presence would
restore the predator-prey balance that was destroyed with its
elimination. At present, Yellowstone's few grizzlies and coyotes
cannot contain the exploding populations of their hoofed prey.
Without evolutionary pressure, "the inflated ungulate [hoofed]   **24**
herds are overgrazing and destroying the range" (Gallagher 37).   **25**
There is little wisdom to allowing the herds to multiply in the
absence of a predator, only to starve due to overpopulation. Far
from posing an unfair threat to the hoofed herds of Yellowstone,
wolves would restore a natural cycle of population control.

9   John Weaver's optimism about the biological suitability of
Yellowstone for wolf recovery is far more reasonable than any
confidence in the political climate surrounding such action.
Concerned that the return of the predator will bring economic
disaster upon them, sheep and cattle ranchers have lobbied for
political support from officials in the states surrounding the

20. From outline to essay. Paragraphs 7 and 8 constitute part III of Ericka's outline. In them, she presents the environmentalists' point of view.

21. Use of authority. In paragraph 5 Ericka used authority to undercut her opposition (see annotation 18). In paragraph 6, she used an authority from an environmentalist organization she had located on the Internet. In paragraph 7, she also uses authority to strengthen her position favoring the reintroduction of wolves.

WRITING HINT   Strengthen your case by citing authorities, but be sure to include their credentials as Ericka does for L. David Mech, "America's leading wolf expert" (see 44i on incorporating evidence).

22. Parenthetical citation for an indirect source. Ericka found this quotation of Mech's in an article by Williams. To acknowledge that she is citing one writer's report of someone else's words, she uses the abbreviation *qtd. in* (meaning "quoted in"). In Ericka's Works Cited entry for this quotation, Mech is not cited.

WRITING HINT   When citing indirectly always name the author of the original source either in your paragraph, as Ericka does, or in a parenthetical citation. Placing the authority's name and credentials in the text of the essay is often more effective than placing the authority's name within parentheses.

23. Evaluating evidence. Ericka relies primarily on articles written by journalists and researchers for her evidence. In paragraphs 7 and 8, she uses three of those sources (articles by Williams in *Audubon,* by Satchell in *U.S. News & World Report,* and by Gallagher in *Mother Earth*) to present the environmentalists' case.

WRITING NOTE   Ericka realizes that two of her sources are environmental publications that may appear biased. To strengthen her claim in her paragraphs about the need for predators, she provides factual information; to keep the presentation balanced, she uses a summary from an environmental publication and a quotation from a more neutral publication. This fair and reasonable presentation makes Ericka's point clear: reintroducing the wolf makes ecological sense.

WRITING HINT   You will need to decide what sources to consider (see 44b), what sources to read critically (see 44c), and then what evidence to incorporate into your essay (see 44i). As a general rule, use evidence that will support your thesis and help your readers understand it. But do not ignore contradictory evidence.

24. Altering quotations. Using brackets, Ericka provides a definition of the unusual word *ungulate.*

25. Reflecting. Your research essay should not be a compilation of the ideas of other writers and researchers. It should contain what you think about your sources. After you have cited evidence, be sure to reflect on how that evidence supports your idea. Your reflections make the essay your own (see 44d-4 and 44i-2 on reflecting).

WRITING NOTE   Notice how effectively Ericka ends paragraph 8; she restates and reflects on her idea about the need for wolves in the park.

Kostka 5

park. They have emphasized their fear of having no recourse   **26**

against wolves that might stray from the park and threaten live-

stock. Bob Budd, director of the Wyoming Stockgrowers' Asso-

ciation in Cheyenne, explains the concern:

> We're not antiwildlife, we're the people who've pre-   **27**
>
> served the open spaces that provide their food and
>
> habitat, but we don't want wolves at Yellowstone for
>
> the simple reason that there's no way to control
>
> them when they inevitably move outside the park.
>
> There are no legal mechanisms in place that specify
>
> what will happen when we have some stock killed
>
> by wolves. (qtd. in Gallagher 41)

The legal mechanism that ranchers and their lobbyists are seek-   **28**

ing is removal of the wolf from the endangered species list. If

the wolf were declassified to "threatened" or removed from the

list entirely, wolves that kill livestock could be killed.

10   Joe Helle, the influential spokesman for the National Wool

Growers Association, has indicated that wolf recovery would be

acceptable only if unrestricted killing of wolves were permitted

in the outer zone of the proposed management areas. Under the

recovery guidelines, wolves would have complete protection in

Zone One, Yellowstone Park and four adjacent wilderness areas,

and equal protection with other interests so that management

decisions could go either way in Zone Two, the national forest

lands surrounding Yellowstone. Beyond these areas, in Zone

Three, ranching and other interests would take priority over

wolves. As endangered animals, wolves could be captured and

relocated from Zone Two or Three by wildlife management offi-

cials should they come into conflict with other interests. They

could not, however, be killed either by officials or by the public

26. **From outline to essay.** Paragraphs 9 and 10 constitute part IV of Ericka's outline. In these paragraphs she presents the concerns of the stockgrowers. As Ericka presents their argument, she also notes the conditions they will insist on if wolves are reintroduced into Yellowstone.

WRITING NOTE　In paragraphs 9 and 10, Ericka offers a clear and logical presentation of the stockgrowers' concerns, showing that she understands both sides in this complicated debate. She also begins to intensify her argument and to use information about the Endangered Species Act. By stating the stockgrowers' conditions for accepting wolf repopulation, she effectively limits their objections and lays the groundwork for the solution she offers later in the essay.

27. **Incorporating a long quotation.** Quotations longer than four typed lines must be indented ten spaces from the left margin and set off from the rest of the essay. Do not enclose these block quotations in quotation marks. Double-space, and place the parenthetical citation at the end of the block quotation after the closing punctuation. (Place parenthetical citations for shorter quotations within the sentence, before the closing punctuation.)

　　Introducing long quotations. To introduce the block quotation within paragraph 9, Ericka states the name of her source and his credentials, followed by a colon. She makes it clear that her source is an authority; it is also clear where the source material begins (after the colon) and where it ends (just before the parenthetical citation).

WRITING HINT　Use long quotations sparingly because too many of them interrupt the flow of your essay and give the impression that you are relying more on your sources than on your own thinking and reflection.

28. **Reflecting.** Ericka's ending for paragraph 9 is effective. Instead of concluding with Budd's long quotation, she reflects on it, putting his concerns in perspective and highlighting the consequences of declassification. She ends the paragraph with her own concerns rather than with Budd's.

Kostka 6

under their present classification. Should wolves become declassified, they could expect no federal protection in Zone
Three. Such action would allow private citizens to shoot, trap,
or poison wolves that stray into this outer zone (Cauble 26-27).

11   Some biologists regard declassification as an acceptable   **29**
compromise to get past a political stalemate on the issue. I fear
that this would set a dangerous precedent. The species is endangered, and the Endangered Species Act mandates that recovery plans be in place to restore the wolf population. Removing
the gray wolf from federal protection could only be a hindrance
to recovery. Yes, it could grease the political gears, but at the
expense of an open season on still-endangered animals.

12   Bill Schneider claims there is little doubt that most wolves,   **30**
given their nomadic nature and their propensity to travel hun-
dreds of miles, will eventually reach the grazing lands of the
outer zone. "As surely as the wolf howls at night, this will happen," Schneider believes (9). But it would be self-defeating to kill
wolves who stray into Zone Three when they do so as a condi-
tion of a recovery act. Only under federal protection will wolves   **31**
have a chance of surviving in the inevitable event that their pio-
neering instincts lead them into the outer zone of recovery.

13   I find the alternative compromise of reintroducing wolves   **32**
as an experimental population, as allowed for under a 1986
amendment to the Endangered Species Act (Parnall 83), more
acceptable. This would leave wolves under federal protection
from the public, while allowing agents to remove or destroy
wolves that become an excessive problem for ranchers. Collaring wolves will permit effective control over nuisance animals.
As wildlife biologist John Weaver explains, radio tracking   **33**
collars could be equipped with "remote-controlled tranquilizing

29. From outline to essay.   Paragraphs 11 and 12 constitute part V of Ericka's outline. In them, she argues against declassification and asserts that the wolf will need federal protection to survive.

Using personal pronouns.   In paragraphs 11 and 12, Ericka begins to present her own solution to the wolf problem using the personal pronoun "I" for the first time since her introduction to the essay.

WRITING HINT   Using "I" in a formal, objective research essay must always be weighed carefully. Does it show acceptance of responsibility for one's own ideas or does it seem too personal and inappropriate? Ericka's use of "I" is effective. Her readers know just where she stands and why, and her objective tone is not undermined. Consult your instructor about using "I" in formal research writing.

30. Being reasonable.   In earlier paragraphs, Ericka acknowledges the legitimacy of the stockgrowers' claims. Careful and reasonable consideration of opposing points of view can only strengthen her argument. In paragraph 12, Ericka reiterates the reasonableness of the stockgrowers' concern but objects to their solution, pointing to the contradiction of "killing" wolves as part of a "recovery" plan.

31. Ericka's solution.   The final sentence of paragraph 12 stirs readers' interest as it provides a transition to Ericka's solution to the wolf repopulation problem; everything in the essay has been leading to this solution, and everything that follows will justify and explain it.

32. From outline to essay.   Paragraphs 13–15 constitute part VI of Ericka's outline. In these three important paragraphs, she argues for federal protection of the wolf—her solution to the wolf repopulation problem.

33. Combining summary and quotation to eliminate a block quotation.   In paragraph 13 Ericka combines summary and quotation. She quotes only the part of Weaver's explanation that she cannot summarize effectively. But as you can see in an excerpt from an earlier draft, Ericka originally quoted more of Weaver. She decided to revise this draft to eliminate the block quotation because the language in it was not cogent or memorable, and she suspected that she might be using too many long quotations. Compare this draft with the final version.

EARLY DRAFT

Wildlife biologist John Weaver made this observation:

> Each wolf released in Yellowstone would be wearing a radio collar, enabling researchers to keep tabs on its wanderings. The collars may be equipped with remote-controlled tranquilizing darts, a new device that could greatly facilitate the capture of problem animals. (Cauble 29)

Under this proposal, wolves would be subject to reasonable federal control, rather than to the vengeance of ranchers whose hatred tends to be deeply rooted.

(See also annotation 27 on incorporating long quotations.)

Kostka 7

darts . . . that could greatly facilitate the capture of problem animals" (qtd. in Cauble 29). Under this proposal, wolves would be
subject to reasonable federal control, rather than to the
vengeance of ranchers whose hatred for them tends to be
deeply rooted.

14   Because wolves will probably kill livestock in their ventures   **34**
onto grazing lands, economic damage suffered by ranchers is an
important concern. Although I believe it is unreasonable to allow
a rancher to kill an endangered animal, I believe that ranchers
should be compensated for losses as part of the program. Reim-
bursement for livestock damage is an economically sound provi-
sion of recovery. The cost of such compensation would be quite
low, considering how few stock animals would likely be lost to
wolves. Ranchers' predictions of extensive losses tend to be
greatly exaggerated. In Minnesota, which boasts a successful
recovery program and an established wolf population, only one-
fifth of 1 percent of the 12,000 farms lose even one animal to   **35**
wolves in any year (Begley 74). Ordinarily, only about ten animals
are killed each year by wolves (Edwards 378).[1]   **36**

15   The Yellowstone area has less livestock than Minnesota,
and will have fewer wolves. Stock losses can therefore be expected to be even smaller than those affecting Minnesota farmers (Gallagher 41). In the rare instances that stock damage
occurs, ranchers will be compensated from a $100,000 fund es-
tablished by the Defenders of Wildlife (Skow 13). I believe that
a compensation program similar to that used in Minnesota is a
more direct and consistent way to deal with any economic loss
that may affect western sheep and cattle growers as a result
of wolf recovery than allowing ranchers to kill an endangered
species. Diane Edwards, writing in Science News, explains that

34. **Evaluating evidence.**   As Ericka explains her solution to the wolf repopulation problem in paragraphs 14 and 15, she cites five sources, more than she has used in any other section of her essay. This was a calculated decision on her part. She clearly has her opponents, the stockgrowers, in mind as she brings together information from these sources. Notice how her use of evidence is sensitive and fair even as she rebuts the stockgrowers' argument.

WRITING HINT   Ericka evaluated her evidence in order to come to a decision about how best to use it to suit her purpose and make her point. You will also need to assess your evidence and decide about how much of it to use and where to place it.

35. **Incorporating numerical data.**   Ericka's discussion of the Minnesota program, which begins here in paragraph 14 and continues in paragraph 15, involves the introduction of numerical data or statistics that serve her argument in two ways: (1) the data suggest that her proposal is reasonable because it has worked successfully elsewhere; and (2) the data allow her to further undercut the stockgrowers' exaggerated predictions about losses. Such statistical data can be persuasive because the numbers are verifiable and carry scientific weight.

WRITING HINT   Numerical data can be integrated into the text, or they can be presented in table, chart, or graph form when their complexity or importance warrants an illustration within the text. Whatever way you decide to present your data, introduce them as you would other material from sources and document them properly.

36. **Using an explanatory note.**   The superscript arabic number 1 in paragraph 14 refers readers to an explanatory note that provides additional information about the Minnesota experiment; the note appears at the end of Ericka's essay on a page titled *Notes*.

WRITING HINT   Use explanatory notes when you want to provide incidental information, whether definitions or explanations, that would be disruptive if placed in the body of your essay. (See 45b for guidelines on preparing explanatory notes in MLA style.)

Kostka 8

biologists "have set a goal of 10 breeding pairs" producing off-   **37**
spring for three consecutive years (379). Declassification must
only be allowed after the recovery goal has been reached and
the gray wolf is no longer considered to be on the verge of extinction. Until then, stock loss can be matched with cash.

16   Volatile western politics has provided an enduring obsta-   **38**
cle to a realistic public image of the wolf. Political pressure has
hindered the park's educational programs on the issue of wolf
recovery. Influential members of Congress from surrounding
states have criticized the park's efforts as being biased in favor
of repopulation. Montana Representative Pat Williams further
questioned "the appropriateness of providing the public with
information . . . about wolf reintroduction" (qtd. in Williams 38).
Our national parks are supposed to provide information to visitors about aspects of the ecosystem. I would certainly expect
the park to have a bias in favor of reintroduction, given that
its function is to preserve wildlife for future generations. Yellowstone should uphold the interests of the wild, not those of the
prevailing political view. But the park buckled under the political pressure. According to Ted Williams, the park not only   **39**
stopped mailing educational material, it also canceled its slide
show on the wolf, stopped writing about restoring the wolf population, and prohibited selling wolf posters at the park (38).

17   Political figures opposing park education programs find
them to be biased because accurate information and evidence
on the subject support repopulation. These officials, with an eye
to special interest groups, would prefer the public to be exposed
to the unsupported rhetoric that they offer as testimony on the
wolf, testimony such as Montana Representative Ron Marlenee's declaration that wolves are "cockroaches" (qtd. in

37. Revising.   Always think about the best way to present evidence to your audience; revise to clarify or improve your presentation.

WRITING NOTE   Compare the way Ericka incorporated Edwards's quotation in an earlier draft with her revised use of it in paragraph 15 of the final draft.

EARLY DRAFT

Biologists "have set a goal of 10 breeding pairs": producing offspring for three consecutive years (Edwards 379). Declassification must only be. . . .

Ericka decided to revise the introduction to the Edwards quotation. She named Edwards and the source (*Science News*) in the text rather than parenthetically, sensing that such a revision would make the quotation more persuasive.

38. From outline to essay.   Paragraphs 16–18 constitute part VII of Ericka's outline. In these paragraphs she argues against the political opposition and points to the public's approval of wolves in the park.

39. Incorporating a paraphrase and avoiding plagiarism.   Use a paraphrase when you want to convey in your own words the essence of a source and a sense of its structure or order (see 44d-2).

WRITING NOTE   Ericka makes effective use of Williams's emphatic order in this paraphrase that concludes paragraph 16. Realizing that she needed evidence to support her contention about the park caving in to political pressure, she took her paraphrase from the following note card:

Williams, "Waiting for Wolves," p. 38   Effects of
                                                            Politics

P / As a result of political opposition, the Park Service stopped mailing
educational material about wolves, canceled its slide show on the wolf,
stopped writing about restoring the wolf population, and prohibited selling
wolf posters in the park. / P

// This is the essence of Williams's case about the effects of politics on the
educational program. He makes this case convincingly, citing considerable
details. No hesitation on my part to accept these conclusions. //

Notice how Ericka wove the material into her paragraph. The text flows smoothly, and you can distinguish her ideas from those of her source. However, it took Ericka a few drafts to get it right. When working on an earlier version of the paragraph, she double-checked the paraphrase against her note card and discovered that she had not properly acknowledged Williams and that she was combining her reflections with his ideas. She was running the risk of unintentionally plagiarizing from her source. Here is the first draft of the paragraph:

Kostka 9

Williams 36). Ted Williams reports that despite lack of evidence   **40**
to support his claim, Wyoming Senator Alan Simpson "has asserted that wolves eat people" (Williams 36). Misinformation
about the wolf, even among elected officials, makes it especially
critical that the National Park Service adhere to its educational
efforts so the public can make informed judgments.

18   Despite political pressure that has curbed the National
Park Service's educational programs, public support for wolf recovery is high. A recent poll of the park's visitors showed that
74 percent agreed "having wolves in the park would improve the
Yellowstone experience," and 60 percent agreed "if wolves can't
return to Yellowstone on their own, then we should put them
back ourselves" (McNamee).[2] The public has the right idea.

19   Returning wolves to Yellowstone would return natural bal-   **41**
ance to its ecosystem and spare the gray wolf from endanger-
ment. In the words of wildlife ecologist Renee Askins, "If we
can't preserve wildness in Yellowstone, where can we preserve
it?" (qtd. in Skow 13). Even Joe Helle, a vocal critic of the repopulation program, has indicated that he does not object to the concept of recovery. "If wolves were declassified in Zone Three and
if the [zone boundaries] were acceptable," he says, "we probably
wouldn't oppose reintroduction of wolves in Yellowstone" (qtd. in
Cauble 27). Helle's words give hope that the stalemate between
restorationists and their opponents might be broken through a
carefully designed recovery program that would offer stockgrowers economic compensation for losses but would not allow
wholesale killing of wolves that wander out of the park's boundaries. If ranchers and restorationists show willingness to make
compromises, we could make room for the wolf to join us again
under the embracing western sky. We certainly ought to.[3]   **42**

The park, however, buckled under the pressure and stopped mailing educational packets. It also canceled its slide show on the wolf, stopped writing about restoring the wolf population, and prohibited the selling of pro-wolf-restoration posters at the park (Williams 38).

To address these problems, Ericka revised to introduce the paraphrase with the words *According to Ted Williams* and she replaced Williams's words with her own.

40. Working with indirect citations.   See annotation 22, which explains indirect citations. Notice here, in paragraph 17, the difference in the citation for Marlenee's declaration and Simpson's assertion. Williams actually quoted Marlenee in his article; he did not quote Simpson.

41. Ending the essay.   An essay's ending should provide a fresh, closing perspective rather than merely restate the thesis and supporting points (see 9b on ending paragraphs).

WRITING NOTE   Ericka's ending is especially effective because she brings in an ecologist and a stockgrower from sources she has already cited to provide a final perspective on her thesis—proposing the reintroduction of wolves into Yellowstone. She also reminds readers that she seeks consensus between the "restorationists and their opponents." Hers is a plea for reasonable compromise under that "embracing western sky" that she introduces in paragraph 1 of her essay and that she returns to so skillfully here in her ending.

42. Using reference notes.   The superscript arabic numbers 2 and 3 refer to reference notes that appear on a page titled Notes at the end of Ericka's essay. Reference notes refer to supplementary sources that can provide additional information for interested readers. (See 45b on preparing notes in MLA style.)

Kostka 10

Notes

¹ L. David Mech believes that public attitudes about the   **43**
wolf have "changed dramatically" over the last decade or so.
Mech managed the recovery program in Minnesota, and he
makes this strong claim: "Even Minnesota farmers, some of
whom actually sustain livestock losses to wolves, showed surprising tolerance of the animal." Mech's survey showed that
"only 24 percent" thought wolves should be forced to live elsewhere than Northern Minnesota.

² In the <u>Harvard Environmental Law Review</u>, Harry R.   **44**
Bader argues convincingly that public support is crucial to effective implementation of recovery plans; he is especially thorough in his analysis of the legal obligations associated with the
recovery plan for reintroducing wolves into Yellowstone. See
Harry R. Bader, "Wolf Conservation: The Importance of Following Endangered Species Recovery Plans," the <u>Harvard Environmental Law Review</u> 13 (1989): 517-33.

³ Since I completed my research, Rick McIntyre has pub-   **45**
lished an extensive study of the battle over reintroducing
wolves into our national parks. He confirms much of what I have
written and provides a comprehensive examination of the larger
problem across America. See Rick McIntyre, <u>A Society of
Wolves: National Parks and the Battle over the Wolf</u> (Stillwater:
Voyageur, 1993) 106-09.

43. Explanatory notes. Use explanatory notes for incidental comments or for information that does not relate directly to your thesis or idea and that would be disruptive if placed in the body of your essay. You can use these notes to clarify, illustrate, or further explain your idea; to provide definitions; and to identify individuals and events.

WRITING NOTE   Ericka chose to include this additional information in an explanatory note because it is related to the topic of her paragraph (see paragraph 14 of the essay), but it does not address directly the paragraph's main idea. Including the information in the paragraph would have been disruptive.

WRITING HINT   Always add a Works Cited entry for sources discussed in explanatory notes. The source for the note (the foreword to *Wolves*) appears in the Works Cited list under Mech's name (see annotation 45 for more on formatting notes).

44. Reference notes. Use reference notes to direct readers to additional supplementary sources.

WRITING NOTE   Ericka included these sources because they confirmed her research. She wanted her readers to be aware of the sources.

WRITING HINT   Be aware that you need to provide a Works Cited entry for each source that appears in the reference notes (as Ericka does on p. 11 of her essay). Note, however, that the format for citing a source in the reference note in MLA style differs from the format for citing that source in the Works Cited list (see 45b–c for details).

45. Formatting explanatory and reference notes. To identify these notes in the body of your essay, insert a superscript arabic number immediately after the term or passage you wish to comment about, as Ericka does on pages 7 and 9 of her essay. That number corresponds to this listing of notes placed on a separate page at the end of the essay. Head this page *Notes* (centered, 1 inch below the top of the page) and place the page or pages immediately before your Works Cited list. The first line of each note should be indented five spaces, and a superscript number followed by a space should mark the beginning of the note. Double-space within and between the notes and place them in numerical order. (See 45b for more details on using and formatting explanatory and reference notes.)

Kostka 11

Works Cited   **46**

Bader, Harry R. "Wolf Conservation: The Importance of Following   **47**
    Endangered Species Recovery Plans." <u>Harvard Environmen-</u>
    <u>tal Law Review</u> 13 (1989): 517-33.

Begley, Sharon. "Crying Wolf in Yellowstone." <u>Newsweek</u> 16 Dec.   **48**
    1985: 74.

Cauble, Christopher. "Return of the Native." <u>National Parks</u> July-   **49**
    Aug. 1986: 24-29.

Edwards, Diane. "Recall of the Wild Wolf." <u>Science News</u> 13 June
    1987: 378-79.

Gallagher, Winifred. "Return of the Wild." <u>Mother Earth</u> Sept.-Oct.
    1990: 34+.

Lopez, Barry. <u>Of Wolves and Men</u>. New York: Scribner's, 1978.   **50**

McIntyre, Rick. <u>A Society of Wolves: National Parks and the Battle</u>
    <u>over the Wolf</u>. Stillwater: Voyageur, 1993.

McNamee, Tom. "Yellowstone's Missing Element." <u>Audubon</u> Jan.
    1986: 12+.

Mech, L. David. Foreword. <u>Wolves</u>. By Candace Savage. San   **51**
    Francisco: Sierra Club, 1988.

Parnall, Peter. "A Wolf in the Eye." <u>Audubon</u> Jan. 1988: 78+.

Satchell, Michael. "The New Call of the Wild." <u>U.S. News & World</u>
    <u>Report</u> 29 Oct. 1990: 29.

Savage, Candace. <u>Wolves</u>. San Francisco: Sierra Club, 1988.

Schneider, Bill. "The Return of the Wolf." <u>National Parks</u> July-Aug.
    1981: 7+.

Skow, John. "The Brawl of the Wild." <u>Time</u> 6 Nov. 1989: 13-14.

Williams, Ted. "Waiting for Wolves to Howl in Yellowstone."
    <u>Audubon</u> Nov. 1990: 32+.

"Yellowstone Wolf Recovery Plan is Blocked." Sept. 1991. <u>EDF-Letter</u>.   **52**
    Vol. 22. No. 4. Online. Internet. 27 Oct., 1993. Available gopher://
    gopher.igc.apc.org/edf.org/pubs/EDF-Letter/1991/Sep/c_wolf.html

46. Formatting the Works Cited list. A list of the sources cited in your essay—commonly called a bibliography—appears at the end of all research papers. In the MLA style, this list of sources is titled *Works Cited*. Entries appear in alphabetical order by the author's last name (if no author's name is provided, alphabetize by the first letter of the title). Entries are double-spaced. The first line of the entry should be typed flush with the left margin; subsequent lines should be indented five spaces. (See 45c for detailed formatting guidelines and examples.)

47. Entry for an article in a journal paged consecutively throughout an annual volume. Invert the author's name (last name, first name). Include the title of the article in quotation marks, followed by the name of the journal, underlined. Give the volume number followed by the year of publication (in parentheses), a colon, and the inclusive page numbers for the article.

48. Entry for an article in a weekly magazine. Invert the author's name. Include the name of the article in quotation marks followed by the name of the periodical, underlined. Give the date of publication and then page number(s) for the entry. If the pages of the article are discontinuous (interrupted by other articles), use a plus sign after the page number—75+.

49. Entry for an article in a monthly magazine. Use the same format as for a weekly magazine (see annotation 48).

50. Entry for a book with one author. Invert the author's name. Underline the title. Include the city of publication, publisher, and year of publication.

51. Foreword. Invert the name of the foreword's author, followed by the word *Foreword* (without underlining or quotation marks, but followed by a period). Include the title of the book, underlined, the book's author preceded by the word *By*, and publication information. At the end of the entry, identify inclusive page numbers in lowercase roman numerals if such numerals are used in the source. No page numbers are given in this entry because the foreword has no page numbers.

52. Entry for an electronic source. This entry is for a letter published by the Environmental Defense Fund that is available on the Internet. The format for this citation is derived from that for a collected letter and an electronic source. The Internet address, added for the reader's convenience, reflects the document's online location in 1993. This document's Internet location in Fall 1996 had been changed to a Web address: http://www.edf.org/pubs/EDF-letter/1991/Sep/c_wolf.html.

46b Sample research essay in APA style

In an independent research class, Rosette Schleifer was asked to write a research paper related to social or organizational psychology; she decided to focus on the development of intimate relations. Rosette's instructor asked her to consider early and more recent studies in the field as a way of learning how experiments in psychology are conducted and how theories evolve as a result of criticism, questioning, and new experiments. Rosette's audience would be the instructor and the members of her class, and her purpose would be to inform her audience about the adequacy of theories that attempt to account for intimate relations and to demonstrate an awareness of the specialized vocabulary associated with these theories.

Excerpts from Rosette's essay follow. It is documented in APA style and is accompanied by annotations that highlight the organization and format of her paper and her findings. (See 48a–d for more on social science writing, and 45d–f for more on APA style.)

Relationships

1

Shortened title and page number

Intimate Relationships:

A Review and Analysis of Research in the Field

Rosette Schleifer

Title and author, centered

Psychology 201

Professor Robert Eisenberger

December 19, 1994

Course information, if required

Place
abstract on
a separate
page; center
heading

Abstract

Researchers over the last two decades have attempted to construct frameworks to account for the development of intimate
relationships between humans. A review and analysis of this research suggest that no single framework or theoretical perspective adequately accounts for the complexity of intimate
Conclusion
relationships; researchers interested in understanding the phenomenon must depend on a number of these frameworks rather
than any single one.

Abstract
summarizes
subject,
methods,
findings, and
conclusion

Relationships

3

Introduction
presents an
overview of
the paper

Intimate Relationships:

A Review and Analysis of Research in the Field

People tend to take the development of intimate personal relationships for granted. Trying to understand these relationships
based exclusively on the nature of their intimacy (whatever that
intimacy may indicate) can cause investigators to ignore the
evolutionary process that leads to the formation of intimacy and
to the many factors that contribute to its development. Focusing
on development rather than on the fact of intimacy reveals how
the level and depth of relationships change over time and how
those changes are related to the way in which the relationships
developed in the first place. "Relationships develop in steps, not
in slopes" (Duck, 1988, p. 48).

Description
of how the
research was
conducted

Method

Over the last two decades, researchers have formulated a
number of theoretical frameworks to account for intimacy in
personal relationships. This review of the work of eleven researchers focuses on whether any single framework provides a
comprehensive explanation of the nature of intimacy in personal
relationships and a sense of just how intimacy develops.

Summary of
data collected
and how they
were analyzed

Results

Several psychological processes underlie the development of
intimate relationships. As these close relationships develop over
time, several changes take place as interaction between people
increases and as partners increase their investment in the relationship. In time, a sense of "WE-NESS" develops (Perlman &
Duck, 1987, p. 31). Investigators trying to understand this

Relationships

4

complex development try to determine just how people exchange information when they first meet and how these exchanges alter relationships over time. While several different
frameworks may partially explain how these intimate relationships develop, a multiplicity of existing theories is needed to
understand the process. Therefore, researchers cannot rely exclusively on one framework; instead, they need to study several.

Presentation of conclusions
based on an interpretation
of the surveyed literature

Discussion

Theory of
social
pene-
tration
intro-
duced

Both early and recent studies regard the theory of social penetration as a basis for understanding the formation of relationships. According to Taylor (1968), social penetration "provides a
framework for describing the development of interpersonal relationships" (p. 79). The theory suggests that "reciprocal behaviors transpire between individuals during the development of an
intimate relationship" (p. 79). These behaviors include the exchange of information and the exchange of expressions of both
positive and negative affects and mutual activities (p. 79). Furthermore, two dimensions affect our understanding of penetration and interpersonal development. The breadth of penetration
describes the amount of interaction per unit of time. The depth
of penetration refers to the degree of interaction in an allotted
exchange.

Concept
of self-
disclo-
sure
intro-
duced
and ex-
plained

Jourard and Lasakow (1958) conducted considerable research related to the social penetration theory, focusing on self-
disclosure, which involves how much people are willing to make
themselves known to others. Jourard and Lasakow developed a
self-disclosure rating scale that has been used in studies other
than their own. They found that in terms of self-disclosure,

Relationships

5

whites disclosed more information than blacks, and females

disclosed more than males. Their results did not indicate a dif-

ference in self-disclosure between married and unmarried sub-

jects. But married subjects did tend to disclose more to their

spouses than to others with whom they had intimate relation-

ships. Jourard and Lasakow concluded that married subjects

"redistributed self-disclosure to their respective spouses"

(p. 96). Their studies helped indicate that self-disclosure is, in

fact, measurable. Other studies stemmed from their work, and

the results of these subsequent studies turned out to be both

critical and supportive. . . .

APA-style reference list
appears on a separate
page; heading is centered

Relationships

6

References

Aron, A., Aron, E., Tudor, M., & Nelson, G. (1991). Close relationships as including other in the self. Journal of Personality and Social Psychology, 60(2), 241-253.

Certner, B. (1973). Exchange of self-disclosure in same sexed groups of strangers. Journal of Counseling and Clinical Psychology, 40(2), 292-297.

Cozby, P. (1973). Self-disclosure: A literature review. Psychology Bulletin, 79, 73-91.

Duck, S. (1988). Handbook of personal relationships: Theory, research and inventions. New York: Wiley.

Jourard, S. M., & Lasakow, P. (1958). Some factors in self-disclosure. Journal of Abnormal and Social Psychology, 56, 91-98.

Pearlman, D., & Duck, S. W. (Eds.). (1987). Intimate relationships: Development, dynamics, and deterioration. Newbury Park, CA: Sage.

Stephen, T. (1984). A symbolic exchange framework for the development of intimate relationships. Human Relations, 37(5), 393-408.

Taylor, D. (1968). The development of interpersonal relationships: Social penetration processes. Journal of Social Psychology, 75, 79-90.

VanLear, C., Jr. (1987). The formation of social relationships: A longitudinal study of social penetration. Human Communication Research, 13(3), 299-322.

Entries in alphabetical order, by authors' names

Last names first; initials only for first names

First line of each entry is flush with left margin

Subsequent lines of each entry are indented three spaces

Writing in the Disciplines

What Writers in the Disciplines Need to Know

The writing you do in many of your college courses shares broadly described goals and purposes. For example, clarity, logical organization, effective style, and convincing arguments cut across disciplinary lines. Aspects of writing important to all disciplines also include identifying your audience and considering your purpose. Whether you are analyzing a pattern of behavior for a psychology course, explaining your observations of a scientific experiment, or describing a work of architecture or sculpture, you will need to be clear not only about your purpose in writing, but also about your audience—your instructor, your classmates, or some larger audience.

Whatever discipline you are writing within, you will also need to draft, revise, edit, and proofread. You will need to discover an idea about your subject, provide evidence in its support, and make connections among your observations—whether of scientific data, literary works, or historical documents or events. And, of course, you will aim to make your writing clear and convincing for your audience.

At the same time, you will need to learn the specific conventions that govern writing within different disciplines. For example, you will use different documentation styles for social sciences, such as psychology and sociology, and for natural sciences, such as biology and physics. Business writing has specific requirements that distinguish it from academic writing. Chapters 47–49 explain the conventions of writing in literature and art, the social and natural sciences, and business.

CHAPTER 47

Writing about Literature and the Arts

T he humanities include the fine arts of drawing, painting, sculpture, and architecture; the performing arts of music, drama, dance, and film; literature, including poetry, fiction, and the essay; and the disciplines of history, philosophy, and religion. This chapter focuses on writing about literature and art, though its approach to writing can be applied to other areas in the humanities as well.

Why write about the humanities, especially literature and the arts? First, writing about a literary or other work of art encourages you to attend to it more carefully, to notice things you might overlook during a more casual reading or viewing. Second, writing stimulates thinking; it helps you discover what you think and why you think what you do. Third, writing provides occasions to state your views about the ideas and values the work suggests. And fourth, writing about works of literature and art can deepen your understanding of their significance and enhance your appreciation of their artistry. The accompanying chart outlines some of the ways of writing about works of literature and art covered in this chapter and in Chapter 2.

Ways to Write about Works of Literature and Art

- Writing to understand a work (47a and 2b)
- Writing to interpret a work (47b and 2d)
- Writing to evaluate a work (47c and 2e)

Writing to understand a work

When you write about literature or art, you need to enter its world of language and images. If you are reading a poem, identify its speaker and situation. If you are listening to a musical work, characterize its dominant sounds and rhythms. If you are looking at a sculpture, consider how the artist is using the medium (e.g., of wood, metal, stone) to convey an image of a person, an action, or an idea. If you are watching a film, observe the pace of action, the changes in setting, and the use of space, camera angles, and light.

In writing to understand a work, open yourself to it. Give the work a chance to make itself felt. Your first writing about a work, then, should be the writing you do for yourself—to discover what you feel and think, to see how you respond. In such writing your aim is not to prove a point or demonstrate a conclusion, but simply to find out more about how the work affects you. This initial personal writing is preliminary, exploratory, and informal. Use the techniques in the accompanying chart to begin writing and understanding works of literature and art.

Techniques for Doing Preliminary Writing about Literature and Art

- Annotate (47a-1 and 2b-1)
- List (47a-2)
- Question (47a-3 and 4a)
- Freewrite (47a-4 and 2b-2)
- Keep a double-column notebook (47a-5 and 2b-3)

   Annotating

Annotations are the notes or questions you make when reading a work of literature or when reading about or looking at a work of art. You can annotate literary works in the margins or within the text by underlining words, circling phrases, bracketing passages, or using exclamation marks, arrows, question marks, or other forms of shorthand. By annotating a text, you can highlight what strikes you as interesting, important, exciting, or puzzling. Annotation can stimulate you to think and feel—to respond to a work directly and honestly. (See 2b-1 for an example of annotation.)

EXERCISE 47–1   **Annotating a Literary Work**

Read the following poem, "Those Winter Sundays," by Robert Hayden, and annotate it. Or, write annotations for Pablo Picasso's *Guernica* (6c-1) or Virginia Woolf's "Old Mrs. Grey" (6b-1).

Those Winter Sundays

Robert Hayden

Sundays too my father got up early
and put his clothes on in the blueblack cold,
then with cracked hands that ached
from labor in the weekday weather made
banked fires blaze. No one ever thanked him.

I'd wake and hear the cold splintering, breaking.
When the rooms were warm, he'd call,
and slowly I would rise and dress,
fearing the chronic angers of that house,

Speaking indifferently to him,
who had driven out the cold
and polished my good shoes as well.
What did I know, what did I know
of love's austere and lonely offices?

---

2 Listing

Listing is the process of recording details from a work in columns or lists. As you identify a work's features—a poem's images, for example, or a painting's colors—you jot them down as a group, vertically. Listing can help you notice details and record observations that provide the foundation for interpretation. Listing also can lead you to discover connections among details scattered throughout a work.

Consider how you might list your observations about Hayden's poem "Those Winter Sundays." Here is one possible list—one in which the writer has grouped related words. Organizing a list this way (with headings for different kinds of details) helps you begin relating the different categories of details you notice in the work.

The father		The cold	The speaker
cracked hands	his call	blueblack	no thanks
labor (work)	love	fires	indifference
fires	lonely	splintering the cold	angers (fear?)
polished shoes	austere	rooms warm	

Reacting to a text with annotations and recording details and observations in a list are complementary techniques you can use together. You may discover that each technique leads you to discover different aspects of a work. However, you may find that you are more comfortable or successful with one technique than the other. Do what works best for you.

Annotating and listing should be followed with additional writing. One possibility is to ask yourself questions about the details you listed or annotated. Jot down those questions and answer them in writing. Another possibility is to develop your preliminary observations and responses through freewriting or a double-column notebook entry.

EXERCISE 47–2   Listing

1. Add two other category headings to the sample list in 47a-2 about "Those Winter Sundays." List at least three relevant details for each new category.
2. Use the listing technique to examine Picasso's *Guernica* (6c-1) or Woolf's "Old Mrs. Grey" (6b-1). Use category headings to separate the details you list.

---

3   Questioning

Asking yourself questions about a work is one way to continue thinking about it and to enrich your understanding of it. Your questions may concern the action described in or implied by a work. They may concern characters. Or they might focus on aspects of meaning and technique. Ask questions about a work's action, characters, language, and situation.

Look again at Robert Hayden's poem in Exercise 47–1 and at the list of details about it in 47a-2. Then consider the kinds of questions you might ask about the poem's details. Here are a few possibilities.

What does the word *offices* mean?

Why does the poet mention the polished shoes?

Who is the speaker?

When does the action of the poem occur?

How can the tone of the poem be described?

Why does the poem end with a question? Why is it repeated?

How would the poem's meaning change if its last sentence were omitted?

Answering such questions will often push you toward a better understanding of a work by helping you notice details and think about their significance. To get the most from the questioning technique, use it in conjunction with the other techniques for preliminary writing. Look also at the questioning checklist in 4a and consider how one student questioned his way to an understanding about a photograph.

EXERCISE 47–3   Thinking about Your Questions

Answer the questions listed in 47a-3 about Hayden's "Those Winter Sundays." Consider your responses as tentative and subject to revision—a good place to start thinking about the poem's meaning and possibly to begin making notes for a more formal paper.

---

4 Freewriting

Freewriting is a technique that helps you explore your thinking. It is more continuous than annotating, listing, and questioning. You usually freewrite in paragraphs and complete sentences, though without a concern about grammar, style, spelling, and punctuation. When you freewrite about a work of art or literature, you should react to features that strike you as interesting or engaging. Write out your thoughts on the work without worrying about whether you will be able to substantiate them. Focus instead on writing about your initial responses informally, on discovering what you feel and think about the work. (For an example of freewriting, see 2b-2.)

EXERCISE 47–4 Freewriting about a Text

On one or more pages, freewrite about Hayden's "Those Winter Sundays." You may use one of the questions in 47a-3 or an item from the list in 47a-2 to get started. Write for five or ten minutes without stopping.

EXERCISE 47–5 Responding to a Painting

Vincent van Gogh painted *The Starry Night* in 1889 in St. Rémy, located in the south of France. (The painting is reproduced on the color plate.) After spending a few minutes looking at the painting, use the following questions to formulate a reaction to van Gogh's work. Use one or more of the techniques covered thus far (annotating, listing, questioning, freewriting) to record your reactions.

1. What is your first reaction to van Gogh's painting? Why?
2. What strikes you most about it now—after looking at it for a while?
3. What is your overall impression of the painting? How can you characterize its mood?
4. Do you like van Gogh's choice of colors? Their intensity? Why or why not?
5. How do you respond to the painting's swirling cyclical lines? To the thick brushstrokes?
6. Would you prefer a painting of the night sky that more closely resembled a photograph? Why or why not?

5 Keeping a double-column notebook

Keeping a journal is a good way to ensure continued thinking and writing about works of literature and art. In a journal you can record your thoughts and responses and summarize details of different works. You can

Vincent van Gogh, *The Starry Night* (1889). Oil on Canvas. 29" × 36¼". Collection, the Museum of Modern Art, New York. Acquired through the Lillie P. Bliss Bequest.

use your journal to record your developing understanding of the works you view and read. (See 1e-1 and 1e-2 on journals.)

One especially useful kind of journal is the double-column notebook. To create a double-column notebook, divide your page in half to make space for two kinds of notes. On one side take notes, recording what you think a work expresses. On this side you should summarize the work and perhaps quote briefly from it. On the other side, react to the work by noting your questions and personal responses. On this more personal side, record what you think and how you feel about the work. Here you can question and criticize the work and relate it to your own knowledge and experience. (For an example of the double-column notebook, see 2b-3.)

After making annotations, creating a list, asking and answering a series of questions, doing some freewriting, writing a double-column notebook entry, or using some combination of these techniques, you are ready to write a draft of your essay, paper, or report. (See 1g on writing a draft.) Depending on the kind of writing assignment as well as on your purpose, you might begin writing your draft from your double-column notebook entry or from the notes you compiled using other preliminary writing techniques. You can use your annotations, questions, and preliminary writing to move into more formal kinds of writing—writing to interpret and to evaluate.

EXERCISE 47–6   Using the Double-Column Notebook

Write a double-column notebook entry based on Robert Hayden's "Those Winter Sundays," Exercise 47-1, or another work, such as Gretel Ehrlich's "About Men" (2h); Pablo Picasso's *Guernica* (6c); or Sylvia Plath's "Mirror" (47e).

47b   Writing to interpret a work

When you write to interpret a work of literature or art, you must go beyond first impressions. It is not enough simply to state your opinion of the work or to express your feelings about it. Nor is it enough to offer an interpretation without providing evidence in its support. You need to explain why readers or viewers should understand the work as you do. Your evidence derives from your analysis or close scrutiny of the work's elements. This section illustrates how to discover ideas about works of literature and art first by analyzing the work and then by developing ideas into thoughtful interpretations. (For more on analysis and interpretation, see 2c–d and Chapter 6.)

In using the preliminary writing techniques discussed in 47a, you began the process of analysis that leads to an interpretation. Annotating, listing, questioning, freewriting, and using the double-column notebook can help you react to a work, observe its details, discover relationships, see patterns, make connections, and think about the work's significance. This preliminary effort is crucial for interpretation. But to arrive at an interpretation you must also come up with an *idea* about the work. That idea will be based on connections you discover among your observations about the work's details and inferences you draw from those observations.

When you interpret, you ask what a work *means,* not how you feel about it. Interpretation aims at understanding, at intellectually comprehending a work rather than simply reacting to it. To arrive at an interpretation, you will need to move beyond your personal reaction to a broader understanding of the work's significance. One way to do this is to relate the work you are interpreting to other works by the same writer or artist, to similar works by different writers and artists, and to your own knowledge—what you know about the subject being analyzed. Another approach is to do some research on the writer or artist. Use the method outlined in the accompanying chart to begin interpreting works of literature and art.

A condensed version of the interpretive process follows. Here you will see how these steps can be applied in an interpretation of Vincent van Gogh's painting *The Starry Night*. You can apply these steps or techniques to any works of literature or art, such as the poem by Robert Hayden (see Exercise 47–1). You may also wish to consider the use of these techniques in 2c–d.

Steps in Interpreting Works of Literature and Art

1. Make observations about the work's details (47b-1 and 2c-1).
2. Establish connections among your observations (47b-2 and 2c-2).
3. Develop inferences based on those connections (47b-3 and 2d-1).
4. Formulate an interpretation based on your inferences (47b-4 and 2d-2).
5. Relate the work (and your interpretation of it) to other works (2b).

---

1 Observing

To begin understanding a work, you must *observe* its details closely. In reading a story, for example, you notice details about the characters' lives, their surroundings, experiences, and thoughts. You attend to dialogue and action, noticing not only what characters say and do but their manner of speaking and acting as well. In listening to a song or other musical work, you pay attention to its melody and harmony, its instrumentation, its changes of tempo and dynamics (its degree of loudness). In looking at a painting or photograph, you observe the shape, size, and color of its figures. You notice their relative positions in the foreground or background. You pay attention to shape, line, and color (and in a painting like van Gogh's *The Starry Night*, to brushstroke as well). You look, in short, at the elements or characteristic features of works of literature and art.

The accompanying chart lists some basic elements of works of literature and art. Some of the listed terms are used in the sample papers at the end of this chapter (see 47e) and in the excerpts about van Gogh's painting in 47b-4. You can use the terms in formulating your own interpretations of works of literature and art.

As you have already learned, it is not enough simply to observe details or elements in a work if your goal is analysis leading to interpretation. In viewing Vincent van Gogh's painting *The Starry Night*, for example, you will likely notice the intensity of its colors. You might notice as well the thickness of its brushstrokes. And you might also observe the way van Gogh surrounds each star with a circular burst of light, the cypress trees in the left foreground, and the whitish disc of the sun. You are likely to notice many other details as well. To interpret *The Starry Night*, however, you will also need to establish connections and discover patterns among your many observations.

What to Look for in Interpreting Works of Literature and Art

Literature

character   An imaginary person who inhabits a literary work.

characterization   The means by which writers present and reveal character.

conflict   A struggle between opposing forces in a work that is usually resolved by the end.

diction   A writer's selection of words.

image   Words that evoke a picture or other sense impression.

imagery   The pattern of related images in a work.

irony   A discrepancy between what is said and what is meant, or between what happens and what is expected.

metaphor and **simile**   A comparison between unlike things. Metaphor says "*x* is *y*"; simile says "*x* is *like y*."

narrator   In fiction the voice that tells the story.

paradox   An apparent contradiction that contains a truth that can be explained.

personification   The endowment of inanimate objects or abstract concepts with human qualities.

plot   The unified structure of incidents in a literary work.

point of view   The angle of vision from which a story or novel is narrated, such as first person, third person limited, or omniscient.

protagonist   The main character of a literary work.

rhyme   The matching of final vowel or consonant sounds in two or more words.

rhythm   The recurrence of accent or stress in a line of verse or prose.

setting   The time and place of a work's action.

speaker   In poetry, the "I" or voice speaking.

stanza   A division or unit of a poem often repeated in the same form.

theme   The idea of a literary work abstracted from its details of language, character, and action cast in the form of a generalization.

tone   A writer's attitude toward the subject and characters of a work.

Art

brushstroke   The thickness and appearance of the paint on a canvas or wood panel (or a reproduction).

color   The way pigment reflects and absorbs light to give a work of art a strong part of its visual identity.

foreground   The part of a painting or other work of art that appears closest to the viewer. A work's **background** appears behind the figures or forms depicted in the foreground.

line   A series of connected marks left by a moving point of a pencil or paintbrush. *Linear* suggests a single dimension rather than two or three dimensions.

perspective   A technique for imitating, on a flat surface, three dimensionality or the appearance of depth.

scale   Relative or proportional size.

(continued)

General

Some terms apply to both literature and art. Here are a few of them.

motif A recurring feature in a work—of color, design, shape, phrase, or subject.

structure The design, form, or organization of a work.

style The way authors and artists use the elements of their art to express themselves. A writer's style refers to his or her choices of words, images, sentence patterns, and methods of organization. A painter's style refers to his or her way of using line, color, brushstroke, and materials to convey an idea, attitude, or feeling.

symbol An object or action in a work that stands for something beyond itself.

2   Connecting

Once you observe the details and other aspects of a work, whether a painting or a work of art or literature, you should look for *connections* among your observations. Try to relate the things you see to one another as you look for both similarities and differences. Making connections is essential to analysis and interpretation: it helps you begin thinking about works of literature and art. Without connections you have only a series of fragmented observations.

In the van Gogh painting, for example, you might notice how the dark and quiet village in the bottom quarter of the painting contrasts with the bright sky. You might relate the shape of the cypress trees to that of the stars since both convey an intense image of burning. You might notice that the village's scale is small compared with the sky and stars. And you might begin to reflect on the significance of such connections, asking yourself why the artist depicted these things as he did.

3   Inferring

By considering the significance of a work's related details, you will be leaping to the third interpretive stage—*inference* (see 4a-1). There is no way around drawing inferences when you interpret a work of literature or art. If you do not draw inferences, you may wind up saying "I have no idea what this writer or artist is doing." And while particular works may stump you, you need to move beyond making observations and connections to thinking about their significance.

In the van Gogh painting, for instance, you might notice how much of the painting is occupied by moon, stars, and sky and how little space is accorded the village. On the basis of that contrast in scale you might wonder whether van Gogh's painting describes the overwhelming power of nature, its potential to wreak destruction on helpless human inhabitants. In connecting van

Gogh's portrayal of the stars, moon, and sun with his depiction of the cypress as a flame shooting into the sky, you might see the painting as an image of an imminent conflagration. But you might see it in other ways as well.

EXERCISE 47–7   Analyzing and Interpreting *The Starry Night*

Answer the following questions about van Gogh's *The Starry Night*. Try to use the questions in conjunction with your own observations about the painting and the connections you make among those observations.

1. Since van Gogh does not depict the night sky realistically, what feeling or attitudes might he be expressing with his bright colors, thick brushstrokes, and swirling forms?
2. What can you infer from the painting about the artist's state of mind?
3. How might someone from a culture in which stars are seen as sacred symbols, perhaps even as supernatural beings, interpret van Gogh's work?
4. How might knowledge about van Gogh's life and work aid you in understanding what he is portraying in *The Starry Night?* What kinds of information might be helpful in interpreting his painting?

---

4   Interpreting

Once you make observations, establish connections among those observations, and start to draw inferences, you are ready to formulate an interpretation of the work. Your interpretation should convey your understanding of the work. The evidence that supports your interpretation should come from the work's details, whether you are interpreting van Gogh's painting or another work of art or literature. In accumulating evidence for your interpretation you may use logical thinking and creative thinking (see Chapter 3). Your interpretation may also be informed by what you have learned from consulting secondary sources.

Following is a short sample interpretation of *The Starry Night*. It is based on an analysis of the work's elements along with information and ideas gleaned from reading about van Gogh's life and work. Notice how the interpretation is organized. The authors begin by describing what they see. They then build on those observations to arrive at an interpretation, which they place in the final sentence of their paragraph for emphasis.

> The artist is looking down on a village from an imaginary viewpoint. It [the painting] is framed by his newly discovered motifs: at left a cypress towers skywards, at right a group of olive trees clusters into a cloud, and against the horizon run the undulating waves of the Alpilles [a mountain range]. Van Gogh's treatment of his motifs prompts associations with fire, mist and the

sea; and the elemental power of the natural scene combines with the intangible cosmic drama of the stars. . . . The church spire seems to be stretching up into the elements, at once an antenna and a lightning conductor, like some kind of provincial Eiffel Tower. . . . van Gogh's mountains and trees (particularly the cypresses) seemed to crackle with an electric charge. Confident that he had grasped their natural appearance, van Gogh set out to remake their image in the service of the symbolic. Together with the firmament, these landscape features are singing the praises of Creation in this painting.

—Ingo F. Walther and Rainer Metzger, *Van Gogh: The Complete Paintings II*

Although the authors did research to arrive at their interpretation of *The Starry Night,* you do not necessarily need to know a great deal about the artist's life, about his other paintings, or about how his work relates to that of other artists. Such additional knowledge, however, can give you a different understanding of a work.

Here, for example, is some additional information about the painting, taken from one of van Gogh's letters.

To look at the stars always makes me dream as simply as I dream over the black dots of a map representing towns and villages. Why, I ask myself, should the shining dots of the sky not be as accessible as the black dots on the map of France? . . .

I go out at night to paint the stars. . . . I have a terrible lucidity at moments when nature is so beautiful; I am not conscious of myself any more, and the pictures come to me as in a dream . . .

That does not keep me from having a terrible need of—shall I say the word—religion. Then I go out at night to paint the stars.

—*The Complete Letters of Vincent van Gogh*

Sources such as van Gogh's letters and Walther and Metzger's comments can help you better understand van Gogh's work. They may lead you to see *The Starry Night* (or another work) in a way you might not have arrived at by simply viewing the painting. Consider, too, how the following interpretations that have been made of van Gogh's painting influence your own interpretation of *The Starry Night.*

1. The painting is a realistic account of the position of the stars in June 1889 in St. Rémy, France (where van Gogh painted this nocturnal scene).
2. The painting expresses van Gogh's personal agony and suffering during an especially trying time of his life.
3. The painting is an attempt to express a state of shock, to convey the inner turmoil of the artist's mind and spirit.
4. The painting portrays the power and grandeur of nature, conveying simultaneously a sense of its beauty and its terror.

5. The painting expresses van Gogh's sense of apocalypse, of the biblical end, and the imminent destruction of the world.

To arrive at your own understanding of the painting, you could consider these interpretations along with your own observations. You could also go to the library to read more of van Gogh's letters as well as books about his life and art.

EXERCISE 47–8   **Interpreting *The Starry Night***

Use your own observations along with the information and interpretive leads presented in 47b to develop a 500–750-word interpretation of van Gogh's *The Starry Night*. Use the artist's own remarks if you wish, or do additional research.

EXERCISE 47–9   **Writing an Interpretation of a Work**

---

1. Read a poem, short story, essay, song, or short play, and write an interpretation of it. Focus on an aspect of the work you consider important. Follow the four interpretive stages outlined in Steps in Interpreting Works of Literature and Art. If you use secondary sources, be sure to document them accurately according to the guidelines in Chapter 45.
2. Write a 500–750-word interpretation of Robert Hayden's poem "Those Winter Sundays." You can use the questions on p. 782 as a start.
3. Write a 500–750-word interpretation of Picasso's *Guernica*. You may research the painting or use the background information in 6c-2–3 to get started.
4. Look carefully at a work of fine art—a painting, sculpture, or work of architecture. Using the four stages of interpretation discussed in 47b, develop an interpretation of the work. Document any secondary sources you use, following the guidelines in Chapter 45.

47c   Writing to evaluate a work

When interpreting a work of art or literature, you aim to understand it, not to judge it. In writing to evaluate a work of art or literature, however, you make a judgment about it. Your judgment may concern its quality, its persuasiveness, or its implied cultural and social values. Although interpretation and evaluation differ, evaluation depends on interpretation. You cannot make a sound judgment about a work of art or literature until you understand it. In evaluating van Gogh's *The Starry Night,* for example, you might consider the artist's success in conveying a particular image of nature or a particular expression of the relationship between nature and civilization. Or you might consider to what extent the painting reflects van Gogh's religious attitudes and how successfully it expresses his artistic or religious vision. (See 2e for a detailed discussion and example of evaluation.)

47d   Writing papers on literary works: The assignment

In writing a paper about a literary work, you should be clear about just what kind of essay or paper you want to write or have been assigned. There are various types of papers: a personal response (in which you express your feelings about a work), an analysis of an element or part of a work (a character analysis or an analysis of some other aspect of a work, such as its imagery or structure), an interpretation, a review, or an evaluation, to name several. You also should be clear about whether you need to consult secondary sources.

Primary sources include original works of writers and artists, original historical documents, data, and observations based on experiments and case studies. **Secondary sources** are interpretations and explanations of primary sources, often in the form of books and articles. In literature, for example, primary sources include poems, plays, novels, stories, and essays. In art, primary sources are paintings, drawings, etchings, engravings, sculptures, and works of architecture. Other primary sources in the arts include musical scores and the scripts of plays. The texts of Shakespeare's plays, for example, are primary sources, whereas interpretations of the plays constitute secondary sources. (For information on using primary and secondary sources, see 43c.) Check with your instructor if you have questions about the requirements of a writing assignment or about the use of primary and secondary sources.

WRITING HINT   In any writing you do about literature and art, you will need to describe the work. In doing so you will use present tense, past tense, or both. In most instances, it is conventional to use present tense when describing literary works and works of art. Consider the following examples.

> Vincent van Gogh's *The Starry Night* depicts a brilliantly lit night sky, in which stars *shine* with a burning light and the moon *glows* fiercely. [The verbs are all in the present tense because they describe the painting, which exists in a single time frame.]

> In Robert Hayden's "Those Winter Sundays," the speaker *reflects* on his father and *remembers* how much his father loved his family. [The verbs describing the speaker's actions are in the present tense; the verb describing the father (*loved*) is in the past—because the father's action is in the past, whereas the speaker's action occurs in the poem's present.]

In his classic film *Battleship Potemkin,* the director, Sergei Eisenstein, *used* extreme close-up shots and other cinematic techniques such as montage to create startling visual effects. [The verb is in the past tense because the sentence describes the efforts of the director, not the work proper.]

47e Two sample interpretations of literary works

The following two student essays were written in response to an assignment requiring an interpretation of an aspect of a literary work. The first paper interprets a poem by the modern American poet Sylvia Plath. In developing her interpretation of Plath's poem "Mirror," Jennifer Stepkowski analyzes the poet's diction and images. Jennifer does not use any outside sources for her paper, relying instead on her own careful analysis of the poem. Jennifer also uses quotations from the poem to support her interpretation.

The second paper interprets James Joyce's short novel "The Dead," from his collection, *Dubliners.* In developing her interpretation of Joyce's work, Michele Carerra analyzes the character of Gabriel Conroy, the protagonist. In addition to her own attentive reading of Joyce's work, Michele uses secondary sources. She documents these sources according to the Modern Language Association guidelines (MLA style), outlined in Chapter 45. Michele has been careful to avoid plagiarism, the use of others' words or ideas as if they were one's own (see 44j). Michele also uses quotations from both Joyce's story and the secondary sources to support her interpretation. For additional guidance in using quotations from primary and secondary sources in your writing, see 36d and 44i.

LITERARY INTERPRETATION WITHOUT SECONDARY SOURCES

Mirror

Sylvia Plath

I am silver and exact. I have no preconceptions.
Whatever I see I swallow immediately
Just as it is, unmisted by love or dislike.
I am not cruel, only truthful—
The eye of a little god, four-cornered.
Most of the time I meditate on the opposite wall.
It is pink, with speckles. I have looked at it so long
I think it is a part of my heart. But it flickers.
Faces and darkness separate us over and over.

Now I am a lake. A woman bends over me,
Searching my reaches for what she really is.
Then she turns to those liars, the candles or the moon.
I see her back, and reflect it faithfully.

She rewards me with tears and an agitation of hands.
I am important to her. She comes and goes.
Each morning it is her face that replaces the darkness.
In me she has drowned a young girl, and in me an old woman
Rises toward her day after day, like a terrible fish.

Jennifer Stepkowski
Professor O'Leary
English 201
April 10, 1994

Reflections on Sylvia Plath's "Mirror"

Sylvia Plath's short poem, "Mirror," presents a portrayal of womanhood that is both accurate and upsetting. The mirror in Plath's poem reflects honestly both inanimate objects and the faces of those who peer into it. As the poem's speaker puts it: "Whatever I see I swallow immediately / Just as it is, unmisted by love or dislike" (3-4).

To convey the mirror's uncompromising accuracy in reflecting what shows in its glass surface, Plath uses such words as <u>exact</u>, <u>truthful</u>, <u>really</u>, and <u>faithfully</u>. Plath personifies her mirror and makes it the poem's speaker. "I am silver and exact," the speaker begins. "I have no preconceptions" (1). This exactness of the mirror's reflection of reality coupled with Plath's precise diction presents a harsh reality in which women grow old inexorably. Women have old age to look forward to, an old age in which the young girls they once were have been "drowned" (17).

This image of drowning follows logically from the opening of the poem's second stanza in which the mirror is compared to a lake. It is in this lake (or mirror as lake) that a woman searches for her self, reaching, as Plath writes, "for what she really is" (10). What the woman finds, however, so disconcerts her that she responds with "an agitation of hands" (14), which calls up a vision of the woman's hands in flurried motion around her face. Yet even though she is upset by what she sees in the mirror, the woman returns repeatedly. The reason for her repeated return the woman partly understands and perhaps also partly fears:

I am important to her. She comes and goes.
Each morning it is her face that replaces the darkness.
In me she has drowned a young girl, and in me an
    old woman
Rises toward her day after day. . . . (14-18)

Marginal notes:

Introduction or beginning identifies poet and poem and states the thesis

Two-line quotation with slash separating lines of the poem

Refers to Plath's diction— her use of a pattern of related words

Quotation and line reference

Thesis or idea

Paragraph develops the idea by discussing images

Three-line quote indented in block form without quotation marks

Sentence reinforces the idea	Plath is uncompromising in portraying women's need to see themselves, a need fed by a powerful concern with their appearance. She also conveys without compromise the inevitable process of aging, rendered powerfully
Refers to simile	in the simile that concludes the poem. Plath conveys a sense of the woman at three stages of life: as she is now, growing older in the poem's present; as she was once as a young girl; and as she will be as an old woman who rises toward her "like a terrible fish" (18).
Refers to structure by relating two stanzas	The images of the second stanza--of lake and tears and agitated hands, of a drowning girl and old woman rising like a fish--reflect concretely the general statements made in the first stanza. There Plath describes the mirror as having "no preconceptions" (1), as "swallow[ing]" immediately "just as it is," whatever it sees, "unmisted by
Conclusion or ending reasserts the writer's idea and offers an evaluation	love or dislike." Soon the woman will be swallowed by the mirror as has the young girl she once was. Only the old woman will remain, coming and going from the mirror, staring into it and looking for the middle-aged woman and the young girl who will have long since vanished.

Work Cited

Plath, Sylvia. "Mirror." <u>The Collected Poems of Sylvia
   Plath</u>. Ed. Ted Hughes. New York: Harper, 1963. 173.

LITERARY INTERPRETATION WITH SECONDARY SOURCES

Michele Carerra
Professor Krickstein
English 120
October 15, 1993

The Awakening of Gabriel Conroy

Thesis stated immediately	Like the stories in <u>Dubliners</u> that lead up to it, "The Dead" dramatizes a moment of self-realization. The story portrays the gradual awakening of Gabriel Conroy, whose vision of his wife, Gretta, at the end of the story is at once a frustrating disappointment and a touching movement toward understanding and love. Robert Adams voices the view of more than one critic when he writes of "The Dead"
Direct quotations of secondary sources properly documented	that this "greatest of the stories in <u>Dubliners</u> stands apart from the rest, being warmer in tonality, richer in writing, and more intimate in its subject matter" (83). Florence Walzl concurs when she writes that "'The Dead' is markedly different from the earlier stories. . . . It is not only a longer, more fully developed narrative, but it presents a more kindly view of Ireland" (428).
Implications of the story's title	In one sense the "dead" of the title are all those who have lived and died, those who have gone before the festive inhabitants of Dublin who celebrate the Christmas season, Gabriel Conroy and Gretta among them. In another sense the dead are all those who, though alive and
Beginning of character analysis	breathing, have lost their naturalness, their spontaneity, and most importantly, their passion. Gabriel, one of these, has lost touch with his past and with traditional Irish val-
Summary of secondary source	ues. He looks instead toward Continental Europe, toward the future, and toward change for an escape from the outmoded and restrictive attitudes of the past (Ellmann 395).
Link established between symbolism and character analysis	We glimpse Gabriel arriving at the party as a man coming in from the dark, here the symbolic darkness of Gabriel's ignorance (Walzl 433). Gabriel appears to be something of a gentleman as he slips a coin into the hand of the servant Lily. With the gesture of good will, Gabriel attempts to buy his way out of further conversation with Lily, but she makes him uncomfortable by commenting that
Direct quotation from story, with page citation	"The men that is now is only all palaver and what they can get out of you." It is a remark, Joyce's narrator notes, that Lily delivers "with great bitterness" (Joyce 178).

Analysis of early
scene with
explanation of its
significance

Gabriel deflects further discussion by attending to his coat, scarf, and shoes. He then presses the tip into Lily's hand and disappears up the stairs. Our first impression of Gabriel is of a man, who though cultivated, and cultured, is nonetheless naive. This small scene sets the tone for Gabriel's more serious errors in understanding, which Joyce saves for a later revelation.

Analysis continues:
contrasts protag-
onist with his wife

Early in the story, Gabriel is distinguished from his wife, Gretta, his emotional opposite. Gabriel describes Gretta as someone who would walk home in the snow if she were allowed. Gabriel, on the other hand, will not go out in snow or rain without his galoshes. Unlike her more cultured husband, Gretta is without pretension, and she is more spontaneous. She retains the youthful romantic nature she possessed when a young man named Michael Furey died, according to her version of the event, for love of her. And even in middle age, Gretta appears more comfortable with the memory of the boy from her past than with the presence of her more cultivated husband.

Connection
established between
characters and
setting

Gabriel's difference from the others at the party is revealed during a conversation with Miss Ivors. When Miss Ivors suggests that Gabriel and Gretta accompany her and some friends on a vacation to the primitive Irish-speaking Aran Islands off the western coast of Ireland, Gabriel does not accept. He tells her that he has already planned to travel in the other direction--east to France and Belgium. These countries represent for Gabriel the world of culture and civilization. The Irish islands, by contrast, represent what he considers uncivilized and repugnant. Ironically, however, his wife's family came from one of those islands--a fact that Gabriel prefers to ignore.

Character contrast
(Gretta and Gabriel)
with reference to
Ireland

Other important scenes put Gabriel on display, increasing our perception of him as more concerned with surface than with substance, more impressed by the sound of his voice than the truth of his words or the value of his actions. Gabriel's clichéd after-dinner speech, for example, is filled with outlandish praise of his old aunts, whom he flatters beyond their comprehension. Gabriel sees the old Irish past as dead, paying it only a token and insincere tribute. His thoughts and energies are directed elsewhere--to the future and to the Continent. Yet Gabriel

Summary of
another scene, its
significance
explained

points ironically toward what seems most true--the power of the past to continue living into the future; the inability of individuals to completely escape their past and their cultural roots. In rejecting those things, Gabriel is rejecting the essential part of himself. It is unclear how much of this he understands. At the time he gives his speech, however, it is clear he believes none of his lofty sentiments.

We begin to see how much Gabriel is shut out of his wife's inner life in still another scene at the party. After dinner there is singing by Mr. Darcy. When he sings an Irish ballad called "The Lass of Aughrim," Gretta listens enraptured, lost in memory:

Block quotation of an important passage indented without quotation marks

> She was standing right under the dusty fan-light and the flame of the gas lit up the rich bronze of her hair which he had seen her dry-ing at the fire a few days before. She was in the same attitude and seemed unaware of the talk about her. At last she turned towards them and Gabriel saw that there was colour on her cheeks and that her eyes were shining. (Joyce 212)

Transition to final climactic scene

At this moment Gabriel feels an immense tender-ness toward his wife and a strong sexual desire for her. Both his tenderness and his desire grow as the party winds down and Gabriel accompanies Gretta to the hotel. His desire increases as he rehearses mentally how he will approach Gretta and how he will express his feelings.

Analysis of climactic scene

The critical point of this scene concerns the thoughts Gretta has as Gabriel watches her. He expects her to tell him that she has been thinking of him and of their life together. Instead, she tells Gabriel about Michael Furey, whose image she had conjured up when Mr. Darcy sang "The Lass of Aughrim," a song Michael Furey him-self sang before he died. As Gabriel listens to Gretta remi-nisce about the poor delicate boy with the big sad eyes, he experiences, with a shock, a moment of self-realization:

Block quotation of critical moment in story

> Gabriel felt humiliated by the failure of his irony and by the evocation of this figure from the dead, a boy in the gasworks. While he had been full of memories of their secret life to-gether, full of tenderness and joy and desire,

she had been comparing him in her mind with another. A shameful consciousness of his own person assailed him. He saw himself as a ludicrous figure, acting as a pennyboy for his aunts, a nervous well-meaning sentimentalist, orating to vulgarians and idealising his own clownish lusts, the pitiable fatuous fellow he had caught a glimpse of in the mirror. Instinctively he turned his back more to the light lest she might see the shame that burned upon his forehead. (Joyce 219-20)

Gabriel's humiliation is increased further when he learns the circumstances of Michael Furey's death. With that knowledge comes a second revelation accompanied by Joyce's description of the snow falling over all of Ireland. The beauty of the language, which matches the beauty of the snow-filled scene, also suggests the beauty of Gabriel's perception that all people share life and death, that the dead live and the living shall join the dead in a shared humanity. "The time had come," as the narrator puts it, "for Gabriel to set out on his journey westward" (Joyce 223), a statement that has been characterized as "an enigmatic sentence that has bothered many readers of 'The Dead'" (Benstock 167).

But as Joyce's biographer Richard Ellmann has explained (396), it is not really so puzzling. According to Ellmann, this westward journey is the journey back to Gabriel's past, to his cultural roots. The tone of Joyce's sentence suggests resignation and relinquishment, as Gabriel gives up his "sense of the importance of civilized thinking, of Continental tastes" (Ellmann 397) and other nice distinctions he prides himself in making. Moreover, this journey westward is the ultimate journey toward the setting sun, toward the close of life. For Gabriel, the journey toward what he previously saw as death is a journey into life, the real life of feeling as experienced by those more sincere and authentic than he has ever been. For although Gabriel had indeed been sick of his country, as he had told Miss Ivors, he nevertheless finds himself drawn into a silent tribute to it. The story, ultimately, turns on a paradox: that to go forward one has to go back. Gabriel's

Connection of final scene with earlier events only referred to

Direct quotation from story

Two source citations with page references

Use of secondary source in analysis of symbolism (the journey)

Direct quotation of story's final words

soul swoons as he hears the snow "falling faintly through the universe and faintly falling, like the descent of their last end, upon all the living and the dead" (Joyce 224).

Concluding (ending) paragraph

During Gabriel's vision, Joyce slows down the narrative pace (Loomis 150). Time slows as we are presented a vision of humanity's common fate. It is a vision we share rather than one we merely analyze. For we too know that like Gabriel and Gretta and Michael Furey, everyone is subject to the experiences of love and sorrow, pain and joy, passion and tenderness, living and dying. And like Gabriel, in realizing and reminding ourselves of the inevitability of this simple truth, our sympathies are enlarged and deepened for Gabriel, for Gretta, for Michael Furey, and for one another as well.

Here are the primary and secondary sources that Michele Carerra cites in her essay.

Works Cited

Adams, Robert. James Joyce. New York: Octagon, 1980.

Benstock, Bernard. "The Dead." Dubliners: Critical Essays. Ed. Clive Hart. London: Faber, 1969. 156-69.

Ellmann, Richard. "The Backgrounds of 'The Dead.'" Dubliners: Text, Criticism, and Notes. Ed. Robert Scholes and A. Walton Litz. New York: Viking, 1969. 388-403.

Joyce, James. "The Dead." Dubliners: Text, Criticism, and Notes. Ed. Robert Scholes and A. Walton Litz. New York: Viking, 1969. 175-224.

Loomis, C. C. "Structure and Sympathy in Joyce's 'The Dead.'" PMLA 75 (1960): 149-51.

Walzl, Florence. "Gabriel and Michael: The Conclusion of 'The Dead.'" Dubliners: Text, Criticism, and Notes. Ed. Robert Scholes and A. Walton Litz. New York: Viking, 1969. 423-79.

CHAPTER 48

Writing in the Social
and Natural Sciences

The social sciences include cultural anthropology, economics, political science, psychology, sociology, and other subject areas that focus on the study of human behavior. Social scientists study how human beings relate to each other and to their environment; their studies are grounded in the belief that human behavior can be explained and interpreted.

The natural sciences include biology, chemistry, geology, physics, mathematics, and various specializations (such as immunology, crystallography, hydrology, and astrophysics). Complementing these natural sciences are integrated fields of study such as biochemistry, which merges biology with chemistry. Natural scientists study natural and technological phenomena through observation and experiment; their experiments yield data that are analyzed and interpreted to explain natural processes.

Both social and natural scientists write to explain their findings. For example, a sociologist or psychologist might write about the results of a survey on the behavioral characteristics of twins; a biologist might record the results of a laboratory experiment on the mating habits of fruit flies; and an engineer would develop proposals for designing dams and levees. Scientists also write to interpret or describe the findings of other scientists. In addition, a good deal of writing in the sciences is done by "popular science" writers, who translate technical matters into language nonexperts can understand. Articles on current scientific research appear regularly in newspapers, in weekly news magazines (e.g., *Newsweek*), in weekly scientific magazines (*Science News*), and in monthly periodicals (*Discover* and *Scientific American*).

This chapter provides an overview of the methods and procedures to follow when writing papers and reports in the social and natural sciences. Use the accompanying chart to locate the information you need.

48a Understanding methodology and using evidence in the social sciences

Unlike the humanities, in which inquiry is based on the interpretation of texts, inquiry in the social sciences involves collecting, analyzing, and inter-

What You Need to Know to Write in the Social and Natural Sciences		
	SOCIAL SCIENCES	NATURAL SCIENCES
Methodology and use of evidence	48a	48e
Purposes and audiences for writing	48b	48f
Documentation	48c	48g
Assignments and formats	48d	48h

preting data culled from observations, interviews, questionnaires, and experiments. Social scientists commonly observe human behavior and record what they see in **field notes**—comprehensive and accurate notes made while doing research in the field rather than in the library. Observations can also be recorded in photographs and on audio- or videotape. Social science researchers often conduct interviews—which can be recorded in writing or on tape—to accumulate data about people's understanding of events, their attitudes, and their behavior. Social science researchers can also use questionnaires and surveys to invite responses to questions about people's beliefs and behavior. And finally, social scientists use controlled experiments—those performed in a laboratory—to carefully structure the environment in which a particular behavior is studied.

In researching work habits and work environments, for example, social scientists would visit work sites and record their observations. They would interview workers with varying responsibilities and degrees of authority. They would use questionnaires to supplement their observations and interviews, asking the questions in personal interviews or distributing questionnaires for response at a later time. They would also design experiments to measure workers' responses to work environments in which light, sound, space, or population density are varied.

In doing such field research, social scientists formulate a **hypothesis,** or testable generalization. On the basis of data collected through observations, interviews, surveys, and experiments, they draw conclusions that support, refute, or qualify their hypotheses.

Two types of data are collected for use in assessing a hypothesis: quantitative data and qualitative data. **Quantitative data** are number based; they usually result from experiments, polls, and surveys. A poll, for example, designed to estimate the percentage of registered voters in Montana who will vote Democratic in the next gubernatorial election elicits quantitative data. So does a survey asking about the number of weekly hours worked by employees in various fields.

Qualitative data are subjective rather than numerical; they usually result from firsthand observations in the field—from interviews, case studies, and ethnographies. A *case study* is a detailed analysis of a person, group, or corporate unit, which may serve as a model of a particular kind of social phenomenon. An *ethnography* is a study of the cultural heritage of a subject. Qualitative data typically involve measuring respondents' attitudes or evaluating their feelings. Interviewing attorneys about their choice of profession would provide qualitative data in the form of personal explanations, from which common principles about motivation and job satisfaction might emerge.

48b Considering purpose and audience for writing in the social sciences

When writing in the social sciences, as in any type of writing, you need to consider your purpose and audience (see 1d). Your purpose might be to **inform** your readers of your observations about a particular phenomenon, such as worker behavior. Or you might wish to **persuade** your readers to adopt your point of view—for example, about the benefits of a work environment with plenty of natural light or one that includes soft background music.

If your purpose is to inform, be sure to describe your findings carefully and accurately. For example, rather than stating that "workers appeared happy" or that they "worked well together," which would reflect a subjective assumption, state that "workers smiled when they greeted one another" or that they "spoke with one another frequently and courteously." Also, use any specialized terms of a discipline with precision. For example, use terms such as *sublimation* in a psychology report, or *mobility* in a sociology paper, with the appropriate specialized meaning those words have within their respective disciplines. When confusion may result from terms that have both specialized and general meanings, be sure to clarify which meaning you intend. In addition, social scientists often define terms *operationally*—that is, they define the terms in the special ways they wish to use these terms in their reports. You may wish to do the same.

If your purpose is to persuade, you need to apply the same care in describing your findings and in using language. When writing to persuade, you should also familiarize yourself with the strategies of argumentation described in Chapter 7 and with the techniques of logical thinking discussed in Chapter 3. For example, if you find that many lawyers seem dissatisfied with their profession, you might argue that increased competition and decreased prestige are responsible. To be convincing, however, you need to establish this cause-and-effect relationship (see 3e and 8e-4) and to support your argument with evidence. That evidence can include statistical information gleaned from surveys, qualitative data culled from interviews and questionnaires, and your own observations. Always be sure to present your research methods and observations thoroughly and carefully to bolster your credibility with your readers.

Social science writing, however, is rarely limited to either informing or persuading. Most social science writing requires that you do both: inform readers about research and persuade them to accept the researcher's analysis and interpretation. For example, you would carefully detail the findings that led to your conclusions about lawyers' dissatisfaction with their work in order to inform your readers. At the same time, you would want to persuade readers of your hypothesis about the causes of that dissatisfaction.

Along with your purpose for writing, you should always consider the nature and needs of your audience. If you are preparing a report for specialists in a particular field, such as economics or clinical psychology, present your data and choose your language to suit that audience of knowledgeable specialists. You might want to use the jargon or specialized vocabulary of the field. However, if you are preparing a report or writing an essay for a general audience of nonexperts, avoid jargon; select details, arrange evidence, present information, and develop your argument in ways more readily understandable by a nonexpert audience (see 28d).

Finally, make sure you understand your instructor's views on using the first person (*I, we, our*) in your social science writing. Much (but not all) writing in the social sciences strives for an objective tone and thus relies on the third person (*he, she, it, one, they*) rather than the more subjective first person. This apparent objectivity of tone may be achieved by using the passive voice ("objects *were watched*"; "changes *were recorded*"), which emphasizes what is being observed or described rather than the action of observing or describing. (See 11j–k on using active and passive voice verbs.) Instructors have different preferences about these stylistic elements, as shown in the very different sample papers in this chapter (see 48d and 48h-2).

 Documenting sources in the social sciences

Although you may derive evidence for your own writing in the social sciences from observations, interviews, questionnaires, and experiments, you may also need to consult additional sources—in books, reports, or journals—about the subject you are investigating. When you consult such sources, you will need to document them—that is, to acknowledge information and ideas taken from your sources—to avoid plagiarism (see 44j).

The documentation style most commonly used for writing in psychology is that outlined in the *Publication Manual of the American Psychological Association* (APA). This style of documenting sources requires using parenthetical citations (see 45d) within your text and a References list at the end (see 45f). Because currency of research is important in the social sciences, the date is cited first. Entire works are cited rather than specific pages because social science research reports are read as complete entities. (For a student research essay formatted according to the conventions of APA documentation style, see 46b.)

There are alternatives to APA documentation style. You may be required to follow the guidelines of another discipline, such as the American Sociological Association as presented on the inside front cover of the *American Sociological Review*. (For a list of various documentation style manuals, see 45i.) It is also possible that you may not need to document at all if your paper is based solely on your own field research (as in the sample paper in 48d, based on a team of students' survey results). If you are in doubt about how to document, be sure to check with your instructor.

48d   Understanding assignments and formats in the social sciences

When you write in the social sciences, you will also need to decide on an appropriate format for your writing. The format you choose will vary, depending on the type of paper or report you write.

Four types of reports are commonly assigned in the social sciences.

1. **Summary or research review.** Provides an overview of the published research on a subject, such as the effectiveness of eating disorder treatments.

2. **Case study.** Analyzes a specific instance of a larger general event, such as opening a megabookstore or moving a sports franchise from one location to another. A case study can be combined with problem-solution analysis, in which the causes of a problem such as yo-yo dieting are explored and a solution proposed.

3. **Research paper.** Presents and sometimes analyzes or evaluates the published work on a subject. Often includes an idea or thesis and supporting evidence. (See Rosette Schleifer's paper on intimate relationships in 46b for an example of a research paper.)

4. **Research report.** Describes the writer's own research. See the sample research report in this section.

The format of your social science papers will vary based on the subject area and your instructor's requirements. Always check the style guide for your subject area. In writing a research report, for example, you may need to follow the guidelines established by the APA. The accompanying chart outlines the APA manual's recommended format for a research report. Be aware, however, that the order of items listed in the format does not reflect the order in which they are written. For example, the Abstract, which comes first in the format, is actually written last.

The following research report on attitudes toward recycling was prepared by a team of four students from Brigham Young University. Excerpts from the

Format for a Social Science Research Report

- **Abstract.** A brief summary (100–150 words) of the subject, research method, findings, and conclusions.
- **Introduction.** An overview of the problem, research method and purpose, hypothesis, and background information (such as previous studies).
- **Method.** A precise description of how the research was conducted, including a discussion of the individuals involved or materials used and an explanation of research procedures.
- **Results.** A summary of the data collected along with a description of how the data were analyzed. This section may also include detailed charts, graphs, or tables.
- **Discussion.** An interpretation, an evaluation, and a conclusion about the data. The conclusions should include further implications of the study.

A social science research report may be prefaced with a title page and may conclude with a References list.

introduction, methods, results, and discussion sections have been included. Notice in particular how the writers use a table to display their quantitative information. Notice as well how the students consistently use the first person (*we*) and active voice verbs.

Excerpts from a research report (sociology)

Place the following information on a separate title page.

Kirsten Olsen, David Barlow, Nathan Benson, and Jon Thompson
Sociology 101
Professor Hoff
March 1, 1994

Begin the paper on a new page. If an abstract is required, place it on a separate page before starting the paper.

Disparity between Recycling Attitudes and Actions
Since the environmental movement began in the United States a few decades ago, citizens have become increasingly concerned about the environment. Although they remain divided on many issues, recycling is one issue that nearly all Americans seem to support. We wondered, however, whether that support is the result of social pressure.

When we began our research project, the members of our research group hypothesized that there would be disparity among students' attitudes and actions regarding recycling. While students say that recycling is important, most participate in it only moderately. We assumed this to be the case because as we talked with fellow students at Brigham Young University (BYU), most seemed committed to recycling. Yet we frequently saw recyclable items in the trash cans rather than in the recycling bins. We even noticed newspapers and aluminum cans in trash cans next to recycling bins. What also surprised us was that of the aluminum cans bought on campus (vending), only 1.4% of them were put in recycling bins. We decided to find out whether BYU students are as strongly committed to recycling as they say they are.

Methods

We administered a written survey to the students in one section of BYU's introductory sociology class. A total of 98 students completed the survey. We asked the respondents 12 questions about their recycling attitudes and actions. Once all the data were collected, we compared responses to see if students' attitudes and actions coincided.

Results

Of the 98 people surveyed, 9 considered themselves to be avid recyclers, 70 moderate recyclers, and 19 nonrecyclers. Of the avid recyclers, 100% often or always go out of their way to recycle. Of the moderate recyclers, 22% often or always go out of their way, 60% sometimes go out of their way, and 18% rarely go out of their way to recycle. None of the nonrecyclers often or always goes out of his or her way to recycle, 24% sometimes go out of their way, 57% rarely go out of their way, and 24% never go out of their way.

Of the avid recyclers, 89% look exclusively for a recycling bin when discarding an empty aluminum can while 11% dispose of the can in the first available receptacle. Forty-seven percent of the moderate recyclers seek out a recycling bin and 53% dispose of the cans in the first available receptacle or in a trash can specifically. Among the nonrecyclers, none looks for a recycling bin: 100% of them place their empty cans in the first available receptacle or in a garbage can specifically.

We also evaluated the willingness of students to purchase and use recycled products. Of the avid recyclers, 33% said that they would be willing to pay an additional 10% or more for recycled products. Of the moderate recyclers, 12% indicated that they would do the same. Among the nonrecyclers, none stated that they would be willing to pay the extra 10%.

Finally, we examined the data regarding items people recycle. Of the avid recyclers, 66% say they recycle all of the four items mentioned in our survey (aluminum, newsprint, white office paper, colored office paper). None of the moderate recyclers say they recycle all of the items, but 63% claim to recycle newspaper and 44% reportedly recycle aluminum. Among the nonrecyclers, none recycles all four items but 38% say they recycle newspaper and 14% claim to recycle aluminum.

(See Table 1.) Twelve of the respondents indicated that they never recycle anything. Of those twelve, ten (83%) listed "personal inconvenience" as the reason for not recycling.

Table appears on a separate page by itself.

Table 1: What Items Are Recycled and by Whom

Category (and number of respondents)	Aluminum	Newsprint	White office paper	Colored office paper
Avid recycler (9)	9	9	8	5
Moderate recycler (70)	43	52	32	9
Nonrecycler (19)	3	8	12	2
Total	55	69	52	17

Discussion

The data from our survey support our hypothesis that a disparity exists between students' attitudes and actions toward recycling. However, the disparity is more complex than originally thought. We also wish to note that though we feel that the students we surveyed represent an excellent cross section of the BYU student body, if we had the chance to readminister the survey, we would add a managerial communications class to our survey pool in order to include business students. However, we do not feel that the lack of input from this sector has skewed the results since we found no variance of statistical significance among the disciplines in the other fields surveyed.

The actions of avid recyclers are quite consistent with their attitudes about recycling. All of them often or always go out of their way to recycle; all but one look exclusively for recycling bins for their cans and recycle all of the items included in our survey. Nevertheless, we did find one interesting inconsistency: while avid recyclers recycle frequently even when it is inconvenient, they are not, as a group, willing to pay much more for recycled products. In fact, only 33% of the avid recyclers indicated that they were willing to pay as much as 10% extra for recycled products.

Moderate recyclers' attitudes and actions varied significantly more than those of avid recyclers. While all of the moderates agree that recycling is an important issue, over half throw their aluminum cans in the trash rather than recycle. This disparity is further evidenced in that only 22% of the moderate recyclers often or always go out of their way to recycle. Like the avid recyclers, the moderates indicated a general unwillingness to pay more for recycled products: only 12%

stated that they would pay an additional 10% or more for recycled items. Nevertheless, about half of them noted that they do recycle aluminum and newsprint.

The gap between attitude and action is greatest in the nonrecycler group. While 81% of nonrecyclers feel that recycling is important, none specifically seeks out recycling bins or goes out of their way to recycle. In addition, none of the nonrecyclers said that they would pay 10% more for recycled products than for nonrecycled items. In spite of this, 14% indicate that they sometimes recycle aluminum, 38% recycle newspaper, 57% recycle white office paper, and 10% recycle colored office paper.

The disparity between students' attitudes and actions on recycling varies from avid to moderate to apathetic; however, three general conclusions transcend group boundaries:

(1) Very few people are willing to pay more for recycled products, even avid recyclers.

(2) Since 83% of those who do not recycle indicate that they are motivated by personal inconvenience, it seems reasonable to infer that efforts to increase recycling should focus on making recycling easier or on encouraging students to look beyond their own convenience.

(3) A significant disparity exists between students' attitudes and actions on recycling. This disparity is immediately obvious in the moderate and nonrecycler groups. Although it is much smaller, the gap also exists in the avid recycler group since the individuals showed a general unwillingness to purchase higher-priced recycled products.

References would follow on a separate page. Because this paper is based on the students' own field research, no references are included.

48e Understanding methodology and using evidence in the natural sciences

Natural scientists study natural phenomena. A botanist, for example, might study particular types of flowering plants, an entomologist the mating habits of various species of beetles, and an astrophysicist the formation and deterioration of stars. Regardless of their areas of specialization, natural scientists share a common approach to inquiry, grounded in scientific thinking.

Scientific thinking is based upon a pair of related assumptions: (1) that the universe is an ordered and organized system that can be understood through careful, systematic observation and analysis; and (2) that understanding one aspect of the universe is relevant to understanding other aspects. In other words, most scientists believe the universe is not random but is a highly organized series of interrelated systems—stellar, molecular, ecological, among many others.

The primary method of inquiry in the natural sciences is known as the *scientific method*. It involves observation leading to a hypothesis, which is then tested by additional observation and experiment. (See the accompanying chart.) A hypothesis is supported or refuted based on evidence, which in the natural sciences consists almost entirely of *empirical data* derived from observation and direct experience. Empirical data are verifiable, or capable of being proved (or disproved) by observation or experiment. They are often, though not always, quantifiable (capable of being measured) as well.

The Scientific Method

- Make observations.
- Question your observations in an effort to look for patterns and relationships.
- Formulate a tentative hypothesis or preliminary generalization about the subject you will investigate.
- Collect evidence for your hypothesis through systematic experimentation and direct observation.
- Reformulate your hypothesis based on your evidence and on the inferences you make about that evidence.
- Test your reformulated hypothesis further with additional observations and experiments.
- Analyze the results of your experiments and observations.
- Develop a theory to explain your hypothesis.

More often than not, scientists work from a **theory,** a systematically organized body of knowledge and thinking, which typically serves as the basis for both hypotheses and observations. (See the discussion of scientific thinking in 3d-1.)

Another method of inquiry in the natural sciences is library research on the scientific studies of other researchers. For example, an extensive scientific report or a science research paper would involve summarizing existing research and reviewing the relevant literature, usually as a prelude to presenting your own findings.

48f Considering purpose and audience for writing in the natural sciences

Scientists often write to inform readers of the results of their experiments and to persuade readers of their conclusions. As a student taking a college science course, you may be asked to inform readers, to persuade them, or to do both. You may also be asked to explain scientific phenomena, for example, the formation of black holes in outer space or the mating behavior of a particular type of fish. Or you may be asked to argue the merits of one theory over another, such as creationism versus evolution as an explanation of human origins. Or you may be asked to inform readers about the latest attempts to develop an AIDS vaccine while persuading them about the merits of one or another approach. Ask your instructor about the required purpose and audience for a particular writing assignment.

Keep in mind that the audiences for scientific writing will vary. Scientists write for one another in their professional journals. They also write for a general audience of nonexperts as well as for scientists outside their own fields. In your science courses, you may be asked to write for an expert or nonexpert audience. You will, of course, need to choose your language and select your details to suit your audience.

You will need to decide, for example, whether charts, graphs, tables, or statistics should be included or not. This will typically depend on the complexity of your topic, the clarity of your visual material, and the nature of your audience. You might decide to use statistical charts and diagrams in one instance because they illustrate a complex relationship more clearly than words do. In another instance, you may decide to omit displayed numerical data for a nonexpert audience and provide a verbal summary in its place.

The same is true for technical language. When you write for an audience of experts, you can use the verbal shorthand (the abbreviations) common to a particular scientific discipline along with its special vocabulary or jargon. In some instances you may be able to substitute nontechnical language for technical terms. But when you need to use technical language—where its precision, elegance, or efficiency are essential—be sure to define and explain the terms carefully and accurately. Further, in using the specialized vocabulary of a scientific discipline (words such as *atom, proton,* or *quark*), or words that have specialized meanings within them (such as *work, energy,* and *power,* whose meanings in physics differ from their everyday meanings), be sure to use that vocabulary with precision.

In addition, always take notes accurately and record your procedures and results carefully. If you are thorough and exacting in describing your work, you will enable other experimenters to repeat your experiments either to verify or challenge your results. (See the guidelines in 48h-2 for keeping a lab notebook.)

Finally, maintain an objective tone, using third-person pronouns and passive voice verbs. Also be aware of one additional convention when writing in the natural sciences: verb tense. Use the guidelines in the following excerpt to help you decide when to use past or present tense. (Also see 48h, especially 48h-2, on formatting science papers.)

> When a scientific paper has been validly published in a primary journal, it thereby becomes knowledge. Therefore, whenever you quote previously

published work, ethics requires you to treat that work with respect. You do this by using the *present* tense. It is correct to say "Streptomycin inhibits the growth of *M. tuberculosis* (13)." Whenever you quote or discuss previously published work, you should use the present tense; you are quoting established knowledge.

Your own present work must be referred to in the *past* tense. Your work is not presumed to be established knowledge until *after* it has been published. If you determined that the optimal growth temperature for *Streptomyces everycolor* was 37°C, you should say "*S. everycolor* grew best at 37°C." If you are citing previous work, possibly your own, it is then correct to say "*S. everycolor* grows best at 37°C."

In the typical paper, you will normally go back and forth between the past and present tenses. Most of the Abstract should be in the past tense, because you are referring to your own present results. Likewise, the Materials and Methods and the Results sections should be in the past tense, as you describe what you did and what you found. On the other hand, most of the Introduction and much of the Discussion should be in the present tense, because these sections usually emphasize previously established knowledge.

—Robert Day, *How to Write and Publish a Scientific Paper*

48g   Documenting sources in the natural sciences

Documentation styles for writing in the natural sciences vary with the discipline, sometimes significantly. It is important, therefore, to ask your instructor which documentation style is preferred. If your instructor has no preference, consult the following brief list as well as the more extensive list of style manuals in 45i. An alternative is to imitate the documentation style of a reputable journal in the relevant discipline.

Three commonly used documentation styles for papers and reports in the sciences are recommended by the Council of Biology Editors (CBE) in the *CBE Style Manual*, 6th ed. (Chicago: CBE, 1994). CBE documentation styles (see Chapter 45) are used by scientists in a number of fields, including botany, biochemistry, geography, geology, and zoology. Other style manuals in the sciences include the following:

AIP [American Institute of Physics] Style Manual. 4th ed. New York: AIP, 1990.

The ACS [American Chemical Society] Style Guide: A Manual for Authors and Editors. Washington: ACS, 1985.

A Manual for Authors of Mathematical Papers. Rev. 8th ed. Providence: American Mathematical Society, 1990.

You may also find the following publications helpful.

> Day, Robert. *How to Write and Publish a Scientific Paper.* 3rd ed. Phoenix: Oryx, 1988.
> Michaelson, Herbert B. *How to Write and Publish Engineering Papers and Reports.* 2nd ed. Philadelphia: ISI, 1986.

48h Understanding assignments and formats in the natural sciences

The format you select for your writing in the natural sciences will depend on the type of report or paper assigned and on your instructor's requirements. Among the more common assignments made in undergraduate science courses are a literature review and a lab report.

1 Literature reviews

The purpose of a *literature review* (also known as a *research review*) is to summarize the available research on a topic. The review writer's tasks include collecting, reading, and analyzing research reports. The review writer may evaluate the research on the basis of its importance to general readers or to specialists pursuing their own research on the subject. A review writer may also reinterpret previous research. If you are asked to do a literature review in a science course, keep the accompanying guidelines in mind.

A review of the literature on a specific topic may be included as part of a lab report (48h-2), but is not always necessary. For longer lab reports that discuss recent research in the context of previous studies, a review of the literature is essential. To see how science writers present reviews of research, consult specialized science journals, such as the *Journal of Microbiology,* and periodicals, such as *Science Review.*

Guidelines for Preparing a Literature Review

- Select a topic and limit it to a specific issue or problem.
- Read current journals, periodicals, and books.
- Summarize and paraphrase what you read.
- Analyze and interpret the researchers' claims.
- Format according to the appropriate style manual or your instructor's guidelines. Observe requirements for length.
- Carefully document your sources.

2 Lab reports

A *laboratory report* describes observations made during an experiment. If your report is based on an experiment conducted outside a laboratory (e.g., during field research), you may wish to call it a *research report*.

Wherever your experiment is performed, it is important to take careful and thorough notes. A good place to record empirical data as well as your own ideas about your experiments and observations is in a lab notebook or research journal. Follow the accompanying guidelines when you make notes in your lab notebook or research journal. (You may also wish to consult 2b-3 on keeping a double-column notebook.)

Guidelines for Keeping a Lab Notebook or Research Journal

- Jot down observations made in class as well as in the lab.
- Take notes on relevant reading; perhaps designate a special section of the notebook for your reading notes.
- Record the purpose of any lab experiment as well as the materials and the method or procedures used.
- Record the results of your experiments in detail, especially the different results of repeated experiments.
- Reserve a section of your notebook or journal for your own thinking about your reading and research. This is a good place to pose questions and begin formulating hypotheses.
- Be systematic in recording the details of your experiments. Write down results of your experiments at various stages of the process so that you can keep track of the sequence of events.
- Be sure to include mathematical calculations and other statistical data and to record them accurately.
- Keep track of your errors and doubts as you go along.

Once you are ready to write, you will find your lab or research notebook to be a valuable resource. In it you will have your preliminary thinking, facts and figures relating to experiments you may have performed, evaluations of other research, and perhaps summaries and reflections about your experiments and any outside reading. Be sure, however, to separate your own thoughts from the ideas of other writers (see 44d on note taking).

Whether you are writing a lab or research report, it typically includes the sections outlined in the accompanying chart. The lab report may be prefaced by a title page and followed with a list of references. (Consult your instructor

or the appropriate style manual about these formatting details.) Label your tables and figures separately, putting the label for a table (*Table 1*) above and that for a figure (*Figure 1*) below. Depending on the report's length and complexity, you may place any graphs, tables, and other illustrations in an appendix rather than in the body of the report.

Parts of a Research or Lab Report

- A **title**
- An **abstract** or summary of the report
- An **introduction** that states the purpose of the report, the reason the research was conducted, a summary of relevant background, and a statement of the problem investigated, including the writer's hypothesis
- The **method** (or **procedures**) followed, along with the **materials** used, including any statistics
- The **results**, or a description of the findings, including any tables, graphs, or other illustrations
- A **discussion** that analyzes and interprets the results and explains how the results relate to the hypothesis. This section may also include new or additional hypotheses that require testing
- Any additional **conclusions** not previously discussed

Sample student paper in the natural sciences

An example of a lab report written for a physics mechanics course follows. The report is based on the student's own lab experiment and therefore does not contain citations to other research or a list of references. Note the use of objective language throughout, especially the writer's use of third-person pronouns and passive voice verbs.

Michael D. Robertson
Physics Lab
Prof. Carlson
April 22, 1994

The Conservation of Energy

Abstract

An experiment to verify the conservation of energy demonstrated that energy is conserved in the absence of friction. Measurements of the total energy at the starting and stopping points of a cart on a track were made and compared. The slight conversion of energy measured is attributed to friction.

Introduction

The purpose of this lab experiment was to verify that when friction is absent, energy is conserved. The research was conducted as part of a series of experiments dealing with energy in its different forms. The hypothesis was that due to the relative lack of friction present in the measuring device, the results would show a near-perfect symmetry between the original and final energy measurements.

Method

Materials included a spring, a ruler, a hanging mass, and a lab cart on a track. The constant of the spring was measured by hanging the mass (M) from the spring, stretching it over a distance (X). The formula $F = kx$ was used to determine the spring constant. After the spring was attached to the hook at the top of the test track, the lab cart was hooked up to the spring and allowed to roll down the test track until it stopped. Its distance of travel (X) was then measured.

The SPE at both the release point and the stopping point of the cart was found using the formula Spring Potential Energy (SPE) = $1/2kx$. Also calculated was the Gravitational Potential Energy (GPE), which is equal to an object's mass (m) times the acceleration of gravity (g) times the height of the object from the ground (h). The formula is, thus, Mgh. The SPE and GPE at the release point and the stopping point of the cart were added and the total energy at each point was compared.

The following definitions were used:

Gravity (g) = 9.8 meters/second (the acceleration of gravity on earth).

A newton is a measurement of force (mass x acceleration) equal to 1 kilogram accelerated at one meter per second.

A joule is the ability to move one newton one meter.

Results

The results of the experiment are summarized in the following lists of calculations:

Calculations for finding k:

Mass used to find k = .106 kilograms

.105 meters = length of spring hanging limp

.715 meters = length of spring stretched

.610 meters = delta x

$F = kx$ $f = .106(9.8) = k(.61)$

$k = 1.7029$

Calculations for finding Gravitational Potential Energy:

Height at release = .134 meters

Height at bottom = .058 meters

Mass of lab cart = .5125 kilograms

Acceleration of gravity = 9.8 m/s/s

GPE = Mgh = .5215(9.8)(.134) at top = .6848 joules

GPE at bottom = .5215(9.8)(.058) = .2964 joules

Calculations for finding Spring Potential Energy:

SPE = 1/2kx^2

Spring = 8.5 cm limp

Spring = 16.5 cm at start (8 cm total stretch)

Spring = 76.5 cm at finish (68 cm total stretch)

1/2kx^2 at top = .5(1.7029)(.08)(.08) = .005449 joules

1/2kx^2 at bottom = .5(1.7029)(.68)(.68) = .3937 joules

Total energy at top and bottom:

Total energy = GPE + SPE + KE + . . . = GPE + SPE in this case

At top GPE = .6848 joules

At top SPE = .005449 joules

Total energy at top = .6848 + .005449 = .690249 joules

At bottom GPE = .2964 joules

At bottom SPE = .3937 joules

Total energy at bottom = .2964 + .3937 = .6901 joules

Calculations for % error:

% error = 100 (energy1 − energy2)/energy1

% error = 100(.690249 − .6901)/.690249

% error = .0201%

Discussion

The results indicate that energy is conserved to the extent that friction does not impede its conservation. The greater the friction, the greater is the energy converted. It is apparent that the lab cart-track system used in the experiment was nearly devoid of friction, and, therefore, the anticipated results were produced. Possible sources of error include inaccuracies in measurements and in the measuring device--though these proved negligible in this experiment.

Conclusions

Newton's First Law of Thermodynamics applies in this as in all measurements of energy in isolated systems. Since energy can be neither created nor destroyed, the slight amount of friction generated by the cart rolling on the track created heat energy that compensated for the kinetic energy lost. The total amount of energy remained the same, though a small amount of one form of energy was converted to another form. This shifting or transferral of energy is inescapable in the real world since in the absence of friction, the cart would roll on the track forever.

CHAPTER 49

Business Writing

The business world requires a great deal of writing. This writing is typically task oriented and time constrained. Reports, letters, and responses to memos, job postings, and e-mail require quick and efficient response. Deadlines are critical. Equally important, business writing needs to be concise, direct, and purposeful.

This chapter explains the conventions of business writing and shows how to write memos, letters, reports, and proposals. It also explains how to write a résumé. In writing for business and the professions follow the basic principles presented in the accompanying chart.

Principles of Business Communication

- **Know your audience.** Be aware of who will receive and read what you write. Try to use his or her name—at the very least you should know the individual's title and level of authority. Avoid outdated forms of address such as *Dear Sir.*

- **Express your purpose.** Explain quickly and clearly your reason for writing.

- **Be polite.** Use a courteous and civilized tone. Be friendly but not overly informal. Put yourself in your reader's place to gauge the tone of your writing.

- **Be concise.** Say what you have to say as directly and briefly as possible. Express your ideas without unnecessary words.

- **Be clear.** Make sure your language can be easily understood. Avoid complicated constructions and confusing sentences. Use the active voice.

- **Use correct grammar, punctuation, and mechanics.** Take pains to ensure that your writing follows the conventions of standard English. Doing so will indicate your concern for accuracy and your attention to detail.

- **Consider appearances.** Be neat. Use high-quality bond paper. Make your work look pleasing to the eye. If you are working on a word processor, experiment with various formatting options to produce an attractive document.

49a   Writing business memos and letters

Business letters and *memorandums* (or *memos*) are the most frequently used types of writing in business. Memos are used to communicate within a company. When writing to a company or organization and for communication between them, business letters are the appropriate form of correspondence.

Business letters are more formal than memos, whose informality typically reflects the closer relationship between writers and readers. In selecting the tone for both memos and letters, use common sense. Let your relationship with your reader determine how formal you need to be. In cases where you are unsure, use a more formal rather than a less formal tone. In all your letters and memos, however, be courteous.

As with most business writing, you need to follow certain conventions of formatting. The following sections will help you determine the appropriate tone and format for your business memos and letters.

1   Memos

Memos serve a number of purposes. Primarily, they maintain open channels of communication within a company—colleagues keep one another apprised of events with informal memos. Memos are also used to call meetings or to announce changes in policy. In addition, memos serve as a permanent record of decisions made and actions undertaken. They may contain information regarding approaches to problems, or they may express attitudes toward company policies.

Memos contain evidence that can be used to enhance or diminish your job performance. Thus, it is a good idea to avoid writing anything ungracious or unkind in your memos. In particular, be careful to avoid biased language (see Chapter 29). In writing memos, keep the accompanying conventions in mind.

Conventions of Business Memos

- Follow the proper format, identifying the date of the memo, its audience, sender, and subject at the top of the page.
- Single-space long memos; double-space short ones.
- Initial the memo next to your name.
- Keep the memo brief and to the point.
- Engage your readers by focusing on essential matters, one idea per paragraph. Begin with the most important idea.
- Conclude with a gesture of goodwill.

---

2   Business letters

Unlike memos, which are the preferred form of written correspondence within a company, business letters serve as a company's primary means of external communication. A business letter is also the appropriate form of communication for an individual writing to a company. Whether you are writing to seek information, place an order, request an adjustment, lodge a complaint, or attend to some other business matter, you should follow the principles of business communication listed in the accompanying chart.

Guidelines for Writing Business Letters

- Direct your letter to an individual.
- Use a courteous opening and maintain a polite tone.
- State your reason for writing at the outset.
- Be clear about what you want.
- State your appreciation of the reader's concern and interest.
- Conclude with a polite gesture of thanks.
- Indicate an enclosure with the abbreviation *enc.* (plural *encs.*)
- Identify anyone else receiving a copy of the letter. Use *c.* for one copy to a single individual and *cc.* for copies to two or more people.
- Be consistent in using the block or modified block format.
- Single-space within paragraphs and double-space between paragraphs.
- Proofread your letter carefully.
- Always remember to sign your letter.

You should also use one of the standard formats for business letters: block or modified block. *Block format* aligns everything at the left margin. *Modified block* format indents as illustrated in 49b. Whichever format you use, be sure to observe the conventions of spacing as illustrated in the sample letters.

SAMPLE ENVELOPE

Boris Rodzinski
1234 Gray Street
Glen Ellyn, IL 54321

Ms. Angela Hernandez
Publicity Department
Cannon Electric Company
35 Harvest Drive
Chicago, IL 35791

SAMPLE BUSINESS LETTER IN BLOCK FORMAT

return address	1234 Gray Street Glen Ellyn, IL 54321
date	April 25, 1994
line space	
inside address	Ms. Angela Hernandez Publicity Department Cannon Electric Company 35 Harvest Drive Chicago, IL 35791
line space	
salutation	Dear Ms. Hernandez:
line space	

I am writing to request information about your company's products and services for a research paper I am preparing for my marketing course at Northwestern University. The instructor suggested that in addition to the usual library research, we could gain a different perspective by reading publications produced by various companies. Hence my request.

line space

I am a senior marketing major with a special interest in electrical products and services. I am particularly interested in research and development your company may be engaged in as well as in your company's relationship with suppliers and clients.

line space

I appreciate your taking the time to send me any company publications you think suitable. And if there were the slightest chance you would have time to speak with me in person, I would be happy to come to Cannon Electric at a time convenient for you.

line space

closing	Sincerely yours,
4 line spaces	*Boris Rodzinski*
signature	
name, typed	Boris Rodzinski

c. Professor K. Evancie

49b Writing job application letters

Like business letters and memos, **job application letters** require a clear sense of purpose, a courteous tone, and care in observing conventions of formatting. An application letter should be more than a mere cover letter announcing that you are sending a résumé and applying for a job. Instead, let your application letter indicate who you are, what you have accomplished, and how you can contribute to a company or organization.

Tailor your letter to each job you apply for. Be sure to indicate where you heard about the job opening, why you are applying, and how your education and experience qualify you for it. And always include a request for an interview. The accompanying guidelines summarize the essential considerations in writing a job application letter.

Guidelines for Writing a Job Application Letter

- Indicate how you learned of the job opening.
- Identify the job or position you are applying for.
- Provide evidence of your qualifications for the job.
- Provide specific information about your background and accomplishments.
- Ask for an interview.
- Note that a copy of your résumé is enclosed.
- Be courteous and confident.
- Pay attention to appearances. Use high-quality 8½ × 11-inch bond paper (for both your letter and résumé). Be sure your letter is neat and error free.
- Type your name below your signature, and do not forget to sign your letter.

SAMPLE JOB APPLICATION LETTER IN MODIFIED BLOCK FORMAT

April 21, 1994
North Hall
Pace University
Pleasantville, NY 10530

Dr. Adrienne Cherloux
Assistant Superintendent for Personnel
Dover High School
300 West McFarland Street
Dover, NJ 07801

Dear Dr. Cherloux:

Professor Samantha Darby, an instructor at Pace, recently conducted research in your school. She suggested I write you about the teaching position in psychology opening up in the fall. I will graduate next month with Honors, with a B.A. in psychology supplemented by a teaching certificate. Bilingual in Spanish and English, I am eager to teach in a public school. My résumé is enclosed.

During my four years at Pace, I focused on educational and social psychology, with a special interest in adolescent development. Having grown up in Puerto Rico, I wish to work in a high school with a large number of Spanish-speaking students. I understand their needs and would like to help them develop.

While pursuing my formal education, I coordinated a student network of volunteers to support the annual blood drive, provided child care for one of the local churches, and staffed a teen shelter one night a week. My volunteer work has given me insight into children's needs as well as a clear sense of how to organize groups of community helpers.

I would like to discuss my qualifications at an interview. I am especially interested in hearing more about your special programs for minorities. Please let me know where and when we can meet to discuss this exciting prospect. I look forward to hearing from you.

Sincerely,

Martha Kilmer

Martha Kilmer

enc. résumé

49c   Writing and formatting résumés

Your job application letter should be accompanied by a *résumé*, a succinct outline of your educational background and work experience, coupled with information about your related extracurricular activities and special skills or interests. Résumés may be arranged according to your specific job skills (a functional résumé) or according to the jobs you have held, beginning with the most recent (a chronological résumé). Functional résumés are suitable when you have acquired significant work experience, well-developed skills, and significant accomplishments. Chronological résumés are more common for someone entering the marketplace for the first time or for those with only modest work experience. The accompanying sample résumé is arranged chronologically. Notice that the educational background and work experience begin with the most recent items and work backward. Employers will be more interested in your most recent work experience.

Also be sure to include reference to the specific job for which you are applying or a general career objective. This will indicate precisely what you are interested in and will increase the likelihood that your letter and résumé will get into the hands of the right person.

And finally, if you include references, provide the names, addresses, and full titles of three professors, supervisors, or employers who have agreed to speak or write on your behalf. You have the option, however, of simply indicating that references can be furnished upon request. Use the accompanying guidelines in preparing your résumé.

Guidelines for Writing a Résumé

- Place your name, address, and phone number at the top of the page.
- Include clearly labeled categories for career objective, education, work experience, special skills, activities, and references.
- Include dates for graduation and for time at each job.
- If you are preparing a chronological résumé, place educational and work experience in reverse chronological order, beginning with the most recent job.
- Provide a brief description of your responsibilities at each job.
- Include a title for each job or position held.
- Try to keep the résumé to a single page so it can be scanned quickly.
- Use a uniform type size for headings, a different type size for information beneath the headings. If you are working on a word processor, take advantage of the available lettering and formatting options.
- Space your categories evenly and make your résumé as pleasing to the eye as you can. Leave ample space between entries, avoid crowding, and be sure the résumé is perfect in appearance.

SAMPLE RÉSUMÉ

Martha T. Kilmer
North Hall
Pace University
Pleasantville, NY 10530
914-555-3286

CAREER OBJECTIVE
To obtain a teaching position requiring Spanish/English language skills.

EDUCATION
Pace University, Pleasantville, New York
  B.A. in Psychology with Honors; anticipated graduation 5/94
  New York State Teaching Certificate, Grades 7-12
Flores High School, Hato Bay, Puerto Rico, diploma 1990
  Salutatorian; Recipient of Principal's Award for Leadership

EXPERIENCE
Pace University, Psychology Department, Pleasantville, NY
  Research Assistant, Professor Samantha Darby. Recruited and processed subjects in a cross-sectional computerized study of mental imagery in adults, children, and teenagers. June 1993 to March 1994.

Rindge Teen Shelter, Department of Human Services, Mt. Kisco, NY
  Youth Coordinator. Staffed the shelter one night a week. Served as friend and counselor to drop-in teenagers. Prepared weekly workshops on issues of adolescence. September 1992 to May 1993.

SPECIAL SKILLS
Fully bilingual in Spanish and English.

ACTIVITIES
Coordinator for Neighborhood Development Program, a public service and community action program.

REFERENCES
Furnished upon request.

CHAPTER 50

Writing with a Computer

A computer can save you time and give you flexibility you do not have composing with pen or typewriter. With a touch of a key or the click of a mouse, you can delete an entire page, move sentences and paragraphs, underline and boldface key words. The computer frees you to experiment because you know that what you write can be easily changed, moved, stored, recalled, deleted, restored, and revised.

Since computers are available in university computer labs, libraries, and writing centers, you need not own a computer to use one. Find out where you can use a computer, when you can use one, and how to sign up to use one.

50a Working with a word-processing program

Most word-processing programs are easy to use once you become familiar with basic commands. You need not master an entire program to begin using it effectively. Nor do you have to know how the computer's hardware works, except to turn it on and access the word-processing software you want to use. You will learn about the computer itself and about the capabilities of your word-processing program as you work. The accompanying chart describes the most important guidelines to follow when you write with a computer.

Guidelines for Writing with a Computer

- Always **save** your documents. As you work, you should pause frequently (every 15 or 30 minutes) to store or save what you have written. You can save either on the computer's hard drive or on a disk. Saving enables you to store permanently the work you have generated. Saving also prevents you from losing large amounts of work because of a computer malfunction or a power outage. Your program's user manual, or its self-help menu, describes how to save your documents.

(continued)

- Before saving or storing any document, you need to give it a **file name.** When you wish to continue working on a document, use this file name to retrieve it from storage on your disk or from your computer's hard drive.
- Familiarize yourself with the basic commands or computer terminology: *insert, delete, block, move, scroll, search.*

    To **delete** a document or a portion of it means to erase it.
    To **block** a portion of text means to highlight it in preparation for doing something else with it, such as underlining, boldfacing, or deleting it.
    To **move** a portion of text means to shift it from one place to another.
    To **scroll** through a document means to move its lines quickly up the screen.
    To **search** a document means to have the computer locate specific words or phrases.

- Protect your work by creating a **backup** system for your documents. Make extra copies of your work on duplicate disks and print out hard copy of your work to serve as an additional backup in case something happens to your disks. Also, take care of your disks. Keep them clean, and store them away from electrical appliances, which might demagnetize or damage them.
- Familiarize yourself with the **formatting** options your program provides. Computer word-processing programs provide options for attractive design of documents. You can choose among typefaces or fonts, vary type size, use bold or italics, and insert bullets, arrows, or other symbols and figures.
- Learn how to **print** your documents, or arrange to have someone print them for you. Consider the capabilities and limitations of the different types of printers available such as dot matrix, ink jet, and laser printers.

50b Using a computer to generate ideas and organize

Use the computer to brainstorm ideas, to make lists, and to jot questions and brief notes in the way you might prepare to write with a pencil and paper. Store these preliminary jottings in a prewrite file, and retrieve them when you work on a draft. You may wish to print them out so you can look through them as you write your drafts.

Using a computer is a good way to do brainstorming, list making, and idea generating because it is easy to add, delete, move, and correct what you write. With a word-processing program you can pull passages of freewriting into your lists and place them with your questions if you like. You can also use the computer to create columns for double-column notebook entries.

You can use a computer to make a preliminary outline, print it out, and then use it as a map to guide your writing. You can organize the notes you take when doing research by providing appropriate headings for each page, and create a working list of works cited or references.

50c Using a word processor for drafting and revising

Some writers suffer from an unreasonable fear of making a mistake when they draft, a fear that can inhibit thinking. With correction just a click of the mouse or a keystroke away, developing your idea and thinking about what you are writing become more important than getting every detail correct the first time.

Word processors offer numerous other advantages for drafting and revising. You can use your word-processing program to move sections of your work, delete passages, rewrite sentences, replace words and phrases, and add paragraphs—all without having to rewrite or retype your draft. With many programs, you can delete a passage, see how your writing reads without it, and immediately restore it should you prefer to retain it. You can also store the deleted text in a file for later use, should you change your mind. You can thus experiment with different forms of your essay, moving sections around to see where they are most effective. Be sure, however, to save each of your drafts under its own file name in case you decide to scrap a later draft and instead use an earlier one.

Once you have completed (and stored) a draft of your writing, it is a good idea to print it out. Most writers find it easier to get a sense of the whole draft and spot errors or problems when reading a printed copy than when reading on a computer screen.

WRITING HINT   A word processor also gives you the freedom to create space between sections or paragraphs of your draft. If you need to add examples to a paragraph, for example, or to explain an idea more fully, use the enter key to add space on the page. You can fill that space with examples, details, and explanations right away, or you can return to it later when you have completed the draft.

50d Benefiting from available features

Computers have additional features you will find helpful when you write. You should be aware, however, that they have limitations.

Computer networks

You may be able to store and post drafts of your essays on your school's computer network for responses from your instructor or your peer group. If you have access to electronic mail (e-mail), communicate with your instructor or fellow students, asking questions and offering suggestions and advice about your own and your classmates' writing. You may also be able to transfer data from online databases, hook into other computer networks, and access university and public library holdings.

Spell-checker programs

A word-processing *spell-check* feature identifies typographical errors and misspelled words, providing a list of correctly spelled alternatives. For example, if you type *kno* in your draft and use the spell-check function, it provides options such as: *knee, knew, knot, know,* and *no.* If you had typed *homogenius,* it might offer you the following possible corrections: *homogeneous, homogeny, homogeneity.* But these programs have their limits, and you will have to recognize the correct spellings of the words you use. You should also know that the spell-check function cannot distinguish among homonyms such as *there, they're,* and *their; it's* and *its; to, two,* and *too.* If you use the wrong word but spell it correctly, the spell checker will not know that you have made a mistake.

Thesaurus programs

A *thesaurus* is a dictionary of synonyms and related words. When you wish to substitute another word for one you have chosen, the thesaurus program can offer you a list of alternatives. But since the words it lists differ not only in denotation and connotation but also in idiomatic usage, be careful when substituting words based on a thesaurus list. Consult a dictionary when deciding among related words, and avoid using unfamiliar words.

Style-checking programs

The *style checker* is most often a style, grammar, and usage guide that identifies common errors such as wordiness, incorrect pronouns, and inappropriate punctuation. Although you may make corrections suggested by a style-checking program, your writing may not be free of error. Some programs, for example, may not be able to identify garbled syntax or misused homonyms.

Other writing programs

In addition to the popular and familiar types of writing and editing programs already described, you may find others. Two of these kinds of programs can be helpful: invention (or discovery) programs and organization programs. Invention programs help you generate ideas for your writing. They help you get started thinking by inviting you to consider your subject from different angles and with different questions in mind. Organization programs can help you order and arrange your ideas and evidence logically.

Finally, *outlining* programs can be used as you plan your drafts and when you complete them. In addition, this book exists in an online format that you can store on your computer's hard drive or work with from the program's floppy disks.

50e   Designing documents

In writing for academic and professional purposes, your primary concern is to communicate information and convey ideas. You accomplish these goals through carefully selected language and tightly organized structures. In ordering your words, however, you should also consider how they appear on the page. The visual appearance of your writing affects your audience just as your words do. Your manner of presentation is part of your message, just as the matter you present is.

The first consideration about the visual appearance of your written text should be your audience. In writing essays, papers, and reports for your college courses, you should follow the conventions of manuscript form as described in Appendix A. In addition, follow any other specific instructions your teachers provide.

1   General design considerations

Titles

Titles should be centered on the page. They may be printed in the same size and font of type as the essay or paper, or in a larger or bolder typeface. Positioning the title and emphasizing it draws readers' attention to your paper's central concern.

Headings

Headings within a paper or report break the text into chunks, which are more easily digested by your readers. Page after page of print is less inviting than pages that include the visual "breaks" of headings and subheadings. Strategically placed headings focus your readers on specific aspects of your general topic. By glancing at your headings, readers can gain a quick overview of the specific content elements you have included.

Block quotations

Quotations of more than four lines of prose and three lines of poetry are set off visually as a *block* rather than being run into the text of your writing. This visual separation indicates that you are quoting more than a few words or sentences. The block of quotation enables the reader to shift gears and prepare to hear the voice of another writer.

Graphs and charts

Graphs and charts add to the communicative possibilities of your papers and reports. Such visual aids display information efficiently in far less space than it would take to explain their information content in words. In addition, graphs and charts provide an alternative way of presenting data. They allow you to introduce variety into your papers and reports. They can provide visual relief for readers, and they can make a strong impression as well.

2 Designing documents for academic contexts

Pagination

Number the pages of your document, omitting a page number from the title page. Begin numbering the first page of text consecutively with arabic numerals, usually in the upper right corner. Do not put parentheses around your numbers or periods after them. Many word-processing programs can paginate your document for you.

Margins and spacing

Most often, your academic papers should be typed and double-spaced. You should indent your paragraphs one-half inch, or five spaces. In some circumstances, such as preparing science lab reports or reports for business courses, you may use single-spacing.

You should always *justify* or align the lines of print to the left margin of your writing. You can indent for new paragraphs and for lists and block quotations. Check with your instructor about aligning or justifying the right margin. In printed books such as this one, both right and left margins are justified. In academic papers, however, it is common to leave the right margin *unjustified* or ragged to avoid overlarge spaces between words to create a right-column alignment, and also to avoid hyphenation for line breaks. (Many word-processing programs can be formatted to run with or without hyphenation.)

Type size and style

Almost all word-processing programs provide options for selecting various type sizes and typefaces, or *fonts*. When you write papers and reports for your courses, it is generally best to select a standard size and font. A common easy-to-read 10- or 11-point size in a simple font keeps the emphasis on your writing. Using script fonts or italics may seem appealing, but these are difficult to read for more than a few lines at a time. In addition, stick with a single font and type size for your academic papers and reports—except for headings and titles, as explained earlier.

Highlighting

You may occasionally highlight words with italics, boldface, or capital letters. Using these techniques of emphasis too often, however, can be distracting. Most often, it is best to use these features only for headings and titles. In this book **boldface** is used to introduce key terms and *italics* to highlight words and phrases in textual illustration and exercise examples. Blocks of CAPITAL LETTERS are used to designate chapters.

Headings

Use headings to announce the focus of sections within your writing. Most of your academic papers will probably not require headings. For longer reports and research papers, however, headings can help focus readers' attention on particular aspects of your topic. Some disciplines, moreover, have established conventions for report headings. See Chapter 48 on the parts of a report in the sciences and in the social sciences.

Lists

You may wish to use a list in a paper or report. Bulleted lists allow you to isolate and emphasize key points. They can also enhance the visual appeal of a document.

In using bulleted lists, however, be careful not to make them too long. Lists of more than ten items should be grouped into two categories. Also, try to keep the items in the list to a single line each. And be sure that the items are grammatically parallel.

You may use a bullet (•), a dash (-), or an asterisk (*) for each item in your list. In some instances, you may wish to number the items rather than bullet them.

White space

The space around the print on a page acts like a frame for a picture. It focuses the reader's attention on the printed text; it also creates a contrast between the dark print and the complementary white background against which that print stands out. For most academic writing, frame your pages with margins of 1 to 1 ½ inches all around, depending on the audience, purpose, and content of your document. Avoid creating lines of type that run nearly across the entire page or from top to bottom. Long lines of print and tiny margins give the page a crowded, unappealing look.

Use white space generally to create a clean, neat, balanced appearance for your documents. Breaking your print text with space makes it both more attractive to readers and easier for them to comprehend. Besides using white space around your words, consider its use around any visuals you may include.

3　Designing documents for nonacademic contexts

When you write for nonacademic audiences, be attentive to the visual appearance of your writing. A carefully designed résumé and an attractively presented letter can help you stand out from a crowd of job applicants. A thoughtfully designed report for a project at work can impress your co-workers and superiors not only in its effective presentation of information but also in the way it conveys your careful attention to details of appearance.

You do not have to go outside the university environment to see the importance of visual design for documents. Look at the various bulletins, notices, newsletters, and posters plastered around your campus. You will find public announcements, advertisements, and other attempts to grab the attention of readers and persuade them to attend a lecture or concert, join a club, support a cause.

You can find concern for the visual dimension of documents in the many publications produced by your college or university. Look at the various functional pieces you encounter, such as course enrollment forms, financial aid forms, class admit forms, as well as the publications produced by your school's support offices—counseling, tutoring, cooperative education, career services, language and computer labs, and the like.

In designing your own documents outside course-required essays, papers, and reports, be attentive to the clarity, coherence, and persuasiveness of your writing. Use design features to reinforce your purpose in writing. Be sure that the design features you select enhance rather than detract from the information and ideas conveyed by your written text.

Remember that readers outside the academic environment are pressed for time. They may skim what you write rather than read it through completely. They may also not have the time or inclination to read long sentences, elaborate paragraphs, and lengthy chunks of written text. You can use a number of design features to respond to such real-world reading realities.

You can use these guidelines in preparing many kinds of documents, including educational materials, training manuals, and textbooks such as this one. You can use them for business reports and academic reports like those included in Chapters 48 and 49 of this book. You can also use them for newsletters and bulletins, such as those published by your college or university. And you can use them as well for promotional and public relations materials designed for marketing purposes.

Imagine, for example, that the Richard Avedon photograph used as the basis for a student essay in Chapter 4 was to be used as a marketing image for

---

How to Design Documents for Nonacademic Contexts

- **Break your text** into chunks, by using white space and headings.
- **Boldface** and/or use **CAPS** to highlight key words and phrases.
- **Include visual images**—icons, photographs, visual design elements, art reproductions—to attract and focus your readers' attention.
- **Use generous margins** and clear, **dark type** that stands out readily against a simple clean background.

---

an exhibition of the photographer's work. That image, accompanied by a catchy headline and carefully prepared and presented body copy would make a striking advertisement. The Avedon photograph might also be included in a promotional brochure or foldout piece with yet another kind of attention-getting, persuasive printed text.

Finally, you can find examples of effective document design in the magazines on display at newsstands around your community. With a visit to a good newsstand display and an hour sifting through a variety of magazines, you can discover many and varied ways to combine written text with visuals. You will discover as well many different ways text can be attractively laid out for reader-friendly perusal.

50f Creating and using visuals

Visuals can help you present your ideas with clarity and emphasis. You can use them as support for a mostly written document, or you can make them the centerpiece of a document that is supported by a brief written text.

The kinds of visuals most frequently used in academic writing include tables, charts, and graphs. Tables present information in columns and rows, usually in numerical form. Charts and graphs present information so that relationships among different elements are apparent. Drawings, diagrams, and other more common images can be used to illustrate a process or describe the parts of something.

Tables and charts are familiar visual elements in business and scientific writing—as, for example, those in Chapters 48 and 4 of this book. When you include tables and charts in your academic papers and reports, it is standard procedure to number your tables and to provide titles for charts and graphs. The specific elements described in the tables and graphs should be made clear for your readers. In addition, you should provide a link between your visuals and your written text, either in the text itself or in a caption or subtitle to accompany the visuals you include.

In preparing your visuals, strive for a neat, clean appearance, with plenty of white space around them to increase their attractiveness and ability to communicate. Your visuals should complement your written text, add to it, or summarize information more efficiently than words can express rather than repeating in visual form what you say in writing.

Consider the following examples of visuals—a pie chart, a line graph, and a bar graph. Notice how the information presented is clearly labeled.

Pie Chart

This *pie chart* illustrates how state lottery proceeds for a thirty-year period 1964–1995 were allocated. Although the information could be presented in alternative formats such as a list, table, or bar graph, the pie chart lets readers see the relative weight in percentages for each area of allocation. In general, use pie charts to portray relationships among parts and a whole.

Percent distribution of 1964–1995
cumulative State lottery proceeds
($93 billion)

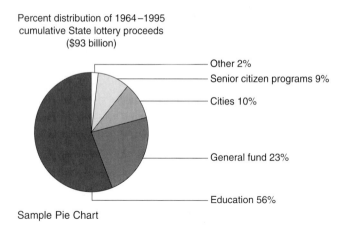

Other 2%
Senior citizen programs 9%
Cities 10%
General fund 23%
Education 56%

Sample Pie Chart

Line Graph

The sample *line graph* represents media usage by consumers for a ten-year period. Each line represents a different type of media. The direction of each line indicates an increase or decrease in the use of particular media. Use line graphs to display trends and multiple line graphs to compare trends over time.

Bar Graph

The sample *bar graph* describes software sales for 1994 and 1995 in millions of dollars. Different types of software programs are included with the most used on top and the less used on the bottom. Use bar graphs to display comparative information visually.

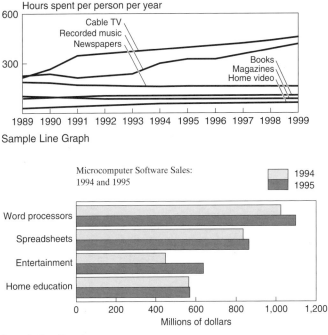

Media Usage by Consumers: 1989 to 1999

Sample Line Graph

Microcomputer Software Sales: 1994 and 1995

Sample Bar Graph

All charts adapted from the U.S. Bureau of the Census. From *The American Almanac 1996–1997 Statistical Abstract of the United States,* Hoover's, Inc., Austin Texas, 1997, 296, 558.

Guidelines for Using Visuals

- Provide a caption or legend for each visual.
- Make sure the details of your visuals are clear and readable.
- Number your visuals.
- Provide a lead-in comment in your written text to introduce each visual.
- For complex visuals that contain multiple kinds of information, explain what the visual illustrates.
- Credit the source for visuals you do not create yourself.

Preparing the Final Manuscript for Submission

A reader's first impression of your writing is often formed by the physical appearance of your manuscript. A neat, crisp, clean essay or report suggests that you have taken care with your work. This appendix offers a survey of what to look for when you have a near final or final manuscript in hand. Be sure to consult the appropriate *Handbook* sections or chapters for additional guidelines, explanations, and examples.

A1 Preparing the final manuscript

The following guidelines will help you prepare a final manuscript that is suitable for submission. However, be sure to follow any other instructions your instructor may give you for manuscript preparation.

Paper

If you are typing your paper or printing it out, use 8½ × 11-inch white bond paper, sixteen to twenty pound. Do not use erasable paper, which smudges easily and is difficult for you or your instructor to write on. Remove hole-punched or perforated edges from the computer printout and separate any connected pages. If you plan to submit a handwritten paper (if your instructor accepts it), use 8½ × 11-inch white, lined paper. Avoid tearing pages from a notebook or using unlined paper.

Clear, readable type

Use a fresh, black typewriter ribbon or be sure the cartridge or ribbon in your computer's printer prints dark and clear. If you are using a computer, select letter quality as the printer option. Handwritten papers should be written legibly in blue or black ink—avoid using pencil or other colored inks. Always double-space your typed or printed papers (unless your instructor prefers 1½-line spacing), and type or print on only one side of the page. If you are working with a printer or typewriter with a variety of fonts, select a clear and legible typeface (the standard 10- or 12-point type). Avoid scripts or other elaborate typefaces that might be difficult to read.

Cover page

If you are required to include a cover page, use the standard format. Center the title a third of the way down. Double-space and center your name on the next line (preceded by *By*) followed by the course number and/or section, your instructor's name, and the date. See Chapter 46 for examples of cover page formats.

Margins, page numbers, and paragraph indents

Set up your paper with 1-inch margins all around. However, use a 1¼-inch margin if you plan to put your work in a binder. (Note that instructor preferences for binding a final paper vary—some prefer staples, paper clips, or simply folding the paper in half; ask your instructor what is recommended.) Number all pages consecutively in the upper right-hand corner, ½ inch from the top of the page. Use arabic numerals. You may include your last name before each page number. In addition, be sure to indent all paragraphs five spaces from the left margin. For an example of a properly formatted essay in MLA style, see 46a.

Documenting sources

Be sure to credit your sources according to the documentation style recommended by your instructor. Most likely your essay will include both in-text and end-of-text citations. (See Chapter 45 for information on documentation. To see how two students documented their papers, turn to Chapter 46.)

A2 Formatting considerations

The following guidelines are based on MLA style. If your instructor requires you to set up your paper according to another documentation style, consult the appropriate style manual for information.

Check the spacing in your manuscript

- Have you left *one space* after commas, semicolons, and colons?
- Have you left *no space* before commas, semicolons, colons, periods, question marks, or exclamation points?

- Did you leave *one space* after a closing quotation mark, parenthesis, or bracket when these marks occur before a period at the end of a sentence? But, did you leave *two spaces* when any of these marks falls after a period?
- Did you leave *two spaces* after a period, question mark, or exclamation point that ends a sentence?
- Have you left *no space* before or after hyphens or apostrophes that fall within words?
- Have you left *no space* before, after, or between dashes that fall among words?
- Have you consulted 45a and 45c (MLA), 45d and 45f (APA), or 45h and 45i (CBE) for detailed guidelines on spacing your parenthetical and end-of-paper documentation?
- (For additional advice, see Part Eight on punctuation and mechanics.)

Check your treatment of titles

- Have you underlined titles of books, plays, book-length (epic) poems, ships, periodicals, films, recordings, and paintings?
- Did you enclose titles of poems, essays, articles, short stories, and chapters within quotation marks?
- Have you omitted underlining and quotation marks from the title of your essay or report (unless you have used another title as part of your own)?

(For additional advice on working with titles, see 36f, 38e, and 39a.)

Check your treatment of quotations

- Have you checked all quotations against your notes or the original sources to ensure accuracy?
- Have you made it clear for readers where quoted material begins and ends?

INCORPORATING PROSE QUOTATIONS

- Have you identified clearly all quoted material of four lines or less by enclosing it within quotation marks, and have you run these quotations into the body of your essay?
- Have you separated out quotations longer than four lines by indenting them ten spaces from the left margin? Have you omitted the quotation marks from these long, block quotations?

INCORPORATING QUOTATIONS FROM POETRY

- Have you run in poetry quotations of fewer than four lines and enclosed them within quotation marks? Did you include a slash to indicate where each poetry line breaks (with a space on each side of the slash)?

Shakespeare ends a sonnet with this couplet: "For thy sweet love remembered such wealth brings / That then I scorn to change my state with kings."

- If your poetry quotation exceeds three lines, have you set the lines of the poem off from the text and omitted quotation marks?

Shakespeare begins one of his sonnets with this quatrain:

> Shall I compare thee to a summer's day?
> Thou art more lovely and more temperate.
> Rough winds do shake the darling buds of May,
> And summer's lease hath all too short a date.

For advice on working with quotation marks and quotations, see 33j, 34h, Chapter 36, 37c-2, 44d-3, and 44i-1.

A3   Making final corrections

Read and edit your manuscript carefully, checking for errors in punctuation, mechanics, spelling, grammar, and format. If you are writing with a word-processing program, use its available features such as the spell checker to help with this process.

Make your corrections on the hard copy and then enter them into your computer file. If you are typing the paper and there are many corrections, retype the page. Proofread your final document using the guidelines in 1i. If you need to make one or two small corrections (e.g., correcting a spelling error or changing a word) on a page, enter those changes neatly in black ink. See the chart of correction symbols at the back of the *Handbook* for a list of correction symbols.

~~Without question,~~ @ trade war with Japan will benefit niether country and, more likely, will have harmful economic consequences for both.

If your changes are many or start to get sloppy, print out or type up a new, clean page or rewrite the page.

Writing Essay Examinations

Writing strong essay exams is essential for success in many college courses. Time constraints make answering essay examination questions a challenge. To write essay exam answers that demonstrate your grasp of a subject, you will have to write efficiently and effectively. This appendix provides advice to help you do just that. It begins with some advice about pre-exam preparation, continues with tips about key words found in typical exam questions, and concludes with guidelines for writing and reviewing your exam response.

B1 Preparing for the essay exam

Effective preparation for an exam includes careful note taking during class and in doing assigned reading. In reviewing your notes for an essay exam, look for patterns and connections among facts, examples, theories, and other forms of information. Essay exams typically require students to synthesize information gleaned from lectures and readings, to explain relationships among important events and ideas, and to evaluate information.

Before the test, study the course material carefully. Form a study group with a few other students, and compare both your notes and your understanding of the important concepts and skills taught in the course. Try to rehearse for the test by anticipating and composing possible essay exam questions. Creating and answering test questions gives you an opportunity to prepare yourself for the types of questions you will be asked. It may also help you feel less nervous when faced with the actual test.

Throughout your preparation—note taking, independent study, group work—try to collect evidence to support your ideas. Identify key concepts you are likely to be asked about, and develop your own thesis or idea to explain and elaborate on each of them. Remember that good essays involve both a clear thesis or a strong idea and ample evidence to support it.

B2 **Considering the exam question and planning your answer**

Read each question on the exam carefully, at least twice. Avoid jumping to a hasty conclusion about its intent. Look carefully at the directions—at the specific words of each question. Does the question ask you to "identify"? To "explain"? To "compare"? To "evaluate"? To do more than one of these or other things? The accompanying chart outlines the common terms to look for as you read the exam question.

Key Terms to Look for in Essay Exam Questions

Identify means to name, indicate, or specify. Some essay exams include *identify* as part of a question that asks you to do more to answer the question: "identify and explain" or "identify and discuss."

> Identify three prominent African-American scientists and explain their contributions to their respective fields.

Explain means to provide reasons for, to lay out causes, effects, implications, ramifications. Explanations can be simple or complex, general or specific; they can include sparse or full detail. The time limit for an essay response will determine how much or how little explanation you should provide. If you are unsure about how much information to include in an explanation, ask your instructor for clarification.

> Explain how a legislative proposal becomes a law.

Discuss means to talk or write about. The instruction is not specific, and as a result, it is important to know how much flexibility you have with your answer. *Discuss* is often used to mean *explain*.

> Discuss Thoreau's reasons for leaving Walden Pond.

Define means to provide a definition, to point out characteristic features, to identify limits, or to put something into a category. Definitions can be brief or extended. An essay question that asks you to define a term or concept may also require that you examine, explain, elucidate, exemplify, list, characterize, or discuss the various aspects or elements of your definition.

(continued)

Define the concept of multiculturalism. Discuss the social and political issues the debate about multiculturalism has raised.

Compare and contrast means to consider the similarities and differences between two items or ideas.

Compare and contrast Woody Allen's movie comedies with those of Mel Brooks. Consider Allen and Brooks as both actors and directors.

Analyze means to break into parts in order to yield insight. To do an analysis of something involves examining it closely and carefully, looking at its details and at its component parts.

Analyze the structure and function of a red blood cell.

Evaluate means to assess or make a judgment about. You may be asked to evaluate the claims made by competing theories or to evaluate the performance of a nonprofit organization. Evaluation often involves comparison and explanation.

Evaluate Mel Gibson's performance in the 1991 film of Shakespeare's *Hamlet*.

Once you have read the question and understood what you are being asked to do, allow yourself a few minutes to think before you begin writing your answer. Spend some time considering what you want to say and how you might go about using what you know to support your idea. You will find that you can remember quite a bit in even a few minutes of thinking—if you are well prepared. Collect your thoughts and begin to sort them. Also consider how much time you have to answer the question, and then allot your time sensibly. For example, if your exam includes two essay questions in a 50-minute period, and if the questions are equally weighted, plan to devote 25 minutes to answering each question.

Begin with some preliminary writing—jotting a few rough notes in no special order. You can arrange your notes later by numbering them as you prepare to write your response. The very act of putting pen on paper should stimulate further thought and help you make connections among all the material that you have studied and learned. You can also order your notes in a rough outline, noting how you can begin and end your essay and identifying some points to cover in between. By making a rough sketch of where you are heading and how you plan to get there, you will decrease the chances of forgetting an important point. You will also enhance the organization and readability of your answer. Even in your rough preliminary notes, try to include a thesis statement that responds concretely and specifically to the question.

B3 Writing and reviewing your answer

As you write, be sure to respond directly to the question. Avoid vagueness and bland generalizations. Also avoid trying to throw everything you can think of into your answer; instead, tackle the question head on. Avoiding a direct response to the question will deprive your answer of clarity and focus and will diminish the point you wish to make.

For example, consider the following question: Discuss the economic factors that led up to the Civil War. This very specific question requires an answer that addresses economic factors only—not political, military, or religious ones (unless, of course, you can show how those other kinds of factors directly relate to the economic issues the question calls for). You also do not want to answer a broad question too narrowly. Respond to a question that asks how divorce affects children in the United States by providing information, statistics, evidence, and arguments specifically about all kinds of effects of divorce on children (social and psychological effects as well as financial and other effects). You should not stray from the question, however, by discussing the causes of divorce or its effects on divorcing couples. The most important thing you can do in writing an essay exam is to attend carefully to what the question asks for and then to be specific and thorough in providing an answer that demonstrates what you know.

ESSAY EXAM NOTE   When you find yourself running short of time in an essay exam, map out the direction your essay would take if you had time to complete it. Provide an outline for the instructor, showing him or her what you intended to discuss. Depending on how specific you can make the outline and on how accurate and thorough you have been up to that point, you should receive a better grade than if you simply stop in midstream.

Essay Exam Checklist

- Prepare for the exam in advance.
- Consider the question, pace yourself, and plan your answer.
- Think before you write.
- Jot some rough notes and perhaps sketch an outline.
- Devise a thesis for your response.
- Write quickly, and be sure you respond to the question.
- Leave time to review your answer.

Glossary of Usage

This glossary provides guidance for using commonly confused words and phrases. The advice offered reflects standard usage for academic and professional writing. It also reflects current opinion among practicing writers on what is considered appropriate for publication. For additional guidance on matters of usage, consult a current dictionary.

a, an Use *a* before words that begin with consonant sounds: *a* book, *a* historical argument. Use *an* before words beginning with a vowel sound: *an* argument, *an* honest mistake.

accept, except *Accept* is a verb that means "to receive." She *accepted* his apology. As a preposition, *except* means "to leave out." *Except* for anchovies, he enjoyed all kinds of pizza toppings.

advice, advise *Advice,* a noun, means a "suggestion": Their *advice* was to take a double major. The verb *advise* means "to give advice": I *advise* you to write a letter expressing your appreciation for the special scholarship.

affect, effect The verb *affect* means "to influence" or "move emotionally": Excessive drinking *affected* their judgment. As a verb, *effect* means "to bring about": She wished to *effect* radical change. As a noun, *effect* signifies a result: The *effects* of the war were staggering.

aggravate, irritate *Aggravate* is sometimes used colloquially to mean *irritate*. Restrict this sense of aggravate to informal situations; in other writing situations observe the following distinction: To *aggravate* means "to make worse." He *aggravated* his back injury when he moved the refrigerator. To *irritate* means "to annoy." His behavior *irritated* her.

agree to, agree with *Agree to* indicates approval; *agree with* suggests shared views. They did not *agree with* every detail in the contract, but they *agreed to* its provisions and decided to sign it.

all ready, already *All ready* means "fully prepared"; *already* means "previously" or "before now." We were *all ready* to leave for our trip, having *already* made plane and hotel reservations.

all right, alright Spell *all right* as two words rather than as *alright*.

all together, altogether *All together* means that all are gathered in a group in one place: The committee had never been *all together*. *Altogether* means "entirely": They were *altogether* opposed to the idea.

allude, elude *Allude* means "to refer to": During her lecture the professor *alluded* to numerous historical events. *Elude* means "to evade or avoid": The runner *eluded* tacklers as he ran down the field.

allusion, illusion An *allusion* is an indirect reference to a person, event, or thing: The *allusion* was to Elvis Presley's habit of gyrating his pelvis in performance. An *illusion* is a deceptive appearance: *Illusions* about the glamor of movie acting draw many to Hollywood.

a lot, alot Spell *a lot* as two words rather than as *alot.* Avoid using the colloquial *a lot* in formal writing to mean "a large amount" or "many."

a.m., p.m. Use these abbreviations only with numbers to indicate time (*2 a.m., 4 p.m.*), not to replace the words *morning* and *afternoon.*

among, between *Among* indicates relationships among three or more people or things; *between* indicates relationships between two people or things. The proposals were considered *among* the club's four officers; they had to decide *between* retaining their present mission or going in an entirely new direction. You may, however, use *between* for three or more people or things to emphasize relationships of each to another. The chess tournament progressed with exciting games *between* the club's ten best players.

amount, number *Amount* indicates a quantity of something noncountable; *number* refers to things that can be counted. A large *number* of people expended a significant *amount* of effort.

and/or This construction is sometimes used in business or legal writing to indicate that either or both of two things apply: We wanted to buy a new car *and/or* truck. Avoid using *and/or* in formal writing. Instead, write out the options: We wanted to buy a new car, a new truck, or both.

anxious, eager *Anxious* means "uneasy or worried": He was *anxious* about his upcoming interview. *Eager* lacks the apprehension of *anxious,* indicating instead "being desirous of something": They were *eager* to begin eating.

anybody, any body; anyone, any one *Anybody* and *anyone* are indefinite pronouns that refer to people but not to particular individuals. Can't *anybody* here play this game? Isn't there *anyone* who can tell me how to get to the Brooklyn Bridge? *Any body* and *any one* both refer to specific though unidentified things or individuals: *Any body* of information can be used as a starting point for research. *Any one* of you may begin. Follow the same guidelines for *nobody, no body,* and *no one.* Note: *no one* is always two words (not *noone*).

as Avoid using *as* to mean *because, since,* or *while;* using *as* to substitute for these more precise words can result in vagueness or ambiguity. *As* they were preparing for the long journey, they decided to have a hearty breakfast. (It is not clear here whether *as* means *because* or *while.*)

as, like Use *as* to indicate equivalence; use *like* to indicate resemblance. *As* a lecturer, Dr. Benton is outstanding. (Dr. Benton = a lecturer.) *Like* other art historians who offer seasonal lecture series, she has an avid following. (*Like* = similar to.) Use *as* (not *like*) in clauses: You should do *as* I say, not *as* I do.

assure, ensure, insure These related words have particular areas of reference. *Insure,* for example, means "to protect against financial loss": They were *insured* against damages from earthquakes and hurricanes. *Ensure* does not carry this specialized meaning but signifies more generally "to make certain": To *ensure* your place in the class, you must pay your tuition on time. *Assure* generally means "to promise": They were *assured* that there would be no additional charges.

awful, awfully Avoid *awful* to mean "bad" and *awfully* to mean "very"—at least in formal and academic writing, even though you may use these words this way in casual conversation. Literally, if something is *awful* it suggests that it inspires awe or wonder.

awhile, a while *Awhile* means "for a short time"; *a while* means "a time." *Awhile* is an adverb and *while* is a noun: We relaxed *awhile* before studying for *a while* longer. The article and noun (*a while*) can be an object of a preposition (*for*).

bad, badly *Bad* is an adjective and *badly* an adverb: They had not been treated *badly*, but they nonetheless felt *bad* about what had happened.

being as, being that Avoid using these expressions in place of *since* or *because*: Because [not *being that*] she completed her work early, she was able to go home.

beside, besides *Beside* is a preposition meaning "next to": Place the chair in the corner *beside* the small table. *Besides,* as an adverb, means "moreover": *Besides,* there is always tomorrow. As a preposition, *besides* means "in addition to": *Besides* an excellent emergency room, the hospital boasts a state-of-the-art neonatal unit.

burst, bust *Burst* is a verb whose principal parts are *burst, burst, burst*. It means "to explode or break apart." *Bust* is a slang word meaning "to be locked up." It is also a nonstandard form for the verb *break*. The bubble *burst* (not *busted* or *bursted*).

but, however, yet Any of these words can be used to express contrast. They should never be combined.

can, may *Can* indicates an ability to do something; *may* suggests possibility. We *can* learn how to play chess. We *may* even become grand masters. Use *may* rather than *can* to request permission: *May* I go now?

can't, couldn't Reserve these contractions for informal writing. In formal writing, use *cannot* and *could not*.

center around Avoid this expression in formal writing; instead use *center on*. The proposal *centers on* increased spending for public works.

cite, sight, site *Cite* means "to mention" or "to identify a source": In her speech she *cited* a recent article published in the *New England Journal of Medicine*. *Sight* means "to view" (verb) or "a view" (noun): Astronomers recently *sighted* what they believe is a previously undiscovered planet. A *site* is a place or location: This is a perfect *site* to pitch a tent.

compare to, compare with Use *compare to* when stressing similarities only: Robert Burns *compares* his love *to* a red, red rose. Use *compare with* for noting similarities and differences: The class was asked to *compare* Vincent van Gogh's self-portraits *with* the self-portraits of Frida Kahlo.

complement, compliment *Complement* means "to add to" or "to go well with": Their trip north *complemented* their southern journey of the summer before. *Compliment* means "to praise": He *complimented* her on the outstanding speech she gave as valedictorian.

comprise, compose *Comprise* is sometimes mistakenly used to mean *consist*. *Comprise* means "to embrace or include"; *compose* means "to make up or consist." The main proposal *comprises* numerous subproposals; the whole plan is *composed* of four parts.

continual, continuous *Continual* means "repeated at frequent or regular intervals": The *continual* attempts to persuade me to buy were unsuccessful. *Continuous* means "ongoing": The music was *continuous*, never stopping for more than the normal break between songs.

credible, credulous *Credible* means "believable"; *credulous* means "believing too easily." His story was hardly *credible*. Some who heard it, however, were *credulous* and wanted to hear more.

criteria, criterion The words refer to standards of evaluation. *Criterion* is singular; *criteria* is plural. The *criteria* used to evaluate candidates were numerous and diverse.

data It has recently become acceptable to use *data* with a singular verb as well as in the plural: The *data was* gathered under the auspices of the American Council of Churches. The *data were* not clearly supportive of either position.

device, devise *Device,* a noun, refers to an instrument; *devise,* a verb, means "to fashion." Together, they invented a *device* to extract paper entangled in computer printers. They worked a long time before they were able to *devise* a solution to the problem.

different from, different than Though the preferred form, *different from* is being joined more and more by *different than* in print as well as in conversation. Their statistics were not very *different from* ours. His statistics were not very *different than* what we had expected.

disinterested, uninterested To be *disinterested* is to be "impartial"; to be *uninterested* means "to be not interested." The judge in the case was *disinterested.* He remained *uninterested* in politics all his life.

due to Use as an adjective following a form of the verb *to be:* The victory *was due to* a persistent and unyielding defense. Avoid using this phrase as a preposition: The committee chair canceled the meeting *because of* (not *due to*) the hurricane.

eager See *anxious, eager.*

effect See *affect, effect.*

elicit, illicit *Elicit* means "to evoke" or "to draw out": The advertisement for subsidized housing *elicited* many applications. *Illicit* means "illegal": The gang had been involved in *illicit* activities for years.

elude See *allude, elude.*

eminent, imminent *Eminent* means "distinguished or prominent": They sought to hire one of the most *eminent* scholars in the field. *Imminent* means "about to happen": The arrival of the performer was *imminent.*

ensure See *assure, ensure.*

especially, specially *Especially* means "particularly"; *specially* means "for a particular reason." She *especially* wanted to visit the Louvre, where she expected to buy a *specially* chosen gift for her grandfather.

every day, everyday Use *every day* to mean "each day"—an adjective with a noun. Use *everyday* as an adjective that modifies another noun. It was an *everyday* outfit, comfortable and simple—one that could be worn *every day.*

every one, everyone *Everyone* is an indefinite pronoun referring to a group as a whole: *Everyone* participated. *Every one,* an adjective followed by a noun, refers to each member of a group individually: *Every one* of the committee members favored the new plan.

except See *accept, except.*

explicit, implicit *Explicit* means "expressed directly or outright": Her *explicit* instructions were to deposit the money by noon in the savings account. *Implicit* means "implied or suggested": They had an *implicit* understanding between them.

farther, further *Farther* indicates distance only: The museum was *farther* away than I thought. *Further* indicates either distance or degree: When he took office in January 1992, President Clinton attempted to stimulate the economy *further.*

fewer, less Use *fewer* for countable items and *less* for noncountable ones: *Fewer* television programs today portray people smoking than those of a decade ago. There is *less* attention paid to survival skills than there used to be. See also *amount, number.*

flaunt, flout To *flaunt* means "to display" or "to show off": If you've got it, *flaunt* it. To *flout* means "to defy": Georgia O'Keeffe *flouted* many conventions of the art world.

former, latter These words work together to refer to the first and second of two things respectively: Louis Armstrong and Duke Ellington were both important American jazz musicians. The *former* was a trumpet player, the *latter* a pianist.

further See *farther, further.*

good, well *Good* is an adjective: He continued in *good* health *well* into his nineties. *Well* is often an adverb (though it can function as an adjective with verbs denoting a state of being or feeling): She performed *well* during the gymnastics competition. He did not feel *well* after eating a *good* two pounds of cole slaw.

hanged, hung The past participle of *hang* is both *hanged* and *hung.* Use *hanged* when referring to executions; use *hung* to mean "suspended." People are *hanged;* pictures are *hung.*

herself, himself, myself, yourself These *-self* pronouns are both reflexive (they refer to an antecedent) and intensive (they intensify an antecedent): I, *myself,* could not go. Do not use these pronouns in place of subjective or objective pronouns: The award went to Barbara and her (not *herself*). No one but you (not *yourself*) can make that decision.

hopefully *Hopefully* means "with hope": The quarterback watched his last pass *hopefully.* Avoid using *hopefully* to mean "it is hoped": We *hoped* the pass would not be intercepted. *Not: Hopefully* the pass would not be intercepted.

however, but, yet See *but, however, yet.*

hung See *hanged, hung.*

if, whether To express doubt, use *whether:* They were uncertain *whether* the game would be telecast in their region. To express an alternative, use *whether or not: Whether or not* you can come, please call next week. Use *if* in an adverbial clause expressing a condition: *If* you can make it, we'd very much like to have you join us.

illicit See *elicit, illicit.*

illusion See *allusion, illusion.*

imminent See *eminent, imminent.*

implicit See *explicit, implicit.*

imply, infer *Imply* means "to suggest"; *infer* means "to interpret or make a guess based on evidence." Readers *infer* what writers *imply.*

in, into, in to *In* suggests a stationary place or position; *into* indicates movement toward a place or position. While she was *in* the pool, the phone rang. When he dived *into* the pool, he made a terrific splash. Use *in to* when *to* is part of an infinitive: She went *in to* answer the phone.

infer See *imply, infer.*

insure See *assure, insure.*

irregardless, regardless *Irregardless* is nonstandard for *regardless. Regardless* (not *irregardless*) of their political connections, they still had to obey the traffic laws.

irritate See *aggravate, irritate.*

its, it's Use *its* only as a possessive adjective: The cat licked *its* fur. Use *it's* to mean "it is" or "it has": *It's* only a ten-minute walk. *It's* been raining steadily.

kind of, sort of Both expressions are informal for "rather." You may use them in formal writing, if *kind* and *sort* function as nouns: The panda is related to the raccoon; it is not a *kind of* bear. Avoid informal usages like the following in college writing: It was *kind of* an intriguing explanation. Instead write: It was an intriguing explanation.

later, latter *Later* means "after some time," or "more late": It was *later* than we thought. *Latter* refers to the second of two things mentioned: It is the *latter* date that I prefer. Do not use *latter* when referring to the last of three or more items. See also *former, latter.*

latter See *former, later* and *later, latter.*

lay, lie *Lie* means "to recline"; *lay* means "to put or place." I wanted to *lie* down and take a nap. Please *lay* the eyeglass case on the bookcase.

leave, let *Leave* means "to depart from" or "to let remain": She had to *leave* early. *Let* means "to allow to" or "to permit": The instructor *let* the class go early.

less, fewer See *fewer, less.*

lie, lay See *lay, lie.*

like See *as, like.*

lose, loose *Lose* is a verb with many meanings, including "to suffer defeat": I hope our team doesn't *lose* the game. *Loose* is usually an adjective, meaning "not firmly attached": This knot is too *loose*. As a verb *loose* means "to set free": They *loosed* the hounds for the foxhunt.

may, can See *can, may.*

maybe, may be *Maybe* is an adverb meaning "perhaps"; *may be* is a verb. *Maybe* I'll travel this summer. It *may be* more difficult than you think.

might of Use *might have*. They *might have* come early. (*Of* is never used as a verb, only a preposition.)

Ms. This abbreviation was invented during the 1960s to provide women with a title parallel to Mr. for men. Midway between *Mrs.* and *Miss, Ms.* is deliberately ambiguous about a woman's marital status. When using *Ms.* with a full name, use the woman's first name and not her husband's name: *Ms.* Emily Beauford (*not* Ms. John Beauford).

nor Use with *neither* within a sentence: *Neither* Joanne *nor* her sister had ever gone abroad. When *nor* begins a sentence, place the verb before the subject: *Nor* had their parents been informed. Do not use *nor* when the verb is already in the negative: I am *not* offended *or* angry. You may also write: I am *neither* offended *nor* angry (since the verb *am* is positive).

number See *amount, number.*

OK, O.K., okay All of these are informal expressions suitable for conversation, but not for formal writing.

percent, percentage *Percent* suggests a specific figure; *percentage* is a more general term. The retention rate at Notre Dame is nearly 99 *percent*. A high *percentage* of college students are not graduated from the schools they attended as freshmen.

phenomena Plural of *phenomenon*: Certain ocean *phenomena* baffle biologists.

principal, principle *Principal* refers either to a sum of money or to the leader or head of an entity such as a school: They collected their interest each month but they left the *principal* untouched. The *principal* decided to hold an assembly to address disciplinary problems in the school. *Principle* means "a fundamental belief": They refused to comply as a matter of *principle*.

quotation, quote *Quotation* is a noun and *quote* is a verb. Former President Bush was *quoted* as saying, "Read my lips; no new taxes." It was a *quotation* that would haunt him during his unsuccessful campaign for reelection.

raise, rise *Raise* means "to lift": Please *raise* the shade. *Rise* means "to get up": I will *rise* tomorrow before 6 a.m.

real, really *Real* is an adjective; *really* is an adverb. Avoid using *real* to mean "very." The purchase they made was a *real* value. The dinner was *very* good. It was a *really* exciting game.

reason is because This is a redundant construction to be avoided. Use either *because* or the *reason . . . that* instead. The *reason* they couldn't come was *that* they had a prior commitment. They couldn't come *because* they had a prior commitment. *Not:* The reason they couldn't come was because they had a prior commitment.

respectively, respectfully *Respectively* means "in the order given." *Respectfully* means "with respect." Alpha and omega are, *respectively,* the first and last letters of the Greek alphabet. The children behaved *respectfully* in the presence of their family's guests.

rise See *raise, rise.*

set, sit *Set* means "to put or place": Would you *set* this cup on the counter? *Sit* means to "seat oneself": May I *sit* on this antique chair?

shall, will Use *shall* for polite questions in the first person: *Shall* we go? *Shall* I begin? Use *will* for other instances involving future tense: We *will* not be able to meet you tomorrow. We *will* be leaving for vacation.

should of Use *should have.* We *should have* avoided the freeway at rush hour.

sight, site See *cite, sight, site.*

somebody, some body; someone, some one *Somebody* and *someone* refer to people but not to particular individuals: *Somebody* ought to fix that wheel. Would *someone* please close the door? *Some body* is a noun modified by an adjective; *some one* is a pronoun modified by an adjective: *Some* governing *body* will decide the issue. *Some one* of you will be the new club president.

sometime, some time, sometimes *Sometime* means "at an indefinite future time": We will get around to seeing them *sometime*. *Some time* means "a period of time": We would like to spend *some time* with them on our next vacation. *Sometimes* means "occasionally": *Sometimes* I lose my concentration.

specially See *especially, specially.*

sure, surely *Sure* is an adjective; *surely* is an adverb. She was *sure* of one thing at least. *Surely,* you have made a mistake. Avoid using *sure* as an intensifier or as an adverb in formal writing. Not: She was *sure* clever. Or: *Sure,* I agree. (Though such usage is fine in conversation.)

than, then The conjunction *than* is used in comparisons; the adverb *then* indicates time. Throughout the 1980s, the Mets had a better baseball team *than* the Yankees. *Then* in the next decade, things changed.

that, which, who *That, which,* and *who* are all relative pronouns. Use *that* to refer to things or people, *which* to refer only to things, and *who* to refer only to people. For his thirtieth birthday, she bought him the gift *that* he had not wanted to buy for himself. The opportunity, *which* will not readily come again, must not be passed by. Among the many attendees were some *who* couldn't wait to leave.

their, there, they're *Their* is a possessive pronoun; *there* is an adverb indicating place and is used in the common expressions "there is" and "there are"; *they're* is a contraction meaning "they are." When George Eliot and Jane Austen wrote *their* great novels, *there* were few creative opportunities for women, besides writing. Please put the books over *there. They're* unable to come until after the game begins.

then See *than, then.*

'til, till, until The contraction *'til* should be avoided in formal writing. *Till* and *until* are both acceptable, though many writers prefer to use *until* in academic writing.

to, too, two *To* is a preposition; *too* means "also" or "excessively"; *two* is a number. The quarterback faked a handoff *to* the fullback and threw over the middle *to* the tight end. You *too* may one day enjoy a chance to travel. You ate *too* much and you ate *too* fast. You'd better take *two* antacids.

toward, towards Both are acceptable.

uninterested See *disinterested, uninterested.*

unique *Unique* means "the only one of its kind." Avoid using modifiers or intensifiers with *unique.* "Very unique" or "the most unique" are meaningless expressions.

use, utilize *Utilize* means "to put to use." Avoid the term *utilize* when *use* will convey your meaning equally well. The mayor urged city residents and commuters to *use* (not *utilize*) public transportation during the week of the festival.

well See *good, well.*

whether, if See *if, whether.*

which, that Although *which* may be used before both restrictive and nonrestrictive clauses, many writers prefer to use it only with nonrestrictive clauses containing nonessential information: The car, *which* was parked behind the house, had been badly damaged. (The essential point here is that the car had been badly damaged. Where it was parked is not as important.) *That* is used only with restrictive clauses: The car *that* was parked behind the house had been badly damaged. (In this case where the car was parked is essential information identifying which car had been badly damaged: that is, the car parked behind the house.)

who, whom Use *who* when a sentence requires a subject pronoun: *Who* will be able to come? Use *whom* when a sentence requires an object pronoun: *Whom* did you tell? In most instances, for relative clauses, use *who* before a verb: Mariela, *who* is Danish, speaks four languages. Before a noun or pronoun, use *whom:* Mariela, *whom* I have just met, speaks four languages.

whose, who's *Whose* is a possessive adjective; *who's* is a contraction meaning "who is." *Whose* umbrella is this? *Who's* responsible for this wonderful dessert?

your, you're *Your* is a possessive adjective; *you're* is a contraction for "you are." *Your* idea was well received by the committee. *You're* one of the most courageous people I've ever met.

Glossary of Terms

This glossary lists and defines selected grammatical and rhetorical terms used throughout the *Handbook*. For fuller explanations of terms and additional examples, see the relevant sections cited within most definitions.

absolute phrase A group of words often consisting of a participle and its subject. An absolute phrase modifies an independent clause as a whole. *The game over,* the team left the field. See 33g.

abstract noun A noun that names concepts, ideas, or qualities: *justice, democracy, generosity.* See 28b.

acronym A word formed from the initial letters of a group of words: *NAFTA* (or *Nafta*) for North American Free Trade Agreement. See 28e and 40b.

active voice The verb form in which the grammatical subject is the agent and the direct object is the receiver of the verb's action. See 11j. See also *passive voice.*

adjective A word that modifies a noun or pronoun: a *bright* light. See 13a.

adjective clause A clause modifying a noun or pronoun in another clause. See 10d.

adjective phrase A prepositional phrase that functions as an adjective. See 10c-1. See also *prepositional phrase.*

adverb A word that modifies a verb, an adjective, or another adverb: *quickly, now.* See 13a.

adverb clause A clause that modifies a verb, adjective, another adverb, or an entire sentence. See 10d.

adverb phrase A prepositional phrase that functions as an adverb. See 10c-1. See also *prepositional phrase.*

agreement Correspondence of a verb with its subject in person and number, and of a pronoun with its antecedent in number and gender. See *subject–verb agreement,* 15a–j; and *pronoun–antecedent agreement,* 15k–n.

analogy A comparison of similar features of two different things in order to clarify, illustrate, or explain an idea. See 3b-3 and 8e-9.

antecedent The noun that a pronoun refers to: Bill and *his* friends. See 12b and 15k–n.

appositive A noun, noun phrase, or pronoun that renames the noun or pronoun it immediately follows: my favorite day, *Saturday.* See 12f.

archaism An obsolete word: *gadzooks.* See 28e.

article A type of determiner that precedes a noun: *a, an,* or *the.* See 12a and 16c.

auxiliary verb Also called a *helping verb,* an auxiliary verb combines with a main verb to form a complete verb or verb phrase: We *will* attend. See 11b, 16i, and 16j.

balanced sentence A sentence that includes two clauses in grammatically parallel structure: *We retreated* while *they advanced.* See 24b.

base form The main form of the verb that indicates an action or state of being in the present: (I) *do,* (you) *hear,* (they) *go.* See 11a.

biased language Prejudiced language that stereotypes or unfairly denigrates members of a group. See Chapter 29.

bibliography A list of primary and secondary sources used in writing an essay, paper, or report. In MLA documentation style, this list is called *Works Cited;* in APA documentation style it is called *References.* See 45c and 45f.

case The changes in form a noun or pronoun undergoes to indicate whether it functions as subject, object, or possessor: *they, them, their; Tom, Tom's.* See 12c–d and 35a.

clause A group of words that contains a subject and a predicate. See 10d. See also *dependent clause; independent clause.*

cliché A trite expression: *last but not least.* See 28h.

collective noun A noun that names a group of people or things: *team, family, committee.* See 12a and 15e.

colloquialism A word or expression appropriate to ordinary conversation, especially in informal situations, but not to academic writing. See 28c-1.

comma splice Two independent clauses incorrectly separated by a comma instead of a period. See Chapter 18.

common noun A noun that refers to classes—to any person, place, thing, concept, or general quality: *student, city, cloud, idea, wisdom.* See 12a.

comparative The form of an adjective (*more eager*) or adverb (*less quickly*) involving a comparison of more or less, greater or lesser. See 13e.

complement A word or group of words that completes the meaning of a subject or a direct object by renaming or describing it. See 10b-3.

complete predicate The verb in a sentence plus its modifiers, complements, and objects. See 10a-2.

complete subject The simple subject plus any additional modifying words or phrases. See 10a-1.

complex sentence A single independent clause with one or more dependent clauses. See 10f-2.

compound-complex sentence Two or more independent clauses and at least one dependent clause. See 10f-2.

compound noun Two nouns combined to form a single word: *moonstone.* See 12a and 31d-3.

compound predicate Two or more verbs that have the same subject. See 10a-2.

compound sentence Two or more independent clauses joined by a coordinating conjunction, without any dependent clauses. See 10f-2.

compound subject Two or more simple subjects joined by a coordinating or correlative conjunction. See 10a-1 and 15c.

concrete noun A noun that names things recognizable through the sense of sight, hearing, touch, taste, or smell: *salt, pumpkin.* See 28b.

conjunction A word that links words, phrases, and clauses to one another: *bread and butter.* See 14c.

conjunctive adverb An adverb that emphasizes the relationship in meaning between two independent clauses: *therefore, however.* See 14c-4.

connotation Secondary associations of a word beyond its primary dictionary meaning. See 28a. See also *denotation*.

contraction A shortened form of a word or group of words: *can't* for *cannot* and *wouldn't* for *would not*. See 35c.

coordinating conjunction A conjunction that joins words and phrases as well as independent clauses: *and, but, or, nor, for, so,* and *yet*. See 14c-1.

coordination The arrangement of two or more words, phrases, or clauses to indicate equal importance. See 23a.

correlative conjunction A paired conjunction that links words, phrases, and clauses: *both . . . and*. See 14c-2.

count noun A noun that can be counted and can take both a plural and singular form: *acorns, oaks, pens*. See 16a–d.

cumulative sentence A sentence that begins with the independent clause and adds modifying phrases as the sentence goes along. See 25c-1. See also *periodic sentence*.

dangling modifier Words, phrases, or clauses that do not modify anything in a sentence while seeming to do so: *Concerned about hurricane-force winds,* the dinner was postponed. See 19i–j.

declarative sentence A sentence that makes a statement. See 10f-1.

deductive reasoning Also called *deduction*. The process of reasoning from a general principle to a particular instance. See 3d-1.

definite article The definite article *the* refers to particular nouns. See 16c. See also *indefinite article*.

demonstrative adjective An adjective that points to the nouns they replace: *this* poster; *these* flyers.

demonstrative pronoun A pronoun that points to a particular thing: *This* is an ugly poster; *those* are useless flyers. See 12b.

denotation The dictionary meaning of a word. See 28a. See also *connotation*.

dependent clause A group of words that begins with a relative pronoun or a subordinating conjunction: *before the game begins*. A dependent clause has both a subject and a verb but cannot stand alone as a sentence. See 10d and 17d.

determiner A word or group of words that introduces a noun. Some determiners signal that a noun is to follow: *a, an, the*. Other determiners indicate quantity by indicating how much or how many: *three, few, some*. See 12a and 16b.

dialect Language that uses expressions distinctive to a particular group or region. See 28f-2.

diction A writer's selection of words. See Chapter 28.

direct address Speech or writing directed at some individual or group: *I'll speak to you later, Sean*. See 16p, 20e, and 36a.

direct discourse Also called *direct quotation*. Reproducing the exact words of a real or imagined speaker in writing, requiring the use of quotation marks: W. T. Sherman once said, *"War is hell."* See 16p, 20e, and 36a. See also *indirect discourse*.

direct object A noun or pronoun that receives the action of a transitive verb in a sentence. See 10b-1. See also *indirect object*.

direct question A sentence that asks a question and ends with a question mark. See 32b and 36i-3. See also *indirect question*.

double comparison A nonstandard form using two comparative adjectives where only one is necessary: *more better*, for example. See 13e-2.

double negative A nonstandard form using two negatives where only one is necessary: *wouldn't never,* for example. See 13f.

double superlative A nonstandard form using two superlatives where only one is needed: *most best,* for example. See 13e-2.

ellipses Three equally spaced dots signifying that words have been omitted from a quotation: *And I have miles . . . before I sleep.* See 37d.

elliptical construction A grammatical construction that deliberately omits words for the sake of economy and emphasis. See 12g and 22c.

enthymeme An argument with an unstated premise. See 3d-1.

etymology The origin or historical derivation of words. See 27a, 30a–b, and 30d.

euphemism An evasive, inoffensive term used as a substitute for a more direct and possibly offensive one. See 28g.

exclamatory sentence A sentence that expresses strong feeling by making an exclamation: *Oh what a moment that was!* See 10f-1.

expletive A construction that begins with the word *here, there,* or *it* and is followed by a form of the verb *to be: There is* an expletive in this sentence. See 26b-5.

faulty predication A sentence error in which subject and predicate do not make sense together, resulting in an illogical construction and a mixed sentence. See 22b.

figurative language Language that is not meant literally. See 28i. See also *irony; metaphor; simile.*

finite verb A verb that combines with a subject to make an independent clause that expresses action, occurrence, or a state of being. Finite verbs indicate tense, person, number, voice, and mood. See Chapters 11 and 17. See also *verbal.*

formal language Represents the standard level of discourse suitable for academic writing. See 28c. See also *informal language.*

fused sentence Also known as a *run-on sentence.* A sentence error in which two sentences are run together without a punctuation mark between them. See Chapter 18. See also *comma splice.*

future perfect progressive tense A verb tense that indicates a continuing action that will end at a future time: *We will have been playing.* See 11h-6.

future perfect tense A verb tense that indicates that an action will be completed at some future time: *We will have played.* See 11g-3.

future progressive tense A verb tense that suggests continuing action in the future: *We will be playing.* See 11h-3.

future tense A verb tense indicating action that has not yet begun: *We will play.* See 11f-3.

gerund A verbal ending in *-ing* that functions as a noun in a sentence: *Smoking* is prohibited. See 10c-2.

gerund phrase A group of words consisting of a gerund with related modifiers, objects, or complements. See 10c-2.

grammar Principles or conventions that govern the way a language works by describing the system of relationships among words and conveying acceptable language patterns. See Chapters 10–16.

helping verb An auxiliary verb that accompanies the main verb in a sentence: We *were* driving. See 11b.

homonyms Words that sound alike but are spelled differently: *one* and *won.* See 31b.

hyperbole A type of figurative language involving excessive exaggeration. See 28i. See also *figurative language*.

hypothesis A generalization that a researcher or writer tests by observation or experiment. See 48a and 48e.

idiomatic expression (or idiom) An expression whose meaning differs from the meaning of its individual words: *get into the swing*. See 16r.

imperative mood A form of a verb that gives directions or expresses a request or command: *Come at noon*. See Chapter 11 and 20c.

imperative sentence A sentence that gives directions or expresses a request or a command. See 10f-1.

incomplete sentence A sentence missing essential words, phrases, or clauses. See 22c–e.

indefinite article The indefinite articles *a* and *an* refer to generalized nouns. See 16c. See also *definite article*.

indefinite pronoun A pronoun that refers to an unspecified person (*somebody*) or thing (*anything*). See 12b, 15d, and 15k.

independent clause A group of words consisting of a subject and a predicate. An independent clause can stand alone as a sentence. See 10d.

indicative mood The mood of verbs in which they state a fact, declare an opinion, or ask a question: The bird *has flown* from the nest. See Chapter 11 and 20c.

indirect discourse Also called *indirect quotation*. A paraphrased comment that does not repeat exactly what someone has said or written and that does not take quotation marks: Francis Macomber said that *he was no longer afraid*. (See 16p, 20e, and 36a.) See also *paraphrase; direct discourse*.

indirect object A noun or pronoun that indicates *to whom* or *for whom* the action of a verb in a sentence is performed. See 10b-1. See also *direct object*.

indirect question A sentence that reports a question and ends with a period rather than a question mark: *We asked if they could come*. See 16p, 32b, and 36h. See also *direct question*.

inductive reasoning Also called *induction*. The process of reasoning from the specific instance to the general case. See 3d.

inference A tentative conclusion based on observation of facts and details. See 4a, 2d-1, and 47b-3.

infinitive In the present, a verbal consisting of the base form of the verb and *to* (*to win*); in the past, a verbal that includes *to*, the past participle of *have*, and the past participle of the verb (*to have won*). Infinitives can function as nouns, adjectives, or adverbs. See 10c-2.

infinitive phrase A group of words consisting of an infinitive with its related modifiers, objects, or complements. Infinitive phrases can function as nouns, adjectives, or adverbs. See 10c-2.

informal language Casual and conversational language, typically used in everyday situations. See 28c. See also *formal language*.

intensifier A word that emphasizes another word or phrase, sometimes unnecessarily: *very* nice. See 26b-1.

intensive pronoun A *-self* form of a pronoun that emphasizes its antecedent: *yourself*. See 12b.

interjection An emphatic word or phrase that expresses surprise or emotion: *Wow!* or *Hey!* See 14d.

interrogative pronoun A pronoun that introduces a question (*who, which, what*). See 12b.

interrogative sentence A sentence that asks a question. See 10f-1.

interrupting modifier A misplaced modifier that disrupts the continuity of thought in a sentence. See 19e–h.

intransitive verb A verb that does not take a direct object: The whistle *blew*. See 11d-2. See also *transitive verb*.

invention techniques The ways that writers generate ideas. See also *mapping*.

inverted word order Reversing the order of subject and verb (so that the subject follows rather than precedes the verb) for variety and emphasis. *From our combined efforts came a new idea*. See 15h and 26a-5. See also *standard word order*.

irony A type of figurative language in which the intended meaning is the opposite of the words used: *War is kind*. See 28i. See also *figurative language*.

irregular verb A verb that forms the past tense and past participle in ways other than adding *-d, -ed*, or *-t: begin, began, begun*. See 11c.

jargon Specialized or technical language that a general audience might not understand. See 28d.

linking verb A verb that joins the subject of a sentence to a subject complement. Linking verbs indicate conditions, states of being, or sense experience: It *will* rain; He *was* tired; They *are* cold. See 11d-1.

main clause See *independent clause*.

mapping Also called *mind map*. An invention technique used to generate ideas and to organize them. See 1f-2.

mass noun Also called a *noncount noun*. Names things that cannot be counted: *sugar, dust, music*. Mass or noncount nouns are used only in the singular. See 16a–d. See also *count noun*.

mechanics Conventions governing the use of abbreviations, capital letters, hyphens, italics, and numbers. See Chapters 38–42.

metaphor A type of figurative language involving a direct comparison of dissimilar things: *He is a dynamo*. See 28i-1. See also *figurative language*.

misplaced modifier A modifier that is positioned in a sentence so that it is unclear which word, phrase, or clause is modified: Writers who read *often* will make use of that reading. See 19a–d.

mixed metaphor A type of figurative language involving an inconsistent or a ludicrous comparison. See 28i-1. See also *figurative language*.

mixed sentence A sentence that combines incompatible grammatical structures or includes an illogical relationship between subject and predicate, resulting in a confusion of meaning. See 22a–b.

modal auxiliary verbs Also called *modals*. Combine with main vbs to indicate necessity (*must*), obligation (*should, ought*), permission (*may*), or possibility (*might*). See 11b.

modifier A word or phrase that functions as an adjective or adverb to limit or qualify the meaning of a word, phrase, or clause. See Chapter 13 and Chapter 19.

mood A writer's or speaker's attitude indicated by a verb's action, whether imperative, indicative, or subjunctive. See Chapter 11 and 20c.

morpheme The smallest meaningful unit into which a word can be divided. In the word *prehistoric*, the prefix *pre-* (meaning "before") is a morpheme. See Chapter 30.

neologism A newly coined word that is not yet widely used. See 28e.

nominalization Using nouns rather than verbs to carry the meaning of a sentence. See 26b-6.

noncount noun See *mass noun*.

nonfinite verb See *verbal*.

nonrestrictive element A word, phrase, or clause that does not limit the element it modifies while providing information not essential to understanding the main clause of the sentence. A nonrestrictive element is set off with commas. See 33c. See also *restrictive element*.

nonstandard Words, expressions, or constructions that do not conform to the conventions of spoken and written English.

noun Names a person, place, thing, concept, or quality. Nouns can be common (*disk*), proper (*Sharon*), abstract (*innocence*), concrete (*ketchup*), collective (*class*), or mass (*weather*). See 12a and 28b.

noun clause A clause that typically begins with a relative pronoun and functions as a subject, an object, or a complement in a sentence. See 10d.

noun phrase A group of words consisting of a noun and its modifiers that functions as a subject, an object, or a complement in a sentence. See 10c-1.

number The quantity indicated by a verb, whether singular or plural. See 15a–j.

object A word or group of words, functioning as a noun or pronoun, that is influenced by a verb (direct object), a verbal (indirect object), or a preposition (object of a preposition). See 10b.

object complement A noun or adjective that follows a direct object and describes or renames it. See 10b-3.

objective case The case or function of a pronoun when it is the direct or indirect object of a verb or verbal, the object of a preposition, the subject of an infinitive, or an appositive to an object. See 12c and 12c-2.

object of a preposition A noun or pronoun that follows a preposition and completes its meaning. See 10b-2.

parallelism The use of a similar grammatical form for two or more coordinate words, phrases, or clauses to achieve clarity, elegance, or equivalence. See 8c-5, Chapter 24, and 26a-1.

paraphrase A restatement of another person's ideas or evidence in different words. See 44d-2. See also *indirect discourse*.

parenthetical citation A form of citing sources in parentheses directly after the source has been quoted, summarized, or paraphrased. See 45a, 45d, and 45h.

participial adjective A participle that functions as an adjective: the *growing* child, for example. See 10c-2.

participial phrase A group of words consisting of a present or past participle and accompanying modifiers, objects, or complements that functions as an adjective. See 10c-2.

participle A verbal that functions as an adjective. Present participles end in *-ing* (*burning*); past participles of regular verbs end in *-d* or *-ed* (*burned*). See 10c-2 and 11a.

parts of speech The categories into which words are grouped according to their grammatical function in sentences: verbs, nouns, pronouns, adjectives, adverbs, prepositions, conjunctions, and interjections. See Chapters 10–16.

passive construction A construction in which the subject of a sentence receives the action of a verb: *The ball was thrown.* See 11k.

passive voice The verb form in which the grammatical subject receives the verb's action, rather than directing that action as in the *active voice*. See 11k. See also *active voice*.

past participle The third principal part of the verb that includes qualities of both an adjective and a verb. The past participle usually ends in *-d* or *-ed*. See 11a, 11i-2, and 16h.

past perfect progressive tense A verb tense that suggests a continuing action that ended before another action: *They had been skiing.* See 11h-5.

past perfect tense A verb tense that designates an action that has been completed prior to another past action: *They had hiked.* See 11g-2.

past progressive tense A verb tense that conveys a continuing past action: *They were walking.* See 11h-2.

past tense A verb tense indicating action that occurred in the past, and which does not extend into the present: *They watched; They ate.* Regular past tense verbs take the ending *-d*, *-t*, or *-ed*; irregular verbs do not. See 11a, 11c, and 11f-2.

perfect tenses Verb tenses that indicate an action that has been completed before another action begins or an action finished by a specific time. See 11g and 16j.

periodic sentence A sentence that begins with modifiers and ends with an independent clause that is emphasized at the end of the sentence. See 25c-2. See also *cumulative sentence*.

person The form of a verb or pronoun that shows whether the subject is speaking (first person—*I, we*), being spoken to (second person—*you*), or being spoken about (third person—*he, she, it, they*). See 11a, 12b, and Chapter 15.

personal pronoun A pronoun that refers to a person or a thing: *we, you, they, him, her, it.* See 12b.

phrasal verb A verb that combines with prepositions to form a multi-word verb: *give up*, for example. See 16m.

phrase A group of related words that does not form a complete sentence and that functions as a noun, verb, or modifier. See 10c.

plagiarism The act of misrepresenting another person's words or ideas as your own by using those words or ideas without giving credit to the source. To avoid plagiarism, sources must be acknowledged with accurate documentation. See 44j.

positive The simple form of an adjective that does not suggest comparison. See 13e. See also *comparative; superlative.*

possessive adjective A personal pronoun that functions as an adjective by modifying nouns and indicating ownership: *their* house; *her* car. See 13h and 16f.

possessive case Indicates when a pronoun shows ownership: *your, yours.* See 12c-3.

predicate The part of a sentence containing the finite verb. The predicate describes what the subject is doing or experiencing or what is being done to the subject: The car *rolled; We were asleep.* See 10a. See also *simple predicate; complete predicate; compound predicate.*

predicate adjective An adjective used as a subject complement: Hillary was *elated.* See 10b-3.

predicate nominative Also called *predicate noun.* A noun or pronoun complement: Bill is a nonstop *talker.* See 10b-3.

prefix A letter or group of letters attached to the beginning of a word that partly indicates its meaning: *pre*bake, meaning bake in advance. See 30c.

premise An assumption basic to an argument. A syllogism consists of a major premise, a minor premise, and a conclusion. See Chapter 3d-1 and Chapter 7.

preposition A word that indicates the relationship between a noun or pronoun and other words in a sentence. See 10c-1 and 14a–b.

prepositional phrase A group of words consisting of a preposition, its object, and any of the object's modifiers. Prepositional phrases function as adjectives or adverbs. See 10c-1.

present participle The -*ing* form of the verb, which functions as an adjective: *sewing, speaking*. See 11a.

present perfect progressive tense A verb tense that indicates action that began in the past and continues into the present: *I have been reading*. See 11h-4.

present perfect tense A verb tense that indicates that an action or its effects, begun in the past, either ended at some time in the past or continues into the present: *He had listened*. See 11g-1.

present progressive tense A verb tense that conveys a sense of ongoing action: *We are eating*. See 11h-1.

present tense The verb tense that designates action occurring at the time of speaking or writing; also used to indicate habitual actions and to express general truths: When you *speak*, they *listen*. See 11f-1.

primary source An original work of art or literature, a diary, speech, film, interview, correspondence, or other firsthand account. See 43c. See also *secondary source*.

principal parts Three forms of a verb: base form, past tense form, and past participle. See 11a and 11c.

progressive tenses Verb tenses indicating action that is continuing in the present, past, or future. See 11h.

pronoun A word that takes the place of a noun. See 12b.

proper noun Names specific persons, places, things, concepts, or qualities. See 12a.

purpose A writer's reason for writing, such as to inform, explain, or persuade. See 1d-3.

quotation An exact repetition or report of the words another has spoken or written. See 44d-3. See also *direct discourse; indirect discourse.*

reciprocal pronoun A pronoun that indicates each of two things has the same relationship toward the other: *each other*. See 12b.

reflexive pronoun A -*self* form of the pronoun that refers to the subject of the clause in which it appears. See 12b.

regionalism A word or expression commonly used in a particular geographic region. See 28f-1.

regular verb A verb that forms its past tense and past participle by adding -*d* or -*ed* (or in some cases -*t*) to the base form. See 11c.

relative clause A clause introduced by a relative pronoun. See 10d.

relative pronoun A pronoun that introduces a clause that modifies a noun or pronoun: *who, which, that*. See 12b and 15g.

restrictive clause A clause serving as an adjective or adverb that limits or restricts the meaning of the word(s) modified. See 33c.

restrictive element A word, phrase, or clause that limits or restricts the meaning of the element it modifies while providing information essential to understanding the main clause of a sentence. It is never set off with commas. See 33c. See also *nonrestrictive element.*

root The unchanging part of a word that takes a prefix or a suffix: inter*vene;* bi*lingual.* See 30b.

run-on sentence See *fused sentence.*

schwa An unstressed vowel sound in a word: comp*e*tent. See 31e.

secondary source A source or reference that explains or describes an original work or other type of primary source. See 43c. See also *primary source.*

sentence A group of words that includes a subject and a predicate. A sentence begins with a capital letter and ends with a mark of end punctuation. See 10a, Chapters 17–26, and Chapter 32.

sentence fragment A group of words that begins with a capital letter and ends with end punctuation but is grammatically incomplete. See Chapter 17.

sexist language A type of biased or prejudiced language that discriminates against females or males on the basis of gender. See 29b.

shift An abrupt change from one verb tense, mood, or voice to another, or from one pronoun person or number to another, which results in confusing writing. See Chapter 20.

simile A type of figurative language involving a comparison using *like, as,* or *as though: They sing like angels.* See 28i-2. See also *figurative language.*

simple predicate The verb of a sentence. See 10a-2.

simple sentence A single independent clause. See 10f-2.

simple subject A subject consisting of a single noun or pronoun. See 10a-1.

simple tenses Verbs in the past, present, and future tenses. See 11f.

slang Informal usage in vocabulary and idiom, often playful, and quickly outdated. See 28c-2.

split infinitive Separating an infinitive by putting one or more words between *to* and the verb: *to boldly go.* Avoid split infinitives in writing. See 19g.

squinting modifier An ambiguous modifier that appears to modify both the words before and after it: The decision we made *ultimately* concerns me. See 19d.

standard English English as used by educated speakers and writers in the business and academic worlds. See also *nonstandard.*

standard word order The usual word order of the English sentence: subject, predicate, object: *We saw the movie.* See also *inverted word order.*

stereotypes Unfair assumptions made about members of a group based on insufficient evidence. See 3e-2 and Chapter 29.

subject The grammatical part of a sentence indicating what it is about. See 10a. See also *complete subject; compound subject; simple subject.*

subject complement A noun or adjective that follows a linking verb and identifies or describes the subject of the sentence. See 10b-3.

subjective case The case of a pronoun when it is the subject of a clause, a subject complement, or an appositive to a subject or a subject complement. See 12c–d.

subject–verb agreement See *agreement.*

subjunctive mood The mood of a verb expressing wishes, stipulating demands or requirements, or making statements contrary to fact: I wish I *were* rich. See Chapter 11.

subordinate clause See *dependent clause.*

subordinating conjunction A conjunction that introduces a dependent (or subordinate) clause indicating the relationship of the dependent clause to the main or independent clause of a sentence. See 10d and 14c-3.

subordination The arrangement of two or more words, phrases, or clauses to distinguish a main term, action, or idea from less important ones. See 23b.

suffix A letter or group of letters attached to the end of a word that partly indicates its meaning: regard*less*, meaning without regard. See 30c-2.

summary A compressed version of a text in which writers explain the text's meaning in their own words. See 2b-4 and 44d-1.

superlative The form of an adjective that suggests the most or least of something: *highest; least*. See 13e. See also *comparative*.

syllogism An argument arranged in three parts: a major premise, a minor premise, and a conclusion. See Chapter 3 and Chapter 7.

synonym Words with the same or similar meaning: *joy* and *happiness.*

syntax The sequence of words in a sentence. See also *inverted word order; standard word order.*

tag question A question added on to the end of a sentence: It was a good film, *wasn't it?* See 33h.

tense The time of a verb's action or state of being, such as past, present, and future. See 11f–i.

thesis The main idea of an essay or report written as a single declarative sentence. See 7b and 44e.

tone A writer's attitude toward the subject conveyed to readers through diction, syntax, and other stylistic elements. See 1d-3 and 4b-2.

topic The broad subject of a piece of writing. See 5b and 43b.

topic sentence The sentence that expresses the main idea of a paragraph. See Chapter 8.

transitional expression A word or phrase that signals connections among ideas and creates coherence in a piece of writing: *for instance; on the other hand.* See 8c-3, 25b-1, and 33-f.

transitive verb A verb that takes a direct object: He *washed* the car. See 11d-2. See also *intransitive verb.*

usage The conventional ways of using words, phrases, and expressions.

verb A part of the predicate of a sentence that describes an action or occurrence or indicates a state of being. Verbs change form to indicate tense, voice, mood, person, or number. See Chapter 11.

verbal A verb form that functions as a noun or a modifier rather than as a verb in a sentence. Verbals may be infinitives, present or past participles, and gerunds. See 10c-2 and 11d-3.

verbal phrase A group of words consisting of a verbal and related modifiers, objects, or complements. Verbal phrases function as nouns or modifiers. See 10c-2.

verb phrase A group of words consisting of a main verb and its auxiliary verbs. A verb phrase functions as the predicate in a sentence or clause. See 10c-1.

voice The attribute of a verb that indicates whether its subject acts (*active voice*) or is acted upon (*passive voice*). See 11j–k. See also *active voice; passive voice.*

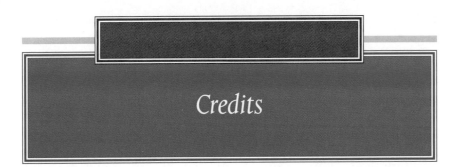

Credits

865

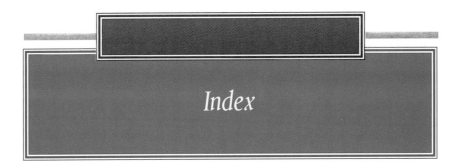

Index

a vs. *an*, 323, 326–327
Abbreviations, 604–610
  acronyms, 605–606
  checklist, chart, 609–610
  initial, 605
  Latin, 607
  periods with, 534–535
  for reference information, 609
  for states, chart, 608
  of titles, 604–605
Abridged dictionaries, 474–475
Absolute phrases, 229, 230, 548
Abstract nouns, 270
Abstracts, 639–640, 731
Abstract words, 481–483
Academic courses, 607
Academic degrees, 604
Academic institutions, 597
Acknowledging sources. *See* Source
    acknowledgement
Acronyms, 486–487, 535, 605
Active voice
  defined, 262–263
  preferring to passive, 465–466
  shifts in, 396–397
A.D., 606
Ad hominem fallacy, 168, 171
Ad populum fallacy, 168, 170–171
Addresses, Internet, 648, 649, 650, 717–719,
    733–734
Addresses, street, 550
Adjective clauses, 232, 543–544
Adjectives, 286–298
  vs. adverbs, 286–289
  as antecedents, 408–409
  comparative form, 292–294
  compound, 617
  coordinate, 546–547
  defined, 286–287
  double comparisons and, 293
  infinitive phrases as, 229
  irregular, chart, 294
  linking verbs and, 289

  managing, 298
  participial phrases as, 228
  participles as, 242, 251, 287, 336–337
  positive form, 292
  possessive, 296–297
  proper, capitalization of, 594–597
  superlative form, 292–294
  word order and, 334–336
Adjective suffixes, chart, 512
Adverb clauses, 232–233, 543–544
Adverbs, 286–298
  vs. adjectives, 286–289
  comparative form, 292–294
  conjunctive, 303–304, 558–559, 561
  as dangling modifiers, 390
  defined, 286, 288
  irregular, chart, 294
  managing, 298
  placement of, 352–354
  positive form, 292
  sentence position of, 288, 448
  superlative form, 292–294
  with two forms, 289–290
Age bias, 501
Agreement, 306–322. *See also* Pronoun-
    antecedent agreement; Subject-verb
    agreement
  defined, 306
  maintaining, 322
  pronoun-antecedent, 317–321
  subject-predicate, 412–416
  subject-verb, 306–317
  summary, charts, 316, 319
Aircraft names, 602
-ally vs. *-ly*, 522
Alta Vista, 647
Alternatives, quota of, 51–52
a.m., 606
America Online, 647, 717
American Psychological Association. *See*
    APA style
American vs. British/Canadian spellings,
    520–521

an vs. *a*, 323, 326–327
Analogy
    in arguments, 70–71
    in creative thinking, 53–54
    false, 168, 171
    paragraph development and, 202
Analysis. *See also* Text analysis
    cause-and-effect, 196–197
    division and, 200–201
    process, 197–198
Analytical essays, 123–142
    analyzing texts for, 124–134
    audience for, 124
    beginning of, 135–136, 206–208
    collaboration and, 134–135
    critical reading for, 124–125, 128–131
    developing, 128–139
    ending of, 136–139, 210–212
    features of, 123–124
    guidelines for, 129
    middle of, 136–137
    purpose for, 123–124
    questioning and, 131–132
    textual details and, 132–134
Analyzing texts. *See* Text analysis
Anglo-Saxon, 505
Annotation of texts, 10, 26–27, 626,
        781–782
Anonymous work, citation of, 699, 703,
        705, 723, 727, 730
Antecedents
    adjectives as, 408–409
    agreement with pronouns, 317–321
    collective nouns as, 318
    compound, 318–320
    defined, 271, 317
    indefinite pronouns as, 318
    possessives as, 408–409
    pronoun reference to, 403–411
    proximity to pronouns, 404–405
    third-person, 320
Anthology, citation of, 705–706, 727
Antonyms, 473
APA style, 719–734. *See also* References list
    for block quotations, 687
    for content notes, 725
    directory of citation types, 720–721
    guidelines for source documentation,
        721–722
    for parenthetical citations, 721–725
    for References list, 725–734
    sample research essay in, 772–777
Apostrophes, 566–572
    with contractions, 569
    incorrect use of, 571
    with omissions of letters and numbers,
        570
    with possessives, 566–568
    with plurals, 570–571

Appalachian English, 489
Appeal to ignorance, 168, 170
Appositive phrase fragments, 367
Appositive phrases, 230
Appositives
    defined, 281, 367, 544
    delayed, 563–564
    nonrestrictive, 544
    pronouns as, 275, 281
    restrictive, 545
Archaisms, 486
Argumentative essays, 143–172
    audience for, 144, 149–150
    developing from experience, 152–158
    developing from sources, 158–167
    fallacies, avoiding, 167–172
    features of, 143–144, 145
    guidelines for, 151
    linking thesis and evidence in, 160–165
    organizing, 150–151, 156–158
    preparing to write, 145–150
    purpose for, 144
    thesis of, 145, 146–150
    troubleshooting, 148–149, 167–172
Arguments, 146–149
    claims of fact, 147
    claims of policy, 147
    claims of value, 147
    fallacies, avoiding, 167–172
    thesis of, 147, 149
    troubleshooting, 148–149
    warrants, 148
Art collections, 640
Articles
    choosing correct, 326
    defined, 271, 325
    definite, 271, 326–328
    indefinite, 271, 326–327
    subject-verb agreement and, 312
    use of, 325–329
    when to omit, 328–329
Articles, periodical. *See* Periodicals
Arts. *See* Literature and the arts
Art works. *See also* Literature and the arts
    citation of, 714
    what to look for in, chart, 788–789
    writing about, 780–793
Asking questions. *See* Questioning
Assignment, research, 623–624
Assumptions, 64
Audience
    for analytical essays, 124
    for argumentative essays, 144, 149–150
    assessing feedback from, 6–7
    checklist for, 9
    defined, 6
    for exploratory essays, 102–103
    influencing, 7–9
    for research essays, 624, 680–681, 751

Audio collections, 640
Authors, citation of. *See* Source
    documentation
Auxiliary verbs, 243–245
  be, 243, 245, 338–341
  defined, 243–244
  do, 243, 245, 338–341
  have, 243, 245, 338–341
  modal, 244–245, 342–343
  in negative sentences, 341
  in passive voice, 340–341
  in perfect tenses, 339–340
  in progressive tenses, 338–339
  in questions, 341
  in verb phrases, 338–341

bad vs. *badly*, 291
Balanced sentences, 435–436. *See also*
    Parallelism
Bar graph, 836–837
Base verb form, 241
B.C., 606
be
  as auxiliary verb, 243, 245, 338–341
  excessive use of, 463–464
  forms of, 337–338
  past tense of, 307
  present participles and, 241
  with *when* and *where*, 414–416
Begging the question, 168, 169
Beginning of an essay, 12–13, 108–109, 111,
    116, 135–136
Beginning paragraphs
  in analytical essays, 206–208
  in argumentative essays, 206–208
  defined, 203
  in exploratory essays, 204–206
  guidelines for, 205
  linking, 216, 218
Biased language, 496–503
  avoidance of, 501–503
  ethnically biased, 496–497
  kinds of, 501–503
  racially biased, 496–497
  sexually biased, 320–321, 497–500
Bibliographic Retrieval Service (BRS), 636,
    644
Bibliographies, reference, 632–633
Bibliography. *See also* Works Cited List;
    References List
  cited vs. consulted works, 661
  in CMS style, 735
  information to record in, chart, 663–664
  in MLA style, 663, 735
  source cards for, 662–664, 671
  working, 661–664
Biographical reference books, 632
Black English, 488–489
Block format, 821–822

Block quotations, 687–688, 759, 761,
    831–832
Blocks to thinking, 58–63
  cultural, 59–60
  emotional, 60–61
  intellectual, 60–61
  perceptual, 58–59
  polarization as, 62–63
Book indexes, 634
Books, citation of, 663, 698–709, 703–709,
    722–729
Books, reference. *See* Reference books
Brackets, 587–588, 757
Brainstorming with computer, 828–829
Break in thought, 582
British spellings, 520–521
Browsing the Web, 647–650. *See also* World
    Wide Web
BRS (Bibliographic Retrieval Service), 636,
    644
Business writing, 819–826
  basic principles, chart, 819
  job applications, 823–824
  letters, 821–822
  memos, 820
  résumés, 825–826

Call number system, 641–642
Canadian spellings, 520–521
Capitalization, 592–599
  commonly capitalized words, chart,
    595–597
  of first word in poetry, 594
  of first word of quotation, 593–594
  of first word of sentence, 592–593
  of *I*, 597
  misuse of, 598
  of *O*, 597
  of proper nouns and adjectives,
    594–597
  of titles and subtitles, 597
Card catalog, 641–642
Cards. *See also* Note taking
  note, 671–672
  source, 662–664, 671
Cartoons, citation of, 715
Case forms. *See* Pronoun case
Catalogs, library
  card, 641–642
  key word searches of, 643–644, 645
  online, 642–644
  serials, 635
Causality
  in argumentative essays, 159–160
  defined, 159
  illogical, 168, 169
  reasoning and, 68–70
  showing with subordination, 429
Cause-and-effect analysis, 196–197

CBE (Council of Biology Editors) style,
738–741. *See also* References list
name-and-year system of citation, 738
number system of citation, 739
order-of-first mention in, 739
for parenthetical citations, 738–739
for References list, 739–741
CBE Style Manual, 738, 813. *See also* CBE
style
CD-ROM (compact disc, read-only
memory)
abstracts on, 640
book indexes on, 634
citation indexes on, 640
databases on, 645
defined, 629
documenting sources from, 663,
716–717, 733
periodical indexes on, 635–638
-*cede, -ceed, -sede*, 522
Character attack, 168, 171
Charts, citation of, 715, 733
Charts, computer, 832, 836–837
Chicago Manual of Style, The, 734–737
Choice, showing with subordination, 429
Chronological sequencing, 191–192
Circular reasoning, 168, 170
Citation indexes, 639–640
Citations. *See also* References list;
Source documentation; Works
Cited list
APA style for, 719–734
CBE style for, 738–742
CMS style for, 734–737
guidelines for, 698
MLA style for, 695–719
in References list, 725–734, 739–741
style manuals for, listed, 742
in Works Cited list, 703–719
Claims, in argument, 145, 146–150
Classification, as writing technique,
199–200
Clauses
adjective, 232
adverb, 232–233
connecting, 303–304, 422–433
defined, 232
dependent, 232, 237–238, 277–280,
369–371, 448
independent, 232, 237–238, 303–304,
422–426
linking dependent with independent,
427–433
linking two independent, 422–427
misplaced, 385–386
noun, 233
relative, 232
Clichés, 481–482
Climactic order, 13, 190–191

CMS (Chicago Manual of Style) style,
734–737. *See also* Works Cited list
bibliographies in, 735
notes in, 735–737
shortened citation forms in, 737
Coherence
defined, 174
guidelines for, 182
paragraph, 174–176, 181–188
parallelism and, 438–441
ways to achieve, 181–188
Coined compounds, 617
Collaboration
defined, 20–21
in evaluating texts, 40–41
guidelines for, 20–21
in idea development, 98–100, 106
in revising, 20–21
Collective nouns, 271, 311–312, 318
Colloquialisms, 399, 483–484. *See also*
Idiomatic expressions
Colons, 562–565
capitalization of following sentences,
592–593
with delayed appositives, 563–564
with hours/minutes, 564
with lists, 563
misuse of, 564
with quotations, 563, 578
with salutations, 564
vs. semicolons, 556
summary of uses, chart, 556
with titles/subtitles, 654
Commas, 539–555
with absolute phrases, 548
as comprehension aid, 552
with coordinate adjectives, 546–547
with coordinating conjunction, 540–541
with introductory elements, 541–542
between items in series, 545–546
with nonrestrictive elements, 542–545
with parenthetical expressions, 547, 585
with phrases, 229, 230
with quotations, 551, 577–578
with series, 554
summary of uses, charts, 539, 555
with transitional expressions, 547
unnecessary uses, 553–554
Commercial online services, 717, 733
Common knowledge, 690, 753
Commonly confused words, glossary,
846–853
Common nouns, 270
Compact disc, read-only memory. *See* CD-
ROM
Company names, 609
Comparatives, adjectives and adverbs,
292–294
double comparisons, 293

incomplete comparisons, 294
  irregular, chart, 294
Comparison and contrast, as writing
  technique, 198–199, 435–438
Comparisons. *See also* Comparison and
  contrast
  clear, 419
  complete, 419
  defined, 418
  double, 293
  incomplete, 294, 418–420
  logically consistent, 419
Compass directions, 598
Complements
  defined, 225
  object, 226
  subject, 225–226, 275, 280, 289
  subject-verb agreement and, 312–313
Complete subject, 222
Complex sentences, 237–238
Compound adjectives, 617
Compound antecedents, 318–320
Compound-complex sentences, 238
Compound nouns, 527
Compound numbers, 617
Compound phrases, 567
Compound predicates, 222, 368–369
Compound prepositions, 299; chart, 300
Compound sentences, 237
Compound structures, 280–282, 553–554
Compound subjects, 222, 309–310
Compound words
  apostrophes with, 567
  chart, 530
  hyphenation of, 616–617
Compuserve, 717
Computerized databases, 644–646
Computer networks, 829–830
Computer use, 827–837. *See also* CD-ROM;
  Electronic sources; Internet; Online
  sources; Word processing
  programs; World Wide Web
  creating charts with, 832, 836–837
  creating graphs with, 832, 836–837
  creating visuals with, 835–837
  formatting papers with, 531–532, 704,
    831–835
  guidelines for writing with, 827–828
  idea generation with, 828–829
  online research sources, 635–640,
    646–657
  outlining programs, 831
  spell checking programs, 531–532, 830
  style checking programs, 830
  thesaurus programs, 830
  useful features of, 829–831
  writing with, 827–837
Concession, showing with subordination,
  429

Conciseness, 459–468
  avoiding overuse of *be*, 463–464
  avoiding overuse of prepositions, 466
  avoiding negating words, 461–462
  avoiding redundancy, 462–463
  avoiding unnecessary intensifiers,
    459–460
  avoiding wordy phrases, 460–461
  defined, 459
  preferring active to passive voice,
    465–466
  preferring verbs to nouns, 464–465
  ways to write with, chart, 460
Conclusion of an essay. *See* Ending of an
  essay
Concrete nouns, 270
Concrete words, 481–483
Condition, showing with subordination,
  429
Conditional sentences, 267–268, 356–357
Conference proceedings, citation of, 708
Conjunctions
  conjunctive adverbs, 303–304
  controlling, 305
  coordinating type, 301–302, 422–427,
    436, 540–541
  correlative type, 302–303, 424, 436–427
  defined, 301
  subordinating type, 303, 366, 369,
    430–431, 437
Conjunctive adverbs
  chart of, 304
  in coordinating sentences, 423
  defined, 303–304
  semicolon with, 558–559, 561
Connections
  between details, 34–35
  guidelines for making, 94
  idea development and, 88–95, 789
  between stories of experience, 103–104,
    106–107, 117–122
  between texts, 117–122
Connotation, 478–481
Consistency, sentence, 393–402. *See also* Shifts
Consonants
  doubling, 524–525
  unstressed (silent), 527–529
Content notes, 725
Context clues to words, chart, 515–516
Contractions
  apostrophes with, 569–570
  avoidance of, 399
  most frequently used, chart, 569
Contrast and comparison, 198–199, 435–438
Controversy
  in argumentative essays, 159–160
  checklist for considering, 98
  defined, 5
  idea development and, 95–98

Coordinate adjectives, 546–547
Coordinate conjunctions. *See* Coordinating
conjunctions
Coordinate structure. *See* Coordination
Coordinating conjunctions
chart of, 302
commas with, 540–541, 553
in coordinate structures, 422–427
defined, 301–302
in parallel structures, 436
Coordination, 422–427, 433
checking, 426
conjunctive adverbs in, 423, 424, 426
coordinating conjunctions in, 422–426
correlative conjunctions in, 424
defined, 422
excessive, 425
illogical, 425–426
semicolons in, 423, 426
as writing technique, 422–426, 433
Corporate author, citation of, 699–700, 706,
723, 727
Corrections, on final manuscript, 841
Correlative conjunctions
chart of, 303
in coordinate structures, 424
defined, 302–303
in parallel structures, 436–437
Council of Biology Editors. *See* CBE style
Count nouns
articles with, 326–327
defined, 271
demonstratives with, 331–332
vs. noncount nouns, 323–325
quantifiers with, 329–331
Cover page, 744, 745, 839
Creative thinking. *See* Thinking, creative
Critical reading. *See* Reading, critical
Cultural blocks, 59–60
Cumulative sentences, 450–451

Dangling modifiers, 390–392
Dashes, 581–584
capitalization with, 593
to insert comment, 581–582
with lists, 582
with parenthetical expressions, 582–583
quotation marks with, 578
Data, 763, 803–804
Databases, computerized, 644–646
Dates, commas with, 549
Days, 607
Declarative sentences, 235–236
Deductive reasoning, 64–68; chart, 66
Definite articles
choosing, 326–328
defined, 271, 325, 326
the, when to use, 327–328
Definition, as writing technique, 195–196

Definitions, 576
Degree, in creative thinking, 62
Delayed appositives, 563–564
Demonstrative pronouns, 272–273
Demonstratives, 325, 331–332
Denotation, 478–479, 481
Denying the negative, 55
Dependent clauses
defined, 232
elliptical, 391
linking with independent, 427–428,
430–431
in sentence fragments, 369–371
in sentence openings, 448
sentence types and, 237–238
who vs. *whom* in, 277–280
Description, as writing technique, 201–202
Descriptors, 645
Designing documents. *See* Document
design
Desk dictionaries, 474–475
Details
listing, 34–35, 129, 132–134, 782–783
logical relationships between, 428–429
textual, 34–35, 129, 132–134
visual, 186–187, 218
Determiners. *See also* Articles
articles, 325–329
defined, 271, 325
demonstratives, 325, 331–332
possessive adjectives, 325, 332–333
quantifiers, 325, 329–331
use of, 325–333
Developing ideas. *See* Idea development
Dewey Decimal System, 641
Dialects, 488–490
Appalachian English, 489
Black English, 488–489
Hispanic English, 489
DIALOG, 636, 644, 645, 717
Dialogue, 575. *See also* Direct discourse
Diction, 470–532
abstract words, 481–483
acronyms, 486–487
archaisms, 486
biased language, 496–503
checking your own, chart, 494
clichés, 481–482
concrete words, 481–483
connotation, 478–481
consistency in, 399–401
defined, 399
denotation, 478–479, 481
dialect, 488–490
dictionary use, 470–477
euphemisms, 490–491
figurative language, 492–495
formal language, 483–484
general words, 481–483

informal language, 483–484
jargon, 485
neologisms, 486
regionalisms, 487–488
specific words, 481–483
vocabulary, 504–516
word characteristics, 478–495
Dictionaries, 470–477
abridged, 474–475
information in, 470–473, 633
specialized, 476
types of, 474–477
unabridged, 475
Direct address, 548
Direct discourse
converting to indirect, 354–355
defined, 354, 397
vs. indirect, 398
question mark use, 535–536
shifts in, 397–399
Directed research, 623. See also Research
Direction prefixes, 510
Direct objects, 223–224, 387–389
Direct questions, 573
Direct quotations. See also Direct discourse
defined, 397
question mark use, 535–536
shifts in, 397–399
Discourse
direct, 354–355, 397–399, 535–536
indirect, 354–355, 398–399
Diskettes, citation of, 716–717, 733
Dissertations, citation of, 713, 723
Dividing words at end of line, chart,
615–616
Division and analysis, as writing
technique, 200–201
do
as auxiliary verb, 243, 245, 338–341
forms of, 337–338
Document design, 831–835
of academic documents, 832–834
block quotations in, 831–832
headings in, 831, 833
highlighting in, 833
lists in, 833
margins in, 832
of nonacademic documents, 834–835
pagination in, 832
spacing in, 832
titles in, 831
type size and style in, 832–833
white space in, 833–834
Documents, government, 640
Domain Name System, 648, 650
Double-column notebook, 10, 29–31,
784–786; chart, 29
Double comparisons, 293
Double negatives, 295

Downloading from the Internet, 657
Drafting
defined, 17
essays, 683–684
guidelines for, 19
idea development and, 79–88
revising and, 17–19

e, final, 521–522
Easily confused words, glossary, 846–853
Editing guidelines, 21–22
Editorials, citation of, 711, 731
Educational Resources Information Center
(ERIC), 645
ei vs. ie, 521
Either-or thinking, 168, 169
Electronic sources. See also Internet; World
Wide Web
CD-ROM, 629, 634–638, 640, 645, 663,
715–717, 733
commercial services, 717–718, 733
diskette, 715–717, 733
e-mail, 646, 719, 829–830
evaluating, 648, 650–657
FTP sites, 647, 719
gopher sites, 648, 719, 734
Internet sites, 646–657, 718–719, 733–733
Listservs, 649, 650, 719
online guide to citing, 716
newsgroups, 649, 650, 719
subscription services, 717–718, 733
synchronous communications, 719
Telnet sites, 719
Usenet postings, 649, 650, 719
World Wide Web sites, 646–657, 719, 734
Ellipses, 589–590, 676
Elliptical clauses, dangling, 391
Elliptical constructions, 281–282, 416–417,
418
E-mail, 646, 719, 829–830
Embedded quotations, 593–594
Emotional blocks, 61–62
Emphasis, 453–459, 468
defined, 453
inversion for, 457–458
italics for, 602
parallelism for, 440–441
repetition for, 455–456
short paragraphs for, 458
short sentences for, 454–455
ways to write with, chart, 453
word placement for, 456–457
Encyclopedias, 630–632
Ending of an essay, 12–13, 115–117,
136–139, 165–166
Ending paragraphs
in analytical essays, 210–212
in argumentative essays, 210–212
defined, 209

Ending paragraphs, *(continued)*
  in exploratory essays, 209–210
  guidelines for, 210
  linking, 216, 218
Endnotes, 735–737
End punctuation, 534–538
  exclamation point, 537
  period, 534–535
  question mark, 535–537
English
  Appalachian, 489
  Black, 488–489
  dialects of, 488–490
  Hispanic, 489
  history of, 504–507
English as a second language. *See* ESL writers
Enthymeme, 65
Enumeration, as writing technique, 194
ERIC (Educational Resources Information
      Center), 645
ESL (English as a second language)
      writers, grammar for, 323–362
  adverb placement, 352–354
  articles, 326–329
  auxiliary verbs, 338–343
  be, use of, 337–341
  conditional sentences, 356–357
  count vs. noncount nouns, 323–325
  demonstratives, 331–332
  determiners, 325–326
  direct vs. indirect discourse, 354–356
  gerunds, 344–348
  idiomatic expressions, chart, 358–361
  infinitives, 344–348
  modal auxiliaries, 342–343
  modifiers, 334–336
  past vs. present participles, 336–337
  plural verbs, 348–351
  possessives, 332–333
  prepositions, 351–352
  quantifiers, 329–331
  verb tenses, 356–357
  word order, 334–336
Essay exams, 842–845
  checklist, chart, 845
  key terms in questions, chart, 843–844
  preparing for, 842
  reviewing, 845
  writing, 845
Essays. *See also* Analytical essays;
      Argumentative essays; Exploratory
      essays; Research essays
  analytical, 123–142
  argumentative, 143–172
  beginning, 12–13, 108–109, 111, 116,
      135–136
  critical reading for, 124–125, 128–131,
      668–670
  defined, 5

developing, 128–139, 152–167
ending, 12–13, 115–117, 136–139,
      165–166
exam, 842–845
exploratory, 102–122
guidelines for, 104, 129, 151
incorporating evidence in, 146, 152–153,
      160–165, 680–681, 684–688
middle, 12–13, 109–115, 116, 136–137,
      212–215
organizing, 12–17, 150–151, 156–158,
      681–683
overview, 101
preparatory strategies, 9–12
research, 665–694
Ethnically biased language, 496–497
Etymology, 471
Euphemisms, 490–491
Eureka, 647
Evaluating sources
  electronic, 648, 650–657
  essays and, 757, 759
  guidelines for, 39, 668
  texts, 37–39, 792–793
Evidence
  accumulating, 4–5
  analyzing, 33–35, 124–125
  in argumentative essays, 146, 152–153,
      160–165
  audience and, 680–681
  incorporating in essays, 146, 152–153,
      160–165, 680–681, 684–688
  in informational paragraphs, 213
  linking with thesis, 160–165
  questioning for ideas, 55–56, 72–79,
      131–132, 139–140, 626, 783
  in research essays, 680–681, 684–688,
      757, 759
Examinations. *See* Essay exams
Examples. *See also* Evidence
  in argumentative essays, 152–153
  illustration by, 194–195
Exclamation points
  placement with parentheses, 585
  quotation marks with, 578
  use of, 537
Exclamatory sentences, 235, 236
Experience, stories of, 103–117; guidelines
      for use, 104
Explanatory notes, 701, 763, 769
Expletives, 463–464
Exploratory essays, 102–122
  audience for, 102–103
  beginning of, 108–109, 111, 116, 204–206
  collaboration and, 106
  creative thinking and, 107–108
  ending of, 115–117
  features of, 102–103
  guidelines for, 104

idea development and, 105–117
making connections in, 103–104,
    106–107, 117–122
middle of, 109–115, 116
purpose for, 102
revising, 110–111
stories of experience in, 103–117
text analysis in, 141–142
Expressions
idiomatic, 358–361, 418, 473
slang, 399, 483–484
transitional, 185, 547

Fallacies, logical
appeal to ignorance, 168, 170
avoidance of, 148–149, 167–172
begging the question, 168, 169
character attack, 168, 171
checklist of, 168
circular reasoning, 168, 170
defined, 167
either-or thinking, 168, 169
false analogy, 168, 171
hasty generalization, 149, 168
illogical causality, 168, 169
non sequitur, 168, 169
playing prejudices, 168, 170–171
red herring, 168, 170
special pleading, 168, 170
stereotyping, 168, 169
False analogy, 168, 171
Faulty predication, 414–416
Field labels, 472
Field notes, 803
Field research, 657–661
defined, 657
interviews as, 657–659
observation as, 660–661
questionnaires in, 659–660
surveys as, 658–660
Figurative language, 492–495
metaphor, 492–493
simile, 493–494
Figures, conventions for use, chart,
    612–613
File Transfer Protocol (FTP), 647, 719
Films, citation of, 714, 732
Finite verbs, 251, 364
First person, 273, 274, 306–307
Focusing question, 669–670
Footnotes. *See also* Source documentation
APA style for, 725
CMS style for, 735–737
Foreign words and phrases, 602
Formal language, 483–484
Formal outline, 14–15
Format, computer. *See also* Word
    processing programs
of documents, 827–837, 839–841

of References list, 725, 777
of Works Cited list, 704, 770
Fractions, 617
Fragments, sentence. *See* Sentence
    fragments
Freewriting, 10, 27–29, 626, 784
FTP (File Transfer Protocol), 647, 719
Functional sentence types, 235–236, 396
Future perfect progressive tense, 259
Future perfect tense, 257
Future progressive tense, 258
Future tense, 255

Gazetteers, 634
Gender-specific language, 320–321, 497–500
Generalizations, 149, 168, 328–329
General-to-specific order, 189
General words, 481–483
Geographical bias, 502
Geographical designations, 608
Gerund phrases, 229
Gerunds
defined, 228, 229, 251
vs. infinitives, chart, 346–347
as objects, chart, 345–346
possessive case forms with, 283–284
present participles as, 242
Glossaries
of grammatical and rhetorical terms,
    854–865
of usage, 846–853
good vs. *well*, 291
Gopher, 648, 719, 734
Government documents, 640, 709, 729
Grammar, 219–362. *See also* Sentence
    grammar
adjectives in, 286–298
adverbs in, 286–298
basic, 220–239
conjunctions in, 301–305
defined, 219
for ESL writers, 323–362
incompatible grammatical patterns,
    413–414
interjections in, 304–305
nouns in, 270–271, 282–283
prepositions in, 299–301, 305
pronoun-antecedent agreement, 317–321
pronouns in, 271–285
sentence, 220–239
subject-verb agreement, 306–317
terms of, glossary, 854–865
verbs in, 240–269
Grammar tips
achieving clear and complete sentences,
    420
achieving emphasis and conciseness, 468
achieving sentence variety, 452
avoiding sexist pronouns, 321

Grammar tips, *(continued)*
  controlling prepositions and
      conjunctions, 305
  controlling pronoun case, 285
  controlling pronoun reference, 410–411
  correcting sentence fragments, 372
  for ESL writers, 362
  maintaining agreement, 322
  maintaining consistency, 401–402
  managing modifiers, 298
  placing modifiers, 392
  using coordination and subordination, 433
  using different sentence types, 239
  using parallelism, 442
  using strong verbs, 269
Grammatical "persons", 273, 274, 306–307,
      393–394
Grammatical sentence types, 237–238
Grammatical structures
  coordinate, 423–427, 433
  parallel, 434–442
  subordinate, 431–433
Graphs, computer, 832, 836–837

Hasty generalization, 149, 168
have
  as auxiliary verb, 243, 245, 338–341
  forms of, 337–338
Headings, formatting on computer, 831
Helping verbs. *See* Auxiliary verb forms
Hesitation, 582, 590
Hispanic English, 489
History of English, 504–507
Holidays, 607
Home page, 647
Homonyms, 518–521
  American vs. British/Canadian
      spellings, 520–521
  commonly confused, chart, 519–520
  frequently confused, chart, 518
  with more than one form, 520
Hours, 564
Http (hypertext transfer protocol), 650
Humanities, writing in, 780–801. *See also*
      Literature and the arts
Hyperbole, 492
Hypertext links, 647
Hypertext transfer protocol (http), 650
Hyphens, 615–619
  with compound words, 616–617
  to divide words at end of line, chart,
      615–616
  with prefixes and suffixes, 618–619
  spelling words with, chart, 529–530
Hypothesis, 803

I, capitalization, 597
Idea development, 72–100
  through collaboration, 98–100, 106

through controversy, 95–98
through drafting, 79–88
guidelines for, 75, 79, 83
through letter-writing, 117–119
through making connections, 34–35,
    88–95, 103–104, 106–107, 117–122,
    789
through questioning, 55–56, 72–79,
    131–132, 139–140, 626, 783
through revising, 79–88
through stories of experience, 103–117
through writing, 79–88, 106–108
Ideas
  coordinating in sentences, 422–426
  defined, 5
  development of, 72–100
  formulating, 4–5
  pairing, 435–438
  subordinating in sentences, 427–433
Idiomatic expressions, 358–361, 418, 473
ie vs. *ei*, 521
Illogical causality, 168, 169
Illustration by example, as writing
      technique, 194–195
Images, visual, 186–187, 218
Imperative mood, 265, 396
Imperative sentences, 235, 236
Implied thesis, 159–160
Incompatible grammatical patterns, 413–414
Incomplete comparisons, 294
Incomplete sentences, 416–420
  elliptical constructions and, 416–417
  incomplete comparisons and, 418–420
  missing words and, 417–418
  revising, 416–420
  sentence fragments and, 364–372
Indefinite articles
  a vs. *an*, 326–327
  apostrophes with, 566
  choosing, 326–327
  defined, 271, 325, 326
Indefinite pronouns
  common, chart, 311
  defined, 272–273
  subject-verb agreement and, 310–311
Indentation of paragraphs, 839
Independent clauses
  commas with, 540–541
  connecting, 303–304, 422–433, 540–541
  defined, 232
  linking in coordinate structures, 422–427
  linking in subordinate structures,
      427–433
  semicolons with, 557–559, 560, 561
  sentence types and, 237–238
Indexes
  of books, 634
  of citations, 639–640
  of periodicals, 635–640

specialized bibliographies, 632–633
Indicative mood, 265, 396
Indirect citation, 700, 757, 767
Indirect discourse, 354–355, 397–399. *See also* Indirect quotations
Indirect object, 223–224
Indirect quotations
  defined, 398
  vs. direct discourse, 398
  periods with, 536
  shifts in, 397–399
Indo-European language, 504–505
Inductive reasoning, 64–68; chart, 64
Inferences, 35–36, 73–74, 789–790
Infinitive phrases, 229
Infinitives
  vs. gerunds, chart, 346–347
  as objects, chart, 344–345
  pronouns with, 276, 283
  split by modifiers, 388
  in tense sequences, 261
  as verbals, 228, 229, 251
Informal language, 483–484
Informal outline, 14
Informational paragraphs, 212–214
Info*Seek*, 647
InfoTrac, 636, 645
Initialisms, 605
Inseparable transitive phrasal verbs, 350
Intellectual blocks, 60–61
Intensity, adverbs indicating, 353
Intensive pronouns, 272–273
Interface card, 647
Interjections, 304–305
Interlibrary loan, 640
Internal interface card, 647
Internet, 646–657. *See also* World Wide Web
  accessing, 647
  addresses on, 648, 649, 650
  benefits of, 649–650
  citation of sources from, 664, 716, 717–719, 733–734
  commercial services on, 717–718, 733
  defined, 646
  domain name system on, 648, 650
  downloading from, 657
  e-mail on, 646, 719, 829–830
  evaluating sources from, 648, 650–657
  FTP sites, 647, 719
  gopher sites, 648, 719, 734
  guidelines for searching, 649
  limitations of, 648–649
  Listservs on, 649, 650, 719
  navigating, 647–650
  newsgroups on, 649, 650, 719
  printing from, 649, 650
  research on, 646–657
  synchronous communications on, 719
  Telnet sites on, 719

URLs on, 650, 718
Usenet postings on, 649, 719
Internet Explorer, 647
Internet service provider (ISP), 647
Interpretation, of texts, 35–37, 42–47
Interrogative pronouns, 272–274
Interrogative sentences, 235, 236
Interrupted quotations, 594
Interrupting comments, 581–582
Interrupting modifiers, 387–389
Intertextual reading, 41–42
Interviews, 657–659; tips for, 658–659
Intransitive verbs
  defined, 250
  examples, 251–253
  phrasal, 350
Introduction. *See* Beginning of an essay
Introductory elements, 541–542
Invented words, 576
Inverted sentences, 313–314, 457–458
IRCs, citation of, 719
Ironically used words, 576
Irregular comparatives, chart, 294
Irregular superlatives, chart, 294
Irregular verbs
  be, 243, 245, 337–341
  chart of common, 246–249
  defined, 242, 246
  do, 243, 245, 337–341
  have, 243, 245, 337–341
  lie vs. *lay*, 251, 252
  past tense and, 242
  rise vs. *raise*, 251, 252
  sit vs. *set*, 251–252
it
  antecedent reference of, 406–407
  indefinite use of, 407–408
Italics, 600–603
  for emphasis, 602–603
  with foreign words and phrases, 602
  with titles, chart, 600–601
  with vehicle names, 602
Italic type, defined, 600

Jargon, 485
Job application letters, 823–824
Joint possession, 567
Journals
  personal, 10–11, 626
  reading, 10, 624, 626
  research, 624, 815
Justification, right-side, 704

Key positions, 454, 456–457
Key terms, 183–184, 218
Key word searches, 643–644, 645

Lab notebook, chart, 815
Laboratory reports, 815–818

Language. *See also* Diction; Words
    biased, 496–503
    English, history of, 504–507
    figurative, 492–495
    formal vs. informal, 483–485
Latin abbreviations, 607
lay vs. *lie*, 251, 252
LCSH (Library of Congress Subject
    Headings), 642
Lectures, citation of, 712–713
Length of sentences, 443–446, 452, 454–455
Letters
    within lists, 584–585
    missing, 570
Letter-writing
    for business, 821–822
    and idea development, 117–119
    for job applications, 823–824
LEXIS-NEXIS, 717
Libraries
    computer resources in, 629, 634–640,
        642–646
    general orientation, 628–629
    interlibrary loan, 640
    periodicals in, 634–640
    reference books in, 629–634
    resources of, 628–641
    searching for sources in, 641–646
    special resources in, 640–641
Library catalog, 641–644
Library of Congress Subject Headings
    (LCSH), 642
Library of Congress System of call
    numbers, 641–642
lie vs. *lay*, 251, 252
Limiting modifiers, 383
Line graph, 836–837
Linking paragraphs, 215–218
Linking verbs, 249–250
    adjectives with, 289
    agreement with subjects, 312–313
    defined, 249
    subject complements and, 225–226
Listing details and observations, 34–35,
        129, 132–134, 782–783, 828
Lists
    colons with, 563
    on computer, 828, 833
    dashes with, 582
    organizing with parallelism,
        441–442
    parentheses with, 584–585
Listserv, 649, 650, 719
Literary present. *See* Present tense
Literary works. *See also* Literature
        and the arts
    citation of, 700
    what to look for in, chart, 788–789
    writing about, 780–801

Literature and the arts, interpreting,
        786–792
    connection, 789
    inference, 789–790
    interpretation, 790–792
    observation, 787–789
    sample, 794–801
    steps in, chart, 787
    what to look for, chart, 788–789
Literature and the arts, writing about,
        780–801
    evaluation, 792–793
    interpretation, 786–792
    sample papers, 793–801
    techniques for, chart, 781
    understanding, 780–786
Literature reviews, scientific, chart, 814
Litotes, 492
Location, showing with subordination,
        429
Logical fallacies. *See* Fallacies, logical
Logical relationships, showing, 428–429
Logical thinking. *See* Thinking, logical
Lurking, 651
-ly vs. *-ally*, 522

Magazines. *See* Periodicals
Major premise, 64–65
Making connections. *See* Connections
Manner, adverbs indicating, 353
Manuscript preparation, 838–841
    corrections, 841
    cover page, 744, 745, 839
    explanatory notes, 763, 769
    formatting, 751, 831–835, 839–841
    headings, 831, 833
    highlighting, 833
    lists, 833
    margins, 704, 751, 832, 839
    outlines, 746–747
    page numbers, 839
    paper, 838
    paragraphs, 839
    quotations, 831–832, 840–841
    reference notes, 767, 769
    source documentation, 839
    spacing, 832, 839–840
    thesis placement, 751
    title, 694, 751, 831
    type for, 832–833, 838–839
    white space, 833–834
Map, mind, 15–16
Mapping, 11, 15–17
Maps, citation of, 715, 733
Margins, of research papers, 704, 751, 832,
        839
Mass nouns, 271, 323–325
Meanings of words, in dictionary, 471
Measurement units, 609

Mechanics, 533, 592–619. *See also* Punctuation
abbreviations, 604–610
capitalization, 592–599
defined, 533
hyphens, 615–619
italics, 600–603
numbers, 611–614
Memo headings, 564
Memos, business, 820
Metaphors, 492–495
Microcomputer center, 641
Microfiche, 635
Microfilm, 635
Microform, 635
Microprint, 635
Microsoft Internet Explorer, 647
Microsoft Network, 647
Middle English, 505–506
Middle of an essay, 12–13, 109–115, 116, 136–137, 212–215
Middle paragraphs
defined, 212
guidelines for, 213, 215
informational, 212–214
linking, 216, 218
transitional, 214–215
Mind map, 15–16
Minor premise, 64–65
Minutes, colons with, 564
Misplaced modifiers, 382–387
defined, 382
misplaced clauses, 385–386
misplaced phrases, 384–385
misplaced words, 383
squinting modifiers, 386–387
Missing letters, 570
Missing numbers, 570
Misspelled words, chart, 532
Mixed metaphors, 493, 495
Mixed sentences, 412–416
causes of, chart, 412
defined, 412
with faulty predication, 414–416
with incompatible grammatical patterns, 413–414
revision of, 412–416
MLA Handbook for Writers of Research Papers, 695–696, 743
MLA (Modern Language Association) style, 695–719. *See also* Works Cited list
for block quotations, 687
directory of citation types, 696–697
for explanatory notes, 701, 763, 769
guidelines for formatting, 839–841
guidelines for source documentation, 698
for parenthetical citations, 697–701
for reference notes, 702–703
sample research essay in, 743–771
for Works Cited list, 703–719, 770–771

Modal auxiliaries, 244–245, 342–343; chart, 342
Modem, 647
Modern Language Association. *See MLA Handbook;* MLA style
Modifiers, 286–298
adjectives, 286–287, 289, 291–296, 334–336
adverbs, 286, 288, 289–296, 298
bad vs. *badly,* 291
comparative form, 292–294
dangling, 390–392
defined, 286, 382
distinguishing between, 286–299
double negatives, 295
good vs. *well,* 291
interrupting, 387–389
irregular, chart, 294
limiting, 383
linking verbs and, 289
managing, 298
misplaced, 382–387
nouns as, 295–296
placement of, 392
positive form, 292
redundant, 462
revision of, summary, 391–392
superlative form, 292–294
word order and, 334–336
Months, 607
Mood, verb, 265–268
conditional, 267–268
consistency in, 396–397
defined, 265
imperative, 265, 396
indicative, 265, 396
subjunctive, 265–266, 268, 396
MOOs, citation of, 719
Morphemes, 473
Motion, prepositions indicating, 351
Ms., period with, 535
MUDs, citation of, 719
Multivolume work, citation of, 699, 707, 728
Musical compositions, citation of, 714

Name-and-year system of citation, 738
Names, capitalization of, chart, 595–596
Natural sciences writing, 810–818
audience for, 811–813
described, 802
formats, 814–818
lab reports, 815–818
literature review, 814
methodology, 810–811
purpose of, 811–813
sample student paper, 816–818
source documentation, 813–814
Negating words, 461–462
Negation prefixes, 509

Negative sentences, 341, 352
Negatives, double, 295
Neologisms, 486
Netscape, 647
Networks, computer, 829–830
Newsgroups
    access to, 650
    citation of, 719
    defined, 649
Newspapers. *See* Periodicals
no, comma with, 548
Nominalization, 464–465
Noncount nouns
    articles with, 323, 326–329
    categories of, chart, 324
    vs. count nouns, 323–325
    defined, 271, 323
    demonstratives with, 331–332
    quantifiers with, 329–331
Nonessential information, 584, 586
Nonfinite verbs, 251, 364. *See also* Verbals
Nonprint source, 663, 701
Nonrestrictive adjective and adverb
        clauses, 543–544
Nonrestrictive appositives, 544–545
Nonrestrictive elements, 542–545
Nonrestrictive phrases, 544
Non sequitur, 168, 169
Notebook, double-column, 10, 29–31,
        784–786; chart, 29
Note cards, 671–672
Notes, documentation. *See also* Source
        documentation
    content, 725
    endnotes, 735–737
    explanatory, 701, 763, 769
    footnotes, 725, 735–737
    reference, 702–703, 767, 769.
Note taking, 670–678
    combining techniques of, 677–678
    guidelines for, 671–672
    note cards for, 671–672
    organizing notes, 681–682
    paraphrases in, 674–675
    quotations in, 676–677
    reflections in, 677
    source cards for, 662–664, 671
    summaries in, 672–674
Notion of degree, 62
Noun clauses, 233
Noun modifiers, 334–336. *See also* Modifiers; Adjectives; Determiners
Noun object, 350
Noun phrase fragments, 367
Noun phrases, 227
Nouns
    abstract, 270
    adjectives formed from, 287
    apparently plural, 314–315

appositive phrases as, 230
capitalization of, chart, 594–597
collective, 271, 311–312, 318
common, 270
compound, 527
concrete, 270
count, 271, 323–331
defined, 270
determiners with, 271, 325–326
gerund phrases as, 229
infinitive phrases as, 229
mass, 271, 323–331
as modifiers, 295–296
modifiers for, 286–298, 334–336
noncount, 271, 323–331
in phrases, 227, 367
plural forms of, 270–271, 314–315, 527
preferring verbs to, 464–465
proper, 270
word order and, 334–336
Noun suffixes, chart, 512
Number, grammatical
    maintaining consistency of, 393–394
    of persons, 307
    of pronouns, 394
Number prefixes, 509
Numbers, 611–614
    commas with, 550
    within lists, 584–585
    missing, 570
    spelling out, 611–612
    using figures according to convention,
        chart, 612–613
Number system of citation, 739
Numerical data, 763

O, capitalization, 597
Object complement, 225–226
Objective case form, 275–276, 277–279,
        283
Objects, 223–225
    defined, 223
    direct, 223–224, 387–389
    indirect, 223–224
    of prepositions, 224–225, 275
    pronouns and, 275, 281
Observation
    checklist for, 661
    of details in texts, 34–35, 129, 132–134,
        782–783, 787–789
    as field research, 660–661
Obstacles to thinking, 58–63
    cultural blocks, 59–60
    emotional blocks, 60–61
    intellectual blocks, 60–61
    overcoming, 59
    perceptual blocks, 58–59
    polarization, 62–63
Occupational stereotypes, 498–499

OCLC (Online Computer Library Center), 642
Old English, 505
Online Computer Library Center (OCLC), 642
Online sources. *See also* Internet; World Wide Web
  abstracts, 640
  book indexes, 634
  citation indexes, 640
  citation of sources from, 664, 716–719, 733–734
  commercial services, 717–718, 733
  computerized databases, 644–646
  e-mail, 646, 719, 829–830
  evaluating, 648, 650–657
  FTP sites, 647, 719
  gopher sites, 648, 719, 734
  Internet, 646–657, 718–719, 733–734
  key word searching of, 643–644
  library catalogs, 642–644
  Listservs, 649, 650, 719
  newsgroups, 649, 650, 719
  periodical indexes, 635–638
  synchronous communications, 719
  Telnet sites, 719
  Usenet postings, 649, 650, 719
  World Wide Web, 646–657, 719, 734
Openings, sentence, 447–449
Order
  adverbs indicating, 353
  climactic, 190–191
  of an essay, 12–13
  general-to-specific, 189
  of a paragraph, 188–193
  spatial, 192–193
  specific-to-general, 189–190
  time, 191–192
Order-of-first mention, 739
Organizing essays, 12–17. *See also* Paragraph organization
  beginning, middle, and ending, 108–117, 135–139, 156–158
  mapping, 15–17
  ordering, 13, 188–193
  organizing notes for, 681–682
  outlining, 13–15, 682–683
Outlines
  on computer, 831
  in final manuscript, 746–749
  formal, 14–15, 746–749
  informal, 14, 747
  organizing with parallelism, 441–442
  as preliminary writing tool, 13–15, 682–683
  revising and, 155–156

Pagination, 832, 839
Pairing ideas, 435–438

Pairs, word, 462
Pamphlet, citation of, 708
Paper, for final manuscript, 838
Paragraph development techniques, 193–202
  analogy, 202
  cause-and-effect analysis, 196–197
  classification, 199–200
  comparison and contrast, 198–199
  definition, 195–196
  description, 201–202
  division and analysis, 200–201
  enumeration, 194
  illustration by example, 194–195
  process analysis, 197–198
Paragraph indentation, 839
Paragraph organization, 188–193
  climactic order, 190–191
  general-to-specific order, 189
  spatial order, 192–193
  specific-to-general order, 189–190
  time order, 191–192
Paragraphs, 173–218
  beginning, 203, 204–208, 218
  coherent, 174–176, 181–188
  defined, 173
  development of, 193–202
  ending, 203, 209–212, 218
  functions of, 203–218
  fundamentals of, 172–202
  guidelines for, 178, 182, 189, 205, 210, 213, 215
  informational, 212–214
  linking, 215–218
  middle, 203, 212–215, 218
  organizing, 188–193
  parallelism in, 440–441
  topic sentence of, 176, 178–181, 755
  transitional, 214–215
  types of, 203–218
  unity between, 215–218
  unity within, 174–181
Parallelism, 434–442
  checking for, 440
  coherence and, 187–188, 438–441
  coordinating series with, 435
  defined, 434
  elliptical constructions and, 417
  emphasis and, 440–441, 453–454
  organizing lists with, 441–442
  organizing outlines with, 441–442
  pairing ideas with, 435–438
  uses of, chart, 434
  as writing technique, 442
Paraphrases
  defined, 31–32, 674–675
  guidelines for, 675
  integrating in essays, 686, 765
Parentheses, 584–587, 593

Parenthetical citations
    APA style for, 721–725
    CBE style for, 738–739
    guidelines for, 698
    MLA style for, 697–701
Parenthetical expressions
    brackets with, 588
    commas with, 547
    dashes with, 582–583
Participial phrases, 228, 384–385
Participles
    as adjectives, 242, 251, 336–337
    defined, 251
    past, 242, 261–262, 336–337
    present, 241–242, 261, 336–337
    present perfect, 261
    pronoun case forms with, 283–284
    as verbals, 228, 251
    verb tenses and, 256–259, 261–262
Parts of speech
    chart, 221
    in dictionary, 471
Passive voice
    auxiliary verbs and, 340–341
    defined, 263–265
    preferring active to, 465–466
    shifts in, 396–397
Past participle
    as primary verb form, 242
    used as adjective, 336–337
    verb tenses and, 256–257, 261–262
Past perfect progressive tense, 258–259
Past perfect tense, 256
Past progressive tense, 257–258
Past tense, 242, 255
Patterns, sentence, 234–235
Pause, ellipses used with, 590
Perceptual blocks, 58–59
Perfect tenses
    auxiliary verbs in, 339–340
    future perfect, 257
    past perfect, 256
    present perfect, 256
Performances, citation of, 713
Periodical indexes, 635–640
    abstract, 639–640
    citation, 639–640
    general, 636–637
    specialized, 637–639
Periodicals, 634–640
    abstracts from, 639–640
    citation of, 709–712, 729–731
    indexes to, 635–640
    on microform, 635
    in working bibliography, 663
Periodic sentences, 451
Periods
    placement with parentheses, 585
    quotation marks with, 577–578

    use of, 534–535
Person, grammatical, 273, 274, 306–307,
        393–394
Personal adjectives, 568
Personal communications, citation of, 724
Personal journal, 10–11
Personal pronouns, 272–274, 280–282, 568,
        761
Personal titles, 604
Personification, 492
Photocopying sources, 678
Phrasal verbs
    chart, 439
    defined, 348
    inseparable, 350
    as intransitive verbs, 350
    prepositions and, 481
    separable, 350
    as transitive verbs, 350
    use of, 348–351
Phrase fragments, 366–368
Phrases, 226–232
    absolute, 229, 230
    appositive, 230, 367
    defined, 226, 366
    gerund, 229
    infinitive, 229
    misplaced, 384–385
    noun, 227, 367
    participial, 228
    prepositional, 227–228, 367, 466
    restrictive vs. nonrestrictive, 544
    in sentence openings, 448–449
    use of, 231–232
    verb, 227, 243
    verbal, 228–230, 366–367
    wordy, list, 460–461
Physical and mental characteristics, bias
        about, 502
Pie chart, 836
Place, indication of, 351, 353
Placement of words for emphasis, 454,
        456–457
Place names, commas with, 550
Plagiarism, 688–692
    defined, 688
    tips for avoiding, 691
    what to acknowledge, 689–690
    what not to acknowledge, 690
Pleading, special, 168, 170
Plurals
    apostrophes with, 567
    contractions used to form, 570–571
    forming, 526–527
    irregular, 527
    of nouns, 270–271, 527
    regular, 526
    subject-verb agreement and, 306–317
p.m., 606

Poetry
  capitalization of first line, 594
  quotation marks with, 574–575
  quotations from, 840–841
Polarization, 62–63
Position prefixes, 510
Positive form of adjectives and adverbs, 292
Possessive adjectives, 296–297, 325, 332
Possessive case form, 276, 283–284
Possessive nouns, 566
Possessives, 332–333, 566–568
Post hoc, ergo propter hoc fallacy, 169
Predicate adjective, 225
Predicate noun, 225
Predicates, 220–223
  in clauses, 232
  complete, 222
  compound, 222
  defined, 220
  relation to subject, 412–416
  simple, 222
Predication, faulty, 414–416
Prefixes
  common, chart, 509–510
  hyphens with, chart, 618
  meanings of, 509–511
Prejudices, playing, 168, 170–171
Preliminary writing techniques
  annotating, 10, 26–27, 781–782
  double-column notebook method, 10,
    29–31, 784–786
  freewriting, 10, 27–29, 784
  journal method, 10–11, 784–786
  listing details and observations, 129,
    132–134, 782–783
  making connections, 34–35, 88–95,
    103–104, 106–107, 117–122, 789
  mapping, 15–17
  outlining, 13–15
  overview, 9–12
  questioning, 55–56, 72–79, 131–132,
    139–140, 626, 783
  using controversy, 95–98
  writing for ideas, 79–88, 106–108
Premises, 64–65, 153
Preparation of final manuscript. *See*
    Manuscript preparation
Preparatory strategies. *See* Preliminary
    writing techniques
Prepositional phrase fragments, 367
Prepositional phrases
  excessive use of, 466
  format of, 299
  function of, 227–228
  misplaced, 384
  as sentence openings, 448–449
Prepositions
  common, chart, 300
  compound, chart, 299, 300

controlling, 305
  defined, 299
  excessive use of, 466
  indicating time, place, or motion,
    351–352
  objects of, 224–225, 299
  use of, 299–301
Present participle
  as primary verb form, 241–242
  used as adjective, 336–337
  verb tenses and, 257–259, 261
Present perfect participle, 261
Present perfect progressive tense, 258
Present perfect tense, 256
Present progressive tense, 257
Present tense
  defined, 254–255
  in describing literature and art, 793–794
  as primary verb form, 241
  use of, 395
Primary sources, 627, 793
Primary verb forms, 241–243
  base, 241
  past participle, 242
  past tense, 242
  present participle, 241–242
  present tense, 241
  simple, 241
Printing from the Internet, 657
Process analysis, 197–198
Prodigy, 647, 717
Professional titles, 604
Progressive tenses
  auxiliary verbs in, 338–339
  future, 258
  future perfect, 259
  past, 257–258
  past perfect, 258–259
  present, 257
  present perfect, 258
Pronoun-antecedent agreement, 317–321
  with collective noun antecedents, 318
  with compound antecedents, 318–320
  defined, 317
  gender-specific pronouns and, 320–321
  with indefinite pronoun antecedents,
    318
  summary, chart, 319
Pronoun case
  chart of, 274
  controlling, 285
  objective, 275–276, 277–279, 283
  possessive, 276, 283–284
  subjective, 275, 277–279
  we vs. *us*, 282–283
  who vs. *whom*, 277–280
Pronoun reference, 403–411
  adjectives as antecedents, 408–409
  checking, chart, 409

Pronoun reference, *(continued)*
  controlling, 410–411
  it, they, and *you,* 401–408
  possessives as antecedents, 408–409
  proximity to antecedents, 404–405
  revising ambiguous, chart, 403
  to a single antecedent, 403–404
  this, that, which, and *it,* 406–407
  who, which, and *that,* 408
Pronouns, 271–285
  agreement with antecedents, 271, 317–321
  appositives and, 281
  case forms of, 274–277, 283–285
  in compound structures, 280–282
  defined, 271
  demonstrative, 272–273
  elliptical constructions and, 281–282
  gender-specific, 320–321, 498
  gerunds and, 283–284
  indefinite, 272–273, 310–311, 318, 566
  infinitives and, 283
  intensive, 272–273
  interrogative, 272–274
  number of, 394
  paragraph coherence and, 182–183
  person of, 394
  personal, 272–274, 280–282, 568, 761
  possessive forms of, 323–333
  reciprocal, 272–273
  reference of, 403–411
  reflexive, 272–273
  relative, 272–274, 313, 366, 369
  shifts in person and number, 394
  subject-verb agreement and, 310–311, 313
  types of, chart, 272
  we vs. *us,* 282–283
  who vs. *whom,* 277–280
Pronunciation, dictionary on, 472
Proofreading, 21–22
Proper adjectives, 594–596
Proper nouns, 270, 594–596
ProQuest, 645, 646
Publication information, 704, 726, 740
*Publication Manual of the American
    Psychological Association,* 719–720,
    743, 805–806. *See also* APA style
Punctuation, 533–591
  apostrophes, 566–572
  brackets, 587–588
  colons, 556–557, 562–565
  commas, 539–555, 586
  ellipses, 589–590
  end punctuation, 534–538
  exclamation point, 537
  dashes, 581–584, 586
  quotation marks, 573–580
  question marks, 535–537
  parentheses, 584–587
  periods, 534–535

semicolons, 556–562
  slashes, 590–591
Purpose, showing with subordination, 429
Purpose in writing
  for analytical essay, 123–124
  for argumentative essay, 144
  defined, 7–9
  for exploratory essay, 102
  for research essay, 623–624

Quantifiers
  choosing correct, 330
  defined, 325, 329
  use of, 329–331
Quantity prefixes, 509
Questioning
  in creative thinking, 55–56
  guidelines for, 79
  in idea development, 72–79, 131–132,
      139–140, 626, 783
Question mark, 535–537, 578, 585
Questionnaires, 659–660
Questions
  do in, 341
  on exams, chart, 843–844
  including quotations, punctuation of,
      536
  quotation marks with, 573
  tag, 548
  who vs. *whom* in, 277–279
Quota of alternatives, 51–52
Quotation marks, 573–580
  for dialogue, 575
  for direct quotations, 573
  to enclose titles and definitions, 575–576
  for lengthy quotations, 574
  misuses of, 577
  with other punctuation, 573
  placement with parentheses, 585
  with poetry, 574–575
  for quotes within quotes, 574
  single marks, 574
  summary of uses, chart, 580
Quotations
  block, 687–688, 759, 761
  brackets with, 588
  brief, 686–687
  capitalization with, 593–594
  colons with, 563
  commas with, 551
  defined, 676
  direct, 354–355, 397–399
  ellipses with, 589, 676
  embedded, 593–594
  formatting, 831–832, 840–841
  indirect, 354–355, 397–399
  interrupted, 594
  integrating in essays, 685–688, 840–841
  lengthy, 574, 687–688, 759, 761

maintaining consistency in, 397–399
vs. paraphrases, 674–675, 686, 765
within quotations, 574
vs. summaries, 672–674, 686, 755, 761
use of, 676–677, 753–755, 757
when to quote, chart, 677

Racially biased language, 496–497
Radio programs, citation of, 714, 732–733
raise vs. *rise,* 251, 252
Reading, critical, 24–48. *See also* Literature
and the arts; Writing from reading
adjusting to texts in, 24–25
analyzing texts in, 33–35, 124–134
discussing texts in, 40–41
evaluating texts in, 37–39
example of, 42–47
guidelines for, 43, 669
formulating interpretations in, 35–37,
786–792
of literature, 780–793
reflecting in, 41–42
of research sources, 668–670
writing from reading and, 25–33
Reading journal, 10, 624, 626
Reasonableness, 97, 145–146, 149–150, 761
Reasoning, circular, 168, 170
Reciprocal pronouns, 272–273
Recordings, citation of, 715
Red herring, 168, 170
Redundancy, 462–463
Reference, pronoun. *See* Pronoun reference
Reference books, 629–634. *See also* Sources,
types of
biographical works, 632
book indexes, 634
citation of, 708
dictionaries, 633
encyclopedias, 630–632
gazetteers, 634
guides to, 629–630
specialized bibliographies, 632–633
yearbooks, 634
Reference information, abbreviations for,
609
Reference notes, 702–703; guidelines for,
702
References list, 725–734
abstracts in, 731
APA style for, 725–734, 777
articles in, 729–731
books in, 726–729
CBE style for, 739–741
CD-ROMs in, 733
charts in, 733
commercial online services in, 733
diskettes in, 733
dissertations in, 732
electronic sources in, 733–734

films in, 732
gopher sites in, 734
interviews in, 731
maps in, 733
online sources in, 733–734
periodicals in, 729–731
radio programs in, 732–733
reports in, 732
sample, APA style, 777
tapes in, 733
television programs in, 732–733
videocassettes in, 732
videotapes in, 732
web sites in, 734
Reflecting, 41–42, 677, 757, 759
Reflexive pronouns, 272–273
Regionalisms, 487–488
Regular verbs, 246
Relationships
logical, among details, 428–429
reversing for creative thinking, 52–53
Relative clauses, 232
Relative pronouns, 272–274, 313, 366,
369
Reliability, of online sources, 651–652
Religions, bias about, 501
Repetition, 437, 455–456, 462–463
Reports
citation of, 732
in natural sciences, 815–818
in social sciences, 806–810
Rereading, 42
Research, 621–742. *See also* Libraries;
Online sources; Sources, types of
defined, 622
field, 657–661
on the Internet, 646–657
journal of, chart, 815
in libraries, 628–641
preliminary stages of, 623–625
overview, chart, 625
scheduling, 624–625
source documentation, 661–664,
695–742
source searches, 641–657
topic selection, 626–627
Research essays, 665–694
acknowledging sources in, 689–690
audience for, 624, 680–681, 751
collaboration and, 692–693
critical reading for, 668–670
documenting sources in, 657, 661–664,
695–742
drafting, 683–684
evaluating sources for, 648, 650–657,
667–668, 757, 763
incorporating evidence in, 684–688
manuscript of, 694
note taking for, 670–678

Research essays, *(continued)*
  numerical data in, 763
  organizing, 681–683
  outlining, 682–683
  paraphrasing sources in, 765
  plagiarism, avoiding, 688–692, 765
  purpose for, 623–624
  quoting sources in, 753–755, 757, 759
  reasonableness of thesis of, 679–681, 751
  restricting topic for, 665–667
  rethinking, checklist, 693–694
  revising, 692–694, 765
  sample, APA style, 772–777
  sample, MLA style, 743–771
  selecting topic for, 626–627
  summarizing sources in, 755, 761
  title of, 694, 751
Research journal, 624, 626, 684; chart, 815
Research Libraries Group (RLG), 645
Research Libraries Information Network
      (RLIN), 644–645
Research reports, 807–810
Restrictive elements, 542, 553
Résumés, 825–826
Reversing relationships, 52–53
Reviews, citation of, 711, 731
Revising, 17–19
  defined, 17
  guidelines for, 19
  idea development and, 79–88
  from the middle, 109–115
  and reflection, 154–155
  rethinking and, 692–694, 765
Rhetoric
  cumulative sentences, 450–451
  periodic sentences, 451
  sentence variety and, 450–451
  terms of, glossary, 854–865
rise vs. *raise,* 251, 252
RLG (Research Libraries Group), 645
RLIN (Research Libraries Information
      Network), 644–645
Roots of words, 471, 506–508; chart, 508

Salutations, colons with, 564
Schedule, research, 624–625; chart, 625
Schwa, 527–528
Scientific method, chart, 810–811
Search engines, 647
Searching for sources. *See also* Libraries;
      Research; Sources, types of
  with card catalogs, 641–642
  in computerized databases, 644–646
  with key words, 643–644, 645
  in libraries, 641–646
  with library catalogs, 641–644
  online, 646–657
Seasons of year, capitalization, 598
Secondary sources, 627–628, 793

Second person, 273, 274, 306–307
Semicolons, 556–562
  avoiding errors in use, 560–561
  vs. colons, 556
  with conjunctive adverbs, 561–562
  with independent clauses, 423, 426,
      557–559
  with items in a series, 559–560
  overuse of, 560–561
  quotation marks with, 578
  summary of uses, chart, 556
Sentence fragments, 364–372
  acceptable, 371–372, 458
  causes of, chart, 370
  checking for, 366
  compound predicate, 368–369
  correcting, 364–366
  defined, 364
  dependent clause, 369–371
  phrase, 366–368
Sentence grammar, 220–239
  clauses in, 232–233
  complements in, 225–226
  defined, 220
  modifiers in, 382–392
  nouns in, 270–271, 282–283
  objects in, 223–225
  parts of speech in, 221
  patterns of, 234–235
  phrases in, 226–232
  predicates in, 222–223
  pronoun reference in, 403–411
  pronouns in, 271–285
  subjects in, 220–222
  types of, 235–239
  verbs in, 240–269
  verb tenses in, 394–397
Sentences, 363–420
  capitalization of first word in, 592
  clear and complete, 420
  comma splices in, 373–381
  consistency in, 393–402
  fragments of, 364–372
  length of, 443–446, 452, 454–455
  shifts in, 393–402
Sentence types
  balanced, 435–436
  classified by function, 235–236
  classified by grammatical construction,
      236–238
  complex, 237–238
  compound, 237
  compound-complex, 238
  conditional, 267–268, 356–357
  coordinate, 422–427, 433
  declarative, 235–236
  exclamatory, 235, 236
  fused, 373–381
  imperative, 235, 236

incomplete, 416–420
interrogative, 235, 236
inverted, 313–314, 457–458
mixed, 412–416
negative, 341
rhetorical, 450–451
sentence variety and, 449–452
simple, 237
subordinate, 422–427, 433
topic, 176, 178–181, 755
use of, 239
Separable transitive phrasal verbs, 350
Separated subjects and verbs, 308–309
Sequencing. *See* Order; Paragraph
    organization
Serials catalog, 635. *See also* Periodical
    indexes
Series
    capitalization of, 593
    commas with, 545–546, 554
    hyphens with, 617
    ordering for emphasis, 454
    semicolons with, 559–560
set vs. *sit*, 251–252
Sexist pronouns, 320–321, 498
Sexually biased (sexist) language, 497–500
Sexual orientation, 503
shall vs. *will*, 255
Shifting attention, in creative thinking, 54–55
Shifts
    avoidance of, 393–402
    defined, 393
    in diction, 39–401
    logical use of, 396
    in mood, 396
    in person and number, 393–394
    in pronoun person and number, 394
    in quotations, 397–399
    in tone, 399–401, 582
    unnecessary, chart, 393
    in verb tenses, 394–396
    in voice, 396–397
Ship names, 602
sic, 676
SilverPlatter, 645
Similes, 493–494
Simple predicate, 222
Simple sentences, 237
Simple subject, 221–222
Simple tenses, 254–255
Simple verb form, 241
Singular nouns ending in -*s*, 566–567
sit vs. *set*, 251–252
Site, web, 646, 719, 734
Slang, 399, 484
Slashes, 590
Social acceptability of words, 490
Social class, bias about, 501
Social sciences writing, 802–810

audience for, 804–805
methodology, 802–804
purpose for, 804–805
research reports, 807–810
source documentation, 805–806
types of reports, 806–807
Sociology research report, 807–810
Software search engines, 647
Solidus, 590
Source acknowledgement, 688–692. *See also*
    Plagiarism; Source documentation
    common knowledge and, 690, 753
    plagiarism, tips for avoiding, 691
    what to acknowledge, 689–690
    what not to acknowledge, 690
Source cards, 662–664, 671
Source documentation, 695–742. *See also*
    References list; Works Cited list
    in APA style, 719–734
    in bibliographies, 703–719, 735
    in CBE style, 738–742
    in CMS style, 734–737
    in content notes, 725
    directory of citations, 696–697, 720–721
    of electronic sources, 715–719, 733–734
    in endnotes, 734–737
    in explanatory notes, 701, 763, 769
    in final manuscript, 839
    in footnotes, 725, 734–737
    in MLA style, 695–719
    in natural sciences, 813–814
    in parenthetical citations, 697–701,
        721–725, 738–739
    in reference notes, 702–703, 767, 769
    in References list, 725–734, 739–741
    in social sciences, 805–806
    style manuals for, listed, 742
    in Works Cited list, 703–719
Sources
    acknowledging, 689–690
    critical reading of, 24–48, 668–670
    defined, 96
    developing arguments from, 158–167
    documenting, 163, 657, 661–664, 695–742
    evaluating, 37–39, 648, 650–657, 667–668
    integrating into essays, 684–688
    note taking from, 670–678
    plagiarism of, avoiding, 688–692
    quoting from, 685–688
    searching for, 641–657
    in text analysis, 140
Sources, types of
    CD-ROM, 634–638, 640, 645, 663,
        715–717, 733
    field research, 657–661
    Internet, 646–657, 718–719, 733–734
    online, 634–640, 646–657, 718–719,
        733–734
    primary, 627, 793

Sources, types of, *(continued)*
  reference books, 629–634
  secondary, 627–628, 793
  special, 640–641
  World Wide Web, 646–657, 719, 734
Spacecraft names, 602
Space prefixes, 510
Spacing, manuscript, 832, 839–840
Spatial order, 192–193
Specialized bibliographies, 632–633
Specialized periodical indexes,
    637–639
Special pleading, 168, 170
Specific-to-general order, 189–190
Specific words, 481–483
Speech, direct vs. indirect, 354–355
Speeches, citation of, 712–713
Spell checker programs, 531–532, 830
Spelling, 517–532
  American vs. British/Canadian,
    520–521
  common rules, 521–526
  dictionary entries, 470–471
  frequently misspelled words, 532
  homonyms, chart, 518–521
  of numbers, 611–612
  plurals, 526–527
  tips to better, 529–532, chart, 532
  word meanings as aid to, 517–518
  words with hyphens, chart, 529–530
  words with unstressed vowels and
    consonants, 527–529
Split infinitives, 388
Squinting modifiers, 386–387
State abbreviations, chart, 608
Stereotypes, 168, 169, 496, 498–499
Stories, in exploratory essays, 103–117
Structures, grammatical. *See* Grammatical
    structures
Style, 421–468
  conciseness, 459–468
  coordination and, 422–427, 433
  defined, 421
  emphasis, 453–459, 468
  parallelism and, 434–442
  subordination and, 427–433
  variety, 443–452
Style-checking programs, 830
Style manuals, listed, 742
Subject complement, 225–226, 275, 280,
    289, 387–388
Subjective case form, 275, 277–279
Subjects, sentence
  agreement with verbs, 306–317
  in clauses, 232–233
  complements and, 225–226
  complete, 222
  compound, 222, 319–310
  defined, 220

indefinite pronoun, 310–311
pronouns in, 280, 310–311, 313
relation to predicates, 412–416
role in grammar, 220–222
separated from their verbs, 387
simple, 221–222
Subject-verb agreement, 306–317
  with apparently plural nouns, 314–315
  with collective noun subjects, 311–312
  complements and, 312–313
  with compound subjects, 309–310
  with indefinite pronoun subjects,
    310–311
  in inverted sentences, 313–314
  maintaining, 322
  with relative pronoun subjects, 313
  with separated subjects and verbs,
    308–309
  summary of, chart, 316
  with third-person singular subjects,
    306–308
  in titles, 315
  with words used as words, 315
Subjunctive mood, 265–266, 268, 396
Subordinate conjunctions. *See*
    Subordinating conjunctions
Subordinate structures. *See* Subordination
Subordinating conjunctions
  chart of, 303
  in parallel structures, 437
  sentence fragments and, 366, 369
  in subordinate structures, 430–431
Subordination, 427–433
  checking, 431
  defined, 422, 427
  excessive, 430, 432
  illogical, 430–432
  relationships implied by, 428–429
  as writing technique, 427–431, 433
Subscription online services, 717, 733
Subtitles, 564, 597
Suffixes, 511–513
  adjectives and, 287
  adverbs and, 288
  hyphens with, 618
  meanings of, chart, 512
  nominalization and, 464
Summaries
  defined, 31, 672
  guidelines for, 673
  integrating in essays, 686
  in research process, 672–674
  writing of, 31–33, 686, 755, 761
Superlative form of adjectives and
    adverbs, 292–294
Superscript, 701, 702, 725
Surveys, 658–660
Syllogism, 64–65
Symbols, 606–607

Synchronous communications, citation of, 719
Synonyms, 472, 473

Tag questions, 548
Tapes, citation of, 716–717, 733
Television programs, citation of, 714, 732–733
Telnet sites, 719
Tenses of verbs
 chart of, 255
 in conditional sentences, 356–357
 defined, 253
 future, 255
 future perfect, 257
 future perfect progressive, 259
 future progressive, 258
 infinitives and, 261
 maintaining consistency in, 394–396
 participles and, 261–262
 past, 255
 past perfect, 256
 past perfect progressive, 258–259
 past progressive, 257–258
 perfect, 256–257, 339–340
 present, 254–255
 present perfect, 256
 present perfect progressive, 258, 338–339
 present progressive, 257
 progressive, 257–260
 sequences, 260–262
 shifts in, 394–396
 simple, 254–255
Terminal punctuation. *See* End punctuation
Terminology glossary, 854–865
Text analysis
 in critical reading, 33–35, 124–128
 methods and objectives of, chart, 125
 writing about literature and, 780–793
Texts
 annotation of, 10, 26–27, 626, 781–782
 critical reading of, 24–48
 defined, 25
 writing from, 10–11, 25–33
that, use of, 406–408
the
 subject-verb agreement and, 312
 when to use, chart, 327–328
Theory, 811
Thesaurus programs, 830
Thesis
 in argumentative essays, 145, 146–150
 audience and, 149–150
 defined, 5
 finding in controversy, 96–97
 implied, 159–160
 reasonableness of, chart, 679–681
 in research essays, 679–681, 751

they, use of, 407–408
Thinking, 49–71
 analogy and, 53–54, 70–71
 avoiding polarization, 62–63
 causality and, 68–70
 cultural blocks to, 59–60
 either-or, 168, 169
 emotional blocks to, 60–61
 intellectual blocks to, 60–61
 overcoming obstacles to, 58–63
 overview, chart, 49–50
 perceptual blocks to, 58–59
Thinking, creative
 through analogy, 53–54
 defined, 49–50
 through denying the negative, 55
 vs. logical, 49–50, 60
 overcoming obstacles to, 58–63
 through questioning, 55–56
 through quota of alternatives, 51–52
 through reversing relationships, 52–53
 through shifting attention, 54–55
 techniques for, 50–58
Thinking, logical, 63–68
 deductive reasoning, 64–67
 defined, 49–50, 63
 enthymemes, 65
 inductive reasoning, 64
 syllogisms, 64–67
Third person, 241, 273, 274, 306–307
this, use of, 406–407
Time
 adverbs indicating, 353
 prepositions indicating, 351
 showing with subordination, 429
Time order, 13, 191–192
Time prefixes, 510
Titles, of people
 abbreviations of, 604–605
 capitalization of, 596–597
 colons with, 564
 commas with, 550
Titles, of works
 capitalization of, 597
 for essays, 694, 751, 831, 840
 italics with, chart, 600–601
 quotation marks with, 575–576, 597
 verb agreement in, 315
Tone of writing
 changing, 83–85, 86–87
 consistency in, 399–401
 defined, 7–9, 400
 punctuation of, 582
 shift for special effect, 400
Topics, research
 focusing question of, 669–670
 guidelines for, 666
 selecting, 626–627
 restricting, 665–667

Topic sentences
  defined, 176
  implied, 180–181
  placement of, 178–181
  relation to thesis, 755
Train names, 602
Transitional expressions, 185, 547
Transitional phrases, semicolons with,
    558–559
Transitions
  paragraph coherence and, 184–186
  paragraphs as, 214–215
  in sentence openings, 447–448
Transitive verbs
  defined, 250
  examples, 251–253
  inseparable, 350
  object complements and, 225–226
  objects of, 223–224
  phrasal, 350
  separable, 350
Translations, citation of, 707, 728
Type, for manuscript, 832–833, 838–839

Underlining, 600
Understatement, 755
Units of measurement, 609
Unity
  defined, 174
  guidelines for, 178
  between paragraphs, 215–218
  within paragraphs, 174–181
  ways to achieve, 176–181
Universal resource locator (URL), 650, 718
Unstressed consonants, spelling of,
    527–529
Unstressed vowels, spelling of, 527–528
Uppercase letters. *See* Capitalization
URL (universal resource locator), 650, 718
us vs. *we* , 282–283
Usage glossary, 846–853
Usage labels, 472
Usenet Discussion Groups (newsgroups),
    649, 650, 719

Variety, 443–452
  defined, 443
  in rhetoric 450–451
  in sentence length, 443–446, 452
  in sentence openings, 447–449, 452
  in sentence type, 449–451, 452
  ways to achieve, chart, 443
Vehicle names, italics with, 602
Verbal phrase fragments, 366–367
Verbal phrases, 228–230, 366–367, 448–449
Verbals
  defined, 228, 250
  gerunds, 228, 229, 242, 251, 283–284,
    344–348

infinitives, 228, 229, 251, 261, 283–284,
    344–348, 388
  participles, 228, 251, 261–262
  in phrases, 228–230, 366–367
  in tense sequences, 261–262
Verb forms
  auxiliary, 243–245, 338–341
  base, 241
  modal auxiliary, 244–245, 342–343
  past participle, 242
  past tense, 242
  present participle, 241–242
  present tense, 241
  primary, 241–243
  simple, 241
Verb phrases, 227, 243, 348–351, 388–389
Verbs, 240–269. *See also* Subject-verb
    agreement; Tenses of verbs
  adjectives formed from, 242, 251, 287,
    336–337
  agreement with subjects, 306–317
  characteristics of, 240
  complements and, 225–226
  defined, 240
  finite, 251
  forms of, 241–253
  infinitive, 388
  intransitive, 250, 251–253, 350
  irregular, 246–249, 251–253, 337–341
  linking, 225–226, 249–250, 289, 312–313
  mood of, 265–269, 396
  nonfinite, 251
  objects of, 223–224, 348–351
  in phrases, 227, 338–341, 348–351
  preferring to nouns, 464–465
  primary forms, 241–243
  principal parts of, 246
  regular, 246
  separated from their objects, 387–388
  separated from their subjects, 387
  subjunctive, 265–266, 268
  tenses of, 253–262
  transitive, 223, 225, 250, 251–253, 350
  using strong, 269
  voice of, 262–265, 340–341
Verb suffixes, chart, 512
Videocassettes, citation of, 715, 732
Videotapes, citation of, 715, 732
Viewpoint, adverbs indicating, 353
Virgules, 590
Visual details, 186–187, 218
Visuals, computer, 835–837
Vocabulary, 504–516. *See also* Words
  context clues, 515–516
  English language history, 504–507
  prefixes, 509–511
  roots of words, 507–508
  stories behind words, 513–515
  strategies for developing, chart, 504

suffixes, 511–513
Voice, verb, 262–265
  active, 262–263, 396–397
  consistency in, 396–397
  defined, 262
  passive, 263–265, 340–341, 396–397
Vowels, unstressed, 527–529

WAIS (Wide Area Information Server), 648
Warrants, 148
we vs. *us*, 282–283
Web. *See* World Wide Web
Webcrawler, 647
Web page, 646
Web sites, 646, 719, 734
well vs. *good*, 291
when, use of, 414–415
where, use of, 414–415
which, use of, 406–408
White space, 833–834
will vs. *shall*, 255
who vs. *whom*, 277–280, 408
Wide Area Information Server (WAIS), 648
WILSON-LINE, 717
Word division, 471
Wordiness, 459–468. *See also* Conciseness
Word order, 313–314, 334–336
Word origins, 471, 506–508; chart, 508
Word processing programs
  academic documents and, 832–834
  block quotations in, 831–832
  document design in, 531–532, 704, 831–835
  drafting papers with, 829
  guidelines for writing with, 827–828
  headings in, 831, 833
  highlighting in, 833
  lists in, 833
  margins in, 832
  nonacademic documents and, 834–835
  pagination in, 832
  revising papers with, 829
  spacing, 832
  titles in, 831
  type size and style in, 832–833
  white space in, 833–834
Words. *See also* Diction; Language; Spelling; Vocabulary
  appropriate, 478–495
  characteristics of (diction), 478–495
  characteristics of, summary chart, 478
  commonly confused, glossary, 846–853
  compound, apostrophes with, 567
  context clues to, chart, 515–516
  division at end of line, 615–616
  inserted into quotations, 588
  misplaced, 383
  missing, 417–418

negating, 461–462
  placement for emphasis, 454, 456–457
  redundant, 462
  referred to as words, 576
  related, 472
  repetition for emphasis, 455–456
  roots of, 471, 506–508
  social acceptability of, 490
  spelling of, 517–532
  stories behind, 513–515
  transitional, 184–186, 447–448
  used as words, 315, 570–571
  varied forms of, 472
Wordy phrases, list, 460–461
Working bibliography. *See* Bibliography, working
Works Cited list, 703–719
  articles in, 708, 709–712, 771
  art work in, 714
  books in, 703–709, 771
  cartoons in, 715
  CD-ROMs in, 715–717
  charts in, 715
  diskettes in, 715–717
  dissertations in, 713
  electronic sources in, 715–719, 771
  e-mail in, 719
  film in, 714
  format of, 704, 771
  FTP sites in, 719
  Internet sources in, 716, 718–719
  interviews in, 712
  lectures in, 712–713
  letters in, 712
  Listserv discussions in, 719
  maps in, 715
  MLA style for, 703–719, 770
  musical compositions in, 714
  newsgroups in, 719
  online sources in, 716, 717–719
  performances in, 713
  periodicals in, 708, 709–712
  radio programs in, 714
  recordings in, 715
  sample, MLA style, 770
  speeches in, 712–713
  synchronous communications in, 719
  tapes in, 716–717
  television programs in, 714
  Telnet sites in, 719
  Usenet postings in, 719
  videocassettes in, 715
  videotapes in, 715
  web sites in, 719
Works of art. *See* Art works
World Wide Web, 646–657. *See also* Internet
  accessing, 647
  addresses on, 648, 649, 650
  benefits of, 649–650

World Wide Web, *(continued)*
 citation of sources from, 664, 716–719,
  733–734
 defined, 646
 domain name system on, 648, 650
 downloading from, 657
 evaluating sources from, 648, 650–657
 guidelines for searching, 649
 limitations of, 648–649
 navigating, 647–650
 printing from, 649, 650
 research on, 646–657
Writing
 analytical essays, 123–142
 argumentative essays, 143–172
 in business, 819–826
 with a computer, 827–837
 critical reading and, 24–48
 exam essays, 842–845
 exploratory essays, 102–122
 grammar in, 219–362
 idea development for, 72–100
 in literature and the arts, 780–801
 mechanics of, 592–619
 in natural sciences, 810–818
 paragraphs, 173–218
 punctuation in, 533–591
 research for, 621–664
 research essays, 665–694
 sentences, 363–420
 in social sciences, 802–810

source documentation in, 695–742
 with style, 421–468
 thinking and, 49–71
 word usage in, 469–532
Writing process, 1–23
 assessing the audience, 6–9
 becoming a writer, 2–3
 collaborating, 20–21
 drafting, 17–19
 editing, 21–22
 formulating ideas, 4–5
 organizing, 12–17
 overview, 3–4
 preparing to write, 9–12
 proofreading, 21–22
 revising, 17–19
Writing from reading, 25–33
 annotations, 10, 26–27, 781–782
 double-column notebook method, 10,
  29–31, 784–786
 freewriting, 10, 27–29, 784
 journal method, 10–11, 784–786
 summaries, 31–33, 672–674
WWW. *See* World Wide Web

y, final, 523
Yahoo, 647
Yearbooks, 634
yes, comma with, 548
you, 407–408

REVISION SYMBOLS

Boldface numbers and letters refer to *Handbook* chapters and sections.

ab	abbreviation **40**
ad	form of adjective/adverb **13**
agr	agreement **15**
awk	awkward diction or construction **20, 22, 28**
bias	biased language **29**
ca	case **12**
cap	capitalization **38**
coh	coherence **8, 9**
coord	coordination **23**
cs	comma splice **18**
d	diction, word choice **28, 30**
dm	dangling modifier **19i–j**
dev	development needed **1–4, 5–7, 8–9, 43–44, 47–49**
doc	check documentation **44, 45**
emph	emphasis needed **26**
frag	sentence fragment **17**
fs	fused sentence **18**
hyph	hyphen **42**
idea dev	develop ideas, thinking, or reading **1–4, 5–7, 47, 48**
int m	interrupting modifier **19e–h**
inc	incomplete construction **17, 22**
ital	italics **39**
k	awkward diction or construction **20, 22, 28**
lc	lower-case letter **38**
log	logic **3d–f, 7f**
mm	misplaced modifier **19a–d**
ms	manuscript form **45–50, App. A**
mix	mixed construction **22**
no ¶	no paragraph needed **8, 9**
num	number **41**
¶	paragraph **8, 9**
¶ dev	paragraph development needed **8, 9**

¶ type	paragraph type inappropriate **9**
prep	inappropriate preposition **14, 16n**
pron	incorrect pronoun form **12**
ref	unclear pronoun reference **21**
rep	unnecessary repetition **26b**
search	check research or citation **43, 44, 45**
sp	spelling error **31**
shift	inconsistent, shifted construction **20**
sub	sentence subordination **23**
t	verb tense error **11f–i, 20b**
trans	transition needed **23, 24, 25**
var	sentence variety needed **25**
vb	verb form error **11a–e**
w	wordy **26b, 28b–d**
ww/wc	wrong word; word choice **27–30**
/ /	faulty parallelism **24**
. ? !	end punctuation **32**
:	colon **34f–k**
'	apostrophe **35**
—	dash **37a**
( )	parentheses **37b**
[ ]	brackets **37c**
. . .	ellipses **37d**
/	slash **37e**
:	semicolon **34a–e**
" "	quotation marks **36**
,	comma **33**
⌣	close up
∧	insert a missing element
ℐ	delete
∿	transpose order

USEFUL CHECKLISTS

THINKING, READING, AND WRITING

THINKING AND DEVELOPING IDEAS

Common Fallacies   168
Creative vs. Logical Thinking   50
Creative Thinking: Obstacles   59
Critical Reading Overview   24
Critically Reading Sources   669
Deductive Thinking   66
Developing Ideas in Paragraphs   194
Double-Column Note-Taking   29
Evidence: Questions to Ask   75

Inductive Thinking   64
Interpretation   37
Making Connections: A Guide   94
Reading & Thinking   43
The Reading Experience   48
Researching to Find Ideas   98
Strategies to Get Ideas   11
Writing to Discover Ideas   83

READING AND RESEARCH

APA Sample Entries   720–21
Critical Reading Overview   24
Critically Reading Sources   669
Double-Column Note-Taking   29
Evaluating Sources   668
Interviewing Tips   658–59
Literature & Art: Preliminary Writing   781
MLA Sample Entries   696–97
Note-Taking: Guidelines   671–72
Observing: A Checklist   661
Paraphrasing: Guidelines   675

Quote? When?   677
Reading & Thinking   43
The Reading Experience   48
Research Essays: Rethinking   693–94
The Research Process   625
Researching to Find Ideas   98
The Scientific Method   811
Social and Natural Sciences   803
Style Manuals in Disciplines   742
Summarizing: Guidelines   673
Working Bibliography   663–64

AIMS AND PURPOSES IN WRITING

The Analytical Essay   124
Analytical Essay Development   129
Analytical Methods & Objectives   125
Analytical/Argumentative Beginnings   207
The Argumentative Essay   145
Argumentative Essay Development   151
Business Communication   819
Business Letters   821
Business Memos   820
The Exploratory Essay   103

Exploratory Essays: Development   104
Job Application Letters   823
Literature & Art: Writing Steps   787
A Literature Review   814
A Research Journal   815
The Research Process   625
Research Report Sections   816
Résumé Writing   825
Social & Natural Sciences: Writing   803
Social Science Research Reports   807

WRITING PROCESSES

Analytical Essay Development   129
Analytical Methods & Objectives   125
Analytical/Argumentative Beginnings   207
Argumentative Essay Development   151
Audience Checklist   9
Avoiding Plagiarism   691
Beginnings, Middles, Endings   116
Business Communication   819
Business Letters   821
Business Memos   820
Coherent Paragraph Writing   182
Collaboration Guidelines   21
Computers & Writing: Guidelines   827–28
Drafting & Revising   19–20
Editing Guidelines   22
Essay Exam Checklist   845
Essay Exams: Key Terms   843–44
Exploratory Essays: Beginnings   206
Incorporating Evidence   685
Interpreting: What to Look for   788–89
Interpreting Literature: Steps   787

Job Application Letters   823
Literature & Art: Preliminary Writing   781
Literature & Art: Writing Steps   787
A Literature Review   814
Paragraph Types   203
Paragraphs for Beginnings   205
Paragraphs for Endings   210
Paragraphs for Information   213
Paragraphs for Transitions   215
Research Essays: Rethinking, Revising   693–94
A Research Journal   815
The Research Process   625
Research Report Sections   816
Résumé Writing   825
Social & Natural Sciences: Writing   803
Social Science Research Reports   807
Strategies to Get Ideas   11
The Thesis: Gauging Reasonableness   679
Topic Restriction   666
Unified Paragraph Writing   178